WISC-IV clinical
assessment and
2008.

WISC-IV
CLINICAL
ASSESSMENT
AND
INTERVENTION

WISC-IV

CLINICAL

ASSESSMENT

AND   250201

INTERVENTION

SECOND EDITION

EDITED BY

AURELIO PRIFITERA
Pearson Assessment
San Antonio, TX, USA

DONALD H. SAKLOFSKE
University of Calgary
Calgary, AB, Canada

LAWRENCE G. WEISS
Pearson Assessment
San Antonio, TX, USA

AMSTERDAM • BOSTON • HEIDELBERG • LONDON • NEW YORK • OXFORD
PARIS • SAN DIEGO • SAN FRANCISCO • SINGAPORE • SYDNEY • TOKYO
Academic Press is an imprint of Elsevier

ELSEVIER

AP

Academic Press is an imprint of Elsevier
525 B Street, Suite 1900, San Diego, CA 92101-4495, USA
30 Corporate Drive, Suite 400, Burlington, MA 01803, USA
84 Theobald's Road, London WC1X 8RR, UK
Radarweg 29, PO Box 211, 1000 AE Amsterdam, The Netherlands

First edition 2005. Second edition 2008.

Notice
No responsibility is assumed by the publisher for any injury and/or damage to persons
or property as a matter of products liability, negligence or otherwise, or from any use
or operation of any methods, products, instructions or ideas contained in the material
herein. Because of rapid advances in the medical sciences, in particular, independent
verification of diagnoses and drug dosages should be made

Library of Congress Cataloging in Publication Data
A catalog record for this book is available from the Library of Congress

British Library Cataloguing in Publication Data
A catalogue record for this book is available from the British Library

ISBN–13: 978-0-12-373626-0

For information on all Academic Press publications
visit our website at books.elsevier.com

Printed and bound in the United States of America

08 09 10   10 9 8 7 6 5 4 3 2 1

Working together to grow
libraries in developing countries
www.elsevier.com | www.bookaid.org | www.sabre.org
ELSEVIER   BOOK AID International   Sabre Foundation

CONTENTS

PART 2

INTERFACING WISC-IV ASSESSMENT AND INTERVENTION: CLINICAL APPLICATIONS

2

RESEARCH-SUPPORTED DIFFERENTIAL DIAGNOSIS OF SPECIFIC LEARNING DISABILITIES AND IMPLICATIONS FOR INSTRUCTION AND RESPONSE TO INSTRUCTION

VIRGINIA W. BERNINGER, LOUISE O'DONNELL AND JAMES HOLDNACK

3

WISC-IV INTERPRETATION FOR SPECIFIC LEARNING DISABILITIES IDENTIFICATION AND INTERVENTION: A COGNITIVE HYPOTHESIS TESTING APPROACH

JAMES B. HALE, CATHERINE A. FIORELLO,
JEFFREY A. MILLER, KRISTEN WENRICH,
ANNEMARIE TEODORI AND JULIE N. HENZEL

4

LANGUAGE DISABILITIES

ELISABETH H. WIIG

5

ATTENTION-DEFICIT/ HYPERACTIVITY DISORDER: USING THE WISC-IV TO INFORM INTERVENTION PLANNING

VICKI L. SCHWEAN AND ADAM MCCRIMMON

6

THE USE OF THE WISC-IV IN ASSESSMENT AND INTERVENTION PLANNING FOR CHILDREN WHO ARE GIFTED

TINA M. NEWMAN, SARA S. SPARROW
AND STEVEN I. PFEIFFER

7

Assessment of Mental Retardation/Intellectual Disability with the WISC-IV
Jean Spruill and Patti L. Harrison

8

Autism Spectrum Disorders: WISC-IV Applications for Clinical Assessment and Intervention
Janine M. Montgomery, Danielle I. Dyke and Vicki L. Schwean

9

ASSESSMENT OF CHILDREN WITH EMOTIONAL DISTURBANCE USING THE WISC-IV

LINDA C. CATERINO, AMANDA L. SULLIVAN AND SEAN C. McDEVITT

10

THE COGNITIVE IMPACT OF SYSTEMIC ILLNESS IN CHILDHOOD AND ADOLESCENCE

R. GRANT STEEN AND FRANCES CAMPBELL

11

CONSIDERATIONS IN USING THE WISC-IV WITH HISPANIC CHILDREN

JOSETTE G. HARRIS, MARÍA R. MUÑOZ AND ANTOLIN M. LLORENTE

PART 3

INTERFACING WISC-IV ASSESSMENT AND INTERVENTION: SOME FURTHER CONSIDERATIONS

12

NEUROPSYCHOLOGICAL APPLICATIONS OF THE WISC-IV AND WISC-IV INTEGRATED

DANIEL C. MILLER AND JAMES B. HALE

LIST OF CONTRIBUTORS

Numbers in parentheses indicate the pages on which the authors' contributions begin.

Tracy Packiam Alloway (3), Durham University, School of Education, Durham, DH1 1TA, United Kingdom

A. Lynne Beal (3), Private Practice, Reaching Your Achievement Potential, Toronto, ON, Canada, M4E 3E8

Virginia W. Berninger (69), University of Washington, Seattle, WA, USA

Frances A. Campbell (365), Frank Porter Graham Child Development Institute, University of North Carolina at Chapel Hill, Chapel Hill, NC, 27599-8180, USA

Linda C. Caterino (339), Arizona State University, Tempe, AZ, 85283, USA

Dean C. Delis (497), Psychology Service, San Diego, CA, 92161, USA

Danielle I. Dyke (299), Division of Applied Psychology, University of Calgary, Calgary, AB, T2N 1N4, Canada

Catherine Fiorello (109), Temple University, College of Education, Philadelphia, PA, 19122-6091, USA

James Georgas (517), University of Athens, Athens 10674, Greece

Linda S. Gottfredson (545), School of Education, University of Delaware, Newark, DE, 19716, USA

Jacques Grégoire (517), Catholic University of Louvain, Laboratory of Educational and Developmental Psychology, 1348 Louvain-la-Neuve, Belgium

James B. Hale (109), Department of Psychology, Philadelphia College of Osteopathic Medicine, Philadelphia, PA, 19131, USA

S. Duke Han (497), Department of Psychology, Loyola University Chicago, Chicago, IL, 60626, USA

Josette G. Harris (409), Departments of Psychiatry and Neurology, University of Colorado School of Medicine, Denver, CO, 80262, USA

Patti L. Harrison (273), Department of Educational Studies in Psychology, Research Methodology and Counseling, School Psychology Program, The University of Alabama, Tuscaloosa, AL, 35487-0231, USA

Julie Henzel (109), Philadelphia College of Osteopathic Medicine, Philadelphia, PA, 19131, USA

James A. Holdnack (69), Pearson Assessment, San Antonio, TX, 78259-3701, USA

Antolin M. Llorente (409), Department of Pediatrics, University of Maryland School of Medicine, Baltimore, MD, USA

Adam McCrimmon (193), Division of Applied Psychology, University of Calgary, Calgary, AB, Canada

Sean C. McDevitt (339), Behavioral-Developmental Initiatives, Scottsdale, AZ, 85254, USA

Daniel C. Miller (445), Texas Woman's University, Department of Psychology and Philosophy, Denton, TX, 76204, USA

Jeffrey A. Miller (109), Duquesne University, Department of Counseling, Psychology, and Special Education, Pittsburgh, PA, 15282-0502, USA

Janine M. Montgomery (299), Department of Psychology, University of Manitoba, Winnipeg, Manitoba, R3T 2N2, Canada

Maria Muñoz (409), Pearson Assessment, San Antonio, TX, 78259-3701, USA

Tina M. Newman (217), Yale Child Study Center, Burnaby, BC, V5A 4Y5, Canada

Louise O'Donnell (69), University of Texas Health Science Center, San Antonio, TX, USA

Steven I. Pfeiffer (217), Florida State University, Educational Psychology and Learning Systems, Tallahassee, FL, 32306-4453, USA

Aurelio Prifitera (3), Pearson Assessment, San Antonio, TX, 78259-3701, USA

Donald H. Saklofske (3), Division of Applied Psychology, University of Calgary, Calgary, AB, T2N 1N4, Canada

Vicki L. Schwean (193), Division of Applied Psychology, University of Calgary, Calgary, AB, T2N 1N4, Canada

Sara S. Sparrow (217), Yale Child Study Center and Pace Center, Department of Psychology, New Haven, CT, 06520, USA

Jean Spruill (273), Department of Psychology, The University of Alabama, Northport, Tuscaloosa, AL, 35475, USA

R. Grant Steen (365), Department of Psychiatry, University of North Carolina at Chapel Hill, Chapel Hill, NC, 27517, USA

Amanda L. Sullivan (339), Mesa, AZ, 85201, USA

Annemarie Teodori (109), Philadelphia College of Osteopathic Medicine, Philadelphia, PA, 19131, USA

Fons J. R. Van de Vijver (517), Faculteit Sociale Wetenschappen, Psychologie en Maatschappij, 5000 LE Tilburg, The Netherlands

Lawrence G. Weiss (3), Pearson Assessment, San Antonio, TX, 78259-3701, USA

Kristen Wenrich (109), Philadelphia College of Osteopathic Medicine, Philadelphia, PA, 19131, USA

Claudine Wierzbicki (517), ECPA, 75980 Paris Cedex 20, France

Elisabeth H. Wiig (173), Arlington, TX, 76016-3517, USA

Jianjun Zhu (517), Pearson Assessment, San Antonio, TX, USA

PREFACE

This is the third edited volume on the WISC-IV that we have co-authored or co-edited. The first volume published in 2005 focused on the use of the WISC-IV with different clinical groups and the second book published in 2006 presented an advanced interpretation of this test. The main theme to date has been on the WISC-IV as an assessment tool that is used in the context of psychological and educational diagnostic and assesssment activities. In all the volumes, including this one, we have asked contributors to take a scientist-practitioner perspective in presenting information in their respective chapter. Tests and assessment measures must be used in the context of a clinical perspective which includes and integrates objective test information, biographical data, and clinical judgment and experience.

In this current volume, we asked the contributors to focus less on the mechanics of test interpretation of the WISC-IV, which are now widely known and written about, and more on how this information on a child's cognitive abilities, together with other test and clinical information, can help to inform interventions. In addition we have included chapters that are not covered in the previous WISC-IV books including, for example, autism and medical disorders. As well there are new chapters addressing cross-cultural factors, general interpretive principles, as well as a chapter on the nature and continued relevance and importance of measuring "g" or general intelligence. Other chapters have been revised to include both new material (e.g., extended norms for gifted children) and a focus on intervention planning.

Unlike the WISC-IV which has strong empirical support and validation as an assessment tool, many psychoeducational interventions, while possessing some empirical validation, are quite often more based on clinical judgment, case studies, and the experience of clinicians who use them with their clients and patients. Also unlike tests which can more easily be given in a standardized manner, often times interventions need to be modified to fit with the uniqueness of a particular client (multiple client characteristics or aptitudes interacting with various treatments). Therefore empirical validation of interventions may be less robust. There are some interventions discussed in this volume with strong empirical validation (e.g., see Berninger's chapter) but many have less rigorous scientific support. This spectrum from "some to strong" empirical validation should not necessarily be viewed as negative. Rather, this breadth allows for exploring new and potentially more effective approaches to interventions, especially when there are not empirically based interventions available or those that are often used don't "work" for a particular case. If a scientist/practitioner perspective is applied throughout the clinical process (from assessment to intervention), then one will apply sound, informed, and critical judgment, grounded in best and ethical practices, in the selection and monitoring of therapeutic effectiveness. In the long run, more evidence-based psychoeducational interventions will also become the norm as the science of interventions progresses as we have seen with interventions for psychological disorders (e.g., *Childhood Mental Health Disorders*, Brown et al., 2008; American Psychological Association; also see Canadian Psychological Association website *Your Health "Psychology Works" Fact Sheets*). Similar approaches are being tried for academic interventions (e.g., see APA Division 16 website).

The need for empirical validation of interventions will become even more important as RTI becomes commonplace in the schools in the identification and treatment of learning disabilities. Ideally the clinician will have available evidence-based treatments to determine whether or not there truly is a response to the intervention. Tests like the WISC-IV may or may not be directly linked to treatments since they were not originally intended to do that. Rather cognitive ability tests measure important traits and abilities in supporting the diagnosis of an individual and that, in turn, can have implications for treatment and outcomes. Testing and assessment, as always, is a part of a complex clinician activity whose orchestrator and leader is still the clinician who practices their art and science in an ethical manner. The editors of this volume hope this series of articles helps in that endeavor.

We are most grateful to many people who have contributed to this book. First, the authors have provided a wealth of psychological knowledge and clinical expertise to the chapters contained in this volume. To each of you we are indebted; thank you. Special thanks to Nikki Levy and Barbara Makinster at Elsevier for their continued support and superb advice in bringing this book to completion. Our appreciation is also extended to the project manager, Mageswaran BabuSivakumar, who has overseen all of the editorial and printing aspects of this book.

Aurelio Prifitera
Don Saklofske
Larry Weiss

PART 1

INTERFACING WISC-IV ASSESSMENT AND INTERVENTION: FOUNDATIONS FOR PRACTICE

1

INTERPRETATION AND INTERVENTION WITH WISC-IV IN THE CLINICAL ASSESSMENT CONTEXT

LAWRENCE G. WEISS[1], A. LYNNE BEAL[2], DONALD H. SAKLOFSKE[3], TRACY PACKIAM ALLOWAY[4] AND AURELIO PRIFITERA[5]

[1]*Pearson, San Antonio, Texas, USA*

[2]*Private Practice, Toronto, Ontario, Canada*

[3]*Division of Applied Psychology, University of Calgary, Calgary, Alberta, Canada*

[4]*Durham University, Durham, UK*

[5]*Pearson, San Antonio, Texas, USA*

OVERVIEW: THE INTERACTION BETWEEN INTELLIGENCE TESTS AND THE CLINICIAN

Assessment is too often viewed as synonymous with testing, and diagnosis as synonymous with test scores. Throughout the chapters that follow, we strongly propose that these are misguided assumptions in both clinical work and research. The purpose of this book is to present new information, research findings, and "critical" clinical thinking related to psychological and psychoeducational assessment issues in which the *Wechsler Intelligence Scale for Children* – Fourth Edition (WISC-IV) is part of the assessment battery. Each chapter contains both research and evidence-based clinical findings pertaining to the use of WISC-IV that are related to assessment issues, or to the most often referred clients for both assessment and intervention planning. Thus, recognition that good assessment data also inform our recommendations and action plans for addressing the psychological and educational needs of children has been moved to the forefront of this book. Each chapter also discusses the links between assessment and intervention planning with a particular focus on how the WISC-IV may inform this continuum of assessment to intervention.

Employing an evidence-based and best practices approach in assessment and using these results in planning interventions is the theme of this book. What constitutes best practice, however, varies across the many specialty areas within psychology – as it should. For example, considerable variability is evident in the assessment needs and practice patterns of neuropsychologists, school psychologists, clinical psychologists, rehabilitation psychologists, intellectual disability evaluators, family counselors, and those working in juvenile justice settings – to name just a few. The different clinical groups and issues discussed in this volume address much of this variability. Despite the variability and heterogeneity of both practice patterns and disorders, the Wechsler scales are used by many psychologists with different areas of expertise engaged in solving quite different clinical questions.

The types of referral questions addressed in each specialty area of practice are unique and present unique challenges for the assessment – yet most psychology practitioners incorporate the WISC-IV as part of the assessment. Thus, the WISC-IV is used in different ways by different types of psychologists for different purposes. Neuropsychologists, for example, might be asked to estimate a patient's cognitive ability prior to a traumatic brain injury (TBI) based on a combination of spared cognitive abilities and demographic factors. Juvenile justice psychologists may be asked to determine if a teenaged offender is cognitively and emotionally able to stand trial as an adult. School and educational psychologists may be asked to predict a student's ability to profit from special educational programming or to determine if a learning disability underlies a child's poor school achievement. In school-based practices, response to intervention (RTI) and the associated movement toward curriculum-based measurement has challenged the role of assessment and particularly the place of intelligence and cognitive assessment in psychoeducational practice. The chapters in this volume address the unique aspects of cognitive assessment in many of these diverse areas of practice, based in the central theme that test scores do not diagnose but must be interpreted by an informed practitioner in light of an evidence base that relates to the specific referral question being addressed, while respecting the needs and rights of the child.

Throughout our previous two books on the WISC-IV, and in this current volume, we underscore that tests and test scores, no matter how psychometrically sound, in and of themselves are not sufficient for a proper, comprehensive, and meaningful psychological assessment. Tests don't assess, clinicians do. Test scores must be interpreted by properly trained clinicians operating within particular areas of professional competency and expertise. This is because best assessment practices differ somewhat across specialty areas based on the varying nature of the clinical questions being asked. Still, best assessment practice always includes interpretation of scores in broader context with relevant cultural, personality, clinical, medical, and other information – all of which may not be clear and objective but relies in part on the integrative skills and professional expertise of the evaluator. This is one of the main themes in Matarazzo's (1990) APA presidential address in which he describes psychological assessment as an activity that:

> is not, even today, a totally objective, completely science-based activity. Rather, in common with much of medical diagnosis . . . the assessment of intelligence, personality, or type or level of impairment is a highly complex operation that involves extracting diagnostic meaning from an individual's personal history and objectively recorded test scores. Rather than being totally objective, assessment involves a subjective component. Specifically, it is the activity of a licensed professional, an artisan familiar with the accumulated findings of his or her young science, who in each instance uses tests, techniques, and a strategy, that, whereas also identifying possible deficits, maximizes the chances of discovering each client's full ability and true potential (p. 1000).

A HISTORICAL PERSPECTIVE ON ASSESSMENT THAT REMAINS CONTEMPORARY

In all too many cases, there is overreliance on scores and not enough on the clinician and clinical judgment. In Wechsler's approach to clinical assessment, understanding of the individual is paramount and test scores are subservient to that end (see Tulsky et al., 2003a, b).This theme can be traced back to the famous personologists, Gordon Allport and Henry Murray. They provided theoretical and clinically rich descriptions of the person by employing both the nomothetic and the idiographic dimensions of personality. In the nomothetic approach, one searches for general rules and laws that apply to all individuals. In the idiographic approach, strongly advocated by Allport, the best way to understand the person is to view the person as having unique characteristics or personal dispositions. The combinations and interactions of these unique characteristics allow nearly infinite variations of individuals.

According to Allport, "each individual is an idiom unto himself, an apparent violation of the syntax of the species" (Allport, 1955, p. 22). Note that in such a view of the person, issues like subtest score scatter are viewed not as psychometric anomalies due to unfortunate vagaries and the confound of measurement error but rather as an expression of individuality that should be explored and understood. While it might be cleaner to have all scores line up as one would expect due to factor structure or other theoretical premises, it just may be that people express abilities and subabilities in different ways that are not necessarily uniform. Furthermore Allport said "all the animals of the world are psychologically less distinct from one another than one man is from other men" (p. 23). This radical idiographic view underscores the notion in Allport's mind that generalizations are limited in helping us understand the uniqueness of the individual.

If all subtests were the same and correlated perfectly with each other, there would be no capacity to differentiate individuals from one another. So the lack of perfect correlation is actually positive and gives the clinician a richer sense of the individual. Of course other psychometric characteristics need to be taken into account but variability across subtests and index scores actually helps in the utility and validity of a test much like in a multi-trait, multi-method approach.

So what does a discussion of personology have to do with the Wechsler tests and intellectual assessment? Everything! Wechsler maintained that intelligence is part of the expression of the whole of personality. This is consistent with personology, which seeks to understand the whole person, which obviously included his or her intelligence. Also, Wechsler maintained that his tests measure only part of intelligence, the intellective aspects and that the nonintellective aspects were not measured well by his scales. Wechsler at heart was a personologist who was most interested in understanding the person in all his or her complexity. In his article (Wechsler, 1950), "Cognitive, Conative, and Non-Intellective Intelligence" written in 1950, Wechsler said:

> factors other than intellectual contribute to achievement in areas whereas in the case of learning, intellectual factors have until recently been considered uniquely determinate, and, second, that these other factors have to do with functions and abilities hitherto considered traits in personality. Among those partially identified so far are factors relating primarily to the conative functions like drive, persistence, will and perseveration, or in some instances, to aspects of temperament that pertain to interests and achievement. . . . that personality traits enter into the effectiveness of intelligent behavior, and hence, into any global concept of intelligence itself" (pp. 45–46).

So if Wechsler viewed himself as a personologist and clinician first and the test as a tool to understand the person, to what uses is it best to put intelligence tests and scores? First of all, regardless of the referral question, users of intelligence tests need to remember that tests yield information that is part of the diagnostic and decision-making process and they are not that process in and of themselves. In both psychology and education, it is rare that one test or score is diagnostic of a specific disorder or disability. Even a very low score on the WISC-IV FSIQ is not diagnostic of mental retardation. The approaches to test interpretation and assessment advocated by Matarazzo (1990), Kamphaus (1993), Kaufman (1994) and others speak to the need to view test results as tools used by a clinician in the evaluation process whether for diagnosis, intervention planning, classification, description, etc.

Test results need to be viewed in the context of other information and knowledge about the person. The psychologist, then, based on multi-source, multi-method knowledge of the client, only one of which is test information, looks across the information to confirm or disconfirm hypotheses of either an a priori or a posteriori nature.

Think of what happens when we go to a medical doctor complaining of headaches. The physician takes our temperature, blood pressure, medical history, and perform other aspects of a physical examination. Then let's say the result is that we have a high blood pressure reading. Is the diagnosis of hypertension given by the physician based on the results of the scores derived from the sphygmomanometer reading alone? Probably not because the physician may want to rule out many other factors before simply saying that an abnormally high blood pressure reading is definitive for a diagnosis of essential hypertension. Even then, various medical conditions can produce a short lived or chronic elevation in blood pressure that will need to be investigated before the final diagnosis is made. In this scenario, note that the test instrument yielding a high blood pressure reading was giving an accurate result. Thus it may be highly accurate (or reliable) in describing the high level of blood pressure; but the high pressure reading may be due to essential hypertension or to numerous other conditions such as heart disease, toxemia, kidney dysfunction, or anxiety. Without other corroborative and/or exclusionary evidence, basing a diagnosis on one test score alone can lead to false conclusions. However, the physician does use his or her knowledge base about the relationship of high blood pressure reading and essential hypertension in the diagnostic activity even though this knowledge does not make the diagnosis in and of itself. Similarly, a relationship between low scores on WISC-IV PSI and WMI scores and attentional disorder is not in and of itself diagnostic of attention deficit hyperactivity disorder (ADHD), but the knowledge of this relationship should be included when trying to understand the person who is the object of the assessment.

If one accepts the tenet that tests do not diagnose but clinicians do and that most psychological tests are not in and of themselves conclusive diagnostic indicators (true of tests in medicine as well), then the large number of articles in the literature that criticize tests such as the WISC-III and WISC-IV for failing to properly diagnose a disorder with a high level of accuracy are misguided in their emphasis. Much of the criticism of intelligence testing surrounding the diagnosis of specific learning disabilities (SLD) and ability–achievement discrepancies discussed previously is based on such misconceptions of the role of tests in diagnosis. Perhaps these studies were needed to point out to practitioners that just looking at profiles of test scores (e.g., McDermott et al., 1990) leads to erroneous diagnostic decisions because subtest patterns in and of themselves are not conclusively diagnostic of a disorder. The thrust of these articles seems to admonish clinicians for even looking at and comparing scores. More balanced and critical clinical assessment such as the approach advocated by Hale et al. (2004) and Fiorello et al. (2001) yields richer and more useful test application results.

Would one want a physician, for example, not to look at patterns of test results just because they in and of themselves do not diagnose a disorder? Would you tell a physician not to take your blood pressure and heart rate and compare them because these two scores in and of themselves do not differentially diagnose kidney disease from heart disease?

The Kavale and Forness article (Kavale and Forness, 1984) is often cited as evidence that profile analysis of the Wechsler scores is not useful in the differential diagnosis of learning disorders. The value of this type of research has been helpful to put the brakes on cookbook, simplistic interpretations of test results devoid of the contextualism of the individual's unique life characteristics. However, the criticism of the practice of profile analysis as the sole piece of information used to make a diagnostic decision has often become a "straw man" argument and has been used to justify elimination of IQ and other psychoeducational tests, which is tantamount to the proverbial throwing out the baby with the bath water. What well-trained clinicians simply rely on test results or patterns as their sole source of information when performing an assessment? If clinicians do not practice in this simplistic way, then to say that a test is not useful because it does not accurately diagnose a disorder is a specious argument because it does not take into account the richness of other sources of information that the clinician is likely to use in arriving at a diagnosis. For example, if a child has a large VCI/PRI discrepancy with a lower VCI, and, based solely on this information, one concludes that left hemisphere functioning is impaired, this would most certainly be viewed as naive and poor practice. Kaufman (1994a, b) demonstrated many years ago, for example, that discrepancies between verbal intelligence quotient (VIQ) and performance intelligence quotient (PIQ) are not uncommon in the normal population. However, there is a sufficient body of research supporting the notion that injuries to the left hemisphere result in lower verbal compared to perceptual scores. Well, if we have additional information that our client recently suffered a head injury, that perhaps other areas of functioning related to verbal abilities are impaired, and that previous functioning in relevant cognitive areas was higher, then the test results are certainly strong evidence that help corroborate a hypothesis of left hemisphere impairment that has resulted in cognitive impairment of certain types. It would appear that studies looking at the validity of test scores and profiles in the assessment process need to also look at the other variables that clinicians use in their assessment including the criterion and not just at test results. Also, studies that conclude that test results are not helpful in such assessments ignore the value of the descriptive nature of tests (e.g., this person has these types of strengths and weaknesses).

WHAT DO WE CONCLUDE?

Good practice in using tests should also include looking at test results in the context of multiple sources of information which include the WISC scores. If we accept this type of notion as a necessary condition of sound clinical practice, then the idea of simply looking at patterns of test scores in isolation from other pieces of information, whether in clinical assessment or research, is limited and probably wrong in most cases. Truly multivariate thinking is needed, which is what the good clinician does.

The WISC-IV, like other key diagnostic and assessment instruments used by psychologists, should be viewed and used for what it is, a useful tool to help the clinician "understand" the child before them. The body of research on the Wechsler scales and the improvements and innovations made particularly in the WISC-IV make it an especially useful measure of children's intellectual abilities and its psychometric and clinical properties are well known and have been scrutinized more than any other scales of their kind. Like other professionals who use assessment tools as part of practicing their profession, psychologists need to understand how to use the scale, its strengths, and limitations. Above all, the clinician remains the ultimate clinical instrument who uses such tools as part of their clinical work.

INTRODUCTION TO INTERPRETATION AND INTERVENTION WITH WISC-IV IN THE CLINICAL ASSESSMENT CONTEXT

A central tenet of this chapter is that differences among the four-factor-based WISC-IV index scores are clinically meaningful and worthy of study within the context of the complete individual. Another central tenet is that strengths and weaknesses in each of the four domains of ability measure by the WISC-IV index scores can be observed in characteristic classroom behaviors which lend themselves to specific instructional modifications and accommodations. Parts I and II of this chapter address these two tenets, interpretation and intervention, respectively. These two tenets are intertwined in that clinically meaningful interpretation underlies clinically meaningful intervention.

The psychometric properties of the WISC-IV and the cultural and social–economic context of the child have been described extensively by Prifitera et al. (2005). Therefore, the next sections discuss the interpretation and application of the major scores obtained from the WISC-IV. In our previous two books on the WISC-IV, we have suggested that WISC-IV interpretation should be both a "top–down" and "bottom–up" process. However, we continue to argue that the basis for understanding a child's cognitive abilities and how this relates to their particular needs is best served, not by the Full Scale Intelligence Quotient (FSIQ) alone, but by the index scores tapping Verbal Comprehension (VCI), Perceptual Reasoning (PRI), Working Memory (WMI), and Processing Speed (PSI). While the FSIQ is especially useful in the assessment and classification of children who are intellectually gifted or cognitively impaired, the index scores allow for a better understanding of how a child is "alike all others, some others, and no others". This is especially the case when so many of the children referred for assessment fall in the ± 1.5 to 2 standard deviation range but show considerable variability between the index scores. We also discuss the use of the General Ability Index (GAI) and the Cognitive Proficiency Index (CPI), reflecting more composite abilities, as they contribute to diagnosis and intervention planning. The GAI is a summary of VCI and PRI. The CPI is a summary of WMI and PSI.

The clinical interpretation and use of the WISC-IV index scores requires an in-depth awareness of clinically meaningful test score patterns in the performance of diagnostic groups, as well as the careful observation and full case history of the child (Prifitera et al., 1998). Such decisions relevant to the goals of assessment are best made with the sound clinical knowledge of how meaningful patterns in performance may vary among diagnostically relevant groups. Thus we briefly review how to calculate strengths and weaknesses across the four index scores.

This introductory chapter is not intended to give an extensive overview and description of the WISC-IV. Because of the widespread use of the Wechsler scales by graduate level trainers, practitioners, and researchers, properties of these scales are well known and full descriptions of the Wechsler scales can be found in multiple sources (e.g., Sattler, 1988, 1992, 2001; Wechsler, 1991, 1997; Kaufman, 1994; Anastasi & Urbina, 1997) and the WISC-IV in particular in Flanagan and Kaufman (2004), Sattler and Dumont (2004), and Wechsler (2003, 2004). Furthermore, the clinical use of the WISC-IV in the assessment of referred children has been extensively addressed in our earlier book (Prifitera et al., 2005). The advanced clinical interpretation of WISC-IV as a process instrument is thoroughly discussed in our companion book (WISC-IV Advanced Clinical Interpretation; Weiss et al., 2006a, b) along with an in-depth discussion of social, economic, and cultural factors that impact the assessment of intelligence. We invite all readers to please consult both of these volumes and particularly to reread their introductory chapters. These chapters provide the foundational underpinnings for using the WISC-IV as a valuable clinical instrument in the comprehensive diagnostic assessment of children's cognitive abilities but also present compelling data that should very much impact the interpretation of test data as it leads to thinking about and planning for intervention. This book, as a revision and extension of the *WISC-IV Clinical Use and Interpretation,* "completes the circle" by placing intervention planning clearly into our description of the WISC-IV.

As a brief visual reminder of the organizational structure of WISC-IV, Figure 1.1 shows the factor-based index structure and corresponding subtests with accompanying descriptions of each subtest, and Table 1.1 gives brief descriptions of each subtest.

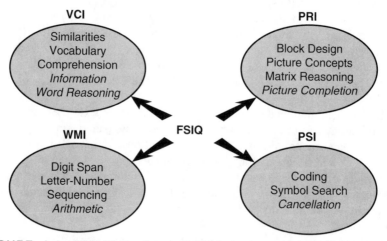

FIGURE 1.1 WISC-IV Test Framework italicized subtests are optional subtests. From Wechsler *Intelligence Scale for Children* – Fourth Edition. Copyright © 2003 by The Psychological Corporation. Used by permission. All rights reserved.

TABLE 1.1 Abbreviations and Descriptions of Subtests

Subtest	Abbreviation	Description
Block Design	BD	While viewing a constructed model or a picture in the Stimulus Book, the child uses red-and-white blocks to recreate the design within a specified time limit.
Similarities	SI	The child is presented with two words that represent common objects or concepts and describes how they are similar.
Digit Span	DS	For Digit Span Forward, the child repeats numbers in the same order as presented aloud by the examiner. For Digit Span Backward, the child repeats numbers in the reverse order of that presented aloud by the examiner.
Picture Concepts	PCn	The child is presented with two or three rows of pictures and chooses one picture from each row to form a group with a common characteristic.
Coding	CD	The child copies symbols that are paired with simple geometric shapes or numbers. Using a key, the child draws each symbol in its corresponding shape or box within a specified time limit.
Vocabulary	VC	For Picture Items, the child names pictures that are displayed in the Stimulus Book. For Verbal Items, the child gives definitions for words that the examiner reads aloud.
Letter–Number Sequencing	LN	The child reads a sequence of numbers and letters and recalls the numbers in ascending order and the letters in alphabetical order.
Matrix Reasoning	MR	The child looks at an incomplete matrix and selects the missing portion from five response options.
Comprehension	CO	The child answers questions based on his or her understanding of general principles and social situations.
Symbol Search	SS	The child scans a search group and indicates whether the target symbol(s) matches any of the symbols in the search group within a specified time limit.
Picture Completion	PCm	The child views a picture and then points to or names the important part missing within a specified time limit.
Cancellation	CA	The child scans both a random and a structured arrangement of pictures and marks target pictures within a specified time limit.
Information	IN	The child answers questions that address a broad range of general knowledge topics.
Arithmetic	AR	The child mentally solves a series of orally presented arithmetic problems within a specified time limit.
Word Reasoning	WR	The child identifies the common concept being described in a series of clues.

Note: From *Wechsler Intelligence Scale for Children – Fourth Edition*. Copyright © 2003 by The Psychological Corporation. Used by permission. All rights reserved.

PART I: INTERPRETING THE WISC-IV INDEX
SCORES

CALCULATING INDEX STRENGTHS AND WEAKNESSES

The domains measured by the four indices are robust clinical constructs with strong psychometric properties. A central tenet of this chapter is that individual differences among the factor-based index scores are clinically important and worthy of study. Interpretation of subtest scores is also noted, but considered secondary to qualitative analysis of the unique response patterns the child utilizes in approaching each task.

Interpretation begins with a comparison of each of the four domain specific index scores (i.e., VCI, PRI, WMI, and PSI) with the mean of the four index scores to determine relative strengths and weaknesses. This process is described in the section "Tables to compare WISC-IV index scores against overall means". The minimum difference required for statistical significance between the mean

TABLE 1.2 Required Difference Between Index Scores and the Mean Index Score at Significance Level by Age Groups

Ages 6–7		Significance level		
Index	Pooled SEM	.15	.05	.01
Verbal Comprehension	4.37	8.25	9.92	11.98
Perceptual Reasoning	4.37	8.25	9.92	11.98
Working Memory	4.50	8.40	10.10	12.19
Processing Speed	6.36	10.69	12.85	15.52

Ages 18–13		Significance level		
Index	Pooled SEM	.15	.05	.01
Verbal Comprehension	3.77	7.10	8.53	10.31
Perceptual Reasoning	3.97	7.33	8.81	10.64
Working Memory	4.29	7.71	9.27	11.20
Processing Speed	4.93	8.50	10.21	12.34

Ages 14–16		Significance level		
Index	Pooled SEM	.15	.05	.01
Verbal Comprehension	3.35	6.58	7.91	9.55
Perceptual Reasoning	4.33	7.72	9.28	11.21
Working Memory	4.06	7.39	8.89	10.74
Processing Speed	4.89	8.41	10.11	12.21

and each index scores is available in Table 1.2, by age and overall. Because strengths and weaknesses across cognitive domains are common among normally developing children, it is essential to determine the frequency with which such a difference is observed in the standardization sample. Table 1.3 shows the base rates for the difference between the mean and each index scores for the entire

TABLE 1.3   Abnormality of Differences between WISC-IV Index Scores and Overall Mean Index Score

				Cumulative percentile				
Difference	VCI < M*	VCI > M	PRI < M	PRI > M	WMI < M	WMI > M	PSI < M	PSI > M
30	0.0	0.1	0.0	0.0	0.2	0.2	0.2	0.0
29	0.0	0.1	0.0	0.0	0.2	0.2	0.3	0.2
28	0.1	0.1	0.0	0.0	0.3	0.3	0.4	0.3
27	0.2	0.1	0.1	0.0	0.4	0.4	0.4	0.4
26	0.3	0.1	0.1	0.0	0.5	0.4	0.6	0.5
25	0.3	0.2	0.1	0.1	0.6	0.5	0.7	0.6
24	0.4	0.2	0.1	0.3	0.7	0.7	0.9	0.9
23	0.6	0.3	0.2	0.4	1.0	1.0	1.1	1.3
22	0.9	0.5	0.3	0.5	1.5	1.3	1.5	1.6
21	1.2	0.9	0.4	0.8	2.0	1.6	2.1	2.0
20	1.5	1.2	0.7	1.0	2.4	2.0	2.7	2.7
19	1.9	1.6	1.2	1.4	2.8	2.5	3.1	3.6
18	2.2	2.1	1.5	2.0	3.6	3.1	4.0	4.5
17	2.8	2.8	2.2	2.5	4.3	3.5	5.2	5.8
16	3.8	3.5	2.9	3.1	5.0	4.4	6.1	7.0
15	5.2	4.1	3.5	4.2	6.0	5.0	7.7	8.0
14	6.3	4.9	4.6	5.4	7.7	6.1	9.1	9.2
13	7.7	6.0	5.7	6.8	8.8	7.4	10.7	11.3
12	9.3	8.0	7.5	8.4	10.8	9.5	12.5	13.4
11	11.7	9.7	9.1	10.3	12.5	11.0	14.6	16.3
10	14.6	12.3	11.5	13.0	15.4	13.4	17.2	19.0
9	17.2	15.0	13.9	15.2	18.0	15.8	19.6	21.8
8	20.0	18.0	17.0	18.3	21.0	18.5	22.1	24.0
7	23.6	21.1	20.5	21.8	25.5	21.9	25.4	27.0
6	27.7	24.9	24.7	26.4	29.3	25.6	28.4	30.1
5	31.7	28.1	29.4	30.2	33.2	29.2	31.0	33.5
4	36.0	31.1	33.2	34.5	37.0	33.6	35.2	37.0

(*continues*)

TABLE 1.3   (*continued*)

	Cumulative percentile							
Difference	VCI < M*	VCI > M	PRI < M	PRI > M	WMI < M	WMI > M	PSI < M	PSI > M
3	40.2	35.0	37.5	39.0	40.7	37.6	39.6	40.0
2	44.7	39.5	42.0	44.0	45.3	41.5	44.1	43.7
1	50.5	44.0	46.8	48.4	49.7	46.1	47.9	47.5
Mean	7.2	7.2	6.8	7.0	7.8	7.5	8.3	8.7
SD	5.2	5.1	4.7	4.9	5.7	5.6	6.1	6.0
Median	6.0	6.0	6.0	6.0	7.0	6.0	7.0	8.0

*M stands for the overall mean of 4 WISC-IV index scores.

standardization sample. As a rule of thumb, these critical base rates are often near 12 points. In these cases, the specific indexes are discussed and interpreted as relative strengths or weaknesses in the child's profile of cognitive abilities.

TABLES TO COMPARE WISC-IV INDEX SCORES AGAINST OVERALL MEANS

The WISC-IV provides guidelines and interpretative values to describe overall level of performance, as well as strategies to identify individual patterns of performance on the subtests and index scores (Wechsler, 2003). Index scores are compared in pairwise fashion, VC to PR, VC to PS, etc., while subtest scores are generally compared against the overall mean. As originally described by R. Stewart Longman (2005) in chapter 2 of first edition of this book, there are good statistical and practical reasons to compare index scores to their overall mean, instead of comparing pairs of scores.

Statistically, the six pairwise comparisons lead to an increased risk of falsely identifying differences between pairs of indexes (Knight & Godfrey, 1984). As a consequence, it is rare to find a WISC-IV profile without at least one significant difference between index scores. As well, some differences may be significant, while an equally large difference between another set of indexes may not be statistically significant. Comparing index scores against the overall mean allows us to make fewer comparisons, use appropriate corrections for overall comparisons, and identify a particular index as showing a relative strength, relative weakness, or no difference from the overall mean. These features all make use of overall comparisons easier to use and easier to communicate to other professionals and to the public (Naglieri, 1993).

Research with the WISC-III (Wechsler, 1991), WAIS-III and WISC-IV (Wechsler, 2003) has shown several common profiles in the general population and in specific clinical groups (described here using the WISC-IV labels for the index scores). Research with the general population has found several common profiles, including no relative strengths or weakness, a single strength or weakness on the PSI (Donders, 1996; Pritchard et al., 2000; Donders et al., 2001a, b) or a relative imbalance between the PRI and the WMI (Pritchard et al., 2000), with one being relatively high and the other relatively low. In clinical populations, specific patterns include a relative weakness in WM for individuals with learning disabilities (Daley & Nagle, 1996; Wechsler, 1997), or a relative weakness in PS after TBI or in ADHD without other concerns (Donders, 1997; Donders et al., 2001a, b; Wechsler, 2003, pp. 88, 92–93). However, a specific index profile is not invariably found with a particular condition, and index profiles should be considered a shorthand description of general patterns of cognitive strengths and weaknesses, rather than providing a definitive diagnosis.

Derivation of Tables for Statistical Significance and Abnormality of Differences

The formula given by Davis (1959) was used to compare index scores to the overall mean of index scores for statistical significance. Because the reliabilities of the various indexes vary across age groups, the data were combined into three age groups with more homogeneous reliabilities: ages 6 and 7, ages 8–13, and ages 14–16. The average standard errors of measurement (SEMs) were calculated by averaging the sum of squared SEMs for each age and obtaining the square root of the results. The average SEMs and corresponding critical values for each index are presented in Table 1.2 using Bonferroni corrected values to correct for the multiple comparisons and keep overall significance levels of .15, .05, and .01.

To assess the relative infrequency of differences between a specific index and the overall mean, the cumulative percentages of differences were calculated using the WISC-IV standardization sample and reported in Table 1.3. Because data analysis revealed that the prevalence of the difference is not identical for an index score that is greater than the overall mean and for an index score that is less than the overall mean, the values are reported by the direction of the difference.

Example

For example, consider a 9-year old referred for suspected learning disabilities, with the following index scores: VC of 97, PR of 105, WM of 84, and PS of 102. Her average index score is 97, and her relative strength on PR (at 8 points) is significant at the .15 level, while her relative weakness on WM (by 13 points) is significant at the .01 level. Inspection of Table 1.3 indicates that her strength on PR is commonly found because 18.3% of the standardization sample obtained PR scores that are 8 points or higher than their average index scores. On the other hand, her weakness on WM is relatively rare because only 8.8% of children show such a relative weakness. This profile can be described as showing a relative weakness on WM, with a possible strength on PR as compared to her overall functioning, a common pattern in children diagnosed with learning disabilities. Of course, to make any such diagnosis, academic achievement would need to be assessed and other possibilities evaluated, but the additional information from the WISC-IV may help select what areas require further evaluation.

A discussion of each of the four index scores follows: VCI, PRI, WMI, and PSI. Each section reviews the theoretical constructs assessed by the index, research related to specific diagnostic groups, clinical interpretation, and suggested strategies for intervention. Understanding the different cognitive abilities being tapped by these indexes is fundamental to sound clinical interpretation of this test and selecting appropriate interventions. This chapter will also revisit the GAI as a composite of VCI and PRI, and addresses issues related to its appropriate use. Finally, the CPI is introduced as a composite of WMI and PSI.

INTERPRETING THE WISC-IV VCI

The VCI is composed of subtests measuring verbal abilities utilizing reasoning, comprehension, and conceptualization. The composition of this index involves tasks that require crystallized knowledge, verbal fluid reasoning, long-term memory, and comprehension. Several authors have written extensively about interpretive issues with each of the verbal and perceptual subtests (Flanagan & Kaufman, 2004; Sattler & Dumont, 2004).

Consensus opinion of the fit of the WISC-IV to the Cattell-Horn Carroll (CHC) model classified all subtests and supplementary subtests of the VCI as measures of crystallized intelligence. These classifications were also found through a factor analytic study by Keith and associates (Flanagan & Kaufman, 2004). At the same time, however, Flanagan, et al. acknowledged the contribution of fluid reasoning to Similarities and Word Reasoning by suggesting that these two subtests can form a composite called verbal fluid reasoning (p. 151). Crystallized intelligence is a broad ability in the CHC model. It is defined as "the breadth and depth of a person's acquired knowledge of a culture and the effective application of this knowledge. This store of primarily verbal or language-based knowledge represents those abilities that have been developed largely through the "investment" of other abilities during educational and general life experience (McGrew & Flanagan, 1998, p. 20).

Crystallized intelligence, as measured by the VCI, shows a strong and consistent relationship with the development of reading and math achievement. Contributions of crystallized intelligence to writing achievement are important primarily after age 7. Its contributions to reading, math, and writing achievement become increasingly important for reading and math achievement with age (Flanagan & Mascolo, 2005, quoting work from their colleagues).

The Information (In) subtest, primarily a measure of crystallized knowledge, is a supplemental subtest. Word Reasoning (WR) was designed to assess reasoning with words, or fluid verbal reasoning. Reasoning with words assumes knowledge of the target words, however, and WR therefore requires some amount of crystallized knowledge as background. The Vocabulary (VC) subtest is a measure of crystallized knowledge which requires that the meaning of a word was learned, can be recalled, and expressed coherently. There is no apparent demand to reason in this subtest. At the same time, however, VC is one of the highest "g" loaded subtests, and one of the best predictors of overall intelligence. Perhaps this is because higher-order thinking requires that more pieces of related information are chunked into a coherent whole for quicker processing. Individuals with larger vocabularies can chunk larger concepts into a single word. Individuals with larger vocabularies may have enjoyed a more linguistically and cognitively enriched environment, but must also be able to apply their knowledge appropriately. Use of advanced vocabulary words in conversation requires the individual to accurately comprehend nuances of the situation. For example, do we say that the AIDS vaccine was "discovered" or "invented"? Consider that to use the word "obviate" appropriately in conversation, one must first perceive that some action will make another action unnecessary. Finally, how intelligent does one need to be to tell the difference between "placating" and "appeasing" another person? Thus, vocabulary is not a simple matter of reciting definitions of words. In spite of these considerations, however, the conventional wisdom is that a strong vocabulary is simply an indication of a high degree of crystallized knowledge. While Vocabulary and Information subtests primarily draw from the child's knowledge base, appropriate use of the stored information requires a good grasp of the situation.

Now, compare the underlying abilities required when the examiner asks the child to describe how "war and peace" are alike on the Similarities (SM) subtest. A correct response requires prior knowledge of each of these words. More specifically, both concepts must have been acquired and stored in long-term memory. Further, the child must be able to access that knowledge from semantic memory upon demand. Once these words are recalled, the child can begin the reasoning process to determine how they are similar. This reasoning process appears to take place within a transitory working memory space, and the ability to reason may be related to working memory capacity and the speed at which ideas are processed in working memory before the trace fades (see section below). Similar issues may be at play with WR.

The SM, CM, and WR subtests require a higher level of reasoning for successful performance than the Vocabulary and Information subtests. Thus it may be useful to examine IN and VC in tandem and compare these scores jointly to SM, CO (Comprehension), and WR. Children with deficits in crystallized knowledge, or in retrieval from long-term memory of previously acquired information, or both, may score higher on SM, CO, and WR than on VC and IN if they have adequate verbal reasoning ability. Conversely, children with an age-appropriate knowledge base that is readily accessible but deficits in higher-order categorization of abstract verbal concepts may show the reverse score pattern. In these cases, it may then also be instructive to compare performance on SM with Picture Concepts (PCn). Both subtests require categorization of abstract verbal concepts, but PCn relieves the child of the demand to verbally explain his or her thinking. Thus, children with good abstract reasoning skills but poor verbal expression may perform better on PCn than SM.

Prior to making an interpretation of low verbal ability, the psychologist should ask: was the knowledge encoded but cannot now be recalled (for several possible reasons), or was it never acquired in the first place? The methodology for addressing this issue is the "recognition paradigm." The VC subtests involve free recall which is a much more difficult cognitive task than cued recognition. How many times have each of us been unable to recall an associate's name, but when others suggest a name we easily recognize if the suggestion was correct? This shows that the name was acquired and stored in long-term memory, but could not be accessed.

The WISC-IV Integrated is a useful assessment tool in such cases. It contains multiple choice versions of the core WISC-IV Verbal Comprehension subtests. Children who answered incorrectly because they could not recall the information will more readily recognize the correct information in the multiple choice paradigm. In this way, the examiner can explore if the incorrect responses were a function of lack of knowledge or lack of access to knowledge. Clearly, this makes a critical difference in interpretation. We are reminded of a young girl who was referred because initial assessments and poor school performance suggested mental retardation (initial WISC-III FSIQ in the 50–60 range). Upon retesting, her VC score was 2, but on the Integrated, her Multiple Choice VC score was 8 and her Picture Vocabulary score was 12. Together with other clinical data, it became clear that mental retardation was not the basis for her poor classroom achievement.

INTERPRETING THE WISC-IV PRI

The PRI is composed of subtests primarily measuring perceptual reasoning with some visual–spatial organization. Block Design (BD), Matrix Reasoning (MR), and Picture Concepts (PCn) primarily tap fluid reasoning. BD and MR also involve an element of perceptual organization whereas PCn seems to require little perceptual organization. PCn may invoke verbal mediation, but there is no demand for a verbal response. Basic interpretative strategies of individual PR subtests have been well documented elsewhere (Sattler & Dumont, 2004), and will not be repeated here.

Consensus evaluation of the fit of the WISC-IV to the CHC model classified BD as a measure of Visual Processing, the supplementary Picture Completion as a measure of Visual Processing and Crystallized Intelligence, MR as a measure of Fluid Reasoning, and PCn as a measure of Fluid Reasoning and Crystallized Intelligence. These classifications were also found through a factor analytic study by Keith and associates (Flanagan & Kaufman, 2004).

Visual Processing is the ability to generate, perceive, analyze, synthesize, manipulate, transform, and think with spatial patterns and stimuli. The visual processing domain includes a broad array of diverse visual abilities that emphasize different aspects of the process of image generation, storage, retrieval, and transformation (McGrew & Flanagan, 1998, p. 23).

Fluid intelligence (Gf) refers to "mental operations that an individual may use when faced with a relatively novel task that cannot be performed automatically. These mental operations may include forming and recognizing concepts, identifying relations, perceiving relationships among patterns, drawing inferences, comprehending implications, problem solving, extrapolating, and reorganizing or transforming information. The narrow abilities of inductive and deductive reasoning are generally considered to be the hallmark narrow ability indicators of Gf" (McGrew & Flanagan, 1998, p. 14).

Fluid reasoning, as measured by the PRI shows a strong and consistent relationship with the development of math achievement. It also contributes moderately to the development of reading skills. In the elementary grades it contributes moderately to basic writing skills, and at all ages it relates to written expression (Flanagan & Mascolo, 2005, quoting work from their colleagues). Visual Processing as measured by the PRI may be important for doing higher-level or advanced mathematics, such as geometry and calculus (Flanagan & Mascolo, 2005, quoting work from their colleagues).

Psychologists have raised concerns in the past about the negative impact of time bonuses on performance subtests with gifted and talented students, and with various minority populations. The BD subtest may be scored with and without time bonuses, while only the score with time bonuses is used in the calculation of PRI and FSIQ. The impact of speed on the child's performance can be determined by comparing performance in these two conditions. Yet, contrary to popular belief, there is very little difference in children's scaled scores on BD with and without time bonuses. As shown in Table B.10 of the *WISC-IV Administration and Scoring Manual*, even a difference of two scaled score points between BD with and without time bonuses occurred in less than 10% of the standardization sample.

The WISC-IV Integrated may prove useful to psychologists in their efforts to "understand" atypical WISC-IV scores. The Integrated includes a multiple choice version of the BD subtest (BDMC) to help parse out the impact of motor demands on the child's performance. For children with BD < BDMC discrepancies, it is possible that performance on BD was limited by the child's ability to construct the design, rather than difficulties with perceptual integration. Higher scores on Block Design than Block Design Multiple Choice (i.e., BD > BDMC) may occur for a number of reasons. Children with visual discrimination problems may fail to appreciate subtle differences among the distracters within the response options. There are no such competing visual stimuli in the BD subtest. Impulsive children may select a response without fully considering or scanning all response options.

Other cognitive functions, such as organization, planning, and other executive functions can impact performance on the WISC-IV. Executive functions are a domain of cognitive skills comprising many discrete abilities that influence higher-order reasoning. As measured by the WISC-IV Integrated subtest Elithorn Mazes (EM), executive functioning focuses narrowly on immediate planning, self-monitoring, and ability to inhibit impulsive responding. Thus, EM allows a preliminary evaluation of some of these important influences and correlates highly with other measures of executive functioning, even though it does not provide full construct coverage of the domain of executive functioning.

The child's performance on MR and BDMC may be compared directly to EM. EM < MR suggests better developed visual discrimination and reasoning abilities than spatial planning. Difficulties with motor control and processing speed may also account for this difference and need to be investigated directly. EM > MR suggests well-developed spatial planning abilities, visual–spatial sequencing, and execution; however, difficulties with detailed visual discrimination and reasoning may be present.

The BDMC–EM comparison enables clinicians to rule out deficits in basic visual identification and discrimination that may impact performance on Elithorn Mazes. EM < BDMC may indicate that visual–perceptual processes do not account for poor performance on EM but that poor spatial planning is affecting perform-ance. Visual scanning and processing speed may also account for this disparate performance and need to be evaluated further. EM > BDMC may indicate intact planning ability despite difficulties with visual discrimination and integration.

The child's approach to these tasks is equally important to informed interpre-tation. Qualitative scores found to be useful with the EM subtest include motor planning, motor imprecision, and backward errors. Motor imprecision errors on EM reflect a rule violation in which the child significantly deviates from the maze pathway perhaps due to poor graphomotor control. Poor graphomotor con-trol may be evident on other tasks such as coding and coding copy. If the child displays good graphomotor control elsewhere but many errors on EM, the errors likely reflect planning problems, difficulties negotiating the small tracks (motor precision problem), or inability to maintain the solution in working memory.

INTERPRETING THE WISC-IV WMI

Working memory is the ability to hold information in mind temporarily while performing some operation or manipulation with that information, or engaging in an interfering task, and then accurately reproducing the information or correctly acting on it. Working memory can be thought of as mental control involving rea-sonably higher-order tasks (rather than rote tasks), and it presumes attention and concentration. Thus, this index measures the ability to sustain attention, concen-trate, and exert mental control.

Flanagan & Kaufman (2004) classify Letter–Number Sequencing (LNS) and Digit Span Backwards (DSB) as measures of working memory – considered in the CHC model to be a narrow ability within the broad ability called short-term memory (p. 152). Short-term memory is defined as the ability to attend to and immediately recall temporally ordered elements in the correct order after a single presentation. They define working memory as the ability to apprehend and hold information in immediate awareness and to use it within a few seconds. Flanagan et al. consider Digit Span Forward (DSF) as a measure of short-term memory. They classify Arithmetic as part of the broad domain of fluid reasoning, and more narrowly as a measure of general sequential reasoning (deduction) – which is the ability to start with stated rules, premises, or conditions, and to engage in one or more steps to reach a solution to a novel problem. In addition, Arithmetic is considered to tap the domains of math achievement and quantitative reasoning within the CHC model.

However, classification of working memory as a "narrow-band CHC ability" belies its importance to intelligence and reflects an approach to understanding the nature of intelligence based on factor analysis alone while ignoring a large body of clinical research in neuropsychology. The work of Alan Baddeley is seminal to understanding the role of working memory in intelligence. He proposes a phonological loop and a visual–spatial sketchpad in which verbal and visual stimuli respectively are stored and refreshed, and a central executive that controls attention directed toward these sources. More recently, he proposed a fourth component of the model known as the episodic buffer. This buffer is assumed to be attentionally controlled by the central executive and to be accessible to conscious awareness. Baddeley regards the episodic buffer as a crucial feature of the capacity of working memory to act as a global work space that is accessed by conscious awareness. According to this model, when working memory requires information from long-term storage, it may be "downloaded" into the episodic buffer rather than simply activated within long-term memory (Baddeley, 2003).

Models of working memory are still being actively researched and refined, and the associated terminology will continue to evolve for some time. For purposes of this chapter we use the term "registration" to convey the process by which stimuli are taken in and maintained in immediate memory. Capacity for registering information in immediate memory can be measured by the length of the person's immediate forward memory span. We use the term "mental manipulation" to imply a transformation of information active in immediate memory, and involving higher-order cognitive resources. The precise point in this process at which working memory resources are invoked is debatable. These processes may be more of a continuum as the point at which one moves from passive registration of auditory stimuli to active strategies for maintenance is not always clear, as we will see next.

Digit Span (DS) and Letter–Number Sequencing (LNS) are excellent examples of tasks designed to tap working memory. As a case in point, DSF requires initial registration of the verbal stimuli – a prerequisite for mental manipulation of the stimuli. In some cases, DSF also requires auditory rehearsal to maintain the memory trace until the item presentation is concluded. To the extent that longer spans of digits require the application of a method for maintaining the trace, such as rehearsal or chunking, then some degree of mental manipulation of the stimuli is also involved. The point in the DSF item set at which this is required will vary as a function of age and ability level, and the response processes utilized by the examinee. In DSB, the student must hold a string of numbers in short-term memory store while reversing the given sequence, and then correctly reproduce the numbers in the new order. This is a clear example of mental manipulation. Yet, shorter spans of digits may tax working memory resources only marginally in older or brighter children. Again, the point at which these children substantially invoke working memory resources on DSB will vary by age and ability. Tables B.7 and B.8 of the *WISC-IV Administration and Scoring Manual* provide base rate comparisons for DSF and DSB by age.

The Arithmetic (AR) subtest is a more ecologically valid working memory task than DSB. We are frequently called upon to mentally calculate arithmetic problems in real-life situations. Some examples include, estimating driving time, halving a cake recipe, and changing US to Canadian dollars or Euros. The AR subtest assesses a complex set of cognitive skills and abilities, and a low score may have several appropriate interpretations depending on the clinical context. It may not be an accurate indication of working memory for students who have not learned grade-level skills related to arithmetic calculation and mathematical operations, or for students with a primary mathematical disability.

All three of these subtests tap only verbal short term and working memory, and not spatial or visual short term and working memory. Working memory does not involve only numbers. Other examples include writing the main points of a teacher's lecture in a notebook while continuing to attend to the lecture, or keeping a three part homework assignment in mind while recording the first two parts in an assignment pad, or keeping in mind the next points you want to make in a conversation while explaining your first point. Clearly, a serious deficit in working memory can have major implications in the academic life of a student, and create difficulties in daily life functioning as well as in many vocational settings.

Children with learning or attention disorders may be more likely to experience problems with working memory as suggested by significantly lower scores on this index (Wechsler, 1991, 2003). However, this must be demonstrated to be the case with an individual rather than being assumed to apply to all children with a particular diagnosis or being used as a diagnostic "marker" (see Kaufman, 1994a, b). Children with serious deficits in working memory are academically challenged, but not necessarily because of lower intelligence. A weakness in working memory may make the processing of complex information more time-consuming and tax the student's mental energies more quickly compared to other children of the same age, perhaps contributing to more frequent errors on a variety of learning tasks. Deficits in the executive function system of planning, organization, and the ability to shift cognitive sets should also be evaluated with these children using such clinical measures as the NEPSY-II and DKEFS. Examiners should also be alert to the social and behavioral consequences of these disorders and assess the level of parental support and emotional resiliency possessed by the child.

Individual differences in the capacity of working memory appear to have important consequences for children's ability to acquire knowledge and learn new skills. We review a number of studies in which working memory skills impact learning throughout the school years.

Reading disabilities can be characterized by marked difficulties in mastering skills including word recognition, spelling, and reading comprehension. Current evidence suggests that although verbal short-term memory is significantly associated with reading achievements over the early years of reading instruction, its role is as part of a general phonological processing construct related to reading development rather than representing a causal factor per se (Wagner et al., 1997; Wagner & Muse, 2006). In a 5-year longitudinal study of several hundred children who were followed from kindergarten through fourth grade, multiple measures of phonological awareness, verbal short-term memory, and rapid naming were administered (Wagner et al., 1997). A key finding was that at three different time periods, phonological awareness skills predicted individual differences in word-level reading, while verbal short-term memory skills did not. While studies such as these and others (e.g., Wagner et al., 1999; also Wagner et al., 1993, 1994) have found a high correlation between phonological awareness and short-term memory, why is it that only phonological awareness ability predict early reading skills? One explanation is that although the memory demands of phonological awareness tasks are similar to those of verbal memory tasks, letter knowledge and other aspects of lexical information play an important role in the performance of phonological awareness tasks (see Wagner & Muse, in press, for further discussion). Indeed phonological short-term memory tasks that draw on lexical knowledge, such as nonword repetition, have a similarly close relationship to vocabulary acquisition (e.g., Gathercole & Baddeley, 1989; Gathercole et al., 1992; Swanson et al., 2004).

It is well established that children with reading disabilities show significant and marked decrements on verbal working memory tasks relative to typically developing individuals (Siegel & Ryan, 1989; Swanson, 1994, 1999; Swanson et al., 1996). In typically developing samples of children, scores on working memory tasks predict reading achievement independently of measures of verbal short-term memory (e.g., Swanson & Howell, 2001; Swanson, 2003) and phonological awareness skills (e.g., Swanson & Beebe-Frankenberger, 2004). This dissociation in performance has been explained as the result of limited capacity for simultaneous processing and storage of information characteristic of working memory tasks, rather than a processing deficiency or specific problem with verbal short-term memory in poor readers (De Jong, 1998). It is important to note that studies have found that working memory skills of children with reading disabilities do not improve over time, indicating that a sustained deficit, rather than a developmental lag, best explains their memory impairment (e.g., Swanson & Sachse-Lee, 2001).

Associations between working memory and mathematical skills vary as a function of sample age as well as mathematical task. The age disparity in the contribution of working memory to mathematical skills is most pronounced with respect to verbal working memory tasks. For example, Bull and Scerif (2001) found a relationship between memory and math in 7-year olds (see also Gathercole & Pickering, 2000), but this association was no longer significant in an adolescent population (Reuhkala, 2001). One possibility is that verbal working memory plays a crucial role in mathematical performance when children are younger. However, as they get older, other factors such as number knowledge and strategies play a greater role (e.g., Thevenot & Oakhill, 2005). This view is supported by recent evidence that working memory is a reliable indicator of mathematical disabilities in the first year of formal schooling (e.g., Gersten et al., 2005).

There is growing evidence that mathematical deficits could result from poor working memory abilities. For example, low working memory scores have been found to be closely related to poor computational skills (Wilson & Swanson, 2001), and reliably differentiate children with mathematical deficits from same-age controls (e.g., Geary et al., 1999; Bull & Scerif, 2001). Weak verbal working memory skills are also characteristic of poor performance on arithmetic word problems (Swanson & Sachse-Lee, 2001). Common failures include impaired recall on both word and number-based working memory stimuli and increased intrusion errors (e.g., Passolunghi & Siegel, 2001). As with reading deficits, mathematical abilities do not improve substantially during the course of schooling, suggesting that such deficits are persistent and cannot be made up over time (e.g., Geary, 1993).

Visuo-spatial working memory is also closely linked with mathematical skills. It has been suggested that visuo-spatial working memory functions as a mental blackboard, supporting number representation, such as place value and alignment in columns, in counting, and arithmetic (Geary, 1990; McLean & Hitch, 1999; D'Amico & Guarnera, 2005). Children with poor visuo-spatial working memory skills have less room in their blackboard to keep in mind the relevant numerical information (e.g., Heathcote, 1994). Specific associations have been found between visuo-spatial working memory and encoding in visually presented problems (e.g., Logie et al., 1994), and in multi-digit operations (e.g., Heathcote, 1994). Visuo-spatial working memory skills also uniquely predict variability in performance in nonverbal problems (operands presented with blocks) in pre-school children (Rasmussen & Bisanz, 2005).

A key question regarding the relationship between working memory and learning disabilities is whether working memory is simply a proxy for IQ. Research suggests that working memory and reasoning (or general ability) are highly similar constructs that are highly correlated (Kyllonen & Christal, 1990). Yet, there is some evidence that working memory is dissociable from general abilities (e.g., Siegel, 1988; Cain et al., 2004), and may still explain individual differences in memory and scholastic attainment (Stothard & Hulme, 1992; Nation et al., 1999). Recent research has confirmed that the specificity of associations between working memory and attainment persist after differences in IQ have been statistically controlled in children with learning difficulties (Gathercole et al., 2006a, b; Alloway, 2007; see also Swanson & Saez, 2003, for a review). Further evidence that verbal working memory taps a unique domain of general ability is provided by reports of differences in working memory scores in children with reading comprehension problems and other learning disabilities even after verbal IQ has been accounted for (e.g., Siegel & Ryan, 1989; Cain et al., 2004).

Research on children with learning disabilities has focused primarily on the primary impairment by which the children are identified (e.g., reading, language, etc.). Any working memory deficits have been taken as secondary, associated characteristics. As a result, little is known about the consequences of low working memory capacity per se, independently of other associated learning difficulties. In particular, we do not know either what proportion of children with low working memory capacities has significant learning difficulties or their behavioral characteristics.

To examine this situation, Alloway et al. (2007a) recently identified, via routine screening, a large sample of children aged 5–6 years and 9–10 years with very low working memory scores. Over 3,000 children were screened on two standardized tests of verbal working memory from the Automated Working Memory Assessment (AWMA; Alloway, 2007) and approximately 300 children were identified as having poor working memory skills (see Alloway et al., 2007b for convergence between AWMA and WISC-IV WMI scores). Selected children each completed a battery of standardized assessments of working memory, language, IQ, reading and mathematics abilities.

A key characteristic of these children was their poor academic progress. About two-thirds of them performed poorly in the two key areas of learning assessed in the study, reading, and mathematics. In one-third of the sample the severity of their learning problems was reflected in formal recognition by their schools that they required additional classroom support. This provides the most substantial evidence to date that low working memory skills constitute a high risk factor for educational underachievement for school children across the primary school years. These findings are entirely consistent with findings of subsequently poor academic progress in children with low memory skills at school entry (Gathercole et al., 2003; Alloway et al., 2005), and of substantial working memory problems for the majority of children identified on the basis of learning disabilities (e.g., Swanson & Beebe-Frankenberger, 2004; Gathercole et al., 2006a, b), including language impairments (Archibald & Gathercole, 2006a).

INTERPRETING THE WISC-IV PSI

The PSI is composed of subtests measuring the speed of mental and graphomotor processing. On the surface, the Coding (CD), Symbol Search (SS), and Cancellation (CA) subtests are simple visual scanning and tracking tasks. A direct test of speed and accuracy, the CD subtest assesses ability in quickly and correctly scanning and sequencing simple visual information. Performance on this subtest also may be influenced by short-term visual memory, attention, or visual-motor coordination. The SS subtest requires the student to inspect several sets of symbols and indicate if special target symbols appeared in each set. It is also a direct test of speed and accuracy and assesses scanning speed and sequential tracking of simple visual information. Performance on this subtest may be influenced by visual discrimination and visual-motor coordination. The supplemental CA subtest also requires these skills, and a minor degree of decision-making. Examinees must decide if each stimulus is a member of the target class of stimuli (e.g., animals). While the decisions are generally simple, the psychologist must take care not to underestimate the cognitive load for the youngest children, especially those without preschool experience, or who are developmentally delayed.

Processing Speed has been described as the ability to fluently and automatically perform cognitive tasks, especially when under pressure to maintain focused attention and concentration. "Attentive speediness" has been said to encapsulate the essence of processing speed which is measured typically by fixed-interval, timed tasks that require little in the way of complex thinking or mental processing (McGrew & Flanagan, 1998; Flanagan & Kaufman, 2004). Processing Speed is a broad ability in the CHC model. Consensus opinion determined that CD measures Rate-of-Test-Taking. A narrow domain under Processing Speed in the CHC model, rate-of-test-taking is defined as the ability to rapidly perform tests that are relatively easy or that require very simple decisions. Consensus opinion determined that SS measures Rate-of-Test-Taking (R9) and Perceptual Speed: the ability to rapidly search for and compare visual symbols presented side by side or separately in a visual field (McGrew & Flanagan, 1998). CD and SS on the WISC-IV were evaluated to measure the same abilities (Flanagan & Mascolo, 2005).

Classification of these tasks according to CHC theory is based on a description of the external behaviors (e.g., how fast does one take a test) and do not reflect the neuro-cognitive processes underlying these behaviors or the relation of those processes to general intellectual ability. In this regard, as with the classification of working memory as a narrow ability discussed above, the CHC classification scheme may not well serve a brain-based understanding of the structure of intelligence. This point is elaborated in the remainder of this section and the next section.

Although the PSI subtests are easy visual scanning tasks for most children, it is our view that it would be a mistake to think of the PSI as a measure of simple clerical functions that influence one's score on an intelligence test but are not integrally related to intelligence. While PSI is traditionally listed last in any representation of the WISC-III or WISC-IV factor structure, it actually emerges third in most factor analyses and accounts for greater variance in intelligence than does the working memory factor. Further, there is consistent evidence that both simple and choice reaction time correlate about .20 or slightly higher with scores from intelligence tests. Inspection time (hypothesized by some to be a measure of the rate that information is processed) correlates about .40 with intelligence test scores (see Deary, 2001; Deary & Stough, 1996). Performance on the PSI is an indication of the rapidity with which a student can process simple or routine information without making errors. Many learning tasks involve a combination of routine information processing (such as reading) and complex information processing (such as reasoning). A weakness in the speed of processing routine information may make the task of comprehending novel information more time-consuming and difficult. A weakness in simple visual scanning and tracking may leave a child less time and mental energy for the complex task of understanding new material. In this way, these lower-order processing abilities are related to higher-order cognitive functioning.

The pattern of lower processing speed abilities than reasoning abilities is more common among students who are experiencing academic difficulties in the classroom than among those who are not (Wechsler, 1991, 2003). Research studies with the WISC-III have also indicated that children with ADHD earn their lowest scores on the PSI (Prifitera & Dersh, 1993; Schwean et al., 1993). Processing Speed, as measured by tests of perceptual speed, shows a strong and consistent relationship with the development of reading and math achievement, particularly during the elementary school years (Flanagan & Mascolo, 2005). Elementary school children are learning the skills in reading and math, and developing speed and automaticity in their use. Older school children use these basic academic skills with automaticity, while integrating them with more complex tasks, like problem solving, subject-focused writing, and complex reading.

Lacking direct research, we hypothesized that children with processing speed deficits may learn less material in the same amount of time, or take longer to learn the same amount of material compared to those without processing speed deficits. These children may also mentally tire more easily because of the additional cognitive effort required to perform routine tasks. In turn, this could lead to more frequent errors, less time spent studying, and possible expressions of frustration. Conversely, a strength in the speed of processing information may facilitate the acquisition of new information.

THE INTERACTION OF WORKING MEMORY AND PROCESSING SPEED

The Working Memory and Processing Speed subtests generally have lower "g" loadings than the Verbal Comprehension and Perceptual Reasoning subtests. In considering this, keep in mind that "g" is more properly referred to as "psychometric g" because it can only be assessed in relation to the mix of tasks included in the analysis. The concept of pure "g" can never be assessed for a variety of technical reasons, but most importantly because intelligence and environment are inexorably linked. While the "g" loadings for these subtests are lower, they represent abilities that play a critical role in overall intellectual functioning including the acquisition of new learning and the ability to utilize encoded (crystallized) knowledge to solve new problems. Thus, Working Memory and Processing Speed may be central to Wechlser's definition of intelligence as the ability to learn and adapt to a changing environment. From the beginning, his tests have included tasks that tap these abilities (Digit Span, Coding, and Arithmetic), although the terminology has changed over time as understanding of the underlying constructs continues to evolve.

The evidence in support of Working Memory and Processing Speed is increasingly convincing. There are large and obvious age-related trends in processing speed that are accompanied by age-related changes in the number of transient connections to the central nervous system and increases in myelination. Several investigators have found that measures of infant processing speed predict later IQ scores (e.g., Dougherty & Haith, 1997). WISC-IV PSI scores have been shown to be potentially sensitive to neurological disorders such as epilepsy (Wechsler, 1991). In samples of students with learning disabilities and attention deficit, both PSI and WMI were found to be lower compared to their VCI and PRI scores, as well as compared with the normal population (Prifitera & Dersh, 1993; Schwean et al. 1993).

Of clinical relevance for school psychologists and specialists is the finding that the WMI contributes the second largest amount of variance, after VCI, to the prediction of reading, writing, and mathematics scores on the WIAT and other measures of achievement (Konold, 1999; Hale et al., 2001). High correlations between working memory and reading comprehension have been replicated numerous times (see Daneman & Merikle, 1996). Similar findings have been observed for a range of variables important to academic functioning in school including spelling (Ormrod & Cochran, 1988), the acquisition of logic (Kyllonen & Stephens, 1990), note taking (Kiewra & Benton, 1988), and following directions (Engle, et al., 1991). Generally, the magnitude of these correlations is near .50 (Baddeley, 2003), suggesting a moderate relationship between working memory and various academic outcomes. Kyllonen & Christal (1990) reported high correlations between these working memory research tasks and traditional measures of intelligence believed to tap reasoning ability. This study also found that high scores on these reasoning tasks were differentially sensitive to the extent of previous knowledge held by the subject, whereas successful performance on pure working memory tasks was more dependent on the person's ability to process information rapidly. The interrelatedness between working memory, reasoning, prior knowledge, and processing speed led Kyllonen & Christal (1990) to conclude that reasoning ability is little more than working memory capacity. In this regard, Baddeley's (2003) proposal for an episodic buffer in which crystallized knowledge is downloaded from long-term storage for further manipulation is rather intriguing for the study of reasoning ability. These models could continue to evolve with future research. This area of study is clearly central to the development of a more neuropsychologically informed understanding of the structure of intelligence.

With their integral contributions to human cognitive functioning, it is not surprising that speed of information processing and immediate memory are included as components of most psychometric models of intelligence such as the Gf-Gc theory (Carroll, 1993). Working memory involves the manipulation of information in temporary storage and, as such, is very closely related to reasoning. Working memory is much more complex than the temporary storage and retrieval of auditory or visual information. It should not be confused with many of the short-term memory measures included in the Gf–Gc model.

Some factor analytically derived models of intelligence suggest that each factor is a unique source of variance, contributing independently to general intelligence. However, this would not seem to be the case, from two perspectives. First a "g" factor tends to emerge whenever a number of cognitively complex variables are factor analyzed (Carroll, 1993). The basis for the FSIQ on the WISC-IV is grounded in the fact that the four index scores, while tapping variance that is unique or exclusive to each, are all positively correlated. Further, the subtests are all more or less positively correlated (while also demonstrating subtest specificity), with those subtests defining a particular factor correlating even more highly.

Secondly, clinical research in developmental cognitive neuropsychology suggests a more dynamic picture, one that practicing psychologists attempt to construct in their every day clinical assessment practice. Fry and Hale (1996) administered measures of processing speed, working memory, and fluid intelligence to children and adolescents between 7 and 19 years of age. Age-related increases in speed of processing were associated with increases in working memory capacity, which, in turn, were associated with higher scores on measures of fluid reasoning. This study suggests that, as children develop normally, more rapid processing of information results in more effective use of working memory space, which enhances performance on many reasoning tasks. Kail (2000) concluded that:

> Processing speed is not simply one of many different independent factors that contribute to intelligence; instead processing speed is thought to be linked causally to other elements of intelligence.

This dynamic model of cognitive information processing suggests that language and reading impairments which interfere with the rapid processing of information may burden the working memory structures, and reduce the student's capacity for comprehension and new learning. This area is ripe for research.

INTERPRETING THE WISC-IV COMPOSITE SCORES

The GAI

The General Ability Index (GAI) is a "composite" index score that summarizes performance on the VCI and PRI into a single number. These two indexes contain the more highly "g" loaded subtests within WISC-IV that tend to correlate best with achievement. The WISC-IV GAI excludes the contributions of the WMI and PSI to intelligence which will later be discussed as an estimate of Cognitive Proficiency. Thus, GAI and FSIQ can lead to different impressions of children's overall ability when there is variability across the four indexes. Therefore, GAI should not be considered as a substitute for FSIQ. Table 1.4 contains the GAI

TABLE 1.4   GAI Equivalents of Sums of Scaled Scores

Sum of scaled scores	GAI	Percentile rank	Confidence level 90%	Confidence level 95%	Sum of scaled scores	GAI	Percentile rank	Confidence level 90%	Confidence level 95%
6	40	<0.1	38–47	37–48	38	77	6	73–83	72–84
7	40	<0.1	38–47	37–48	39	78	7	74–84	73–85
8	40	<0.1	38–47	37–48	40	79	8	75–85	74–85
9	40	<0.1	38–47	37–48	41	81	10	77–86	76–87
10	40	<0.1	38–47	37–48	42	82	12	78–87	77–88
11	40	<0.1	38–47	37–48	43	83	13	79–88	78–89
12	41	<0.1	39–48	38–49	44	84	14	80–89	79–90
13	42	<0.1	40–49	39–50	45	85	16	81–90	80–91
14	43	<0.1	41–50	40–51	46	86	18	82–91	81–92
15	44	<0.1	42–51	41–52	47	87	19	83–92	82–93
16	45	<0.1	42–52	42–53	48	88	21	84–93	83–94
17	46	<0.1	43–53	43–54	49	89	23	85–94	84–95
18	47	<0.1	44–54	43–55	50	90	25	86–95	85–96
19	49	<0.1	46–56	45–57	51	91	27	87–96	86–97
20	51	0.1	48–58	47–59	52	92	30	88–97	87–98
21	52	0.1	49–59	48–60	53	93	32	89–98	88–99
22	53	0.1	50–60	49–61	54	94	34	90–99	89–100
23	55	0.1	52–62	51–62	55	95	37	90–100	90–101
24	57	0.2	54–63	53–64	56	96	39	91–101	91–102
25	58	0.3	55–64	54–65	57	97	42	92–102	91–103
26	59	0.3	56–65	55–66	58	98	45	93–103	92–104
27	61	0.5	58–67	57–68	59	99	47	94–104	93–105
28	63	1	60–69	59–70	60	100	50	95–105	94–106
29	64	1	61–70	60–71	61	101	53	96–106	95–107
30	65	1	62–71	61–72	62	102	55	97–107	96–108
31	67	1	64–73	63–74	63	103	58	98–108	97–109
32	69	2	66–75	65–76	64	104	61	99–109	98–109
33	70	2	66–76	66–77	65	105	63	100–110	99–110
34	71	3	67–77	67–78	66	106	66	101–110	100–111
35	73	4	69–79	68–80	67	107	68	102–111	101–112
36	74	4	70–80	69–81	68	108	70	103–112	102–113
37	75	5	71–81	70–82	69	110	75	105–114	104–115

(continues)

TABLE 1.4   (*continued*)

Sum of scaled scores	GAI	Percentile rank	Confidence level 90%	Confidence level 95%	Sum of scaled scores	GAI	Percentile rank	Confidence level 90%	Confidence level 95%
70	111	77	106–115	105–116	93	140	99.6	134–143	133–144
71	112	79	107–116	106–117	94	142	99.7	136–145	135–146
72	113	81	108–117	107–118	95	143	99.8	137–146	136–147
73	115	84	110–119	109–120	96	144	99.8	138–147	137–148
74	116	86	111–120	110–121	97	146	99.9	139–149	139–150
75	117	87	112–121	111–122	98	147	99.9	140–150	139–151
76	119	90	114–123	113–124	99	148	99.9	141–151	140–152
77	120	91	114–124	114–125	100	150	>99.9	143–153	142–154
78	121	92	115–125	115–126	101	151	>99.9	144–154	143–155
79	122	93	116–126	115–127	102	153	>99.9	146–156	145–157
80	123	94	117–127	116–128	103	154	>99.9	147–157	146–157
81	124	95	118–128	117–129	104	155	>99.9	148–158	147–158
82	126	96	120–130	119–131	105	156	>99.9	149–158	148–159
83	127	96	121–131	120–132	106	157	>99.9	150–159	149–160
84	128	97	122–132	121–133	107	158	>99.9	151–160	150–161
85	129	97	123–133	122–133	108	159	>99.9	152–161	151–162
86	130	98	124–134	123–134	109	160	>99.9	153–162	152–163
87	132	98	126–135	125–136	110	160	>99.9	153–162	152–163
88	133	99	127–136	126–137	111	160	>99.9	153–162	152–163
89	135	99	129–138	128–139	112	160	>99.9	153–162	152–163
90	136	99	130–139	129–140	113	160	>99.9	153–162	152–163
91	138	99	132–141	131–142	114	160	>99.9	153–162	152–163
92	139	99.5	133–142	132–143					

norms tables for use with WISC-IV based on the US standardization data (Canadian users should refer to the equivalent tables available on the PsychCorp website in Canada available at http://www.harcourtassessment.com/NR/rdonlyres/ 9C577ACC-75C0-4F2F-BA3E-F7B94CF4175F/0/WISCIV_41_Re1.pdf). To use this table, add the subtest scaled scores for the three subtests that enter the VCI and the three subtests that enter the PRI. Use this sum of scaled scores to look up the GAI score.

The GAI was developed originally for use in ability–achievement discrepancy analyses. It was developed because many learning disabled students exhibit cognitive processing deficits in working memory and processing speed concomitant with their learning disabilities. Depressed performance on WM and PS tasks

TABLE 1.5 Differences Between WISC-IV GAI Scores and WIAT-II Subtest and Composite Scores Required for Statistical Significance (Critical Values): Simple-Difference and Predicted-Difference Methods by Age-Band

Subtest/ Composite	Significance level	Ages 6–11		Ages 12–16	
		Simple-difference GAI	Predicted-difference GAI	Simple-difference GAI	Predicted-difference GAI
Word Reading	.05	7.20	4.87	8.32	6.92
	.01	9.48	6.41	10.95	9.11
Numerical Operations	.05	13.15	12.01	9.75	8.59
	.01	17.31	15.81	12.84	11.31
Reading Comprehension	.05	8.32	6.52	8.82	7.52
	.01	10.95	8.59	11.61	9.90
Spelling	.05	9.75	8.24	9.75	8.38
	.01	12.84	10.85	12.84	11.03
Pseudoword Decoding	.05	7.78	5.42	7.78	5.91
	.01	10.24	7.14	10.24	7.78
Math Reasoning	.05	10.18	8.91	9.75	8.80
	.01	13.41	11.72	12.84	11.58
Written Expression	.05	12.47	11.18	12.47	11.59
	.01	16.42	14.72	16.42	15.25
Listening Comprehension	.05	13.79	12.77	14.10	13.41
	.01	18.15	16.81	18.56	17.65
Oral Expression	.05	11.76	10.21	12.82	11.73
	.01	15.48	13.44	16.87	15.44
Reading	.05	7.20	5.03	7.20	5.65
	.01	9.48	6.62	9.48	7.43
Math	.05	10.18	8.91	8.32	7.18
	.01	13.41	11.72	10.95	9.45
Written Language	.05	9.75	8.24	11.76	10.82
	.01	12.84	10.85	15.48	14.24
Oral Language	.05	11.00	9.66	9.75	8.72
	.01	14.48	12.72	12.84	11.48
Total	.05	7.78	6.25	7.20	5.93
	.01	10.24	8.23	9.48	7.81

lowers the FSIQ for many learning disabled children, making a large discrepancy between ability and achievement less likely, and often resulting in denial of needed special education services. In this situation, the GAI may be used in the AAD analysis in order to aid in the determination of eligibility for special education. (The section "Tables to compare WISC-IV index scores against overall means" – Tables 1.5–1.8 provide the data necessary to utilize the GAI in AAD analyses.) Readers interested in professional issues surrounding use of AAD analyses in LD assessments are referred to the chapter by James B. Hale in this volume.

Other uses for the GAI have since been identified. For example, GAI may be an appropriate estimate of overall ability when physical or sensory disorders invalidate performance on the working memory or processing speed tasks, or both. Another appropriate use is in estimating the pre-injury cognitive status and memory abilities of children with TBI. This is because TBI is known to impair processing speed and short-term memory more than verbal knowledge and some perceptual abilities. However, better methodologies for estimating pre-injury ability presently exist based on pseudoword reading tasks combined with demographic variables to estimate pre-injury ability (see *WAIS-III/WMS-III Technical Manual*).

TABLE 1.6   Differences Between Predicted and Obtained WIAT-II Subtest and Composite Scores for Various Percentages of the Theoretical Normal Distribution (Base Rates): Simple-Difference Method Using WISC-IV GAI

Subtest/Composite	Percentage of theoretical normal distribution (base rates)								
	25	20	15	10	5	4	3	2	1
Word Reading	8	10	12	14	18	19	21	23	26
Numerical Operations	9	11	13	16	21	22	23	26	29
Reading Comprehension	8	9	11	14	18	19	20	22	25
Spelling	8	10	13	16	20	21	23	25	28
Pseudoword Decoding	10	12	14	18	23	24	26	28	32
Math Reasoning	8	9	11	14	18	19	20	22	25
Written Expression	9	11	13	16	21	22	24	26	29
Listening Comprehension	7	8	10	13	16	17	18	20	23
Oral Expression	10	12	15	19	24	25	27	29	33
Reading	7	9	11	14	17	18	20	21	24
Mathematics	8	9	11	14	18	19	20	22	25
Written Language	8	10	12	15	19	20	22	24	27
Oral Language	7	9	11	14	17	18	20	21	24
Total	6	7	9	11	14	15	16	17	20

Note: Percentages represent the proportions of the sample who obtained WIAT-II scores lower than their WISC-IV GAI scores by the specified amount or more.

TABLE 1.7 WIAT-II Subtest and Composite Scores Predicted from WISC-IV GAI Scores

WISC-IV GAI	WIAT-II														WISC-IV GAI
	Subtest scores									Composite scores					
	WR	NO	RC	SP	PD	MR	WE	LC	OE	RD	MA	WL	OL	TA	
40	56	60	55	59	64	54	60	52	66	54	55	57	54	49	40
41	56	60	56	59	65	55	61	53	67	55	56	58	55	50	41
42	57	61	57	60	65	56	62	54	68	55	57	58	55	51	42
43	58	62	57	61	66	57	62	54	68	56	57	59	56	52	43
44	59	62	58	61	66	57	63	55	69	57	58	60	57	52	44
45	59	63	59	62	67	58	64	56	69	58	59	60	58	53	45
46	60	64	60	63	68	59	64	57	70	58	60	61	58	54	46
47	61	64	60	63	68	60	65	58	70	59	60	62	59	55	47
48	62	65	61	64	69	60	66	58	71	60	61	63	60	56	48
49	62	66	62	65	69	61	66	59	71	61	62	63	61	57	49
50	63	67	63	66	70	62	67	60	72	62	63	64	62	58	50
51	64	67	63	66	71	63	68	61	73	62	63	65	62	58	51
52	64	68	64	67	71	64	68	62	73	63	64	65	63	59	52
53	65	69	65	68	72	64	69	62	74	64	65	66	64	60	53
54	66	69	66	68	72	65	70	63	74	65	66	67	65	61	54
55	67	70	66	69	73	66	70	64	75	65	66	68	65	62	55
56	67	71	67	70	74	67	71	65	75	66	67	68	66	63	56
57	68	71	68	70	74	67	72	66	76	67	68	69	67	63	57
58	69	72	69	71	75	68	72	66	76	68	69	70	68	64	58
59	70	73	69	72	75	69	73	67	77	68	69	70	68	65	59
60	70	73	70	72	76	70	74	68	78	69	70	71	69	66	60
61	71	74	71	73	77	70	74	69	78	70	71	72	70	67	61
62	72	75	72	74	77	71	75	70	79	71	72	73	71	68	62
63	73	75	72	74	78	72	76	70	79	72	72	73	72	69	63
64	73	76	73	75	78	73	76	71	80	72	73	74	72	69	64
65	74	77	74	76	79	73	77	72	80	73	74	75	73	70	65
66	75	77	75	77	80	74	78	73	81	74	75	76	74	71	66
67	76	78	75	77	80	75	78	74	82	75	75	76	75	72	67
68	76	79	76	78	81	76	79	74	82	75	76	77	75	73	68
69	77	79	77	79	81	76	80	75	83	76	77	78	76	74	69
70	78	80	78	79	82	77	80	76	83	77	78	78	77	75	70
71	79	81	78	80	83	78	81	77	84	78	78	79	78	75	71

(continues)

TABLE 1.7 (*continued*)

WISC-IV GAI	WIAT-II														WISC-IV GAI
	Subtest scores									Composite scores					
	WR	NO	RC	SP	PD	MR	WE	LC	OE	RD	MA	WL	OL	TA	
72	79	81	79	81	83	79	82	78	84	78	79	80	78	76	72
73	80	82	80	81	84	79	82	78	85	79	80	81	79	77	73
74	81	83	81	82	84	80	83	79	85	80	81	81	80	78	74
75	82	83	81	83	85	81	84	80	86	81	81	82	81	79	75
76	82	84	82	83	86	82	84	81	87	82	82	83	82	80	76
77	83	85	83	84	86	83	85	82	87	82	83	83	82	80	77
78	84	85	84	85	87	83	85	82	88	83	84	84	83	81	78
79	84	86	84	86	87	84	86	83	88	84	84	85	84	82	79
80	85	87	85	86	88	85	87	84	89	85	85	86	85	83	80
81	86	87	86	87	89	86	87	85	89	85	86	86	85	84	81
82	87	88	87	88	89	86	88	86	90	86	87	87	86	85	82
83	87	89	87	88	90	87	89	86	90	87	87	88	87	86	83
84	88	89	88	89	90	88	89	87	91	88	88	88	88	86	84
85	89	90	89	90	91	89	90	88	92	88	89	89	88	87	85
86	90	91	90	90	92	89	91	89	92	89	90	90	89	88	86
87	90	91	90	91	92	90	91	90	93	90	90	91	90	89	87
88	91	92	91	92	93	91	92	90	93	91	91	91	91	90	88
89	92	93	92	92	93	92	93	91	94	92	92	92	92	91	89
90	93	93	93	93	94	92	93	92	94	92	93	93	92	92	90
91	93	94	93	94	95	93	94	93	95	93	93	94	93	92	91
92	94	95	94	94	95	94	95	94	96	94	94	94	94	93	92
93	95	95	95	95	96	95	95	94	96	95	95	95	95	94	93
94	96	96	96	96	96	95	96	95	97	95	96	96	95	95	94
95	96	97	96	97	97	96	97	96	97	96	96	96	96	96	95
96	97	97	97	97	98	97	97	97	98	97	97	97	97	97	96
97	98	98	98	98	98	98	98	98	98	98	98	98	98	97	97
98	99	99	99	99	99	98	99	98	99	98	99	99	98	98	98
99	99	99	99	99	99	99	99	99	99	99	99	99	99	99	99
100	100	100	100	100	100	100	100	100	100	100	100	100	100	100	100
101	101	101	101	101	101	101	101	101	101	101	101	101	101	101	101
102	101	101	102	101	101	102	101	102	101	102	102	101	102	102	102
103	102	102	102	102	102	102	102	102	102	102	102	102	102	103	103

(*continues*)

TABLE 1.7   (*continued*)

WISC-IV GAI	WR	NO	RC	SP	PD	MR	WE	LC	OE	RD	MA	WL	OL	TA	WISC-IV GAI
				WIAT-II											
			Subtest scores								Composite scores				
104	103	103	103	103	102	103	103	103	102	103	103	103	103	103	104
105	104	103	104	103	103	104	103	104	103	104	104	104	104	104	105
106	104	104	105	104	104	105	104	105	103	105	105	104	105	105	106
107	105	105	105	105	104	105	105	106	104	105	105	105	105	106	107
108	106	105	106	106	105	106	105	106	104	106	106	106	106	107	108
109	107	106	107	106	105	107	106	107	105	107	107	106	107	108	109
110	107	107	108	107	106	108	107	108	106	108	108	107	108	109	110
111	108	107	108	108	107	108	107	109	106	108	108	108	108	109	111
112	109	108	109	108	107	109	108	110	107	109	109	109	109	110	112
113	110	109	110	109	108	110	109	110	107	110	110	109	110	111	113
114	110	109	111	110	108	111	109	111	108	111	111	110	111	112	114
115	111	110	111	110	109	111	110	112	108	112	111	111	112	113	115
116	112	111	112	111	110	112	111	113	109	112	112	112	112	114	116
117	113	111	113	112	110	113	111	114	110	113	113	112	113	114	117
118	113	112	114	112	111	114	112	114	110	114	114	113	114	115	118
119	114	113	114	113	111	114	113	115	111	115	114	114	115	116	119
120	115	113	115	114	112	115	113	116	111	115	115	114	115	117	120
121	116	114	116	114	113	116	114	117	112	116	116	115	116	118	121
122	116	115	117	115	113	117	115	118	112	117	117	116	117	119	122
123	117	115	117	116	114	117	115	118	113	118	117	117	118	120	123
124	118	116	118	117	114	118	116	119	113	118	118	117	118	120	124
125	119	117	119	117	115	119	117	120	114	119	119	118	119	121	125
126	119	117	120	118	116	120	117	121	115	120	120	119	120	122	126
127	120	118	120	119	116	121	118	122	115	121	120	119	121	123	127
128	121	119	121	119	117	121	118	122	116	122	121	120	122	124	128
129	121	119	122	120	117	122	119	123	116	122	122	121	122	125	129
130	122	120	123	121	118	123	120	124	117	123	123	122	123	126	130
131	123	121	123	121	119	124	120	125	117	124	123	122	124	126	131
132	124	121	124	122	119	124	121	126	118	125	124	123	125	127	132
133	124	122	125	123	120	125	122	126	118	125	125	124	125	128	133
134	125	123	126	123	120	126	122	127	119	126	126	124	126	129	134

(*continues*)

TABLE 1.7 *(continued)*

	WIAT-II														
	Subtest scores									Composite scores					
WISC-IV GAI	WR	NO	RC	SP	PD	MR	WE	LC	OE	RD	MA	WL	OL	TA	WISC-IV GAI
135	126	123	126	124	121	127	123	128	120	127	126	125	127	130	135
136	127	124	127	125	122	127	124	129	120	128	127	126	128	131	136
137	127	125	128	126	122	128	124	130	121	128	128	127	128	131	137
138	128	125	129	126	123	129	125	130	121	129	129	127	129	132	138
139	129	126	129	127	123	130	126	131	122	130	129	128	130	133	139
140	130	127	130	128	124	130	126	132	122	131	130	129	131	134	140
141	130	127	131	128	125	131	127	133	123	132	131	130	132	135	141
142	131	128	132	129	125	132	128	134	124	132	132	130	132	136	142
143	132	129	132	130	126	133	128	134	124	133	132	131	133	137	143
144	133	129	133	130	126	133	129	135	125	134	133	132	134	137	144
145	133	130	134	131	127	134	130	136	125	135	134	132	135	138	145
146	134	131	135	132	128	135	130	137	126	135	135	133	135	139	146
147	135	131	135	132	128	136	131	138	126	136	135	134	136	140	147
148	136	132	136	133	129	136	132	138	127	137	136	135	137	141	148
149	136	133	137	134	129	137	132	139	127	138	137	135	138	142	149
150	137	134	138	135	130	138	133	140	128	139	138	136	139	143	150
151	138	134	138	135	131	139	134	141	129	139	138	137	139	143	151
152	138	135	139	136	131	140	134	142	129	140	139	137	140	144	152
153	139	136	140	137	132	140	135	142	130	141	140	138	141	145	153
154	140	136	141	137	132	141	136	143	130	142	141	139	142	146	154
155	141	137	141	138	133	142	136	144	131	142	141	140	142	147	155
156	141	138	142	139	134	143	137	145	131	143	142	140	143	148	156
157	142	138	143	139	134	143	138	146	132	144	143	141	144	148	157
158	143	139	144	140	135	144	138	146	132	145	144	142	145	149	158
159	144	140	144	141	135	145	139	147	133	145	144	142	145	150	159
160	144	140	145	141	136	146	140	148	134	146	145	143	146	151	160

WR = Word Reading; NO = Numerical Operations; RC = Reading Comp; SP = Spelling;
PD = Pseudoword Decoding; MR = Mathematics Reasoning; WE = Written Expression;
LC = Listening Comp; OE = Oral Expression; RD = Reading; MA = Mathematics; WL = Written
Language; OL = Oral Language; TA = Total Achievement.

TABLE 1.8   Differences Between Predicted and Obtained WIAT-II Subtest and Composite Scores for Various Percentages of the Theoretical Normal Distribution (Base Rates): Predicted-Difference Method Using WISC-IV GAI

Subtest/Composite	Percentage of theoretical normal distribution (base rates)								
	25	20	15	10	5	4	3	2	1
Word Reading	7	9	11	13	17	18	19	21	24
Numerical Operations	8	10	12	15	19	20	21	23	26
Reading Comprehension	7	9	11	13	17	18	19	21	24
Spelling	8	10	12	14	18	20	21	23	26
Pseudoword Decoding	9	11	13	16	20	22	23	25	28
Math Reasoning	7	9	11	13	17	18	19	21	23
Written Expression	8	10	12	15	19	20	22	24	27
Listening Comprehension	7	8	10	12	15	16	17	19	21
Oral Expression	9	11	13	16	21	22	24	26	29
Reading	7	9	10	13	16	17	19	20	23
Mathematics	7	9	11	13	17	18	19	21	24
Written Language	8	9	11	14	18	19	20	22	25
Oral Language	7	9	10	13	16	17	19	20	23
Total	6	7	9	11	13	14	15	17	19

Note: Percentages in Table 1.8 represent the proportions of the sample who obtained WIAT-II scores lower than their WISC-IV GAI scores by the specified amount or more.

In the first edition of this book we suggested that some practitioners may prefer the GAI as an alternative way of summarizing overall ability. This suggestion has led to an increasing number of psychological evaluations in which the GAI is reported as a better estimate of overall ability than FSIQ whenever the WMI or PSI score are significantly lower than the VCI or PRI scores. This is not what we intended and can be a very problematic practice. We intended GAI to be used only when there are sound clinical reasons to exclude WMI and PSI, such as those reasons mentioned above. We believe that working memory and processing speed are essential components of overall intelligence, and discarding them simply because they are low will result in an unrealistically high estimate of intelligence for these children.

The CPI

The Cognitive Proficiency Index (CPI) summarizes performance on the Working Memory and Processing Speed indices of the WISC-IV into a single score. Creating a new index by combining WMI and PSI was first suggested by

Dumont & Willis (2001), and subsequently extended by Weiss et al. (2006a, b). The CPI represents a set of functions whose common element is the proficiency with which one processes certain types of cognitive information. Proficient processing – through quick visual speed and good mental control – facilitates fluid reasoning and the acquisition of new material by reducing the cognitive demands of novel or higher-order tasks (Weiss et al., 2006a, b). More simply, efficient cognitive processing facilitates learning and problem-solving by "freeing up" cognitive resources for more advanced, higher level skills.

The WISC-IV CPI excludes the contributions of Verbal Comprehension and Perceptual Reasoning to intelligence. Thus, CPI and GAI provide different views into children's cognitive abilities when there is variability across the four indexes. Both views are sometimes necessary to form a complete picture of the child's individual set of strengths and weaknesses that is not distorted by averaging diverse abilities into a single overall score.

Norms tables for CPI are provided in Table 1.9. To use this table, add the subtest scaled scores for the two subtests that enter the WMI and the two subtests that enter the PSI to obtain the sum of scaled scores. Locate this sum of scaled scores in the table, and read across the row to obtain the CPI score.

Table 1.10 shows the base rates of GAI/CPI differences by direction. In general, differences that occur in 10% or less of the population should be considered rare and interpretable. Before interpreting GAI, CPI, or the difference between the two indexes, however, practitioners should ensure that there are not large differences between VCI and PRI, or between WMI and PSI. In such instances, the VCI, PRI, WMI, and PSI scores should be interpreted individually.

Comparing GAI and CPI to each other and to school achievement may be useful in the identification of psychological processing deficits in children with certain learning disabilities. Weiss, et al. (2006a, b) examined the prevalence of large CPI > GAI profiles occurring simultaneously with large Achievement > GAI profiles. Two (2) percent of the nonclinical sample met both criteria. That is, only 2% of normal children obtained a large CPI > GAI difference in combination with a large Achievement > GAI difference. The frequency of these dual criteria was examined in the reading disorder, writing disorder, and combined reading and writing disorder samples, described in the *WISC-IV Technical and Interpretive Manual*. The percentage of students receiving LD services that met both criteria ranged between 45% and 50% in the various reading and writing disorder samples. These findings suggest that these combined criteria may hold some promise in the identification of psychological processing disorders which underlie some types of learning disabilities.

Results of this study are consistent with recent research which supports the practice of going beyond FSIQ to examine a pattern of cognitive strengths and weaknesses among the four WISC-IV index scores in psychoeducational evaluations. Konold (1999) found that when the four index scores were entered simultaneously into a regression equation predicting academic achievement, the resulting variance explained was larger than that for FSIQ in all academic

TABLE 1.9   CPI Equivalents of Sums of Scales Scores

Sum of scaled scores	CPI	Confidence interval 90% CI	95% CI	Percentile rank	Sum of scaled scores	CPI	Confidence interval 90% CI	95% CI	Percentile rank
4	40	38–50	37–51	<0.1	35	91	86–98	84–99	28
5	42	40–52	39–53	<0.1	36	93	87–99	86–100	31
6	44	42–54	41–55	<0.1	37	94	88–100	87–102	34
7	46	44–56	43–57	<0.1	38	96	90–102	89–104	39
8	48	46–58	44–59	<0.1	39	98	92–104	91–105	44
9	50	47–60	46–61	<0.1	40	100	94–106	93–107	50
10	52	49–61	48–63	0.1	41	101	95–107	94–108	53
11	54	51–63	50–64	0.1	42	102	96–108	95–109	56
12	56	53–65	52–66	0.2	43	104	98–110	97–111	62
13	58	55–67	54–68	0.3	44	106	99–111	98–112	65
14	60	57–69	56–70	0.4	45	107	101–113	100–114	69
15	62	59–71	57–72	1	46	109	102–114	101–116	73
16	63	60–72	58–73	1	47	112	105–117	104–118	79
17	65	61–74	60–75	1	48	113	106–118	105–120	81
18	67	63–75	62–77	1	49	116	108–121	107–122	85
19	68	64–76	63–77	2	50	117	110–122	109–123	87
20	70	66–78	65–79	2	51	119	112–124	111–125	90
21	71	67–79	66–80	3	52	121	113–125	112–126	92
22	72	68–80	67–81	3	53	123	115–127	114–128	93
23	73	69–81	68–82	4	54	125	117–129	116–130	95
24	75	71–83	70–84	5	55	127	119–131	118–132	96
25	76	72–84	70–85	5	56	129	121–133	120–134	97
26	77	73–85	72–86	7	57	131	123–135	122–136	98
27	79	74–87	73–88	8	58	133	125–137	124–138	99
28	80	75–87	74–89	9	59	136	127–140	126–141	99
29	81	76–88	75–90	10	60	138	129–141	128–143	99
30	83	78–90	77–91	12	61	140	131–143	130–144	99.6
31	84	79–91	78–92	14	62	142	133–145	132–146	99.7
32	86	81–93	80–94	18	63	144	135–147	134–148	99.8
33	87	82–94	81–96	20	64	146	137–149	136–150	99.9
34	89	83–95	82–97	22	65	148	139–151	137–152	99.9

(*continues*)

TABLE 1.9   *(continued)*

Sum of scaled scores	CPI	Confidence interval 90% CI	95% CI	Percentile rank	Sum of scaled scores	CPI	Confidence interval 90% CI	95% CI	Percentile rank
66	150	140–153	139–154	>99.9	72	160	150–162	149–163	>99.9
67	152	142–154	141–156	>99.9	73	160	150–162	149–163	>99.9
68	154	144–156	143–157	>99.9	74	160	150–162	149–163	>99.9
69	156	146–158	145–159	>99.9	75	160	150–162	149–163	>99.9
70	158	148–160	147–161	>99.9	76	160	150–162	149–163	>99.9
71	160	150–162	149–163	>99.9					

TABLE 1.10   Cumulative Percentages of Standardization Sample (Base Rates) Obtaining GAI–CPI Score Discrepancies by Direction

	GAI–CPI		
Amount of discrepancy	GAI > CPI (−)	GAI < CPI (+)	Amount of discrepancy
40	0.0	0.1	40
39	0.1	0.1	39
38	0.1	0.2	38
37	0.1	0.3	37
36	0.3	0.4	36
35	0.3	0.5	35
34	0.3	0.6	34
33	0.4	0.7	33
32	0.6	0.7	32
31	0.7	0.8	31
30	0.8	0.8	30
29	1.0	1.1	29
28	1.3	1.4	28
27	1.4	1.6	27
26	1.7	2.0	26
25	2.1	2.5	25
24	2.5	2.9	24
23	3.1	3.5	23

(continues)

TABLE 1.10   (*continued*)

Amount of discrepancy	GAI > CPI (−)	GAI < CPI (+)	Amount of discrepancy
22	3.8	4.3	22
21	4.4	5.0	21
20	5.2	6.0	20
19	6.3	7.2	19
18	7.3	8.3	18
17	8.7	9.5	17
16	10.1	11.0	16
15	11.2	12.5	15
14	12.5	14.1	14
13	14.0	16.8	13
12	16.5	18.5	12
11	18.3	20.6	11
10	20.7	22.9	10
9	22.9	25.0	9
8	25.2	27.7	8
7	27.7	30.8	7
6	30.8	33.7	6
5	33.5	37.0	5
4	37.0	40.7	4
3	40.0	43.6	3
2	43.1	46.8	2
1	47.1	50.1	1
Mean	9.8	10.2	Mean
SD	7.4	7.5	SD
Median	8.0	8.0	Median

Note: Wechsler Intelligence Scale for Children – Fourth Edition (WISC-IV). Copyright © 2003 by Harcourt Assessment, Inc. Reproduced with permission. All rights reserved.

areas examined. Using WISC-III, he found that the variance accounted for by the four index scores was 61% for reading, 65% for math, and 48% for writing. Similarly, Meyes and Calhoun (2007) showed that when all four WISC-IV index scores are entered simultaneously into a regression equation predicting academic achievement, the resulting variance explained was 68% for basic reading, 70% for reading comprehension, 77% for numerical operations, and 58% for written expression. Our results are consistent with these studies in the areas of reading and writing. Taken together, our data in combination with these two studies provide empirical support for an approach to evaluating LD which involves a pattern of cognitive strengths and weaknesses among the WISC-IV index scores.

ISSUES IN ESTIMATING OVERALL ABILITY WITH THE FSIQ

Unlike every other Wechsler interpretative system that has been written, we discuss FSIQ last, rather than first. This is not to devalue the explanatory and predictive power of the FSIQ, but to emphasize the descriptive clinical power of the WISC-IV indexes and to place FSIQ in its proper role as a summary statement at the end of the psychological evaluation. The FSIQ has strong explanatory power at the group and individual level. Still, the use of an overall summary score sometimes may mask individual differences among the broad domains of general ability. This is why we suggest that the first line of clinical interpretation rests with the index scores.

Some authors have argued that a large amount of subtest scatter invalidates the FSIQ (Fiorello et al., 2007). Consequently, some practitioners refuse to report an FSIQ when there is significant scatter among the index scores. They label the FSIQ as invalid, and even appear disappointed in the test. However, our view is that fractured profiles are rich with clinically meaningful information that provides skilled practitioners an opportunity to understand the cognitive drivers of the child's behavior and make more targeted recommendations for assisting them. Thus scatter can be useful both diagnostically and prescriptively. In fact, when all four index scores "hang together" within a few points of each other and the FSIQ is "valid", there is little to say in the report about the child's unique set of abilities and how those individual differences serve to shape her or his perceptions of and relationship to the academic and social worlds in which they live.

The child's overall level of cognitive ability provides a critical backdrop to interpretation of individual differences among the various domains of ability as assessed by the index scores. The calculation of an FSIQ continues to be important for this and several other reasons. From a purely psychometric perspective, a general factor tends to emerge in studies of intelligence (Carroll, 1993). In fact, the correlations between the FSIQ and the 10 core subtests range from .46 to .72; while the four index scores correlated between .70 and .86 with the FSIQ. This makes a psychometrically compelling case for the interpretation of the FSIQ.

Further, recent studies suggest that FSIQ may be an equally valid measure of general ability for individuals or groups having highly variable index scores as for those having consistent index scores (Daniel, 2007), and that there may be no difference in the predictive validity of FSIQ for low-scatter and high-scatter groups (Watkins et al., 2007).

FSIQ is an especially strong predictor of achievement and memory. FSIQ and achievement correlate more strongly than any other two variables known to the behavioral sciences, typically around .70. This means that FSIQ explains about half the variance in achievement. There is no known variable or collection of variables that can fully account for the other half. There is no stronger relationship in the psychological sciences than that between IQ and achievement. Beyond the relationship with achievement, there is considerable ecological and criterion validity for the use of an overall estimate of general intelligence (Gottfredson, 1997, 1998; Kuncel et al., 2004). In the last chapter of this volume, Linda Gottfredson summarizes a vast body of research demonstrating that IQ is related to a wide array of important life outcomes.

SUMMARY AND COMMENT ON WISC-IV INDEX AND COMPOSITE SCORE INTERPRETATION

Each revision of the original 1939 Wechsler-Bellevue scale for the assessment of children's intelligence (WISC, 1949 – Wechsler (1949); WISC-R, 1974 – Wechsler (1974); WISC-III, 1991 – Wechsler, 1991; WISC-IV, 2003 – Wechsler, 2003) has added to the Wechsler legacy and tradition. A number of significant improvements and modifications have been made to the Wechsler family of tests, driven by the demands of clinical practice but also reflecting advances in theory, research, and measurement sophistication. In Wechsler's original model VIQ and PIQ combined to form FSIQ. His original model included as part of the VIQ two subtests designed to measure what we now call working memory (i.e., Arithmetic and Digit Span). Similarly, the original model included as part of the PIQ one subtest designed to measure what we now call processing speed (i.e., Coding). Ongoing neuropsychological research and psychometric advances have highlighted the clinical import of these constructs, and subsequent editions of the test have systematically added more subtests in these areas. Over the years, the Wechsler model has systematically expanded the domain coverage of the FSIQ to more fully represent these clinically important constructs. Other advances include revision of the verbal subtests to include more verbal reasoning than crystallized knowledge, and the revision of the performance subtests to include more fluid reasoning than visual–spatial skills.

The focus of interpreting the WISC-IV now rests solidly on a four-factor structure that is grounded in a wide body of research in clinical neuropsychology. While the psychometric fit of the WISC-III and WISC-IV to a four-factor model is now beyond question, the evolution of the Wechsler scales has been guided less by factor analysis – as in the CHC model – and more by ongoing neuro-cognitive research. Nevertheless, there is a fair amount of overlap between these models and this congruence among independent research groups is ultimately confirming of the progress our science continues to make in building increasingly advanced models of intelligence.

PART II: INTERVENTION SUGGESTIONS
RELATED TO THE WISC-IV INDEX SCORES

Understanding what ability is measured by an index score is the first step toward planning accommodations for a student who is weak in that ability. Knowing how this weakness would be manifested in daily activities in the classroom is the next step to validating the hypothesized weak ability indicated by the test score. A first line of intervention is to draw upon the student's strong abilities, be they personal strengths or normative strengths, to compensate for weaker abilities. In Part II of this chapter we suggest classroom modifications and teacher oriented accommodations for children with weaknesses in each of the four main abilities measured by WISC-IV (Verbal Comprehension, Perceptual Reasoning, Working Memory, and Processing Speed). In this regard, weaknesses can either be defined normatively or ipsatively, but it is not necessary that the student be achieving below potential (i.e., discrepancy approach) to be considered for one or more of these modifications or accommodations.

Modifications are changes made in the age-appropriate grade-level expectations for a subject or course in order to meet a student's learning needs. These changes might involve developing expectations that reflect knowledge and skills required in the curriculum for a different grade level, or increasing or decreasing the number and/or complexity of the regular grade-level curriculum expectations, or both. The term *accommodations* is used to refer to the special teaching and classroom assessment strategies, human supports, or individualized equipment, or both, required to enable a student to learn and to demonstrate learning. Accommodations do not alter the local curriculum expectations for the grade. The accommodations that the student requires in connection with instruction, assessment, and functioning in the physical environment may be conceptualized as instructional, environmental, or assessment. *Instructional accommodations* are adjustments in teaching strategies required to enable the student to learn and to progress through the curriculum. *Environmental accommodations* are changes or supports in the physical environment of the classroom or the school, or both. *Assessment accommodations* are adjustments in assessment activities and methods required to enable the student to demonstrate learning. Throughout Part II of this chapter, many of the bulleted lists of classroom indicators, modifications, accommodations, and assessment strategies are reprinted with permission from *The Special Education Handbook: A Practical Guide for All Teachers* (Elementary Teachers Federation of Ontario, 2007).

This approach is rooted in a belief that deficits in specific cognitive processes restrict the student's access to the curriculum, and that the cognitive deficit likely cannot be remediated directly so the teacher must find ways to teach around the deficit. Empirical support for some of the intervention ideas made in this section is emerging (see Gathercole et al., 2006a, b; Gathercole & Alloway, 2008) and will likely continue and inform practice. Yet, many of these intervention ideas are simply suggested teaching tips intended to be tried if there is some support from the convergence of clinical data (tests, observations, previous intervention data, etc.) and used only if they can be demonstrated to work for an individual student. Thus, single case studies are recommended as one method of providing empirical support for the strategies suggested below on a student by student basis. Methodologies for single case designs exist and are well accepted. In this case, the methodology would include tracking the student's progress on a series of brief academic probes before and after implementation of one or more of the accommodations or modifications suggested below. This can be an effective and powerful methodology for demonstrating empirical support at the student level, and collections of these studies begin to build a body of evidence. If implemented on a school wide scale, a data management system that charts progress on frequent academic probes as a function of a series of attempted interventions can be a very powerful administrative and scientific tool. One such software system is AIMSweb (The Psychological Corporation, 2007).

Selection from among the tips offered below can be made based on the pattern of classroom behaviors observed (see below) for struggling learners who have not responded to standard group level educational interventions (i.e., Tier II of a three tier RTI model), or based on patterns of WISC-IV test scores for students in special education or being considered for special education (i.e., Tier III of a three tier RTI model).

The hardest part of the job of assessment for the purposes of intervention is to translate test results into appropriate modifications and accommodations to the student's work in the classroom. Yet, this is the function that teachers rely on the most when they refer their student for a psychological assessment. The interventions provided here follow directly from the abilities that are measured by the WISC-IV index scores. Additional interventions would also be useful. Examples are interventions to address weaknesses found in the academic skills of reading, written language, and mathematics. Excellent sources for such interventions are Mather and Jaffe (2002) and Naglieri and Pickering (2003). Further examples are interventions to address executive skills, such as organization, time management, self-regulation, and others. Excellent resources for interventions on executive functions are Dawson and Guare (2004) and Hale and Fiorello (2004).

INTERVENTION SUGGESTIONS RELATED TO WISC-IV VCI

The VCI measures crystallized knowledge and verbal fluid reasoning. Crystallized intelligence, as measured by the VCI, shows a strong and consistent relationship with the development of reading and math achievement. Contributions of crystallized intelligence to writing achievement are important primarily after age 7. Its contributions to reading, math, and writing achievement become increasingly important for reading and math achievement with age (Flanagan & Mascolo, 2005, quoting work from their colleagues).

A student with needs in these areas has difficulty in understanding oral language, or in expressing himself or herself through oral language, or in both.

Classroom indicators of this need in the student's daily performance related to verbal comprehension include:

- Having a limited receptive vocabulary to understand words and their meaning, or having a limited expressive vocabulary to express thoughts and ideas using language in terms of correct word meanings, or both.
- Having difficulty in listening and comprehending oral language, including gleaning the meanings of phrases, sentences, idiom, and colloquialisms, despite adequate attention and auditory processing skills.
- Having difficulty in speaking in "real-life" situations in an age-appropriate manner.
- Having difficulty with language comprehension and usage, evident in their native language and impacting their learning of a second language in similar ways.
- Having a limited range of general knowledge and subject-specific knowledge, despite indicators of adequate memory functioning. This limitation is evidenced by limited expression of the ideas and knowledge through oral language.

Instructional accommodations for children with low verbal comprehension abilities include:

- Keep the language of instruction as simple as possible.
- Provide definitions for all new terms and concepts before teaching the lesson. Be alert for subject-specific terms that the student does not know. Teach the student to keep a separate page at the back of each subject's notebook to write the new terms and their definitions. Advise the student to study the list regularly.
- Teach new vocabulary in the context of information that the student already knows about the topic. Make explicit links to known vocabulary, information, and concepts.
- Provide models for more elaborate language usage when conversing with the student. Respond to their statements by repeating their utterances with revised vocabulary and sentence structure that is more age-appropriate.
- Teach the student how to use the dictionary to look up words to find their meanings. Use grade-appropriate resources, both in book form and electronic format.
- Teach the student how to use a thesaurus to look up words to find synonyms and related words. Use grade-appropriate resources, both in book form and electronic format.
- Ask the student whether he or she understood instructions that were given orally. If he or she did not understand, then:
  - Paraphrase the instruction using more simple language.
  - Explain the terms used in the instruction.
  - Reduce the complexity of the instruction by breaking it down into parts.

- Teach the student to recognize when he or she has not understood an oral instruction or lesson, and to ask for clarification to build understanding.
- Use instructional strategies that are not reliant on language, or that include other formats, such as:
  - Demonstrations and modeling to teach concepts and procedures.
  - Hand over hand guidance for young students, coupled with verbal explanations.
  - Pictures, graphs, charts.
  - Maps, diagrams, flow charts, logic models.
  - Semantic webbing maps.
- Teach the student to create a visual image of what he or she hears to supplement the language with visual and procedural representations.
- Communicate with parents in writing through notes, the student's agenda book, postings on the class website, or by e-mail.
- Check for knowledge gaps when teaching new information and concepts that rely on prior knowledge. Where gaps occur, teach the material as though it were new.
- Permit the student to make an audio recording of explanations given to clarify assignments and projects so he or she can replay it while working and getting assistance from a parent or tutor.

Environmental accommodations for children with low verbal comprehension abilities include the following considerations:

- Seat the student near the teacher and away from noise sources.
- Reduce the background noise against which oral language is heard in order to reduce the possibility of distortions of the speech stream.

Classroom assessment strategies for children with low verbal comprehension abilities include:

- Confirm that the student understand the instructions and directions before beginning a test or project.
- Use assessment methods with reduced demands on verbal output, such as True/False, multiple choice, or short answer.
- Reduce the demands for language comprehension when assessing competencies in mathematics and sciences. Use language and structures that scores low in reading level.
- Minimize the requirement for oral presentations.
- Assign projects whose products are visual representations, models, charts, and other constructions.

INTERVENTION SUGGESTIONS RELATED TO THE WISC-IV PRI

The PRI measures fluid reasoning and visual processing. Fluid reasoning shows a strong relationship with the development of math achievement, and contributes moderately to the development of reading skills. In the elementary grades it contributes moderately to basic writing skills, and at all ages it relates to written expression (Flanagan & Mascolo, 2005, quoting work from their colleagues). Visual Processing as measured by the PRI may be important for doing higher-level or advanced mathematics, such as geometry and calculus (Flanagan & Mascolo, 2005, quoting work from their colleagues).

Before recommending instructional accommodations based on low PRI scores the practitioner must first determine if the low ability is primarily due to poor visual processing or fluid reasoning, as described above. A student with educational needs related to visual processing has difficulty in organizing visual information into meaningful patterns and understanding how they might change as they rotate and move through space. A student with needs related to fluid reasoning has difficulty when faced with relatively novel tasks that require reasoning, recognizing and forming concepts, and drawing inferences (Elementary Teachers' Federation of Ontario, 2007).

Indicators of a need in the student's daily performance related to visual processing components of Perceptual Reasoning may include the following behaviors:

- Having difficulty making visual images to "see something in the mind's eye."
- Having difficulty remembering and differentiating left and right.
- Having difficulty manipulating simple visual patterns or maintaining their orientation to see things in space.
- Having difficulty mentally manipulating objects or visual patterns to see how they would appear if altered or rotated in space.
- Having difficulty in combining disconnected, vague, or partially hidden visual information patterns into meaningful wholes.
- Having difficulty finding a path through a spatial field or pattern.
- Having difficulty in estimating or comparing visual lengths and distances without measuring them.
- Having difficulty understanding math concepts in geometry, calculus, and other higher math.
- Having difficulty in remembering letter formations and letter patterns.
- Having difficulty in reading charts, maps, and blueprints and extracting the needed information.
- Having difficulty arranging materials in space, such as in their desks or lockers or rooms at home.
- Missing visual details.
- Having difficulty copying information from far point, like the blackboard or from near point, like texts.

Indicators of this need in the student's daily performance related to fluid reasoning components of Perceptual Reasoning may include:

- Having difficulty recognizing, forming, and understanding concepts.
- Having difficulty perceiving relationships among patterns.

- Having difficulty drawing inferences from information that is presented.
- Having difficulty understanding the implications of an issue or an action.
- Having difficulty with complex problem solving and concept formation.
- Having difficulty understanding and using "and logic."
- Having difficulty understanding and using "or logic."
- Having difficulty with extrapolating, or following a logical pattern through to another conclusion.
- Having difficulty with quantitative reasoning needed for understanding and computing mathematics.
- Relying heavily on the use of language to aid in their comprehension of concepts and to solve problems that are new to them and cannot be solved automatically.
- Having difficulty understanding the Piagetian concepts of conservation and classification.
- Having difficulty transferring and generalizing information to new situations.

Instructional accommodations for a weakness in visual processing abilities include:

- Reduce the number of visual displays involving manipulative materials, drawings, diagrams, and charts that could overwhelm the student, and replace them with clear verbal instructions.
- Explain in words all new skills and concepts, and all graphics and visually based concepts and tasks.
- Provide the support of clear verbal instructions for tasks requiring spatial organization.
- Encourage student to use verbal mediation to talk themselves through visual or spatial work.
- Teach the student to write from left to right. Use a green for "go" margin on the left side of paper where the student begins to write. Use a red for "stop" line at the right edge of the paper.
- Do not require the student to use any visual strategies that he or she finds confusing, such as webs, diagrams, charts, and schemas for math operations.
- Provide activities with manipulative materials, particularly in the primary grades.
- Replace copying from the blackboard with providing copies of the notes or assignments.
- When copying is required, do not require speed. Allow extra time for the student to proofread for accuracy.
- Provide math exercises on worksheets with only a few questions and plenty of white space. Do not require the student to copy problems from the blackboard or textbook.
- Teach the student to use verbal mediation, by saying each word or number or detail when copying from far point to paper.

- Provide extra visual structure on worksheets and assignments. Use organizers like numbered boxes, or color codes where instructions and similar questions have the same color.
- Provide graph paper and lined paper to use for completing math exercises while the student learns how to line up numbers by place value.
- Teach the student how to interpret the organization of a page of text having an unusual format by using numbers to identify the sequence, or colors to link related information.
- Provide direct instruction in reading and interpreting maps, graphs, charts, and diagrams.

Environmental Strategies that may be considered when working with children who have visual processing deficits are:

- Keep work space free from extraneous distractions, by removing all visual clutter that is not necessary to the task.
- Ensure that the student clears his or her desk completely before beginning a task. Remove all visual clutter from the work space before assembling the materials needed for the current task.
- Ensure that presentations using colors have enough contrast to be distinguishable in all light conditions.
- Modify color usage in visual presentations to avoid reliance on color coding for students with deficits in color vision.

Classroom assessment strategies for children with weaknesses in visual processing abilities include the following suggestions:

- Put few math questions on each page, with a lot of white space for calculations on math tests.
- Provide manipulative materials when testing concepts involving spatial relationships.
- Emphasize verbal and written answers, rather than charts, diagrams and maps, where possible.
- Permit students to explain spatial information from their perspective without the requirement to rotate it to the examiner's point of regard.
- Reduce the emphasis on charts and mapping, unless that is the skill being taught and evaluated.
- Relax standards of production for art assignments and accept approximations of accepted criteria.
- Do not penalize the student for placing information incorrectly on a page.

Consider the following instructional strategies when working with children who demonstrate a weakness in fluid reasoning in the perceptual domain:

- Provide verbal instructions to all tasks (assuming verbal skills are adequate).
- Use teaching approaches that promote the development of self-talk to mediate all tasks.

- Rely on the student's verbal memory skills to teach problem-solving through repetition and rote recall.
- Present concepts and procedures verbally, in a straightforward fashion to ensure comprehension.
- Teach strategies for solving problems, paying close attention to the proper sequence of events that can be memorized as verbal instructions.
- Provide repetition and review of concepts to ensure over-learning. Check that a student's memory for material includes comprehension.
- Teach mechanical arithmetic in a systematic, verbal, step-by-step fashion.
- Use real objects and manipulative materials, along with verbal descriptions to teach concepts.
- Teach strategies to increase understanding and retention of concepts, including:
  - self-talk, so the student guides himself or herself through the problem verbally;
  - lists of procedures or steps to follow.
- Teach problem-solving techniques in the contexts in which they are most likely to be applied.
- Teach and emphasize reading comprehension skills as early as possible so the student may rely on reading and rereading to ensure comprehension of concepts.
- Teach verbal strategies that will help them to organize their written work into sequential steps.
- Structure and adjust the difficulty level of the task, where possible.
- Explain homework and assignments in a sequential, step-by-step, fashion.
- When teaching concepts or providing instructions, avoid:
  - complicated and lengthy instructions and directions;
  - figurative language, since the student is likely to interpret language literally;
  - complex instructions.
- Watch for associated problems with organizational skills and follow instructional strategies for organization, if needed.
- Watch for associated problems with social skills, and provide interventions, if needed.

For children with deficits in fluid reasoning in the perceptual domain, there are no obvious environmental strategies. However, the following classroom assessment strategies may be considered:

- Initially, rely more on verbal instructions and less on charts, maps, and diagrams.
- Pair verbal explanations with visual material to make use of the child's relative strength in verbal reasoning to help them learn how to interpret and organize visual information.

- Ask clear, specific questions, rather than asking open-ended questions or asking students to make inferences.
- Rely more on verbal responses and less on the production of charts, maps, and diagrams.
- Test for knowledge of the material, where possible.
- Ask student to show all of their work (e.g., complete math calculations, or the outline for a long answer). Give partial marks for the process they followed.
- Provide a scoring rubric to the student so he or she knows how many marks they got for their knowledge, and how many they got for applications and problem solving using the knowledge.

INTERVENTION SUGGESTIONS RELATED TO THE
WISC-IV WMI

How do marked working memory deficits affect classroom activities? Two observational studies are informative. The first study involved a group of children with low working memory but typical scores in general ability measures (Gathercole et al., 2006a, b). Compared with classmates with typical working memory skills, the low working memory children frequently forgot instructions, struggled to cope with tasks involving simultaneous processing and storage, and lost track of their place in complex tasks. The most common consequence of these failures was that the children abandoned the activity without completing it. A detailed description of common characteristics of low working memory children in the classroom is in Gathercole and Alloway (2008) and Gathercole et al., (2006a, b). The second observational study by these authors drew a selection of children from the screening study described above. They were observed in mainstream primary classrooms in demographically diverse areas that included children with either low or average working memory skills. Examples of frequently observed behaviors that corresponded to working memory deficits included: "The child raised his hand but when called upon, he had forgotten his response;" "She lost her place in a task with multiple steps;" and "The child had difficulty remaining on task." Children with poor working memory struggled in many classroom activities, simply because they were unable to hold in mind sufficient information to allow them to complete the task. Losing crucial information from working memory caused them to forget many things: instructions they are attempting to follow, the details of what they are doing, where they have got to in a complicated task.

In the observational study described above (Gathercole et al., 2006a, b), children with poor working memory function often gravitated toward lower level strategies with lower processing requirements resulting in reduced general efficiency. For example, instead of using number aids such as blocks and number lines that are designed to reduce processing demands, these children relied on more error-prone strategies like simple counting instead.

Frequent failures of children with low memory to meet the working memory demands of classroom activities may be at least one cause of the poor academic progress that is typical for them. In order to reach expected attainment targets, the child must succeed in many different structured learning activities designed to build up gradually across time, the body of knowledge and skills that they need in areas of the curriculum such as literacy and mathematics. If the children frequently fail in individual learning situations simply because they cannot store and manipulate information in working memory, their progress in acquiring complex knowledge and skills in areas such as literacy and mathematics will be slow and difficult.

The ideal solution to ameliorate the learning difficulties resulting from impairments of working memory would be to remediate these memory impairments directly. However, there is little evidence that training working memory in children with low working memory skills leads to substantial gains in academic attainments (e.g., Turley-Ames & Whitfield, 2003). Thus, we recommend a number of classroom management techniques to minimize memory-related failures in classroom-based learning activities frequently experienced by children with working memory impairments.

Indicators of a need in the student's daily performance related to difficulties with working memory may include the following behaviors:

- Having difficulty following directions beyond the first steps.
- Forgetting what they have to do next.
- Difficulty with sentence writing.
- Losing his or her place in complex activities.
- Having difficulty with writing sentences or paragraphs.
- Having difficulty with mathematics computations that involve more than one step, such as long division.
- Having difficulty attending to and immediately recalling information they have just seen or heard.

Instructional accommodations for children with working memory difficulties:

- First, ensure that the child can remember what he or she is doing, to avoid failure to complete all steps of a learning activity. Strategies include:
  - Use instructions that are as brief and simple as possible. Break instructions down into individual steps where possible.
  - Repeat the instructions frequently.
  - For tasks that take place over an extended period of time, remind the child of crucial information for that phase of the task instead of repeating the original instruction.
  - Ask the child to repeat critical instructions back to you.
  - Since children often have good insight into their working memory failures, check with the child to make sure he or she remembers what to do.

- To help students to follow instructions:
  - Give brief and simple instructions with limited extraneous verbalization.
  - Break down instructions into simple steps when possible. Use numbered points for any sequence.
  - Reduce the number of steps given at one time.
  - Repeat instructions frequently.
  - Ask the child to repeat the instructions to ensure that they are remembered.
  - Give specific reminders targeted to the current step – a multi-step task.
- To prevent a child from losing his or her place in a complex task:
  - Break down tasks into separate steps.
  - Encourage older students to practice and actively use memory aids.
  - Provide support for use of external memory aids.
  - Encourage student to ask for forgotten information.
- To improve the learning successes of individuals with poor working memory skills teach them self-help strategies to promote their development as independent learners who can identify and support their own learning needs. Teach them to develop effective strategies to cope with working memory failures, including:
  - Encourage the child to ask for forgotten information where necessary.
  - Train the child in the use of memory aids.
  - Encourage the child to continue with a complex task rather than abandoning it, even if some of the steps are not completed due to memory failure.
- Provide supports for spelling frequently occurring words. This will prevent children from losing their place in the complex task of writing activities.
  - Reducing the processing load and opportunity for error in spelling individual words will increase the child's success in completing the sentence as a whole. However, reading off information from spellings on key words on the teachers' board was itself observed to be a source of error in low memory children in our study, with children commonly losing their place within the word.
  - Making available spellings of key words on the child's own desk rather than on a distant board may reduce these errors by making the task of locating key information easier and reducing opportunities for distraction.
  - Develop ways of marking the child's place in word spellings as a means of reducing place-keeping errors during copying.
- For writing tasks:
  - Reduce the linguistic complexity of sentences to be written.
  - Simplify the vocabulary of sentences to be written.
  - Reduce length of sentences to be written.
  - For older students, introduce use of outlines and techniques to keep place in the outline when writing.

- Teach memory aids, such as verbal mediation or rehearsal, and mnemonic strategies, such as:
  - Dracula's Mother Sucks Blood, to cue the order of operations in long division (Divide, Multiply, Subtract, and Bring down).
  - Every Good Boy Deserves Fudge, for the names of the lines in the treble clef music staff.
  - The method of loci to match items with landmarks on the route to school.
- Teach student to use lists, advance organizers, personal planners as aids to memory.
- Communicate frequently with parents about school activities, equipment needed, homework, and assignments through a communication book or regular e-mail.
- Provide notes to the student from presentations and lectures.

Environmental accommodations for children with working memory problems:

- Reduce opportunities for distraction and reduce the number of distractions in the vicinity.
- Provide visual reminders and other memory supports for multi-step tasks.
- Attach the student's daily schedule or timetable to the notebook cover that the child takes home every day.
- Post the student's daily schedule or timetable on the student's desk or classroom wall. Send a copy of the schedule or timetable home for posting in the student's room or on the fridge.

Assessment accommodations:

- Allow the student to use appropriate memory supports during testing. Supports would typically provide information about procedures to use, rather than providing content that the student should know.
- Use open-ended questions with more than one correct answer to allow for marks for anything the student remembers.
- Reduce the demands on working memory on tests by providing a structure and outline for responding.

INTERVENTION SUGGESTIONS RELATED TO THE WISC-IV PSI

Processing speed shows a strong relationship with the development of reading and math achievement, especially during the elementary school years when children are learning the skills in reading and math, and developing speed and automaticity in their use (Flanagan & Mascolo, 2005). Older school children use these basic academic skills with automaticity, and integrate them with more complex tasks such as problem solving, subject-focused writing, and complex reading. When mental efficiency in focusing concentration is required, students with processing speed needs have difficulty performing simple cognitive tasks fluently and automatically. Indicators of this need in the student's daily performance related to the speed with which he or she processes information and completes tasks include:

- Being slow to perform basic arithmetic operations, not learning the times tables, and not attaining automaticity in calculations and so uses fingers or counters.
- Taking longer to complete assignments in class.
- Not finishing tests and exams within the time allotted.
- Not finishing a copying exercise within the time allotted.
- Reading slowly.
- Taking even more time to complete tasks under pressure.
- Coming to the right answer, but taking longer to do it.

Consider the following instructional accommodations when processing speed is a weakness:

- Allow the student longer response times:
  - To respond orally to questions asked in class.
  - To make decisions when offered a choice of activities.
  - To complete assignments in class.
- Do not require the student to work under time pressure.
- Reduce the quantity of work assigned in favor of quality productions.
- When copying is required, do not require speed. Allow extra time for the student to proofread for accuracy.
- Provide the student with ample time to complete his or her work, or shorten the assignment so it can be accomplished within the time allotted.
- Provide extra time for the student to complete in-class assignments in a way that does not bring negative attention to him or her.
- Shorten drill and practice assignments that have a written component by requiring fewer repetitions of each concept.
- Provide copies of notes rather than requiring the student to copy from the board in a limited time.
- Provide instruction to increase the student's reading speed by training reading fluency, ability to recognize common letter sequences automatically that are used in print and sight vocabulary.
- Teach the student how to monitor time spent on each task. The student could use a stopwatch or timer. He or she could record the start and end times on paper. Set a goal for the student to gradually reduce the time needed to do each tasks.
- Provide timed activities to build speed and automaticity with basic skills, such as:
  - reading a list of high-frequency words as fast as possible,
  - calculating simple math facts as fast as possible,

- learning simple math calculations through flash cards and educational software exercises,
- charting daily performance for speed and accuracy.

In the classroom and other settings where the student does tasks such as homework provide environmental accommodations:

• Reduce environmental distractions to improve performance.

When taking tests in the classroom consider the following strategies for assessment accommodations to obtain maximum performance:

• Emphasize accuracy rather than speed in evaluating the student in all subject areas.
• Do not use timed tests for evaluation. Instead, use assessment procedures that do not rely on speed.
• Allow a specified amount of extra time for tests and exams (usually time and a half).
• Provide supervised breaks during tests and exams.
• Break long tests into more sittings of shorter duration across a few days.
• Provide a reader or text-to-voice software to read test and exam questions to a student to accommodate for slow reading fluency.
• Provide a scribe or voice-to-text software to record the student's answers on tests to accommodate for slow writing fluency.
• Use test and exam formats with reduced written output formats to accommodate for slow writing fluency.
  – Examples include: multiple choice formats; True/False formats; and short answer formats where a student fills in the blank.

A COMMENT ON INTERVENTION SUGGESTIONS

Younger children have a lot of support available in the classroom in the form of various aids, such as visual displays of number lines, letters, and rhymes. Once children get older, learning becomes more autonomous and there are fewer opportunities to rely on external supports. For instance, while memory aids such as dictionaries and spelling charts are still available, there is less repetition of instructions, fewer visual cues such as number lines or multiplication tables, and more individual rather than group or supervised activity. At the same time, instructions get lengthier, classroom lessons more complex, and specific cognitive demands become greater. The combination of these factors can serve to widen the gap in performance between children with average abilities and those with specific impairments as they grow into adolescence and enter middle and high school settings.

The strategies described above for modifying the environment and class-room assessment demands, and differentiating the style of instruction are appropriate for children of all ages. For some children with cognitive processing deficits these modifications and accommodations are necessary to ensure that they have equal access to the curriculum. As these children age, however, they need to be directly taught compensatory strategies that they can employ on their own across environments. Thus, general recommendations for improving the learning successes of children with a weakness in one or the domains of cognitive ability are: to encourage them to develop their own learning strategies; and to take advantage of available classroom resources. Strategies may include encouraging the child to ask for forgotten information where necessary, training the child in the use of memory aids, and encouraging the child to continue with complex tasks rather than abandoning them, even if some of the steps are not completed due to memory failure. Arming the child with such self-help strategies will promote their development as independent learners able to identify and support their own learning needs. The following case example provides a clear demonstration.

POST SCRIPT: A CASE EXAMPLE

Ellen is a 10-year old girl with an impairment of working memory. A psychoeducational assessment conducted at the start of this school was initiated by the teacher's observation that Ellen's achievement and progress in class was somewhat variable. She especially was seen to have difficulty when required to use both new and previously acquired information to address new questions and especially to then continue to build on these themes by revisiting and modifying previous solutions. This was observed in subjects ranging from social studies to mathematics and seemed to occur mainly when the task involved more "mental" than "paper and pencil" work.

The psychologist reported that Ellen's earned average scores on both the WISC-IV VCI (104) and PRI (110). Her PSI score was also average (99). However, WMI (82) was significantly lower compared to her average scores on the other index scores. The base rate tables (B.2) showed that only 3–5% of children in the average ability range demonstrated such a large discrepancy between the WMI and VCI and PRI. As well, the WMI > PRI discrepancy is observed in about 15% of 10-year old children in the average ability range. Of particular interest was that DSB and LNS were both relatively weak scores for Ellen in contrast to average DSF. Furthermore, Ellen did not show the same difficulty with the Spatial Span and Visual Digit Span subtests from the WISC-IV Integrated. Comparing the AR subtest on the WISC-IV and WISC-IV Integrated further confirmed that Ellen's WM difficulty was mainly observed during auditory tasks. Thus her classroom achievement, under particular learning conditions, was being compromised by her WM difficulties. While Ellen's classroom learning was supported with visual prompts and cues, as well as the pacing of material, she was also helped to develop strategies for managing tasks that required greater demands on working memory.

Ellen was observed in a numeracy lesson in which there were 10 pupils of relatively similar ability who were split into 2 groups. The lesson began with the children sitting at their tables for the "mental math" session in which the class played "What number am I?" The teacher reminded the children how to play the game as she encouraged them to ask focussed questions about the number she was thinking of. She modeled examples of questions that could be asked to help the children work out her number, for example, "Is the number less than 20?" and emphasized the use of specific mathematical vocabulary before giving volunteers the opportunity to lead the game.

Ellen participated well when asking questions about other pupils' numbers, though she did ask the same type of question each time which was based on an example that had been modeled by the teacher, for example, "If I partition it, will it be 30 and 3? Does it partition into 20 and 4? Does it partition into 70 and 2?" She was also keen to take the leading role part-way through the game. However, as soon as the other pupils began to ask questions about her number, she quickly lost her enthusiasm to participate. When asked, "Does the number have 8 tens?" Ellen did not respond. The teacher repeated the question and reminded her to think of the place value of her number, giving the prompts "Does your number have tens? Do you know how many tens there are?" But Ellen was evidently struggling to hold the number in mind whilst attempting to answer questions about it and eventually told the teacher that she had forgotten it. At this point, the teacher spent a few minutes revisiting the concept of place value. She referred the children to the 100 square and the place value chart as she asked key questions such as "How many tens does a number in the eighties have?" and "If a number has six tens, which row do we to point to on the 100 square?" Ellen successfully answered this question, making good use of the visual aids available.

As this took place, the teacher constantly repeated crucial information such as the key vocabulary (more than/less than) and asked target questions to help the children gain greater understanding of the concepts being taught, for example, "If we are working out ten more/less than a number, which part of the number changes?" She often directed such questions toward Ellen to support her thinking processes. For instance, "When thinking about 10 less than 307 Ellen, which part of the number will stay the same?"

> Ellen correctly stated, "7."
> "Which part of the number will change?"
> Ellen replied, "The 30. It gives 29."

As this main part of the lesson developed, Ellen became increasingly more distracted and appeared to lose total concentration. She began to swing on her chair, talk to her neighbor, and shout out random comments unrelated to the task. The teacher reminded Ellen on several occasions to follow the usual classroom routines and actually stopped the class at one point to reinforce her expectations of behavior: "Stop talking. Put your pens down. Listen to me when I'm talking and put your hand up if you have something to say."

These instructions were clearly broken down by the teacher as she simultaneously pointed to the classroom rules displayed on the wall, thus allowing the children time to store and process the information. During the lesson, students were challenged to perform simple calculations using some of the mental strategies taught in previous lessons. They were encouraged to use the tables' charts, number lines, and 100 square and to note key information on their whiteboards to help them in their calculations. Ellen responded well and made excellent use of strategies to support her working memory. For example, she regularly referred to the poster to help her remember multiplication facts, used her fingers to count on from a given number when performing additions, and used diagrams to calculate divisions.

Here, we see that the teacher regularly repeated key questions to Ellen so that she would not fall behind in understanding the mathematical concepts. This is also a good example of how to encourage children to develop and use strategies to support their learning as Ellen was able to complete the activity on her own.

REFERENCES

Alloway, T. P. (2007). *The Automated Working Memory Assessment*. London: Pearson Assessment.

Alloway, T. P., Gathercole, S. E., Willis, C., & Adams, A. M. (2005). Working memory and special educational needs. *Educational and Child Psychology*, 22, 56–67.

Alloway, T. P., Gathercole, S. E., Kirkwood, H. J., & Elliott, J. E. (2007). The cognitive and behavioural characteristics of children with low working memory, Manuscript submitted for publication.

Alloway, T. P., Gathercole, S. E, Kirkwood, H. J., & Elliott, J. E. (in press). Evaluating the validity of the automated working memory assessment. Educational Psychology.

Allport, G. W. (1955). *Becoming: Basic Considerations for a Psychology of Personality*. New Haven: Yale University Press.

Anastasi, A., & Urbina, S. (1997). *Psychological Testing* (7th ed.). Upper Saddle River, NJ: Prentice Hall.

Archibald, L. M., & Gathercole, S. E. (2006). Short-term and working memory in specific language impairment. *International Journal of Language and Communication Disorders*, 41, 675–693.

Baddeley, A. (2003). Working memory: Looking back and looking forward. *Nature Reviews/ Neuroscience*, 4, 829–839.

Beal, A. L. (1988). Canadian content in the WISC-R: Bias or jingoism. *Canadian Journal of Behavioral Science*, 20, 154–166.

Bull, R., & Scerif, G. (2001). Executive functioning as a predictor of children's mathematics ability. Shifting, inhibition and working memory. *Developmental Neuropsychology*, 19, 273–293.

Cain, K., Oakhill, J., & Bryant, P. (2004). Children's reading comprehension ability: Concurrent prediction by working memory, verbal ability and component skills. *Journal of Educational Psychology*, 96, 31–42.

Carroll, J. B. (1993). *Human cognitive abilities: A survey of factor-analytic studies*. New York: Cambridge University Press.

D'Amico, A., & Guarnera, M. (2005). Exploring working memory in children with low arithmetical achievement. *Learning and Individual Differences*, 15, 189–202.

Daley, C. E., & Nagle, R. J. (1996). Relevance of WISC-III indicators for assessment of learning disabilities. *Journal of Psychoeducational Research*, 14, 320–333.

Daneman, M., & Merikle, M. (1996). Working memory and language comprehension: A meta-analysis. *Psychonomic Bulletin Review*, 3, 422–433.

Daniel, M. H. (2007). "Scatter" and the construct validity of FSIQ: Coment on Fiorello et al. (2007). *Applied Neuropsychology*, 14(4), 291–295.

Davis, F. B. (1959). Interpretation of differences among averages and individual test scores. *Journal of Educational Psychology*, 50, 162–170.

Dawson, P., & Guare, R. (2004). *Executive Skills in Children and Adolescents: A Practical Guide to Assessment and Intervention*. New York: The Guilford Press.

Deary, I. J. (2001). *Intelligence: A very short introduction*. Oxford: Oxford University Press.

Deary, I. J., & Stough, C. (1996). Intelligence and inspection time: Achievements, prospects, and problems. *American Psychologist*, 51, 599–608.

De Jong, P. F. (1998). Working memory deficits of reading disabled children. *Journal of Experimental Child Psychology*, 70, 75–96.

Donders, J. (1996). Cluster subtypes in the WISC-III standardization sample: Analysis of factor index scores. *Psychological Assessment*, 8, 312–318.

Donders, J. (1997). Sensitivity of the WISC-III to injury severity in children with traumatic head injury. *Assessment*, 4, 107–109.

Donders, J., Tulsky, D. S., & Zhu, J. (2001a). Criterion validity of new WAIS-III subtest scores after traumatic brain injury. *Journal of the International Neuropsychological Society*, 7, 892–898.

Donders, J., Zhu, J., & Tulsky, D. (2001b). Factor index score patterns in the WAIS-III standardization sample. *Assessment*, 8, 193–203.

Dougherty, T. M., & Haith, M. M. (Jan 1997). Infant expectations and reaction times as predictors of childhood speed of processing and IQ. *Developmental Psychology*, 33(1), 146–155.

Dumont, R., & Willis, J. (2001). Use of the Tellegen & Briggs formula to determine the Dumont – Willis Indexes (DWI-I & DWI-II) for the WISC-IV. http://alpha.fdu.edu/psychology/

Elementary Teachers' Federation of Ontario (2007). *Special Education Handbook: A Practical Guide for All Teachers*. Toronto: Elementary Teachers' Federation of Ontario (ETFO).

Engle, R. W., Carullo, J. J., & Collins, K. W. (1991). Individual differences in working memory for comprehension and following directions. *Journal of Educational Research*, 84, 253–262.

Fiorello, C. A., Hale, J. B., McGrath, M., Ryan, K., & Quinn, S. (2001). IQ interpretation for children with flat and variable test profiles. *Learning & Individual Differences*, 13, 115–125.

Fiorello, C. A., Hale, J. B., Holdnack, J. A., Kavanagh, J. A., Terrell, J., & Long, L. (2007). Interpreting intelligence test results for children with disabilities: Is global intelligence relevant? *Applied Neuropsychology*, 14, 2–12.

Flanagan, D. P., & Kaufman, A. S. (2004). *Essentials of WISC-IV Assessment*. New York: Wiley.

Flanagan, D. P., & Mascolo, J. T. (2005). Psychoeducational assessment and learning disability diagnosis. In: D. P. Flanagan, & P. Harrison (Eds.), *Contemporary Intellectual Assessment: Theories, Tests, and Issues, Second Edition* (pp. 521–544). New York: The Guilford Press.

Fry, A. F., & Hale, S. (1996). Processing speed, working memory, and fluid intelligence: Evidence for a developmental cascade. *Psychological Science*, 7(4), 237–241.

Gathercole, S., & Baddeley, A. (1989). Evaluation of the role of STM in the development of vocabulary of children: A longitudinal study. *Journal of Memory & Language*, 28, 200–213.

Gathercole, S. E., & Pickering, S. J. (2000). Assessment of working memory in six- and seven-year old children. *Journal of Educational Psychology*, 92, 377–390.

Gathercole, S. E., Willis, C., Emslie, H., & Baddeley, A. (1992). Phonological memory and vocabulary development during the early school years: A longitudinal study. *Developmental Psychology*, 28, 887–898.

Gathercole, S. E., Brown, L., & Pickering, S. J. (2003). Working memory assessments at school entry as longitudinal predictors of National Curriculum attainment levels. *Educational and Child Psychology*, 20, 109–122.

Gathercole, S. E., Alloway, T. P., Willis, C., & Adams, A. M. (2006a). Working memory in children with reading disabilities. *Journal of Experimental Child Psychology*, 93, 265–281.

Gathercole, S. E., Lamont, E., & Alloway, T. P. (2006b). Working memory in the classroom. In: S. Pickering (Ed.), *Working Memory and Education* (pp. 219–240). Elsevier Press.

Gatherecole, & Alloway, (2008). *Working Memory and Learning: A practical guide.* London: Sage Press.

Geary, D. C. (1990). A componential analysis of an early learning deficit in mathematics. *Journal of Experimental Child Psychology*, 49, 363–383.

Geary, D. C. (1993). Mathematical disabilities: Cognition, neuropsychological and genetic components. *Psychological Bulletin*, 114, 345–362.

Geary, D. C., Hoard, M. K., & Hamson, C. O. (1999). Numerical and arithmetical cognition: Patterns of functions and deficits in children at risk for a mathematical disability. *Journal of Experimental Child Psychology*, 74, 213–239.

Gersten, R., Jordan, N. C., & Flojo, J. R. (2005). Early identification and interventions for students with mathematics difficulties. *Journal of Learning Disabilities*, 38, 293–304.

Gottfredson, L. S. (1997). Why g matters: The complexity of everyday life. *Intelligence*, 24, 79–132.

Gottfredson, L. S. (1998). The general intelligence factor. *Scientific American Presents*, 9, 24–29.

Hale, J. B., Fiorello, C. A., Kavanagh, J. A., Hoeppner, & Gaither, (Spring 2001). WISC–III predictors of academic achievement for children with learning disabilities: Are global and factor scores comparable? *School Psychology Quarterly Special Issue*, 16(1), 31–55.

Hale, J. B., Naglieri, J. A., Kaufman, A. S., & Kavale, K. A. (2004). Specific learning disability classification in the new Individuals with Disabilities Education Act: The danger of good ideas. *The School Psychologist, Winter*, 6–13.

Hale, J. B., & Fiorello, C. A. (2004). *School Neuropsychology: A Practitioners' Handbook.* New York: The Guilford Press.

Heathcote, D. (1994). The role of visuospatial working memory in the mental addition of multi-digit addends. *Current Psychology of Cognition*, 13, 207–245.

Kail, R. (Spring 2000). Speed of Information Processing: Developmental change and links to intelligence. *Journal of Psychology Special Issue: Developmental perspectives in intelligence*, 38(1), 51–61.

Kamphaus, R. W. (1993). *Clinical Assessment of Children's Intelligence.* Needham Heights, MA: Allyn & Bacon.

Kaufman, A. S. (1994). *Intelligent testing with the WISC–III.* New York: Wiley.

Kavale, K. A., & Forness, S. R. (1984). A meta-analysis of the validity of Wechsler scale profiles and recategorizations: Patterns or parodies? *Learning Disability Quarterly*, 7, 136–156.

Kiewra, K. A., & Benton, S. L. (1988). The relationship between information processing ability and note taking. *Contemporary Educational Psychology*, 13, 3–44.

Knight, R. G., & Godfrey, H. P. D. (1984). Assessing the significance of differences between subtests on the Wechsler Adult Intelligence Scale – Revised. *Journal of Clinical Psychology*, 40, 808–810.

Konold, T. R. (1999). Evaluating discrepancy analysis with the WISC–III and WIAT. *Journal of Psychoeducational Assessment*, 17, 24–35.

Kuncel, N. R., Hezlett, S. A., & Ones, D. S. (2004). Academic performance, career potential, creativity, and job performance: Can one construct predict them all? *Journal of Personality and Social Psychology*, 86, 148–161.

Kyllonen, P. C., & Christal, R. E. (1990). Reasoning ability is (little more than) working memory capacity? *Intelligence*, 14, 389–433.

Kyllonen, P. C., & Stephens, D. L. (1990). Cognitive abilities as the determinant of success in acquiring logic skills. *Learning and Individual Differences*, 2, 129–160.

Logie, R. H., Gilhooly, K. J., & Wynn, V. (1994). Counting on working memory in arithmetic problem solving. *Memory & Cognition*, 22, 395–410.

Matarazzo, J. D. (1990). Psychological assessment versus psychological testing: Validation from Binet to the school, clinic, and courtroom. *American Psychologist*, 45, 999–1017.

Mather, N., & Jaffe, L. E. (2002). *Woodcock-Johnson III Reports, Recommendations and Strategies.* New York: John Wiley & Sons.

McGrew, K., & Flanagan, D. P. (1998). *The Intelligence Test Desk Reference (ITDR) Gf – Gc Cross-Battery Assessment*. Boston: Allyn and Bacon.

McLean, J. F., & Hitch, G. H. (1999). Working memory impairments in children with specific mathematics learning difficulties. *Journal of Experimental Child Psychology*, 74, 240–260.

Meyes, S. D., & Calhoun, S. L. (2007). Wechsler Intelligence Scale for children – Third and Fourth Edition Predictors of academic achievement in children with attention-deficit/hyperactivity disorder. *School Psychology Quarterly*, 22(2), 234–249.

Naglieri, J. A. (1993). Pairwise and ipsative comparisons of WISC-III IQ and index scores. *Psychological Assessment*, 5, 113–116.

Naglieri, J. A., & Pickering, E. B. (2003). *Helping Children Learn: Intervention Handouts for Use in School and at Home*. Baltimore: Paul H. Brookes Publishing Co.

Nation, K., Adams, J. W., Bowyer-Crane, C. A., & Snowling, M. J. (1999). *Journal of Experimental Child Psychology*, 73, 139–158.

Ormrod, J. E., & Cochran, K. F. (1988). Relationship of verbal ability and working memory to spelling achievement and learning to spell. *Reading Research Instruction*, 28, 33–43.

Passolunghi, M. C., & Siegel, L. S. (2001). Short-term memory, working memory, and inhibitory control in children with difficulties in arithmetic problem solving. *Journal of Experimental Child Psychology*, 80, 44–57.

Pearson, Inc (2002). *AIMSweb*. San Antonio, TX: Author.

Price, L., Tulsky, D., Millis, S., & Weiss, L. (2002). Redefining the factor structure of the Wechsler Memory Scale-III: Confirmatory factor analysis with cross validation. *Journal of Clinical and Experimental Neuropsychology*, 24(5), 574–585.

Prifitera, A., & Dersh, J. (1993). Base rates of WISC-III diagnostic subtest patterns among normal, learning-disabled, and ADHD samples. Advances in psychological assessment: Wechsler Intelligence Scale for children – Third Edition. *Journal of Psychological Assessment monograph series*, , 43–55.

Prifitera, A., Weiss, L. G., & Saklofske, D. H. (1998). The WISC-III in context. In: A. Prifitera, & D. H. Saklofske (Eds.), *The WISC-III in Clinical Use and Interpretation: Scientist–Practitioner Perspectives*. San Diego: Academic Press.

Prifitera, A., Saklofske, D. H., & Weiss, L. G. (2005). *WISC-IV Clinical Use and Interpretation*. San Diego: Academic Press.

Pritchard, D. A., Livingston, R. B., Reynolds, C. R., & Moses, J. A. (2000). Modal profiles for the WISC-III. *School Psychology Quarterly*, 15, 400–418.

Rasmussen, C., & Bisanz, J. (2005). Representation and working memory in early arithmetic. *Journal of Experimental Child Psychology*, 91, 137–157.

Reuhkala, M. (2001). Mathematical skills in ninth-graders: Relationship with visuospatial abilities and working memory. *Educational Psychology*, 21, 387–399.

Roid, G. H., & Worrall, W. (1996). Equivalence of factor structure in the U.S. and Canada editions of the WISC-III. Paper presented at the annual meeting of the American Psychological Association; Toronto.

Saklofske, D. H., Gorsuch, R. L ,Weiss, L. G., Zhu, J. J., & Patterson, C. (2005). General ability index for the WAIS-III: Canadian norms. Canadian Journal of Behavioural Science, 37(1), 44–48.

Sattler, J. M. (1988). *Assessment of Children* (3rd ed.). San Diego: Jerome M. Sattler Publisher, Inc.

Sattler, J. M. (1992). *Assessment of Children* (3rd ed.). San Diego: Jerome M. Sattler Publisher, Inc.

Sattler, J. M. (2001). *Assessment of Children: Cognitive Applications* (4th ed.). San Diego: Author.

Sattler, J. M., & Dumont, R. (2004). *Assessment of Children: WISC-IV and WPPSI-III Supplement*. San Diego: Author.

Schwean, V. L., Saklofske, D. H., Yackulic, R. A., & Quinn, D. (1993). WISC – III performance of ADHD boys: Cognitive, intellectual, and behavioral comparisons. *Journal of Psychoeducational Assessment, Special ADHD Issue Monograph*, 6–21.

Siegel, L. S. (1988). Evidence that IQ scores are irrelevant to the definition and analysis of reading-disability. *Canadian Journal of Psychology*, 42, 201–215.

Siegel, L. S., & Ryan, E. B. (1989). The development of working memory in normally achieving and subtypes of learning disabled children. *Child Development*, 60, 973–980.

Stothard, S. E., & Hulme, C. (1992). Reading comprehension difficulties in children. *Reading and Writing: An Interdisciplinary Journal*, 4, 245–256.

Swanson, H. L. (1994). Short-term memory and working memory: Do both contribute to our understanding of academic achievement in children and adults with learning disabilities? *Journal of Learning Disabilities*, 27, 34–50.

Swanson, H. L. (1999). Reading comprehension and working memory in skilled readers: Is the phonological loop more important than the executive system? *Journal of Experimental Child Psychology*, 72, 1–31.

Swanson, H. L. (2003). Age-related differences in learning disabled and skilled readers' working memory. *Journal of Experimental Child Psychology*, 85, 1–31.

Swanson, H. L., & Howell, M. (2001). Working memory, short-term memory, and speech rate as predictors of children's reading performance at different ages. *Journal of Educational Psychology*, 93, 720–734.

Swanson, H. L., & Sachse-Lee, C. (2001). Mathematical problem solving and working memory in children with learning disabilities: Both executive and phonological processes are important. *Journal of Experimental Child Psychology*, 79, 294–321.

Swanson, H. L., & Saez, L. (2003). Memory difficulties in children and adults with learning disabilities. In: H. L. Swanson, S. Graham, & K. R. Harris (Eds.), *Handbook of Learning Disabilities* (pp. 182–198). New York: Guildford Press.

Swanson, H. L., & Beebe-Frankenberger, M. (2004). The relationship between working memory and mathematical problem solving in children at risk and not at risk for math disabilities. *Journal of Education Psychology*, 96, 471–491.

Swanson, H. L., Ashbaker, M., & Lee, C. (1996). Learning disabled readers' working memory as a function of processing demands. *Journal of Experimental Child Psychology*, 61, 242–275.

Swanson, H. L., Saez, L., Gerber, M., & Leafstedt, J. (2004). Literacy and cognitive functioning in bilingual and nonbilingual children at or not at risk for reading disabilities. *Journal of Educational Psychology*, 96, 3–18.

Thevenot, C., & Oakhill, J. (2005). The strategic use of alternative representations in arithmetic word problem solving. *Quarterly Journal of Experimental Psychology*, 58A, 1311–1323.

Tulsky, D. S., Saklofske, D. H., & Ricker, J., (2003a). Historical overview of intelligence and memory: Factors influencing the Wechsler scales. In: D. S. Tulsky, D. H. Saklofske *et al.* (Eds.), *Clinical Interpretation of the WAIS-III and WMS-III*. San Diego: Academic Press.

Tulsky, D. S., Saklofske, D. H., & Zhu, J. J., (2003b). Revising a standard: An evaluation of the origin and development of the WAIS-III. In: D. S. Tulsky, D. H. Saklofske *et al.* (Eds.), *Clinical Interpretation of the WAIS-III and WMS-III*. San Diego: Academic Press.

Turley-Ames, K. J., & Whitfield, M. M. (2003). Strategy training and working memory task performance. *Journal of Memory and Language*, 49, 446–468.

Wagner, R. K., & Muse, A. (2006). Working memory deficits in developmental dyslexia. In T. P. Alloway, & S. E. Gathercole (Eds.), *Working Memory in Neurodevelopmental Conditions* (pp. 41–58). East Sussex, UK: Psychology Press.

Wagner, R. K., Torgesen, J. K., Laughon, P., Simmons, K., & Rashotte, C. A. (1993). Development of young readers' phonological processing abilities. *Journal of Educational Psychology*, 85, 13–83.

Wagner, R. K., Torgesen, J. K., & Rashotte, C. A. (1994). Development of reading-related phonological processing abilities: New evidence of bi-directional causality from a latent variable longitudinal study. *Journal of Educational Psychology*, 85, 83–103.

Wagner, R. K., Torgesen, J. K., Rashotte, C. A., Hecht, S. A., Barker, T. A., Burgess, S. R., Donahue, J., & Garon, T. (1997). Changing relations between phonological processing abilities and word-level reading as children develop from beginning to skilled readers: A 5-year longitudinal study. *Developmental Psychology*, 33, 468–479.

Wagner, R., Torgesen, J., & Rashotte, C. (1999). *Comprehensive Test of Phonological Processing*. Austin, TX: Pro-Ed.

Wagner, R. K., & Muse, A. (2006). Working memory deficits in developmental dyslexia. In: T. P. Alloway, & S. E. Gathercole (Eds.), *Working memory in neurodevelopmental conditions* (pp. 41–58). East Sussex, UK: Psychology Press.

Watkins, M. W., Glutting, J. J., & Lei, P. W. (2007). Validity of the full-scale IQ when there is significant variability among WISC-III and WISC-IV factor scores. *Applied Neuropsychology*, 14, 13–20.

Wechsler, D. (1949). *Wechsler Intelligence Scale for Children*. New York: Psychological Corporation.

Wechsler, D. (1950). Cognitive, Conative, and Non-intellective Intelligence. *American Psychologist*, 5, 78–83.

Wechsler, D. (1974). *Manual for the Wechsler Intelligence Scale for Children – Revised*. San Antonio: The Psychological Corporation.

Wechsler, D. (1991). *Manual for the Wechsler Intelligence Scale for Children – Third Edition*. San Antonio: The Psychological Corporation.

Wechsler, D. (1997). *WAIS-III/WMS-III Technical Manual*. San Antonio: The Psychological Corporation.

Wechsler, D. (2003). *Wechsler Intelligence Scale for Children – Fourth Edition Technical and Interpretive Manual*. San Antonio: The Psychological Corporation.

Wechsler, D. (2004). *WISC-IV Integrated Technical and Interpretation Manual*. San Antonio: The Psychological Corporation.

Weiss, L. G., Harris, J. G., Prifitera, A., Courville, T., Rolfhus, E., Saklofske, D. H., & Holdnack, J. A. (2006a). WISC-IV interpretation in societal context. In: L. G. Weiss, D. H. Saklofske, A. Prifitera, & J. A. Holdnack (Ed.), *WISC-IV Advanced Clinical Interpretation*. San Diego: Academic Press.

Weiss, L. G., Saklofske, D. H., Prifitera, A., & Holdnack, J. A. (2006b). *WISC-IV: Advanced Clinical Interpretation*. San Diego: Academic Press.

Wilson, K. M., & Swanson, H. L. (2001). Are mathematical disabilities due to a domain-general or domain-specific deficit? *Journal of Learning Disabilities*, 34, 237–248.

INTERFACING WISC-IV ASSESSMENT AND INTERVENTION: CLINICAL APPLICATIONS

2

RESEARCH-SUPPORTED DIFFERENTIAL DIAGNOSIS OF SPECIFIC LEARNING DISABILITIES AND IMPLICATIONS FOR INSTRUCTION AND RESPONSE TO INSTRUCTION

VIRGINIA W. BERNINGER[1], LOUISE O'DONNELL[2] AND JAMES HOLDNACK[3]

[1]*University of Washington, Seattle, WA, USA*

[2]*University of Texas Health Science Center, San Antonio, TX, USA*

[3]*Pearson, San Antonio, TX, USA*

BACKGROUND

When over 30 years ago federal legislation in the United States first mandated that children with learning disabilities receive a free, appropriate education program (FAEP), the focus was on criteria for qualifying students for services rather than differential diagnosis of specific learning disabilities. Moreover, the experts were not able to agree upon *inclusionary criteria for defining what each specific kind of learning disability is*. Rather, a generic category of learning disabilities was created based on *exclusionary criteria for what a learning disability is not*. The federal law stipulated that a learning disability was not due to mental retardation, sensory or physical disability, lack of opportunity to learn, or cultural difference.

Because many children were known to underachieve relative to their IQ (intellectual or cognitive ability – not really an intelligence quotient in the mathematical sense of the term), the federal law defined learning disability on the basis of a discrepancy between IQ and academic achievement. However, no one could agree on how to calculate the discrepancy (e.g., simple standard score difference or regression-based discrepancy measure, Prifitera et al., 1998) or how large the discrepancy had to be. Consequently, the various states implemented the federal definition in different ways. Some states even used grade level as an index for expected achievement and ignored IQ altogether.

With the reauthorization of the federal law in 2004 and the implementation of it in various states, the definitions of specific learning disabilities remain blurred. Although current regulation calls for comprehensive assessment, of which response to intervention (RTI) may be a part, the focus is still on qualifying students for special education. The issue of how specific learning disabilities may be defined on the basis of inclusionary rather than exclusionary criteria has not been addressed. At a time in American education when educators are increasingly being encouraged to use research-supported instruction, it is puzzling why federal and state laws for educationally handicapping conditions such as learning disabilities are not emphasizing adoption of research-based definitions of specific learning disabilities for identifying affected children, planning treatment, and evaluating response to the treatment. For further discussion of these issues, see Berninger and Holdnack (2008).

The purposes of this chapter are four-fold. First, we explain a research-supported approach that recognizes the importance of including cognitive measures (from tests for assessing intelligence like *Wechsler Intelligence Scale for Children*, Fourth Edition – WISC IV but not based exclusively on Full Scale IQ), along with achievement, language, and neurodevelopmental measures in comprehensive assessment. We question rigid use of only one formula for IQ-achievement discrepancy in identifying specific learning disabilities and think cognitive assessment with its strong neuroscience research basis has an integral place in comprehensive assessment by scientist-practitioners. To ignore the information neurocognitive assessment can provide is a scientific step-backward. We advocate for a *flexible approach* (Berninger et al., 1992a) that is based on research, much of it conducted at the University of Washington since 1989 through grant support from the National Institute of Child Health and Human Development (NICHD) for investigator-initiated projects and a multidisciplinary learning disabilities research center, but also by other research groups supported by federal funding.

Second, we present research-supported definitions for four specific learning disabilities: dysgraphia, dyslexia, oral and written language learning disability (OWL LD), and dyscalculia. The first three are based on the NICHD-funded research since 1989 that had as its specific aims research-supported definitions of specific learning disabilities involving writing and/or reading. The last is based on extensive clinical observations over a 3-year period in outpatient pediatric clinics of children solving math problems and a Javitz award from the United States Department of Education to study math development in typically developing children and those with math talent.

Third, we describe assessment procedures for differential diagnosis to distinguish among these four learning disabilities and distinguish them from other kinds of developmental and learning disorders found in school age populations. We also note that these four specific learning disabilities may occur alone or in combination with each other (often referred to as comorbidity). The assessment procedures draw for the most part on the WISC IV (The Psychological Corporation, 2003), the *Wechsler Individual Achievement Test*, Second Edition (WIAT II) (The Psychological Corporation, 2001), the *Process Assessment of the Learner*, Second Edition *Diagnostic for Reading and Writing* (PAL II RW) and *Diagnostic for Math* (PAL II M) (Berninger, 2007a, b) (see Tables 2.1–2.4 for an overview), Clinical Evaluation of Language Fundamentals (CELF 4) (Semel, Wiig & Secord, 2003), and the Delis-Kaplan Executive Functions Survey (D-KEFS, Delis et al., 2001).

Fourth, we discuss the treatment implications of the differential diagnosis – why it matters that the nature of the specific learning disability be identified and why it is important to monitor RTI. We take the position that the appropriate use of RTI is to assess response to instructional intervention for the purpose of evaluating whether the current treatment is effective or needs to be modified. We also strongly believe that RTI alone is not an appropriate diagnostic procedure for identification of the underlying learning disability (or disabilities) nor does it pinpoint the appropriate treatment needed. Research-supported diagnostic assessment can pinpoint appropriate treatment or modification of curriculum (Berninger et al., 2004a, 2004b). Case studies are also provided to illustrate the diagnostic, treatment, and progress monitoring issues for specific learning disabilities.

The definitions, assessment procedures, and instructional interventions are based on research. References for that research are provided for interested practitioners to consult. However, the intended audience for this chapter is practitioners – psychologists working in schools, community or hospital clinics, or private practices – who are committed to grounding their practice in research-supported assessment and intervention. Thus, the main focus is on the practical issues of implementing research-supported procedures for assessment, translating assessment findings into instructional intervention, and assessing response to instruction (RTI). We begin with a research-supported approach to incorporating cognitive measures and related diagnostic procedures within a comprehensive assessment model for specific learning disabilities.

RESEARCH-SUPPORTED APPROACH TO
INCORPORATING COGNITIVE MEASURES

Full Scale IQ is not used for reasons discussed by Prifitera et al. (1998). To begin with, part of the Full Scale IQ score is based on reasoning abilities (verbal and nonverbal), which tend to fall at least within the lower limits of the normal range and are often much higher in students with specific learning disabilities, and on other cognitive abilities, which are often impaired in children with learning disabilities (working memory and/or processing speed). Thus inclusion of all subtests may lower the overall Full Scale IQ. Use of Verbal Comprehension Index or Perceptual Reasoning Index may provide a better estimate of expected achievement if the student can overcome the learning disability.

For dyslexia, Verbal IQ (or prorated Verbal IQ or Verbal Comprehension Index) is used as the index of expected achievement because Verbal IQ (verbal reasoning) has been shown in research to be a better predictor of reading achievement in referred (Greenblatt et al., 1990) and unreferred (Vellutino et al., 1991) samples than is Performance IQ (nonverbal reasoning). The lower limit for the Verbal IQ is set at 90 (25th percentile) and individuals in the top 75% of the population in cognitive ability are evaluated for a possible diagnosis of dyslexia. The reason is that the probability of known and unknown comorbid neurogenetic and neurodevelopmental disorders (e.g., fragile X, autism, Williams, Downs, etc. and various kinds of pervasive developmental disorders in which two or more domains of development fall outside the normal range) increases in the population with an IQ below 90 ($-2/3$ standard deviation). Consequently, research findings for treating dyslexia, which assumes cognitive functioning in the normal range or higher, may not generalize to all students with reading problems who may have different profiles of developmental, neurodevelopmental, and academic skills than those with dyslexia. For students whose IQ falls in the bottom quartile, another neurogenetic or neurodevelopmental condition, rather than dyslexia, may be relevant to the etiology, treatment, and prognosis of the reading problem.

This chapter focuses on three specific learning disabilities that affect learning written language – dysgraphia, dyslexia, and OWL LD – and one that affects learning arithmetic and math – dyscalculia. Each of these disabilities is best conceptualized as the result of impairment in one or more of a set of related skills in a functional system. Affected individuals share a common set (constellation) of behavioral symptoms but also display some individual variation as to which of these symptoms in the set are expressed (Berninger & O'Donnell, 2004; Berninger & Holdnack, 2008). Also changes may occur across development in expression of these symptoms as a function of interactions of areas of vulnerability with changing curriculum requirements (Berninger, 2006). For example, for students with dyslexia learning to decode is a major problem in the primary grades, but a persisting problem in the intermediate grades and the high school and college years may be spelling (for recent findings, see Berninger et al., 2008a, which also cites the earlier studies by Pennington and colleagues and by Bruck and colleagues pointing to a similar conclusion).

Dysgraphia which affects handwriting and/or spelling, is the result of impaired orthographic, fine motor planning, and working memory processes (Berninger, 2004, 2006, in press). *Dyslexia,* which affects accuracy and rate of word decoding, word reading, and spelling, is the result of impaired orthographic, phonological, and working memory processes (Berninger, 2001, 2006, in press; Berninger et al., 2001, 2006a). In general, listening comprehension and reading comprehension, once adequate word decoding and word reading skills are achieved, are spared in dyslexia, that is, they are within the normal limits. *OWL LD*, which affects learning oral language and then using oral language to learn written language, is the result of impaired phonological, orthographic, morphological, syntactic, and working memory processes (Berninger & O'Donnell, 2004; Berninger, 2006, in press). Even after word decoding is brought up to adequate levels, reading real words and reading comprehension tends to be very impaired until treated. The WISC IV Processing Speed Index or Coding subtest (an index of orthographic loop) may also be impaired in any of the three specific learning disabilities. See Figure 2.1 and PAL II User Guide for the prism that illustrates how these three disabilities affecting acquisition of written language can be differentiated on the basis of whether orthographic coding only is impaired (dysgraphia), orthographic and phonological coding are impaired (dyslexia), or orthographic, phonological, and morphological/syntactic coding are impaired (OWL LD); for evidence see, Berninger et al. (in press).

Dyscalculia is impairment in rapidly accessing and retrieving math facts from memory, applying algorithms or steps of calculation to solve math problems, and expressing answers orally and in writing. Dyscalculia may result from (a) lack of conceptual understanding of counting, place value, or part–whole relationships, (b) difficulty with the visual notation system (automatic numeral

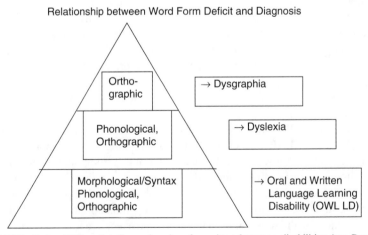

FIGURE 2.1   Differential diagnosis prism for written language disabilities (see Berninger et al., in press). *Process Assessment of the Learner – Second Edition (PAL-II).* Copyright © 2007 by NCS Pearson, Inc. Reproduced with permission. All rights reserved.

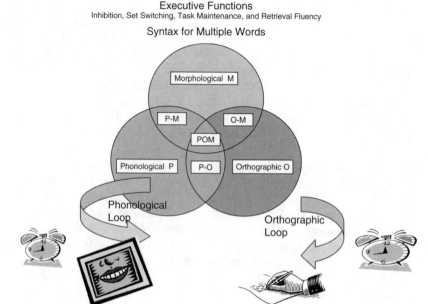

Executive Functions
Inhibition, Set Switching, Task Maintenance, and Retrieval Fluency

Syntax for Multiple Words

Morphological M

P-M   O-M

POM

Phonological P   P-O   Orthographic O

Phonological Loop   Orthographic Loop

Working Memory for Reading and Writing

FIGURE 2.2   Working memory architecture underlying functional reading and writing systems. *Process Assessment of the Learner – Second Edition (PAL-II).* Copyright © 2007 by NCS Pearson, Inc. Reproduced with permission. All rights reserved.

writing, coding multi-place numerals into working memory, or representing visual problems in two-dimensional space) or with integrating somatosensory information with visual symbols, (c) impaired quantitative or visual-spatial working memory, and (d) inefficient executive functions for switching attention, staying on task over time, or self-monitoring. Affected individuals vary in which of these processes are impaired. Although dyscalculia is first evident during the elementary grades when arithmetic (elementary math with focus on calculation) is taught, children who do not develop these prerequisite skills are likely to struggle with learning intermediate level mathematics beginning with algebra; see The Final Report of the National Mathematics Advisory Panel (National Mathematics Advisory Panel, 2008).

Underlying the PAL II diagnostic system is a *model of working memory* (see Figure 2.2 and PAL II User Guide) for understanding how components of this system supporting conscious, task-related learning (orthographic, phonological, morphological word form storage and processing, syntactic storage and processing, a phonological loop for coordinating phonological representations with output through the mouth, an orthographic loop for coordinating orthographic representations with output through the hand, and executive functions) may affect the acquisition of written language. Likewise, a model of working memory components (see Figure 2.3 and PAL II User Guide) (storage and processing of

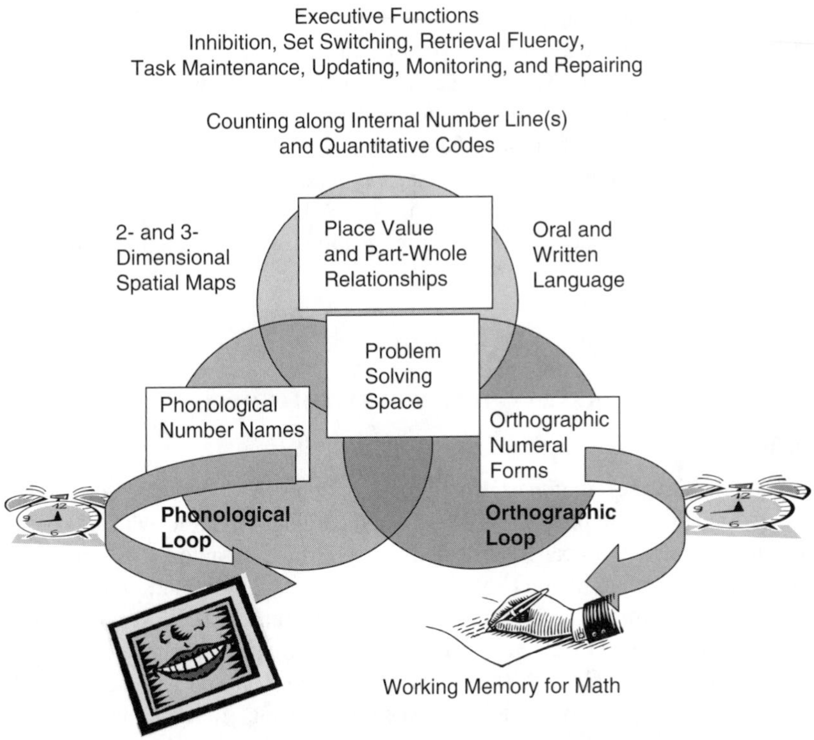

Executive Functions
Inhibition, Set Switching, Retrieval Fluency,
Task Maintenance, Updating, Monitoring, and Repairing

Counting along Internal Number Line(s)
and Quantitative Codes

2- and 3-
Dimensional
Spatial Maps

Place Value
and Part-Whole
Relationships

Oral and
Written
Language

Problem
Solving
Space

Phonological
Number Names

Orthographic
Numeral
Forms

Phonological
Loop

Orthographic
Loop

Working Memory for Math

FIGURE 2.3   Working memory architecture underlying functional math system. *Process Assessment of the Learner – Second Edition (PAL-II)*. Copyright © 2007 by NCS Pearson, Inc. Reproduced with permission. All rights reserved.

numbers, phonological and orthographic loops, and executive functions) may affect the acquisition of math calculation operations. Individuals may vary as to which of these components may be underdeveloped or functioning inefficiently, but if all components are not functionally efficient and in concert with one another, then fluency for reading or writing or performing math calculations is impaired.

The PAL II User Guide also provides a decision tree with downloadable diagnostic flow sheets for deciding whether any of the four diagnoses discussed in this chapter are relevant to the case at hand. At Step 1, the first question is whether the child has had sufficient opportunity to learn English? If not, then the focus should be on teaching the child English so that the child understands the oral language of instruction. The second question is whether, based on the five domains of development (cognitive/memory, receptive/expressive language, gross/fine motor, attention/executive function, or social emotional), does child meet criteria for mental retardation or pervasive developmental disorder, autism spectrum, primary language, or primary social emotional disorder as in the *Diagnostic and Statistical Manual of Mental Disorders*, Fourth Edition (DSM IV) (American Psychiatric Association, 1994)? If so, there are other etiologies, treatment issues, and prognoses than for the four specific learning disabilities covered in this chapter. The third question is whether the child has a known genetic disorder like Downs, fragile X, Williams or if the child had a brain injury or disease that affects brain function? If so, there are other etiologies, treatment issues, and prognoses than for the four specific learning disabilities covered in this chapter. The next steps in the decision tree are explained in each section dedicated to a specific learning disability. See Berninger & Richards (in press) for a brain-based conceptual framework for planning reading, writing, and math instruction.

DYSGRAPHIA

RESEARCH-SUPPORTED DIAGNOSIS

Definition

Dysgraphia is severe impairment in transcription skills, which include handwriting and spelling (Berninger, 2004) and keyboarding. Children with handwriting impairment may be impaired in legible letter formation, automatic letter writing from memory, or handwriting speed (Berninger et al., 2006b) and in motor-related issues such as motor programming for planning and executing motor output, visual-spatial arrangement on paper, and letter formation parameter setting that affects letter sizing (Graham et al., 2006). Although children with severe reading impairment are typically impaired in spelling as well, some children may read reasonably well and still be impaired in spelling; reading impairment with spared spelling is rare but does occur (Fayol, in press). Students whose dysgraphia is not identified are often mistakingly thought to be unmotivated or lazy. Gifted students may have undiagnosed handwriting and/or spelling problems masked by their superb language abilities (Yates et al., 1994).

Relationship to Cognitive Function

Verbal IQ was not related to handwriting in cross-sectional studies of normal writing development (Berninger et al., 1992b, 1994). Measures that uniquely predicted handwriting during this developmental stage included receptive and expressive orthographic coding and finger succession (an imitative sequential finger movement task that reflects grapho-motor planning) (Berninger et al., 1992a, b, 1994). However, when both orthographic coding and finger motor skills were included in the structural model for predicting handwriting, it was the orthographic factor that contributed unique variance, but the model fit best when both the orthographic coding and fine motor factors were included (Abbott & Berninger, 1993). A measure of visual-motor integration, which did not use letter form stimuli, did not uniquely predict handwriting (Berninger et al., 1992a, b). Rapid automatic switching (RAS) also predicted growth trajectories for handwriting in typically developing children (Altemeier et al., 2007).

TABLE 2.1　Diagnosing Dysgraphia – Transcription Disability in Handwriting Disability (HD) Only, Spelling Disability (SD) Only, or Combined Handwriting and Spelling Disability (HSD)

Transcription disability subtype	Cognitive Index	Achievement	Process measures
Handwriting disability (HD)	None	PAL II Alphabet writing Copy A Copy B Score for　　1. Automatic legible letter writing　　2. Total legible letter writing　　3. Handwriting speed	PAL II Receptive and expressive Orthographic Coding Finger succession and finger repetition
Spelling disability (SD)	WISC IV Verbal Comprehension (or WISC IV Vocabulary subtest)	WIAT II Spelling PAL II Word choice – score for accuracy and fluency (rate)	PAL II Phonological Coding Receptive and expressive Orthographic Coding Morphological Coding
Handwriting and spelling disability (HSD)	WISC IV Verbal Comprehension (or WISC IV Vocabulary subtest)	PAL II Alphabet writing Copy A Copy B Score for　　1. Automatic legible letter writing　　2. Total legible letter writing　　3. Handwriting speed WIAT II Spelling PAL II Word choice – score for accuracy and fluency (rate)	PAL II Receptive and expressive Orthographic Coding Finger succession and finger repetition Phonological Coding Morphological Coding

Prorated Verbal IQ (comparable to Verbal Comprehension Index) or the Vocabulary subtest was related to spelling in cross-sectional studies of normal writing development (Berninger et al., 1992a, b, 1994). Measures that uniquely predicted spelling during this developmental stage included receptive and expressive orthographic coding, phonological coding, and morphological coding (Berninger, in press; Berninger et al., in press; Nagy et al., 2003, 2006; Garcia, 2007; Garcia et al., 2008). Based on spelling research by many investigators of

English and French spelling, orthotactic (letter frequency and sequences) and phonotactic (sound frequency and sequences) knowledge, orthographic, phonological, and morphological awareness, and vocabulary knowledge contribute uniquely to spelling (for review, see Berninger & Fayol, 2008). Also word frequency (Fry, 1996) may contribute to spelling. In addition, rapid automatic naming (RAN), an index of automatic integration of orthographic and phonological codes, a phonological loop function, has been shown in growth mixture modeling to identify classes of response to instruction based on children's spelling during composing (Amtmann et al., 2008). RAS, an index of executive functions for managing switching mental sets, has been shown to predict growth trajectories for spelling in typically developing children (Altemeier et al., 2007).

Dysgraphia – Handwriting Disability

Thus, research-supported diagnosis of handwriting disability is based on level of achievement in handwriting independent of cognitive functioning or verbal reasoning. Students in grades 1–6 whose handwriting scores fall at or below one standard deviation below the mean for grade on PAL II measures of legible letter writing, automatic legible letter writing, or handwriting speed (total time) on the Alphabet Writing Task (letter writing from memory) or Copy A (from model sentence) or Copy B (from model paragraph) may be diagnosed with dysgraphia *if* answers to Step 1 questions discussed earlier indicate that there is not another probable cause of the handwriting difficulty. However, in addition to low handwriting achievement, there should be an indicator of a related process deficit if dysgraphia is an appropriate diagnosis; otherwise the low handwriting achievement may be the result of failure to receive instruction in handwriting. However, more boys than girls appeared to be impaired in automatic letter writing even in a sample selected from classrooms providing handwriting instruction (Berninger & Fuller, 1992).

Handwriting-related process measures that should be assessed include PAL II Receptive and Expressive Orthographic Coding, Finger Succession, and RAS. The first assesses ability to store written word forms and analyze letter forms in them in working memory, the second assesses ability to plan and execute sequential finger movements, and the third assesses an executive function for switching mental set (presumably as writers move from one letter form to another). In addition, rating scales are available to evaluate whether the following occur more often than expected on the basis of base rates derived from the national norming sample: letter form errors (e.g., reversals, inversions, omissions, repetitions, transpositions, case confusions – upper and lower, and format confusions – cursive with manuscript) and motor errors (e.g., alignment of letters on lines, letter sizing, and sizing consistency). See Table 2.1 of this chapter and PAL II User Guide (including Diagnostic Flow Sheets for Dysgraphia – Handwriting), Administration and Scoring Manual for PAL RW, and PAL II RW Record Form with Writing Profile and Diagnosis of Dysgraphia – Handwriting.

Dysgraphia – Spelling Disability

Research-supported diagnosis of spelling disability does rely on Verbal IQ or Verbal Comprehension Index (especially the subtest assessing vocabulary knowledge). *If* answers to Step 1 questions discussed earlier indicate no other probable cause of the spelling difficulty, then the following spelling and spelling-related process measures should be administered. To assess spelling achievement, give WIAT II spelling and PAL II word choice. The former assesses ability to spell with handwriting requirements for producing the written word, and the latter assesses knowledge of written spelling without handwriting requirements. To determine if research-supported spelling-related processes are impaired give: PAL II phonological coding, receptive and expressive orthographic coding, morphological coding, and RAN single letters and letter groups. In addition, scaled scores are available for the number of words spelled correctly while composing PAL II narratives and expository essay. See Table 2.1 of this chapter and PAL II User Guide (including Diagnostic Flow Sheets for Dysgraphia – Spelling), Administration and Scoring Manual, and PAL II RW Record Form with Writing Profile and Diagnosis of Dysgraphia – Spelling.

Table 2.1 provides an overview of how cognitive, academic achievement, and process assessment can be combined to identify children with dysgraphia (also referred to as transcription disability) – handwriting disability subtype, dysgraphia – spelling disability subtype, or combined handwriting and spelling disability subtype. The cognitive assessment is always relevant to Step 1 of the diagnostic decision process to show that a student's current cognitive ability falls within the normal range, but discrepancy from that cognitive ability may be more relevant to diagnosing spelling disability than handwriting disability within the broader dysgraphia (transcription disability) category.

Effect of Transcription Skills on Written Composition

Either handwriting disability or spelling disability can interfere with the ability to express one's ideas in writing; individuals who have both handwriting and spelling disability are even more compromised in their ability to express their ideas in writing. For review of the evidence, see Berninger and Amtmann (2003). Thus, it is essential that the written composition skills of students with dysgraphia be assessed. PAL II RW has measures of both narrative (two sets of two prompts each) and of expository (composing a content subject report) genres of composing.

Most school assignments require writing about source material (texts written by others) rather than only creative writing of one's own thoughts; that is, they require both reading and writing and thus executive functions for integrating reading and writing (Altemeier et al., 2006). Therefore, PAL II also assesses note taking ability based on reading source material as well as writing a report based on those notes. Also, PAL II assesses different levels of language within the narrative genre and both the narrative and expository genres combined – number of words and number of complete sentences within the time limits. For expository writing, a PAL II coding scheme also assesses quality and organization of writing and appropriate use of notes about read source material. To evaluate the student's ability to apply transcription skills during composition, for expository report writing, legible letter writing (rating scale) is assessed and, for narrative writing, number of correctly spelled words (scaled score) is assessed.

Individuals with transcription disabilities often make capitalization and punctuation errors. PAL II has a rating scale for capitalization and punctuation errors for this reason; when a specific kind of error exceeds base rates in the standardization sample, instruction can be planned to teach the necessary skills and monitor response to the instruction to evaluate when the skill is mastered. However, contrary to popular belief, capitalization and punctuation errors are not mechanical skills. Rather, they reflect application of translation, an executive function in writing, for marking in written language cognitive units and sequences of cognitive units in the constructed sentences (Fayol, 1997) and should be taught as such.

RESEARCH-SUPPORTED TREATMENT

Handwriting Disability

Handwriting treatments have been validated for letter formation problems (see first study in Berninger et al., 2006b) and for automatic letter writing problems (see first study in Berninger et al., 2006b; also Berninger et al., 1997). An instructional approach that combines study of numbered arrow cues for letter formation, holding letter forms in memory for increasing duration, and frequent naming of letters by the teacher has improved handwriting and transferred to improved compositional fluency (Berninger et al., 1997) and eliminated reversals (third study reported in Berninger et al., 2006b). This instructional treatment, validated in a large, randomized, control study, has been translated into handwriting lessons and composition prompts for teachers to use (Berninger, 1998b, Lesson Set 3 in Berninger & Abbott, 2003; and PAL II User Guide Instructional Resources, which may be downloaded). Also the Alphabet Retrieval Games (writing letters that come before and that come after designated alphabet letters) of Berninger (1998a, p. 193) have been shown to transfer to improved compositional fluency (Berninger et al., 1995). All the handwriting lessons that are downloadable from the PAL II User Guide also contain composition prompts so that students have practice in transferring letter writing to authentic written communication.

Spelling Disability

Spelling treatments have been validated for low achieving spellers that involve making connections between different units of spoken and written words (e.g., phonemes and graphemes, onsets and rimes, syllable types) and for spelling content and function words. Treatments used in these studies are reviewed in Berninger (2008) and Berninger and Wagner (2008) and have been translated into lesson plans for teachers (Lesson Sets 4, 5, 7 in Berninger & Abbott, 2003). See Berninger and Fayol (2008) for comprehensive model of what effective spelling treatment may need to include; also word frequency affects spelling during on-line composing (Fayol, 2008). All the spelling lessons that are downloadable from the PAL II User Guide also contain composition prompts so that students have practice in transferring spelling to authentic written communication.

Handouts for Parents and Teachers

NASP has published handouts for parents and educators to help school age children on a variety of school issues including writing – handwriting and spelling and its relationships to composing early in schooling (Berninger & Dunn, 2004a) and later in schooling (Berninger & Dunn, 2004b). Berninger (1998a) also has reproducible handouts that explain learning disabilities in general as well as those that affect writing (and reading): A Parent's Guide to Learning Disabilities and A Teacher's Guide to Learning Disabilities.

Assessment of Response to Instruction

Of priority is whether students improve on handwriting and/or spelling measures that identified the area of disability before intervention was begun and, if gains have occurred, whether they have transferred to improved composition, for example, on WIAT II Written Expression or PAL II narrative compositions or expository report writing. Only if achievement in handwriting, spelling, and written composition continues to lag behind, do the process measures need to be readministered to identify which of these may be the bottleneck that interferes with writing development.

Also of concern is whether children begin to apply improved handwriting or spelling not only on tests but also in daily work in the classroom. The PAL II Administration and Scoring manual contains a scoring system for legibility of letters that can be applied not only to PAL II subtests but also to any written composing students do in the classroom and to monitor their response to instruction on that basis as well. Children who are impaired in both handwriting and spelling are at the greatest risk for impaired written composition (Berninger & Amtmann, 2003) and should be monitored very closely for response to instruction. Children with dysgraphia plus attention deficit hyperactivity disorder (ADHD) often do not respond to instructional treatment in handwriting until they also receive appropriate medication prescribed by and monitored by a physician (and parents and other professionals on the multidisciplinary team) (see Case 3 below).

CASE STUDIES

Case 1

This second grader succeeded in all areas of the school curriculum except handwriting, which had been a problem for the child since kindergarten. PAL

II assessment showed why reading was a strength, but handwriting was a problem. In contrast to copying letters or words, with a model present (scaled scores of 10 and 11), automatic alphabet letter writing, which requires timed retrieval of letter forms and letter production, was impaired (scaled score 7). Likewise, graphomotor planning for sequential finger movements was impaired on an imitative finger task (Finger Succession, scaled score 6). This child's dysgraphia was specific to handwriting. His spelling (WIAT II standard score of 117) was a strength. Consistent with research findings for writing (Berninger & Amtmann, 2003), this child's problem in automatic handwriting impaired his written composing (standard score of 80 on untimed WIAT II Written Expression, and scaled score of 4 on PAL II narrative fluency). PAL Handwriting Lessons (Berninger, 1998b) were recommended to teach automatic letter writing through teacher-directed handwriting instruction and transfer of letter writing to composition (5-minute writing samples in response to prompts/composition starters in each lesson).

Case 2

This fifth grader was a very strong reader (standard score of 119 on WIAT II Reading Composite). However, spelling was less well developed (standard score of 87 on WIAT II Spelling) than either reading or WISC III Verbal IQ (standard score of 115) or WISC III Full Scale IQ (standard score of 119). Although untimed composition was a relative strength (standard scores of 110 on WIAT II Written Expression), timed rate of composition (scaled score of 8 on PAL II narrative fluency) was a relative weakness. The child did not qualify for learning disabilities services because the IQ-achievement discrepancy, based on a composite of state-approved untimed writing measures, missed the cutoff by 1 point, and the state special education regulations do not allow students to be qualified for specialized instruction on the basis of a spelling disability. Also, traditionally, spelling problems have not been considered as important as reading problems, and the multidisciplinary team that relies on special education procedures mandated by the state were not concerned about the spelling difficulties even though the teacher, parents, and affected child were. Neither copying text nor handwriting automaticity (scaled scores of 10 and 11, respectively) was impaired. Spelling impairment appeared to be related to deficits in receptive and expressive orthographic coding (scaled scores of 5 and 4). Dr. Fry's Spelling Program (Fry, 1996) was recommended with focus on using orthographic spelling strategies (Berninger, Winn et al., 2007) to learn to spell the instant words alone and in the context of daily sentence dictation activities.

Case 3

This third grader had both dysgraphia and ADHD. These developmental disorders co-occur in some but not all children with either dysgraphia or ADHD. This child was receiving special education services under the category of ADHD and was also taking medication under the supervision of a physician. The child's WISC-III Verbal IQ (104) fell in the average range and his most significant impairment was in handwriting automaticity, that is, rapid automatic retrieval and production of alphabet letters (scaled score of 6 on PAL Alphabet Writing). The teacher recommended that the child repeat third grade. The research team identified instructional approaches for dealing with the child's weaknesses in attention and automaticity and proposed an alternative to retention: explicit, systematic, and integrated writing instruction aimed at letter formation, automatic letter writing, spelling, and cognitive strategies for composing different genre (planning, translating, reviewing and revising) (PAL Reading and Writing Lessons, Berninger & Abbott, 2003, Lesson Set 8). The research team also identified the child's strengths in social interaction and the motivating influence of writing with other children and emphasized writing for an audience and sharing with others, which is incorporated in many PAL Reading and Writing Lessons in that children share their compositions with one another.

DYSLEXIA

RESEARCH-SUPPORTED DIAGNOSIS

When the University of Washington Multidisciplinary Research Center (UW LDC) was first funded in 1995, the team decided to focus on developmental dyslexia and adopted a definition that seemed consistent with that used by other investigators who had longstanding research programs on dyslexia (e.g., Maureen Lovett and colleagues at Toronto's Children's Hospital, Richard Olson and colleagues at the University of Colorado, and several other research teams in Canada, England, and the United States). That is, the focus was on the impairments in oral reading – both accuracy and rate (Lovett, 1987) for oral reading of single real words or pseudowords on a list (Stanovich & Siegel, 1994) and passages (Wiederholt & Bryant, 1992) and spelling (Bruck, 1990; Pennington et al., 1990).

The UW LDC conducted seven family genetics studies relevant to phenotyping, which is the behavioral expression of an underlying genotype (inherited individual differences in DNA). In all these studies the probands (children who met research criteria for dyslexia and thus qualified their families for participation in the study) showed a discrepancy of at least one standard deviation between their prorated Verbal IQ (comparable to WISC IV Verbal Comprehension Index) and achievement in accuracy or rate in oral reading of real words or pseudowords on a list or real words in a passage or written spelling. On average they were discrepant by more than the 15 standard score points (one standard deviation unit) and were discrepant in most of these skills rather than a single one. Consistent with previous research (Scarborough, 1984; Bruck, 1990; Pennington et al., 1990; Shaywitz et al., 2003), not only the probands, but also many of their parents, showed the behavioral indicators of dyslexia. Both

TABLE 2.2   Diagnosing Dyslexia

	Cognitive Index	Achievement	Process measure
	WISC IV Verbal Comprehension	WIAT II Word reading PAL II Pseudoword reading Accuracy and rate	
Component of working memory architecture			
Phonological storage and processing			PAL II Rhymes Syllables Phonemes Rimes
Orthographic storage and processing			PAL II Whole words Letters Letter groups
Morphological storage and processing			PAL II Signals Are They Related?
Phonological loop			PAL II RAN letters RAN letter groups RAN words
Orthographic loop			PAL II Expressive Orthographic Coding And finger succession
Executive functions			RAS Words and digits Delis-Kaplan color word form Inhibition and verbal fluency- repetitions

the children and affected adults (parents showing indicators of dyslexia) were included in the phenotyping studies.

In the first UW LDC phenotyping study (Berninger et al., 2001), 102 probands and 122 affected adults were given a half-day battery of reading, writing, and math achievement measures and related processing measures. Results showed that they were not only discrepant from their Verbal IQ on the target reading and spelling skills but also had associated impairments in the following processes: orthographic, phonological, and RAN. The more of these processing measures that were impaired, the more severe was the reading and spelling impairment. Structural equation modeling showed that the orthographic coding factor uniquely predicted accuracy and rate for all reading and writing outcomes except reading comprehension, that phonological coding predicted accuracy of reading and writing outcomes, and RAN predicted rate of reading and writing outcomes. In the adults, but not the children, the prorated Verbal IQ predicted some of the reading and writing achievement outcomes, providing evidence for use of Verbal IQ – achievement discrepancy in developmental dyslexia as an index of what eventual expected reading and spelling achievement might be. This study provided validation not only for the use of IQ-achievement discrepancy (at least for Verbal IQ and one specific learning disability – dyslexia) in diagnosis but also introduced the idea that the learning disability had associated phenotype markers of processing deficits that were part of the inclusionary criteria for defining it.

In 2003, the International Dyslexia Association adopted a definition of dyslexia, consistent with the work of Maureen Lovett and colleagues, Richard Olson and colleagues, Sally Shaywitz and colleagues and others including the UW LDC that dyslexia is a disorder in accuracy and rate of oral reading of single pseudowords or real words on lists or passages and in spelling (Lyon et al., 2003).

In the second UW LDC phenotyping study (Berninger et al., 2006a) behavioral expression of dyslexia was modeled within the theoretical framework of a working memory architecture that has a phonological core process in each of its components. This theoretical framework for working memory is different from, but not inconsistent with, using only behavioral measures of working memory function that have storage and processing requirements. Rather, this model of working memory architecture is brain-based and grounded in recent theoretical and empirical developments in the evolving construct of working memory (e.g., Baddeley, 2002). In this working memory architecture word forms can be stored and processed and accumulated word forms in syntactic structures can be stored and processed (Berninger, in press), but phonological and orthographic loops and a panel of executive functions also are involved in the system for supporting reading and writing. A *phonological core process* (Morris et al., 1998) exists in each of the working memory components:

1. Word form storage and processing (e.g., as assessed by measures of aural nonword repetition and validated in brain imaging studies, Richards et al., 2007).

2. Phonological loop, which can be assessed with RAN (personal communication with Elizabeth Wiig, May, 2004).

3. Executive functions, which involve inhibition or switching attention among tasks that involve phonological processing.

Results showed that this working memory architecture fit the phenotyping data well, consistent with the:

1. Psychological research of Swanson (2000) and Swanson and Siegel (2001) showing that dyslexia is a disorder in working memory as well as phonology.

2. Brain imaging research showing that phonological, orthographic, and morphological word forms and their parts are stored and processed in working memory (Berninger et al., 2006a, b; Richards et al., 2006a, b).

3. Working memory research showing that the phonological loop of working memory does more than sustain information in working memory as originally thought and plays an important role in the cross-code integration involved in language learning (Baddeley et al., 1998).

4. Executive function research showing that executive functions play an important role in literacy learning (Lyon et al., 1996; Swanson, 2000).

The surprise was that of the three components – word form storage and processing, phonological loop, and executive function, more of the individuals with dyslexia fell outside of the normal range on executive functions than on word form storage or phonological loop. This finding was consistent with research showing that children with learning disabilities benefit from explicit instruction in self-regulation, that is, executive functions for managing their literacy learning (e.g., Graham & Harris, 1996). Also, individuals with dyslexia fell outside of the normal range in orthographic and morphological word form storage and processing as well as phonological word form storage and processing and in phonological loop (RAN) as well as aural nonword repetition, which appear to be distinct processes.

In the third UW phenotyping study, Thomson et al. (2005) showed that the inattention factor (but not the hyperactivity factor) had a significant path to the orthographic coding factor but not the phonological coding factor. Brain imaging showed a correlation between activation in the brain regions associated with fast visual motion and rate of visual processing in children with but not without dyslexia (Winn et al., 2006). Berninger and Richards (2002) and Berninger and Wolf (in press) hypothesized that the fast visual motion deficit in dyslexia explains why many individuals with dyslexia have difficulty moving their attention to sequential graphemes (1 and 2 letters in length) within written words when learning to decode – associate phonemes with the graphemes and then synthesize the phonemes into a recognizable word. Instructional strategies that help students with dyslexia overcome this problem in attention to orthographic word forms and their parts include (a) use of color printers to color code grapheme units in written words to be taught, and (b) asking children to write the graphemes in written words in alternating colors (see Berninger et al., 2007).

In the fourth UW phenotyping study, analyses of phenotype expression in dyslexia showed that it is not only a reading disorder but also a writing disorder (Berninger et al., 2008a). With appropriate early intervention in learning to decode words, the reading problems often resolve by the middle of elementary school, but writing problems persist during the middle school and high school and even the college years unless students received explicit instruction in writing and not only accommodations for their writing problems (Berninger, 2006).

In the fifth study, analyses of phenotype expression in dyslexia showed that males are more impaired than females in writing phenotypes (Berninger et al., 2008b). As reported by other research groups (e.g., Shaywitz et al., 1990), major gender differences were not found in reading phenotypes associated with dyslexia.

In the sixth UW phenotyping study, growth mixture modeling (Amtmann et al., 2006) revealed two classes of response across rows on the RAN and RAS measures – slow and steady slow versus slow and slower within the individuals with dyslexia. These findings showed that individuals with this specific learning disability often have difficulty maintaining linguistic information (spoken names or phonological codes for orthographic codes) in working memory over time – that is, sustaining that information in mind until a task is completed. This disability is invisible to others but very real to the affected individuals who have to exert far more mental effort to accomplish the same reading and writing tasks than their classmates. The third author developed norms for not only the total time on PAL II RAN and RAS measures but also change in time across the rows of RAN and RAS. These scaled scores indicate whether an individual student is having difficulty sustaining mental effort for phonological loop functions.

In the seventh UW phenotyping study (third set of studies in Berninger et al., in press), structural equation modeling showed that phonological, orthographic, and morphological word forms and their parts contributed to reading and writing achievement in students with dyslexia just as they did for typically developing readers and writers, but that in general morphological word forms and their parts contributed more unique variance to the literacy learning of students with dyslexia than was the case for the typically developing readers and writers. The instructional implication is that students with dyslexia require explicit instruction in morphological awareness added onto their phonics instruction that emphasizes orthographic–phonological correspondences only.

In the first set of studies in this same phenotyping study (Berninger et al., in press), case study controls were used to identify phenotypes associated with genotypes – gene candidates that have replicated across research groups. A gene candidate on chromosome 6 was associated reliably with RAS, an executive function. A gene candidate on chromosome 15 was associated reliably with the phonological word form and its parts on a task that was also studied in brain imaging and found to differentiate the good readers and children with dyslexia (aural nonword repetition) (Richards et al., 2007). Collectively, these studies support the claim that there is a biological basis for the executive function and phonological word form storage and processing problems in developmental dyslexia (Berninger et al., 2006a, b).

The seventh phenotyping study (Berninger et al., in press) also showed that some individuals have only one specific learning disability – dysgraphia, dyslexia, or OWL LD – while others have combinations of these. Dyslexia occurred with and without dysgraphia. Some children, especially those with high verbal reasoning ability, showed signs of both dyslexia and OWL LD (complete with early preschool history of mild to moderate difficulties in learning oral language).

That is why the PAL II User Guide advised clinicians to use the diagnostic flow charts for differential diagnosis but also to consider whether more than one diagnosis may be appropriate. This study also showed that ADHD occurred rarely with classic dyslexia. Case studies showed that ADHD co-occurred more frequently with OWL LD. Further research is needed on these comorbidities within the specific learning disabilities affecting written language learning and with other developmental disorders that affect school age children and youth.

Table 2.2 summarizes the WISC V cognitive, WIAT II achievement, and PAL II process measures to give to decide if a diagnosis of dyslexia is warranted. In addition, the parent questionnaire on the PAL II User Guide should be given to parents to complete.

Note whether any signs of a learning problem were evident in the preschool years and whether the family has any history of reading or writing problems. Typically with classic dyslexia no signs of a future reading or writing problem are evident during the preschool years. In the UW LDC family genetics study, parents reported the first signs in kindergarten and first grade when their child had unusual difficulty in learning to name and write alphabet letters and then to associate sounds with those letters in learning beginning phonics.

Because dyslexia is a genetic disorder it tends to occur in families across generations and more than one family member is usually affected. Determining whether the family has history of reading and writing problems is useful information in further work with the parents of a child referred by a teacher or parent for possible learning disability.

RESEARCH-SUPPORTED TREATMENT

The PAL II User Guide has downloadable lessons (Lesson Sets 11, 12, 13, 14, and 15) that have been used successfully in published treatment studies for dyslexia. Children in grades 1–9 in the family genetics study for dyslexia just described participated in these studies. More recently, additional treatment studies have shown that attentional training before writing instruction can improve the ability of upper elementary grade students to attend and benefit from writing instruction (Chenault et al., 2006). Also see Berninger and Hidi (2006) and Berninger, Winn et al. (2007) for Writers' Workshops for Students with Dyslexia with Reading and Writing Problems. *Teaching Students with Dyslexia and Dysgraphia: Perspectives from Science and Practice* (Berninger & Wolf, in press) contains instructional strategies for teaching students with specific reading and writing disabilities within the general education classroom; it has four sets of lessons (also downloadable from CD) for one readers' workshop, one writers' workshop, and two reader–writer workshops that were developed for and validated with students with dyslexia who were in the family genetics study or met the same research inclusion criteria as those students. The PAL II User Guide also contains many recommendations of other instructional resources that are based on research.

ASSESSMENT OF RESPONSE TO INSTRUCTION

A multi-modal, leveled approach to monitoring RTI is recommended. These levels are not mutually exclusive and collectively they provide comprehensive progress monitoring that allows schools to evaluate both their curriculum in general and how individual children who have specific learning disabilities are responding to the instruction they receive in general education and possible special education.

At one level, all students in a school should be monitored using a set of common indicators of progress monitoring. For example, in many schools these include (a) the state benchmarks for high stakes standards, and curriculum-based fluency metrics for reading, writing, and math (e.g., Aims Web, Harcourt Assessment, Inc., 2008), which are administered at the beginning, middle, and end of the year. Some schools also give group-administered achievement tests.

At another level, students who are identified on the basis of cognitive, achievement, and process measures that research has shown provide inclusion criteria for identifying specific learning disabilities (as described in this chapter and summarized in Tables 2.1–2.4) should also be monitored for progress on these measures to determine if after identification and treatment they make significant progress and are performing at expected levels.

At yet another level, response to instruction should be monitored on a daily and weekly basis for whether students meet the instructional goals in specific lessons. Specific recommendations for this kind of monitoring are included in the Reading and Writing Lessons in the PAL II User Guide, along with the Growth Graphs for depicting visually for the students and teachers whether each student is meeting the specific goals for taught skills in a lesson. The growth graphs in the Reproducibles Manual for the PAL Reading and Writing Lessons, which are also downloadable from the PAL II User Guide, can be used to record time, frequency correct, percent correct, or rate for whatever probes the teacher decides to collect to assess instructional goals; PAL Reading and Writing Lessons contain recommendations for which probes to collect. Specific suggestions for alternative teaching strategies are provided at the end of each lesson set for students who are not responding adequately to instructional goals in the lesson set.

CASE STUDIES

The following case studies for developmental dyslexia, which is a genetic and brain-based disorder, illustrate how dyslexia presents differently at different stages of literacy development.

Case 1

A first grader participated in an early intervention study for children whose reading skills were behind at the end of first grade. This child, whose family had a history of dyslexia, already met research criteria for dyslexia at the end of first grade. After a year-long university-based intervention, which began during the summer between first and second grade and continued until the end of second grade, the child was reading on grade level (accuracy of decoding, real word reading, and reading comprehension). At the end of third grade, the child met criteria for another university-based study because reading rate was slow and oral reading was not fluent (smooth and coordinated). Mother reported that the child was a reluctant reader who avoided reading. After that summer intervention, the child's reading rate and fluency were grade-appropriate. Six years later the mother wrote the research director a thank-you note and explained the following. After a struggle throughout the primary grades, when the child hated school and faced daily challenges in keeping up with reading assignments, a transformation occurred in fourth grade and the change in attitude toward reading and the improved reading ability were maintained consistently after that. In ninth grade the child was an honor student, loved school, and had very high career aspirations. The mother was not only grateful but surprised that the family history had not repeated itself.

Case 2

A sixth grader, who had no special services previously because of parental fear of labeling, was a nonreader. During sixth grade, a special education teacher initiated specialized instruction using research-generated lessons (Reading Lessons in PAL Intervention Guides, Berninger, 1998a), which are similar to the PAL Lesson Set 11 (Berninger & Abbott, 2003). By eighth grade, the child was reading on grade level and the parents reported that their child now thought of himself as a reader. However, spelling problems persisted. Despite private tutoring, which commenced in high school, for spelling and writing (because special education services were not provided in school at that grade level), problems in spelling persisted. The child attends college but needs accommodations because writing intervention was not initiated early enough and sustained sufficiently until the writing problems were overcome. To qualify for accommodation and special services geared to learning disabilities in college, this student will have to be repeatedly evaluated every 3 years. Just as research-based diagnostic procedures have not been available for dyslexia during childhood, likewise they have not been available for adolescents and young adults for whom diagnostic findings might inform both instructional supports and accommodations after high school.

OWL LD

RESEARCH-SUPPORTED DIAGNOSIS

Many students who struggle in learning to read and write do not show IQ-achievement discrepancy. Thus, many researchers recommended not using

TABLE 2.3   Diagnosing OWL LD – Same as Dyslexia Plus Morphological, Syntactic, and Word Retrieval Measures. WISC IV Perceptual Reasoning Index May be Used in Place of Verbal Comprehension Index

Cognitive	Achievement	Morphological Syntactic	Word retrieval
WISC IV Verbal Comprehension or Perceptual Reasoning Index	WIAT II Reading comprehension PAL II Sentence sense Accuracy and fluency Morphological Decoding: Accuracy and rate 1. Finding the true fixes (silent) 2. Morphological decoding accuracy and fluency (with and without phonological shifts) (oral)	CELF 4 Receptive language age core CELF 4 Expressive language age core PAL II Are they Related? PAL II Does It Fit? PAL II Sentence Structure	Delis-Kaplan Verbal fluency measures or confrontational naming

IQ tests in diagnosis of learning disabilities. The UW LDC adopted a different approach – they conducted careful case studies of students who did not show IQ-achievement discrepancy (e.g., see Berninger & O'Donnell, 2004; Berninger, 2006, in press). They noted many similarities with what speech and language professionals were calling language learning disability (e.g., Butler & Silliman, 2002; Catts & Kamhi, 2005; Wallach & Butler, 1994; Wiig, 1991). These children do not have severe, primary language disorder or developmental aphasia and typically do not qualify for special education services under the category of communication disorders (e.g., for which in the state of Washington a student must be two standard deviations below the mean in receptive or expressive language). Nevertheless a careful preschool history is likely to identify early signs of some difficulty in learning oral language and careful diagnostic assessment during the school years is likely to identify continuing struggles in using oral language to learn written language and in understanding teachers' instructional language across different registers in which language is employed for different reasons (Silliman & Scott, in press; Silliman et al., in press).

The case studies conducted by the UW LDC since 2001 have consistently led to the conclusion that these students have in addition to the orthographic, phonological and RAN and RAS impairments of the students with dysgraphia and/ or dyslexia, additional significant impairment in morphological and syntactic awareness and word retrieval (Berninger & O'Donnell, 2004; Berninger, 2006, in press). These impairments, which sometimes are observed in oral language productions, are consistently observed on linguistic awareness tasks that require reflection about morphemes and syntax. They are sizable and often more than two standard deviations below the mean. PAL II morphological coding subtests (Does It Fit? Are They Related? and Sentence Structure), which do not require reading, and morphological decoding subtests, which do require reading (Finding the Fixes and Morphological Decoding – Phonological Shifts) identify children with OWL LD. So do the age scores on *Clinical Evaluation of Language Fundamentals – Fourth Edition* (CELF 4) (Semel et al., 2003) for receptive and expressive language, which have subtests that assess syntax awareness. Some of these children also have word retrieval difficulties (finding words in long term memory) on confrontation naming tasks or verbal fluency tasks.

What is relevant to differential diagnosis between dyslexia and OWL LD is whether the reading problems are solely in phonological decoding of pseudowords devoid of semantic content and related phonological and orthographic skills, as is the case with dyslexia, or whether real word reading and reading comprehension are also affected as well as related morphological and syntactic awareness and word retrieval, as is the case with OWL LD. In fact, in many cases the fast responders to phonics training for decoding have OWL LD; they are the treatment nonresponders in terms of improvement in real word reading, which does depend on semantic access to long term memory and access to names of real words in long term memory, and in reading comprehension, which depends greatly on morphological and syntactic awareness as a bridge between word meaning and construction of discourse understanding. Like the individuals with dyslexia, those with OWL LD typically have working memory problems too that impair their reading and writing fluency. Because of their syntactic problems, they also write shorter sentences that may contain grammatical anomalies (Scott, 2002).

All too often in the past students with OWL LD were considered slow learners when indeed their language problems interfere with their being language-based thinkers (a concept introduced by Audrey J. Don, a neuropsychologist in Washington State). Their thinking abilities may be masked in conventional assessments and learning environments. Some have amazing art or mechanical or technological skills that are evident in portfolios rather than on standardized test measures. Some show IQ-achievement discrepancy when Perceptual Reasoning Index is used rather than Full Scale IQ. However, in some cases Verbal IQ is higher than Performance IQ, especially in high IQ students with OWL LD. Thus, it cannot always be assumed that their Nonverbal Cognitive Index is the best or only estimate of the intellectual ability of individuals with OWL LD. Language learning disability can occur along with ability to think with language – the problems are in thinking about language and using language to learn.

Differential diagnosis between OWL LD and dyslexia is important for two reasons. First, the diagnosis has treatment implications. The cases being referred to the UW LDC that involve students who are not responding to intervention at school have a common theme. The treatment has focused just on phonological awareness and decoding instruction. The treatment has not focused on morphological and syntactic awareness (and in some cases orthographic awareness). When these missing instructional components in morphological and syntactic awareness are added, students begin to respond to the reading instruction.

Second, children with OWL LD may also have difficulty in using language to self-regulate their behavior. Many students are referred for and placed in special education programs for behavioral disabilities without a thorough assessment of their oral language and written language abilities and disabilities. Such an assessment might meaningfully inform an individual education plan for their behavioral as well as academic needs. Also, those students with OWL LD, who do not have family supports, may be at risk for dropping out of school, for not completing high school graduation requirements, for having social and behavioral problems as well as academic problems, and for getting in trouble with the law and being sent to prison. Many of the incarcerated adolescents the second author has evaluated have OWL LD coupled with ADHD and Conduct Disorder.

RESEARCH-SUPPORTED TREATMENT

Students with OWL LD benefit from explicit instruction in both reading comprehension and word decoding and reading (e.g., Berninger et al., 2003) and phonological, orthographic, and morphological awareness training (unpublished case studies). PAL II User Guide contains a list of instructional resources available for teaching morphological and syntactic awareness and word retrieval skills to students with OWL LD. Preliminary case studies suggest that these approaches to instruction for OWL LD can be very successful. However, more research is needed on identifying and treating this specific learning disability for which there has not been as much large scale, randomized control studies as for dyslexia.

The speech and language professionals have historically focused on oral language learning, although they are increasingly becoming more involved in written language learning and literacy. Psychologists have historically not focused on language issues, believing that language problems were best left to the speech and language professionals. However, now that three decades of research have clearly shown that reading and writing are language too, psychologists need to become more knowledgeable about language and its role in academic learning, behavior, and social emotional development and how incorporating language issues in assessment and treatment may benefit students with learning disabilities.

ASSESSMENT OF RESPONSE TO INSTRUCTION

In general, the same approach to assessing response to instruction as recommended for dyslexia can be applied to OWL LD, with this caveat. It is important to evaluate whether real word reading and reading comprehension are approaching grade level and Verbal IQ-level expectations. It is also important to monitor whether morphological and syntactic awareness and word retrieval are developing appropriately.

CASE STUDIES

Case 1

This boy was mildly delayed in saying his first words (slower than normal but just within the normal limits). During the preschool years he had difficulty focusing and was diagnosed by a medical professional as having an attention deficit disorder, but his parents decided not to use stimulant medication in treating the attentional problems because they noted that he had trouble focusing only when listening to oral language. The mother had heard a speech and language pathologist discuss a specific learning disability called language learning disability. However, during kindergarten and the primary grades, the school provided speech services for developmental articulation errors but not for language processing. Because he did not meet the state criterion for severe ability – achievement discrepancy, he was qualified for special education services under the category of attention deficit disorder (although he did not meet DSM-IV criteria for this ADHD or any of its subtypes). The special education instruction focused on multisensory phonics. Despite considerable help at school and home, he experienced a daily struggle with reading and writing. His spontaneous writing at home, which had interesting content, short sentences, immature handwriting, and phonologically based spelling errors, reflected his sadness at not being able to read and write like his peers.

When initially assessed by the UW research team when he was in third grade, his standard scores for accuracy of phonological decoding (98) and rate of phonological decoding (86) were higher than for accuracy of real word reading (86) and rate of real word reading (76). Typically in children and adults with dyslexia, the reverse pattern is found: phonological decoding is less well developed than real word reading. The rate problem, which is shared by children with both dyslexia and OWL LD, was found in oral reading of text as well (accuracy, 90; rate, 75). This boy had impaired orthographic, phonological, and RAN, as is common in students with dyslexia, but, unlike students with dyslexia, he was severely impaired in morphological and syntactic processing: PAL II Signals (deciding on the basis of suffixes which of four alternatives fits a specific sentence context) (scaled score of 4), Are They Related? (deciding whether a second word with a true morpheme or morpheme foil is semantically related or not to the first word) (scaled score of 5), and Sentence Structure (choosing which of three sets of words are in acceptable syntactic order(scaled score of 3) (Nagy et al., 2003, 2006). None of these morphological or syntactic measures, which may explain his severe problems in reading comprehension (WIAT II standard score of 80), require decoding of written words because they are administered orally (but with visual words and sentences to inspect). Both his reading comprehension and sentence formulation (planning and constructing syntax) fell at the lower limits of the low average range. Although he was not discrepant from his Verbal IQ (96) in phonological decoding, he was in reading comprehension, morphological, and syntactic skills. His verbal and nonverbal reasoning on the WISC-IV fell in the average range (near the population mean) but were not discrepant from each other. Like many other children with OWL LD, his attention problems were specific to his language processing problems.

The clinician recommended that the focus of the instructional program in special education and general education be redirected from an exclusive focus on multisensory phonics to a broader focus on automaticity of real word reading, fluency of text reading, and reading comprehension (reading vocabulary, sentence understanding, and paragraph comprehension). Although phonological decoding instruction is necessary for both dyslexia and OWL LD, it is not sufficient for OWL LD. In addition, she recommended inclusion of morphological and syntactic awareness instructional activities.

Case 2

This boy's language learning problems surfaced when he was a toddler – when most children are learning to combine words, he still had less than 10 words and used gestures to communicate. He received intensive language therapy services during the preschool years, but was exited in kindergarten when he no longer met criteria for needing special education services focused on communication. He became very talkative, but wordy; careful analysis of his language production revealed occasional syntactic anomalies. His CELF-IV profile was notable for better developed expressive than receptive language. Since first grade he continuously received special education services for reading and writing. He received considerable training in multisensory phonics. Teachers noted problems in attentional focus, especially when processing language. When tested at age 6 and 8, his Verbal Comprehension Factor was slightly but not significantly higher than his Perceptual Reasoning Factor, but both increased over time from the lower limits of the average range to the upper limits of the average range. The Processing Speed Factor (21st percentile) was an area of relative weakness compared to his reasoning skills. Like the child in Case 1, this child's phonological decoding skills (standard score of 100) were better developed than his word reading (standard score of 84) and reading comprehension (standard score less than 70); also, the accuracy above was better than rate of phonological decoding (standard score of 93) or real word reading (standard score of 81). Like the child in Case 1, this boy was found to have a severe morphological processing problem (PAL II Signals scaled score 6; PAL II Are They Related? scaled score 5) and a severe syntactic processing problem (PAL II Sentence Structure scaled score 3). The clinician recommended that the instructional program redirect its focus from exclusive focus on multisensory phonics to more focus on morphological and syntactic processing, oral word retrieval, and reading comprehension (reading vocabulary, sentence understanding, and paragraph comprehension).

When tested a year later after daily instruction and reading practice at school, the same pattern of relative strength in word decoding (standard score 100) and relative weakness in reading real words (standard score 85) was found, but reading comprehension had improved to the average range (standard score of 95). This response to instruction illustrates that the student with OWL LD has instructional needs in reading comprehension, as well as decoding. Further research is needed on effective instruction for improving the real word reading (accuracy and rate) for the student with OWL LD.

DYSCALCULIA

RESEARCH-SUPPORTED DIAGNOSIS

Geary (1993) identified three subtypes of math disabilities: impairment in knowledge of math facts, impairment in arithmetic algorithms for calculation, and impaired visual-spatial understanding of math. Fleishner and colleagues (e.g., Garnett & Fleischner, 1983; Fleishner & Manheimer, 1997) emphasized that some children understand the concepts but have difficulty using the visual notation system of math to represent their math knowledge on paper and pencil or have difficulty with automatizing math fact retrieval. While acknowledging the difficulties in automatic math fact retrieval, Swanson (in press) also called attention to the working memory problems that may interfere with math learning and performance. For example, many have difficulty with mental math in internal working memory when they cannot rely on paper and pencil representations and calculations to support processing in working memory. These individuals generally do very poor on WISC IV Arithmetic (now in the supplementary battery), which is a measure of mental math. As such, it can be compared to performance on written math calculation and problem solving on WIAT II to identify those who may do better when written support for calculation is allowed and those who do better when they rely only on mental math without that written support.

Table 2.4 outlines the skills identified in the Final Report of the National Math Advisory Panel (National Mathematics Advisory Panel, 2008) that are recommended as benchmarks for the youth in the United States. WIAT II Numerical Operations and Problem Solving can be used to identify those students whose achievement in arithmetic calculation or application of calculation to problem solving is delayed for grade or WISC IV Verbal Comprehension Index or Perceptual Reasoning Index, both of which are relevant to math learning (Robinson et al., 1996). Table 2.4 outlines how various PAL II subtests can be used then to identify various math skills and math-related processes that may be contributing to the calculation problems including understanding of whole numbers, fractions, and mixed numbers.

TABLE 2.4   PAL II M Diagnostic for Math has Subtests Aligned with Recommendations in the Final Report of the National Mathematics Advisory Panel (NMAP) and the Adding It Up Report of the National Research Council. These Target Math Skills, Any One of Which Might Contribute to Dyscalculia, are Listed Below with the Recommended PAL II M Subtest to Give to Identify Students with Weaknesses in the Target Math Skill for Purposes of Supplementary Instruction to Master the Skill. *Process Assessment of the Learner – Second Edition (PAL-II).* Copyright © 2007 by NCS Pearson, Inc. Reproduced with permission. All rights reserved

National Mathematics Advisory Panel Final Report	
Target skills	**Related PAL II subtest**
1. To prepare K to 6 students for success in algebra in middle school and high school, students need to develop these skills in elementary school (page 19, NMAP)	
• Conceptual understanding	Oral counting Place value Part–whole relationships
• Computational fluency	Fact retrieval Computation operations Finding the bug
• Problem solving	Multi-step problem solving Place value (Part C) Part–whole relationships (time) Quantitative working memory
2. Other targeted skills	
• Number sense (page 27, NMAP)	
Basic counting skills	Oral counting
Place value	Place value
Basic Arithmetic Operations (addition, subtraction, multiplication, division)	Math fact retrieval, computation operations
• Fluency with whole numbers (page 17, NMAP)	
Place value	Place value
Basic operations (algorithms)	Fact retrieval Computation operations Finding the bug
Applying operations to problem solving	Multi-step problem solving Place value (Part C) Part–whole relationships (time) Quantitative working memory
Automatic recall of number facts	Fact retrieval
• Fluency with fractions and decimals (page 18, NMAP)	

(*continues*)

TABLE 2.4 *(continued)*

National Mathematics Advisory Panel Final Report	
Target skills	**Related PAL II subtest**
Part–whole relationships (fractions, mixed numbers)	Part–whole relationships – Part–whole fractions and mixed numbers
Place value (whole numbers + decimals)	Place value
3. Number line representations (page 29, NMAP). Many of the recommended interventions in the PAL II M Test Administration Manual and PAL II User Guides involve number line representations.	
Adding It Up (National Research Council, page 16)	
5 attributes of proficiency	
1. Conceptual understanding	Oral counting Place value Part–whole relationships
2. Procedural fluency	Computational operations – verbal explanations and problem solution
3. Strategic competence (formulate and represent math problems)	Multi-step problem solving Part–whole time
4. Adaptive reasoning (e.g., explanation)	Computation operations – verbal explanation
5. Procedural disposition (seeing math as sensible)	Place value – problem solving written response Finding the bug Part–whole concept

RESEARCH-SUPPORTED TREATMENT

Swanson's meta-analyses (e.g., Swanson, in press; Swanson & Jerman, 2006) showed that explicit math instruction and strategy instruction are effective for students with math disabilities. Thus, PAL II Administration and Scoring Manual and PAL II User Guide contains recommendations for explicit strategy instruction for each math subtest. Thus, if a student scores low on a particular math subtest or math-related subtest, a strategy is described, which if taught to the student is likely to help the student learn the skill or overcome the processing weakness that interfered with math learning or math performance. In addition, instructional resources available at websites or commercially available are provided in the PAL II User Guide for planning treatment for students with math disabilities. Not as many large scale, randomized, controlled studies are available for math instruction in the general or special education population as for reading and much more research is clearly needed (National Mathematics Advisory Panel, 2008), but what does exist points to the importance of teaching skills to mastery before moving on to the next topic in the curriculum. Also, research has not found use of hand-held calculators to be effective. Students need to understand basic concepts about number and to perform mental calculation in working memory. Students with dyscalculia struggle in learning to do so but if identified early and given appropriate instruction may overcome this math disability and succeed later in schooling when algebra is taught.

ASSESSMENT OF RESPONSE TO INSTRUCTION

PAL II subtests in Table 2.4 can be used both in treatment planning and assessing response to treatment for dyscalculia. They can also be used in future research to identify reliable subtypes of dyscalculia and to evaluate effective instructional interventions for the various subtypes of dyscalculia.

CASE STUDIES

Case 1

This third grader had extraordinary difficulty recalling math facts automatically. The child's teacher used a pedagogical approach called Minute Math to promote automatic math fact retrieval. The child, who was significantly impaired in automaticity (scaled score of 5 on PAL RAN for numbers), cried during Minute Math and could not complete more than a few items when asked to retrieve math facts on this timed paper and pencil activity. Assessment revealed that the child had a repertoire of clever strategies for figuring out the math facts, so the problem was indeed automatic production of answers, not in controlled, strategic deduction of the answers. The clinician recommended (1) acknowledging the strength in strategy application, and (2) using alternatives to flash card number fact drill (e.g., selective reminding in which only missed items are practiced on subsequent trials; see Berninger (1998a) and multisensory strategies in which children listen and write, listen and speak, read and write, and read and speak number facts to automatize retrieval of all the numbers in the math fact equation).

Case 2

Assessment showed that this second grader had automatic recall of grade-appropriate number facts, but made many errors during computation. Observation of the child performing PAL II Computational Operations revealed that on multi-place subtraction (including problems involving regrouping) the child could not remember or verbalize the order of the steps in the algorithm. The clinician recommended teaching a strategy with verbal prompts for each step in the algorithm that the child could apply for self-regulated, independent computation.

Case 3

Assessment showed that this fourth grader, a sibling of the child in the second case, also had automatic recall of grade-appropriate math facts, but made many errors during computation. Observation of the child performing multiplication of multi-place numbers and long division of multi-place divisors revealed that the child got lost in the process of continually switching direction in space – from top to bottom (multipliers in one's place), bottom to top (to proceed to ten's place), and right to left (in contrast to reading most math proceeds from right to left) during multiplication; and from left to right (beginning with divisor), top to bottom (multiplying number at top with the divisor and placing the result below the appropriate digits), right to left (subtracting the product from the appropriate digits in the number being divided), and bottom to top (making sure that the difference is less than the divisor) during long division. The clinician also noted on PAL II Computational Operations that the student had difficulty aligning numbers on different rows in the correct column to retain place value of the number.

The clinician recommended teaching a strategy with both verbal and visual prompts for each step in the algorithm that cued both the computational step and the direction of movement in applying the computational steps so that the child could apply the strategy for self-regulated, independent computation. She also recommended that the child complete math calculations on graph paper with small grids and place one digit per square and review the concepts of place value using a combination of manipulatives and written representation of place value.

When the mother of the children in Cases 2 and 3 was asked if she understood the difference between the two recommended strategies, she readily responded that she did: one of her children was lost in time and the other was lost in space while computing. Application of arithmetic algorithms does require application of computational steps in time and space. Children may have requisite quantitative knowledge but have difficulty in negotiating the expression of this knowledge in the temporal and spatial dimensions of paper and pencil calculations.

Case 4

This fourth grader could retrieve math facts automatically and apply arithmetic algorithms reliably during paper and pencil calculations, but could not grasp the concepts of telling time, fractions, and decimals used in measurement. Some children have difficulty in grasping part–whole relationships. Unlike object permanence (objects stay constant despite irrelevant variations), magnitude of quantity may change in relationship to the number of parts in which a whole object is divided. Although increasing magnitude of a whole number signals greater quantity ($5 > 4$), if that number reflects part of a whole, then more is less – increasing absolute magnitude of the number of parts lowers relative magnitude (1 of 4 is more than 1 of 5). Without a grasp of the underlying part–whole relationships, errors will be made in telling time, fractions, decimals, and measurement. The clinician recommended that the conceptual understanding of part–whole relationships should be taught independent of paper and pencil activities that require application of part–whole relationships, for example, by using manipulatives to show the representation of different part–whole relationships.

Case 5

This second grade boy was referred for failure to complete paper and pencil arithmetic. Through administration of a number of visual-spatial reasoning and mental quantitative reasoning tasks on several IQ test batteries, the clinician discovered that the child was thinking algebraically and had advanced understanding of geometry. This child was a budding mathematician, but the teacher did not recognize it, and the second grade curriculum was way behind where this child's mathematical thinking was. The clinician recommended that the child be given an accelerated program of math in an individual progress program for intellectually capable (gifted) children (see Busse et al., 2001).

SUMMARY AND CONCLUSION

The approach described in this chapter differs from that recommended by others in the field of learning disabilities in two important ways. First, rather than ignoring the role of cognitive development in learning written language and math, cognitive assessment is included. Where research shows that cognitive measures are relevant for learning a particular skill (e.g., spelling, composing, reading words, and reading comprehension), then the level of cognitive functioning is considered in deciding whether current achievement is unexpected for cognitive ability. Where research does not establish a relationship between cognitive ability and skill acquisition, only level of achievement is considered (e.g., handwriting). However, the nature of the relevant cognitive ability is also considered. For reading, spelling, and composing WISC IV Verbal Comprehension Index is relevant. For math, both WISC IV Verbal and Perceptual Reasoning Indexes are relevant. However, a discrepancy of at least a standard deviation between the relevant cognitive ability and an academic skill does not alone serve as the basis for diagnosis of a specific learning disability. Rather, it serves as an indicator that further diagnostic assessment is warranted and that measures of processes shown in research to explain specific learning disabilities and to specify relevant treatment planning should be administered. Many of these processes have been shown in research to have not only diagnostic validity but also treatment validity – they predict individual growth curves in response to instruction.

Second, a diagnosis is based on research-supported inclusionary criteria – underachievement based on specific cognitive skill or mean for grade *and* associated research-supported process deficits – and is made when assessment shows that these inclusionary criteria are met. This approach is proactive and preventive because instead of waiting for a student to fail to respond to core curriculum or supplementary instruction in order to qualify for specialized instruction, the student is:

1. Identified through screening and family questionnaires early in schooling and then when appropriate through additional diagnostic assessment.

2. Given early supplementary intervention tailored to the nature of a diagnosed specific learning disabilities so that the student can respond optimally to the general education curriculum.

3. Monitored for response to supplementary instruction until adequate progress is made and student is achieving at expected level for grade and/or ability.

Such approaches instituted during the infant and toddler years have dramatically reduced the developmental pathway to mental retardation and language impairment in individuals who are born deaf. Such approaches at entry to formal schooling and literacy instruction hold great promise for helping to eliminate the chronic academic failure and associated behavioral and emotional problems of children at biological risk for specific learning disabilities. Serving these students does not mean that educational professionals are not also concerned about helping students at risk for reading, writing, and math problems due to the fact that they are English language learners or come from homes unable to provide home literacy and numeracy activities during the preschool years. Scientist-practitioners apply research-supported assessment and treatment to practice to optimize the academic achievement and mental health of ALL students.

NOTES

Dr. O'Donnell was the Research Director for the national standardization of the PAL II and the Research-Based Reading and Writing Lessons. Dr. Holdnack was the Research Director involved with norming, preparation of administration and scoring manuals, summary of technical properties of the PAL II, and validation studies.

ACKNOWLEDGMENT

Dr. Berninger was supported by R01 HD025858 from the National Institute of Child Health and Human Development (NICHD) during the preparation of this chapter.

REFERENCES

Abbott, R., & Berninger, V. (1993). Structural equation modeling of relationships among developmental skills and writing skills in primary and intermediate grade writers. *Journal of Educational Psychology*, 85(3), 478–508.

Altemeier, L., Jones, J., Abbott, R., & Berninger, V. (2006). Executive factors in becoming writing-readers and reading-writers: Note-taking and report writing in third and fifth graders. *Developmental Neuropsychology*, 29, 161–173.

Altemeier, L., Abbott, R., & Berninger, V. (2007). Executive functions for reading and writing in typical literacy development and dyslexia. *Journal of Clinical and Experimental Neuropsychology*, 30, 588–606. First Published on: 09 November 2007 1–19 To link to this article: DOI: 10.1080/13803390701562818 URL: http://dx.doi.org/10.1080/13803390701562818

American Psychiatric Association (1994). *Diagnostic and Statistical Manual of Mental Disorders* (4th ed.). Washington, D.C.: American Psychiatric Association.

Amtmann, D., Abbott, R., & Berninger, V. (2006). Mixture growth models for RAN and RAS row by row: Insight into the reading system at work over time. *Reading and Writing. An Interdisciplinary Journal*, 20, 785–813. Published Springer online: 28 November 2006.

Amtmann, D., Abbott, R., & Berninger, V. (2008). Identifying and predicting classes of response to explicit, phonological spelling instruction during independent composing. *Journal of Learning Disabilities*, 41, 218–234.

Baddeley, A. (2002). Is working memory still working? *European Psychologist*, 7, 85–97.

Baddeley, A., Gathercole, S., & Papagno, C. (1998). The phonological loop as a language learning device. *Psychological Review*, 105, 158–173.

Berninger, V. (1998a). *Process Assessment of the Learner (PAL). Guides for Intervention in Reading and Writing*. San Antonio, TX: The Psychological Corporation.

Berninger, V. (1998b). *PAL Handwriting Lessons*. San Antonio, TX: The Psychological Corporation.

Berninger, V. (2001). Understanding the lexia in dyslexia. *Annals of Dyslexia*, 51, 23–48.

Berninger, V. (2004). Understanding the graphia in dysgraphia. In D. Dewey, & D. Tupper (Eds.), *Developmental Motor Disorders: A Neuropsychological Perspective* (pp. 328–350). New York: Guilford.

Berninger, V. (2006). A developmental approach to learning disabilities. In I. Siegel, & A. Renninger (Eds.), *Handbook of Child Psychology, Child Psychology and Practice* (Vol. IV, pp. 420–452). New York: John Wiley & Sons.

Berninger, V. (2007a). *Process Assessment of the Learner, Diagnostic for Reading and Writing (PAL-II RW)* (2nd ed.). San Antonio, TX: The Psychological Corporation.

Berninger, V. (2007b). *Process Assessment of the Learner Diagnostic for Math (PAL II-M)*. The San Antonio, TX: Psychological Corporation.

Berninger, V. (2008). Evidence-based written language instruction during early and middle childhood. In R. Morris, & N. Mather (Eds.), *Evidence-Based Interventions for Students with Learning and Behavioral Challenges* (pp. 215–235). Lawrence Erlbaum Associates (LEA). Mahweh, NJ.

Berninger, V. (in press). Defining and differentiating dyslexia, dysgraphia, and language learning disability within a working memory model. To appear in E. Silliman, & M. Mody (Eds.), *Language Impairment and Reading Disability-Interactions Among Brain, Behavior, and Experience*. Guilford Press. New York.

Berninger, V., & Abbott, S. (2003). *PAL Research-Supported Reading and Writing Lessons*. San Antonio, TX: The Psychological Corporation.

Berninger, V., & Amtmann, D. (2003). Preventing written expression disabilities through early and continuing assessment and intervention for handwriting and/or spelling problems: Research into practice. In H. L. Swanson, K. Harris, & S. Graham (Eds.), *Handbook of Research on Learning Disabilities* (pp. 345–363). New York: Guilford.

Berninger, V., & Dunn, A. (2004a). Written language interventions for preschool and primary grades. In A. Carter, S. Carroll, L. Page, & I. Romero (Eds.), *Helping Children at Home and*

School: Handouts for Families and Educators. Bethesda, MD: National Association of School Psychologists.

Berninger, V., & Dunn, A. (2004b). Written language interventions for intermediate and secondary school students. In A. Carter, S. Carroll, L. Page, & I. Romero (Eds.), *Helping Children at Home and School: Handouts for Families and Educators.* Bethesda, MD: National Association of School Psychologists.

Berninger, V., & Fayol, M. (2008). Why spelling is important and how to teach it effectively. *Published online:* 2008-01-22 14:57:52 at Canadian Encyclopedia Entry\Encyclopedia of Language and Literacy Development.htm ON-LINE ENCYCLOPEDIA OF LANGUAGE AND LITERACY DEVELOPMENT. National Centres for Excellence Canadian Language and Literacy Research Network (CLLRNet).

Berninger, V., & Fuller, F. (1992). Gender differences in orthographic, verbal, and compositional fluency: Implications for diagnosis of writing disabilities in primary grade children. *Journal of School Psychology,* 30, 363–382.

Berninger, V., & Hidi, S. (2006). Mark Twain's writers' workshop: A nature-nurture perspective in motivating students with learning disabilities to compose. In S. Hidi, & P. Boscolo (Eds.), *Motivation in writing* (pp. 159–179). Amsterdam: Elsevier.

Berninger, V., & Holdnack, J. (2008). Neuroscientific and clinical perspectives on the RTI initiative in learning disabilities diagnosis and intervention: Response to questions begging answers that see the forest and the trees. In C. Reynolds, & E. Fletcher-Janzen (Eds.), *Neuroscientific and Clinical Perspectives on the RTI Initiative in Learning Disabilities Diagnosis and Intervention* (pp. 66–81). New York: John Wiley & Sons.

Berninger, V., & O'Donnell, L. (2004). Research-supported differential diagnosis of specific learning disabilities. In A. Prifitera, D. Saklofske, L. Weiss, & E. Rolfhus (Eds.), *WISC-IV Clinical Use and Interpretation* (pp. 189–233). San Diego, CA: Academic Press.

Berninger, V., & Richards, T. (2002). *Brain Literacy for Educators and Psychologists.* San Diego: Academic Press (Elsevier Imprint).

Berninger, V., & Richards, T. (in press). How brain research informs reading, writing, and math instruction and learning. In E. Anderman, L. Anderman, C. Chinn, T. Murcock, & H. L. Swanson (Eds.), *Psychology of Classroom Learning: An Encyclopedia.* Farmington Hills, MI: The Gale Group.

Berninger, V., & Wagner, R. (2008). Best practices for school psychology assessment and intervention in reading and writing. *Best Practices in School Psychology V,* (Vol. 4, Chapter 74, pp. 1205–1219). Bethesda, WA: National Association of School Psychologists.

Berninger, V., & Wolf, B. (in press) *Teaching students with dyslexia and dysgraphia: Perspectives from science and practice.* Paul H. Brookes.

Berninger, V., Abbott, R., Thomson, J., & Raskind, W. (2001). Language phenotype for reading and writing disability: A family approach. *Scientific Studies in Reading,* 5, 59–105.

Berninger, V., Abbott, R., Thomson, J., Wagner, R., Swanson, H. L., Wijsman, E., *et al.* (2006). Modeling developmental phonological core deficits within a working-memory architecture in children and adults with developmental dyslexia. *Scientific Studies in Reading,* 10, 165–198.

Berninger, V., Abbott, R., Whitaker, D., Sylvester, L., & Nolen, S. (1995). Integrating low-level skills and high-level skills in treatment protocols for writing disabilities. *Learning Disability Quarterly,* 18, 293–309.

Berninger, V., Cartwright, A., Yates, C., Swanson, H. L., & Abbott, R. (1994). Developmental skills related to writing and reading acquisition in the intermediate grades: Shared and unique variance. *Reading and Writing: An Interdisciplinary Journal,* 6, 161–196.

Berninger, V., Dunn, A., & Alper, T. (2004a). Integrated models for branching assessment, instructional assessment, and profile assessment. In A. Prifitera, D. Saklofske, L. Weiss, & E. Rolfhus (Eds.), *WISC-IV Clinical Use and Interpretation* (pp. 151–185). San Diego, CA: Academic Press.

Berninger, V., Dunn, A., Lin, S., & Shimada, S. (2004b). School evolution: Scientist-practitioner educators creating optimal learning environments for ALL students. *Journal of Learning Disabilities,* 37, 500–508.

Berninger, V., Garcia, N., & Abbott, R. (in press). Multiple processes that matter in writing instruction and assessment. In Gary Troia (Ed.), *Writing Instruction and Assessment for Struggling Writers: From Theory to Evidence Based Practices*. Guilford. New York.

Berninger, V., Hart, T., Abbott, R., & Karovsky, R. (1992). Defining reading and writing disabilities with and without IQ: A flexible, developmental perspective. *Learning Disability Quarterly*, 15, 103–118.

Berninger, V., Nielsen, K., Abbott, R., Wijsman, E., & Raskind, W. (2008a). Writing problems in developmental dyslexia: Under-recognized and under-treated. *Journal of School Psychology*, 46, 1–21. Available online Elsevier 8 January 2007. DOI link: http://dx.doi.org/10.1016/j.jsp.2006.11.008

Berninger, V., Nielsen, K., Abbott, R., Wijsman, E., & Raskind, W. (2008b). Gender differences in severity of writing and reading disabilities. *Journal of School Psychology*, 46, 151–172. Corrected Proof, Available online Elesevier 2 April 2007. http://dx.doi.org/10.1016/j.jsp.2007.02.007

Berninger, V., Raskind, W., Richards, T., Abbott, R., & Stock, P. (in press). A multidisciplinary approach to understanding developmental dyslexia within working-memory architecture: Genotypes, phenotypes, brain, and instruction. *Developmental Neuropsychology*.

Berninger, V., Rutberg, J., Abbott, R., Garcia, N., Anderson-Youngstrom, M., Brooks, A., & Fulton, C. (2006b). Tier 1 and Tier 2 early intervention for handwriting and composing. *Journal of School Psychology*, 44, 3–30. Honorable mention as one of the best research articles of the year.

Berninger, V., Vaughan, K., Abbott, R., Abbott, S., Brooks, A., Rogan, L., et al. (1997). Treatment of handwriting fluency problems in beginning writing: Transfer from handwriting to composition. *Journal of Educational Psychology*, 89, 652–666.

Berninger, V., Vermeulen, K., Abbott, R., McCutchen, D., Cotton, S., Cude, J., et al. (2003). Comparison of three approaches to supplementary reading instruction for low achieving second-grade readers. *Language, Speech, and Hearing Services in Schools*, 34, 101–115.

Berninger, V., Winn, W., Stock, P., Abbott, R., Eschen, K., Lin, C., et al. (2007). Tier 3 specialized writing instruction for students with dyslexia. *Reading and Writing. An Interdisciplinary Journal*. Printed Springer online. May 15 2007.

Berninger, V., Yates, C., Cartwright, A., Rutberg, J., Remy, E., & Abbott, R. (1992). Lower-level developmental skills in beginning writing. *Reading and Writing. An Interdisciplinary Journal*, 4, 257–280.

Bruck, M. (1990). Word recognition skills of adults with childhood diagnoses of dyslexia. *Developmental Psychology*, 26, 439–454.

Busse, J., Berninger, V., Smith, D., & Hildebrand, D. (2001). Assessment for math talent and disability: A developmental model. In J. Andrews, H. D. Saklofske, & H. Janzen (Eds.), *Ability, Achievement, and Behavior Assessment. A practical handbook* (pp. 225–253). New York: Academic Press.

Butler, K., & Silliman, E. (Eds.) (2002). *Speaking, Reading, and Writing in Children with Language Learning Disabilities*. Mahwah, NJ: Lawrence Erlbaum Associates.

Catts, H., & Kamhi, A. (Eds.) (2005). *The connections between language and reading disabilities*. Mahweh, NJ: Lawrence Erlbaum Associates.

Chenault, B., Thomson, J., Abbott, R., & Berninger, V. (2006). Effects of prior attention training on child dyslexics' response to composition instruction. *Developmental Neuropsychology*, 29, 243–260.

Delis, D. C., Kaplan, E., & Kramer, J. H. (2001). *Delis-Kaplan Executive Function System*. San Antonio, TX: The Psychological Corporation.

Fayol, M. (1997). On acquiring and using punctuation: A study of written French. In J. Costermans, & M. Fayol (Eds.), *Processing Interclausal Relationships. Studies in the Production and Comprehension of Text*. Mahweh, NJ: Lawrence Erlbaum.

Fayol, M. (2008, February). Toward a dynamic conception of written production. *Santa Barbara Conference* on Writing Research: Writing Research across Borders. Santa Barbara, CA.

Fayol, M., Zorman, M., & Lété, B. (in press). Associations and dissociations in reading and spelling French. Unexpecteadly poor and good spellers. *British Journal of Educational Psychology Monograph.*

Fleishner, J., & Manheimer, M. (1997). Math interventions for students with learning disabilities: Myth and reality. *School Psychology Review*, 26, 397–413.

Fry, E. (1996). *Spelling book: Words Most Needed Plus Phonics for Grades 1–6.* Now distributed as Dr. Fry's Spelling Book (available through Teacher Created Materials, 6421 Industry Way Westminster, CA 92683, 1-800-662-4321).

Garcia, N. (2007, December). *Phonological, orthographic, and morphological contributions to the spelling development of good, average, and poor spellers.* Ph.D. dissertation. University of Washington.

Garcia, N., Abbott, R., & Berninger, V. (2008, February). Contribution of phonological, orthographic, and morphological awareness to good, average, and poor spelling ability in grades 1 to 6. *Santa Barbara Conference* on Writing Research: Writing Research across Borders. Santa Barbara, CA.

Garnett, K., & Fleischner, J. (1983). Automatization and basic math performance of learning disabled children. *Learning Disability Quarterly*, 6, 223–230.

Geary, D. (1993). Mathematical disabilities: Cognitive, neuropsychological, and genetic components. *Psychological Bulletin*, 114, 345–362.

Graham, S., & Harris, K. (1996). Addressing problems in attention, memory, and executive functioning. An example from self-regulated strategy development. In R. Lyon, & N. Krasnegor (Eds.), *Attention, Memory, and Executive Function.* Baltimore: Paul H. Brookes.

Graham, S., Struck, M., Richardson, J., & Berninger, V. (2006). Dimensions of good and poor handwriting legibility in first and second graders: Motor programs, visual-spatial arrangement, and letter formation parameter setting. *Developmental Neuropsychology*, 29, 43–60.

Greenblatt, E., Mattis, S., & Trad, P. (1990). Nature and prevalence of learning disabilities in a child psychiatric population. *Developmental Neuropsychology*, 6, 71–83.

Lovett, M. (1987). A developmental approach to reading disability: Accuracy and speed criteria of normal and deficient reading skill. *Child Development*, 58, 234–260.

Lyon, G., Reid, & Krasnegor, N. (Eds.) (1996). *Attention, Memory, and Executive Function.* Baltimore: Paul H. Brookes.

Lyon, G. R., Shaywitz, S., & Shaywitz, B. (2003). A definition of dyslexia. *Annals of Dyslexia*, 53, 1–14.

Morris, R., Stuebing, K., Fletcher, J., Shaywitz, S., Lyon, G. R., Shakweiler, D., et al. (1998). Subtypes of reading disability: Variability around a phonological core. *Journal of Educational Psychology*, 90, 347–373.

Nagy, W., Berninger, V., Abbott, R., Vaughan, K., & Vermeulin, K. (2003). Relationship of morphology and other language skills to literacy skills in at-risk second graders and at risk fourth grade writers. *Journal of Educational Psychology*, 95, 730–742.

Nagy, W., Berninger, V., & Abbott, R. (2006). Contributions of morphology beyond phonology to literacy outcomes of upper elementary and middle school students. *Journal of Educational Psychology*, 98, 134–147.

National Mathematics Advisory Panel (2008). *Foundations for Success: The Final Report of the National Mathematics Advisory Panel.* Washington, DC: U.S. Department of Education.

Pennington, B., Van Order, G., Smith, S., Green, P., & Haith, M. (1990). Phonological processing skills and deficits in adult dyslexics. *Child Development*, 61, 1753–1778.

Prifitera, A., Weiss, L., & Saklofske, D. (1998). The WISC-III in context. In A. Prifitera, & D. Saklofske (Eds.), *WISC-III Clinical Use and Interpretation: Scientist-Practitioner Perspectives* (pp. 1–38). San Diego: Academic Press.

The Psychological Corporation (2001). *Wechsler Individual Achievement Test. WIATII* (2nd ed.). San Antonio, TX: The Psychological Corporation.

The Psychological Corporation (2003). *Wechsler Individual Intelligence Test for Children WISC-IV* (4th ed.). San Antonio, TX: The Psychological Corporation.

Richards, T., Aylward, E., Berninger, V., Field, K., Parsons, A., Richards, A., et al. (2006a). Individual fMRI activation in orthographic mapping and morpheme mapping after orthographic or morphological spelling treatment in child dyslexics. Journal of Neurolinguistics, 19, 56–86.

Richards, T., Aylward, E., Raskind, W., Abbott, R., Field, K., Parsons, A., et al. (2006b). Converging evidence for triple word form theory in children with dyslexia. Developmental Neuropsychology, 30, 547–589.

Richards, T., Berninger, V., Winn, W., Stock, P., Wagner, R. , Muse, A., et al. (2007). fMRI activation in children with dyslexia during pseudoword aural repeat and visual decode: Before and after instruction. Neuropsychology, 21, 732–747.

Robinson, N., Abbott, R., Berninger, V., & Busse, J. (1996). Structure of precocious mathematical abilities: Gender similarities and differences. Journal of Educational Psychology, 88, 341–352.

Scarborough, H. (1984). Continuity between childhood dyslexia and adult reading. British Journal of Psychology, 75, 329–348.

Scott, C. (2002). A fork in the road less traveled: Writing intervention based on language profile. In K. Butler, & E. Silliman (Eds.), Speaking, Reading, and Writing in Children with Language Learning Disabilities (pp. 219–237). Mahwah, New Jersey: Lawrence Erlbaum.

Semel, E., Wiig, E. H., & Secord, W. (2003). Clinical evaluation of language fundamentals fourth edition (CELF-4). San Antorio, TX: Harcourt Assessment.

Shaywitz, S., Shaywitz, B., Fletcher, J., & Escobar, M. (1990). Prevalence of reading disabilities in boys and girls. Results of the Connecticut longitudinal study. Journal of the American Medical Association, 264, 102–998.

Shaywitz, S., Shaywitz, B., Fulbright, R., Skudlarski, P., Mencl, W., Constable, R. et al. (2003) Neural systems for compensation and persistence: Young adult outcome of childhood reading disability. Biological Psychiatry, 54, 25–33.

Silliman, E., & Scott, C. (in press). Research-based oral language intervention routes to the academic language of literacy: Finding the right road. In S. Rosenfield, & V. Berninger. (Eds.), Handbook on Implementing Evidence Based Academic Interventions. New York: Oxford University Press.

Silliman, E., Wilkinson, L., & Danzak, R. (in press). Putting humpty dumpty together again: What's right with Betsy. In E. Silliman, & L. C. Wilkinson (Eds.), Language and Literacy in Schools. New York: Guilford.

Stanovich, K. E., & Siegel, L. S. (1994). Phenotypic performance profile of children with reading disabilities: A regression-based test of the phonological-core variable-difference model. Journal of Educational Psychology, 86, 24–53.

Swanson, H. L. (in press). Science-supported math instruction for children with math difficulties: Converting a meta-analysis to practice. In S. Rosenfield, & V. Berninger (Eds.), Handbook on Implementing Evidence Based Academic Interventions. New York: Oxford University Press.

Swanson, H. L. (2000). Working memory, short-term memory, speech rate, word recognition and reading comprehension in learning disabled readers: Does the executive system have a role? Intelligence, 28, 1–30.

Swanson, L., & Siegel, L. (2001). Learning disabilities as a working memory deficit. Issues in Education, 7, 1–48.

Swanson, H. L., & Jerman, O. (2006). Math disabilities: A selective meta-analysis. Review of Education Research, 76, 249–274.

Thomson, J., Chennault, B., Abbott, R., Raskind, W., Richards, T., Aylward, E., et al. (2005). Converging evidence for attentional influences on the orthographic word form in child dyslexics. Journal of Neurolinguistics, 18, 93–126.

Vellutino, F., Scanlon, D., & Tanzman, M. (1991). Bridging the gap between cognitive and neuropsychological conceptualizations of reading disabilities. Learning and Individual Differences, 3, 181–203.

Wallach, G., & Butler, K. (Eds.) (1994). Language Learning Disabilities in School-Age Children and Adolescents: Some Principles and Applications (2nd ed.). New York: Maxwell Macmillan International.

Wiederholt, J., & Bryant, B. (1992). *Gray Oral Reading Test* (3rd ed.). Odessa, FL: Psychological Assessment Resources.

Wiig, E. (1991). Language-learning disabilities: Paradigms for the nineties. *Annals of Dyslexia*, 41, 3–22.

Winn, W., Berninger, V., Richards, T., Aylward, E., Stock, P., Lee, Y., *et al.* (2006). Effects of non-verbal problem solving treatment on skills for externalizing visual representation in upper elementary grade students with and without dyslexia. *Journal of Educational Computing Research*, 34, 395–418.

Yates, C., Berninger, V., & Abbott, R. (1994). Writing problems in intellectually gifted children. *Journal for the Education of the Gifted*, 18, 131–155.

3

WISC-IV INTERPRETATION FOR SPECIFIC LEARNING DISABILITIES IDENTIFICATION AND INTERVENTION: A COGNITIVE HYPOTHESIS TESTING APPROACH[1]

JAMES B. HALE[1], CATHERINE A. FIORELLO[2],
JEFFREY A. MILLER[3], KRISTEN WENRICH[4],
ANNEMARIE TEODORI[4] AND JULIE N. HENZEL[4]

[1]Department of Psychology, Philadelphia College of Osteopathic Medicine, Philadelphia, PA, USA

[2]Temple University, College of Education, Philadelphia, PA, USA

[3]Duquesne University, Department of Counseling, Psychology, and Special Education, Pittsburgh, PA, USA

[4]Philadelphia College of Osteopathic Medicine, Philadelphia, PA, USA

[1]*Wechsler Intelligence Scale for Children – Fourth Edition*© and *Wechsler Individual Achievement Test – Second Edition*© standardization linking sample data used by permission of Harcourt Assessment, Inc. All rights reserved.

WISC-IV Clinical Assessment and Intervention

Children can have specific learning disabilities (SLD) that interfere with their academic achievement. With its historical foundations in neurology over a century ago, and codification in special education law, this premise serves as an important foundation for the remainder of this chapter. Inherent in this perspective is the critical word *specific*. Children with SLD have *specific* cognitive deficits that lead to poorer academic performance than would be expected given their *specific* cognitive assets (Hale, Kaufman, Naglieri, & Kavale, 2006). This differentiates children with SLD from those with lower global intelligence, which would be characteristic of those with borderline intellectual functioning or mental retardation (i.e., intellectual disabilities). Although these essential defining characteristics of SLD have been maintained throughout the 40-year history of the disorder, at least in the Federal law, there is no other disabling condition that has sparked more controversy than SLD.

Contentious and sometimes vitriolic debate by scholars and practitioners alike have raged in recent times, with little agreement on how best to identify and serve these children (Willis & Dumont, 2006), with some even questioning the validity of the SLD concept (e.g., Gresham et al., 2005; Ysseldyke & Marston, 2000). The lack of consensus among stakeholders in this SLD debate only serves to undermine our service delivery to children with and without SLD (e.g., Flanagan, Ortiz, Alfonso, & Dynda, 2006). Inextricably entangled in this debate is the relevance of individual differences in understanding and serving children's needs. Is SLD caused by characteristics intrinsic to the individual, environmental determinants such as instruction or contingency management, or (of course) both – the only conclusion that a responsible clinician would consider given the extant empirical evidence (Hale, 2006; Mather & Gregg, 2006; Schrank, Miller, Catering, & Desrochers, 2006).

This chapter examines the literature on several main topics critical to serving children with SLD and other learner needs, and how the WISC-IV can serve as an essential tool in the process. We begin with further examination of the SLD construct within the context of definitional issues, identification methods, and service delivery strategies, arguing for a balanced practice model that incorporates both response-to-intervention (RtI) and comprehensive evaluation (e.g., Fiorello, Hale, & Snyder, 2006; Hale, 2006; Hale et al., 2006, in press) using our Cognitive Hypothesis Testing (CHT) (Hale & Fiorello, 2004) model for comprehensive evaluation and service delivery for children with SLD who do not respond to standard general education interventions.

Arguably a critical feature in this model is the use of a well-standardized measure based on the latest cognitive/intellectual and neuropsychological theories (Hale et al., in press), and the WISC-IV rises to this challenge (e.g., Flanagan & Kaufman, 2004). We conclude that for children who do not respond to standard instruction, the WISC-IV and the Concordance–Discordance SLD identification model (Hale & Fiorello, 2004; Hale, Fiorello, Bertin, & Sherman, 2003; Miller, Getz, & Leffard, 2006) can be used as the "Third Method" of identifying children with SLD under the Individuals with Disabilities Education Improvement Act (IDEA). WISC-IV predictors of reading and math outcomes, and subtypes of reading and math SLD are presented to foster differential diagnosis and intervention for the diverse, heterogeneous, and enigmatic population of children we call SLD. Finally, empirical studies that support the use of cognitive/neuropsychological assessment to guide intervention efforts are reviewed, with implications of WISC-IV CHT-driven intervention offered.

DEFINITIONS OF SLD: LEARNING DELAY OR DEFICIT?

Children can experience classroom success or difficulties for a plethora of reasons, including inadequate instruction, learning delays, and specific learning deficits, which makes identification of children with SLD both difficult and controversial. Although some have advocated transforming SLD into a generic learning difficulty category (e.g., Dombrowski, Kamphaus, & Reynolds, 2004; Fletcher, Coulter, Reschly, & Vaughn, 2004; Stanovich, 1994), thereby serving individuals with learning delays and deficits in the same broad undifferentiated learning problem group, this model inappropriately suggests that all academic problems are temporary, outgrown, and overcome (Mather & Gregg, 2006).

Unfortunately, longitudinal research comparing delay and deficit models has shown that children with SLD have specific learning *deficits* not delays (Francis, Shaywitz, Stuebing, Shaywitz, & Fletcher, 1996) that require individualized assessment and intervention techniques that have greater diagnostic sensitivity and specificity (Holdnack, Kavale, & Mastert, 2005). This conclusion has been codified through expert consensus (Learning Disabilities Roundtable; US Department of Education, 2002, 2005) and the current Federal IDEA Definition of SLD (34 C.F.R. 300.8):

> Specific Learning Disability means a disorder in one or more of the basic psychological processes involved in understanding or in using language, spoken or written, which may manifest itself in the imperfect ability to listen, think, speak, read, write, spell, or do mathematical calculations, including conditions such as perceptual disabilities, brain injury, minimal brain dysfunction, dyslexia, and developmental aphasia.

Inherent in this statutory regulation is the notion that the achievement deficits experienced by children with SLD are caused by a *disorder in the basic psychological processes*, which would be consistent with the plethora of studies demonstrating that many childhood disorders are caused by specific neuropsychological *deficits* not delays (see Berninger & Richards, 2002; Castellanos et al., 2002; Collins & Rourke, 2003; Fiez & Petersen, 1998; Filipek, 1999; Fine, Semrud-Clikeman, Keith, Stapleton, & Hynd, 2007; Francis et al., 1996; Geary, Hoard, & Hamsom, 1999; Hale & Fiorello, 2004; Naglieri & Bornstein, 2003; Nicholson & Fawcett, 2001; Pugh et al., 2000; Shaywitz, Lyon, & Shaywitz, 2006; Simos et al., 2005; Stein, 2001; Tallal, 2006).

The deficit position was also advanced by 14 organizations that composed the Learning Disabilities Roundtable (2002, 2005) advisory panel, which concluded, "The identification of a core cognitive deficit, or a disorder in one or more of the basic psychological processes, predictive of an imperfect ability to learn, is a marker for a SLD (U.S. D. O. E., 2002, p. 5)." In the 2004 session, participants concluded that establishing a pattern of strengths and weaknesses was more important than ability–achievement discrepancy when determining SLD, noting, "...[I]t is important to recognize that the new guideline also acknowledges intra-individual differences as a fundamental concept of SLD (U.S. D. O. E., 2005, p. 13)."

Despite resistance to this essential defining feature of SLD under IDEA, with vocal opposition commencing with the inception of the SLD category (Hammill & Larsen, 1974) and continuing to the present time (Fletcher & Reschly, 2005), practitioners must recognize that adherence to this critical SLD statutory requirement can help differentiate children with SLD from children with other causes of learning problems or delay (Kavale & Flanagan, 2007). There is no doubt that some children with learning problems have limited educational opportunity, experience ineffectual instruction, and/or their academic progress is poorly monitored and accordingly modified, but all these are *environmental causes* for their learning problems. Even with adequate instruction, some children learn at a lower rate than is typical and are considered to be "slow learners" or a "low achievement" (LA) group. In contrast, those with SLD have *specific* cognitive assets in the presence of *specific* cognitive deficits, and this pattern leads to poor academic achievement in one or more domains (Hale et al., 2006). This is not just an opinion, but one substantiated by extensive neurobiological and genetic evidence (Berninger & Richards, 2002; Hale & Fiorello, 2004; Ingalls & Goldstein, 1999).

Although the differentiation of "instructional casualties," LA, and SLD groups has intuitive and empirical appeal, some have argued that there are no relevant or discriminating measures of psychological processing deficits (Gresham et al., 2005), leading some to conclude it is perhaps best to ignore them altogether (e.g., Reschly, 2005), especially when it is obvious that all these children are not acquiring basic academic skills commensurate with their typically achieving peers. Unfortunately, using a low achievement model alone will likely lead to overidentification of children with SLD (Mather & Gregg, 2006), especially ethnic minority and disadvantaged students (McDermott, Goldberg, Watkins, Stanley, & Glutting, 2006) – a traditional criticism levied against the use of intelligence tests and ability–achievement discrepancy (Warner, Dede, Garvan, & Conway, 2002). It is critical to recognize that although ability–achievement discrepancy is controversial and is no longer required under IDEA (2004), this should not be equated with abandonment of the essential marker for SLD – a deficit in the basic psychological processes (Hale et al., 2006; Ofiesh, 2006; Schrank et al., 2006).

Do children with LA and SLD need additional instructional support? Of course both groups need and should receive additional services to reach expected academic competencies or benchmarks, and low achievement models (e.g., Dombrowski et al., 2004; Fletcher, Denton, & Francis, 2005) would serve both. However, we contend that those with SLD differ from children with LA in that the SLD group requires *individualized* instruction tailored to their specific cognitive assets and deficits (Fiorello et al., 2001, 2006, 2007, in press; Hale, 2006; Hale & Fiorello, 2004; Hale et al., 2006, 2007, in press) whereas the latter group requires instruction comparable to typical children but at *greater intensity*. The notion that increasing intervention intensity will serve children at each tier has been the hallmark of several multi-tiered RtI models designed to serve all children with learning difficulties (e.g., Barnett, Daly, Jones, & Lentz, 2004; Brown-Chidsey & Steege, 2005; VanDerHeyden, Witt, & Gilbertson, 2007). However, more *intensive* instruction using the *same* techniques will only work for children with LA. Children with SLD who do not benefit from typical instruction offered at more intense levels need innovative instructional approaches to acquire academic skills commensurate with their higher level cognitive assets. Despite consensus among many leading educators that this heuristic has face validity, in practice differential diagnosis of and service delivery for these LA and SLD groups have been largely ineffectual in the past (Fletcher, Shaywitz, Shankweiler, & Katz, 1994; Stanovich, 1994), which, of course, could be due to evaluation methods that lack diagnostic sensitivity and specificity (Kavale, Holdnack, & Mostert, 2005) or interventions that are seldom individualized based on child cognitive or neuropsychological characteristics (Hale & Fiorello, 2004).

There are numerous reasons why children do not respond to instructional approaches for serving typical children, only one of which may be SLD (Fuchs & Deshler, 2007; Hale et al., 2006; Mather & Gregg, 2006; Schrank et al., 2006). The question of whether learning problems are reflective of a learning delay as opposed to a learning deficit is critical in this analysis. The notion that all children learn similarly, but are not learning due to environmental causes such as ineffective instruction or that some children experience learning delays due to low average intellectual functioning, is intuitively appealing and has an alluring humanistic cachet. In fact, there are many children who primarily have learning delays for these environmental or intellectual causes, and for these children, more intensive, scientifically based instruction should foster their academic achievement.

Unfortunately, not all children fit this mold, and environmental causes of learning problems are listed in the *exclusionary* criteria for determining SLD under IDEA (34 C.F.R. 300.8):

> Specific Learning Disability does not include learning problems that are primarily the result of visual, hearing, or motor disabilities, of mental retardation, of emotional disturbance, or of environmental, cultural, or economic disadvantage.

In addition, our research (Fiorello et al., 2001, 2007; Hale et al., 2001, 2007, in press) shows that cognitive strengths and weaknesses are *common* in typical children and children with learning and other high incidence disabilities, so profile variability in and of itself is *not* an essential marker for SLD or other disorders (although see Mayes, Calhoun, & Crowell, 1998; Mayes & Calhoun, 2004, 2007). Does this suggest that profile variability observed on intellectual measures such as the WISC-IV is clinically meaningless, as has been suggested by others (e.g., Glutting, Youngstorm, Ward, Ward, & Hale, 1997)? On the contrary, it would seem we live in a marvelously diverse cognitive world that can be measured by the WISC-IV, and exploring individual differences in cognitive functioning, academic achievement, and socioemotional functioning can serve as a foundation for providing differentiated instruction in classrooms – not only for those with SLD, but other disorders and typical children as well.

PREVALENCE OF SLD: HETEROGENEITY AND COMORBIDITY

Concerns over the identification of SLD have arisen in part because it is the most common disabling condition, with as much as 15% of the population having some form of SLD, and over 50% of all children with disabilities classified as having SLD (Lerner, 2003; Sattler, 2001). State educational definitions differ in their identification methods, criteria, and as a result, their prevalence rates, ranging from 3% to 9% of the student population (Reschly & Hosp, 2004). Because services have not been typically provided for children with learning difficulties who did not meet SLD discrepancy criteria, the SLD category has become intangible and amorphous. Given that three different SLD identification methods are now available under IDEA (2004), this problem will likely persist and may even become exacerbated (Hale, 2006).

Rigid discrepancy cut-off criteria (e.g. 15-point discrepancy) were typically established in some jurisdictions in an attempt to stem the flow of SLD numbers, where one child would qualify but another would not, even though they only had a one-point difference and had similar causes for their learning difficulties and similar instructional needs. Those with higher IQs tend to meet discrepancy criteria more than those with lower IQs when cut-off scores are used (Reschly & Hosp, 2004), because children with cognitive deficits apparent on both the intelligence and achievement tests have depressed global IQs, and often do not meet discrepancy criteria (e.g., Mark Penalty; Willis & Dumont, 2006). In addition, young children would seldom qualify given the discrepancy rules, so they had to "wait to fail" before being retested several years later and subsequently classified (Lyon, 2005).

As a result of ambiguous and seemingly arbitrary SLD identification methods, many children with learning problems were classified as SLD regardless of whether they had the processing deficit required by federal statutory law. There has been little agreement among teams, schools, districts, and even states regarding the SLD definition and method of determination (Reschly & Hosp, 2004). Disagreements and concerns over the process have often lead to "optional" identification methods typically based on team "judgment."

In other words, there has been nothing "specific" about SLD in the past. In fact, almost any child with learning problems could be identified as SLD, which leads one to conclude that SLD is a very heterogenous group comprised of children with SLD, LA, and many other developmental, medical, or psychological disabilities. In fact, under IDEA, academic difficulties are required for disability entitlement regardless of the category, so in essence, *any* child with learning difficulties could conceivably be labeled as SLD if teams are not careful and judicious in their identification practices.

This may be in part to the failure of states to address both the statutory and regulatory requirements under IDEA (Hale et al., 2006), as only about 25% of the states require identification of a processing deficit when determining SLD, and this requirement has actually *declined* in recent years (Reschly & Hosp, 2004). Finally, even if a child is appropriately classified as SLD, this does little to provide us with a prototypical SLD cognitive or achievement profile, as there are numerous SLD subtypes, even within academic domains (e.g., reading, math, writing), with different cognitive/neuropsychological causes for their academic deficits, and different intervention needs (see Hale & Fiorello, 2004).

For children with reading SLD, classification rates vary from 5% to 17.5% (Semrud-Clikeman, Fine, & Harder, 2005), but for those with reading problems, prevalence rates are much higher, with as many as 25% of the population failing to meet Federal benchmarks for minimal reading competency, and the failure rates are often higher for children of sociocultural, ethnic, and racial differences (Hale et al., 2004). A majority (approximately 80%) of children identified as SLD have a specific reading disability (Shaywitz & Shaywitz, 2006). However, the question remains as to whether more children have reading disability, or whether we are more likely to identify children with the disorder, as math SLD may be just as common as reading SLD (Swanson & Jerman, 2006), with prevalence rates indicating about 6% of the population is affected by math SLD (Geary, Hamson, & Hoard, 2000; Mazzocco, 2001) and approximately 5–8% of typical children have some form of cognitive difficulty that interferes with learning math concepts or procedures (Geary, 2004). A common misconception is that all children with math SLD have "nonverbal" or right hemisphere dysfunction (Hale et al., 2003), but this is not typical, as language-based SLDs – presumed to be due to left hemisphere dysfunction – are far more common causes of math SLD, and often co-occur with reading and written language-based SLDs (Geary, 2004; Hale & Fiorello, 2004; Light & Defries, 1995).

Is language-based SLD more a speech and language disorder, or a SLD? Certainly, language issues are critical to consider when diagnosing SLD (Wiig, 2005), such as a reading comprehension (e.g., receptive language deficits) or written language (e.g., expressive language deficits) SLD. The prevalence of written language disorders has been estimated to be as high as 17% of the population (Hooper et al., 1994), so this further complicates differential diagnosis and comorbidity estimates. Certainly, one can be classified with receptive or expressive language problems leading to SLD in one or more areas, so comorbidity rates are typically high (McLeod & McKinnon, 2007). These issues are further addressed in the Wiig chapter, as we focus primarily on reading and math SLD in this chapter.

When one examines comorbidity in clinical populations, rates tend to be higher than the general population. Prevalence estimates of comorbid emotional/behavioral or psychiatric disorders and SLD are often 40% or higher (Taggart,

Cousins, & Milner, 2007). Mayes and Calhoun (2006) found 65% of their clinical sample had comorbid SLD, with 92% of these children showing a disorder of written expression. Single reading, writing or math LDs were less common, and prevalence rates were comparable for reading (33%) and math (32%) SLD. Comorbid SLD was identified in children with bipolar disorder (79%), attention-deficit/hyperactivity disorder (ADHD) combined (71%) and inattentive (66%) types, and autism spectrum disorders (67%), but was less common in other psychiatric conditions (Mayes & Calhoun, 2006). The high rates of written language SLD in this population could be related to the high rate of frontal–executive dysfunction in psychopathology (see Lichter & Cummings, 2001).

Not surprisingly, high rates of reading, math, and writing SLD are found in children with ADHD (Mayes & Calhoun, 2004; Semrud-Clikeman, 2005), given that ADHD is likely caused by frontal–subcortical circuit dysfunction (Hale et al., 2005). Mayes and Calhoun (2007) reported that 76% of their ADHD population had comorbid SLD, but written language SLD was much more common than reading and math SLD. However, other studies have suggested that reading SLD is more common in children with ADHD than math or written language disorders (Del'Homme, Kim, Loo, Yang, & Smalley, 2007), with as many as 50% showing reading difficulties (Semrud-Clikeman et al., 1992).

Reading SLD is often found among adjudicated delinquents, with estimates suggesting about 40% of that population has significant reading problems (Shelley-Tremblay, O'Brien, & Langhinrichsen-Rohling, 2007). Despite variable findings, these rates suggest considering comorbidity is not only essential for differential diagnosis of SLD, but also for developing successful academic interventions as well. Comorbidity of SLD with other conditions exacerbates achievement deficits and confounds diagnostic results (Smith & Adams, 2006), thereby limiting the utility of both RtI and discrepancy approaches in SLD identification (Fiorello et al., 2006; Hale et al., 2006).

ABILITY–ACHIEVEMENT DISCREPANCY, RTI, OR THE "THIRD METHOD"

When IDEA (2004) was passed by the US Congress, two regulatory methods – ability–achievement discrepancy and failure to RtI – were written into law as methods for determining a SLD. However, the final Federal regulations (34 C.F.R. Parts 300 and 301; 2006) provided a "Third Method" for SLD identification:

> (3) May permit the use of other alternative research-based procedures for determining whether a child has a specific learning disability, as defined in §300.8(c)(10).

Although this "Third Method" appears to be vague and nonspecific, leading some to largely ignore it (e.g., Lichtenstein & Klotz, 2007), it likely reflects similar empirically supported methods as viable alternatives to ability–achievement discrepancy (Flanagan et al., 2006; Hale & Fiorello, 2004; Naglieri, 1999).

Described later, these plausible "Third Method" approaches hold the key to effective SLD identification and service delivery, because neither ability–achievement discrepancy nor failure to RtI addresses both the IDEA (2004) statutory and regulatory SLD requirements or individualized interventions for those who do not RtI (Fiorello et al., 2006; Hale, 2006; Hale et al., 2006).

If neither discrepancy nor RtI are sufficient to determine whether a child has SLD, why are these methods so widely recognized? Despite widespread criticism regarding the use of ability–achievement discrepancy method for determining SLD (see Fletcher et al., 2004), it has endured for over 30 years. Rutter and Yule's (1975) Isle of Wright study and the passage of the P.L. 94–142 (Education of All Handicapped Children Act) in 1975 solidified the use of the ability–achievement discrepancy method of classifying children with SLD.

Since this time, evidence has mounted that discrepancy was not an effective classification method (Meyer, 2000), as ability-discrepant and ability-consistent poor readers have typically differed only on cognitive ability measures (Steubing et al., 2002). Although those who both support and abhor cognitive/intellectual assessment no longer support rigid adherence to ability–achievement discrepancy (e.g., Fletcher et al., 2004; Hale et al., 2006; Shinn, 2002), many have conflated the global IQ with cognitive/intellectual assessment, resulting in a less than useful schism in the field. This was exacerbated by studies that suggested the global IQ was the only relevant measure obtained from intellectual/cognitive tests (e.g., Glutting, Watkins, Konold, & McDermott, 2006; Watkins, Gluting, & Lei, 2007). Thus, the rallying cry for many in the RtI-only position is, "If discrepancy is not useful, then neither are 'IQ' tests!" It should be noted, however, that the "incremental validity" study findings have been empirically challenged, calling into to question whether these tests are indeed just measures of global IQ or "g" (see Fiorello et al., 2007; Hale et al., 2007, in press, for statistical presentation). In fact, these studies have shown that the WISC-IV and Differential Ability Scales – Second Edition (DAS-II) factors uniquely and in combination predict reading and math achievement quite well, but the shared variance among all these constructs (an alternative measure of "g" or general intelligence) is actually quite small (Hale et al., 2007, in press).

As this intelligence/cognitive test interpretive schism has broadened, so did a progressive movement toward more formative evaluation and ongoing curriculum-based measurement (CBM) of child progress, which has in turn strengthened and fueled advocacy for the current RtI method of determining SLD (Hosp, Hosp, & Howell, 2007). Combined with widespread criticism of ability–achievement discrepancy, the idea of empirically supported instructional practices, early identification and remediation of child learning difficulties, and regular progress monitoring of student acquisition of academic benchmarks (Deno, 2002; Fuchs, Deshler, & Reschly, 2004; Shinn, 2002) gained substantial support, even from those who offer a balanced perspective that includes RtI and comprehensive evaluation of cognitive processes for identification and intervention purposes (Berninger, 2006; Hale et al., 2006). Although it can be argued that RtI principles and practices should be mandated to foster the academic performance of all children (Hale, 2006), the extension of RtI to SLD identification presents new challenges, resulting in significant and sometimes vitriolic debate (Willis & Dumont, 2006).

Some RtI advocates oppose the use of norm-referenced, standardized tests for SLD identification (e.g., Reschly, 2005), yet Mastropieri and Scruggs (2005) argue that eliminating the concept and methods of SLD identification because they have been poorly implemented is essentially "throwing the baby out with the bathwater" (p. 155). It is interesting that the tools used in SLD identification (i.e., cognitive and intelligence tests) have been the focus of much criticism, when in reality it is the ineffective use of these tools that is likely the source of the problem (Hale et al., 2006; Mastropieri & Scruggs, 2005; Mather & Gregg, 2006). Despite recognition of the value of comprehensive evaluation in law and professional policy, the RtI position has downplayed the use of standardized measures in the comprehensive evaluation process (Fiorello, Hale, Snyder, Forrest, & Teodori, 2008). However, the final Federal regulations (34 C.F.R. Parts 300 and 301; 2006) specifically state:

> RTI is only one component of the process to identify children in need of special education and related services. Determining why a child has not responded to research-based interventions requires a comprehensive evaluation…An RTI process does not replace the need for a comprehensive evaluation.

The reasons why RtI alone cannot be used to identify SLD are many (Berninger, 2006), including the lack of consistency in curriculum, instruction, and measurement to ensure comparable service delivery across classrooms and schools, limited availability of empirically supported interventions across academic domains and grades, and subjectivity in determining response or failure to respond (see Fiorello et al., 2006; Flanagan et al., 2006; Fuchs & Deshler, 2007; Hale, 2006; Hale et al., 2006; Schrank et al., 2006; Wodrich, Spencer, & Daley, 2006). In an attempt to remedy these RtI inadequacies, RtI proponents apparently have adopted a position that single subject designs can serve the purpose of determining "response to scientific, research-based intervention." This position typically advocates use of a flexible problem-solving model (PSM), a multi-tier approach, and single subject designs using progressively intensive interventions to help children overcome difficulties (e.g., Barnett et al., 2004; Marston, Muyskens, Lau, & Canter, 2003; Tilly, 2002).

Unfortunately, the assumption that single subject designs somehow correct for the subjective nature of RtI decision-making is dubious, especially for the PSM approach, given that this PSM RtI model requires manipulation of multiple independent variables (thereby violating single subject requirements for determining causality), so there is no way to determine why a child did not respond (Hale, 2006). Gerber (2005) further argues that the RtI position suffers from the same circularity problems that IQ advocates have, confusing measurement of the construct with the actual construct itself. Hale et al. (2006) conclude the potential for inaccurate identification is great given that the RtI position cannot specify what a "true positive" is under the model. Without the comprehensive evaluation, the RtI method alone results in the unreliable identification of heterogeneous groups of children as SLD (Fuchs et al., 2003, 2004b). As the dust has settled, it is now generally accepted that a comprehensive evaluation is necessary (National Association of School Psychologists, 2007), with the weight of empirical and legal evidence indicating that RtI alone cannot meet statutory and regulatory SLD requirements under IDEA (Fiorello et al., 2006; Flanagan et al., 2006; Hale, 2006; Hale et al., 2006; Ofiesh, 2006; Schrank et al., 2006; Willis & Dumont, 2006; Wodrich et al., 2006).

An informed reader may wonder why we provide such a detailed analysis of the RtI/comprehensive evaluation debate given this is a book about WISC-IV assessment and intervention. This is because our position has been misconstrued to suggest that we are opposed to RtI (e.g., Reschly & Hosp, 2004). This is inaccurate. The position advocated here and in other writings (Fiorello et al., 2006; Hale et al., 2006; Kavale et al., 2005b), and supported by a majority of practitioners (Machek & Nelson, 2007) and professional organizations (e.g.. Schrank et al., 2006), is that RtI is a critical component of service delivery (Hale, 2006), but it is *not* sufficient for identification of SLD. For children who do not respond to Tier 1 and Tier 2 interventions, the WISC-IV and other cognitive/neuropsychological measures can be particularly useful in differential diagnosis and intervention planning for children with SLD before Tier 3 interventions are undertaken (Berninger & O'Donnell, 2005; Fiorello et al., 2006; Hale, 2006).

There are many good reasons to rigorously adopt RtI principles and practices. As Hale and Fiorello (2004) argue, we must *intervene to assess*. If referrals for comprehensive evaluations are reduced and a majority of children are served through RtI, then children who do not respond to standard or problem-solving interventions (i.e., nonresponders) can be provided with the types of comprehensive evaluations we advocate in this chapter. The days of blindly applying ability–achievement discrepancy to determine SLD eligibility are over, as psychological assessment practices today must serve both identification and intervention purposes (Weiss, 2007). Rather than dogmatically taking an either/or perspective regarding RtI and comprehensive cognitive/neuropsychological assessment, practitioners now recognize the value of multiple models and practices for serving children with and without SLD (e.g., Machek & Nelson, 2007; Schrank et al., 2006). For children who do not RtI, more thorough evaluations using cognitive measures such as the WISC-IV and other data sources must be linked to intervention if we are to ensure better SLD diagnostic and treatment validity.

USING THE WISC-IV FOR CONCORDANCE–DISCORDANCE AND SLD DETERMINATION

Kavale and Forness (2000) are widely recognized as introducing an innovative five-step or level data-based diagnostic procedure – including ability–achievement discrepancy – until a sufficient case can be made for SLD diagnosis. Flanagan et al. (2002, 2006) and Kavale and Flanagan (2007) extended the

Kavale and Forness definition and methods in several ways. First, Flanagan and colleagues introduced the Cattell-Horn-Carroll (CHC) theory of cognitive abilities as a framework for identifying consistencies between cognitive processes thought to account for learning problems and achievement deficits. Second, they recommended using the cross-battery approach (see Flanagan & McGrew, 1997; Flanagan et al., 2007) to measure the cognitive processes. Cross-battery assessment entails averaging subtests to measure cognitive constructs to minimize construct underrepresentation and construct irrelevant variance during an evaluation (Flanagan & McGrew, 1997). Recently, this second aspect has been deemphasized in Flanagan et al. (2006), likely because new cognitive test batteries, including the WISC-IV, are better at measuring CHC factors.

The Flanagan et al. (2006) approach to SLD identification includes seven steps, each of which evaluates a core component of SLD, including identification of academic difficulties, cognitive processing deficits, and intact cognitive processes. Although their SLD diagnostic operationalization provides a good heuristic, it would benefit from a statistically sound method for determining when cognitive processes and achievement scores are consistent or discrepant. The method advocated for determining whether deficient processes and achievement scores are consistent is to determine that "performance is generally outside and below normal limits" (Flanagan et al., 2006, p. 812). A similar approach is recommended for determining adequate ipsative cognitive processes in which functioning is "within normal limits or higher" (Flanagan et al., 2006, p. 812).

The Flanagan et al. (2006) model would benefit from an adequate algorithm to guide decision making – a statistical test that takes into consideration measurement error to determine if obtained test scores are very likely similar or different. Contemporaneously with Flanagan and colleagues' efforts, Naglieri (1999) developed the Discrepancy/Consistency Model where Cognitive Assessment System (CAS; Naglieri, 1997) cognitive processing weaknesses are associated with an academic weakness, but those scores should be different from cognitive and academic strengths. Naglieri (1999) provides tables with critical values for comparing CAS factor scores to major achievement batteries, so an advantage of this model is that statistical criteria can be applied when using the CAS.

Hale and colleagues (2003, 2004) developed the Concordance–Discordance Model (C-DM; see Figure 3.1), which is conceptually similar to the Flanagan et al. (2006) and Naglieri (1999) models. Unlike the others, the C-DM uses the Standard Error of Difference (SED; Anastasi & Urbina, 1997) to provide a statistical test of difference among the three components (i.e., cognitive strengths, cognitive weaknesses, achievement weaknesses), but doesn't require the use of any particular standardized cognitive and achievement measure.

The SED is easily transferable to a variety of different tests, and allows for the same statistical method to be applied when new tests come onto the market. The SED is defined as: $SED = SD\sqrt{2 - r_{xx} - r_{yy}}$. Typical confidence intervals are used to determine level of significance (e.g., 90% Confidence Interval = +/− SED * 1.65; 95% Confidence Interval = +/− SED * 1.96;

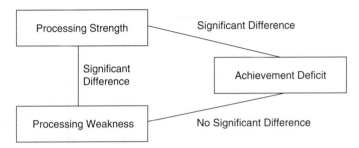

FIGURE 3.1   Concordance-Discordance model of SLD diagnosis. *Source*: Hale & Fiorello (2004).

99% Confidence Interval $= +/-$ SED $*$ 2.58). Thus, the C-DM approach to SLD diagnosis provides the mechanism to apply statistical analysis to previous operationalizations of the multi-step diagnostic approaches pioneered by Kavale and Forness (2000) and extended by Flanagan et al. (2003) and Naglieri (1999).

The C-DM method for SLD classification certainly has face value as an empirically supported practice consistent with IDEA "Third Method" regulations. Although it has been advocated for use in school psychology and neuropsychology practice (Hale & Fiorello, 2004; Hale et al., 2006; Miller et al., 2006), it cannot be blindly or rigidly applied. Hale and Fiorello (2004) note that in addition to the statistical tests, the literature should be examined to ensure the cognitive strength is not typically related to the academic deficit (e.g., Perceptual Reasoning and word reading), and the cognitive deficit should be empirically associated with the academic weakness (e.g., Working Memory and reading comprehension) in the literature.

If extant factors are used for C-DM, then computation is relatively straightforward because standard scores (SS) and reliability coefficients for age level are reported in the manual. For children with SLD, difficulties on Working Memory and Processing Speed are typical (Calhoun & Mayes, 2005), and could represent the "deficit in the basic psychological processes" that lead to the achievement deficit and SLD. However, the cognitive factor concordant or discordant with the academic domain in question may or may not be represented in the standardization manual. For instance, the WISC-IV manual only reports the SS and reliabilities for the four Indices, but alternative factor structures could be the cause of a SLD, such as an auditory-sequential processing score for a child with a reading SLD (e.g., Digit Span Forward, Letter–Number Sequencing) or visual–spatial processing score for a child with a math SLD presumed to be due to right hemisphere visual–spatial dysfunction (e.g., Block Design, Picture Completion).

The preliminary results for the WISC-IV Verbal Comprehension (VC), Perceptual Reasoning (PR), Working Memory (WM), and Processing Speed (PS) factors and WIAT-II reading and math performance using the WISC-IV/WIAT-II Linking Sample (Wechsler, 2003) are reported in Table 3.1 using the

TABLE 3.1   Concordance–Discordance Model Results for WISC-IV/WIAT-II SLD Linking
Sample

Achievement subtest	Number meeting C-DM criteria Achievement standard score				
	>85	70–84	<70	Total (%)	<85(%)
Word Reading	10	18	12	40(27.2)	30(20.4)
Reading Comprehension	3	11	18	32(21.8)	29(19.7)
Numerical Operations	3	9	8	20(13.6)	17(11.6)
Math Reasoning	3	11	5	19(12.9)	16(10.9)
Total	19	49	43	111(75.5)	92(62.6)

95% confidence interval (i.e., SED * 1.96). The children with SLD ($N = 147$) reported in Table 3.1 demonstrated a significant difference between the highest obtained WISC-IV factor score and the lowest WISC-IV factor score (discordance), the highest WISC-IV factor score and the lowest achievement subtest score (discordance), and no significant difference between the lowest WISC-IV factor score and achievement subtest score (concordance). No attempt was made to ensure a child's processing deficits were related to the child's poor academic performance other than by psychometric analysis. Each case is listed only once, and comorbidity of achievement problems was not evaluated. The findings show both the promise and limitations for using C-DM criteria to determine SLD. For the SLD sample, only 75% met C-DM psychometric criteria. If one adds a low achievement (achievement SS < 85) criterion, the rate of C-DM criteria met drops to 63% of the SLD sample, and if impaired achievement (achievement deficit < 70) is used, only 29% of the SLD sample met C-DM criteria.

The results in Table 3.1 suggest the C-DM, when applied using psychometric criteria only, reduces the number of children classified as SLD as compared to discrepancy/district criteria reported in Wechsler (2003). As these results could suggest there are numerous false negatives obtained when using C-DM, it is important to consider several plausible explanations for such findings. Perhaps the C-DM approach can reduce SLD classification rates by adding the additional criteria of a processing deficit in addition to discrepant achievement, as 25% of the SLD sample did not display WISC-IV cognitive strengths and weaknesses, and/or achievement weaknesses relative to cognitive strengths as determined by the SED statistical analyses. Perhaps for these children, the WISC-IV index scores were not sensitive to the processing deficit causing the disability (e.g., phonological processing, WISC-IV ACID profile) or perhaps profile variability at the factor level did not reflect subtest profile variability. For instance, Hale et al. (2006) reported a child with SLD who performed within the average range on all WISC-IV index scores, but had a significant SLD in math and written language. Although subsequent cognitive/neuropsychological testing revealed the child had a significant right hemisphere "nonverbal" LD, the factor scores were comparable because the child had a very low score on Comprehension, thereby depressing VC, and a very high score on Picture Concepts, thereby inflating PR (Hale et al., 2006).

Another plausible explanation is that many of these children were actually false positives given district/ability–achievement discrepancy criteria – they don't have a deficit in the basic psychological processes, and therefore should not be classified as having SLD. Perhaps these children would benefit from a more intensive RtI approach to foster academic growth (e.g., Barnett et al., 2004), and if they were determined to be responders, would never have received a comprehensive evaluation in the first place. Regardless, these findings indicate that simple psychometric calculation of C-DM for SLD classification may not be a sufficient replacement for a balanced practice model that includes both RtI and comprehensive evaluation for nonresponders (Fiorello et al., 2006; Hale, 2006; Hale et al., 2006). For nonresponders, the establishment of C-DM criteria could further strengthen classification criteria, especially if the comprehensive evaluation includes validation of cognitive assets and limitations (e.g., Cognitive Hypothesis Testing; Hale & Fiorello, 2004). In addition to the findings here, these data must be compared to C-DM base rates for typical children, where over 83% of the sample displays significant differences between one or more factors (see Hale et al., 2007).

As noted earlier, the WISC-IV Indices may not represent the pattern of strengths and weaknesses observed for some children, yet these individuals must also be evaluated for C-DM criteria using different clusters of subtests. There are three primary situations that require subtest combinations during cognitive assessment. The first is when subtests are averaged to form a new composite described in the literature, such as is the case when a cross-battery approach is used (e.g., Flanagan & McGrew, 1997). The second is when subtest scores are combined using weights derived from multiple regression to form a new composite (Keith et al., 2006; Sattler, 2001). The third instance is when there is significant inter- or intra-subtest variation within a composite (e.g., WISC-IV Full Scale IQ), thereby calling into question composite validity (e.g., Hale et al., 2007). The eventuality of this latter situation is evidenced by numerous studies demonstrating that variation within and across cognitive domains can have clinical significance (Berninger et al., 2001) and evidence that there is little shared variance among WISC-IV and DAS-II factors in the prediction of reading and math (Fiorello et al., 2008; Hale et al., 2007, in press). Further, there is substantial evidence that, for children with SLD and other neurodevelopmental disorders, there is within subject heterogeneity of cognitive profiles (Fiorello et al., 2007; Saklofske et al., 2005), which must be considered within the context of social, cultural, and ethnic diversity (Harris & Llorente, 2005). In each of these cases the C-DM approach can be applied through averaging or weighting combinations of subtests either from within or across test batteries (e.g., CHC/cross-battery approaches).

Averaging subtest scores using a cross-battery or other approach is not sufficient to determine C-DM significance, as the reliability coefficient must be available for each subtest or composite score that represents the cognitive process or achievement score in question. Although it would seem logical to average the reliability coefficients of the combined subtests, as can be done with SS, a simple arithmetic average of correlation coefficients is not possible because the distributions of correlation coefficients are negatively skewed when they are larger than zero (Feldt & Charter, 2006; Silver & Dunlap, 1987; Strube, 1988). This notion applies to the reliability coefficient because it is a special case of the correlation coefficient (Feldt & Charter, 2006).

In the case of reliability coefficients, it is expected that they be greater than 0.90 for tests used to make decisions about people (Salvia & Yssyldyke, 2001). As such, averaging the reliability coefficients for C-DM would underestimate the combined reliability coefficient. This problem can be solved by applying the Fisher's z transformation to the reliability coefficients prior to averaging them, then converting them back to the original scale for subsequent C-DM computation. Silver and Dunlap (1987) showed that the back-transformation of averaged z is the least biased method for averaging reliability coefficients. Their conclusions are supported by Feldt and Charter's (2006) Monte Carlo study that indicates the back-transformation technique can be used to combine correlations from different tests.

The Fisher's z transformation is defined as:

$$z = 0.5 \log_e[(1 + r_{xx})/(1 - r_{xx})] \tag{A}$$

The back-transformation equation is:

$$r_{xx} = (e^{2z} - 1)/(e^{2z} + 1) \tag{B}$$

Applying these equations, the steps to average reliability coefficients are: (1) transform each reliability coefficient into its respective Fisher's z value, (2) compute the arithmetic mean of the Fisher's z values, (3) transform the averaged Fisher's z value back to the reliability scaling.

Equations (A) and (B) can easily be computed using Microsoft Excel. Table 3.2 provides an example of averaging two reliability coefficients. Simple averaging of the two reliabilities (0.88 and 0.95) would have resulted in a shared reliability coefficient of 0.915, as opposed to 0.922 when computed using the

TABLE 3.2   Excel Example of Averaging Reliability Coefficients

	A	B	C	D	E	F
	r_{xx}	r_{yy}	$z\ r_{xx}$	$z\ r_{yy}$	Mean	z to r
1						
2	0.880	0.950	1.376	1.832	1.604	0.922
3			=0.5 * LN((1 + A2)/ (1 − A2))	=0.5 * LN((1 + B2)/ (1 − B2))		=+EXP((2 * E2) − 1)/ (EXP(2 * E2) + 1)

Note: The relevant equations are below each computed cell. For example, the Fisher's z transformation represented in C2 is described in C3.

Fisher's z transformation. Even though the differences between the averaged reliability coefficient and the Fisher's z transformed computation are sometimes small, the latter is the least biased, and thus most appropriate, method for combining reliability coefficients (Silver & Dunlap, 1987). As suggested above, the Fisher's z averaged reliability coefficient method is also useful when subtest relationships differ from the published factor structure, but fit some other subtest profile reported in the literature.

For instance, on the WISC-IV, the Arithmetic-Coding-Information-Digit Span (ACID) profile may be evident for a particular child, as has been found in several studies of children with reading SLDs (see Fiorello et al., 2006; Helland, 2007), but there is no normative data or reliabilities offered in the manual for such a factor for use in C-DM computation. Cohen et al. (2006) used a Guttman approach (smallest space analysis) to categorize WISC-IV subtests according to input, processing, and output demands, which could form different subtest clusters for C-DM computation. For the processing categorization, Similarities, Matrix Reasoning, Picture Concepts, and Block Design were rule-inferring tasks; Arithmetic, Information, Vocabulary, Comprehension, Word Reasoning and Picture Completion were rule-applying tasks; and Letter-Number Sequencing, Coding, Symbol Search and Cancellation tasks were learning and low inference subtests. This method can also be used when alternative factor structures are reported in the literature, such as the Keith et al. (2006) confirmatory factor analysis of the WISC-IV CHC factor structure. In this study, it was concluded that the Perceptual Reasoning subtests actually measure Visual Processing (Gv) and Fluid Reasoning (Gf). Keith and colleagues provided a formula for computing a short form composite based on Sattler (2001). The average internal consistency reliability coefficients for Matrix Reasoning and Picture Concepts are 0.89 and 0.86, respectively (Wechsler, 2003). Applying Fisher's z transformation, averaging, and then back-transforming results produces a combined r_{xx} of 0.876 for the new Gf factor.

This example of computing the Fisher z averaged reliability can then be extended for use in a C-DM case example. In this case, the child obtained a WISC-IV Matrix Reasoning score of 6 and a Picture Concepts score of 7 that are combined to form a single Gf composite (using the following equation [3.18 * (Matrix Reasoning + Picture Concepts) + 36.35]; Keith et al., 2006) to obtain a SS of 78. As described above, the Fisher z averaged reliability coefficient for this new composite would be 0.876. Continuing with a cross-battery example, if a student evidences well-developed verbal reasoning (WJ-III Comprehension-Knowledge SS = 98) and poor basic math calculation (WIAT-II Numerical Operations SS = 80). The reliability for the WJ-III Comprehension-Knowledge composite is 0.95 and the reliability for the WIAT-II Numerical Operations subtest is 0.91. Thus applying the equation SED = SD * SQRT($2 - r_{xx} - r_{yy}$) Comprehension-Knowledge is found to be discordant with both Fluid Reasoning (1.96 * SED = 12.26, obtained difference = 20) and Numerical Operations (1.96 * SED = 11.00, obtained difference = 18). Fluid Reasoning was found to be concordant with Numerical Operations (1.96 * SED = 13.60, obtained difference = 2), both of which are relative weaknesses in the student's profile.

COGNITIVE HYPOTHESIS TESTING FOR SLD IDENTIFICATION AND INTERVENTION

Our Cognitive Hypothesis Testing model (CHT; Hale & Fiorello, 2002, 2004; Hale et al., 2003; see Figure 3.2) provides a framework for integrating cognitive assessment into a problem-solving RtI model for children with SLD and other disorders who do not respond to standard interventions. Based on scientific method principles, the CHT approach to comprehensive cognitive and neuropsychological assessment for identification and programming for students with neuropsychological learning disorders requires a strong intervention model – such as RtI – for it to be an effective field practice. We argue that you must *intervene* to *assess* (Hale & Fiorello, 2004). As a field, we typically test too much, and intervene too little. By reducing referrals for comprehensive evaluation using a multi-tiered RtI approach, we can then conduct fewer evaluations, but when children do not respond, we can provide more thorough CHT evaluations (Fiorello et al., 2006).

In the Hale et al. (2006) balanced practice model, children receive standard protocol RtI and progress monitoring during Tier 1, and more individualized problem-solving RtI at Tier 2, both of which can be accomplished in the general education setting (Fiorello et al., 2006; Hale, 2006; Hale et al., 2006). This ensures that those referred for comprehensive CHT evaluations have undergone a RtI approach that maximizes external validity (Tier 1) and internal validity (Tier 2) in the decision-making process (Hale, 2006). Although some would argue failure to RtI is sufficient for SLD classification (e.g., Reschly, 2005), we argue that an additional step – a comprehensive CHT evaluation – is necessary

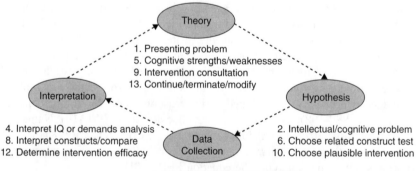

FIGURE 3.2   The cognitive hypothesis testing model. *Source*: Hale & Fiorello (2004).

prior to SLD classification, not only to ensure diagnostic accuracy because there are many reasons why children do not RtI (Mather & Gregg, 2006), but also to inform subsequent intervention efforts (Fiorello et al., 2006; Hale, 2006; Hale et al., 2006; Hale & Fiorello, 2004). With its well-known technical characteristics, the WISC-IV can be particularly useful in neuropsychological evaluation of children with SLD and other childhood disorders (Berninger & O'Donnell, 2005; Yeates & Donders, 2005), so it can be used an intellectual/cognitive process screener to form hypotheses regarding cognitive assets and deficits. However, since individual performance on the multifactorial subtests varies for reasons not easily identified in group studies (Baron, 2005), hypotheses derived from these measures must be confirmed or refuted using additional standardized cognitive/neuropsychological testing and other data using CHT, not only for more accurate diagnoses, but also for developing informed interventions sensitive to child needs (Hale & Fiorello, 2004).

Children with brain-based learning and other disorders experience developmental deficits (e.g., Castellanos et al., 2002; Francis et al., 1996), not delays, suggesting using similar strategies at greater intensities (e.g., Barnett et al., 2004; Reschly, 2005) will not meet their unique needs. Only when those interventions are not sufficient to meet a child's needs does CHT become necessary to determine why the child did not respond, and to identify alternative interventions that might be successful (Fiorello et al., 2006). That "next step" may be SLD classification and Tier 3 special education services provided in a number of possible settings (including general education), but the goal of CHT is to develop individualized single subject interventions that are subsequently monitored to determine their effectiveness (Hale & Fiorello, 2004).

The CHT approach to comprehensive evaluation is necessary for children who do not respond to Tier 1 and Tier 2 interventions because profile interpretation of cognitive tests for determining reading and other types of SLD can be of limited use (e.g., McDermott et al., 1990) unless findings are corroborated through additional evaluation and efforts are made to ensure results have both ecological and treatment validity (Hale & Fiorello, 2004). The CHT model is designed to overcome the limitations of traditional profile analysis, not only to ensure accurate diagnosis (i.e., reducing false positives or negatives), but also to link assessment data to empirically supported interventions. These single subject interventions are subsequently monitored, evaluated, and recycled until treatment efficacy is obtained (Hale & Fiorello, 2004), and case study data supports the utility of such approaches (e.g., Fiorello et al., 2006; Hale et al., 2006; Reddy & Hale, 2007).

Although similar approaches for differential diagnosis are offered in the cross-battery approach (e.g., Flanagan et al., 2006) and neuropsychological process approaches (e.g., Kaplan, 1988), what is innovative about CHT is the use of cognitive and neuropsychological data to guide subsequent development of individualized single subject interventions sensitive to individual needs within the context of a flexible PSM, thereby effectively linking assessment results to intervention.

COGNITIVE HYPOTHESIS TESTING FOR
SPECIFIC READING DISABILITY SUBTYPES

Although many children with reading SLD have a deficit in phonological processes (Shaywitz & Shaywitz, 2005; Torgesen, 2000; Vellutino et al., 1996), this is by no means the only cause of reading SLD (Fiorello et al., 2006), with each reading SLD subtype requiring different interventions to foster reading competency (Hale & Fiorello, 2004). The following section will review reading SLD by detailing the subtype cognitive and neurological features of each, with WISC-IV and WIAT-II profiles provided to help clinicians better understand the psychological processes of the different subtypes, not only for more effective differential diagnosis, but for informing intervention as well.

There are multiple cognitive functions and academic skills involved in reading competency, and as a result, a number of different possible combinations of assets and deficits that can lead to reading SLD. Children with word reading problems can have phonological (sound), orthographic (symbol), phoneme–grapheme correspondence, rapid automatic naming/reading fluency, receptive and/or expressive language, and/or working memory deficits leading to reading SLD (Badian, 1997; Beaton & Davies, 2007; Berninger & Richards, 2002; Demb, Boynton, & Heeger, 1998; Eckert et al., 2003; Fitch & Tallal, 2003; Flowers et al., 2004; Hale et al., 2001; Hale & Fiorello, 2004; Joseph, Noble, & Eden, 2001; Pugh et al., 2000; Richards et al., 2006; Shaywitz & Shaywitz, 2005; Shaywitz et al., 2003; Simos et al., 2005; Stein, 2001; Sunseth & Bowers, 2002; Thomson et al., 2005; Torgesen, 2000; Vellutino et al., 1996; Waber et al., 2000; Wolf, Miller, & Donnelly, 2000). The language system is intertwined with these basic reading skills (Snowling & Stackhouse, 2006), as lexical/semantic (particularly word knowledge or vocabulary) and perception of syntactic relationships also play a role. Finally, comprehension and use of language requires an understanding of the differences between explicit (concordant–convergent) and implicit (discordant–divergent) language, related to left and right hemisphere functions respectively (Bryan & Hale, 2001).

Given that many of these clinically relevant processes are tapped by the WISC-IV factor Indices, which have substantial validity across populations (Prifitera, Saklofske, Weiss, & Rolfnus, 2005), we present the commonality analysis results using factor indices as predictors of achievement for the WISC-IV/WIAT-II linking samples for typical children and children with reading SLD (Wechsler, 2003) in Tables 3.3 and 3.4. All typical children ($N = 846$; 412 Females, 434 Males) and children with reading SLD ($N = 128$; 46 Females, 82 Males) who completed the WISC-IV and WIAT-II, and met rigorous standardization inclusion and exclusion criteria, were included in the analyses (see Wechsler, 2003 for detailed description). As noted in the manual and discussed in Flanagan and Kaufman (2004), the typical children had a higher Full Scale IQ ($M = 100.33$, $SD = 14.25$) than the reading SLD sample ($M = 89.62$, $SD = 11.09$). Similarly, WISC-IV factor scores and WIAT-II reading subtest scores were close to the

TABLE 3.3 WISC-IV Factor Predictors of WIAT-II Word Reading, Pseudoword Decoding, and Reading Comprehension Subtests for Typical Children

	WISC-IV Factor/CHC Classification			
	VC/Gc	PR/Gf-Gv	WM/Gsm-WM	PS/Gs
WISC-IV/WIAT-II Word Reading ($R^2_{Total} = .481$)				
U_{VCI}	.091			
U_{PRI}		.011		
U_{WMI}			.027	
U_{PSI}				.010
$C_{VCI/PRI}$	.031	.031		
$C_{VCI/WMI}$	.060		.060	
$C_{PRI/WMI}$		.012	.012	
$C_{WMI/PSI}$			.010	.010
$C_{VCI/PRI/WMI}$	.068	.068	.068	
$C_{VCI/PRI/PSI}$	.016	.016		.016
$C_{VCI/WMI/PSI}$	.017		.017	.017
$C_{PRI/WMI/PSI}$		.015	.015	.015
$C_{ALL(g)}$	.101	.101	.101	.101
UNIQUE	.091	.011	.017	.010
SHARED	.298	.250	.293	.171
TOTAL	.389	.261	.310	.181
WISC-IV/WIAT-II Pseudoword Decoding ($R^2_{Total} = .361$)				
U_{VCI}	.034			
U_{PRI}		.010		
U_{WMI}			.044	
U_{PSI}				.007
$C_{VCI/PRI}$	.016	.016		
$C_{VCI/WMI}$	.037		.037	
$C_{PRI/WMI}$		.015	.015	
$C_{WMI/PSI}$			.014	.014
$C_{VCI/PRI/WMI}$	.051	.051	.051	
$C_{VCI/PRI/PSI}$	.011	.011		.011
$C_{VCI/WMI/PSI}$	.012		.012	.012
$C_{PRI/WMI/PSI}$		.020	.020	.020
$C_{ALL(g)}$	.079	.079	.079	.079
UNIQUE	.034	.010	.044	.007
SHARED	.209	.200	.228	.147
TOTAL	.243	.210	.272	.154
WISC-IV/WIAT-II Reading Comprehension ($R^2_{Total} = .521$)				
U_{VCI}	.138			
U_{PRI}		.007		
U_{WMI}			.008	
U_{PSI}				.010
$C_{VCI/PRI}$	.039	.039		
$C_{VCI/WMI}$	.056		.056	
$C_{PRI/WMI}$		.010	.010	
$C_{VCI/PRI/WMI}$	.070	.070	.070	
$C_{VCI/PRI/PSI}$	.020	.020		.020

(*continues*)

TABLE 3.3 *(continued)*

	VC/Gc	PR/Gf-Gv	WM/Gsm-WM	PS/Gs
$C_{VCI/WMI/PSI}$	.019		.019	.019
$C_{PRI/WMI/PSI}$		.011	.011	.011
$C_{ALL(g)}$	.109	.109	.109	.109
UNIQUE	.138	.007	.008	.010
SHARED	.321	.267	.283	.183
TOTAL	.459	.274	.291	.193

Notes. Commonalities <.01 omitted. VCI = Verbal Comprehension Index; Gc = Crystallized Ability; PRI = Perceptual Reasoning Index; Gf = Fluid Reasoning; Gv = Visualization; WMI = Working Memory Index; Gsm = Short-term Memory; PSI = Processing Speed Index; Gs = Speediness.

TABLE 3.4 WISC-IV Factor Predictors of WIAT-II Word Reading, Pseudoword Decoding, and Reading Comprehension Subtests for Children with Reading Disabilities

WISC-IV Factor/CHC Classification

	VC/Gc	PR/Gf-Gv	WM/Gsm-WM	PS/Gs
WISC-IV/WIAT-II Word Reading (R^2_{Total} = .230)				
U_{VCI}	.126			
U_{PRI}		.000		
U_{WMI}			.014	
U_{PSI}				.019
$C_{VCI/PRI}$	.018	.018		
$C_{VCI/WMI}$	.029		.029	
$C_{VCI/PRI/WMI}$	.015	.015	.015	
$C_{VCI/PRI/PSI}$	.010	.010		.010
$C_{VCI/WMI/PSI}$	.017		.017	.017
$C_{PRI/WMI/PSI}$		.015	.015	.015
$C_{ALL(g)}$	.007	.007	.007	.007
UNIQUE	.126	.000	.014	.019
SHARED	.073	.051	.051	.009
TOTAL	.199	.051	.065	.028
WISC-IV/WIAT-II Pseudoword Decoding (R^2_{Total} = .173)				
U_{VCI}	.077			
U_{PRI}		.011		
U_{WMI}			.006	
U_{PSI}				.012
$C_{VCI/PRI}$	.029	.029		
$C_{VCI/WMI}$	.014		.014	
$C_{VCI/PRI/WMI}$	.015	.015	.015	
$C_{ALL(g)}$	.010	.010	.010	.010
UNIQUE	.077	.011	.006	.012
SHARED	.063	.061	.036	.011
TOTAL	.140	.072	.042	.023

(continues)

TABLE 3.4   (*continued*)

	WISC-IV Factor/CHC Classification			
	VC/Gc	PR/Gf-Gv	WM/Gsm-WM	PS/Gs
	WISC-IV/WIAT-II Reading Comprehension ($R^2_{Total} = .378$)			
U_{VCI}	.112			
U_{PRI}		.005		
U_{WMI}			.034	
U_{PSI}				.005
$C_{VCI/PRI}$	.039	.039		
$C_{VCI/WMI}$	.082		.082	
$C_{VCI/PRI/WMI}$	.055	.055	.055	
$C_{ALL(g)}$	.022	.022	.022	.022
UNIQUE	.112	.005	.034	.005
SHARED	.196	.138	.177	.039
TOTAL	.308	.143	.211	.044

Notes: Commonalities <.01 omitted. VCI = Verbal Comprehension Index; Gc = Crystallized Ability; PRI = Perceptual Reasoning Index; Gf = Fluid Reasoning; Gv = Visualization; WMI = Working Memory Index; Gsm = Short-term Memory; PSI = Processing Speed Index; Gs = Speediness.

mean for the typical group (range 99.52–100.47), but the reading SLD sample had lower scores on the WISC-IV Verbal Comprehension (VC; $M = 92.26$, $SD = 10.96$), Perceptual Reasoning (PR; $M = 94.21$, $SD = 12.13$), Working Memory (WM; $M = 88.69$, $SD = 12.64$), Processing Speed (PS; $M = 90.73$, $SD = 13.12$), and the WIAT-II Word Reading (WR; $M = 79.55$, $SD = 12.13$), Pseudoword Decoding (PW; $M = 82.92$, $SD = 11.89$), and Reading Comprehension (RC; $M = 82.66$, $SD = 16.37$) subtests.

Commonality analysis is a regression method that partitions the data into unique and shared variance among independent variables in the prediction of outcomes. Unlike hierarchical or other stepwise regression approaches (e.g., Glutting et al., 2006) which artificially inflate the importance of the first variable in predicting the outcome (Pedhazur, 1997), commonality analysis is appropriate when independent variables are highly related (i.e., collinear) in the prediction of meaningful academic outcomes (Hale et al., 2007), as is the case when WISC-IV factors are used to predict WIAT-II reading subtests. Comparing the WISC-IV factor scores in the prediction of reading, for typical children and those with SLD, provides insight into cognitive predictors of reading competency, and why children with SLD struggle to achieve.

For the Typical Group commonality analysis (see Table 3.3), VC accounts for the most unique and total WR and RC variance, but WM also plays an important role, primarily in combination with VC and PR, attesting to its importance in predicting academic success (Gathercole & Pickering, 2000). These data are consistent with the literature that suggests crystallized, lexical/semantic, receptive and expressive language, and auditory–verbal working memory processes all play an important role in the prediction of reading (Fiorello et al., 2006; Richards et al.,

2006; Semrud-Clikeman et al., 2000; Shaywitz & Shaywitz, 2005; Snowling & Stackhouse, 2006; Wolf & Bowers, 1999). The WISC-IV WM Index likely taps three important constructs, auditory attention/discrimination/perception, auditory-sequential processing, and executive mental manipulation of stimuli, which would be important in phonological analysis and synthesis of words not readily recalled from memory (Berninger et al., 2001; Fiorello et al., 2006; Semrud-Clikeman et al., 2000; Waber et al., 2001). Its primary importance in predicting PW performance attests to this combined role for WM. In fact, since VC and higher order commonalities play a less important role in PW performance, clinicians might want to compare/contrast these measures to parse out the influence of language competency/prior knowledge, which would be more evident on WR and RC.

Although visual processing skills are not typically related to reading performance (Nation, Clarke, & Snowling, 2002; Shankweiler et al., 1999), the typical group PR visual–spatial and nonverbal reasoning skills account for reading variance in these and other analyses (e.g., Floyd, Bergeron, & Alfonso, 2006), but mostly in combination with other factors, which could in part reflect problem solving required on these tasks, or general cognitive integrity/intelligence. However, it is important to note that these visual problem-solving skills are predictive of reading performance, even without the influence of VC, and many commonalities cross over the traditional verbal–nonverbal dichotomy, as has been noted in previous studies (Hale et al., 2001, 2007, in press), attesting to the importance of looking at all WISC-IV factors in predicting reading achievement. Although the PS factor appears to play a minor role in reading competency, it is likely important for both symbolic (i.e., orthographic) information and rapid naming of whole words from long-term memory, which is important for reading fluency skills (Bowers, 2001; Fawcett & Nicholson, 2001; Manis & Freedman, 2001; Stein, 2001; Torgesen, Rashotte, & Alexander, 2001; Wolf & Bowers, 1999). The combination of WM and PS could be reflective of executive control of this rapid naming skill, especially when considered in combination with VC variance.

Interestingly, much of the reading variance could be explained by the large amounts of unique and interpretable two-factor commonalities for the prediction of WR (13.9% and 11.3%, respectively), PW (9.5% and 8.2%, respectively), and RC (16.3% and 10.5%). This is in contrast to the shared variance among all four factors, which could be considered as an alternative measure of general intelligence (Fiorello et al., 2001, 2007; Hale et al., 2001, 2007, in press), was very small for WR (10.1%), PW (7.9%), and RC (10.9%).

For children with reading SLD, similar relationships were found, but there was a relative dearth of higher level commonalities, and unique variance was important in the prediction of WR (15.9%), PW (10.6%), and RC (15.6%), higher than results found for the typical children, and consistent with our previous research (Hale et al., 2001, 2007, in press). Perhaps this suggests that children with reading SLD rely on some cognitive functions when reading, but not others; whereas, typical children are likely to use multiple cognitive functions simultaneously when reading successfully (Fiorello et al., 2006; Hale et al., 2007). Especially notable is the relative absence of the higher level commonalities, with the four factor commonality accounting for only about 1% of WR and PW, and 2.2% of RC performance. VC was an important predictor, as it was for the Typical Group, attesting to the importance of vocabulary development, receptive and expressive language (lexical/semantic/syntactic skills), and crystallized abilities in predicting reading for children with and without SLD (Evans, Floyd, McCrew, & Leforgee, 2002; Snowling & Stackhouse, 2006; Wiig, 2005). WM played a lesser unique role for WR and PW in the reading SLD sample, but a greater role in RC than was found for the typical sample. Its relative absence in WR and PW could be evidence of the auditory–phonological–sequential processing deficits common in reading SLD (Nicholson et al., 1995; Ram-Tsur, Faust, & Zivotofsky, 2006; Waber et al., 2001), and the increased demands on the actual working memory/ executive system during reading comprehension, independent of phonological/ articulatory processes (e.g., Semrud-Clikeman, Guy, & Griffin, 2000; Swanson & Ashebaker, 2000). It is especially important to note that WM here reflects auditory–verbal WM, and that the addition of the WISC-IV Integrated *visual* WM subtests could further reveal the nature of WM deficits in children with SLD (e.g., Leffard et al., 2006).

These VC and WM findings are consistent with the literature indicating auditory and crystallized abilities discriminate children with reading SLD from controls (Ganci, 2005). They could in part reflect poor discrimination of temporal and spectral elements of consonants and vowels leading to auditory–temporal processing deficits common in reading SLD (Corbera, Escera, Artigas, 2006; Fitch & Tallal, 2003; Johnson, Nicol, Zecker, & Kraus, 2007). Although some argue only phonological awareness is important in predicting reading competency, it is clear that language (Wiig, 2005) and working memory (Gathercole & Pickering, 2000) also play important roles, suggesting specific interventions are needed for these causes of reading SLD (Fiorello et al., 2006).

PR variance was also minimal for the SLD group, suggesting children with SLD do not adequately use novel problem-solving skills when reading more difficult words or passages, and instead rely on their limited VC and WM skills. In fact, the PR-WM-PS commonalities found for the typical group were absent in those with reading SLD, which would be consistent with findings that children with SLD have deficits on WM and PS tasks (Mayes et al., 1998; Mayes & Calhoun, 2004). However, the lack of unique PR variance was somewhat surprising given previous work showing the importance of PR/fluid reasoning subtests in predicting reading competency (Hale et al., 2001, in press), consistent with findings suggesting right hemisphere functions are used to compensate for left hemisphere deficits in children with reading disability (Breier et al., 2003; Simos et al., 2001; Weekes, Coltheart, & Gordon, 1997). However, it should be noted that some children with reading SLD fail to recruit visual processes when they read (Eden, Van Meter, Rumsey, Maison, & Zeffiro, 1996), and instead might attempt to use their poor phonological and expressive articulation skills when struggling to read (e.g., Pugh et al., 2000; Shaywitz et al., 2003), albeit unsuccessfully.

It should be noted that the VC-PR commonality was twice as large for the SLD group during PW, which could suggest a relationship between problem solving and prior knowledge in attempting to read nonsense words. Perhaps PR subtests are important in combination with other cognitive functions, as was the case in this analysis and the literature on fluid abilities and reading SLD (Breier et al., 2003; Floyd, Bergeron, & Alfonso, 2006; Plaza & Cohen, 2007). This combination could reflect a known tendency for children with reading SLD to avoid attempting phoneme–grapheme decoding skills in favor of a sight word reading approach for word recognition (Farah, 1990; Fiorello et al., 2006; Hale & Fiorello, 2004; Horwitz et al., 1998; Simos et al., 2005). Alternatively, the compensatory functions noted in the neuropsychological literature may be best represented by PS variance, which is a common deficit area in neurodevelopmental disorders (Baron, 2005), and it was present in the SLD sample. Visual attention, symbolic representation, and processing speed are often deficient in children with reading SLD (Solan et al., 2007; Stein, 2001) with and without ADHD (Willcutt, Pennington, Olson, Chhabildas, & Hulslander, 2005), and orthographic processes are directly related to reading fluency and comprehension (Thomson et al., 2005). For some children with reading SLD, helping them develop problem-solving, visual–perceptual, and executive functions during word attack and reading comprehension activities might foster performance, especially if used as a compensatory strategy to help overcome auditory–verbal deficits (Hale & Fiorello, 2004).

Meta-analyses results make it clear that there are many SLD subtypes with different patterns of assets and deficits (Kavale & Nye, 1985–1986), so one plausible reason why variance components reported above are low or absent in the heterogeneous reading SLD sample is that subtypes are collapsed into a single group (e.g., Semrud-Clikeman & Pliszka, 2005). There could be possible cognitive relationships with reading subtests that differ among factors and the constituent subtests, as was suggested in Fiorello et al. (2006). In the Fiorello et al. study, different relationships among cognitive predictors and achievement outcomes were evident, suggesting differential assessment–intervention relationships could be strengthened through subtype examination (Licht, 1994; Zadina et al., 2006). In the Fiorello et al. SLD subtype study, phonological, orthographic, fluency, and global reading SLD subtypes were identified, consistent with the literature (Bakker, Van Strien, Licht, Smit-Glaude, & Sietsia, 2007; King, Giess, & Lombardino, 2007; Masutto, Bravar, & Fabbro, 1994; Morris et al., 1998; Richman & Wood, 2002; Torppa et al., 2007; Zadina et al., 2006). Although the ACID profile (Prifitera & Dersh, 1993; Vargo, Gosnner, & Spafford, 1995) was found for all reading SLD subtypes, and WM and PS deficits are common in SLD (Mayes et al., 1998; Mayes & Calhoun, 2004), it may have limited discriminant validity (Watkins, Kush, & Glutting, 1997). As a result, the Fiorello et al. subtypes warrant further examination.

In Fiorello et al. (2006), children with the phonological subtype were characterized with relative weaknesses on Information, Digit Span (especially Digits Backwards), Arithmetic, Matrix Reasoning and Coding subtests, with deficits in WR and PW. Although the WISC-IV does not tap phonological processes per se, critical to identifying many children with reading SLD (see Berninger & Richards, 2002; Hale & Fiorello, 2004; Thomson et al., 2005), this profile appears to be critical in defining the phonological subtype. The orthographic subtype had lower scores on Coding, Symbol Search, Cancellation, and Arithmetic, consistent with visual attention, symbolic representation, and processing speed deficits in children with reading SLD (Solan et al., 2007; Stein, 2001; Thomson et al., 2005). The fluency/Comprehension subtype had the lowest scores on Digit Span, Letter–Number Sequencing, Arithmetic and Coding, leading to RC deficits, as would be expected (e.g., Wolf & Bowers, 1999). Finally, the Global Subtype had auditory–verbal deficits on both VC and WM factors, with Vocabulary, Information, Digit Span, and Arithmetic, and Coding low relative to PR subtests. Clearly, this suggests that subtypes do not necessarily reflect global delays on particular WISC-IV factors, but instead show within and across factor variability (Fiorello et al., 2006). This variability necessitates further hypothesis testing of findings with multiple sources, including additional standardized cognitive and neuropsychological measures, to ensure concurrent, ecological, and treatment validity of WISC-IV results. These findings also attest to the value of examining optional WISC-IV subtests, such as Information and Arithmetic, because they have strong diagnostic value and predictive validity (e.g., Filippatou & Livaniou, 2005; Hale et al., 2001).

The subtype variability found in Fiorello et al. (2006) argues that considerable variance could be lost when one examines global or composite scores as compared to subtype scores. To examine this possibility, we examined multiple combinations of WISC-IV predictors of WIAT-II reading subtests in separate forced entry multiple regression equations. As can be seen in Table 3.5, the

TABLE 3.5 WIAT-II Reading Subtest Variance Accounted for by Different Predictor Combinations for Typical Children and Children with Reading Disabilities

	Word Reading		Pseudoword Decoding		Reading Comprehension	
	R^2	%Change	R^2	%Change	R^2	%Change
Standardization Sample						
16 Total Subtests	.574	–	.424	–	.589	–
10 Core Subtests	.499	−13%	.377	−11%	.537	−9%
4 Factor Indices	.481	−16%	.361	−15%	.521	−12%
Full Scale IQ	.464	−19%	.350	−17%	.491	−17%
Reading Disability Sample						
16 Total Subtests	.326	–	.295	–	.481	–
10 Core Subtests	.294	−10%	.254	−14%	.449	−7%
4 Factor Indices	.230	−29%	.173	−41%	.378	−21%
Full Scale IQ	.183	−44%	.147	−50%	.326	−32%

most variance was accounted for by all WISC-IV subtests, and the least amount of variance is accounted for by FSIQ. However, when one just examines the 10 subtests that compose the four factors, there is little loss of predictive validity in the standardization sample, but considerable loss of variance occurs when one interprets factors as opposed to subtests in the SLD sample. The consistent finding reported here and elsewhere (Hale et al., 2007, in press) explains some of the limited amounts of variance explained in the SLD sample commonality analysis, and subtest level interpretation may be necessary if considerable subtest variability is found within an Index score.

Of course, as noted earlier, any WISC-IV profile variability should be confirmed using a CHT approach and checked for ecological and treatment validity rather than rely on profile interpretation in isolation. Regardless, these results suggest that the predictive validity of the WISC-IV is heightened when one uses idiographic as opposed to nomothetic interpretation (Fiorello et al., 2001, 2007, in press; Hale & Fiorello, 2004; Hale et al., 2001, 2007, in press). Not only will this foster differential diagnosis of reading SLD, but unlike FSIQ, can serve as a foundation for an individualized CHT-driven intervention.

COGNITIVE HYPOTHESIS TESTING FOR SPECIFIC MATH DISABILITY

There has been comparatively little research conducted that examines the psychological processes involved in math competency for typical children, and the characteristics, etiology, and treatment of children with math SLD (Fleischner, 1994; Geary, Hamson, & Hoard, 2000; Mazzocco, 2001). Many children with math SLD also have problems in reading and written language, and in these cases, there may be similar cognitive/neuropsychological reasons for their difficulties (Ardila, Concha, & Rosselli, 2000; Helland, 2006), but others may have characteristics of "nonverbal" SLD, presumably due to right hemisphere dysfunction (Palombo, 2006; Rourke, 2001; Stein & Krishnan, 2007). Multiple cognitive and neuropsychological functions requiring frontal, left, and right hemisphere systems are necessary for math computation and reasoning skills, consistent with cognitive and neuropsychological literature on math competence and disability (e.g. Geary & Hoard, 2001; Hale & Fiorello, 2004; Hale, Fiorello, Dumont, Willis, Rackley, & Elliott, in press; Hale et al., 2002; Mazzocco, 2001; Palombo, 2006; Proctor et al., 2005; Palombo, 2006; Rourke, 2001). Although some have suggested right hemisphere dysfunction leads to math SLD, previous studies have found auditory–verbal–crystallized abilities (e.g., VC) and executive functions (e.g. WM, PS) to be most predictive of mathematics achievement (Hale, Fiorello, Bertin, & Sherman, 2003). Clearly, neuropsychological research shows that disruption of one or more brain regions can lead to math SLD (Benbow et al., 1997), and can result from both left- and right-hemisphere damage (Grafman, Passaflume, & Faglioni, & Boller, 1982).

Floyd, Evans, and McGrew (2003) used structural equation modeling to show that Woodcock-Johnson III (WJ III; Woodcock, McGrew, & Mather, 2001) specific cognitive abilities predicted math achievement better than general cognitive ability. Similar to earlier large-scale studies (McGrew, Flanagan, Keith, & Vanderwood, 1997), complex relationships among CHC factors and math achievement domains were found for different age levels (Floyd et al., 2003). They found that Gc, Gf, Gsm-WM, and Gs were moderate to strong predictors, with Long-term Retrieval (Glr) and Auditory Processing (Ga) demonstrating moderate relationships at younger ages. Gf or novel problem-solving skills consistently predicted math achievement, and Gc's importance increased with age, and was more related to math reasoning, which would be consistent with the notion that Gc reflects both prior knowledge and language development (Hale & Fiorello, 2004). Gs was related to math calculation more than reasoning, and Glr and Ga were predictive for young children. Although Gsm was an important math predictor in these studies, not all children with math difficulties experience deficits in this area (Proctor et al., 2005).

Hale et al. (2001) similarly showed that VC/Gc, WM/Gsm-WM, Arithmetic/Gq/Gf, and PS/Gs were strong predictors of math computation skills for children with SLD, but some unique and shared variance for Perceptual Organization/Gv and PS/Gs was found, but most of this was in combination with Gc, Gq/Gf, and Gsm-WM factors. Subtest analysis in Hale et al. (2003) revealed most math computation and reasoning variance was accounted for by the Gc/VC and Gs/PS subtests, with some contribution by Block Design. Not surprisingly, the Arithmetic (Gf/Gq/Gsm-WM) subtest accounted for substantial math achievement variance in Hale et al. (2003). However, Arithmetic also predicts reading achievement variance as well (see above; Hale et al., 2001, 2007), so this finding suggests it also measures executive WM (e.g., Leffard et al., 2006) and fluid reasoning (e.g., Keith et al., 2006) skills. For the WISC-IV/WIAT-II Math Composite commonality analysis, Hale et al. (2007) found VC/Gc and PR/Gf to be the strongest predictors, and this predictive validity was enhanced by their combination with WM/Gsm-WM.

To examine WISC-IV predictors for typical children (sample described previously), and Math SLD ($N = 63$), we performed commonality analysis on the WIAT-II Numerical Operations (NO) and Math Reasoning (MR) subtests similar to the reading analyses described above (see Table 3.6). As would be expected given the importance of novel problem solving and visual–spatial relationships (both Gf and Gv) and right hemisphere functions (e.g., Palombo, 2006; Proctor et al., 2005; Rourke, 2001) in predicting math competency, we found that VC relationships were somewhat diminished relative to the reading analyses, and PR and PS relationships were stronger in the prediction of math domains, and a predictive PR-PS commonality was present in the math but not the reading analyses. Both factors contributed substantial portions of variance in the prediction of NO and MR, and PR was especially important for the prediction of MR, which should not be surprising given the relationship between quantitative and fluid reasoning (Flanagan et al., 2006). Gc has been consistently found to predict math performance (Floyd et al., 2003; Hale et al., 2001, 2003, 2007), as it likely reflects both prior knowledge of math concepts and language facility for word problems.

Consistent with other findings (e.g., Floyd et al., 2003; Hale et al., 2003), WM/Gsm-WM demands played a larger role in predicting MR than NO performance, suggesting executive demands are high when children solve math word problems (Hale et al., in press). This finding likely reflects the working memory requirements in translating the linguistic word problems (analysis) into quantitative equations for computation and subsequent oral responding (synthesis). This could also account for the increased PS involvement in math performance (e.g., processing speed and performance monitoring), but since it was more important in NO than MR, PS variance might be more indicative of numeric–symbolic representations, as was suggested with the letter–orthographic explanation for reading. Otherwise, unique and shared variance components in the math analyses were fairly comparable to the reading results, with the primary difference being increased PR and PS and decreased VC and WM variance.

For children with math SLD, there were substantial amounts of unique variance in the prediction of NO (27.7%) and MR (19.4%), and shared variance among all factors was low (1%), attesting to the importance of examining index scores as opposed to global IQ interpretation (see Table 3.7). Interestingly, a substantial portion of unique variance was explained by VC and PS, similar to recent studies using the DAS-II and WISC-IV (Hale et al., 2007, in press), and there was a VC-PS commonality that was absent in the Typical Group. Given that VC likely reflects prior quantitative knowledge (i.e., math facts and algorithms), this finding was expected, but the PS findings reported here and in other studies (Calhoun & Mayes, 2005; Hale et al., 2001, 2007, in press) requires further examination.

Perhaps these findings suggest children with math SLD do not attempt or are unsuccessful at solving more complex math problems, and instead NO performance merely reflects what they have achieved. Children with math SLD may also struggle when asked to quickly and efficiently access math facts and algorithms, leading to difficulty carrying out sequential math algorithm computation steps, which has been found in some children with math SLD (Mammarella et al., 2006). As speeded performance is related to automaticity, this finding would also be consistent with children with math SLD using more immature calculation strategies (Geary & Hoard, 2001). PS measures may have more to do with *processing and decision* speed than speeded motor performance (e.g., Kennedy, Clement, & Curtiss, 2003). However, PS variance separate from PR likely in part reflects fine motor functioning and psychomotor speed (e.g., Baron, 2005), so this PS finding in math SLD is particularly intriguing.

Although PR and WM processes, presumed to reflect "nonverbal" right hemisphere and frontal lobe functioning, respectively (see Hale & Fiorello, 2004; Stein & Krishnan, 2007) were evident in the Typical Group NO performance, they contributed little NO variance in the math SLD group. These findings could indicate that children with math SLD rely on specific cognitive functions or immature strategies (e.g. finger counting) (Geary et al., 1999), have difficulty integrating different brain functions (Smith & Rourke, 1995), and/or have general

TABLE 3.6   WISC-IV Factor Predictors of WIAT-II Numerical Operations and Math Reasoning for Typical Children

	WISC-IV Factor/CHC Classification			
	VC/Gc	PR/Gf-Gv	WM/Gsm-WM	PS/Gs
WISC-IV/WIAT-II Numerical Operations ($R^2_{Total} = .448$)				
U_{VCI}	.047			
U_{PRI}		.037		
U_{WMI}			.009	
U_{PSI}				.022
$C_{VCI/PRI}$	.032	.032		
$C_{VCI/WMI}$	.030		.030	
$C_{PRI/WMI}$		.014	.014	
$C_{PRI/PSI}$		.025		.025
$C_{WMI/PSI}$			.010	.010
$C_{VCI/PRI/WMI}$	.054	.054	.054	
$C_{VCI/PRI/PSI}$	.021	.021		.021
$C_{VCI/WMI/PSI}$	.016		.016	.016
$C_{PRI/WMI/PSI}$		.022	.022	.022
$C_{ALL(g)}$	.103	.103	.103	.103
UNIQUE	.047	.037	.009	.022
SHARED	.262	.271	.249	.203
TOTAL	.309	.308	.258	.225
WISC-IV/WIAT-II Math Reasoning ($R^2_{Total} = .569$)				
U_{VCI}	.058			
U_{PRI}		.048		
U_{WMI}			.049	
U_{PSI}				.012
$C_{VCI/PRI}$	.045	.045		
$C_{VCI/WMI}$	.039		.039	
$C_{PRI/WMI}$		.027	.027	
$C_{PRI/PSI}$		.018		.018
$C_{VCI/PRI/PSI}$	.083	.083	.083	
$C_{VCI/PRI/PSI}$	.022	.022		.022
$C_{VCI/WMI/PSI}$	.015		.015	.015
$C_{PRI/WMI/PSI}$		.024	.024	.024
$C_{ALL(g)}$	.117	.117	.117	.117
UNIQUE	.058	.048	.049	.012
SHARED	.326	.336	.312	.208
TOTAL	.384	.384	.361	.220

Notes: Commonalities <.01 omitted. VCI = Verbal Comprehension Index; Gc = Crystallized Ability; PRI = Perceptual Reasoning Index; Gf = Fluid Reasoning; Gv = Visualization; WMI = Working Memory Index; Gsm = Short-term Memory; PSI = Processing Speed Index; Gs = Speediness.

white matter dysfunction (e.g., Rourke, 2000), especially given their poor mean PR scores. Even children with "nonverbal" right hemisphere SLD can be differentiated on whether they show sequential or simultaneous deficits (Mammarella et al., 2006), so further differentiation of subtypes may elucidate the PR, WM, and math relationships.

It is interesting to note that the "nonverbal" PR factor predicted the auditory–verbal MR subtest, but not the visual–motor NO subtest, similar to DAS-II and WISC-III/WISC-IV findings (Hale et al., 2001, 2007, in press), suggesting PR *psychological processes* are more important than observable input or output demands (Hale & Fiorello, 2004; Hale et al., in press). This could suggest children with math SLD use visualization to solve math word problems, but it is more likely that both PR analysis and synthesis skills are needed when translating verbal content to written math algorithms for subsequent computation, and since PR deficits are found, poor math problem-solving skills are found in children with math SLD. This could explain why WM and PS demands are high for children with math SLD as they struggle to retrieve linguistic, math fact, and math algorithm information from long-term memory. Although these skills are needed, they may not be available or used by children with math SLD. For instance, Cirino, Morris, and Morris (2007) also found a limited role for executive predictors in their referred sample, so perhaps executive function interventions would be important for many children with math SLD.

As was the case with the reading SLD analyses, many variance components were low or absent in the heterogeneous math SLD sample, which could reflect the presence of math SLD subtypes. There could be possible factor and subtest relationships with NO and MR measures that differ for math SLD subtypes, as was the case with reading subtypes in Fiorello et al. (2006). As a result, we used average linkage within groups variant of the UPGMAA (unweighted pair-group method arithmetic average) cluster analysis for NO and MR subtests, which minimizes within group variability, and the Euclidean distance measure. Results revealed five math SLD subtypes (see Figure 3.3) according to the agglomeration schedule coefficient changes from 11.29 to 13.08. Subsequent chi-square analyses revealed no gender (Females = 28; Males = 35) or racial (African-Americans = 23; Caucasian-Americans = 36; Latino-Americans = 4) differences among subtypes, although Latino-American sample size was very small. There were no group age differences ($F(4,58) = 0.06$, $p = 0.994$), but group differences were found for all global scores except WM, which was low for all groups (see Table 3.8).

To examine subtest differences among MLD subtypes displayed in Figure 3.2, we used forced entry discriminant analysis and Tukey's Honestly Significant Difference post-hoc comparisons (see Table 3.9) to determine the best method for identifying math SLD subtypes. The first canonical discriminant function (eigenvalue = 1.22, canonical correlation = 0.742) accounted for 52.7% of the variance. The most effective discriminating variables were Information, Vocabulary, Comprehension, Arithmetic, Word Reasoning, Picture Completion and Symbol Search. Digit Span Backward and Coding did not discriminate subtypes, which

TABLE 3.7   WISC-IV Factor Predictors of WIAT-II Numerical Operations and Math Reasoning for Children with Math Disabilities

	WISC-IV Factor/CHC Classification			
	VC/Gc	PR/Gf-Gv	WM/Gsm-WM	PS/Gs
WISC-IV/WIAT-II Numerical Operations (R^2_{Total} = .357)				
U_{VCI}	.135			
U_{PRI}		.001		
U_{WMI}			.017	
U_{PSI}				.124
$C_{VCI/WMI}$	.033		.033	
$C_{VCI/PSI}$	.017			.017
$C_{VCI/PRI/PSI}$	.013	.013		.013
$C_{ALL(g)}$	.010	.010	.010	.010
UNIQUE	.135	.001	.017	.124
SHARED	.082	.032	.048	.038
TOTAL	.217	.033	.065	.162
WISC-IV/WIAT-II Math Reasoning (R^2_{Total} = .358)				
U_{VCI}	.072			
U_{PRI}		.061		
U_{WMI}			.027	
U_{PSI}				.034
$C_{VCI/PRI}$	.056	.056		
$C_{VCI/WMI}$	.015		.015	
$C_{VCI/PSI}$	.014			.014
$C_{PRI/PSI}$		.015		.015
$C_{VCI/PRI/PSI}$	.037	.037	.037	
$C_{VCI/PRI/PSI}$	.020	.020		.020
$C_{ALL(g)}$	.011	.011	.011	.011
UNIQUE	.072	.061	.027	.034
SHARED	.152	.137	.059	.058
TOTAL	.224	.198	.086	.092

Notes: Commonalities <.01 omitted. VCI = Verbal Comprehension Index; Gc = Crystallized Ability; PRI = Perceptual Reasoning Index; Gf = Fluid Reasoning; Gv = Visualization; WMI = Working Memory Index; Gsm = Short-term Memory; PSI = Processing Speed Index; Gs = Speediness.

suggests these were consistent weaknesses ($M = 8.18$ and $M = 7.89$, respectively) in children with math SLD.

For the subtypes, the fluid/quantitative reasoning subtype had the most difficulty with Matrix Reasoning, Picture Concepts, and Arithmetic, the three subtests that Keith et al. (2005) suggested were Gf. The mild executive/working memory subtype had the highest scores of all subtypes, and only mild deficits on math subtests. Their lowest scores were Information, Digits Backward, Arithmetic, and Matrix Reasoning. The right hemisphere subtype (e.g., "Nonverbal" SLD) had low scores on PR and PS subtests, and also performed poorly on Information, Digits Backward, and Arithmetic. The Digits Forward and Digits Backward difference

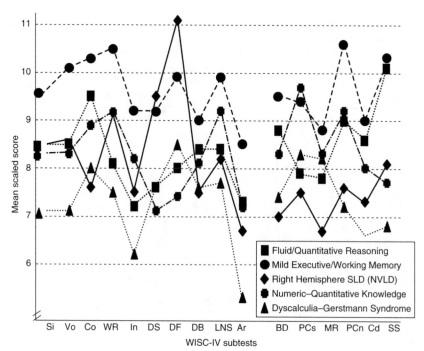

FIGURE 3.3   Math disability subtypes.

was remarkable, with Digits Forward well above average. The Working Memory subtest results could be reflective of a right hemisphere predominance for executive functions, as has been suggested in ADHD studies (Hale, Fiorello, & Brown, 2005) or a primary attention deficit found in children with right hemisphere SLD (Greenham, Stelmach, & van der Vlugt, 2003).

A different pattern was found for the numeric/quantitative knowledge subtype, as they performed poorly on Digits Forward, Arithmetic, and PS subtests. The finding of this subtype provides additional support that not all children with math problems have "nonverbal" SLD, and is consistent with findings supporting a comorbid language, reading and math SLD subtype (Helland, 2006). Finally, the Dyscalculia/Gerstmann Syndrome (see Shalev & Gross-Tsur, 2001) subtype had the lowest performance on multiple verbal and nonverbal measures especially Information, Arithmetic, Block Design, Picture Completion, and PS subtests, which could suggest general verbal–crystallized or left hemisphere dysfunction, which co-occurs with reading SLD (Helland, 2006). Together, these results demonstrate that there are multiple math SLD subtypes with deficits in numeric concepts, computational knowledge, working memory, long-term memory storage and/or retrieval, problem solving, and visual–spatial processes reported in the literature (Geary, Hamson, & Hoard, 2000; Hale & Fiorello, 2004; Hale et al., 2003; Mazzocco, 2005).

TABLE 3.8   Nomothetic Results for WISC-IV/WIAT-II Standardization Math SLD Subtypes

		Dyscalculia/ Gerstmann (n = 16)	Quantitative Knowledge (n = 14)	NVLD/Right Hemisphere (n = 14)	Executive/ WM (mild) (n = 11)	Fluid/Quant. Reasoning (n = 8)	F^1
NO	M	65.69[a, b, c, d]	81.29[c, d]	79.93[c, d]	94.82	94.50	45.08[1]
	SD	5.55	7.78	3.08	6.60	8.86	
MR	M	68.88[a, c, d]	87.93	72.50[a, c, d]	94.55	80.63[d]	41.65[1]
	SD	6.53	7.27	5.21	4.56	5.37	
FSIQ	M	81.06[c]	89.14	83.86[c]	97.82	91.75	7.01[1]
	SD	5.73	9.25	11.51	8.41	8.56	
VC	M	84.50[c]	92.71	89.50[c]	100.18	95.75	5.68[1]
	SD	7.32	8.85	9.46	8.83	11.44	
WM	M	85.94	90.43	91.64	98.09	91.13	2.23
	SD	13.88	8.98	9.81	8.02	8.51	
PR	M	87.94	92.86	81.21[c]	95.45	91.13	3.44[1]
	SD	8.34	11.67	13.28	9.48	9.19	
PS	M	82.13[c]	89.86	88.07	99.82	95.50	3.18[1]
	SD	13.09	13.04	17.01	12.93	8.18	

Notes: [1]F ratios significant at $p < .05$; [a]Less than Subtype2; [b]Less than Subtype3; [c]Less than Subtype4; [d]Less than Subtype5. FSIQ = Full Scale Intelligence Quotient; VC = Verbal Comprehension; PR = Perceptual Reasoning; WM = Working Memory; PS = Processing Speed; NO = Numerical Operations; MR = Math Reasoning.

TABLE 3.9   Significance Tests and Wilks' Lambda Results for WISC-IV Discriminating Variables

Variable	F	p	Wilks' λ
Similarities	2.84	.032	.836
Vocabulary	5.21	.001	.736
Comprehension	4.79	.002	.752
Information	5.93	<.001	.710
Word Reasoning	4.49	.003	.764
Digit Span Forward	3.57	.011	.802
Digit Span Backward	1.31	.276	.917
Letter–Number Sequencing	2.30	.070	.863
Arithmetic	7.50	<.001	.659
Block Design	2.54	.049	.851
Picture Concepts	2.28	.071	.864
Matrix Reasoning	2.03	.102	.877
Picture Completion	3.58	.011	.802
Coding	1.49	.216	.907
Symbol Search	3.53	.012	.804

TABLE 3.10 WIAT-II Math Subtest Variance Accounted for by Different Predictor Combinations for Typical Children and Children with Math Disabilities

	Numerical Operations		Math Reasoning	
	R^2	%Change	R^2	%Change
Standardization sample				
16 Total subtests	.588	–	.679	–
10 Core subtests	.475	−19%	.587	−14%
4 Factor indexes	.448	−24%	.569	−16%
Full scale IQ	.446	−24%	.564	−17%
Math disability sample				
16 Total subtests	.514	–	.295	–
10 Core subtests	.401	−12%	.254	−27%
4 Factor indexes	.357	−31%	.173	−39%
Full Scale IQ	.280	−46%	.147	−41%

Seventy percent of the cases were correctly classified by the WISC-IV discriminating variables, with no particular subtype pattern observed regarding misclassification. Results would be enhanced if the WISC-IV was used in conjunction with other cognitive/neuropsychological measures, as is required in the CHT model (Hale & Fiorello, 2004). Obviously, the WISC-IV variability among math SLD subtypes suggests that there is no one math SLD profile, with each requiring individualized assessment and intervention strategies designed to serve multiple cognitive and academic needs.

As was the case with reading, variance is likely lost when one examines global or composite scores as compared to subtest scores, which are more sensitive to MLD subtype differences. The results of forced entry multiple regression with multiple combinations of predictors of WIAT-II math subtests in separate forced entry multiple regression equations are reported in Table 3.10. Once again, the most variance is accounted for by all WISC-IV subtests, and the least amount of variance is accounted for by FSIQ. Although the loss of variance for the 10 subtest versus FSIQ analysis was not significant for the standardization sample, it was considerable for the math SLD group, demonstrating why commonality analysis for subtypes might reveal important cognitive–achievement relationships not revealed when the entire math SLD sample is used. Again, the point here is WISC-IV predictive validity is enhanced when one uses idiographic as opposed to nomothetic interpretation. Recognizing how children with math SLD solve math problems, and the types of errors they commit, can provide us with understanding of how to remediate or compensate deficient math performance (Hale & Fiorello, 2004).

WISC-IV/WIAT-II ANALYSES CONCLUSIONS

These findings clearly show that multiple cognitive functions as measured by the WISC-IV predict academic performance, and in typical children, substantial portions of achievement variance are accounted for by the predictors. These predictors, and their interrelationships, differ depending on the academic domain in question, so careful idiographic analysis is required, especially for children with SLD, because the predictor relationships with academic domains differed for typical children and those with SLD. This is entirely consistent with previous research, practitioner perspectives, and Federal law that children with SLD have developmental *deficits* – not delays, and that they require individualized interventions – not more intense ones – to meet their unique needs.

A consistent finding reported here using children with SLD, and in previous studies (Hale et al., 2007, in press), is that so much variance is lost when one uses global instead of subcomponent predictors for achievement in clinical populations (Hale et al., 2007), failure to conduct profile analysis might limit the diagnostic utility of the WISC-IV. Many school psychologists (see Pfeiffer et al., 2000) and neuropsychologists (see Kaplan, 1988; Lezak, 1995), routinely analyze patterns of factor, scale, cluster, or subtest scores to determine individual cognitive assets and deficits, and confirmation using CHT would provide meaningful conclusions, not only for determining whether a child has SLD under IDEA (e.g., Hale et al., 2006), but for developing individualized interventions following classification.

USING COGNITIVE HYPOTHESIS TESTING RESULTS TO GUIDE INTERVENTION

A frequent complaint about cognitive and neuropsychological tests is that they do not inform intervention (e.g., Reschly, 2005). In other words, some argue there is no relationship between cognitive "aptitudes" and "treatments" (i.e., ATI). However, we don't have one brain for intelligence tests, another for neuropsychological measures, a third for academic performance, and another for acting within the environment. If the brain is responsible for the learning process, one is left to wonder why these enigmatic assessment–intervention relationships are difficult to document. Perhaps the dearth of ATI studies is related to FSIQ or "g" overemphasis by some researchers (e.g., Watkins et al., 2007), because this number just tells you a child's level of performance and can only lead to ability grouping interventions, which have little value in our diverse society (e.g., Slavin, 1993). Or perhaps the purpose of many psychological evaluations, namely using ability–achievement discrepancy for determining SLD entitlement instead of intervention purposes, is the real problem (Fiorello et al., 2006; Hale, 2006; Hale et al., 2006; Kavale, Holdnack, & Mostert, 2005).

Alternatively, perhaps the problem is related to theoretical orientations or system issues that often dictate practice. Some practitioners may have knowledge about assessment of individual differences, but they primarily use these skills for SLD classification purposes, therefore neglecting the essential neuropsychological–ecological interpretive frameworks necessary to guide intervention efforts (e.g., D'Amato, Crepeau-Hobson, Huang, & Geil, 2005). Others may be well versed in empirically based interventions, but individual cognitive differences are not typically addressed in their intervention efforts (e.g., Ardoin, Witt, Cornell, & Koenig, 2005). Practitioners shouldn't have to "choose sides" and become diagnosticians or interventionists, but instead should be well-trained to do both (Hale et al., 2006; Willis & Dumont, 2006).

As noted earlier, the overwhelming evidence presented in the law, literature, and professional consensus necessitates assessment of cognitive constructs, like those found on the WISC-IV Indices (Fiorello et al., 2006; Hale et al., 2007), and suggests findings should be used to guide subsequent intervention efforts, especially for children who do not respond to standard interventions (Semrud-Clikeman, 2005). Given the high numbers of children who are nonresponders according to national and empirical study epidemiological evidence (see Fuchs et al., 2004; Gerber, 2005; Hale, Naglieri, Kaufman, & Kavale, 2004; O'Connell et al., 2005), it is clear that practitioners must be good at both assessment and intervention (Weiss, 2007) – with knowledge of cognitive, academic, and behavioral functioning intertwined with flexible, adaptive problem solving and intervention skills so that assessment can guide differentiated instruction tailored to individual child needs. The only conclusion given the extant literature (see Hale & Fiorello, 2004) is that there must be these elusive cognitive–intervention relationships, so we must evaluate new cognitive models and practices to see if they have treatment validity (e.g., Braden & Kratochwill, 1997), even if we do so only one child at a time. As discussed previously, one advantage of the Hale and Fiorello (2004) CHT approach is greater diagnostic accuracy, but it also provides for an empirically-based approach to link assessment to intervention within the context of a flexible and adaptive PSM.

Although a common argument against cognitive assessment is that there is no relationship between cognitive functioning and intervention (e.g., Reschly, 2005), this belief is largely inaccurate and outdated. True, few today call the relationship between cognitive/neuropsychological functioning and academic interventions "ATI". The researchers who are demonstrating these relationships are showing meaningful intervention response, not only in academic outcomes as related to cognitive assets and deficits, but changes on neuropsychological and neurophysiological measures as well. In fact, changes in brain functioning following intervention may serve as a method for demonstrating RtI in the future.

LINKING COGNITIVE–NEUROPSYCHOLOGICAL ASSESSMENT RESULTS TO INTERVENTION

Several of the cognitive-assessment intervention relationships reviewed below utilized Wechsler (e.g., WISC-III/WISC-IV) data, but for others, it is important to evaluate these studies for comparable relationships that could be demonstrated on auditory–verbal–crystallized-language skills (e.g., WISC-IV VC), attention, working memory, processing speed, and executive functions (e.g., WISC-IV WM/PS), and visual–spatial–holistic-fluid skills (e.g., WISC-IV PR). As many children with WISC-IV profiles suggestive of auditory–verbal difficulties may experience SLD in reading, mathematics, and/or written language disabilities (Hale & Fiorello, 2004), developing targeted interventions that address this cognitive–achievement deficit concordance may be helpful for some children (i.e., deficit remediation), but for others targeting discordant cognitive strengths may be more useful (i.e., deficit compensation).

Helland (2006) found that phonological, executive, and visual–spatial skills were differentially predictive of children struggling with phonemic and orthographic reading problems, and these children responded differentially to instruction as a result. This was also found in a study comparing phonemic and orthographic subtypes, where remediating respective weaknesses in each resulted in better RtI (measured by word decoding and text reading) than compensation using relative processing strengths (Gustafson, Ferreira, & Ronnberg, 2007). Similarly, Lovett et al. (2000) found response to phonics and metacognition interventions, while beneficial for children with phonological deficits, rapid naming speed deficits, and double-deficit groups, showed differential effects for subtypes. This suggests that WISC-IV WM or PS subtest deficits, reflective of the subtypes described earlier, could yield specific information to tailor phonemic or orthographic remedial interventions accordingly.

Certainly, WISC-IV VC processes play a role in language-related deficits for children with reading and other SLDs, as language deficits are the most common distinguishing population characteristic (Kavale & Nye, 1985, 1986) and phonological and semantic impairments are present even when reading is not required (Corina et al., 2000). Hay (2007) found that teacher–student instructional dialogs focusing on vocabulary, memory, and verbal reasoning skills showed differential effectiveness for children with reading SLD and comorbid language deficits relative to controls, consistent with the findings that language and particularly vocabulary interventions are helpful for children with reading SLD (Bryant, Goodwin, Bryant, & Higgins, 2003; Wiig, 2005). But in a direct comparison of lexical/semantic and phoneme/grapheme correspondence interventions, the latter was found to be more successful in ameliorating word reading deficits (Wise, Sevcik, Morris, Lovett, & Wolf, 2007), suggesting language interventions are not sufficient to address all reading SLDs.

Comparing speed of language processing may be relevant, as children with reading SLD have been shown to have temporal and spectral auditory processing speed deficits (Tallal, 2004), which could manifest itself on WISC-IV VC and WM subtests. Pitch discrimination, phonological, and phoneme–grapheme conversion interventions for children with reading SLD normalize event-related evoked potentials, signifying changes in brain function, but the interventions also improve phonological awareness, spelling and irregular word and pseudoword reading (Santos et al., 2007). However, speech and sound segmentation deficits could be due to sound discrimination or perception, so the specific pattern of performance is relevant for intervention (Kujala et al., 2006).

The University of Washington has served as a primary site for several studies showing neuropsychological, neurophysiological, and academic response to reading and writing interventions. Richards et al. (2005) found that the phonological, orthographic, and morphological differences among children with reading SLD and controls apparent during testing and on brain imaging results (fMRI) reflected different *patterns* (not levels) of functioning, and reading SLD group differences were ameliorated or normalized following intervention. Richards et al. (2007) found that phonological–orthographic mapping, not auditory discrimination, characterized children with reading SLD, consistent with Kujala et al. (2006). As a result, the WISC-IV factors involved in both phonological (e.g., VC/WM) and orthographic (e.g., PS) processes may indeed play a more important role in differentiating reading SLD instructional strategies, because it is more likely to tap perceptual/integration processes more than just phonological discrimination. Interestingly, Richards et al. (2007) found that brain changes in children with reading SLD differed in the *amount* (phonological intervention) or *direction* (orthographic intervention), both of which ameliorated dysfunctional brain and achievement patterns. Comparing different instructional approaches for phonology and orthography, Berninger et al. (2000) showed a connectionist approach using phonological–orthographic mapping produces the most generalizable gains. Phonological, orthographic, and morphological word forms are all necessary for reading comprehension (Berninger et al., 2006), and changes in brain function in RtI affect both reading and language processes (Aylward et al., 2003; Corina et al., 2001), suggesting that reading SLD subtypes would benefit from word reading (phonological and orthographic), rapid naming/reading fluency, and/or language comprehension interventions (Stage, Abott, Jenkins, & Berninger, 2003).

A series of studies by Simos and colleagues (see Simos et al., 2006) show specific deficits in reading SLD, and how the deficits are related to intervention. For instance, Simos et al. (2002) found children with reading SLD showed changes in left hemisphere brain functioning associated with language and phoneme–grapheme correspondence in response to phonological and/or phonological–orthographic/alphabetic instruction, and changes in right hemisphere function found at baseline. The authors suggest this remediation reflects a decreased need for compensation; however, as has been suggested elsewhere (Goldberg, 2001; Hale & Fiorello, 2004), this could reflect the typical shift from right to left hemisphere as one gains proficiency. In addition, continued difficulties with reading fluency were noted, which could reflect comorbid ADHD problems inherent in most of the sample. Simos et al. (2007) and Denton, Fletcher, Anthony, and Francis (2006) demonstrated that for children who were nonresponders to reading instruction, intensive phonics, orthographic, and fluency instruction either again resulted in improvement in deficient brain areas commonly associated with phonological reading SLD (i.e., left temporal–parietal regions), or development of compensatory right hemisphere areas found in other studies (i.e., Shaywitz et al., 2003), but responsiveness was associated with normalization of aberrant patterns. Interestingly, unlike the compensatory subtype in Shaywitz et al. (2003), the compensated subtype showed minimal response in Simos et al. (2007), which could suggest persistent disruption in the left temporal–parietal regions as suggested by Pugh et al. (2000).

These studies suggest some children would be unlikely to respond to standard phonological and fluency instruction efforts offered by Simos et al., even at greater intensity as some have suggested (Barnett et al., 2004). As treatment resistant children may not be able to develop phonological representations of words (Elbro & Petersen, 2004), they might benefit from more individualized instruction tailored to their needs, such as a working memory/learning strategy approach for decoding, or a global–holistic sight word approach, capitalizing on their intact right hemisphere processes. The use of semantic/word maps, structural/semantic analysis, keyword methods, and guided/visual imagery would fit nicely with a compensatory approach for children with auditory–verbal and linguistic deficits (Baumann & Kameenui, 1991; Bos & Anders, 1990; Greenwood, 2002; McAndrews, 2002; McCormick & Becker, 1996; Szabo, 2006) that are likely displayed on the WISC-IV VC and WM factors.

One recent subtype study found stimulating visual–spatial/ right hemisphere or language/left hemisphere processes led to differential response to intervention based on initial subtype patterns of reading performance (Smit-Glaude, van Strien, Licht, & Bakker, 2005), which would be consistent with another study that showed auditory–visual stimulation differentially remediated WISC-III SCAD (Symbol Search, Coding, Arithmetic, Digit Span) profile deficits (Olmstead, 2005) – deficits that are commonly reported in SLD populations (Mayes et al., 1998; Mayes & Calhoun, 2004). Structuring tasks for children with PR difficulties, such as providing step-by-step analysis of math word problems, number squares for math concepts, or using graph paper for math computation tasks (Levine, 2001; Mercer & Miller, 1992; Naglieri & Pickering, 2003) could be useful in ameliorating math problems caused by PR deficits.

For attention, working memory, and executive processes (i.e., WM, PS), metacognitive strategies such as mnemonics, goal setting, paired associates, self-monitoring, and imagery are the most commonly used (Bolich & McLaughlin, 2001; Levine, 2001; Miller, Strawser, & Mercer, 1996; Schraw, 1998; Seabaugh & Schumaker, 1994). Shamir and Lazerovitz (2007) showed that peer-mediated tutoring sessions improved analogic reasoning and self-regulation skills in children with SLD over controls. Similarly, metacognitive strategies such as self-management, goal setting, step-by-step problem solving, and self-determination have led to improved math performance and general academic productivity in children with math SLD and ADHD (Konrad et al., 2007; Montague, 2007). Denckla (2007) suggests differential response to intervention for SLD and ADHD populations is based on the types of executive deficits displayed, so differentiating children with WM and PS executive deficits may be essential, as this may interact with instruction. For instance, attention training, while not sufficient to foster fluent reading performance on its own, interacts with instruction to remediate executive deficits found in reading and writing SLD (Chenault Thomson, Abott, & Berninger, 2006). Improvements in executive functions related to social competency, such as hypothesis testing and appreciation of humor can also promote gains in socioemotional functioning among children with SLD (Schnitzer, Andries, & Lebeer, 2007). Naglieri and Pickering (2003) detail the importance of self-monitoring of math calculation and associating math facts with semantically meaningful content.

Related to WISC-IV PS skills (e.g., Hale & Fiorello, 2004), reading fluency is often considered as the "second" deficit in the "double-deficit" hypothesis (Wolf & Bowers, 1999) of reading SLD. Fluency appears to be fostered most by executive-mediated strategies such as goal setting, question generation, and performance feedback more than simply developing better word reading skills (Morgan & Sideridis, 2006; Therrien, Wickstorm, & Jones, 2006), as would be suggested in a "more intensive" remediation approach (e.g., Barnett et al., 2004). Fostering WISC-IV PS skills during reading can also be successfully accomplished through simple repeated readings (O'Connor, White, & Swanson, 2007), with self-charting of progress likely resulting in greater individual investment. PS is likely related to orthographic processing as well as speed of processing, both of which are related to each other, and reading fluency (Thomson et al., 2005). Intervention programs that target multiple areas may hold the greatest promise, such as the RAVE-O program that focuses on building retrieval, automaticity, vocabulary elaboration, and orthography to foster skill development in multiple areas of known reading deficit (Wolf, Miller, & Donnelly, 2000), with the result being improved word reading, reading fluency, and comprehension.

One of the difficulties with establishing strong cognitive assessment–intervention associations may be related to experimental design, as the research questions asked and design chosen are reciprocally determined (Gersten, 2005). Although group designs have strong external validity, randomized experimental group designs are rare (Seethaler & Fuchs, 2005) and may not be feasible in applied settings. In addition, large groups of children used in these designs tend to be cognitively and neuropsychologically heterogeneous, which serves to undermine treatment efficacy, but small homogeneous groups also have limitations regarding generalizability of findings (Semrud-Clikeman & Pliszka, 2005). In a large group, if one subset of children shows a positive assessment–intervention relationship, but the other displays a negative one, then the whole group treatment effect will be absent.

As a result, single subject research designs, with their strong internal validity, are increasingly being used to demonstrate cognitive assessment–intervention associations, both at the neuropsychological and behavioral level. For instance, Bowes and Martin (2007) found bigraph–biphone (CV + VC = CVC) correspondence intervention with increasing word length across conditions fostered reading and writing in phonological SLD. Tuller et al. (2007) found that using strength-based verbal mediation could improve academic performance and brain functioning in individual children with right hemisphere or "nonverbal" SLD.

Single subject approaches have also be used to document gains in attention, executive function, graphomotor problems in children with ADHD and "non-verbal" SLD (Hale et al., 2006; Reddy & Hale, 2007). Naglieri and colleagues (Naglieri & Gottling, 1995; Naglieri & Johnson, 2000) showed that children with low executive planning scores benefitted from self-reflection and strategy verbalization more than children with other cognitive deficits or adequate planning scores. Jitendra et al. (2004) found support for the use of a more frequent and intensive empirically supported reading intervention, which would be consistent with the "greater intensity" RtI approach (e.g., Barnett et al., 2004), but differential response curves were indicative of individual cognitive/neuropsychological differences. These differential cognitive/neuropsychological-assessment relationships would have been absent or attenuated if these children were collapsed into a single heterogeneous group.

Several books are now available for those interested in linking cognitive/ neuropsychological profiles to intervention. The Flanagan and Kaufman (2004) book is especially relevant for use with the WISC-IV, as the authors have a "Suggestions for Intervention" section for different WISC-IV CHC profiles. While some texts are more general, such as the Swanson, Hoskyn, and Lee (1999) meta-analysis of SLD interventions, others are more specifically designed to make cognitive processing relevant for intervention. Dawson and Guare (2004) discuss intervention strategies for children with executive function deficits. Naglieri and Pickering (2003) approach to ameliorating attention, executive, successive, and simultaneous processing deficits as related to achievement domains. Feifer and Della Toffalo (2007) provide specific recommendations for various causes of reading SLD within the context of a PSM that incorporates both RtI and cognitive neuropsychology. Hale and Fiorello (2004) provide the CHT model and interventions for children with reading, math, or written language disorders. Mather and Jaffe (2002) provide many empirically based approaches that can be applied to WISC-IV VC (Gc), PR (Gf/Gv), WM (Gsm-WM), and PS (Gs) Indices. Mastropieri and Scruggs (2000) provide useful recommendations for providing instructional accommodations in inclusive classrooms. Finally, Wong (2004) and Bradley, Danielson, and Hallahan (2002) provide edited volumes that address critical issues in SLD identification and intervention.

Choosing a particular intervention must be based on multiple criteria, including teacher characteristics, curricula, age, and severity of the processing problem. The only way individualized instruction that is sensitive to individual learner differences can be achieved is through tailoring the intervention to the child, and then monitoring, evaluating, and modifying/recycling it until success is achieved. In Hale and Fiorello's (2004) CHT model, the problem-solving approach permeates every aspect of this process, and single subject designs are used to evaluate treatment efficacy. The CHT assessment is a beginning, not an endpoint. For cognitive and neuropsychological data to be truly useful, it must be used to guide intervention in a flexible, adaptive problem-solving approach designed to ensure treatment efficacy. When combined with RtI practices, assessment can guide intervention if multiple tools and practices are incorporated, thereby ensuring differentiated instruction for all children, regardless of disability status.

Recognition that not all children will respond to any given empirically based intervention suggests we must have multiple strategies and tools available if we flexibly adapt instruction to meet diverse learner needs. A responsible clinician must examine multiple possible cognitive processing–academic deficit relationships so that differentiated instruction sensitive to individual differences in learning can be provided. If the subsequent single subject intervention is collaboratively developed with teachers, carefully monitored and evaluated using objective data, and recycled until treatment efficacy is obtained, the fruits of such assessments will be realized (Hale & Fiorello, 2004).

WISC-IV CHT CASE STUDY

RELEVANT BACKGROUND INFORMATION

Luke's gestation and delivery were unremarkable except for a mild case of neonatal jaundice treated with phototherapy. He was described as a healthy child with good hearing and vision. Developmental milestones were said to be acquired within normal limits. Starting preschool at age 4, Luke adjusted well and had no academic problems. However, 1 year prior to evaluation he was suspended for fighting, and then recently he wrote his teacher an "offensive" note apparently because she had corrected him in front of his peers. He was also a "discipline problem" on the bus, but mostly due to his being "overly talkative" with peers. Academic concerns in reading and math also surfaced during this period, and he struggled with spelling and written language at times. But instead of giving up on these tasks, Luke was somewhat perfectionistic in his writing and often took considerable time to complete written assignments. Luke seemed to have particular difficulty with vocabulary or recalling words previously learned, but the teacher said he struggled with decoding and had limited reading and math fact automaticity. Although described as pleasant, affable, and compassionate, Luke was described as inattentive, fidgety, impulsive, and noncompliant at times. His difficulty in reading led to early intervention services in the school for students with learning delays, but he did not effectively respond to their interventions according to informal reading inventory results. Luke lived with his mother and had regular contact with his father. Close to his grandmother, Luke was distraught over her recent cerebral vascular accident (i.e., stroke) and resultant disability, which led to significant family stress. Other than an extended family member diagnosed with depression, there were no other known medical or psychological conditions reported for the family.

ASSESSMENT OBSERVATIONS

Luke presented as an 8-year, 2-month-old boy with adequate health and hygiene. Mostly pleasant and cooperative, Luke regularly attempted to engage the examiner in off-task conversations, and the more she used planned ignoring, the more Luke provided comments that could be considered tangential or bizarre, as if he were trying to get the examiner to feed into his off-task comments. For instance, he told her that he had X-ray vision and was a psychic, and at one point he began using aprosodic robotic speech to indicate he didn't know an answer. He also made personalized comments and self-deprecating remarks during facial memory. During difficult tasks, Luke made several moans, vocalizations, and self-deprecating remarks, and these were typically congruent with his facial grimaces. Although the parent reported adequate behavior, the teacher noted limited attention, impulse control, and executive functions. These behaviors were observed during testing, especially as tasks increased in difficulty, and his persistence was often minimal following failure responding.

ASSESSMENT RESULTS AND CLINICAL IMPRESSIONS

Intellectual Screening

On the WISC-IV, Luke had considerable subtest and factor variability which precludes the interpretation of the Full Scale SS. He scored in the average range on the VC (SS = 93) and PR (SS = 94) Indices, but his WM (SS = 77) and PS (SS = 78) scores were significantly lower. This suggests WM and PS represented cognitive deficits, and the General Ability Index (GAI) using VC and PR should be calculated as an indicator of Luke's cognitive assets, and these scores were significantly different using C-DM calculations. It should be noted that as a result of this profile variability, no one score accurately represents Luke's global intellectual ability. His GAI SS of 93 was in the average range, and at the 32nd percentile compared to his same age peers. However, given his variable profile, the CHT model would appear to be the preferred method of interpretation.

As can be seen in the table below, Luke's profile was variable, with the PR factor the highest stable global score achieved during the evaluation. For visual–perceptual reasoning skills, Luke again showed good perceptual integration and categorization when asked to identify relationships among meaningful pictures. Although in the average range, Luke had some qualitative difficulty putting together blocks according to a visual model. On some items he inverted or reversed the direction of the diagonal, suggesting poor attention to detail or directional confusion. However, this finding was not significant, suggesting overall his perceptual analysis and synthesis of part–whole relationships was otherwise adequate. He also had some difficulty with novel problem solving or discordant/divergent thought and analogic reasoning as suggested by his variable performance on a task that required identifying a missing element of a visual pattern, but his score was still in the average range. He scored quite well on tasks requiring verbal or visual categorization of stimuli, suggesting good verbal concept formation and concordant/convergent thinking. Luke appeared to have fairly adequate crystallized and common sense knowledge, gained through formal and informal experience and education, but his vocabulary knowledge may be somewhat below average, and he had considerable difficulty with retrieval of factual information from long-term memory. Receptive and expressive language appeared to be fairly adequate, but Luke asked to have verbal directions repeated at times, appeared to mishear some items, and tended to produce lengthy and indirect verbal responses, which could suggest difficulty with language formulation or memory retrieval.

Although the VC and PR scores were in the average range, Luke struggled with the WM and PS subtests, with both indices in the borderline range. He had little difficulty recalling orally presented digits in forward sequence (SS = 9), but struggled with attention, concentration, and working memory when asked to mentally manipulate sequences to produce the reverse order (SS = 3). Substitutions, omissions, and sequencing errors were noted, especially on the latter task. Similarly, he struggled with mental manipulation of letters and numbers, often responding by just repeating the stimulus in forward sequence regardless of the working memory demands for a particular item. This difficulty appeared to transcend auditory–verbal stimuli, as Luke had difficulty with quick, efficient, graphomotor reproduction of symbols according to a number–symbol template, and determining if one of two target symbols were contained among a group of distracters. Although accuracy was fairly good on these speeded subtests, his careful methodical style slowed his performance, especially when graphomotor demands were high.

VC (SS = 93)	SS	PR (SS = 94)	SS
Similarities	11	Block Design	8
Vocabulary	7	Picture Concepts	11
Comprehension	8	Matrix Reasoning	8
(Information)	5	(Picture Completion)	10
WM (SS = 77)		PS (SS = 78)	
Digit Span	6	Coding	5
Letter–Number Sequencing	6	Symbol Search	7

Cognitive Hypothesis Testing

On the basis of the WISC-IV testing, Luke appeared to have fairly well-developed visual–spatial–holistic processing, novel problem solving/fluid reasoning, discordant and divergent thinking, receptive and expressive language, vocabulary or lexical/semantic knowledge, concordant and convergent thought processes, categorical thinking, and verbal reasoning. Some qualitative difficulty with language comprehension and expression were noted, but these did not appear to be significant given the intellectual screening results, and could be due to limited crystallized knowledge, especially given his performance on the task requiring retrieval of factual knowledge. Qualitative signs suggested language processes needed further evaluation, because Luke misheard some words and used words that were semantically similar to the correct response, but were inaccurate nonetheless. Luke did appear to have considerable difficulty with attention, working memory, processing speed, and executive function, so further evaluation in these areas was necessary to confirm hypotheses.

Language and Crystallized Abilities

As noted earlier, Luke seemed to have some minor difficulty with receptive and expressive language, and possibly crystallized knowledge. These difficulties were confirmed during hypothesis testing. Luke had difficulty with auditory attention, phonological processing, learning and recalling word lists, understanding directions, and language formulation. Although he struggled providing motoric responses reflective of orally presented instructions, suggesting some comprehension difficulties, his lexical–semantic knowledge appeared to be adequate, as he performed in the average range on a narrative memory task and retrieval of factual information presented in multiple choice format. It appeared that Luke did best when language was meaningful and contextualized. Both phonological awareness and rapid naming skills were impaired, which would be consistent with a "double-deficit" reading disorder negatively affecting both word reading and reading comprehension, which was the case during Luke's performance on the WIAT-II (word reading SS = 78; pseudoword decoding SS = 76; reading comprehension SS = 73), the only impaired achievement subtests. Interestingly, error responses indicated that Luke tended to guess at words based on initial letter or whole word configuration, and when decoding was attempted, he had difficulty with phonological analysis and assembly.

Attention, Working Memory, Fluid Reasoning, and Executive Function

During hypothesis testing, Luke showed some difficulty with sustained auditory and visual attention, working memory, inhibition/interference control, and executive function tasks. Luke performed fairly well on a task requiring novel problem solving, maintaining cognitive set, mental flexibility, and executive control processes necessary to develop multiple different card sorts. However, his auditory attention for naming was limited, which could be due to his difficulty with auditory discrimination and phonological processing, but he also struggled with auditory inhibition and flexibility when asked to provide a competing response, making many errors on this task. Consistent with findings reported earlier, Luke's speeded naming was accurate but slow, consistent with poor retrieval speed, limited auditory–verbal skill automaticity and slow processing speed. He also had difficulty repeating and recalling unrelated word lists, and a series of oral instructions, with several sequential errors observed on this task. In other words, Luke followed all the oral directions or steps, but in the wrong order. However, it should be noted that this pattern appears to be more related to executive dysfunction than a long-term memory storage problem, as lexical–semantic memory storage and retrieval appeared to be adequate. However, when given the WISC-IV multiple choice format for recall of factual information, Luke performed in the average range, which does suggest minor retrieval difficulties. As Luke seems to vacillate between slow, methodical, accurate responding, and quick, impulsive, error responding, the problem appears to be one of consistent self-regulation of performance, and variability in response patterns.

Luke had little difficulty with recognizing affect and the mental states of others, and processing emotional content in facial expressions. When combined with behavior rating scale and parent/teacher reports, these findings suggest Luke's comments during testing probably reflected attention-seeking behavior rather than the bizarre ideation found in some forms of psychopathology.

Visual–Spatial–Holistic Processes and Visual–Motor Integration Skills

Although Luke's WISC-IV Processing Speed Performance appeared to be caused by executive deficits that limit efficient information processing and decision-making speed, it was important to ensure that visual, spatial, and motor skills were adequate. As a result, several tasks of visual–spatial processing, nonverbal memory, visual–motor integration, and motor/graphomotor functioning were administered. Luke had no difficulty with any of these measures, with all scores found to be within the average range. With processing speed demands removed, Luke appears to have adequate spatial-holistic, and visual–motor integration skills, and nonverbal memory. This also suggests minor difficulties with nonverbal reasoning are not due to their visual–spatial test stimuli, but rather the novel problem solving and executive demands required on these tasks.

Recommendations and Intervention Planning

Combined with his poor response to prior intervention attempts, and pattern of performance described here, Luke appeared to have a reading SLD. He demonstrated a discordance between his VC and PR cognitive assets, and his SCAD deficits (Information was also related to SCAD deficits), and WIAT-II reading subtest scores, and the SCAD profile was concordant with his reading performance, suggesting Luke met C-DM criteria for an SLD. Results suggest he has a "deficit in the basic psychological processes" that has resulted in his SLD as determined by C-DM statistics, so he meets both IDEA statutory and regulatory requirements. As a result, Luke was classified as having a reading SLD.

Several recommendations were offered to the team to address Luke's difficulty with reading, attention, working memory, impulse control, processing speed, and general executive function. Recommendations included direct instruction, task analysis of complex tasks, extended time testing, limited use of multiple instructions/sequences, asking Luke to repeat directions back to the teacher, using cue hierarchies and mnemonics to aid memory storage and retrieval, notetaking and supplemental visual aids during oral lecture, improvement of phonological analysis and assembly, orthographic processing, and fluency instruction to help Luke gain speeded access to his lexicon. This intervention included improving phoneme–grapheme correspondence skills, and rapid naming of words and objects to improve automaticity. It was decided that Luke should be further monitored regarding his attention and executive problems, as well as his repetitive thoughts and behaviors because reading problems were the most pressing issue according to the team. However, if monitoring suggested further interference with academics and social adjustment, the team felt a more specific intervention would be necessary.

During the follow-up consultation meeting with the teacher a week later, we brainstormed multiple intervention strategies, and hierarchically arranged them in order of importance. Although both reading and written language were important to address, his difficulty with word attack skills, phoneme–grapheme correspondence, phonological analysis and assembly, rapid naming and reading fluency, and reading comprehension were of greatest concern. We used basic instruction in phonological and orthographic processes, focusing on phoneme–grapheme correspondence in a highly structured phonics program that focused on related word families and morpheme recognition.

During individual biweekly direct service sessions lasting 20 minutes, Luke met with the consultant to improve his word reading skills. For each trial during the sessions, Luke attempted to read 10 words without guidance. He placed words he read correctly in the "Got It!" pile, and the rest in a "Not Yet" pile. He then received systematic instruction in each phoneme, grapheme, and morpheme for the words in the "Not Yet" pile to foster phonological and orthographic

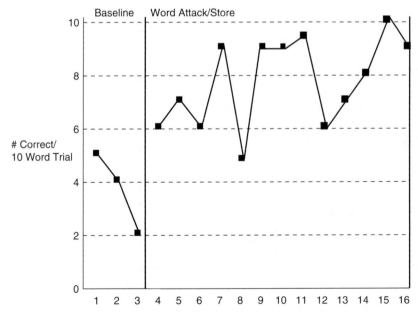

FIGURE 3.4   Luke's word recognition.

rule acquisition. He was then asked to read each word from the "Not Yet" pile again, using his hands to guide the "discovery window" across the word to foster sequencing/scanning (see Fiorello et al., 2006). In each subsequent session for each trial, new words (provided from the teacher) were introduced with the words from the "Not Yet" pile plus two words from the "Got it" pile. This strategy was used to increase successful responding, foster maintenance of known words, and decrease frustration. Self-charting was used as a reinforcer. The results of this intervention are depicted in Figure 3.4. As can be seen, Luke increased his word recognition skills showing fairly steady improvement during initial reading of words. Subsequent testing revealed Luke's word recognition skills were approaching grade level, but fluency was still limited, which was the next step in the individualized intervention program.

REFERENCES

Anastasi, A., & Urbina, S. (1997). *Psychological Testing* (7th ed.). Upper Saddle River, NJ: Prentice-Hall.

Ardila, A., Concha, M., & Rosselli, M. (2000). Angular gyrus syndrome revisited: Acalculia, finger agnosia, right-left disorientation and semantic aphasia. *Aphasiology, 14*, 743–754.

Ardoin, S. P., Witt, J. C., Connell, J. E., & Koenig, J. L. (2005). Application of a three-tiered response to intervention model for instructional planning, decision making, and the identification of children in need of services. *Journal of Psychoeducational Assessment, 23*, 362–380.

Aylward, E. H., Richards, T. L., Berninger, V. W., Nagy, W. E., Field, K. M., Grimme, A. C., et al. (2003). Instructional treatment associated with changes in brain activation in children with dyslexia. *Neurology, 61*, 212–219.

Badian, N. A. (1997). Dyslexia and the double deficit hypothesis. *Annals of Dyslexia, 47*, 69–87.

Bakker, D. J., Van Strien, J. W., Licht, R., & Smit-Glaude, & Sietsia, S. W. D. (2007). Cognitive brain potentials in kindergarten children with subtyped risks of reading retardation. *Annals of Dyslexia, 57*, 99–111.

Barnett, D. W., Daly, E. J., Jones, K. M., & Lentz, F. E. (2004). Response to intervention: Empirically based special service decisions from single-case designs of increasing and decreasing intensity. *The Journal of Special Education, 38*, 66–79.

Baron, I. S. (2005). Test review: Wechsler intelligence scale for children-fourth edition (WISC-IV). *Child Neuropsychology, 11*, 471–475.

Baumann, J. F., & Kameenui, E. J. (1991). Research on vocabulary instruction. In J. Flood, J. Jensen, J. J. Lapp, & J. R. Squire (Eds.), *Handbook of Research on Teaching the English Language Arts* (pp. 604–632). New York: MacMillan.

Beaton, A. A., & Davies, N. W. (2007). Semantic errors in deep dyslexia: Does orthographic depth matter? *Cognitive Neuropsychology, 24*, 312–323.

Benbow, C. P., Lubinski, D., & Hyde, J. S. (1997). Mathematics: Is biology the cause of gender differences in performance? In M. R. Walsh (Ed.), *Women, Men, & Gender: Ongoing Debates* (pp. 271–287). New Haven, CT: Yale University Press.

Berninger, V., & Richards, T. L. (2002). *Brain Literacy for Educators and Psychologists*. Boston: Academic Press.

Berninger, V. W. (2006). Research-supported ideas for implementing reauthorized IDEA with intelligent professional psychological services. *Psychology in the Schools, 43*, 781–796.

Berninger, V. W., Abbott, R. D., Billingsley, F. B., & Nagy, W. (2001). Processes underlying timing and fluency of reading: Efficiency, automaticity, coordination, and morphological awareness. In M. Wolf (Ed.), *Dyslexia, Fluency, and the Brain* (pp. 383–414). Timonium, MD: York Press.

Berninger, V. W., Abbott, R. D., Brooksher, R., Lemos, Z., Ogier, S., Zook, D., et al. (2000). A connectionist approach to making the predictability of English orthography explicit to at-risk beginning readers: Evidence for alternative, effective strategies. *Developmental Neuropsychology, 17,* 241–271.

Berninger, V. W., Abbott, R. D., Jones, J., Wolf, B. J., Gould, L., Anderson-Youngstrom, M., et al. (2006). Early development of language by hand: Composing, reading, listening, and speaking connections. *Developmental Neuropsychology, 29,* 61–92.

Berninger, V. W., & O'Donnell, L. (2005). Research-supported differential diagnosis of specific learning disabilities. In A. Prifitera, D. H. Saklofske, & L.G. Weiss (Eds.), *WISC-IV Clinical Use and Interpretation: Scientist–Practitioner Perspectives* (pp. 189–233). San Diego, CA: Elsevier Academic Press.

Bolich, B., & McLaughlin, T. F. (2001). The use of mnemonic strategies as instructional tools for children with learning disabilities. *International Journal of Special Education, 16,* 40–49.

Bos, C. S., & Anders, P. L. (1990). Effects of interactive vocabulary instruction on the vocabulary learning and reading comprehension of junior-high learning disabled students. *Learning Disability Quarterly, 13,* 31–42.

Bowers, P. G. (2001). Exploration of the basis for rapid naming's relationship to reading. In M. Wolf (Ed.), *Dyslexia, Fluency, and the Brain* (pp. 41–64). Timonium, MD: York Press.

Bowes, K., & Martin, N. (2007). Longitudinal study of reading and writing rehabilitation using a bigraph–biphone correspondence approach. *Aphasiology, 21,* 687–701.

Braden, J. P., & Kratochwill, T. R. (1997). Treatment utility of assessment: Myths and realities. *School Psychology Review, 26,* 475–485.

Bradley, R., Danielson, I., & Hallahan, D. P. (Eds.) (2002). *Identification of Learning Disabilities: Research to Practice.* Mahwah, NJ: Lawrence Erlbaum.

Breier, J. I., Simos, P. G., Fletcher, J. M., Castillo, E. M., Zhang, W., & Papanicolaou, A. C. (2003). Abnormal activation of temporoparietal language areas during phonetic analysis in dyslexia. *Neuropsychology, 17,* 610–621.

Brown-Chidsey, R., & Steege, M. W. (2005). *Response to Intervention: Principles and Strategies for Effective Practice.* New York, NY: Guilford Press.

Bryan, K. L., & Hale, J. B. (2001). Differential effects of left and right hemisphere accidents on language competency. *Journal of the International Neuropsychological Society, 7,* 655–664.

Bryant, D. P., Goodwin, M., Bryant, B. R., & Higgins, K. (2003). Vocabulary instruction for students with learning disabilities: A review of research. *Learning Disability Quarterly, 26,* 117–128.

Calhoun, S. L., & Mayes, S. D. (2005). Processing speed in children with clinical disorders. *Psychology in the Schools, 42*(4), 333–343.

Castellanos, F. X., Lee, P. P., Sharp, W., Jeffries, N. O., Greenstein, D. K., Clasen, L. S., et al. (2002). Developmental trajectories of brain volume abnormalities in children and adolescents with attention-deficit/hyperactivity disorder. *Journal of the American Medical Association, 288,* 1740–1748.

Chenault, B., Thomson, J., Abbott, R. D., & Berninger, V. W. (2006). Effects of prior training on child dyslexics' response to composition instruction. *Developmental Neuropsychology, 29,* 243–260.

Cirino, P. T., Morris, M. K., & Morris, R. D. (2007). Semantic, executive, and visuospatial abilities in mathematical reasoning in referred college students. *Assessment, 14,* 94–104.

Cohen, A., Fiorello, C. A., & Farley, F. H. (2006). The cylindrical structure of the Wechsler Intelligence Scale for Children-IV: A retest of the Guttman model of intelligence. *Intelligence, 34,* 587–591.

Collins, D. W., & Rourke, B. P. (2003). Learning-disabled brains: A review of the literature. *Journal of Clinical and Experimental Neuropsychology, 25,* 1011–1034.

Corbera, S., Escera, C., & Artigas, J. (2006). Impaired duration mismatch negativity in developmental dyslexia. *Neuroreport: For Rapid Communication of Neuroscience Research, 17,* 1051–1055.

Corina, D. P., Richards, T. L., Serafini, S., Richards, A. L., Steury, K., Abbott, R. D., et al. (2001). fMRI auditory language differences between dyslexic and able reading children. *Neuroreport: For Rapid Communication of Neuroscience Research, 12,* 1195–1201.

D'Amato, R. C., Crepeau-Hobson, F., Huang, L. V., & Geil, M. (2005). Ecological neuropsychology: An alternative to the deficit model for serving students with learning disabilities. *Neuropsychology Review, 15,* 97–103.

Dawson, P., & Guare, R. (2004). *Executive Skills in Children and Adolescents: A Practical Guide to Assessment and Intervention.* New York, NY: Guilford Press.

Del'Homme, M., Kim, T. S., Loo, S. K., Yang, M. H., & Smalley, S. L. (2007). Familial association and frequency of learning disabilities in ADHD sibling pair families. *Journal of Abnormal Child Psychology, 35,* 55–62.

Demb, J. B., Boynton, G. M., & Heeger, D. J. (1998). Functional magnetic resonance imaging of early visual pathways in dyslexia. *The Journal of Neuroscience, 18,* 6939–6951.

Denckla, M. B. (2007). Executive function: Binding together the definitions of attention-deficit/ hyperactivity disorder and learning disabilities. In L. Meltzer (Ed.), *Executive Function in Education: From Theory to Practice* (pp. 5–18). New York, NY: Guilford Press.

Deno, S. L. (2002). Problem solving as "best practice". In A. Thomas, & J. Grimes (Eds.), *Best Practices in School Psychology IV* (pp. 37–56). Bethesda, MD: National Association of School Psychologists.

Denton, C. A., Fletcher, J. M., Anthony, J. L., & Francis, D. J. (2007). An evaluation of intensive intervention for students with persistent reading difficulties. *Journal of Learning Disabilities.*

Dombrowski, S. C., Kamphaus, R. W., & Reynolds, C. R. (2004). After the demise of the discrepancy: Proposed learning disabilities diagnostic criteria. *Professional Psychology: Research and Practice, 35,* 364–372.

Eckert, M. A., Leonard, C. M., Richards, T. L., Aylward, E. H., Thomson, J., & Berninger, V. W. (2003). Anatomical correlates of dyslexia: Frontal and cerebellar findings. *Brain, 126,* 482–494.

Eden, G. F., VanMeter, J. W., Rumsey, J. W., Maison, J., & Zeffiro, T. A. (1996). Functional MRI reveals differences in visual motion processing in individuals with dyslexia. *Nature, 382,* 66–69.

Elbro, C., & Petersen, D. K. (2004). Long-term effects of phoneme awareness and letter sound training: An intervention study with children at risk for dyslexia. *Journal of Educational Psychology, 96,* 660–670.

Evans, J. J., Floyd, R. G., McGrew, K. S., & Leforgee, M. H. (2002). The relations between measures of Cattell-Horn-Carroll (CHC) cognitive abilities and reading achievement during childhood and adolescence. *School Psychology Review, 31,* 364–372.

Farah, M. J. (1990). *Visual Agnosia: Disorders of Object Recognition and What They Tell Us About Normal Vision.* Cambridge, MA: MIT Press.

Fawcett, A. J., & Nicholson, R. I. (2001). Speed and temporal processing in dyslexia. In M. Wolf (Ed.), *Dyslexia, Fluency, and the Brain* (pp. 277–306). Timonium, MD: York Press.

Feifer, S. G., & Della Toffalo, D. A. (2007). *Integrating RTI with Cognitive Neuropsychology. A Scientific Approach to Reading.* Middletown, MD: School Neuropsych Press.

Feldt, L. S., & Charter, R. A. (2006). Averaging internal consistency reliability coefficients. *Educational and Psychological Measurement, 66,* 215–227.

Fiez, J. A., & Petersen, S. E. (1998). Neuroimaging studies of word reading. *Proceedings of the National Academy of Sciences USA, 95,* 914–921.

Filipek, P. A. (1999). Neuroimaging in the developmental disorders. The state of the science. *Journal of Child Psychology and Psychiatry, 40,* 113–128.

Filippatou, D. N., & Livaniou, E. (2005). Comorbidity and WISC-III profiles of Greek children with attention deficit hyperactivity disorder, learning disabilities, and language disorders. *Psychological Reports, 97,* 485–504.

Fine, J. G., Semrud-Clikeman, M., Keith, T. Z., Stapleton, L. M., & Hynd, G. W. (2007). Reading and the corpus callosum: An MRI family study of volume and area. *Neuropsychology, 21,* 235–241.

Fiorello, C. A., Hale, J. B., Holdnack, J. A., Kavanagh, J. A., Terrell, J., & Long, L. (2007). Interpreting intelligence test results for children with disabilities: Is global intelligence relevant? *Applied Neuropsychology, 14*, 2–12.

Fiorello, C. A., Hale, J. B., McGrath, M., Ryan, K., & Quinn, S. (2001). IQ interpretation for children with flat and variable test profiles. *Learning and Individual Differences, 13*, 115–125.

Fiorello, C. A., Hale, J. B., & Snyder, L. E. (2006). Cognitive hypothesis testing and response to intervention for children with reading disabilities. *Psychology in the Schools, 43*, 835–854.

Fiorello, C. A., Hale, J. B., Snyder, L. E., Forrest, E., & Teodori, A. (2008). Validating individual differences through examination of converging psychometric and neuropsychological models of cognitive functioning. In S. K. Thurman, & C. A. Fiorello (Eds.), *Applied Cognitive Research in K-3 Classrooms*. New York, NY: Routledge.

Fitch, R. H., & Tallal, P. (2003). Neural mechanisms of language-based learning impairments: Insights from human populations and animal models. *Behavioral and Cognitive Neuroscience Reviews, 2*, 155–178.

Flanagan, D. P., & Kaufman, A. S. (2004). *Essentials of WISC-IV Assessment*. Hoboken, NJ: John Wiley & Sons.

Flanagan, D. P., & McGrew, K. S. (1997). A cross-battery approach to assessing and interpreting cognitive abilities: Narrowing the gap between practice and cognitive science. In D. P. Flanagan, J. L. Genshaft, & P. L. Harrison (Eds.), *Contemporary Intellectual Assessment* (pp. 314–325). New York: Guilford Press.

Flanagan, D. P., Ortiz, S. O., & Alfonso, V. C. (2007). *Essentials of Cross Battery Assessment* (2nd ed.). Hoboken, NJ: John Wiley & Sons, Inc.

Flanagan, D. P., Ortiz, S. O., Alfonso, V. C., & Dynda, A. M. (2006). Integration of response to intervention and norm-referenced tests in learning disability identification: Learning from the Tower of Babel. *Psychology in the Schools, 43*, 807–825.

Flanagan, D. P., Ortiz, S. O., Alfonso, V. C., & Mascolo, J. T. (2002). *The achievement test desk reference (ATDR): Comprehensive assessment an learning disabilities*. Boston: Allyn & Bacon.

Fleischner, J. (1994). Diagnosis and assessment of mathematics learning disabilities. In G. R. Lyon (Ed.), *Frames of Reference for the Assessment of Learning Disabilities* (pp. 441–458). Baltimore, MD: Brookes.

Fletcher, J. M., Coulter, A. W., Reschly, D. J., & Vaughn, S. (2004). Alternative approaches to the definition and identification of learning disabilities: Some questions and answers. *Annals of Dyslexia, 54*.

Fletcher, J. M., Denton, C., & Francis, D. J. (2005). Validity of alternative approaches for the identification of learning disabilities: Operationalizing unexpected underachievement. *Journal of Learning Disabilities, 38*, 545–552.

Fletcher, J. M., & Reschly, D. J. (2005). Changing procedures for identifying learning disabilities: The danger of perpetuating old ideas. *The School Psychologist, 59*(1), 10–15.

Fletcher, J. M., Shaywitz, S. E., Shankweiler, D. P., Katz, L., Liberman, I. Y., Stuebing, K. K., et al. (1994). Cognitive profiles of reading disability: Comparisons of discrepancy and low achievement definitions. *Journal of Educational Psychology, 85*, 1–18.

Flowers, D. L., Jones, K., Noble, K., VanMeter, J., Zeffiro, T. A., Wood, F. B., et al. (2004). Attention to single letters activates the left extrastriate cortex. *NeuroImage, 21*, 829–839.

Floyd, R. G., Bergeron, R., & Alfonso, V. C. (2006). Cattell-Horn-Carroll cognitive ability profiles of poor comprehenders. *Reading and Writing, 19*, 427–456.

Floyd, R. G., Evans, J. J., & McGrew, K. S. (2003). Relations between measures of Cattell-Horn-Carroll (CHC) cognitive abilities and mathematics achievement across the school-age years. *Psychology in the Schools, 40*, 155–171.

Francis, D. J., Shaywitz, S. E., Stuebing, K. K., Shaywitz, B. A., & Fletcher, J. M. (1996). Developmental delay versus deficit models of reading disability: A longitudinal, individual growth curve analysis. *Journal of Educational Psychology, 88*, 3–17.

Fuchs, D., & Deshler, D. D. (2007). What we need to know about responsiveness to intervention (and shouldn't be afraid to ask). *Learning Disabilities Research & Practice, 22*, 129–136.

Fuchs, D., Deshler, D. D., & Reschly, D. J. (2004). National research center on learning disabilities: Multimethod studies of identification and classification issues. *Learning Disability Quarterly, 27*, 189–195.

Fuchs, D., Fuchs, L. S., & Compton, D. L. (2004). Identifying reading disabilities by responsiveness to instruction: Specifying measures and criteria. *Learning Disability Quarterly, 27*, 216–227.

Fuchs, D., Mock, D., Morgan, P., & Young, C. (2003). Responsiveness-to-intervention: Definitions, evidence, and implications fro the learning disabilities construct. *Learning Disabilities Research & Practice, 18*, 157–171.

Ganci, M. (2005). The diagnostic validity of a Developmental Neuropsychological Assessment (NEPSY)-Wechsler Intelligence Scale for Children – Third Edition (WISC-III)-based cross-battery assessment. *Dissertation Abstracts International, 65*(10-A), 3772.

Gathercole, S. E., & Pickering, S. J. (2000). Assessment of working memory in six- and seven-year-old children. *Journal of Educational Psychology, 92*, 377–390.

Geary, D. C. (2004). Mathematics and learning disabilities. *Journal of Learning Disabilities, 37*, 4–15.

Geary, D. C., Hamson, C. O., & Hoard, M. K. (2000). Numerical and arithmetical cognition: A longitudinal study of process deficits in children with learning disabilities. *Journal of Experimental Child Psychology, 77*, 236–263.

Geary, D. C., & Hoard, M. K. (2001). Numerical and arithmetical deficits in learning-disabled children: Relation to dyscalculia and dyslexia. *Aphasiology, 15*, 635–647.

Geary, D. C., Hoard, M. K., & Hamson, C. O. (1999). Numerical and arithmetical cognition: Patterns of functions and deficits in children at risk for mathematical disability. *Journal of Experimental Child Psychology, 74*, 213–239.

Gerber, M. M. (2005). Teachers are still the test: Limitations of response to instruction strategies for identifying children with learning disabilities. *Journal of Learning Disabilities, 38*, 516–523.

Gersten, R. (2005). Behind the scenes of an intervention research study. *Learning Disabilities Research & Practice, 20*, 200–212.

Glutting, J. J., McDermott, P. A., Watkins, M. W., Kush, J. C., & Konold, T. R. (1997). The base rate problem and its consequences for interpreting children's ability profiles. *School Psychology Review, 26*, 176–188.

Glutting, J. J., Watkins, M. W., Konold, T. R., & McDermott, P. A. (2006). Distinctions without a difference: The utility of observed versus latent factors from the WISC-IV in estimating reading and math achievement on the WIAT-II. *The Journal of Special Education, 40*, 103–114.

Glutting, J. J., Youngstrom, E. A., Ward, T., Ward, S., & Hale, R. L. (1997). Incremental efficacy of WISC-III factor scores in predicting achievement: What do they tell us? *Psychological Assessment, 9*, 295–301.

Goldberg, E. (2001). *The Executive Brain Frontal Lobes and the Civilized Mind*. New York, NY: Oxford University Press.

Grafman, J., Passafiume, D., Faglioni, P., & Boller, F. (1982). Calculation disturbances in adults with focal hemispheric damage. *Cortex, 18*, 37–50.

Greenham, S. L., Stelmack, R. M., & van der Vlugt, H. (2003). Learning disability subtypes and the role of attention during the naming of pictures and words: An event-related potential analysis. *Developmental Neuropsychology, 23*, 339–358.

Greenwood, S. C. (2002). Making words matter. Vocabulary study in content areas. *ERIC, 75*(5), 258–263.

Gresham, F. M., Reschly, D. J., Tilly, D. W., Fletcher, J., Burns, M., Crist, T., et al. (2005). Comprehensive evaluation of learning disabilities: A response to intervention perspective. *The School Psychologist, 59*(1), 26–29.

Gustafson, S., Ferreira, J., & Ronnberg, J. (2007). Phonological or orthographic training for children with phonological or orthographic deficits. *Dyslexia: An International Journal of Research and Practice, 13*, 211–228.

Hale, J. B. (2006). Implementing IDEA with a three-tier model that includes response to intervention and cognitive assessment methods. *School Psychology Forum: Research and Practice, 1*, 16–27.

Hale, J. B., & Fiorello, C. A. (2004). *School neuropsychology: A practitioner's handbook.* New York, NY: Guilford Press.

Hale, J. B., Fiorello, C. A., Bertin, M., & Sherman, R. (2003). Predicting math competency through neuropsychological interpretation of WISC-III variance components. *Journal of Psychoeducational Assessment, 21*, 358–380.

Hale, J. B., Fiorello, C. A., & Brown, L. (2005). Determining medication treatment effects using teacher ratings and classroom observations of children with ADHD: Does neuropsychological impairment matter? *Educational and Child Psychology, 22*, 39–61.

Hale, J. B., Fiorello, C. A., Dumont, R., Willis, J. O., Rackley, C., & Elliott, C. (in press). Differential Ability Scales – Second Edition (neuro)psychological Predictors of Math Performance for Typical Children and Children with Math Disabilities. Psychology in the Schools.

Hale, J. B., Fiorello, C. A., Kavanagh, J. A., Hoeppner, J. B., & Gaither, R. A. (2001). WISC-III predictors of academic achievement for children with learning disabilities: Are global and factor scores comparable? *School Psychology Quarterly, 16*, 31–55.

Hale, J. B., Fiorello, C. A., Kavanagh, J. A., Holdnack, J. A., & Aloe, A. M. (2007). Is the demise of IQ interpretation justified? A response to special issue authors. *Applied Neuropsychology, 14*, 37–51.

Hale, J. B., Hoeppner, J. B., & Fiorello, C. A. (2002). Analyzing Digit Span components for assessment of attention processes. *Journal of Psychoeducational Assessment, 20*, 128–143.

Hale, J. B., Kaufman, A., Naglieri, J. A., & Kavale, K. A. (2006). Implementation of IDEA: Integrating response to intervention and cognitive assessment methods. *Psychology in the Schools, 43*, 753–770.

Hale, J. B., Naglieri, J. A., Kaufman, A. S., & Kavale, K. A. (2004). Specific learning disability classification in the new Individuals with Disabilities Education Act: The danger of good ideas. *The School Psychologist, 58*(1), 6–14.

Hammill, D., & Larsen, S. (1974). The effectiveness of psycholinguistic training. *Exceptional Children, 41*, 5–15.

Harris, J. G., & Llorente, A. M. (2005). Cultural considerations in the use of the Wechsler Intelligence Scale for Children – Fourth Edition (WISC-IV). In A. Prifitera, D. H. Saklofske, & L. G. Weiss (Eds.), *WISC-IV Clinical Use and Interpretation: Scientist–Practitioner Perspectives* (pp. 381–413). San Diego, CA: Elsevier Academic Press.

Hay, D. B. (2007). Using concept maps to measure deep, surface, and non-learning outcomes. *Studies in Higher Education, 32*, 39–57.

Helland, T. (2007). Dyslexia at a behavioural and a cognitive level. *Dyslexia: An International Journal of Research and Practice, 13*, 25–41.

Hooper, S. R., Montgomery, J., Swartz, C., Reed, M. S., Sandler, A. D., Levine, M. D., et al. (1994). Measurement of written language. In G. R. Lyon (Ed.), *Frames of Reference for the Assessment of Learning Disabilities* (pp. 375–415). Baltimore, MD: Brookes.

Horwitz, B., Rumsey, J. M., & Donohue, B. C. (1998). Functional connectivity of the angular gyrus in normal reading and dyslexia. *Proceedings of the National Academy of Sciences USA., 95*, 8939–8944.

Hosp, M. K., Hosp, J. L., & Howell, K. W. (2007). *The ABCs of CBM: A Practical Guide to Curriculum-Based Measurement.* New York, NY: Guilford Press.

Individuals with Disabilities Education Improvement Act of 2004 (IDEA) P.L. 108-446, 118 Stat. 2647 (2004). [Amending U. S. C. §§ 1400 et. seq.).

Ingalls, S., & Goldstein, S. (1999). Learning disabilities. In S. Goldstein, & C. R. Reynolds (Eds.), *Handbook of Neurodevelopmental and Genetic Disorders in Children* (pp. 101–153). New York, NY: Guilford Press.

Jitendra, A. K., Edwards, L. L., Starosta, K., Sacks, G., Jacobson, L. A., & Choutka, C. M. (2004). Reading instruction for children with reading difficulties: Meeting the needs of diverse learners. *Journal of Learning Disabilities, 37*, 421–439.

Johnson, K. L., Nicol, T. G., Zecker, S. G., & Kraus, N. (2007). Auditory brainstem correlates of perceptual timing deficits. *Journal of Cognitive Neuroscience, 19*, 376–385.

Joseph, J. E., Noble, K., & Eden, G. F. (2001). The neurobiological basis of reading. *Journal of Learning Disabilities, 34*, 566–579.

Kaplan, E. (1988). A process approach to neuropsychological assessment. In T. Boll, & B. K. Bryant (Eds.), *Clinical Neuropsychology and Brain Function* (pp. 125–167). Washington, DC: American Psychological Association.

Kavale, K. A., & Flanagan, D. P. (2007). Ability–achievement discrepancy, response to intervention, and assessment of cognitive abilities/processes in specific learning disability identification: Toward a contemporary operational definition. In S. R. Jimerson, M. K. Burns, & A. M. VanDerHeyden (Eds.), *Handbook of Response to Intervention: The Science and Practice of Assessment and Intervention* (pp. 130–147). New York, NY: Springer.

Kavale, K. A., & Forness, S. R. (2000). What definitions of learning disability say and don't say: A critical analysis. *Journal of Learning Disabilities, 33*, 239–256.

Kavale, K. A., Holdnack, J. A., & Mostert, M. P. (2005). Responsiveness to intervention and the identification of specific learning disability: A critique and alternative proposal. *Learning Disability Quarterly, 28*, 2–16.

Kavale, K. A., Kaufman, A. S., Naglieri, J. A., & Hale, J. B. (2005). Changing procedures for identifying learning disabilities: The danger of poorly supported ideas. *The School Psychologist, 43*(7), 753–770.

Kavale, K. A., & Nye, C. (1985–1986). Parameters of learning disabilities in achievement, linguistic, neuropsychological, and social/behavioral domains. *The Journal of Special Education, 19*, 443–458.

Keith, T. Z., Fine, J. G., Taub, G. E., Reynolds, M. R., & Kranzler, J. H. (2006). Higher order, multisample, confirmatory factor analysis of the Wechsler Intelligence Scale for Children – Fourth Edition: What does it measure? *School Psychology Review, 35*, 108–127.

Kennedy, J. E., Clement, P. F., & Curtiss, G. (2003). WAIS-III processing speed index scores after TBI: The influence of working memory, psychomotor speed and perceptual processing. *Clinical Neuropsychologist, 17*, 303–307.

King, W. M., Giess, S. A., & Lombardino, L. J. (2007). Subtyping of children with developmental dyslexia via bootstrap aggregated clustering and the gap statistic: Comparison with the double-deficit hypothesis. *International Journal of Language & Communication Disorders, 42*, 77–95.

Konrad, M., Fowler, C. H., Walker, A. R., Test, D. W., & Wood, W. M. (2007). Effects of self-determination interventions on the academic skills for students with learning disabilities. *Learning Disability Quarterly, 30*, 89–113.

Kujala, T., Halmetoja, J., Naatanen, R., Alku, P., Lyytinen, H., & Sussman, E. (2006). Speech- and sound-segmentation in dyslexia: Evidence for a multiple-level cortical impairment. *European Journal of Neuroscience, 24*, 2420–2427.

Learning Disabilities Roundtable (2002). *Specific Learning Disabilities: Finding Common Ground.* Washington, DC: U.S. Department of Education. Office of Special Education Programs, Office of Innovation and Development.

Learning Disabilities Roundtable (2005). *Comments and recommendations on regulatory issues under the Individuals with Disabilities Education Improvement Act of 2004 P.L. 108-446.* Washington, DC: U.S. Department of Education Office of Special Education Programs.

Leffard, S. A., Miller, J. A., Bernstein, J., DeMann, J. J., Mangis, H. A., & McCoy, E. L. B. (2006). Sustantive validity of working memory measures in cognitive functioning test batteries. *Applied Neuropsychology, 13*, 230–241.

Lerner, J. (2003). *Learning Disabilities: Theories, Diagnosis, and Teaching Strategies.* Boston, MA: Houghton Mifflin.

Levine, M. D. (2001). *Developmental Variation and Learning Disorders.* Cambridge, MA: Educators Publishing Service.

Lezak, M. D. (1995). *Neuropsychological Assessment* (3rd ed.). New York: Oxford University Press.

Licht, R. (1994). Differences in word recognition between P- and L-type reading disability. In R. Licht G. Spyer (Ed.), *The Balance Model of Dyslexia: Theoretical and Clinical Progress* (pp. 41–55). Assen, Netherlands: Van Gorcum.

Lichtenstein, R., & Klotz, M. B. (2007). Deciphering the federal regulations on identifying children with specific learning disabilities. *Communique, 36*(3), 1.

Lichter, D. G., & Cummings, J. L. (Eds.) (2001). *Frontal–Subcortical Circuits in Psychiatric and Neurological disorders.* New York, NY: Guilford Press.

Light, G. J., & DeFries, J. C. (1995). Comborbidity of reading and mathematics disabilities: Genetic and environmental etiologies. *Journal of Learning Disabilities, 28,* 96–106.

Lovett, M. W., Steinbach, K. A., & Frijters, J. C. (2000). Remediating the core deficits of developmental reading disability: A double-deficit hypothesis. *Journal of Learning Disabilities, 33,* 334–358.

Lyon, G. R. (2005). Why scientific research must guide educational policy and instructional practices in learning disabilities. *Learning Disability Quarterly, 28,* 140–143.

Machek, G. R., & Nelson, J. M. (2007). How should reading disabilities be operationalized? A survey of practicing school psychologists. *Learning Disabilities Research & Practice, 22,* 147–157.

Mammarella, I. C., Cornoldi, C., Pazzaglia, F., Toso, C., Grimoldi, M., & Vio, C. (2006). Evidence for a double dissociation between spatial-simultaneous and spatial-sequential working memory in visuospatial (nonverbal) learning. *Brain and Cognition, 62,* 58–67.

Manis, F. R., & Freedman, L. (2001). The relationship of naming speed to multiple reading measures in disabled and normal readers. In M. Wolf (Ed.), *Dysflexia, fluency, and the brain* (pp. 65–92). Timonium, MD: York Press.

Marston, D., Muyskens, P., Lau, M. Y., & Canter, A. (2003). Problem-solving model for decision making with high-incidence disabilities: The Minneapolis experience. *Learning Disabilities Research & Practice, 18,* 187–200.

Mastropieri, M. A., & Scruggs, T. E. (2000). *The inclusive classroom: Strategies for effective instruction.* Columbus, OH: Prentice Hall/Merrill.

Mastropieri, M. A., & Scruggs, T. E. (2005). Feasibility and consequences of response to intervention: Examination of the issues and scientific evidence as a model for the identification of individuals with learning disabilities. *Journal of Learning Disabilities, 38,* 525–531.

Masutto, C., Bravar, L., & Fabbro, F. (1993). Diagnosis and rehabilitation in childhood dyslexia: A neuropsychological approach. *Archivio di Psicologia, Neurologia e Psichiatria, 54,* 249–262.

Mather, N., & Gregg, N. (2006). Specific learning disabilities: Clarifying, not eliminating, a construct. *Professional Psychology: Research and Practice, 37,* 99–106.

Mather, N., & Jaffe, L. (2002). *Woodcock-Johnson III: Reports, Recommendations, and Strategies.* Hoboken, NJ: Wiley.

Mayes, S. D., & Calhoun, S. L. (2004). Similarities and differences in WISC-III profiles: Support for subtest analysis in clinical referrals. *Clinical Neuropsychologist, 18,* 559–572.

Mayes, S. D., & Calhoun, S. L. (2006). WISC-IV and WISC-III profiles in children with ADHD. *Journal of Attention Disorders, 9,* 486–493.

Mayes, S. D., & Calhoun, S. L. (2007). Challenging the assumptions about the frequency and coexistence of learning disability types. *School Psychology International, 28,* 437–448.

Mayes, S. D., Calhoun, S. L., & Crowell, E. W. (1998). WISC-III profiles for children with and without learning disabilities. *Psychology in the Schools, 35,* 309–316.

Mazzocco, M. M. M. (2001). Math learning disability and math LD subtypes: Evidence from studies of Turner Syndrome, Fragile X Syndrome, and Neurofibromatosis Type 1. *Journal of Learning Disabilities, 34,* 520–533.

Mazzocco, M. M. M. (2005). Challenges in identifying target skills for math disability screening and intervention. *Journal of Learning Disabilities, 38,* 318–323.

McAndrews, S. L. (2006). Linking literacy assessments to diagnostic instructional strategies for children with an APD. In T. K. Parthasarathy (Ed.), *An Introduction to Auditory Processing Disorders in Children* (pp. 95–108). Mahwah, NJ: Lawrence Erlbaum Associates.

McCormick, S., & Becker, E. Z. (1996). Word recognition and word identification: A review of research on effective instructional practices with learning disabled students. *Reading Research and Instruction, 36*, 5–17.

McDermott, P. A., Fantuzzo, J. W., & Glutting, J. J. (1990). Just say no to subtest analysis: A critique on Wechsler theory and practice. *Journal of Psychoeducational Assessment, 8*, 290–302.

McDermott, P. A., Goldberg, M. M., Watkins, M. W., Stanley, J. L., & Glutting, J. J. (2006). A nationwide epidemiologic modeling study of LD: Risk, protection, and unintended impact. *Journal of Learning Disabilities, 39*, 230–251.

McGrew, K. S., Flanagan, D. P., Keith, T. Z., & Vanderwood, M. (1997). Beyond g: The impact of Gf-Gc specific cognitive abilities research on the future use and interpretation of intelligence tests in the schools. *School Psychology Review, 26*, 189–210.

McLeod, S., & McKinnon, D. H. (2007). Prevalence of communication disorders compared with other learning needs in 14,500 primary and secondary school students. *International Journal of Language & Communication Disorders, 42*(Suppl1), 37–59.

Mercer, M. C., & Miller, S. P. (1992). *Strategic Math Series*. Lawrence, KA: Edge Enterprises.

Meyer, M. S. (2000). The ability–achievement discrepancy: Does it contribute to an understanding of learning disabilities? *Educational Psychology Review, 12*, 315–337.

Miller, J. A., Getz, G., & Leffard, S. A. (2006). *Neuropsychology and the diagnosis of learning disabilities under IDEA 2004*. Boston, MA: Poster presented at the 34th annual meeting of the International Neuropsychological Society.

Miller, S. P., Strawser, S., & Mercer, C. D. (1996). Promoting strategic math performance among students with learning disabilities. *LD Forum, 21*, 31–40.

Montague, M. (2007). Self regulation and mathematics instruction. *Learning Disabilities Research & Practice, 22*, 75–83.

Morgan, P. L., & Sideridis, G. D. (2006). Contrasting the effectiveness of fluency interventions for students with or at-risk for learning disabilities: A multilevel random coefficient modeling meta-analysis. *Learning Disabilities Research & Practice, 24*, 191–210.

Morris, R. D., Shaywitz, S. E., Shankweiler, D. P., Katz, L., Stuebing, K. K., Fletcher, J. M., et al. (1998). Subtypes of reading disability: Variability around a phonological core. *Journal of Educational Psychology, 90*, 347–373.

Naglieri, J. A. (1997). Planning, attention, simultaneous, and successive theory and the Cognitive Assessment System: A new theory-based measure of intelligence. In D. P. Flanagan, J. L. Genshaft, & P. L. Harrison (Eds.), *Contemporary Intellectual Assessment: Theories, Tests, and Issues* (pp. 247–267). New York, NY: Guilford Press.

Naglieri, J. A. (1999). *Essentials of CAS Assessment*. New York, NY: John Wiley & Sons.

Naglieri, J. A., & Bornstein, B. T. (2003). Intelligence and achievement: Just how correlated are they? *Journal of Psychoeducational Assessment, 21*, 244–260.

Naglieri, J. A., & Gottling, S. H. (1995). A cognitive education approach to math instruction for the learning disabled: An individual study. *Psychological Reports, 76*, 1343–1354.

Naglieri, J. A., & Johnson, D. (2000). Effectiveness of a cognitive strategy intervention in improving arithmetic computation based on PASS theory. *Journal of Learning Disabilities, 33*, 591–597.

Naglieri, J. A., & Pickering, E. B. (2003). *Helping Children Learn. Intervention Handouts for Use in School and at Home*. Baltimore, MD: Brookes.

Nation, K., Clarke, P., & Snowling, M. J. (2002). General cognitive ability in children with reading comprehension difficulties. *British Journal of Educational Psychology, 72*, 549–560.

National Association of School Psychologists (2007). *Position Statement on Identification of Children with Specific Learning Disabilities*. Bethesda, MD: Author.

Nicholson, R. I., & Fawcett, A. J. (2001). Dyslexia, learning, and the cerebellum. In M. Wolf (Ed.), *Dyslexia, Fluency, and the Brain* (pp. 159–188). Timonium, MD: York Press.

Nicholson, R. I., Fawcett, A. J., & Dean, P. (1995). Time estimation deficits in developmental dyslexia:Evidence of cerebellar involvement. *Proceedings of the Royal Society of London, Series B: Biological Sciences, 259*, 43–47.

O'Connor, R. E., White, A., & Swanson, H. L. (2007). Repeated reading versus continuous reading on reading fluency and comprehension. *Exceptional Children, 74*, 31–47.

Ofiesh, N. (2006). Response to intervention and the identification of specific learning disabilities: Why we need comprehensive evaluations as part of the process. *Psychology in the Schools, 43*, 883–888.

Olmstead, R. (2005). Use of auditory and visual stimulation to improve cognitive abilities in learning-disabled children. *Journal of Neurotherapy, 9*, 49–61.

Palombo, J. (2006). *Nonverbal Learning Disabilities: A Clinical Perspective*. New York, NY: W. W. Norton & Co.

Pedhazur, E. J. (1997). *Multiple Regression in Behavioral Research: Explanation and Prediction* (3rd ed.). Orlando, FL: Holt, Rinehart, & Winston.

Pfeiffer, S. I., Reddy, L. A., Kletzel, J. E., Schmelzer, E. R., & Boyer, L. M. (2000). A practitioner's view of IQ testing and profile analysis. *School Psychology Quarterly, 15*, 376–385.

Plaza, M., & Cohen, H. (2007). The contribution of phonological awareness and visual attention in early reading and spelling. *Dyslexia: An International Journal of Research and Practice, 13*, 67–76.

Prifitera, A., & Dersh, J. (1993). Base rates of WISC-III diagnostic subtest patterns among normal, learning disabled, and ADHD samples. *Journal of Psychoeducational Assesssment (WISC-III Monograph)*, 43–55.

Prifitera, A., Saklofske, D. H., Weiss, L. G., & Rolfhus, E. (2005). The WISC-IV in the clinical assessment context. In A. Prifitera, D. H. Saklofske, & L. G. Weiss (Eds.), *WISC-IV Clinical Use and Interpretation: Scientist–Practitioner Perspectives* (pp. 3–32). San Diego, CA: Elsevier Academic Press.

Proctor, B. E., Floyd, R. G., & Shaver, R. B. (2005). Cattell-Horn-Carroll broad cognitive ability profiles of low math achievers. *Psychology in the Schools, 42*, 1–12.

Pugh, K. R., Mencl, W. E., Shaywitz, B. A., Shaywitz, S. E., Fulbright, R. K., Constable, R. T., et al. (2000). The angular gyrus in developmental dyslexia: Task-specific differences in functional connectivity within posterior regions. *Psychological Science, 11*, 51–56.

Ram-Tsur, R., Faust, M., & Zivotofsky, A. Z. (2006). Sequential processing deficits of reading disabled persons is independent of inter-stimulus interval. *Vision Research, 46*, 3949–3960.

Reddy, L. A., & Hale, J. B. (2007). Inattentiveness. In A. R. Eisen (Ed.), *Clinical Handbook of Childhood Behavior Problems: Case Formulation and Step-by-Step Treatment Programs* (pp. 156–211). New York, NY: Guilford Press.

Reschly, D. J. (2005). Learning disabilities identification: Primary intervention, secondary intervention, and then what? *Journal of Learning Disabilities, 38*, 510–515.

Reschly, D. J., & Hosp, J. L. (2004). State SLD policies and practices. *Learning Disability Quarterly, 27*, 197–213.

Richards, T. L., Aylward, E. H., Field, K. M., Grimme, A. C., Raskind, W., Richards, A. L., et al. (2006). Converging evidence for triple word form theory in children with dyslexia. *Developmental Neuropsychology, 30*, 547–589.

Richards, T., Berninger, V., Nagy, W., Parsons, A., Field, K., & Richards, A. (2005). Brain activation during language task contrasts in children with and without dyslexia: Inferring mapping processes and assessing response to spelling instruction. *Educational and Child Psychology, 22*, 62–80.

Richards, T., Berninger, V., Winn, W., Stock, P., Wagner, R., Muse, A., et al. (2007). Functional MRI activation in children with and without dyslexia during pseudoword aural repeat and visual decode: Before and after treatment. *Neuropsychology, 21*, 732–741.

Richman, L. C., & Wood, K. M. (2002). Learning disability subtypes: Classification of high functioning hyperlexia. *Brain and Language, 82*, 10–21.

Rourke, B. P. (2000). Neuropsychological and psychosocial subtyping: A review of investigations within the University of Windsor Laboratory. *Canadian Psychology, 41*, 34–51.

Rutter, M., & Yule, W. (1975). The concept of specific reading retardation. *Journal of Child Psychology and Psychiatry, 16*, 181–197.

Saklofske, D. H., Prifitera, A., Weiss, L. G., Rolfhus, E., & Zhu, J. (2005). Clinical interpretation of the WISC-IV FSIQ and GAI. In A. Prifitera, D. H. Saklofske, & L. G. Weiss (Eds.), *WISC-IV Clinical Use and Interpretation: Scientist–Practitioner Perspectives* (pp. 33–65). San Diego, CA: Elsevier Academic Press.

Salvia, J., & Yssyldyke, J. E. (2001). *Assessment* (8th ed.). Boston, MA: Houghton Mifflin Company.

Santos, A., Joly-Pottuz, B., Moreno, S., Habib, M., & Besson, M. (2007). Behavioural and event-related potentials evidence for pitch discrimination deficits in dyslexic children: Improvement after intensive phonic intervention. *Neuropsychologia, 45*, 1080–1090.

Sattler, J. M. (2001). *Assessment of Children: Cognitive Applications* (4th ed.). San Diego: Jerome M. Sattler, Publisher.

Schnitzer, G., Andries, C., & Lebeer, J. (2007). Usefulness of cognitive intervention programmes for socio-emotional and behaviour problems in children with learning disabilities. *Journal of Research in Special Education, 7*, 161–171.

Schrank, F. A., Miller, J. A., Catering, L., & Desrochers, J. (2006). American Academy of School Psychology survey on the independent educational evaluation for a specific learning disability: Results and discussion. *Psychology in the Schools, 43*, 771–780.

Schraw, G. (1998). Promoting general metacognitive awareness. *Instructional Science, 26*, 113–125.

Scruggs, T. E., & Mastropieri, M. A. (2002). On babies and bathwater: Addressing the problems of identification of learning disabilities. *Learning Disability Quarterly, 25*, 155–168.

Seabaugh, G. O., & Schumaker, J. B. (1994). The effects of self-regulation training on the academic productivity of secondary students with learning problems. *Journal of Behavioral Education, 4*, 109–133.

Seethaler, P., & Fuchs, L. S. (2005). A drop in the bucket: Randomized controlled trials testing reading and math interventions. *Learning Disabilities Research & Practice, 20*, 98–102.

Semrud-Clikeman, M. (2005). Neuropsychological aspects for evaluating learning disabilities. *Journal of Learning Disabilities, 38*, 563–568.

Semrud-Clikeman, M., Biederman, J., Sprich-Buckminster, S., Lehman, B. K., et al. (1992). Comorbidity between ADDH and learning disability: A review and report in a clinically referred sample. *Journal of the American Academy of Child & Adolescent Psychiatry, 31*, 439–448.

Semrud-Clikeman, M., Fine, J., & Harder, L. (2005). The school neuropsychology of learning disabilities. In R. K. D'Amato, E. Fletcher-Janzen, & C. R. Reynolds (Eds.), *Handbook of School Neuropsychology*. New York, NY: John Wiley & Sons.

Semrud-Clikeman, M., Guy, K. A., & Griffin, J. D. (2000). Rapid automatized naming in children with reading disabilities and attention deficit hyperactivity disorder. *Brain and Language, 74*, 70–83.

Semrud-Clikeman, M., & Pliszka, S. R. (2005). Neuroimaging and psychopharmacology. *School Psychology Quarterly, 20*, 172–186.

Shalev, R. S., Manor, O., Kerem, B., Ayali, M., Badichi, N., Friedlander, Y., et al. (2001). Developmental dyscalculia is a familial learning disability. *Journal of Learning Disabilities, 34*, 59–65.

Shamir, A., & Lazerovitz, T. (2007). Peer mediation intervention for scaffolding self-regulated learning among children with learning disabilities. *European Journal of Special Needs Education, 22*, 255–273.

Shankweiler, D. L., Lundquist, E., Katz, L., Stuebing, K. K., Fletcher, J. M., Brady, S. F., et al. (1999). Comprehension and decoding: Patterns of association in children with reading difficulties. *Scientific Studies of Reading, 3*, 69–94.

Shaywitz, B. A., Lyon, G. R., & Shaywitz, S. E. (2006). The role of functional magnetic imaging in understanding reading and dyslexia. *Developmental Neuropsychology, 30*(1), 613–632.

Shaywitz, S. E., Shaywitz, B. A., Fulbright, R., Skudlarski, P., Mencl, W. E., Constable, R. T., *et al.* (2003). Neural systems for compensation and persistence: Young adult outcome of childhood reading disability. *Biological Psychiatry, 54*, 25–33.

Shaywitz, S. E., & Shaywitz, B. E. (2005). Dyslexia (specific reading disability). *Biological Psychiatry, 57*, 1301–1309.

Shaywitz, S. E., & Shaywitz, B. A. (2006). Dyslexia. In M. D'Esposito (Ed.), *Functional MRI: Applications in Clinical Neurology and Psychiatry* (pp. 61–79). Boca Raton, FL: Informa Healthcare.

Shelley-Tremblay, J., O'Brien, N., & Langhinrichsen-Rohling, J. (2007). Reading disability in adjudicated youth: Prevalence rates, models, traditional and innovative treatments. *Aggression & Violent Behavior, 12,* 376–392.

Shinn, M. R. (2002). Best practices in using curriculum-based measurement in a problem-solving model. In A. Thomas, & J. Grimes (Eds.), *Best Practices in School Psychology IV* (pp. 671–697). Washington, DC: National Association of School Psychologists.

Silver, N. C., & Dunlap, W. P. (1987). Averaging correlation coefficients: should Fisher's z transformation be used? *Journal of Applied Psychology, 72,* 146–148.

Simos, P. G., Breier, J. I., Fletcher, J. M., Foorman, B. R., Mouzaki, A., & Papanicolaou, A. C. (2001). Age-related changes in regional brain activation during phonological decoding and printed word recognition. *Developmental Neuropsychology, 19,* 191–210.

Simos, P. G., Fletcher, J. M., Bergman, E., Breier, J. I., Foorman, B. R., Castillo, E. M., et al. (2002). Dyslexia-specific brain activation profile becomes normal following successful remedial training. *Neurology, 58,* 1–10.

Simos, P. G., Fletcher, J. M., Sarkari, S., Billingsley, R. L., Denton, C., & Papanicolaou, A. C. (2007). Altering the brain circuits for reading through intervention: A magnetic source imaging study. *Neuropsychology, 21,* 485–496.

Simos, P. G., Fletcher, J. M., Sarkari, S., Billingsley, R. L., Francis, D. J., Castillo, E. M., et al. (2005). Early reading development of neurophysiological processes involved in normal reading and reading disability: A magnetic source imaging study. *Neuropsychology, 19,* 787–798.

Slavin, R. E. (1993). Ability grouping in the middle grades: Achievement effects and alternatives. *The Elementary School Journal, 93,* 535–552.

Smit-Glaude, S. W. D., van Strien, J. W., Licht, R., & Bakker, D. J. (2005). Neuropsychological intervention in kindergarten children with subtyped risks of reading retardation. *Annals of Dyslexia, 55,* 217–245.

Smith, T. J., & Adams, G. (2006). The effect of comorbid AD/HD and learning disabilities on parent-reported behavioral and academic outcomes of children. *Learning Disability Quarterly, 29,* 101–112.

Smith, L. A., & Rourke, B. P. (1995). Callosal agenesis. In B. P. Rourke (Ed.), *Syndrome of Nonverbal Learning Disabilities: Neurodevelopmental Manifestations* (pp. 45–92). New York, NY: Guilford Press.

Snowling, M., & Stackhouse, J. (2006). *Dyslexia, Speech and Language: A Practitioner's Handbook.* Hoboken, NJ: John Wiley & Sons.

Solan, H. A., Shelley-Tremblay, J. F., Hansen, P. C., & Larson, S. (2007). Is there a common linkage among reading comprehension, visual attention, and magnocellular processing? *Journal of Learning Disabilities, 40,* 270–278.

Stage, S. A., Abbott, R. D., Jenkins, J. R., & Berninger, V. W. (2003). Predicting response to early reading intervention from verbal IQ, reading-related language abilities, attention ratings, and verbal IQ-word readings discrepancy: Failure to validate discrepancy method. *Journal of Learning Disabilities, 36,* 24–33.

Stanovich, K. E. (1994). Are discrepancy-based definitions of dyslexia empirically defensible? In K. P. van den Bos, L. S. Siegel, D. J. Bakker, & D. L. Share (Eds.), *Current Directions in Dyslexia Research* (pp. 15–30). Lisse, Netherlands: Swets & Zeitlinger.

Stein, J. A., & Krishnan, K. (2007). Nonverbal learning disabilities and executive function: The challenges of effective assessment and teaching. In L. Meltzer (Ed.), *Executive Function in Education: From Theory to Practice* (pp. 106–132). New York, NY: Guilford Press.

Stein, J. F. (2001). The neurobiology of reading difficulties. In M. Wolf (Ed.), *Dyslexia, Fluency, and the Brain* (pp. 3–22). Timonium, MD: York Press.

Strube, M. J. (1988). Averaging correlation coefficients: Influence of heterogeneity and set size. *Journal of Applied Psychology, 73,* 559–568.

Stuebing, K. K., Fletcher, J. M., LeDoux, J. M., Lyon, G. R., Shaywitz, S. E., & Shaywitz, B. A. (2002). Validity of IQ-discrepancy classifications of reading disabilities: A meta-analysis. *American Educational Research Journal, 39*, 469–518.

Sunseth, K., & Bowers, P. G. (2002). Rapid naming and phonemic awareness: Contributions to reading, spelling, and orthographic knowledge. *Scientific Studies of Reading, 6*, 401–429.

Swanson, H. L., & Ashebaker, M. H. (2000). Working memory, short-term memory, speech rate, word recognition and reading comprehension in learning disabled readers: Does the executive system have a role? *Intelligence, 28*, 1–30.

Swanson, H. L., Hoskyn, M., & Lee, C. (1999). *Interventions for children with learning disabilities: A meta-analysis of treatment outcomes.* New York, NY: Guilford Press.

Swanson, H. L., & Jerman, O. (2006). Math disabilities: A selective meta-analysis of the literature. *Review of Educational Research, 76*, 249–274.

Szabo, S. (2006). KWHHL: A student-driven evolution of the KWL. *American Secondary Education, 34*, 57–67.

Taggart, L., Cousins, W., & Milner, S. (2007). Young people with learning disabilities living in state care: Their emotional, behavioural and mental health status. *Child Care in Practice, 13*, 401–416.

Tallal, P. (2004). Improving language and literacy is a matter of time. *Nature Reviews Neuroscience, 5*, 721–728.

Tallal, P. (2006). What happens when 'dyslexic' subjects do not meet the criteria for dyslexia and sensorimotor tasks are too difficult even for the controls? *Developmental Science, 9*, 262–264.

Therrien, W. J., Wickstrom, K., & Jones, K. (2006). Effect of a combined repeated reading andquestion generation intervention on reading achievement. *Learning Disabilities Research & Practice, 21*, 89–97.

Thomson, J. B., Chenault, B., Abbott, R. D., Raskind, W. H., Richards, T., Aylward, E., & Berninger, V. W. (2005). Converging evidence for attentional influences on the orthographic word form in child dyslexics. *Journal of Neurolinguistics, 18*, 93–126.

Tilly, W. D., III (2002). Best practices in school psychology as a problem-solving enterprise. In A. Thomas, & J. Grimes (Eds.), *Best Practices in School Psychology IV* (pp. 21–36). Washington, DC: US: NASP.

Torgesen, J. K. (2000). Individual differences in response to early interventions in reading: The lingering problem of treatment resisters. *Learning Disabilities Research and Practice, 15*, 55–64.

Torgesen, J. K., Rashotte, C. A., & Alexander, A. W. (2001). Principles of fluency instruction in reading: Relationships with established empirical outcomes. In M. Wolf (Ed.), *Dyslexia, Fluency, and the Brain* (pp. 333–355). Timonium, MD: York Press.

Torppa, M., Tolvanen, A., Poikkeus, A., Eklund, K., Lerkkanen, M. K., Leskinen, E., et al. (2007). Reading development subtypes and their early characteristics. *Annals of Dyslexia, 57*, 3–52.

Tuller, B., Jantzen, K. J., Olvera, D., Steinberg, F., & Kelso, J. A. S. (2007). The influence of instruction modality on brain activation in teenagers with nonverbal learning disabilities: Two case histories. *Journal of Learning Disabilities, 40*, 348–359.

VanDerHeyden, A. M., Witt, J. C., & Gilbertson, D. (2007). A multi-year evaluation of the effects of a Response to Intervention model on identification of children for special education. *Journal of School Psychology, 45*, 225–256.

Vargo, F. E., Grosser, G., & Spafford, C. S. (1995). Digit Span and other WISC-R scores in the diagnosis of dyslexia in children. *Perceptual and Motor Skills, 80*, 1219–1229.

Vellutino, F. R., Scanlon, D. M., Sipay, E. R., Small, S. G., Pratt, A., Chen, R., & Denckla, M. B. (1996). Cognitive profiles of difficult-to-remediate and readily remediated poor readers: Early intervention as a vehicle for distinguishing between cognitive and experiential deficits as basic causes of specific reading disability. *Journal of Educational Psychology, 88*, 601–638.

Waber, D. P., Forbes, P. W., Wolff, P. H., & Weiler, M. D. (2004). Neurodevelopmental characteristics of children with learning impairments classified according to the double-deficit hypothesis. *Journal of Learning Disabilities, 37*, 451–461.

Waber, D. P., Weiler, M. D., Wolff, P. H., Bellinger, D., Marcus, D. J., Ariel, R., et al. (2001). Processing of rapid auditory stimuli in school-age children referred for evaluation of learning disorders. *Child Development, 72*, 37–49.

Warner, T. D., Dede, D. E., Garvan, C. W., & Conway, T. W. (2002). One size still does not fit all in specific learning disability assessment across ethnic groups. *Journal of Learning Disabilities, 35*, 501–509.

Watkins, M. W., Glutting, J. J., & Lei, P. W. (2007). Validity of the full-scale IQ when there is significant variability among WISC-III and WISC-IV factor scores. *Applied Neuropsychology, 14*, 13–20.

Watkins, M. W., Kush, J. C., & Glutting, J. J. (1997). Discriminant and predictive validity of the WISC-III ACID profile among children with learning disabilities. *Psychology in the Schools, 34*, 309–319.

Wechsler, D. (2003). *Wechsler Intelligence Scale for Children – Fourth Edition (WISC-IV): Technical and Interpretive Manual*. San Antonio, TX: Psychological Corporation.

Weekes, B., Coltheart, M., & Gordon, E. (1997). Deep dyslexia and right hemisphere reading – a regional cerebral blood flow study. *Aphasiology, 11*, 1139–1158.

Weiss, L. G. (2007). Integrating RTI into SLD determination. In V. Berninger, (Chair) (Ed.), *Developing Differentiated Instruction Through Integration of RTI and Cognitive Assessment*. San Francisco, CA: Symposium presentation at the Annual Convention of the American Psychological Association.

Wiig, E. H. (2005). Language disabilities. In A. Prifitera, D. H. Saklofske, & L. G. Weiss (Eds.), *WISC-IV Clinical Use and Interpretation: Scientist–Practitioner Perspectives* (pp. 333–349). San Diego, CA: Elsevier Academic Press.

Willcutt, E. G., Pennington, B. F., Olson, R. K., Chhabildas, N., & Hulslander, J. (2005). Neuropsychological analyses of comorbidity between reading disability and attention deficit hyperactivity disorder: In search of the common deficit. *Developmental Neuropsychology, 27*, 35–78.

Willis, J. O., & Dumont, R. (2006). And never the twain shall meet: Can response to intervention and cognitive assessment be reconciled? *Psychology in the Schools, 43*, 901–908.

Wise, J. C., Sevcik, R. A., Morris, R. D., Lovett, M. W., & Wolf, M. (2007). The growth of phonological awareness by children with reading disabilities: A result of semantic knowledge or knowledge of grapheme–phoneme correspondences? *Scientific Studies of Reading, 11*, 151–164.

Wodrich, D. L., Spencer, M. L., & Daley, K. B. (2006). Combining RTI and psychoeducational assessment: What we must assume to do otherwise. *Psychology in the Schools, 43*, 797–806.

Wolf, M., & Bowers, P. (1999). The "Double-Deficit Hypothesis" for the developmental dyslexias. *Journal of Educational Psychology, 91*, 1–24.

Wolf, M., Miller, L., & Donnelly, K. (2000). Retrieval, automaticity, vocabulary elaboration, orthography (RAVE-O): A comprehensive fluency-based reading intervention program. *Journal of Learning Disabilities, 33*, 375–386.

Wong, B. Y. L. (Ed.) (2004). *Learning About Learning Disabilities* (3rd ed.). New York, NY: Academic Press.

Woodcock, R. W., McGrew, K. S., & Mather, N. (2001). *Woodcock-Johnson III*. Itasca, IL: Riverside Publishing.

Yeates, K. O., & Donders, J. (2005). The WISC-IV and neuropsychological assessment. In A. Prifitera, D. H. Saklofske, & L. G. Weiss (Eds.), *WISC-IV Clinical Use and Interpretation: Scientist–Practitioner Perspectives* (pp. 415–434). San Diego, CA: Elsevier Academic Press.

Ysseldyke, J. E., & Marston, D. (2000). Origins of categorical special education services in schools and a rationale for changing them. In D. Reschly D. Tilly (Ed.), *Functional and Noncategorical Special Education*. Longmont, CO: Sopris West.

Zadina, J. N., Corey, D. M., & Casbergue, R. M. (2006). Lobar asymmetries in subtypes of dyslexic and control subjects. *Journal of Child Neurology, 21*, 922–931.

4

LANGUAGE DISABILITIES[1]

ELISABETH H. WIIG

Boston University; Knowledge Research Institute, Inc., Arlington, TX, USA

LANGUAGE DISABILITIES DEFINED

Children and adolescents with language disabilities form a large, heterogeneous group, accounting for from 10% to 20% of children (Tallal, 2003). Other prevalence reports for language impairments (LI) indicate a range from 6% to 8% of school-age children (Gilger & Wise, 2004) and an estimated 50% of children with LI later experience reading difficulties. The heterogeneity in this group results from the fact that language and communication disorders can originate in a variety of etiologies, express themselves as different types and be associated with different comorbidities. Furthermore, the nature of language and communication disorders changes with age as cognitive and linguistic demands associated with academic curricula, vocations and professions, and social interaction increase in complexity and diversity (Ratner & Harris, 1994; Lord Larson & McKinley, 2003). Language and communication disabilities are also a part of genetic syndromes such as Down, Fragile X and Tourette Spectrum syndromes (Jung, 1989); Dornbush & Pruitt, 1995; Prestia, 2003). They also exist as comorbidities in developmental disorders such as Autism, Attention Deficit/Hyperactivity Disorder (ADHD) and executive function disorders (EDF) (Singer & Bashir, 1999; Mirrett et al., 2003), or as a result of Traumatic Brain Injury (TBI) (Barkley, 1997, 1998; Brown, 2000; Culatta & Wiig, 2002; Ottinger, 2003; Wetherby, 2002).

The *Diagnostic and Statistical Manual of Mental Disorders* (DSM-IV-TR) (American Psychiatric Association, 2000) defines language and communication disorders as being either of the Expressive or Mixed Receptive–Expressive type. Expressive language and communication disorders are identified by four criteria, three of which relate to inclusion and one of which specifies exclusion. The four criteria are: (1) Expressive language development is significantly below receptive

[1]This chapter is largely based on an earlier chapter published in WISC-IV Clinical Use and Interpretation (Prifitera et al., 2005).

language development and nonverbal intellectual ability; (2) deficits interfere with academic, vocational, and professional achievement and/or social communication; (3) the language difficulties are in excess of those usually observed in cases with cognitive, sensory or motor deficits or environmental deprivation; and (4) symptoms do not meet criteria for Mixed Receptive–Expressive Language Disorders or Pervasive Developmental Disorders (DSM-IV-TR, pp. 58–61). Mixed Receptive–Expressive Disorders are defined against three diagnostic criteria, two of which are inclusive and one exclusionary. The criteria are: (1) Both receptive and expressive language development are significantly below measures of nonverbal intellectual ability; (2) deficits interfere with academic, vocational, and professional achievement and social communication; and (3) symptoms do not meet criteria for Pervasive Developmental Disorders (DSM-IV-TR, pp. 62–64).

Language disabilities can be the primary or secondary source of a student's exceptionality, and the impairments can involve different modalities (e.g., listening/receptive, speaking/expressive), modes (e.g., reading, writing) and dimensions of the language system (e.g., phonology, morphology and syntax, semantics, or pragmatics). Depending on which modalities and components of the language system are involved, the symptomatic manifestations, severity and impact of a language disability on language learning, academic achievement, social competence and emotional stability will vary (Bashir et al., 1987; Culatta & Wiig, 2002; Wetherby, 2002).

The term Specific Language Impairment (SLI) is often used to label school-age children, adolescents and young adults in whom language disability is of a primary nature, do not result from emotional disorders, cognitive delays, sensory impairments or language differences (Leonard, 1991; NJCLD, 1994). Recent research has provided evidence of connections between SLI, speed of processing and verbal working memory deficits (Weismer, Evans & Hesketh, 1999; Montgomery, 2002; Weismer, et al., 2005; Leonard et al., 2007). Furthermore, other learning disabilities in these children and youth may be explained with reference to the nature of existing LI (Ratner & Harris, 1994; Culatta & Wiig, 2002; Lord Larson & McKinley, 2003).

COGNITIVE REFERENCING IN LANGUAGE DISABILITIES

There is an ongoing debate of how to identify language disabilities and differentiate SLI and language differences, and whether or not cognitive referencing is essential or even relevant in the comprehensive assessment of children and adolescents for language disabilities (Paul, 2000). One point of view follows the DSM-IV-TR diagnostic criteria and looks to identify discrepancies between language and nonverbal cognitive abilities on standardized measures. This position has been termed a *neutralist perspective*, as it does not account for ethnic, cultural or social norms or expectations (Fey, 1986). The second depends on evaluating and observing how a child or youth performs in contexts with different demands and constraints (e.g., academic, family, community, and broader social). This perspective is referred to as the *normative position* (Fey, 1986; Merritt & Culatta, 1998; Dornbush & Pruitt, 1995; Nelson, 1998, 2000). The controversy of whether to adopt a neutralist perspective or a normative position for the assessment and identification of language disabilities extends into all branches of special education. Thus, a normative position with Responsiveness-to-Intervention as the focus for identifying children with language-learning impairments or differences is advocated by numerous professional organizations and concept papers abound (Fuchs et al., 2003). The normative position received national support with the 2004 reauthorization of the Education for All Handicapped Children Act (PL 94-142). It stated that schools will *"not be required to take into consideration whether a child has a severe discrepancy between achievement and intellectual ability..."* (Section 1414(b)) (Wrightslaw: IDEA, 2004, p. 88). For children with language disabilities this represents progress, because many children with syndromes, such as Tourette Spectrum Syndrome, previously were unable to meet discrepancy criteria to receive services or accommodations for, for example, expressive language disorders with executive function comorbidities (e.g., attention and working memory deficits, inflexibility in set-shifting and dysnomia).

The Responsiveness-to-Intervention movement is often considered to be of recent origin, however, this is not exactly the case. As an early move toward assessing responsiveness-to-intervention, the Ohio Department of Education, Division of Special Education (1991) issued a handbook for the use of intervention assistance teams (IT) as part of the identification and evaluation of children with language problems. The handbook outlined an assessment and IT process and provided suggestions for teacher accommodations with strategies to use in the classroom with students suspected of having language problems. The IT processes were initiated by using language- and communication-specific behavioral checklists, teacher and student interviews, and other background information. Designating facilitators involved in implementing classroom-based intervention and a monitor of student progress, and specifying educational outcomes and setting timelines for intervention followed this. If stated outcomes were not achieved, students were referred for a multifactor evaluation to determine a least-restrictive special education placement. One model proposed for naturalistic assessment through Responsiveness-to-Intervention provides a three-tiered structure for implementation (Mellard, 2005). In Tier I, teachers provide quality academic instruction and supports as part of the general education program. If a student fails to meet set educational objectives after tracking progress during a specified time period, often of 9 weeks duration, she/he is referred to a study team for possible Tier II invention. At this tier, students receive evidence-based intervention that is supplemental to the core-curriculum, often in small groups. If expected progress cannot be documented by curriculum-based evaluations, a student is referred to Tier III for intensive individualized and research-based intervention or assessment followed by intervention. The expectations are that from 5% to 10% of students will be referred for services or evaluation at this tier. Monitoring of progress is suggested to use curriculum-based evaluations (Bennet & Davis, 2001; Howell & Nolet, 2000) and there are few discussions of how to integrate norm-referenced language and/or cognitive or neuropsychological assessments in the implementation process. The main issue in special education now centers on whether or not norm-referenced testing, including assessment of cognitive or neurocognitive abilities, will have a place in the future.

As a researcher and practitioner in the field of speech–language pathology, I acknowledge the validity of the discussion and the pros and cons of each position. In this context, I shall assume the stance that norm-referenced evaluations of language and cognitive abilities can contribute significantly in a multi-dimensional assessment and identification process. After decades of practice, I have seen many "babies thrown out with the dirty bath water," experienced cycles of fads and fancies in speech–language pathology and education and seen reversals to previously vilified methods and procedures (e.g., phonological awareness testing and training). With this, and recent research of processing speed and working memory capacities as they relate to LI, as backgrounds, I will express and support my views of the relevance of cognitive and neuropsychological referencing in a comprehensive, multi-dimensional assessment of children with potential LI or with syndromes, which include language disabilities.

First, using cognitive and intellectual referencing as an integral aspect of multi-dimensional language assessment does not contradict the current IDEA mandates to describe a student's strengths and weaknesses, relate these to potential for academic achievement or to curriculum objectives which may be compromised. As an example, if norm-referenced language and cognitive assessments indicate significant verbal working memory or word-finding (dysnomia) deficits and/or processing speed deficits, this knowledge contributes to a broadened understanding of contributing factors to the student's LI (Berninger, 2001; McGregor et al., 2002; Montgomery, 2002; Semel et al., 2003; Weiler et al., 2000). The test results can also explain how these deficits may influence performance on academic tasks such as note taking, early and later literacy development, and oral and written presentations of narrative or dialog or study skills acquisition and can indicate needed classroom accommodations (Ratner & Harris, 1994; Storkel & Morrisette, 2002; Lord Larson & McKinley, 2003; Montgomery, 2002).

Secondly, with exclusively "normative" or authentic assessment procedures and without cognitive referencing, the group of students identified to have LI or disabilities will be of high incidence and unmanageable heterogeneity. It would include children with any variety of language and communication problems that may not have underlying neurological or neuropsychological bases. This heterogeneous group cannot be expected to respond similarly to classroom intervention, precision teaching or programmatic language intervention procedures. Furthermore, services which target the deficit areas and foster compensatory strategies may not be provided for students with specific neuropsychological deficits that interfere with language and communication in increasingly complex academic contexts as is the case in, for example, the Tourette Spectrum Syndrome (Dornbush & Pruitt, 1995; Prestia, 2003).

Thirdly, there are educational and theoretical issues that are not addressed by the normative position, Response to Intervention (RtI) or exclusively curriculum-based assessments. Among these issues are the nature-versus-nurture conundrum, the relations considered to exist between the biological basis of language and other cognitive systems, and the practice of treating symptoms in isolation from underlying causal and functional systems. Thus, in the normative position and its implementation, nurture and context appear to take precedence over nature and existing neuroscience-based knowledge of brain–behavior relationships (Gazzaniga, 2004). It also promotes symptomatic intervention over in-depth consideration of the interplay between language, cognition, and neurobiological factors. With rapidly increasing understanding of the biological bases of language and communication and the impact of neurocognitive deficits, attention to underlying causes and neuropsychological bases of disorders should become mandatory. This would assure that specialized services are provided for children, who may otherwise show temporary symptomatic progress, but later experience regression as the demands on language and cognition increase with age and education. The normative position and RtI also appear to be based on the theoretical position that language is a modular system and that language and cognition are dissociated (van der Lely et al., 1998; Marcus & Rabagliati, 2006). This position implies that language can be evaluated and improved within isolated linguistic, pragmatic, or contextual frameworks. An opposite position holds that language is a joint product of hereditary and domain-specific factors and is therefore a reflection of domain-general cognitive systems (see Marcus & Rabagliati, 2006). This theoretical construct is supported by research-based evidence that language disorders, such as SLI, often co-occur with impairments of cognitive functions such as motor control, general intelligence, working memory and other executive function deficits (Hill, 2001; Kovas & Plomin, 2006; Leonard et al., 2007). The following discussion of the role of WISC-IV in the assessment of students with language disorders assumes the position that language is a reflection of domain-general cognitive systems.

WISC-IV AND LANGUAGE DISABILITIES

The third edition of the Wechsler Intelligence Scale for Children (WISC-III) (Wechsler, 1991) provided relevant data about intellectual and neuropsychological abilities in multi-dimensional assessments of student's with language and communication difficulties. With cognitive and intellectual referencing, students with Mental Retardation or Pervasive Developmental Disorders (DSM-IV, 1994) were identified and comprehensive educational and psycho-educational supports, including language stimulation and/or intervention, were provided. Similarly,

LI and learning disabilities with neuropsychological bases and comorbidities (e.g., ADHD, EFD) could be differentiated from language disabilities related to deprivation, language differences or interactions between language codes (e.g., English–Spanish bilingualism) (Payne & Taylor, 2002; Langdon, 2007).

Relationships between WISC-III measures of intellectual ability (Wechsler, 1991) and performances on norm-referenced receptive and expressive language tasks was explored during standardization of the *Clinical Evaluation of Language Fundamentals – 3rd Edition (CELF-3)* (Semel et al., 1995). Correlations between the CELF-3 Total Language standard score and WISC-III Full Scale ($r = .75$), Verbal Scale ($r = .75$) and Performance Scale IQs ($r = .60$) were all significant ($p < .01$), but moderate in degree. The CELF-3 and WISC-III Verbal Scale relationships underscored that the measures shared a general language construct. However, the moderate size of the correlation indicated that the WISC-III Verbal Scale alone did not adequately identify aspects of the expressive or receptive–expressive language syndromes described in DSM-IV-TR.

WISC-IV STUDIES OF CHILDREN WITH LANGUAGE DISABILITIES

The WISC-IV (Wechsler, 2003) and CELF-4 (Semel et al., 2003) were administered concurrently during standardization and the respective manuals report the results from different perspectives. The WISC-IV technical manual reports findings from a comparison of performances by 27 children in the age range from 6 to 16 years with primarily expressive language disorders, as defined by DSM-IV-TR criteria, and 27 age-matched controls. The group mean differences between the WISC-IV Verbal Comprehension and Working Memory Index scores were highly significant ($p < .01$), indicating large negative effects of the expressive language disorder syndrome. There was also a significant, but moderate negative effect of expressive language disorders on WISC-IV Full-Scale IQ. Among subtests, Comprehension and Information showed large negative effects for expressive language disorders ($p < .01$), and Vocabulary and Arithmetic showed significant, but moderate effects.

Performances by a group of 41 children with mixed receptive–expressive language disorders ranging in age from 6 to 16 years and identified according to DSM-IV-TR criteria and 41 age-matched controls were also compared. There were large and significant differences between groups for Verbal Comprehension, Perceptual Reasoning, Working Memory, and Processing Speed, as well as Full-Scale IQ ($p < .01$). Group differences were substantial and significant for all Comprehension and Working Memory subtests, two Processing Speed subtests, and one Perceptual Reasoning subtest ($p < .01$). These findings support that children with mixed receptive–expressive language disorders show global deficits in cognitive functioning, as well as in linguistic aspects of language and communication, working memory and visual-verbal processing speed (e.g., rapid automatic naming, RAN) (Beitchman et al., 1996; Semel et al., 2002; Wiig et al., 2000, 2001).

RELEVANCE AND APPROPRIATENESS

The statistical and clinical properties of WISC-IV and controlled studies of clinical populations support the relevance and appropriateness of its use for cognitive referencing in a multi-dimensional and multi-perspective assessment of language disabilities. From the perspective of the clinical or educational diagnostician, the performance patterns on those subtests that contribute to the Verbal Comprehension and Working Memory Index scores are of immediate relevance. Congruency in language test and WISC-IV Verbal Comprehension measures can serve to validate a diagnosis of a language disorder. Working Memory measures further serve to validate language test results, and identify a potentially critical component of SLI (Montgomery, 2002). Performances on subtests that contribute to the Perceptual Reasoning Index are relevant and appropriate for assessing nonverbal cognitive and reasoning strengths and weaknesses to complete the diagnostic profile. These measures can identify strengths that can be employed in selecting language intervention strategies, such as conceptual mapping with cognitive mediation and determining the use of media to enhance language learning (Hyerle, 1996; Wiig & Wilson, 2001; Lord-Larson & McKinley, 2003). They also contribute to determining "appropriate accommodations," as mandated by IDEA 2004.

Each of the subtests that form the *Verbal Comprehension Index* can provide specific information relevant for identifying strengths and weaknesses and relating performances to social or academic learning content and tasks. Thus, the Similarities subtest probes verbal, semantic abilities that reflect concept formation and the development of semantic networks. Here the student is required to respond to two related words or concepts by referring to shared-meaning features and semantic class membership. This task is often difficult for students with Mixed Receptive–Expressive Language Deficits and the spontaneous responses may indicate a focus on differences in meaning rather than on similarities. Responses may also focus on shared secondary, concrete characteristics (e.g., physical attributes) rather than essential abstract meanings (e.g., class membership). As examples of these response patterns, the student with a language disability may respond to the stimuli "cat" and "mouse" by saying either that they are not alike "because a cat eats a mouse" or that they are alike "because they are both brown, and have fur and a long tail." For the astute clinician, the nature of error responses is as important as the standard score earned on this subtest, as the error pattern points to objectives and procedures for intervention (e.g., developing semantic classification and superordinate naming strategies and skills (Nippold, 1991).

The Picture Concepts subtest reveals information that is similar to that obtained from the Similarities subtest. It requires the student to identify one item from each of two or three rows of pictured stimuli to form a semantic group, and then to explain why the items go together. Students with primarily expressive language disabilities generally perform well on the picture-matching task, but may have problems expressing the reasons for their choices succinctly with, for example, superordinate names. Students with pervasive receptive–expressive language disabilities may show inadequate performance on both the nonverbal pointing and the verbal explanation tasks. Again the nature of the student's error patterns is relevant to the clinician by pointing out strengths and weaknesses and developing a focus and selecting strategies for intervention.

The Vocabulary subtest uses two stimulus-response formats. In response to the picture items, the student is required to name the featured instance. In response to the verbal reasoning items, the student is required to formulate a definition by giving a synonym, major use, primary feature, or category membership. Frequently, students with mixed-receptive expressive language disabilities respond to the Verbal Reasoning items with circumlocutions, vague or terse responses, or concrete interpretations, therefore earning primarily part scores. Students with expressive language disabilities may exhibit word-finding difficulties and substitute words. If the student self-monitors and corrects substitute responses, this should be noted as a positive. In all instances the speech–language pathologist should be informed of error patterns so that appropriate follow-up evaluation of naming and word-finding abilities can be provided (German, 1986, 1990, 1991; German & Newman, 2004).

The Comprehension subtest requires students to give reasons, state the importance, advantages or disadvantages of actions, characteristics or features, or social expectations for behavior. Students with mixed receptive–expressive language disabilities generally have difficulties expressing cause–effect relationships and moral judgment. They typically earn part or no scores on this type of Comprehension test, and it may be difficult to establish basals and ceilings. Their response and error patterns can indicate inadequacies in critical thinking, verbal reasoning, and moral judgment that are important for speech–language pathologists to be aware of. When these deficits are present, intervention procedures that develop critical thinking, abstract reasoning, and moral judgment through cognitive mapping and mediation, guided questioning, scaffolding, or other procedures are appropriate (Hyerle, 1996; Nippold, 1991; Wiig & Wilson, 2001).

The *Working Memory* and *Processing Speed Index* scores are also of importance and relevance to the understanding of language deficits and disorders. Processing and naming speed deficits for highly familiar visual stimuli are prevalent among monolingual English and bilingual English–Spanish speaking students with mixed receptive–expressive language disabilities, who earn language scores in the low to very-low educational range (Wiig et al., 2000, 2001). These rapid naming speed deficits are indicative of inadequate processing speed, implicit (visual) working memory and verbal automaticity, validated by neuroimaging to be mediated by the temporal-parietal regions of the brain (Wiig et al., 2002). They are also predictors of dyslexia and difficulties in literacy acquisition (Wolf et al., 2000). The WISC-IV Working Memory Index provides important validation of the presence of verbal Working Memory and retrieval deficits for academically important materials (e.g., digits, letters, and other familiar sequences). Working Memory and RAN tests, featured in current, comprehensive language assessment tools (e.g., CELF-4), can assist in identifying underlying clinical (neuropsychological) symptoms, such as deficits in attention, working memory, cognitive set shifting, and verbal automaticity. These can have negative effects on language and communication development and the attainment of mature competencies in language, communication, and literacy and in later professional development. The results from these tests can also serve to differentiate students with SLI from those with language differences caused by cultural, ethnic, parental education and socio-economic factors. This differentiation will become increasingly important as funding for language intervention and English as a Second Language (ESL) services must be separated so that students can be assigned to appropriate services immediately following identification and differential diagnosis.

Last, but not least, it is relevant for the clinician to have information about a student's strengths and/or weaknesses in nonverbal cognitive and reasoning abilities. The WISC-IV *Perceptual Reasoning Index* provides this information. If a student shows relative strength in Perceptual Reasoning, this translates to potential success for using cognitive approaches to language intervention such as visual tools for conceptual mapping and cognitive meditation (e.g., Nippold, Esrskine & Freed, 1988; Hyerle, 1996; Wiig & Wilson, 2001) to support development of concepts, linguistic rules, narrative structure, and other organizational strategies.

TESTING CONSIDERATIONS

There are several aspects of WISC-IV administration and interpretation of results that must be considered when testing students with probable language disabilities. First, the psychologist must satisfy that the student understands the test tasks and expectations for responding. This may mean asking direct questions about task characteristics and expected responses. Students with language disabilities of the mixed receptive–expressive type often develop non-adaptive strategies for responding to tasks. They may guess what to do if directions were not understood, an approach which often leads to failure because the various scripts for spoken directions for tasks and tests may not be internalized or automatized.

Secondly, students with language disabilities often give error responses that can point directly to the underlying sources for difficulties in language learning and use. The psychologist should therefore record inaccurate spontaneous responses for, for example, word definitions so that error patterns can be identified and interpreted either for or by a speech–language pathologist. As an example, there is ample research of error types associated with word-finding problems (dysnomia), a characteristic concomitant of language disabilities of the expressive type (German, 1986, 1990, 1991). It is especially important to identify circumlocutions, verbose descriptions, imprecise referencing with overuse of pronouns, word substitutions, and use of similar sounding words in context (e.g., television for telephone), all characteristics of word-finding difficulties.

Thirdly, the psychologist should relate the observed cognitive strengths and weaknesses, to educational expectations, curriculum objectives, and classroom behaviors. A pragmatic interpretation of the WISC-IV results can then be compared to interpretations based on a student's performance on language tests. This can serve as validation or as a means of providing a more complete picture of the student. When cognitive deficits that are commonly linked to language and communication disabilities are observed, a referral to a speech–language pathologist for in-depth language evaluation seems appropriate. It follows, that the psychologist and speech pathologist should then collaborate to interpret and validate the WISC-IV results and integrate these with the language measures that led to a diagnosis of a language disability of a mixed receptive–expressive or predominantly expressive type.

CLINICAL INTERPRETATIONS AND IMPLICATIONS FOR INTERVENTION

CASE STUDIES

The following case studies describe language and cognitive test results for selected students with LI. The three cases were administered the CELF-4 and WISC-IV at the time of standardization. The clinical categories, from which the illustrative cases were selected, represent language disorders of the primarily expressive type (Cases A and C), and mixed receptive–expressive type (Case B). Each case study will follow a descriptive format in which the student's (a) background and prior diagnosis is described, (b) CELF-4 norm-referenced index and selected criterion referenced subtest scores are presented and interpreted, (c) WISC-IV norm-referenced index scores and Full-Scale IQ are reported, and (d) the combined findings are interpreted for clinical and educational implications.

Case Study A: Male, Age 6 Years 5 Months

This study is of a 6 year 5 months old boy with language disorders and learning disabilities. The student was receiving speech and language intervention services at the time of the assessment. His language disorder was initially identified by administering the Preschool Language Scales (PLS) (standard score 58), the Peabody Picture Vocabulary Test (PPVT) (standard score 90) and the CELF-Preschool (Receptive 77; Expressive 65). The prior evaluations indicated performance on comprehensive language tests in the low to very-low educational range for his age and determined eligibility for speech–language resources. The student's CELF-4 Core Language and Index scores are shown in Table 4.1 and WISC-IV Index scores and Full-Scale IQ in Table 4.2.

TABLE 4.1   Overview of CELF-4 Core Language and Index Scores (Age 6 Year 5 Months)

CELF-4 Index scores	Standard score	Confidence interval (90%)	Percentile rank	Educational performance range
Core Language	83	78–88	13	Marginal to average
Receptive Index	101	93–109	53	Average
Expressive Index	83	77–89	13	Marginal to average
Language Content	94	88–100	34	Average
Language Structure	88	82–94	21	Marginal to average
Working Memory	80	71–89	9	Low to marginal

TABLE 4.2   Overview of WISC-IV Index Scores and IQ (Age 6 Year 5 Months)

WISC-IV Index scores	Standard score	Confidence interval (90%)	Percentile rank	Performance range
Verbal Comprehension	95	90–101	37	Average normal
Perceptual Reasoning	94	88–101	34	Average normal
Working Memory	72	64–80	3	Average normal
Processing Speed	97	90–105	42	Average normal
Full-Scale IQ	96	92–100	39	Average normal

This student's CELF-4 Core Language score (83) indicates performance in the marginal to average educational range and supports eligibility for continuation of language resource services. The Receptive Index score (101) indicates performance within the average educational range, while the Expressive Index score (83) indicates performance in the marginal to average range. The Modality Index scores (Receptive–Expressive) differ by 18 points and the discrepancy is significant ($p < .05$). In other words, this boy's language difficulties are primarily expressive in nature based on the Modality Index scores. The Language Content score (94) indicates performance within the average educational range, and the Language Structure score (88) indicates performance in the marginal to average educational range. The Content Index scores (Language Content versus Language Structure) also did not differ significantly ($p > .05$). The Working Memory Index score (80) falls within the low to marginal range, indicating that Working Memory presents an area of relative weakness. The supplementary subtests showed performance within the typical range for Phonological Awareness (56; criterion > 46), Word Associations (22; criterion > 18), and Pragmatics (172; criterion > 125). The RAN time for color–shape combinations was significantly slower than typical (142 s; criterion < 120 s), indicating reduction in cognitive speed (i.e., attention, visual working memory, set shifting). In summary, this student's primarily expressive language difficulties are associated with inadequate Working Memory, as measured by the CELF-4 Index, and attention, Working Memory and set-shifting, as measured by CELF-4 RAN. Without repeated norm-referenced language assessment, language intervention services may have been discontinued for this student. This may have resulted in regression in the language competence gained through early intervention. Similarly, RtI procedures at Tier I might have resulted in dismissal from services. If the RtI process were to progress to Tier II, it may have resulted in symptomatic (expressive language and grammar), curriculum-based interventions.

The student's WISC-IV Full-Scale IQ (96) and the Verbal Comprehension (95), Perceptual Reasoning (94), Working Memory (104) and Processing Speed (97) Index scores are all within the average normal range. There are no significant differences between paired WISC-IV Index scores, indicating no significant areas of cognitive strengths or weaknesses beyond the average normal range. Using the presence of a significant discrepancy between measures of language and cognition as a criterion for eligibility for special education resources may not have resulted in language services for this student. However, the persistence of an expressive language disability qualifies the student for continuation of already initiated resource services.

The combined WISC-IV and CELF-4 test results suggest that the student's relative language and cognitive strengths (Verbal Comprehension and Perceptual Reasoning) should be activated to facilitate internalization and automatization of verbal strategies for expression. Language intervention approaches with picture support and cognitive bases (e.g., visual tools for conceptual mapping, cognitive mediation, and mediated learning) should support activation and use of these cognitive strengths. Time-added accommodations do not appear needed for processing visual information that does not require verbal processing and expression. In contrast, additional response and test-taking time should be allowed to accommodate for the observed expressive language, verbal and visual working memory and verbal fluency deficits.

Case Study B: Female, Age 8 Years 0 Months

This study is of an 8 years 0 months old girl with a diagnosed language disorder, who was receiving language intervention and resource reading services at the time of testing. The language disorder was first identified with the TOLD-P:3 (Newcomer & Hammill, 1997) at age 5. At the time of identification and determination of eligibility for service, Listening (standard score 94) was within the normal range, while Speaking (standard score 67) was significantly lower and indicated a severe expressive deficit. The student's CELF-4 Core Language and Index scores are presented in Table 4.3 below and WISC-IV Index scores and IQ are shown in Table 4.4.

The girl's CELF-4 Core Language score of 56 places her performance within the very low educational range and supports eligibility and continuing needs

TABLE 4.3   Overview of CELF-4 Core language and Index Scores (Age 8 Years 0 Months)

CELF-4 Index scores	Standard score	Confidence interval (90%)	Percentile rank	Educational performance range
Core Language	56	51–62	0.2	Very low
Receptive Index	53	46–60	0.1	Very low
Expressive Index	59	53–65	0.3	Very low
Language Content	60	54–66	0.4	Very low
Language Structure	58	51–65	0.3	Very low
Working Memory	72	64–80	3	Low to marginal

TABLE 4.4   Overview of WISC-IV IQ and Index Scores (Age 8 Years 0 Months)

WISC-IV Index scores	Standard score	Confidence interval (90%)	Percentile rank	Performance range
Verbal Comprehension	89	84–95	23	Average normal
Perceptual Reasoning	106	99–112	66	Average normal
Working Memory	88	83–95	21	Average normal
Processing Speed	65	62–77	1	Very low
Full-Scale IQ	85	81–90	16	Average to marginal

for speech and language resource services. The Receptive Index score (53) falls within the very low educational range, as does the Expressive Index score (59), indicating a severe language disorder of the mixed receptive–expressive type. The Language Content score (60) falls within the very low educational range, as does the Language Structure score (58). Neither the Modality Index (Receptive versus Expressive) nor the Content Index (Language Content versus Language Structure) scores differ significantly ($p > .05$). The Working Memory Index (72) is in the low to marginal educational range, and while it represents an area of relative strength, it appears inadequate for successful compensation. The supplementary subtests showed performance within the typical range for Phonological Awareness (51; criterion > 24), Word Associations (24; criterion > 13), but indicated difficulties in the area of Pragmatics (108; criterion > 125). The CELF-4 RAN time for color–shape combinations was significantly slower than typical (204 s; criterion < 135 s), indicating highly significant attention, working memory, set-shifting, and verbal automaticity deficits. In other words, the student's language and communication difficulties can be related to inadequate acquisition of content and structural linguistic rules in the presence of low to marginal working memory abilities, executive dysfunction (i.e., attention, implicit working memory for visual input, set-shifting) and deficits in verbal automaticity. In this case, the RtI process would be expected to identify the severity of the language disorders at Tier I and this should have resulted in referral for repeated norm-referenced language assessment (Tier III).

The student's WISC-IV Full-Scale IQ (85) is within the marginal to average range, but this measure does not describe the student's cognitive strengths, weaknesses or potential for learning. The student's Perceptual Reasoning (106) is significantly higher than Verbal Comprehension (89), indicating nonverbal reasoning abilities that may assist in building language and communication competence and developing adaptive compensatory strategies. The differences between the index scores for Verbal Comprehension and Processing Speed (24 points); Perceptual Reasoning and Processing Speed (41 points); Perceptual Reasoning and Working Memory (16 points) and Processing Speed and Working Memory (23 points) were all significant ($p < .05$). In other words, this student presents a complex picture of cognitive strengths and weaknesses with clear evidence of executive dysfunction. The very low Processing Speed Index (65) suggests a need for extensive classroom accommodations in form of use of basic technology (e.g., audio taping; word processing) and added time for completing tests and projects.

This student would meet discrepancy criteria between cognitive and language abilities for continuation of language resource services. However, the LI are severe enough to warrant continued intervention to establish linguistic competence. In relation to language intervention, the student's relative strengths in Perceptual Reasoning should be used to develop semantic networks and abstract concepts, as well as structural linguistic (sentence transformation) and pragmatic rules for communicating in context. The use of linguistic structures for communication in context should be developed to a level of automaticity to compensate for working memory and verbal fluency deficits. The nonverbal reasoning strengths should also be activated to develop executive functions (e.g., planning and organization) and compensatory strategies for communication and real-time performance (e.g., studying, working). Visual supports (e.g., pictures, conceptual maps, diagrams, and other organizational structures) and cognitive approaches (e.g., mediated learning, conceptual mapping, and cognitive mediation) should also be used to strengthen critical thinking and the integration and internalization of new knowledge. The very low performance on measures of processing speed, including visual memory, visual discrimination and visual-motor integration, suggests that the students may benefit from accommodations such as extended time for tests and tasks and introduction to basic technology in preparation for producing written products at the higher grades.

Case Study C: Female Age 12 Years 9 Months

This study is of a 12 year 9 months old girl with diagnosed language disorders and learning disabilities. The student was administered the TOLD-I:3

(Hammill & Newcomer, 1997) at age 9 and obtained a listening standard score of 94, speaking standard score of 68, and total standard score of 79. Her test scores on the WISC-III indicated a significant discrepancy between Verbal (92) and Performance IQ (126). The student received special education services with emphasis on reading and writing at the time of testing. The CELF-4 Core Language and Index scores are presented in Table 4.5 and the WISC-IV Index scores in Table 4.6.

This student's CELF-4 Core Language score (87) places her performance in the marginal to average educational range. The overall performance barely supports her eligibility for continuing language intervention. The Receptive Index (93) indicates performance within the average educational range, while the Expressive Index (77) places her performance in the low to marginal educational range. The Language Content Index (78) also places the student's performance in the low to marginal range. In contrast, the Language and Memory Index (92) places her performance within the average range. The Modality (Receptive versus Expressive) and Content Index scores (Language Content versus Language & Memory) both differ significantly ($p < .05$). In other words, there are obvious

TABLE 4.5   Overview of CELF-4 Core Language and Index Scores (Age 12 Years 9 Months)

CELF-4 Index scores	Standard score	Confidence interval (90%)	Percentile rank	Educational performance range
Core Language	87	81–93	19	Marginal to average
Receptive Index	93	86–100	32	Average
Expressive Index	77	70–84	6	Low to marginal
Language Content	78	71–85	7	Low to marginal
Language Memory	92	85–99	30	Average
Working Memory	97	87–107	32	Average

TABLE 4.6   Overview of WISC-IV IQ and Index Scores (Age 12 Year 9 Months)

WISC-IV Index scores	Standard score	Confidence interval (90%)	Percentile rank	Performance range
Verbal Comprehension	87	82–93	19	Average to marginal
Perceptual Reasoning	102	95–108	55	Average normal
Working Memory	110	103–116	75	High average
Processing Speed	97	90–105	42	Average normal
Full-Scale IQ	98	94–102	45	Average normal

modality- and content-related strengths and weaknesses. Thus, receptive language skills are superior to expressive language skills and memory for spoken language is superior to language content acquisition. The student's Working Memory Index (97) is within the average range and this explains why receptive and language and memory abilities are areas of relative strengths for this student. The supplementary subtests showed performance outside the typical range for Phonological Awareness (60; criterion > 67), Word Associations (18; criterion > 30), and Pragmatics (83; criterion > 142). The RAN time for color–shape combinations was in the slower-than-typical range (93 s; criterion < 75 s). The marginal phonological awareness, verbal fluency and severely slowed RAN cognitive speed (i.e., perceptual processing speed + cognitive overhead imposed by demands on executive attention, visual working memory, and set shifting) concur with the student's difficulties in reading and writing. An RtI process would be expected to identify the literacy deficits at Tier I, and the student would probably have been put through procedures associated with Tiers II and III. The final outcome would be expected to lead to recommendations for special education services for reading and writing. The deficits in the acquisition of language content (semantics) and skills that are basic to literacy (i.e., phonological awareness and visual working memory) might have been overlooked, however.

The student's WISC-IV Full-Scale IQ (87) places her performance within the average to below average range. The profile of index scores, however, points to specific strengths and weaknesses among cognitive abilities. Notably, the differences between (a) Perceptual Reasoning (102) and Verbal Comprehension (87), (b) Working Memory (110) and Verbal Comprehension (87) and Processing Speed (97) are all significant ($p < .05$). The student therefore shows strengths in perceptual/nonverbal reasoning and verbal Working Memory, which may support further development of expressive language skills and language content. The CELF-4 Core Language and WISC-IV Verbal Comprehension scores are generally in agreement and validate the persistence of language disabilities in this student. The test results are complementary in that CELF-4 pointed to visual Working Memory deficits, while WISC-IV indicated adequate verbal Working Memory abilities. CELF-4 also pointed to inadequacies in phonological awareness and fluent retrieval of word associations, a measure of executive functions supported by activation of frontal cortical regions. Application of discrepancy criteria between language abilities and WISC-IV Verbal Comprehension and Perceptual Reasoning measures of cognition would support the continuation of resource services for this student. The areas of weakness in oral language abilities suggest that supportive resources should be expanded to include individualized language intervention in addition to the continuation of current reading and writing resource services. In language intervention, the Perceptual Reasoning and verbal Working Memory strengths of the student should be activated in structured, cognitive approaches. The purpose would be to accelerate concept formation, the development of semantic networks and use of higher-level and abstract language content, as well as of complex linguistic structures and pragmatic competence.

The slower-than-typical RAN speed (CELF-4) suggests that time-added accommodations for verbal and written linguistic responses, academic projects and test taking would be appropriate.

CONCLUSIONS

The strength of the WISC-IV as a tool for broadening the assessment and understanding of students with language disabilities resides in the new model for categorizing and interpreting performances. This model stresses the use and interpretation of index scores, validated by factor analysis, rather than using the traditional verbal versus performance IQ categorization. From the perspective of the speech–language pathologist, this model is attuned to current trends in assessment and differentiation of language disabilities (i.e., SLI versus language difference) and responds to the IDEA mandates for language resources. The new model that identifies strengths and weaknesses in Verbal Comprehension, Perceptual Reasoning, Working Memory, and Processing Speed avoids the tendency for static interpretations of IQ. Instead it supports the value of using language versus cognitive function discrepancy measures for determining eligibility for language resources. In combination with results from language tests, the WISC-IV can point to targets for intervention, developing compensatory strategies and providing classroom accommodations for access to content and curriculum. Without in-depth language assessment, including cognitive referencing, a student's cognitive strengths might be overlooked and unaccounted for in language and literacy intervention. As a result, valuable avenues for compensation and accommodation and appropriate strategies for language and literacy intervention may not be put to use. Without assessment and integration of relative strengths and weaknesses in language and cognition, as provided by WISC-IV administration, inappropriate placement, statements of Individualized Educational Program (IEP) objectives, provisions for accommodations, selection of intervention approaches and stipulations of expected educational objectives may result. WISC-IV can provide broad-based cognitive referencing and reliable measures of cognitive strengths and weakness that should be shared with and interpreted for speech–language pathologists in educational and clinical settings. The sharing and integration of norm-referenced and naturalistic observations of students with language disorders would be expected to foster inter- and transdisciplinary collaboration and sharing of responsibilities for intervention across the continuum of special needs.

REFERENCES

American Psychiatric Association (2000). *Diagnostic and Statistical Manual of Mental Disorders, 4th Edition, Text Revision (DSM–IV–TR)*. Washington, DC: American Psychiatric Association.
Barkley, R. A. (1997). *ADHD and the Nature of Self-Control*. New York: Guilford Press.

Barkley, R. A. (1998). Attention-deficit hyperactivity disorder. *Scientific American*, September, 66–71.

Bashir, A. S., Wiig, E. H., & Abrams, J. C. (1987). Language disorders in childhood and adolescence: Implications for learning and socialization. *Pediatric Annals*, 16, 145–158.

Beitchman, J. H., Wilson, B., Brownlie, E. B., Walters, H., & Lancee, W. (1996). Long-term consistency in speech/language profiles: I. Developmental and academic outcomes. *Journal of the American Academy of Child and Adolescent Psychiatry*, 35(6), 804–814.

Bennet, D. E., & Davis, M. A. (2001). The development of computer-based alternate assessment systems. *Assessment for Effective Intervention*, 2(3), 15–34.

Berninger, V. (2001). *The Process Assessment of the Learner-Test Battery for Reading and Writing.* San Antonio, TX: The Psychological Corporation.

Brown, T. R. (2000). *Attention-Deficit Disorders and Comorbidities in Children, Adolescents, and Adults.* Washington, D.C.: American Psychiatric Press.

Culatta, B., & Wiig, E. H. (2002). Language disabilities in school-age children and youth. In G. H. Shames, & N. B. Anderson (Eds.), *Human Communication Disorders* (6th ed., pp. 218–257). Boston, MA: Allyn & Bacon.

Dornbush, M. P., & Pruitt, S. K. (1995). *Teaching the Tiger: A Handbook for Individuals in the Education of Students with Attention Deficit Disorders, Tourette Syndrome, or Obsessive-Compulsive Disorders.* Duarte, CA: Hope Press.

Fey, M. (1986). *Language Intervention with Young Children.* Austin, TX: ProEd.

Fuchs, D., Mock, D., Morgan, P. L., & Young, C. L. (2003). Responsiveness-to-Education: Definitions, evidence and implications for the learning disabilities construct. *Learning Disabilities Research & Practice*, 18, 157–171.

Gazzaniga, M. S. (2004). *The cognitive neurosciences* (Third edition). Cambridge, MA: MIT Press.

German, D. J. (1986). *National College of Education Test of Word Finding.* Austin, TX: Pro-Ed.

German, D. J. (1990). *National College of Education test of adolescent/adult word finding.* Austin, TX: Pro-Ed.

German, D. J. (1991). *Test of Word Finding in Discourse.* Austin, TX: Pro-Ed.

German, D. J., & Newman, R. S. (2004). The impact of lexical factors on children's word-finding errors. *Journal of Speech, Language, and Hearing Research*, 47, 624–636.

Gilger, J. W., & Wise, S. E. (2004). Genetic correlates of language and literacy impairments. In C. A. Stone, E. R. Silliman, B. J. Ehren, & K. Appel (Eds.), *Handbook of Language and Literacy: Development and Disorders* (pp. 25–48). New York: Guilford Press.

Hammill, D., & Newcomer, P. (1997). *Test of Language Development – Intermediate: 3.* Austin, TX: ProEd.

Hill, E. L. (2001). Non-specific nature of specific language impairment: a review of the literature with regard to concomitant motor impairments. *International Journal of Language and Communication Disorders*, 36, 149–171.

Howell, K. W., & Nolet, V. (2000). Tools for assessment. *Curriculum-Based Evaluation, Teaching and Decisions Making.* Scarborough, Ontario: Wadsworth/Thompson Learning.

Hyerle, D. (1996). *Visual Tools for Constructing Knowledge.* Alexandria, VA: Association for Supervision and Curriculum Development.

Jung, J. H. (1989). *Genetic syndromes in communication disorders.* Boston, MA: College Hill Press.

Kovas, Y., & Plomin, R. (2006). Generalist genes: implications for the cognitive sciences. *Trends in Cognitive Science*, 10, 198–203.

Langdon, H. W. (2007). *Assessment and Intervention for Communication Disorders in Culturally and Linguistically Diverse Populations.* Clifton Park, N.Y.: Delmar/Cengage Learning.

Leonard, L. B. (1991). Specific language impairment as a clinical category. *Language, Speech, and Hearing Services in Schools*, 22, 66–68.

Leonard, L. B., Weismer, S. E., Miller, C. A., Francis, D. J., Tomblin, J. B., & Kail, R. V. (2007). Speed of processing, Working Memory, and language impairment in children. *Journal of Speech, Language, and Hearing Research*, 50, 408–428.

Lord Larson, V., & McKinley, N. L. (2003). *Communication Solutions for Older Students: Assessment and Intervention Strategies.* Greenville, NC: Thinking Publications/Super Duper.

Marcus, G., & Rabagliati, H. (2006). What developmental disorders can tell us about the nature and origins of language. *Nature Neuroscience*, 9, 1226–1229.

McGregor, K. K., Newman, R. M., Reilly, R. M., & Capone, N. C. (2002). Semantic representation and naming in children with specific language impairment. *Journal of Speech, Language, and Hearing Research*, 45, 998–1014.

Mellard, D. (2005). Linking early intervening services and responsiveness to intervention with specific learning disabilities determination. *National Research center on Learning Disabilities*, . www.nrcld.org

Merritt, D. D., & Culatta, B. (1998). *Language intervention in the classroom*. San Diego, CA: Singular Publishing Group.

Mirrett, P. L., Roberts, J. E., & Price, J. (2003). Early intervention practices and communication intervention strategies for young males with Fragile X syndrome. *Language, Speech, and Hearing Services in Schools*, 34, 320–331.

Montgomery, J. W. (2002). Understanding the language difficulties of children with specific language impairments: Does verbal Working Memory matter? *American Journal of Speech-Language Pathology*, 11, 77–91.

National Joint Committee on Learning Disabilities (NJCLD) (1994). Position paper. *Reprinted in Topics in Language Disorders*, 16, 69–73. (1996)

Nelson, N. W. (1998). *Childhood Language Disorders in Context: Infancy Through Adolescence*. Boston, MA: Allyn & Bacon.

Nelson, N. W. (2000). Basing eligibility on discrepancy criteria: A bad idea whose time has passed. *ASHA Special Interest Division I, Language, Learning and Education*, 7(1), 8.

Newcomer, P., & Hammill, D. (1997). *Test of Language Development – Preschool: 3*. Austin, TX: ProEd.

Nippold, M. A. (1991). Evaluation and enhancing idiom Comprehension in language-disordered students. *Language, Speech, and Hearing Services in Schools*, 22, 100–106.

Nippold, M. A., Erskine, B. J., & Freed, D. B. (1988). Proportional and functional analogical reasoning in normal and language-impaired children. *Journal of Speech and Hearing Disorders*, 53, 440–448.

Ohio handbook for the identification, evaluation, and placement of children with language problems. (1991). State of Ohio Department of Education, Columbus, Ohio.

Ottinger, B. (2003). *Dictionary: A Reference Guide to the World of Tourette Syndrome, Asperger Syndrome, Attention Deficit Hyperactivity Disorders and Obsessive Compulsive Disorder for Parents and Professionals*. Shawnee Mission, KS: Autism Asperger Publishing Co.

Paul, R. (2000). *Language Disorders from Infancy through Adolescence* (2nd ed.). St. Louis, MO: Mosby.

Payne, K. T., & Taylor, O. L. (2002). Multicultural influences on human communication. In G. H. Shames, & N. B. Anderson (Eds.), *Human Communication Disorders: An Introduction* (pp. 106–140). Boston, MA: Allyn & Bacon.

Prestia, K. (2003). Tourette's syndrome: Characteristics and interventions. *Intervention in Schools and Clinic*, 39, 67–71.

Ratner, V., & Harris, L. (1994). *Understanding Language Disorders: The Impact on Learning*. Eau Claire, WI: Thinking Publications.

Semel, E. M., Wiig, E. H., & Secord, W. A. (1995). *Clinical Evaluation of Language Fundamentals-3*. San Antonio, TX: The Psychological Corporation.

Semel, E. M., Wiig, E. H., & Secord, W. A. (2002). *Clinical Evaluation of Language Fundamentals-4*. San Antonio, TX: Psych Corp.

Semel, E. M., Wiig, E. H., & Secord, W. A. (2003). *Clinical evaluation of language fundamentals – 4*. San Antonio, TX: PsychCorp.

Singer, B. D., & Bashir, A. S. (1999). What are executive functions and self-regulation and what do they have to do with language-learning disorders? *Language, Speech, and Hearing Services in Schools*, 30, 265–273.

Storkel, H. L., & Morrisette, M. L. (2002). The lexicon and phonology: Interactions in language acquisition. *Language, Speech, and Hearing Services in Schools*, 33, 24–37.

Tallal, P. (2003). Language disabilities: Integrating research approaches. *Current Directions in Psychological Science*, 12, 206–211.

Van der Lely, K. H., Rosen, S., & McClelland, A. (1998). Evidence for a grammar-specific deficit in children. *Current Biology*, 8, 1253–1258.

Wechsler, D. (1991). *Wechsler Intelligence Scale for Children* (3rd edition). San Antonio, TX: The Psychological Corporation.

Weiler, M. D., Bernstein, J. H., Bellinger, D. C., & Waber, D. P. (2000). Processing Speed in Children with Attention Deficit/Hyperactivity Disorder, Inattentive Type. *Child Neuropsychology*, 6(3), 218–234.

Weismer, S. E., Evans, J., & Hesketh, L. J. (1999). An examination of verbal Working Memory capacity in children with specific language impairment. *Journal of Speech, Language, and Hearing Research*, 42, 1249–1260.

Weismer, S. E., Plante, E., Jones, M., & Tomblin, J. B. (2005). A functional magnetic resonance imaging investigation of verbal Working Memory in adolescents with specific language impairment. *Journal of Speech, Language, and Hearing Research*, 48, 405–425.

Wetherby, A. M. (2002). Communication and language disorders in infants, toddlers, and preschool children. In: G. H. Shames, & N. B. Anderson (Eds.), *Human Communication Disorders*, (6th ed, pp. 186–217). Boston, MA: Allyn & Bacon.

Wiig, E. H., Langdon, H. W., & Flores, N. (2001). Nominación rápida y automática en niños hispanohablantes bilingües y monolingües. *Revista de Logopedia, Foniatria y Audiologia*, 21(3), 106–117.

Wiig, E. H., Nielsen, N. P., Minthon, L., & Warkentin, S. (2002). *A Quick Test of Cognitive Speed.* San Antonio, TX: Pearson.

Wiig, E. H., & Wilson, C. C. (2001). *Map It Out! Visual Tools for Thinking, Organizing and Communicating.* Grenville, NC: Thinking Publications/Super Duper.

Wiig, E. H., Zureich, P., & Chan, H. N. (2000). A clinical rational for assessing rapid, automatic naming in children with language disorders. *Journal of Learning Disabilities*, 33, 369–374.

Wolf, M., Bowers, P. G., & Biddle, K. (2000). Naming-speed processes, timing, and reading: A conceptual review. *Journal of Learning Disability*, 33, 387–407.

5

ATTENTION-DEFICIT/ HYPERACTIVITY DISORDER: USING THE WISC-IV TO INFORM INTERVENTION PLANNING

VICKI L. SCHWEAN AND ADAM MCCRIMMON

Calgary, AB, Canada

Attention-Deficit/Hyperactivity Disorder (ADHD) is a developmental disorder of behavioral inhibition hindering self-regulation, organization of behavior, and goal-directed thoughts and action. A massive body of research and clinical literature exists on this disorder, given its prevalence and stigma in society. However, despite this large body of research, many clinicians are unaware of, and therefore do not practice, evidence-based assessments and interventions with children in this population. The outcome of this is often a lack of effective recommendations to teachers and caregivers, resulting in the adoption of ineffective behavior management and instructional techniques.

Billy was referred for a psychoeducational assessment by his teacher. Billy's teacher described him as lacking "stick-to-itiveness", noting that he is rarely able to follow through on pedantic tasks. She commented that he does not appear to listen or remember directions. Particular problematic is his tendency to act without reflection or consideration of the consequences. While she perceives that Billy is intellectual capable, accuracy in arithmetic calculations, and expressing himself coherently in both oral and written language are relative weaknesses. His handwriting is extremely poor and co-ordination difficulties are evident on activities requiring balance.

The purpose of this chapter is to specifically examine the role of the WISC-IV in understanding and developing evidence-based interventions for children with Attention-Deficit/Hyperactivity Disorder, Predominantly Hyperactive-Impulsive and Combined types. We will initially examine the historical and conceptual literature on ADHD, with specific focus on the theoretical model outlined by Barkley (1997a, b). Our intent is to use Barkley's model to inform our discussion on the use of the WISC-IV in assessing and treating ADHD in children.

INTRODUCTION

BACKGROUND

According to the *Diagnostic and Statistical Manual of Mental Disorders*, Fourth Edition (American Psychiatric Association, 2000), the essential feature of ADHD is a persistent pattern of inattention and/or hyperactivity–impulsivity. These symptoms must be more severe than is typically observed in normally-developing peers and present before the age of 7. They often persist throughout an individual's lifespan (Barkley, 1990; Barkley et al., 1990; Weiss & Hechtman, 1993). The disorder occurs in approximately 3–7% of the childhood population, with a 3:1 over-representation of boys (Szatmari, 1992). Indeed, it is one of the most commonly diagnosed mental disorders in childhood (Centers for Disease Control (CDC), 2005).

As noted, the disorder as presently defined centers around two primary symptoms: hyperactive-impulsive behavior and inattention. Hyperactive-impulsive behavior is often manifested through restlessness, fidgetiness, running and climbing more than peers, talking excessively, and inability to wait (American Psychiatric Association, 2000). Individuals often cannot control motor movements and demonstrate difficulty in stopping an ongoing movement. The inattentive symptom is typically displayed as an inability to sustain attention on or respond to a task as long as peers (American Psychiatric Association, 2000). As a result, the child exhibiting this symptom will often have difficulty following rules and instructions and appear disorganized and forgetful. In academic settings, complaints of lack of concentration and failure to complete assignments are common (Barkley et al., 1990). Research has shown that hyperactive-impulsive symptoms tend to emerge around 3–4 years of age, whereas the inattentive symptoms tend to emerge later in the development of the disorder, at 5–7 years of age (Applegate et al., 1997). Additionally, the hyperactive symptoms tend to decline during the school years whereas the inattentive symptoms tend to be more stable throughout school age before declining in later adolescence and adulthood (Hart et al., 1995).

ADHD is also associated with several cognitive impairments. Among these are difficulties with digit span and mental computation (Mariani & Barkley, 1997), planning and anticipation (Barkley et al., 1992), verbal fluency (Grodzinsky & Diamond, 1992), development of organizational strategies for complex tasks (Voelker et al., 1989), adherence to rules or instructions (Danforth et al., 1991), and motor co-ordination (Barkley, 1997a, b). An overarching impairment appears to be difficulties involving executive functions, or mental functions mediated by the frontal cortex, which will be explained in greater detail during the introduction and exploration of the theoretical model of ADHD later in this chapter.

This presenting symptomatology is associated with risks for poor academic achievement; impaired family, peer, and adult social relationships; and comorbid conditions such as Oppositional-Defiant Disorder (ODD), Conduct Disorder (CD), depression, anxiety, and drug and alcohol experimentation or abuse (Barkley, 1990). As such, appropriate and early diagnosis of this disorder followed by effective and efficient methods of intervention are of paramount importance to reduce these associated risks.

HISTORY

ADHD has a rich history in the psychological literature. Early descriptions of individuals displaying ADHD-like symptoms can be found as far back as the mid- to late 1800s. However, it was not until 1902 when clinical interest in these symptoms emerged (Still, 1902). The term "hyperactive child syndrome" was adopted, with the common symptom of an excess of motor movement compared to other children. The emerging dominant psychoanalytic view of the time came to modify perceptions of mental disorders as reactions to environmental influences. As a result, hyperactive child syndrome was re-defined as "hyperkinetic reaction of childhood" in the *Diagnostic and Statistical Manual of Mental Disorders*, Second Edition (DSM-II) (American Psychiatric Association, 1968). This re-conceptualization was important in its incorporation of difficulties with attention and inhibition along with hyperactivity, as well as a specification of reduction of symptoms throughout development. This increasing awareness of and clinical sensitivity toward difficulties with attention and inhibition continued to dominate the research literature culminating in the disorder being re-titled as "Attention-Deficit Disorder" (ADD) in the DSM-III (American Psychiatric Association, 1980).

It was this characterization as ADD that provided the framework for the classification structure currently in use. Of importance was the distinction between two subtypes of ADD, namely one with hyperactivity and one without. This distinction in the DSM-III was made primarily to stimulate research to determine the validity of the taxonomy. Such research has concluded that the taxonomy is valid and, as such, the current classification of the disorder continues to reflect subgroups based on these constructs. The DSM-III also switched from a psychodynamic perspective to one focused upon the cognitive and behavioral nature of the disorder. Additionally, the DSM-III provided explicit criteria including definitions of symptomatology and related cutoff scores for diagnosis. As the body of research on this disorder grew, so did the importance of hyperactivity as a differentiating symptom from other disorders of attention. As a result, the disorder was renamed to ADHD in the DSM-III-R (American Psychiatric Association, 1987).

Currently, the DSM-IV (American Psychiatric Association, 1994), and its subsequent text revised version (DSM-IV-TR) (American Psychiatric Association, 2000), provides a classification for ADHD, with three subtypes: (1) the predominantly inattentive subtype (ADHD-I), (2) the predominantly hyperactive-impulsive subtype (ADHD-H), and (3) a combined subtype (ADHD-C).

DIAGNOSTIC CRITERIA

The criteria in the DSM-IV-TR provide symptom lists and cutoff scores required for a diagnosis (Table 5.1).

These criteria provide the appropriate structure for investigating the differential influences of the core symptoms of ADHD, namely inattention and hyperactivity. Thus, an individual may be provided a diagnosis if they meet criteria for inattention (ADHD, predominantly inattentive type), hyperactivity–impulsivity (ADHD, predominantly hyperactive-impulsive type), or both (ADHD, combined type). These symptoms must have been present prior to 7 years of age and evident for at least 6 months, be inconsistent with the individual's developmental level, be present in two or more settings (i.e., school and home), and significantly impair functioning in these settings. The symptoms also cannot result primarily from another disorder such as Pervasive Developmental Disorder.

DIFFERENTIATION OF ADHD-I

The inclusion of an inattentive subtype in the DSM-III and its continued use in the DSM-IV has prompted a growing body of research investigating the differences between these subtypes. While the DSM-IV-TR provides diagnostic criteria for these three subtypes in the same diagnostic category, continuing research evidence is accumulating that ADHD-I is a qualitatively different disorder than ADHD-H and ADHD-C (Barkley, 1997a, b; Milich et al., 2001). While this taxonomy is by no means uncontested, research investigating differences between the subtypes has shown that children diagnosed with ADHD-I demonstrate a sluggish cognitive style combined with a selective inattention deficit, possess a passive social interaction style, are less likely to be diagnosed with comorbid Oppositional-Defiant Disorder (ODD) or Conduct Disorder (CD), and are more

TABLE 5.1   DSM-IV-TR (American Psychiatric Association, 2000) Diagnostic Criteria for Attention-Deficit/Hyperactivity Disorder

---

A. Either (1) or (2):

1. Six (or more) of the following symptoms of *inattention* have persisted for at least 6 months to a degree that is maladaptive and inconsistent with developmental level:

Inattention

(a) Often fails to give close attention to details or makes careless mistakes in schoolwork, work, or other activities.
(b) Often has difficulty sustaining attention in tasks or play activities.
(c) Often does not seem to listen when spoken to directly.
(d) Often does not follow through on instructions and fails to finish schoolwork, chores, or duties in the workplace (not due to oppositional behavior or failure to understand instructions).
(e) Often has difficulty organizing tasks and activities.
(f) Often avoids, dislikes, or is reluctant to engage in tasks that require sustained mental effort (such as schoolwork or homework).
(g) Often loses things necessary for tasks or activities (e.g., toys, school assignments, pencils, books, or tools).
(h) Is often easily distracted by extraneous stimuli.
(i) Is often forgetful in daily activities.

2. Six (or more) of the following symptoms of *hyperactivity–impulsivity* have persisted for at least 6 months to a degree that is maladaptive and inconsistent with developmental level.

Hyperactivity

(a) Often fidgets with hands or feet or squirms in seat.
(b) Often leaves seat in classroom or in other situations in which remaining seated is expected.
(c) Often runs about or climbs excessively in situations in which it is inappropriate (in adolescents or adults, may be limited to subjective feelings of restlessness).
(d) Often has difficulty playing or engaging in leisure activities quietly.
(e) Is often "on the go" or often acts as if "driven by a motor".
(f) Often talks excessively.

Impulsivity

(g) Often blurts out answers before the questions have been completed.
(h) Often has difficulty awaiting turn.
(i) Often interrupts or intrudes on others (e.g., butts into conversations or games).

B. Some hyperactive-impulsive or inattentive symptoms that caused impairment were present before age 7 years.
C. Some impairment from the symptoms is present in two or more settings (e.g., at school (or work) and at home).
D. There must be clear evidence of clinically significant impairment in social, academic, or occupational functioning.
E. The symptoms do not occur exclusively during the course of a Pervasive Developmental Disorder, Schizophrenia, or other Psychotic Disorder, and are not better accounted for by another mental disorder (e.g., Mood Disorder, Anxiety Disorder, Dissociative Disorder, or a Personality Disorder).

(continues)

TABLE 5.1   *(continued)*

Code based on type:

314.01 *Attention-Deficit/Hyperactivity Disorder, Combined Type*: If both Criteria A1 and A2 are met for the past 6 months.

314.00 *Attention-Deficit/Hyperactivity Disorder, Predominantly Inattentive Type*: If Criterion A1 is met but Criterion A2 is not met for the past 6 months.

314.01 *Attention-Deficit/Hyperactivity Disorder, Predominantly Hyperactive-Impulsive Type*: If Criterion A2 is met but Criterion A1 is not met for the past 6 months.

Coding note: For individuals (especially adolescents and adults) who currently have symptoms that no longer meet full criteria, "In Partial Remission" should be specified.

---

likely to have comorbid anxiety and mood disorders. Compared to this, children diagnosed with ADHD-H and ADHD-C tend to have difficulty with task persistence, spatial and verbal working memory, response and motor inhibition, and are rated as more aggressive and oppositional and therefore more likely to be rejected by their peers than children with ADHD-I (Barkley et al., 1992; Morgan et al., 1996; Barkley, 2003). Additionally, as noted earlier, the inattention symptoms emerge later in development (around the age of 5–7) whereas the symptoms associated with hyperactivity-impulsiveness emerge around the age of 3–4. Thus, children diagnosed with the combined subtype most often develop symptoms associated with inattention subsequent to those associated with hyperactivity. ADHD-C is most often a developmental progression from ADHD-H, whereas children diagnosed with ADHD-I tend to follow a different symptom pathway. This differentiation is important to the following discussion of the theoretical model, as it was designed to provide a structure for ADHD-H and ADHD-C. As such, the cognitive processes involved in this model and the resulting symptomology are applicable only to these two subtypes.

THE THEORETICAL MODEL

Over the years, there have been several attempts to conceptualize the underlying mechanisms of ADHD (Douglas, 1972, 1976, 1980a, b, 1983; Denny & Rapport, 2001; Rapport, 2002; Rapport et al., 2000, 2001). The theoretical model to be discussed and analyzed here has been put forth by Barkley (1997a, b) in an effort to conceptualize a heuristic framework of ADHD, primarily hyperactive-impulsive and combined subtypes and their associated symptomology. It has as its premise the notion that the core deficit of ADHD is one of response inhibition. It is this primary deficit which leads to secondary deficits in other mental abilities and the symptoms typically displayed with this disorder. Response inhibition denotes three processes: (1) inhibition of a prepotent, or dominant, response to an event, (2) stopping a current response which allows for a delay in the decision to respond, and (3) the protection of this delay from external competing events and responses. The term "prepotent response" is meant to refer to a response which has been previously reinforced. Therefore, response inhibition involves the conscious restraint or cessation of a response that an individual makes subsequent to that response being rewarded in the past. A deficit in this specific ability is then linked to further higher-order cognitive processes, called executive functions, as these rely upon appropriate response inhibition for their effective execution. It is important to note that a deficit in response inhibition does not *cause* the associated deficits in executive functions. Rather, response inhibition is required for the appropriate execution of these executive processes as a result of the delay provided through response inhibition. Thus, a deficit in response inhibition does not afford the opportunity for these cognitive processes to execute.

Executive functions are cognitive processes carried out by the frontal lobes and primarily by the prefrontal cortex. These processes allow for "the ability to maintain an appropriate problem-solving set for attainment of a future goal" (Ozonoff et al., 1991). Involved in this umbrella are higher mental processes such as selective attention, impulse control, planning, problem-solving, flexibility of thinking, concept formation, working memory, and abstract thinking. Of importance for the current discussion are the executive functions of non-verbal working memory, internalization of speech (verbal working memory), self-regulation of emotions and arousal, and reconstitution.

NON-VERBAL WORKING MEMORY

Non-verbal working memory involves the visual perception of stimuli and temporary preservation of that visual information in memory. The capacity of this process increases throughout development, allowing for more than simple reactivation and maintenance of visual information. Rather, an individual becomes capable of manipulating or acting upon the information by providing a controlled (typically motor) response. It is this development that is critical to the current discussion on ADHD. Specifically, the model posits that specific factors relating to non-verbal working memory are common deficits in individuals with ADHD, namely imitation and vicarious learning, the ability to reactivate past visual information (retrospective function), the reactivation of memory relating to response patterns and contingencies associated with past visual information (prospective function), the ability to anticipate a future based upon past responses (anticipatory set), the retention of a sequence of past events (sequence of time), and the resulting ability to organize and direct behavior based upon past experiences toward future events or goals (cross-temporal organization of behavior). When response inhibition is successfully exercised, a delay in responding is created. It is during this delay that non-verbal working memory is utilized.

Billy's teacher reports that he frequently interrupts the class by blurting out responses without putting his hand up and waiting to be called upon. When Billy is made to wait his turn, he appears to struggle and often becomes agitated or restless.

As well, Billy frequently interferes or interrupts his classmates during recess. Rather than asking to play or accepting their responses, Billy will intrusively join the interaction, which often leads to conflict with his peers.

For example, picture a child in a typical classroom setting who displays a lack of response inhibition. When the teacher asks a question to the class, students are to put up their hand to be called upon to answer. A child who has poor response inhibition is more likely to blurt out the answer, demonstrating a failure to inhibit this prepotent response and create a delay. As a result, this child is likely not to appropriately perceive and store the visual information of other students raising their hands, allowing him/her to process the information and imitate the appropriate behavior of the other students. This failure to imitate and learn vicariously will also result in a failure to demonstrate the correct behavior (putting up his/her hand and waiting to be called upon) in future scenarios, a failure to anticipate when such behavior will be expected of him/her in the future, an inability to temporally sequence events in his/her mind, and an inability to utilize this information to organize his/her thoughts and actions on future scenarios which may require similar behaviors.

INTERNALIZATION OF SPEECH

Internalization of speech, or verbal working memory, denotes "the capacity to converse with oneself in a quasi-dialogic fashion" (Barkley, 1997a, b). This process, similar to non-verbal working memory outlined above, is used to preserve auditory information in memory for processing and later use. The use of the term in the present context is as a method of self-description and reflection upon information, self-questioning, problem-solving, rule generation, and moral reasoning through a process of covert speech to oneself. As with non-verbal reasoning, if a deficit in response inhibition exists, the ability to utilize this cognitive construct will be limited and ineffective.

Billy's mother and teacher both noted that Billy requires that instructions frequently be repeated. For example, before going on a family outing, Billy's mother has to remind him to brush his teeth, put his dishes away, and get his coat and shoes. She noted that he appears to "just forget" what he is supposed to do because he appears to be distracted with other items or events around the house.

A child with poor response inhibition will not take advantage of the delay created by inhibition to covertly speak to him- or herself regarding the scenario. He/she will be unable to utilize this covert speech to describe the situation to him- or herself and reflect upon similar past experiences, problem-solve for more appropriate responses, generate rules to use in future similar situations, and reason about the social and moral implications (appropriateness) of their behavior.

SELF-REGULATION OF AFFECT/MOTIVATION/AROUSAL

Self-regulation of emotions and arousal refer to an individual's ability to govern control over emotional reactions to external stimuli and, as a result, to be guided by internal (rather than external) sources of motivation. Young children tend to be externally motivated by immediate reinforcement. However, this predisposition typically matures throughout childhood as children acquire stronger internal motivation and acceptance of delayed gratification/reinforcement. Individuals diagnosed with ADHD tend to maintain a mindset of external motivation, resulting in a continued need for immediate reinforcement of behavior and a deficit in future-oriented thinking (Barkley, 1997a, b). The current model accounts for this through the deficit in response inhibition. A deficit in inhibition of a prepotent response and the associated delay result in an inability to regulate emotions associated with the prepotent response. Subsequently, an individual with such a deficit is unable to fully regulate their emotions and emotional expression. Effective inhibition of prepotent responses and their associated emotions are often necessary for social acceptance, especially in regards to negative emotions.

Billy's teacher reports that he often interferes with his classmates' abilities to remain task-oriented. He disrupts their ongoing activities through his disruptive behavior and attempts to socialize during structured work time. He sometimes will demonstrate an emotional outburst when asked to sit and focus on his work. Additionally, his mood often changes quickly, and he seems to have difficulties adapting to changes in the classroom. However, his teacher reports that when his desk is moved beside hers, Billy is better able to focus on his work.

The delay caused by inhibition of a prepotent response also allows for secondary emotional regulation in the form of objectivity and social perspective taking. Inhibition creates the opportunity to process event information and comprehend the motivations of others. This understanding in turn allows for consideration of others' perspectives and greater social understanding.

Continuing the example of the child in the classroom, if a deficit in response inhibition exists, then it is likely that emotions associated with those responses will also be uninhibited. As a result, the child will exhibit emotional reactions in an unregulated fashion, such as appearing overly eager with his/her blurting out responses or anger and frustration when he/she is not called upon to answer or is rebuked for not putting his/her hand up. Additionally, the child will not take into consideration the views and emotions of his/her peers in regards to his/her behaviors. Finally, this deficit in inhibition will limit his/her development of internal sources of motivation, leading to a continued requirement for immediate external sources of reward.

RECONSTITUTION

Reconstitution is a term used to denote the analysis and synthesis of behavior. Analysis refers to the "ability to take the units of behavioral sequences apart" (Barkley, 1997a, b). Behavioral units are those that can be combined into sequences of action and organized hierarchically. Synthesis is the development of novel sequences of behaviors comprised of previously learned behavioral units. For example, a pianist is capable of creating novel sequences of previously learned behavioral units (in this case movements of the hands and fingers) to play music. Reconstitution can be verbal (the ability to analyze units of speech individually as well as combine these units into novel and meaningful statements) and non-verbal (or behavioral) in nature. Development of this ability also leads to the creation of rules governing sequences of behavior.

Billy was assessed by and has received the services of an occupational therapist since Kindergarten to assist him with fine motor control and penmanship. He has difficulties with pencil grasp and writing pressure in addition to cutting skills, though he is improving in these areas.

Returning to the child in the classroom, many children affected by ADHD frequently experience difficulties with verbal fluency (i.e., ability to rapidly and effectively assemble the units of language to create a diversity of verbal responses) (Barkley, 1998, p. 187). As a result, he/she may have difficulties when responding to confrontational questioning, solving verbal problem-solving tasks, communicating essential information when engaged in collaborative tasks, and relating narratives in an organized and detailed manner.

MOTOR CONTROL/FLUENCY SYNTAX

Barkley hypothesizes that inhibitory deficits will lead to impairments in behaviors associated with the executive functions (e.g., task-irrelevant activity; less flexible, less diverse, less complex, and more poorly temporally organized goal-directed behavior; poorer goal-directed persistence; patterns of perseverative responding; diminished likelihood of benefiting from feedback about errors in performance; diminished ability to return to goal-directed activities when temporally disrupted; and sluggishness and variability in motor preparation). Handwriting, which involves the complex sequencing of simpler motor movements into complex, novel patterns (Barkley, 1998, p. 295), is a prime example of the observable motor control/fluency syntax products of the executive functions.

SUMMARY OF THE MODEL

Within Barkley's model, a deficit of behavioral inhibition, posited to be the primary deficit in ADHD-H and ADHD-C, leads to secondary deficits in several executive functions, namely verbal and non-verbal working memory, self-regulation of affect and motivation, and reconstitution. Additionally, this primary deficit and the related secondary deficits each impact upon motor control, fluency of responses, and temporal syntax of responses. Barkley has argued that the executive functions hypothesized to be deficient in children with ADHD are critical to the development of self-determination, self-direction, and self-control and regulation.

ADHD, through the delay in behavioral inhibition it represents, serves to delay and disrupt the overall developmental process of the internalization of behavior that creates self-regulation. The forms of thought these internalized behaviors give rise to will be diminished by ADHD, such that forms of thought will be more external than internal in form and behavior will be less internally simulated, selected, guided, and motivated across time than normal. The ADHD person is therefore more under the control of the immediate context, external information and sources of motivation, and the temporal now, and considerably less under the control of time, their past, the future, and the internally generated motivation that drives behavior away from the moment and toward the future (Barkley, 1997b, pp. 348–349).

This model of ADHD-H and ADHD-C is theoretical in nature. However, it is also highly testable and for that reason, it has merit in the assessment and treatment of ADHD. The response inhibition deficit and resulting secondary executive functioning deficits can be examined and evaluated within this population to determine goodness of fit. As well, the model can be used to determine differences between ADHD and other similar populations as a means of external validation of the taxonomy established in the DSM-IV-TR.

ASSESSMENT OF ADHD

IMPLICATIONS FOR ASSESSMENT OF ADHD

There are several assessment implications stemming from Barkley's Hybrid Model of Executive Functions (for a more comprehensive discussion, see Barkley, 1997b, pp. 331–337). These include:

• Measures of behavioral inhibition (i.e., those that evaluate the capacity to inhibit responding, to cease ongoing responding quickly when demanded to do so or when confronted with errors of performance, and interference control) will be more discriminating of ADHD than measures of attention or those of other psychological constructs.

• Measures that assess inhibition, self-regulation, the executive functions, or the capacity to organize behavior across time or over longer temporal durations (e.g., rating scales or clinical measures administered over longer durations or on multiple occasions) will be more effective in the identification of ADHD than those administrated within clinical settings.

• Behavioral observations collected on multiple occasions, within natural situations, and over longer durations are more useful than those taken within clinical settings on single occasions.

• Interviews should probe functioning with respect to behavioral disinhibition, working memory and sense of time, internalized speech, self-control and affect, and goal-directed creativity and persistence rather than symptoms of inattention, impulsivity, or hyperactivity.

• Because Barkley views ADHD not as a disorder of knowing what to do, but of doing what one knows (i.e., disorder of performance or applied intelligence more than a disorder of skills), evaluations of how the individual is performing in meeting daily demands will be more sensitive than those that assess the individual's knowledge about how to do these things (e.g., scales of adaptive functioning rather than tests of IQ or academic achievement).

• Impairments that children with ADHD experience in behavioral inhibition and the executive functions dependent on it could be expected to result in a small but significant and negative relationship between ADHD and IQ, particularly verbal IQ.

ROLE OF INTELLIGENCE TESTING IN ADHD

Given that ADHD is conceptualized as a disorder of performance rather than of knowing, one naturally questions the usefulness of administering an IQ test. In a previous chapter (Schwean & Saklofske, 1998), we discussed why a clinician would routinely administer the WISC-IV in ADHD assessment. Points addressed included:

• IQ and achievement data can contribute to establishing the ADHD diagnosis in more indirect ways because the determination hinges, in part, on documenting severity of impairment. A child's failure to acquire age-appropriate cognitive skills, particularly in areas known to be causal in ADHD (e.g., working memory), may be inferred from results of IQ evaluation.

• An intelligence test such as the WISC-IV can contribute to the diagnosis of ADHD by generating information that may help to rule in or out other possible explanations for presenting complaints and/or aid in identifying co-existing disorders. For example, the attention problems that may be associated with mental retardation can be linked to that condition, in part, through intelligence testing.

IQ results are also useful in establishing the presence of a learning disability or giftedness that may either co-exist with ADHD, or in the case of a learning disability, be explanatory of specific weaknesses in working memory or processing speed.

• As part of a more comprehensive battery, intelligence test results on particular tasks and factors (e.g., working memory and processing speed) may identify patterns of weaknesses that, in combination with other assessment findings, are implicated in or explanatory of the ADHD symptomatology.

• Evaluation of intellectual skills can assist in identifying patterns of strengths and weaknesses that may inform intervention planning, progress evaluations, prognosis, and administrative decision-making (Schwean & Saklofske, 1998, pp. 260–261).

WECHSLER FINDINGS IN CHILDREN WITH ADHD

In our previous chapter (Schwean & Saklofske, 2005), we provided a detailed discussion of WISC findings relative to children presenting with ADHD. A selected summary of that discussion, along with more recent findings, is presented in the following points:

• Given that many children receive pharmacological treatment for the symptoms of ADHD, it is appropriate to question whether medication alters WISC performance. Studies examining the impact of medication on WISC-III performance have not found significant treatment effects for subtest, index, or VIQ (verbal intelligence quotient) and PIQ (performance intelligence quotient) scores (Saklofske & Schwean, 1993; Schwean et al., 1993). As a result, there appears to be no strong reason to temporarily halt medication treatment prior to assessment of intelligence.

• A study examining the stability of WISC-III Full Scale, Verbal, and Performance IQ scores obtained by ADHD children 1–2 years after initial assessment show these scores remained stable, although subtest stability over time was slightly more variable. Specifically, the Processing Speed (PS) demonstrated the lowest correlation between testings due to an increase of almost 9 points (Schwean & Saklofske, 1998).

• The comparability of various versions of the Wechsler scales for children with ADHD has been examined in various studies. Earlier studies comparing the WISC-R and WISC-III IQs in ADHD children report that the WISC-III yielded lower scores on the Full Scale IQ (FSIQ), VIQ, and PIQ (Horn-Alsberge, 1999; Mahone et al., 2003). More recently, Mayes and Calhoun's (2006) study examining the WISC-III or WISC-IV profiles of children with ADHD revealed profiles of strengths and weaknesses that were similar across the measures, with significantly lower mean scores on FDI/WMI (Freedom from Distractibility Index/Working Memory Index) and PSI (Processing Speed Index) than on VCI (Verbal Comprehension Index) and POI/PRI (Perceptual Organization/Perceptual

Reasoning Index). Within the PSI, Coding was significantly lower than Symbol Search on both measures. Mayes and Calhoun report, though, that the magnitude of the profile differences was greater for the WISC-IV than WISC-III. Specifically, the WMI and PSI were significantly more discrepant from the VCI and PRI than were WISC-III FDI and PSI from VCI and POI. Furthermore, 100% of the children in the WISC-IV group scored lowest on SMI (Story Memory Index) or PSI, whereas this was the case for only 88% of the children in the WISC-III group, suggesting that the WISC-IV may have greater sensitivity to ADHD symptoms than the earlier version. Subtest changes to the WISC-IV on the PRI (e.g., elimination of two timed visual-motor subtests and addition of two untimed motor-free tests of visual reasoning) showed the ADHD sample to have a relative strength in visual reasoning which was not evident on the WISC-III.

• Clinical and educational needs may require a re-examination of a child's ability in a short time span to confirm the first test results or to ensure an accurate diagnosis. While the Wechsler scales may be administered more than once to a child, to reduce practice effects, it is often advisable to use a different test if the time interval between testing is fairly brief. It is necessary to "equate" the two tests to determine if they yield equivalent scores and information. If score differences occur, it is necessary to determine how much of this difference is due to "real" change and how much is due to the imperfect correlations between different tests. A study (Saklofske et al., 1994) comparing the short form of the *Stanford-Binet Intelligence Scale*, Fourth Edition (SB:FE; Thorndike et al., 1986) administered at intake with the WISC-III given 4 weeks later showed the WISC-III FSIQ was slightly lower than that obtained for the SB:FE composite. Correlation patterns between the IQ, Index, and Area Scores revealed a fair amount of variance shared by the two tests but also supported the convergent-discriminant validity of these scales.

• In another convergent-discriminant validity study of the WISC-III (Schwean et al., 1993), findings showed that the patterns of correlations for the ADHD sample were similar to those reported in the WISC-III standardization sample across parallel age groupings, suggesting that the measure retains its psychometric characteristics when used in an examination of children with ADHD.

• Research that has examined the effects of co-existing learning disorders on ADHD intelligence profiles has generally shown that the comorbidity results in poorer performance on the FSIQ, WMI, and PSI (WISC-IV Technical Manual).

• The Technical and Interpretive Manual for the WISC-IV provides performance data on 89 children, ages 8–13 years, who were identified as having one of the subtypes of ADHD as outlined in the DSM-IV-TR. Relative to a matched control group, children with ADHD achieved a slightly lower mean performance on the FSIQ (mean 96.6, SD = 14.0 compared to mean 102.7, SD = 102.7 for the control group; see Table 7.1). The differences in FSIQ are statistically significant but the effect size was not large. Only a 1-point scaled score difference was observed between the VCI and PRI. The lowest index scores were observed on the WMI and PSI. As pointed out earlier, Mayes and Collhoun also found that the VCI and PRI were significantly higher than the FDI and WMI and effect sizes were very large. The VCI and PRI were significantly higher than the FSIQ and WMI/PSI was significantly lower than FSIQ. Examination of subtest scatter showed that for both the WISC-IV clinical and the Mayes and Collhoun studies, scores were significantly higher on the Coding than Symbol Search subtest.

• It is important to underscore that statistical significance does not imply clinical significance. Further, although abnormal scores might indicate the presence of a condition, like ADHD, they do not necessarily indicate the presence of ADHD.

• As we have noted, Barkley considers ADHD to be a disorder of behavioral disinhibition that impacts on several types of executive functions. The question as to whether the WISC-IV yields information different from measures of executive functions immediately arises. In a brief review of studies examining the relationship of IQ to performance on executive functions measures in children, Arfi (2007) reported inconsistent results. Although some studies she reviewed found no strong correlations, others highlight the moderating effect of IQ on executive functions, particularly at higher IQ levels. Her own study, which explored the relationship of various measures of executive function to the various factors and subtests of the WISC-III in average, above average, and gifted children, revealed that most executive function measures were primarily related to subtests that comprise the Freedom from Distractibility and Processing Speed factors of the WISC-III (i.e., Arithmetic, Digit Span, and Coding subtests). Referencing future research related to ADHD, Arffi argued that given that these working memory tasks may be the primary source of the covariance between IQ and executive functioning, statistical equations for IQ in studies comparing children with ADHD on executive function measures should be based on a composite of the Verbal and Performance subtests and not those that compromise the working memory and Processing Speed factors.

• Over the years, various Wechsler profiles have been examined as a means for differentiating children with ADHD (e.g., ACID profile, SCAD profile, Deterioration index). Given the neurological underpinnings of ADHD, a new composite based on a combination of the WISC-IV WMI and PSI, the Cognitive Proficiency Index (CPI), which assesses aspects of executive function (i.e., Working Memory and Processing Speed), may have clinical utility. Weiss et al. (2006) explored whether it was possible to identify an adequate cut score for the discrepancy between CPI and General Ability Index (GAI), a composite comprising the VCI and PRI, that correctly identified an acceptable percentage of clinical and non-clinical subjects. Minimally acceptable results were obtained for four clinical groups (learning disabilities; closed traumatic brain injuries; open traumatic brain injuries; Asperger's disorder); however, the GAI–CPI discrepancy alone was not sufficient evidence to diagnose a condition. To date, there is no research exploring the clinical usefulness of the GAI–CPI discrepancy cutoff scores, either alone or in combination with other measures, in children with ADHD.

INTERVENTION

HOW WECHSLER RESULTS INFORM INTERVENTION

Children with ADHD are heterogeneous in their intellectual profiles. While research has shown a decrement in IQ, likely due to impaired performance on those measures assessing aspects of executive functioning, the overall profile pattern can yield evidence of other intellectual strengths and weaknesses that are relevant to both a priori and posteriori hypothesis testing necessary for differential diagnosis. Further, performance patterns across factors and subtests may inform intervention planning by identifying not only areas in need of intervention, but also those that can serve in compensatory capacities. Although often overlooked, the observations made during administration of the test will yield important information about the conditions and tasks that facilitate the child's ability to learn (e.g., how the type of material, rate and modality of presentation, cues, and reinforcement differentially affect learning) which, in turn, can assist in designing more effective intervention programs (Sattler, 2001). Testing-of-limits can further elaborate our understanding of adaptations and modifications that may enhance the child's performance.

Of particular interest to the assessment of children with ADHD will be their performance on those tasks that assess aspects of executive functioning (i.e., Working Memory and Processing Speed). While not diagnostic of ADHD, the work of Mayes and Collhoun suggests that poor performance across these factors may *aide* not only in differential diagnosis, but also in designing intervention supports. For the latter to be fruitful, though, it is important that we heed Barkley's advise: the most useful treatments are those that take place in natural settings at the points of performance where the desired behavior is to occur. In addressing interventions related to psychological processes like working memory, interventions must focus on filling the context with forms of stimuli that are comparable to the internal counterparts that are ineffective (Barkley, 1997a, b).

A number of authors (e.g., Nadeau, 1995; Mastropieri & Scruggs, 2006; Turnbull et al., 2007) have listed interventions for enhancing executive functions that are based on this principal. A sampling of these follows.

WORKING MEMORY INTERVENTIONS

• Using technology memory aid devices or personal data assistants that provide timed prompts to assist children in following routines, taking medications, remembering to perform a new task, and marking when to start or end a task (e.g., Visual Assistant software, AbleLink, Inc. or Schedule Assistant, AbleLink, Inc.). Alternatively, low technology memory aides such as pagers or electronic watchers that produce sounds or visual stimuli to prompt children to engage in a specific activity can be used.

• Using visual prompts (e.g., placing items to be remembered in conspicuous places.

• Providing backups for essential items (e.g., same textbook at home and school).
• Developing daily rituals and routines. Implementing routines that are unvarying will ensure they become overlearned behaviors which place limited demands on the attentional and memory systems. As long as routines are developed and are unvarying, they fall into the category of "overlearned" behaviors which place very little demand on the attentional and memory systems.
• Employing tape recorders to capture essential information.

PROCESSING SPEED INTERVENTIONS

• Pacing instruction (i.e., delivering content in smaller increments or packets of information, modifying the time between their delivery of new information).
• Providing adequate processing time (recognize that children may require varying times to respond given their processing capacities).
• Monitoring responses to ensure that students are mastering the content. Adjust instruction if learning is not optimal.
• Providing supportive and specific feedback on correct and incorrect responses and correcting the latter in "real time" instead of waiting until the lesson is over.
• Employing pre-teaching and advanced organizers to prepare students for upcoming tasks and to direct their attention to specific learning objectives.
• Lesson lower-level cognitive demands so that children can direct all of their cognitive resources toward higher-level learning.

PHARMACOTHERAPY

Although previous research has shown that medication does not enhance intellectual performance per se, there is ample evidence demonstrating its effectiveness at normalizing deficits in behavioral disinhibition and executive functioning. Medication is the most commonly used intervention for children with ADHD. Of these, the most frequently used are stimulant medications, including methylphenidate (Ritalin), dextroamphetamine (Dexedrine), and pemoline (Cylert). It is believed that individuals with ADHD possess a reduced basal level of neural activity, and therefore the displayed behavioral symptoms of inattention and hyperactivity serve the purpose of increasing stimulation and activity level. The stimulant medications act upon the central nervous system by stimulating activity levels, thus providing the required increase in neural activity and reducing stimulatory and sensation-seeking behaviors.

Efficacy studies have shown that 75% of children evaluated respond positively to the use of Ritalin (O'Tool et al., 1997). Improvements have been documented in inhibition and impulse control, working memory, reduction of aggression, and cognitive flexibility, among others (Barkley, 1977a, b; Barkley et al., 1991; Rapport & Kelly, 1993; Swanson et al, 1995; Chronis et al., 2006). Ritalin, the most studied and possibly the most effective stimulant medication in this population, is a fast-acting but short-lived stimulant, with effectiveness typically lasting 4 hours. On the other hand, Dexedrine is longer lasting and therefore requires fewer doses throughout the day to maintain effective levels. Cylert has been found to be effective in reducing ADHD symptoms, though not to the extent of Ritalin. It typically lasts 4–10 hours and so often only a once daily dose is required. However, Cylert has a history of troublesome side-effects and so is not usually the first-choice medication.

Despite the positive effects of stimulant medication, the benefits are most often seen in the school setting, as the medication is administered prior to going to school and then, if so prescribed, throughout the school day. As such, parents often report no change in problematic behavior as the medication's effectiveness has worn off by day's end. Therefore, increased and continued communication between the parent and the teacher will be important in determining a medication's effectiveness.

While stimulant medications appear to be the most effective in treating symptoms of ADHD, side-effects such as short duration requiring multiple doses throughout the day, decreased appetite and anorexia, insomnia, headaches, and irritability often necessitate their discontinuation. In such cases, tricyclic antidepressant medication such as imipramine, amitriptyline, desipramine, or nortriptyline is often used. These medications act upon neurotransmitter supply, inhibiting the reuptake of serotonin and norepinephrine. Research evaluating the effectiveness of this class of medication has shown that most individuals demonstrate a moderate improvement in symptoms with their use (Biederman, 1998).

As we noted above, despite the well demonstrated reduction in ADHD symptoms, such as disinhibition, medications do not resolve the associated problems experienced by children with ADHD. Specifically, areas such as cognitive and academic impairments, social relationships with peers and parents, and development of coping skills and strategies are not addressed by medication. Additionally, while short-term benefits have been well reported, medication use has not been found to produce long-term change in this population (MTA Co-operative Group, 1999a). Therefore, additional, and often combined, interventions are utilized in order to bring about the most effective positive change in children with ADHD. In this regard, behavioral contingency strategies such as parent training and school-based interventions have been found to be most effective.

SCHOOL-BASED INTERVENTIONS

School-based interventions for children with ADHD attempt to minimize symptoms of the disorder and disruptive behaviors in the classroom setting. If left, these typically result in poor academic functioning, leading to poorer outcome in adult life. School-based interventions typically take one of two forms, consultation with the teacher regarding behavior management strategies and academic interventions which focus upon the antecedent conditions such as instructional style and materials in order to improve executive functioning deficits and academic outcomes (DuPaul & Eckert, 1998). The use of a daily schedule for events so that activities can be anticipated, the use of a sign system to inform the child of their appropriate vocal volume and activity level, a color chart providing feedback regarding following of classroom rules, and the establishment of weekly rewarding activities whose access is dependent upon behavior and performance throughout the week have all proved to be effective in the classroom (Anastopoulos et al., 2005). Additionally, peer tutoring, computer assisted instruction, task modification (reducing task length or dividing a task into subtasks with goals), and using increased stimulation within tasks to facilitate children's on-task attention have also shown to be effective (Power et al., 2001). Finally, instruction in note-taking, study skills, and self-reinforcement will also likely be of benefit (DuPaul & Eckert, 1998).

SUMMARY

ADHD is a developmental disorder of behavioral inhibition affecting many young children. Symptoms of this disorder typically present as inattentiveness and/or hyperactivity, which often result in poor academic and social functioning. The diagnostic formulation of this disorder has changed throughout its history in the psychological literature, with current criteria reflecting the inattentiveness and hyperactivity domains. A theoretical model of this disorder has been put forth by Barkley (1997a, b) in order to provide a framework for assessment, diagnosis, and intervention with individuals with ADHD-H and ADHD-C. This theory posits the primary symptom of this disorder to be a deficit in behavioral inhibition of a prepotent response which results in secondary deficits in four executive functioning domains (verbal working memory, non-verbal working memory, self-regulation of emotions/arousal, and reconstitution). These five deficits (behavioral inhibition and the four secondary deficits) all contribute to the observed behavioral symptoms in motor control such as goal-directed behavior, execution of novel motor sequences, sensitivity to response feedback, and internal control of behavior.

In this chapter, we used Barkley's model to explore the utility of the Wechsler scales for informing assessment and interventions for children with ADHD. Relative to assessment, Barkley's framework predicts that ADHD will best be identified through measures that assess behavioral inhibition and the executive functions using multi-modal and multi-source techniques. The WISC-IV is an integral component of such a comprehensive assessment plan: it has utility for the identification of relative cognitive strengths and weaknesses, aides in differential diagnosis, and can identify patterns of weaknesses that, in combination with other assessment findings, are implicated in or explanatory of ADHD. We also examined ways in which WISC-IV results may inform intervention practice. Emphasis was placed not only on how observations made during test administration can assist in intervention planning, but also how standardized scores on particular factors (e.g., working memory and processing speed) can lead to evidence-based intervention practices. We firmly endorse the use of evidence-based assessment and intervention practices as means to promote better understandings of the specific nature of ADHD and facilitate better outcomes for children affected by this condition. Indeed, this disorder currently carries with it a highly negative social stigma, leading many parents and teachers to be resistant to accepting the diagnosis and related intervention strategies. Through better evidence-based practices, hopefully these concerns will become a difficulty of the past.

REFERENCES

American Psychiatric Association (1968). *Diagnostic and Statistical Manual of Mental Disorders* (2nd ed.). Washington, DC: American Psychiatric Association.

American Psychiatric Association (1980). *Diagnostic and Statistical Manual of Mental Disorders* (3rd ed.). Washington, DC: American Psychiatric Association.

American Psychiatric Association (1987). *Diagnostic and Statistical Manual of Mental Disorders* (3rd ed., revision). Washington, DC: American Psychiatric Association.

American Psychiatric Association (1994). *Diagnostic and Statistical Manual of Mental Disorders* (4th ed.). Washington, DC: American Psychiatric Association.

American Psychiatric Association (2000). *Diagnostic and Statistical Manual of Mental Disorders* (4th ed., text revision). Washington, DC: American Psychiatric Association.

Anastopoulos, A. D., Shelton, T. L., & Barkley, R. A. (2005). Family-based psychosocial treatments for children and adolescents with Attention-Deficit/Hyperactivity Disorder. In: E. D. Hibbs, & P. S. Jensen (Eds.), *Psychosocial treatments for child and adolescent disorders: Empirically-based strategies for clinical practice* (2nd ed., pp. 327–350). Washington, D.C.: American Psychological Association.

Applegate, B., Lahey, B. B., Hart, E. L., Biederman, J., Hynd, G. W., Barkley, R. A., Ollendick, T., Frick, P. J., Greenhill, L., McBurnett, K., Newcorn, J. H., Kerdyk, L., Garfinkel, B., Waldman, I., & Shaffer, D. (1997). Validity of the age-of-onset criterion for ADHD: A report from the DSM-IV field trials. *Journal of the American Academy of Child and Adolescent Psychiatry*, 36(9), 1211–1221.

Barkley, R. A. (1990). *Attention-Deficit Hyperactivity Disorder: A Handbook for Diagnosis and Treatment*. New York: The Guilford Press.

Barkley, R. A. (1997a). Behavioral inhibition, sustained attention, and executive functions: Constructing a unifying theory of ADHD. *Psychological Bulletin*, 121, 65–94.

Barkley, R. A. (1997b). *ADHD and the Nature of Self-control*. New York: Guilford Press.

Barkley, R. A. (1998). *Attention-Deficit Hyperactivity Disorder: A Handbook for Diagnosis and Treatment* (2nd ed.). New York: The Guilford Press.

Barkley, R. A. (2003). Attention-deficit/hyperactivity disorder. In E. Mash (Ed.), *Child Psychopathology* (2nd ed., pp. 75–143). New York: Guilford Press.

Barkley, R. A., DuPaul, G. J., & McMurray, M. B. (1990). A comprehensive evaluation of attention deficit disorder with and without hyperactivity. *Journal of Consulting and Clinical Psychology*, 58, 775–789.

Barkley, R. A., DuPaul, G. J., & McMurray, M. B. (1991). Attention deficit disorder with and without hyperactivity: Clinical response to three doses of methylphenidate. *Pediatrics*, 87, 519–531.

Barkley, R. A., Grodzinsky, G., & DuPaul, G. (1992). Frontal lobe functions in attention deficit disorder with and without hyperactivity: A review and research report. *Journal of Abnormal Child Psychology*, 20, 163–188.

Barkley, R. A., Fischer, M., Edelbrock, C. S., & Smallish, L. (1990). The adolescent outcome of hyperactive children diagnosed by research criteria: I: An 8-year prospective study. *Journal of the American Academy of Child and Adolescent Psychiatry*, 29, 546–557.

Biederman, J. (1998). Attention-deficit/hyperactivity disorder: A life-span perspective. *Journal of Clinical Psychiatry*, 59(Suppl. 7), 4–16.

Centers for Disease Control (CDC) (2005). Mental health in the United States: Prevalence of diagnosis and medication treatment for attention-deficit/hyperactivity disorder – United States, 2003. *Morbidity and Mortality Weekly Report*, 54, 842–847.

Chronis, A. M., Jones, H. A., & Raggi, V. L. (2006). Evidence-based psychosocial treatments for children and adolescents with attention-deficit/hyperactivity disorder. *Clinical Psychology Review*, 26, 486–502.

Danforth, J. S., Barkley, R. A., & Stokes, T. F. (1991). Observations of parent–child interactions with hyperactive children: Research and clinical implications. *Clinical Psychology Review*, 11, 703–727.

Denney, C. B., & Rapport, M. D., (2001). Cognitive pharmacology of stimulants in children with ADHD. In: M. V. Solanto, A. F. Torrance *et al.* (Eds.), *Stimulant drugs and ADHD: Basic and clinical neuroscience* (pp. 283–302). London: Oxford University Press.

Douglas, V. I. (1972). Stop, look and listen: the problem of sustained attention and impulse control in hyperactive and normal children. *Canadian Journal of Behavioural Science*, 4, 259–282.

Douglas, V. I. (1976). Perceptual and cognitive factors as determinants of learning disabilities: A review chapter with special emphasis on attentional factors. In: R. M. Knights, & D. J. Baker (Eds.), *The neuropsychology of learning disorders: Theoretical approaches* (pp. 413–421). Baltimore: University Park Press.

Douglas, V. I. (1980a). Higher mental processes in hyperactive children: Implications for training. In: R. M. Knights, & D. J. Baker (Eds.), *Rehabilitation, treatment, and management of learning disorders* (pp. 65–92). Baltimore: University Park Press.

Douglas, V. I. (1980b). Treatment approaches: Establishing inner our outer control? In: C. K. Whalen, & B. Henker (Eds.), *Hyperactive children: The social ecology of identification and treatment*. New York: Academic Press.

Douglas, V. I. (1983). Attentional and cognitive problems. In: M. Rutter (Ed.), *Developmental neuropsychiatry* (pp. 280–329). New York: The Guilford Press.

DuPaul, G. J., & Eckert, T. L. (1998). Academic interventions for students with attention deficit hyperactivity disorder: A review of the literature. *Reading & Writing Quarterly: Overcoming Learning Difficulties*, 14, 59–82.

Grodzinsky, G. M., & Diamond, R. (1992). Frontal lobe functioning in boys with attention-deficit hyperactivity disorder. *Developmental Neuropsychology*, 8, 427–445.

Hart, E. L., Lahey, B. B., Loeber, R., Applegate, B., & Frick, P. J. (1995). Developmental changes in attention-deficit hyperactivity disorder in boys: A four-year longitudinal study. *Journal of Abnormal Child Psychology*, 23, 729–750.

Horn-Alsberge, M. M. (1999). Stability of WISC-R and WISC-III IQs and subtest scores for a learning disabled sample. *Dissertation Abstracts International: Section B: The Sciences and Engineering*, 60(5-B), 2344.

Kaufman, A. S., & Kaufman, N. L. (1983). *Kaufman Assessment Battery for Children*. Circle Pines, MN: American Guidance Services.

Mahone, E. M., Miller, T. L., Koth, C. W., Mostofsky, S. H., Goldberg, M. C., & Denckla, M. B. (2003). Differences between WISC-R and WISC-III performance scale among children with ADHD. *Psychology in the Schools*, 40(4), 331–340.

Mariani, M., & Barkley, R. A. (1997). Neuropsychological and academic functioning in preschool children with attention deficit hyperactivity disorder. *Developmental Neuropsychology*, 13, 111–129.

Mastropieri, M. A., & Scruggs, T. E. (2006). *The inclusive classroom: Strategies for effective instruction* (3rd ed.). Columbus, OH: Pearson Merrill Prentice Hall.

Mayes, S. D., & Calhoun, S. L. (2006). WISC-IV and WISC-III profiles in children with ADHD. *Journal of Attention Disorders*, 9, 486.

Milich, R., Ballentine, A. C., & Lynam, D. R. (2001). ADHD combined type and ADHD predominantly inattentive type are distinct and unrelated disorders. *Clinical Psychology: Science and Practice*, 8, 463–488.

Morgan, A. E., Hynd, G. W., Riccio, C. A., & Hall, J. (1996). Validity of DSM-IV ADHD predominantly inattentive and combined types: Relationship to previous DSM diagnoses/subtype differences. *Journal of the American Academy of Child and Adolescent Psychiatry*, 35, 325–333.

MTA Co-operative Group (1999a). Fourteen-month randomized clinical trial of treatment strategies for attention-deficit hyperactivity disorder. *Archives of General Psychology*, 56, 1088–1096.

Nadeau, K. G. (Ed.) (1995). *A comprehensive guide to attention deficit disorder in adults: Research, diagnosis, and treatment*. New York: Brunner/Mazel Publishers.

O'Tool, K., Abramowitz, A., Morris, R., & Dulcan, M. (1997). Effects of methylphenidate on attention and nonverbal learning in children with attention-deficit hyperactivity disorder. *Journal of the American Academy of Child and Adolescent Psychiatry*, 36, 531–538.

Ozonoff, S., Pennington, B., & Rogers, S. (1991). Executive function deficits in high-functioning autistic individuals: Relationship to theory of mind. *Journal of Child Psychology and Psychiatry*, 32(7), 1081–1105.

Power, T. J., Harustis, J. L., & Habboushe, D. F. (2001). *Homework success for children with ADHD*. New York: The Guilford Press.

Rapport, M. D. (2001). Attention-deficit/hyperactivity disorder. In: M. Hersen, & V. B. Van Hasselt (Eds.), *Advanced abnormal psychology* (2nd ed., pp. 191–208). Dordrecht, Netherlands: Kluwer Academic Publishers.

Rapport, M. D., Chung, K. M., Shore, G., Denney, C. B., & Isaacs, P. (2000). Upgrading the science and technology of assessment and diagnosis: Laboratory and clinic-based assessment of children with ADHD. *Journal of Clinical Child Psychology*, 29(4), 555–568.

Rapport, M. D., Chung, K. M., Shore, G., & Isaacs, P. (2001). A conceptual model of child psychopathology: Implications for understanding attention deficit hyperactivity disorder and treatment efficacy. *Journal of Community Psychology*, 30(1), 48–58.

Rapport, M. D., & Kelly, K. L. (1993). Psychostimulant effects on learning and cognitive function. In: J. L. Matson (Ed.), *Handbook of hyperactivity in children* (pp. 97–135). Boston: Allyn & Bacon.

Saklofske, D. H., & Schwean, V. L. (1993). Standardized procedures for measuring the correlates of ADHD in children: A research program. *Canadian Journal of School Psychology*, 9, 28–36.

Saklofske, D. H., Schwean, V. L., & Ray, D. O. (1994). WISC-III and SB:FE performance of children with attention deficit hyperactivity disorder. *Canadian Journal of School Psychology*, 10, 167–171.

Sattler, J. M. (2001). *Assessment of children: Cognitive applications* (4th ed.). San Diego, CA: Jerome M. Sattler, Publisher, Inc.

Schwean, V. L., & Saklofske, D. H. (1998). WISC-III assessment of children with attention deficit/hyperactivity disorder. In A. Prifitera, & D. H. Saklofske (Eds.), *WISC-III clinical use and interpretation: Scientist–practitioner perspectives* (pp. 92–118). San Diego, CA: Academic Press.

Schwean, V. L., & Saklofske, D. H. (2005). Assessment of attention deficit hyperactivity disorder with the WISC-IV. In A. Prifitera, D. H. Saklofske, & L. G. Weiss (Eds.), *WISC-IV Clinical Use and Interpretation: Scientist–practitioner perspectives* (pp. 236–281). Burlington, MA: Elsevier Academic Press.

Schwean, V. L., Saklofske, D. H., Yackulic, R. A., & Quinn, D. (1993). WISC-III performance of ADHD children. *Journal of Psychoeducational Assessment, WISC-III Monograph*, 56–70.

Still, G. F. (1902). The Coulstonian lectures on some abnormal physical conditions in children. *Lancet*, 1, 1008–1012. 1077–1082, 1163–1168

Szatmari, P. (1992). The epidemiology of attention-deficit hyperactivity disorders. In G. Weiss (Ed.), *Child and Adolescent Psychiatric Clinics of North America: Attention deficit disorder* (pp. 361–372). Philadelphia, PA: W.B. Saunders.

Thorndike, R. L., Hagen, E., & Sattler, J. M. (1986). *Stanford-Binet Intelligence Scale* (4th ed.). Chicago: Riverside.

Turnbull, A., Turnbull, R., & Wehmeyer, L. (2007). *Exceptional Lives: Special Education in Today's Schools* (5th ed.). Columbus, OH: Pearson Merrill Prentice Hall.

Weiss, L. G., Saklofske, D. H., Prifitera, A., & Holdnack, J. A. (Eds.) (2007). *WISC-IV advanced clinical interpretation*. Burlington, MA: Academic Press.

Voelker, S. L., Carter, R. A., Sprague, D. J., Gdowski, C. L., & Lachar, D. (1989). Developmental trends in memory and metamemory in children with attention deficit disorder. *Journal of Pediatric Psychology*, 14, 75–88.

6

THE USE OF THE WISC-IV

IN ASSESSMENT AND

INTERVENTION PLANNING

FOR CHILDREN WHO ARE

GIFTED

TINA M. NEWMAN[1,3], SARA S. SPARROW[1]
AND STEVEN I. PFEIFFER[2]

[1]*Yale University Child Study Center and British Columbia Children's Hospital*

[2]*Yale University Child Study Center*

[3]*Florida State University*

INTRODUCTION

Ever since Terman published his seminal work on gifted children in 1925 (Terman, 1925), scientists, educators, and parents have sought to better understand, identify, and provide for, gifted children. Assessment and identification of gifted children and adolescents has been a major focus of studies undertaken in the interest of providing the educational needs of these special children and adolescents.

This chapter addresses the assessment of gifted children using the *Wechsler Intelligence Scale for Children* – Fourth Edition (WISC-IV) and the ways in which information from the WISC-IV can inform intervention with gifted children within the new "Response to Intervention (RTI)" model of special education. The Wechsler Scales, in general, have been the most widely used instrument for this purpose, in part, because they represent the most widely used intelligence tests in schools in the United States today, and because most school systems usually view the gifted child or adolescent as gifted either intellectually, academically, or both. Klausmeier et al. (1987) conducted a national survey of assessment practices among school psychologists, and found that the Wechsler Scales had also become the overwhelming first choice for the assessment of gifted children. Additionally, a short discussion of the recently developed extended norms for the WISC-IV is included here along with the tables of extended norms developed by the publisher (Zhu et al., 2008). In addition to the WISC-IV, we also plan to discuss a complementary instrument, the Gifted Rating Scales (*GRS*) (Pfeiffer & Jarosewich, 2003). This scale is designed to be completed by teachers that will assist in the identification of gifted children and adolescents.

Finally, we will make recommendations for how the WISC-IV and the GRS may be used to identify gifted children and adolescents.

DEFINITION OF GIFTEDNESS

One issue facing the gifted field is a lack of consensus on how to define giftedness. The federal definition has undergone a number of revisions, in 1972, 1978, 1988, and 1994. States have crafted their own definitions based on modifications of the different versions of the federal definition (Pfeiffer, 2002).

Most states are using a version of the 1978 modification of the 1972 federal definition, known as the Marland definition. The majority of states use the term "gifted and talented" in describing highly capable students, although 13 states restrict their definition to the term "gifted." Almost all states include superior intelligence as a characteristic of giftedness. Specific academic ability is considered a type of giftedness by 33 states, creative ability a type of giftedness by 30 states, and leadership a type of giftedness by 18 states (Stephens & Karnes, 2000).

Experts in the gifted field do not agree on how to define giftedness (Pfeiffer, 2001, 2003, 2007). The lack of agreement among experts should come as no great surprise since authorities in almost all applied fields, including education, psychology, and medicine, rarely reach consensus in defining social constructs of interest. The lack of professional consensus in how to define "giftedness," in conjunction with inconsistent state definitions, can make the identification of gifted students particularly challenging for the practitioner.

Exceptional general intelligence was once thought to be the hallmark of giftedness, but now is regarded by most authorities as only one manifestation of giftedness (Gardner, 1983; Sternberg, 1997; Pfeiffer & Jarosewich, 2003). New theories of giftedness emphasize the multi-dimensionality of outstanding abilities (Gardner, 1983; Sternberg, 1997; Gagné, 1993). For example, the Munich

Model of Giftedness and Talent includes the following manifestations of talent: intelligence, creativity, social competence/leadership, and musical–artistic abilities (Zigler & Heller, 2000).

Gifted children can display many talents, such as esthetic, artistic, athletic, creative, dramatic, interpersonal, musical, and others. The number and types of gifts is only limited by what a given society recognizes and values as culturally important (Pfeiffer, 2002, 2007). Research suggests that different types of talents are moderately inter-correlated for many gifted children; however, there are many gifted children for whom this is not the case (Pfeiffer & Jarosewich, 2003).

Most, if not all, multi-dimensional conceptual definitions of giftedness include some reference to intelligence. Intelligence is viewed as goal-directed mental activity marked by efficient problem solving, critical thinking, and effective abstract reasoning (Pfeiffer, 2002).

This chapter will restrict its discussion to the use of the WISC-IV in the assessment of one type of giftedness, intellectual. Robert Sternberg succinctly states that "intelligence comprises the mental abilities necessary for adaptation to, as well as shaping and selection of, environmental context (Sternberg, 1997, p. 1030)." Intellectual giftedness includes cognitive abilities such as verbal and/ or non-verbal abstract reasoning, effective and efficient problem solving, insight, mental speed, and memory (Pfeiffer & Jarosewich, 2003).

REVIEW OF THE LITERATURE

INTELLIGENCE AND GIFTEDNESS

Although the WISC-IV has been in use for a number of years, no research studies were available that investigated the use of the WISC-IV with gifted individuals except those carried out on the standardization sample and that were reported in the *Technical and Interpretive Manual* (Wechsler, 2003). Therefore, the most relevant literature concerning assessment of highly intelligent children with the Wechsler Scales, deals with the WISC-III (Wechsler, 1991). Since there are considerable differences between the WISC-III and the WISC-IV, in both content and structure, caution must be taken when comparing results from the WISC-III to the most recent revision. Data from the *WISC-IV Technical and Interpretive Manual* (Wechsler, 2003) will be presented later in this chapter.

Quite aside from the use of the Wechsler Scales to identify individuals who are gifted, there has also been debate over the use of *any* intelligence tests to identify gifted children. Tyerman (1986) argued that the cultural bias of intelligence tests unfairly places gifted children of "deprived or immigrant background(s)" at a disadvantage, even when conventional methods for reducing cultural bias are employed. He advocated instead the use of ability tests such as Raven's Progressive Matrices and Kohs' Block Design Test.

Others have not opposed the use of intelligence tests for the identification of gifted children, but have cautioned against the misapplication or misinterpretation of IQ scores. Harrington (1982), for example, cited a host of dangers in intelligence testing with gifted children. He pointed out that gifted children's IQ scores can be depressed by ceiling effects, the use of recently revised tests, or cultural bias. In addition, the use of arbitrary "cutoff scores" and the instability of IQ scores among preschool children can lead to misidentification of gifted children. Furthermore, intelligence tests can penalize gifted children by rewarding convergent-type responses, but granting no credit for divergent-type responses. Sparrow and Gurland (1998) in discussing the WISC-III and its use in identification of children and adolescents who are gifted, cautioned psychologists to be aware of ceiling effects and the emphasis of speed of performance that can penalize individuals with reflective cognitive styles.

Like Harrington, Sternberg (1982) identified widely used, but not necessarily sound practices in intelligence testing. Specifically, he questioned the premises: that speed is an indication of intelligence, the claim that intelligence tests measure only intelligence, and not achievement, the practice of administering intelligence tests in anxiety-provoking or stressful test-taking environments, and the tendency to treat a precise score as a necessarily valid score. In a similar vein, Barona and Pfeiffer (1992) cautioned that standard test administration procedures may compromise the maximal performance of students from culturally diverse backgrounds.

Still other psychologists and educators have acknowledged the limitations of intelligence tests, but stress their value, when used properly, as a clinical tool for evaluating a child's intellectual abilities and as a predictor of future educational achievement. Robinson and Chamrad (1986), for example, took note of the valuable information yielded by intelligence tests, such as a child's scores, mental age estimates, predictions regarding the child's future academic achievement, and clinical observations made during the testing session. At the same time, they acknowledged that intelligence tests are not perfect and will not result in 100% accurate identification of gifted children, and that intelligence tests measure only intelligence and not other worthwhile characteristics of a child, such as creativity and other artistic talents.

Kaufman and Harrison (1986), too, acknowledged the limitations of intelligence tests, but argue convincingly in favor of their use for identifying gifted children. Intelligence tests, they argue, are very good predictors of academic achievement and academic success, and they have the most solid psychometric properties of all other kinds of tests used with gifted individuals. In addition, they pointed out that intelligence tests can identify as gifted, children who might otherwise go undetected because of behavior problems, learning disabilities, physical handicaps, or other attention-demanding characteristics that might cause educators or other professionals to overlook the child's intellectual abilities.

In addition, Kaufman and Harrison (1986) cautioned psychologists and educators to use intelligence tests responsibly. In particular, they cited the importance of using multiple criteria, not a single intelligence test score, in determining eligibility for gifted programs, and they stress that standard errors of measurement should always be taken into account. Further, they caution against making placement decisions in the absence of educational planning. That is, a child who is identified as gifted may be placed in a gifted program, but this placement should be made in the context of longer term educational planning for that child.

Despite the numerous cautions against misuse of, or over reliance on, intelligence tests for identification of gifted children, Kaufman and Harrison's (1986) point is well taken that there currently exists no method that has been demonstrated to be superior to intelligence tests for this purpose.

Pfeiffer (2002) echoed many of Kaufman and Harrison's (1986) suggestions in an article proposing best practices in identifying gifted students. The article included the following recommendations for psychologists and educators: gain familiarity with gifted children and their families, recognize the multiple manifestations of giftedness, appreciate the developmental nature of talent development and the developmental trajectories unique to the different domains of giftedness, and assess academic motivation when evaluating giftedness.

INTELLIGENCE AND THE WISC-III

Seiver et al. (1994) investigated the relationship between the WISC-R and the WISC-III with gifted children by administering the WISC-III to 35 elementary school students in a gifted program who had previously been administered the WISC-R. They found the students' WISC-III global scores to be significantly lower than the WISC-R scores, such that 14 children (or 40%) in their sample would not have been placed in the local gifted program if the WISC-III had been used to determine eligibility. Sabatino et al. (1995) conducted a similar investigation, employing a more robust methodology. They administered both tests in a counterbalanced design, to 51 gifted children. They found very high agreement between the two tests, such that all 51 of their subjects who were found eligible for a gifted program with one test, also would have been found eligible had the other test been used.

Without comparing it to other tests, Kaufman (1992) evaluated the psychometric strength of the WISC-III for gifted children. He found that the WISC-III places unduly high emphasis on the speed of the child's performance, and that low subtest stability can complicate an educator's or psychologist's efforts to interpret children's profiles. Overall, however, he stated that the WISC-III is quite useful for identifying gifted children in that it is a "carefully constructed, technically superior instrument with attractive materials, sensitive items (by gender and ethnicity), exceptional standardization(s), strong construct validity, reliable and stable IQ scores, and intelligently written manuals that facilitate test interpretation" (p. 158). Furthermore, he pointed out that the majority of subtests have ceiling ranging "from adequate to exceptional" (p. 158).

Watkins et al. (2002) recently conducted a factor analytic study of WISC-III performance of 505 gifted students. Results indicated a two-factor solution that approximated the Verbal Comprehension and Perceptual Reasoning indexes best demonstrated the strengths of the gifted students. Furthermore, Arithmetic, Coding and Picture Arrangement did not contribute to this solution. It is of interest that Arithmetic is no longer a part of the core battery and Picture Arrangement has been deleted from the WISC-IV.

WISC-IV STANDARDIZATION SAMPLE: PROFILES OF GIFTEDNESS

The changes from the WISC-III to the WISC-IV are substantial in both structure and content. Structurally, the WISC-IV has dropped the verbal intelligence quotient/performance intelligence quotient (VIQ/PIQ) designation to fully adopt the more valid four-factor model. The new model retains the previous factors Verbal Comprehension and Processing Speed, and adds in a reconceptualized Perceptual Reasoning factor. A new factor, Working Memory completes the four-factor model. With respect to content, there are new subtests in the core assessment including Perceptual Reasoning subtests – Matrix Reasoning and Picture Concepts, and a Working Memory subtest – Letter–Number Sequencing. The supplemental subtests have been reconfigured to include previous core subtests, Arithmetic, Picture Completion, and Information, with two new subtests Cancellation and Word Reasoning. A full discussion of these changes appear earlier in this volume.

For the purposes of the WISC-IV standardization sample, giftedness was defined based on an existing score of two standard deviations above the mean on the WISC-III (60% of the gifted sample) or another standardized measure of cognitive abilities either individual (SB-IV, WJ-R/III, or KABC) (Thorndike et al., 1986; Woodcock & Johnson, 1989; Woodcock et al., 2001; and Kaufman & Kaufman, 1983 respectively) or group administered (Otis-19% of the sample, or CogAT-10% of the gifted sample) (Otis & Lennon, 1997; and Lohman& Hagen, 2001 respectively). In all, 63 children ages 6–16 from the standardization sample were categorized as gifted and their results in comparison to a matched control sample on the WISC-IV are summarized in the *WISC-IV Technical and Interpretative Manual* (Wechsler, 2003, p. 77). In general, students in the gifted sample significantly outperformed students in the matched control sample on the WISC-IV subtests. However, on two subtests, the optional Cancellation subtest and the required Coding subtest, the differences between the two groups were non-significant, indicating that these subtests did not distinguish students identified as gifted from the control sample. Both of these subtests fall under the Processing Speed factor and these non-significant findings are consistent with previous reports that suggest that processing speed is not a distinguishing characteristic of gifted individuals (Kaufman, 1993). In this regard, the new framework of the WISC-IV, with the lowered emphasis on Processing Speed in the Verbal Comprehension, Perceptual Reasoning, and Working Memory factors may actually assist psychologists in identifying gifted individuals whose gifts fall predominantly in the verbal or perceptual domains of intelligence. However, with the new factor structure, two measures of Processing Speed (Coding and Symbol Search) are included in the Full Scale IQ (FSIQ), as opposed to the WISC-III where only Coding (or optionally Symbol Search) contributed. This may be a disadvantage in identifying gifted individuals if an FSIQ is used.

Of note in the standardization sample is the large number of students previously identified as gifted who are not performing two standard deviations above the mean on any factor of the WISC-IV. It is unclear if this discrepancy is a product of the considerable changes to both the content and the structure from the WISC-III to the WISC-IV, or of there being a large number of students (29%) who are included in the WISC-IV gifted sample based solely on a group-administered cognitive ability test that offers a less valid measure of abilities than an individually administered one. If we consider only the 34 students from the gifted sample who performed two standard deviations above the mean on a WISC-IV factor, the results in comparison to their matched controls indicate that although the four factors still discriminate between the two groups, the subtests Cancellation (Randomized, Structured, and Total), Coding, Digit Span Backward, and Word Reasoning demonstrate no significant differences between gifted and matched controls (see the table below).

Subtest	Mean score for students with at least one index score over 130	Mean score for matched control students	F	p-value
Arithmetic	14.83	11.42	23.974	.000
Block Design – no time bonus	14.61	11.08	25.846	.000
Block Design	15.17	11.42	22.929	.000
Cancellation – randomized	10.50	10.63	.021	.886
Cancellation – structured	10.56	10.92	.205	.654
Cancellation – total	10.72	11.04	.127	.723
Coding	11.83	10.96	.727	.399
Comprehension	14.83	11.46	17.328	.000
Digit Span – bwd	11.78	11.04	.710	.405
Digit Span – fwd	12.56	10.25	6.127	.018
Digit Span – total	12.78	10.67	4.625	.038
Information	14.56	12.54	7.571	.009
Letter–Number Sequencing	13.56	10.71	13.591	.001
Matrix Reasoning	14.89	11.33	23.312	.000
Picture Completion	13.72	11.17	12.161	.001
Picture Concepts	13.17	11.21	8.372	.006
Similarities	15.28	12.00	19.946	.000
Symbol Search	13.22	11.08	5.258	.029
Vocabulary	15.39	12.00	21.451	.000
Word Reasoning	12.56	12.17	1.556	.615

In addition, of the 34 students who scored greater than 130 on a factor of the WISC-IV, 27 achieved this score on the Verbal Comprehension factor, 4 additional (9 total) students achieved greater than 130 on the Perceptual Reasoning factor, and one additional student attained a score greater than 130 in each of the Working Memory, Processing Speed, and Full Scale factors. For this sample, Verbal Comprehension was the important defining factor in determining giftedness, although we do not wish to discount other areas of giftedness that may be less prevalent, but are still important to success in school and beyond. The inability of Processing Speed subtests Coding and Cancellation to discriminate between the groups was expected based on previous findings and assertions that speed is not a defining characteristic of intelligence (Sternberg, 1982). It was surprising to note that the new Working Memory factor, often conceptualized as a higher-level skill than processing speed was not more influential in defining this gifted group and in addition, that the optional subtest Word Reasoning, from the Verbal Comprehension factor did not discriminate between the two groups. The information regarding both the subtests and factor scores will be important to take into consideration in determining which subtests and/or factors to administer when assessing a child for giftedness.

HOW THE CHANGES TO THE WISC-IV IMPACT GIFTED IDENTIFICATION

Although the WISC-III also had an optional four-factor structure, the dropping of the VIQ/PIQ structure from the WISC-IV will result in the widespread use of the more descriptive and discriminating four-factor model. For gifted students the new structure appears to provide a more discriminating means of identification for gifted programming. The greater weighting of the Verbal Comprehension and Perceptual Reasoning factors (3 subtests each) into the Full Scale score is of benefit to students with strengths in these higher-level cognitive areas. In addition, the separation of speed-based tasks into a separate factor allows students who have strengths in the higher-level cognitive demands of the verbal comprehension and perceptual reasoning tasks to demonstrate their skills with time to reflect. It is interesting to note in the standardization sample that although these students did not perform significantly better than controls on the traditional processing speed tasks such as Coding and Cancellation, on the higher-level task, Block Design, which now offers options for scoring with and without time bonuses, the gifted students did not show any benefit from the no time bonus option. Still, the option of scoring Block Design without time bonuses will be important for students who demonstrate high ability on solving the problems, but who are more reflective in their approach to the task.

The four factors have all been changed to some degree. Verbal Comprehension has remained very similar to the WISC-III factor of the same name. For the gifted population, the skills required in the Verbal Comprehension factor are traditionally the strongest indicators of giftedness and this was found to be true with the standardization sample. The core subtests that comprise this high-level, language-based factor are all familiar subtests from the WISC-III – Comprehension, Similarities, and Vocabulary. Two subtests are designated as supplemental in the Verbal Comprehension factor. Information is relegated from core status and Word Reasoning was brought in as a new subtest. However, Word Reasoning, did not turn out to be a highly discriminating subtest with the above 130 gifted standardization sample, suggesting that this supplemental subtest should be used with caution in gifted identification.

Perceptual Reasoning has changed significantly from the old Perceptual Organization factor. It includes, two new core reasoning subtests – Matrix Reasoning and Picture Concepts, in addition to Block Design. All of these subtests were found to discriminate between the gifted and control standardization samples. Although all the factors have undergone some degree of change, the only new factor is the Working Memory factor. Before looking at the standardization sample, we hypothesized that Working Memory would be a better discriminating factor than Processing Speed for students who were gifted. Although both Processing Speed and Working Memory did discriminate between the gifted and control samples, in both of these factors there were component tasks (Digit Span Backward, Cancellation, and Coding) for which there were no differences between the two groups. In addition, only one student would have been identified as gifted based solely on the Processing Speed or Working Memory factors.

Given the discrepancies often seen in gifted children between the stronger higher-level Verbal Comprehension or Perceptual Reasoning tasks and the relatively weaker skills, especially in Processing Speed, it will be important to carefully consider scores obtained on the WISC-IV. One important consideration is the use of the General Ability Index or GAI (see Raiford et al., 2005 for the US GAI norms and Saklofske et al., 2005 for the Canadian GAI norms). The option of calculating the GAI that comprises only the Verbal Comprehension and Perceptual Reasoning scores into a single composite may often be more advisable to use than the FSIQ in identifying children who are gifted. The decision to use the GAI in place of the FSIQ in determining program eligibility should likely be made a priori and correspond to the goals of the gifted program. A second consideration in identifying students who are gifted is assessing which discrepancies may be clinically important. A superior Verbal Comprehension score and a high average Processing Speed score may create a significant discrepancy that bears little or no clinical relevance or validity for the child. Fortunately, the *WISC-IV Manual* offers tables indicating base rates of discrepancies for aiding in the interpretation of index differences. Finally, as we move forward in our understanding of giftedness, investigations into WISC-IV profiles and their relationship with success in gifted programs will be of interest. While it is clear that many identified gifted students have stronger Verbal Comprehension and Perceptual Reasoning performance and relatively weaker Working Memory and Processing Speed performance, it will be interesting to see how the academic performance of these students compares to the performance of students with more uniform superior profiles of ability on the WISC-IV.

CEILING EFFECTS AND POTENTIAL SOLUTIONS

One issue that has received a great deal of attention in cognitive ability testing and extremely gifted students is the potential impact of ceiling effects in determining valid estimates of "intelligence." One solution that has been proposed to mediate the impact of possible underestimates of IQ is the use of Ratio IQ scores. Ratio IQ scores are calculated based on age equivalent scores (e.g., mental age/biological age $\times$ 100). However, age equivalent scores are less reliable in general than standard scores and become even less reliable with advanced test-takers (Bracken, 1988) – thus their use for children who are gifted and in particular, older gifted students seem ill advised.

A second potential solution to the problem of ceiling effects is the use of extended norms that have been developed by the publishers of the WISC-IV (Zhu et al., 2008). These norms, developed in response to the identified problem of differentiating highly gifted students (IQ or GAI above 150) from gifted students (IQ or GAI 130–150) offer administrators a means to quantify exceptional performances (see Appendix A for extended norms tables provided by the WISC-IV publishers). Specifically, the extended norms were developed using the standardization data and a set of data provided by the National Association for Gifted Children and offer scaled subtest scores as high as 28 and composite scores up to 210 (Zhu et al., 2008). The authors of the technical report on these norms caution that this approach is only applicable for extremely gifted students and recommend that extended norms be used only when a student achieves ceiling performance (score of 18 or 19) on two subtests (Zhu et al., 2008). While exciting in its potential, it is important to consider some of the current limitations of the use of extended norms. Given the natural ceiling of the test, maximum extended scaled scores are not the same across the subtests and not the same across different ages. Greater range of scaled scores is available at younger ages, presenting potential problems in comparing the performance of children of different ages and the same child's performance at different points in time. Finally, as identified by the authors of the extended norms, scores at these extreme levels are very rare (1 in 20,000,000 expected to obtain a score above 180) (Zhu et al., 2008) and therefore great care should be taken in interpreting what meaning these scores have clinically. As very few individuals will perform at these high levels on these measures we have little understanding of meaningful differences in obtained scores.

CASE STUDY OF KATE

A case study of a gifted student highlights some of the resolved and unresolved issues in the WISC-IV. Kate is a fifth grade student who was assessed at the age of 6 years 4 months with the WISC-III and determined to have very superior general ability. For the purposes of educational planning, Kate was assessed again at the age of 10 years 2 months with the Woodcock-Johnson Tests of Cognitive Abilities. Two months later, at the age of 10 years 4 months, she was administered the WISC-IV for the purposes of providing information for this chapter. The WISC-III and WISC-IV scores presented below are very similar despite the significant changes that were made to the newer measure. Kate's Verbal Comprehension performance remained virtually the same and although the perceptual tasks changed from having an emphasis on visualization to having an emphasis on reasoning, her scores remained highly similar. The Freedom from Distractibility Index changed from the WISC-III to the WISC-IV to a purely Working Memory measure and Kate's performance decreased slightly with this new change. Interestingly, with the virtually identical Processing Speed Index (PSI), Kate's performance increased.

There are a number of issues to note in Kate's WISC-IV performance. As with the standardization sample, Kate performed best in the Verbal Comprehension domain and had a relatively weaker performance in Processing Speed, with the Coding subtest score only in the average range. In this case, the GAI score may better reflect Kate's highest level of potential when speed of performance is not a factor. Her performance also highlights the issue of statistical significance versus clinical significance. Although there is a significant difference between her higher Verbal Comprehension score and her lower Processing Speed score, it is clear that Processing Speed is not an area of deficit for Kate. Her score is still within the superior range indicating that this is not a difference of clinical importance. Finally, as with the WISC-III, ceiling effects continue to be an issue with the WISC-IV. Kate's performance on the Vocabulary measure in particular yielded a raw score of 63. However, any raw score between 55 and 68 yields a standard score of 19 for her age group. This ceiling effect is most significant at the younger ages, where raw score point spreads of up to 35 can yield the same score at the highest level. For children who are highly gifted, this can underestimate their true ability. With the extended norms recently developed, Kate's performance on the Vocabulary subtest would yield a scaled score of 24 for her age group and her score on the Similarities subtest would yield a scaled score of 21. This would raise her Verbal Comprehension standard score from 144 to 160. On the WJ-III administered to Kate 2 months prior to the WISC-IV, Kate scored 170 on a measure of Verbal Ability (including Verbal Comprehension and General Information subtests), indicating that without the extended norms the WISC-IV may be underestimating her verbal ability. Kate is an individual whose WISC-IV Verbal Comprehension performance may be better understood with the use of the recently developed extended norms. Of course, in practical terms, both of these scores will allow Kate access to most if not all special programs or resources serving the gifted. However, for students who demonstrate significant discrepancy in their profile, one or more subtest scores that underestimate their true potential may have a deleterious effect on their program eligibility and in these cases the extended norms may have more practical applications.

The use of WISC-IV as part of global assessment of gifted children is shown in the table given below.

Kate 6 years 4 months

WISC-III	Factor scores	Subtest scores
Full Scale	146	
Verbal Comprehension	143	
Information		19
Similarities		19
Vocabulary		19
Comprehension		13
Perceptual Organization	124	
Picture Completion		11
Picture Arrangement		14
Block Design		14
Object Assembly		17
Freedom from Distractibility	150	
Arithmetic		19
Digit Span		19
Processing Speed	114	
Coding		8
Symbol Search		17

Kate 10 years 4 months

WISC-IV	Factor scores	Subtest scores
Full Scale	142	
Verbal Comprehension	144	
Similarities		19
Vocabulary		19
Comprehension		14
Perceptual Reasoning	129	
Block Design		16
Picture Concepts		14
Matrix Reasoning		14
Working Memory	135	
Digit Span		18
Letter–Number Sequencing		14
Processing Speed	123	
Coding		12
Symbol Search		16

As mentioned earlier, a number of authorities have recommended the use of multiple measures in the identification of giftedness (Kaufman & Harrison, 1986; Pfeiffer, 2001). A single test score should never be used alone in making a diagnostic or classificatory decision. Overall *predictive accuracy* (i.e., the overall probability that the result of an assessment procedure accurately identifies individuals as having a certain condition – in this instance, giftedness) is increased with the judicious use of technically meritorious, multiple measures, and clinical procedures (Pfeiffer, 2002).

TREATMENT AND INTERVENTION PLANS INFORMED BY WISC-IV RESULTS

In the recent reauthorization of Individuals with Disabilities Education Improvement Act (IDEA), there was a major shift in identification of the largest group of students in special education, those students with learning disabilities. The approach introduced is referred to as "Response to Intervention" or RtI and promotes the idea that students can best be identified as having special educational needs by observing how they respond to appropriate interventions. This theoretical shift from reliance on testing as the sole determinant of special education status has had a large impact on special education as a whole and this section will focus on the potential role the WISC-IV can play within this model, particularly with respect to students who are gifted.

RtI offers an alternative means of identifying students' educational needs earlier and intervening with research-based methods of intervention, however, it does not discount the use of standardized assessments in the process. When students do not respond to the scientific, research-based interventions, standardized assessment can provide valuable insights into the specific needs of the individual child. Within the population of students who are gifted, the use of standardized measures of cognitive ability, and in particular, the WISC-IV, continue to have important implications for (1) identification, (2) understanding of responsiveness or non-responsiveness to interventions, and (3) planning of more individually tailored and therefore effective programs.

IDENTIFICATION

Within the population of students with special needs, there is a subset of children who remain under-identified. Studies have indicated that students who have both high ability and learning difficulties are an often unidentified and underserved population within our school systems (Brody & Mills, 1997; Ferri et al., 1997; Bianco, 2005). These students may use their high ability to compensate or hide their areas of difficulties and end up underachieving and possibly experiencing emotional difficulties as they struggle to keep up with their peers. While some of these students may underachieve sufficiently to be identified as at-risk and receive services under RtI, others may never be identified as at-risk under the RtI model and therefore not receive the appropriate interventions. For both these groups of students, appropriate intervention that addresses both their areas of strength and areas of need may never be made available.

For example, consider the case of Sarah, a third grade student who was achieving at grade level, however, her parents noted that she cried each night at being placed in a lower reading group and that her oral language abilities appeared to be much higher than her basic reading and spelling skills. Sarah was given the WISC-IV as part of a psychoeducational assessment and her results on the WISC-IV are presented below.

WISC-IV	Factor scores	Subtest scores	Percentile
Full Scale	130		98
Verbal Comprehension	144		99.8
Similarities		16	
Vocabulary		18	
Comprehension		18	
Perceptual Reasoning	121		92
Block Design		13	
Picture Concepts		14	
Matrix Reasoning		13	
Working Memory	102		55
Digit Span		10	
Letter–Number Sequencing		11	
Processing Speed	121		92
Coding		13	
Symbol Search		14	

As can be seen, Sarah is a student with superior cognitive ability in the area of verbal comprehension and high average perceptual reasoning. She also demonstrated the ability to process information quickly and average working/short-term memory ability. In summary, she demonstrated no significant weaknesses in her cognitive profile and superior verbal comprehension ability.

On measures of academic achievement it was noted that Sarah had visually memorized a large sight vocabulary and with her strong verbal comprehension ability was able to use meaning to assist in filling in words in connected text. However, she experienced significant difficulty in decoding unfamiliar single words and nonsense words. Her teachers had considered her an average student as her reading comprehension was in the average range, however, Sarah was a child who had the potential to be achieving at a higher level and was experiencing a specific difficulty in reading decoding that she was able to hide with her strong verbal comprehension ability. With the new information from the psychoeducational assessment, Sarah was provided a research-based reading decoding intervention and was eligible for a gifted program. Her academic achievement, confidence, and engagement in school increased significantly with the appropriate interventions. Sarah is a child who was achieving at grade level, was not reported to be at-risk by her teachers, and therefore may not have been identified by an RtI approach, however, through standardized testing, she became eligible for the reading intervention services offered through RtI and quickly improved her reading decoding and overall academic achievement. In addition, she was identified for gifted programming and interventions that supported the development of her strong verbal cognitive abilities.

UNDERSTANDING RESPONSIVENESS AND NON-RESPONSIVENESS TO INTERVENTION

In addition to the possible contribution of the WISC-IV to identification of students with special educational needs, standardized tests may also play a role in the RtI model in understanding responsiveness and non-responsiveness to the interventions being provided to students who are gifted. In a review of the literature, Fuchs and Young (2006) found that IQ is a frequent predictor to responsiveness to reading intervention, in particular, interventions that offer a combination of decoding, fluency, and comprehension instruction were found to be more mediated by IQ than just phonological awareness instruction. With its multiple factors (Verbal Comprehension, Perceptual Reasoning, Working Memory, and Processing Speed), the WISC-IV may provide a means to better understand individual student's strengths and weaknesses and their degree of RtI.

For example, consider the case of Warren, a fifth grade student who although was receiving above average grades in his classes and was in a gifted program, he was demonstrating difficulties expressing his ideas, especially in written assignments. He also performed poorly on group-administered standardized tests in school and required longer to complete assignments. Warren's teachers reported that if he was asked to perform tasks quickly, he "shut down" and would not do the work. Warren had received numerous interventions throughout his school career, particularly focusing on developing his written expression, however, he continued to experience difficulties and anxiety regarding his academic work. Standardized testing with the WISC-IV revealed the following factor scores:

WISC-IV	Factor scores	Percentile
Verbal Comprehension	132	98
Perceptual Reasoning	141	99.7
Working Memory	135	99
Processing Speed	78	7

Warren's performance on the WISC-IV, and the extreme discrepancy between his low processing speed and his other factor scores, provided his teachers and himself with insight into his learning needs. This insight may otherwise be unavailable or may be attributed to social-emotional difficulties, such as test anxiety.

In addition to processing speed, students may have discrepancies within specific other domains of learning that are revealed by performance on the WISC-IV factor scores. One factor of the WISC-IV that has received particular attention with regards to learning disabilities is the Working Memory factor. In the WISC-IV, the Working Memory factor has been strengthened by the addition of the Letter–Number Sequencing subtest. A 3-year longitudinal study found that working memory growth in students with reading disability is slower and that working memory is related to growth in reading comprehension and reading fluency (Swanson & Jerman, 2006). For a student who is struggling to read, understanding their cognitive profile can provide insight into what interventions may be most effective. For example, for a student with an early reading difficulty, if they also have a working memory deficit, it may be important to focus on reading decoding, as well as comprehension and reading fluency development as the student progresses through school. In addition, the instructor may benefit from knowing that this student may have difficulty holding onto and working with information in immediate awareness, for example, sounding out a word, holding all those sounds in immediate awareness and blending the sounds to decode a word.

For a student who has a working memory deficit and also has high ability in other domains, intervention may focus not only on developing areas of weakness, but also developing and using areas of strength to motivate the student. Cara is a student in third grade with a significant reading decoding and spelling difficulty who has been receiving a scientific, research-based intervention since kindergarten as promoted by RtI. She is continuing to struggle with reading decoding and spelling despite receiving this intervention and is beginning to demonstrate signs of frustration and resistance to trying. A psychoeducational assessment, including the WISC-IV revealed the following profile:

WISC-IV	Factor scores	Subtest scores	Percentile
Verbal Comprehension	134		99
Similarities		15	
Vocabulary		13	
Comprehension		19	
Perceptual Reasoning	106		66
Block Design		11	
Picture Concepts		12	
Matrix Reasoning		10	
Working Memory	83		13
Digit Span		7	
Letter–Number Sequencing			
Processing Speed	112		79
Coding		10	
Symbol Search		14	
(Cancellation)		(14)	

The WISC-IV revealed that not only does Cara have a weakness in working memory, she has very superior verbal comprehension. Cara's teachers had focused their efforts on developing her reading decoding and spelling and her strength in verbal comprehension had been overlooked. The WISC-IV provided a different way of looking at Cara's learning and by offering her programming designed to highlight her strengths, her frustration decreased and her effort in improving her decoding and spelling increased. In addition, the reading teacher was able to revise the way the reading program was being delivered to compensate for Cara's working memory difficulties and take advantage of her verbal comprehension strengths. Cara is a student who may only have qualified for services for her reading disability without the standardized testing that revealed she was also a student who would benefit from a gifted program.

DEVELOPING INDIVIDUALLY TARGETED INTERVENTIONS

RtI often relies on understanding the learning strengths and weaknesses of the individual child and what is motivating to them. Many of the programs designed for students with learning difficulties require the student to engage in tasks that are inherently not as interesting or motivating for many students, for example, repetition, reading of phonetically controlled texts, flash cards. Finding strategies to keep a student engaged, motivated, and learning skills that are difficult for them is a challenge for educators. For students who are gifted, frustration may occur even faster and the challenge may be even greater to keep them engaged. The WISC-IV may provide insights for educators on best ways to reach students who are gifted and have learning difficulties.

Student's who are gifted may become frustrated more quickly with interventions that focus exclusively on their areas of weakness. Acknowledging students areas of strength and supporting the development of these strengths may increase a student's motivation to develop their areas of weakness (e.g., Baum et al., 2001). Students who have both gifts and learning difficulties have been found to benefit from programs that both develop their areas of strength as well as their areas of weakness (Shevitz et al., 2003; Cooper et al., 2004). In addition, strengths can often be used to help compensate for areas of weakness. Interventions that take advantage of a student's areas of strength may provide more benefit to the child. For example, for a child with strong verbal comprehension skills, ensuring that they are being exposed to reading material, stories, information, and discussions that continue to develop their vocabulary and general information may increase their motivation to read and keep learning in their areas of interest. In addition, providing these challenging activities helps to ensure that students are not falling behind their peers in vocabulary and general information even if they are not able to read the books at their level of understanding.

In addition, students with gifts are often more aware of their learning, have a greater understanding, and their self-esteem may suffer more quickly if placed in a remedial reading or learning group. For example, a student with high verbal comprehension may understand books at a very high level, but if they also have a reading disability, they may only be able to decode very simple text. This discrepancy between books they enjoy and comprehend and books they can read independently may be very apparent to them when compared to their peers. Understanding the emotional impact of how interventions are implemented with this group will be important to their success.

Finally, there is evidence to suggest that students with gifts differ in their approach to their areas of weakness and may develop different compensatory strategies than students who have lower IQ's. For example, one study found that students with higher IQ (mean 117.7) have more severe phonological difficulties than those students whose IQ is lower (Johnston & Morrison, 2007). This study found that higher IQ students had more difficulty taking a phonological approach to tasks when compared to reading-age-matched controls, including having more difficulty decoding non-words. The authors suggest that higher IQ students with reading difficulties are taking a visual approach for reading high frequency words and not using the more effective orthographic–phonological–semantic approach that is most effective in fluent reading (Johnston & Morrison, 2007). Understanding possible differences in approach and compensatory strategies of students who are gifted will assist in developing the most effective approach for intervening.

SUMMARY OF THE WISC-IV AND INTERVENTION

Although recent trends in education have focused on using an RtI model in identifying students with special educational needs, the WISC-IV continues to hold a valuable place in identifying the learning needs of students, understanding their responsiveness to interventions, and assisting in planning effective interventions. This is particularly true for students who are gifted. Students who are gifted have special educational needs, particularly if they also have learning difficulties. The WISC-IV provides a means to better understand the learning profiles of these unique students, so that more effective intervention programs can be implemented to both address their areas of strength and develop their areas of weakness.

THE GRS: PART OF A COMPREHENSIVE GIFTED ASSESSMENT

Recognizing the value of a well-designed teacher-completed rating scale to complement the WISC-IV (and WPPSI-III) in the identification of gifted students, and as a stand-alone screening tool, The Psychological Corporation supported the development of the *GRS*. Published in 2003, standardization of the *GRS* was linked with the standardization of the WISC-IV and WPPSI-III. The following principles guided the development of the *GRS*:

- *User-friendly*: the *GRS* requires minimal training to administer, score and interpret.
- *Scientifically sound*: the *GRS* is reliable and accurate in identifying gifted students.
- *Simple interpretation*: the *GRS* conceptualizes giftedness in a straightforward, direct, and conceptually meaningful way.
- *Flexible*: the *GRS* can be used as a stand-alone screening instrument, with other diagnostic procedures such as auditions and portfolio samples, and with the WISC-IV as part of a comprehensive test battery.

The *GRS* includes a School Form (*GRS-S*) and a Preschool/Kindergarten Form (*GRS-P*) in order to account for developmental differences in giftedness across the age range from 4:0 years to 13:11 years. Although the two forms are similar in format, item overlap is only 29%.

Item development began with an exhaustive review and critique of existing rating scales (Jarosewich et al., 2002). This was followed by a survey of experts in the gifted field (Pfeiffer, 2003) and a review of the talent development and gifted literatures. Experts in child development, education, school psychology, giftedness, and talent development were then invited to react to an initial pool of items, which subsequently went through a number of revisions as a result of a pilot test, field testing, and final item editing.

Since this chapter focuses on the assessment of gifted children with the WISC-IV, we will only discuss the *GRS-S*, designed for children in elementary and middle school, grades 1–8, ages 6:0–13:11. (The reader interested in testing gifted preschool and kindergarten students is encouraged to read the *GRS Manual* (Pfeiffer & Jarosewich, 2003)). The *GRS-S* consists of six scales. Each scale has twelve items. Each item is rated on a nine-point scale divided into three ranges: 1–3 below average, 4–6 average, and 7–9 above average. This format permits the rater to determine first whether the student is below average, average, or above average for a specific behavior, compared to other students of the same age. The teacher then determines, within the range, whether the child is at the bottom, middle, or top of the given range. Ratings of 1, 2, and 3 are part of the below average category; ratings of 4, 5, and 6 the average category; and ratings of 7, 8, and 9 the above average category.

The six scales on the GRS represent five types of giftedness (intellectual ability, academic ability, creativity, artistic talent, and leadership ability) as well as motivation. Motivation refers to the student's drive or persistence, desire to succeed, tendency to enjoy challenging tasks, and ability to work well without encouragement. Motivation is not viewed as a type of giftedness but rather as a clinically useful and psychometrically reliable measure of how hard the student is working, whether or not s/he is gifted. The *GRS-S* yields five scale scores indicating the likelihood that a student is gifted in one or more of five areas of giftedness.

For each of the 72 items on the *GRS-S*, the teacher is asked to rate the student compared to other children of the same age. An illustrative item is provided for each of the six scales. These items are copyrighted and should not be reproduced or transmitted, without written permission from the publisher.

- Intellectual ability: *Learns difficult concepts easily*
- Academic ability: *Completes academic work unassisted*
- Creativity: *Approaches the world "as a scientist" or explorer*
- Artistic talent: *Performs or produces art marked by detail, complexity, sophistication, and/or richness*
- Leadership ability: *Gets others to work together*
- Motivation: *Reacts to challenges enthusiastically*

GRS-S raw scores are converted to *T*-scores with a mean of 50 and a standard deviation of 10. The student's *T*-score on each of the gifted scales indicates the degree to which the student's ratings deviate from the standardization sample's average score. The *T*-scores were computed based on each age group and are age adjusted so that the ranges may be applied across age bands and *GRS* forms.

Standardization samples were collected across the United States. For the *GRS-S*, 600 children ages 6:0–13:11 were rated by their teachers. This sample was stratified within eight 12-month age bands from 6:0 to 13:11. Samples were stratified to match the US census by ethnicity and parent education level.

The *GRS Manual* (Pfeiffer & Jarosewich, 2003) includes detailed information on the reliability and validity of the test. We encourage the interested reader to review the manual. The manual reports that a sample of 406 students ages 6:0–13:11 participated in a *GRS-S*: WISC-IV validity study. The average age was 9.9 years, 49.3% were female, 50.7% male. Distribution by race/ethnicity was: 67% White, 17% African American, 10% Hispanic, 5% Asian, and 1% others. Distribution by parent level of education was: 3%, 8 years or fewer; 8%, 9–11 years; 27%, 12 years; 33%, 13–15 years; 29%, 16 years or more.

The great majority of correlations between the *GRS-S* scale scores and WISC-IV full scale and subscale scores were significant: 44 of the 120 correlations were significant at the $p < .001$ level (36.6%) and 61 of the 120 correlations were significant at the $p < .01$ level (50.8%). As one might predict, the *GRS-S* Intellectual and Academic Ability Scales correlated most strongly with the WISC-IV subtest and composite scores. The *GRS-S* Intellectual Ability Scale correlated .53 with WISC-IV FSIQ, .45 with Verbal Comprehension Index (VCI), .42 with Perceptual Reasoning Index (PRI), .39 with Working Memory Index (WMI), and .32 with Processing Speed Index (PSI). All of these correlations are significant at $p < .001$ level.

Only 15 of the 120 *GRS-S*: WISC-IV correlations were not significant (12.5%); 9 of these 15 non-significant correlations were WISC-IV subtests not correlating significantly with the *GRS-S* leadership ability scale score.

Data from the standardization sample that included *all* subjects with *both* GRS and WISC-IV data was used to analyze the diagnostic accuracy of the rating scale. The sub-sample consisted of 196 boys and 185 girls and closely matched the US population on race/ethnicity, parent education level, and geographic representation.

Multiple statistical analyses were conducted, including: *sensitivity*, the proportion of children which the *GRS-S* correctly detected as intellectually gifted; *specificity*, the proportion of children correctly identified by the *GRS-S* as *not* intellectually gifted; *likelihood ratio*, an index of the accuracy of a test which depicts what the odds are that a positive test result comes from a youngster who is gifted; and *overall correct classification*.

The *GRS-S* was successful in both correctly identifying individuals who are intellectually gifted (test sensitivity) and correctly identifying individuals who are not intellectually gifted (test specificity), especially when intellectually gifted was operationally defined as intellectual ability in the top 5%. Using a *T* score of 60, as suggested in the test manual as demarcating a *high probability of gifted*, the overall correct classification rate for intellectually gifted was .82 with a WISC-IV IQ of 130 and .80 with a WISC-IV IQ of 115 (Pfeiffer & Jarosewich, 2007).

In addition to its use in the screening and identifying of multiple manifestations of giftedness, the *GRS* was designed to measure change over time in a student's profile of abilities. The *GRS* as a measure of reliable change over time is helpful in determining gifted program eligibility when an academically precocious student comes close but doesn't quite make the district or state cut-score for gifted eligibility (Pfeiffer et al., 2006). The GRS as a measure of reliable change over time can also be used to measure a student's progress in a gifted program.

The procedure to measure change using the *GRS* is fairly straightforward. The practitioner simply compares a student's original *GRS* scale score(s) with a range of scores that take into account the variability expected by both regression to the mean and measurement error (Atkinson, 1991). Standard error of prediction (*SEp*) scores provide confidence bands for *T* scores so that a second and more recent set of *T* scores can be compared with an original set of *T* scores (Pfeiffer et al., 2006).

The *GRS-S* can be easily used as a first-stage, screening instrument to screen an entire class, school, or school district. The *GRS-S* also can be used as a second-stage screening device with a target subgroup of the school population who have already been identified using another method (e.g., students nominated by their last year teacher or scoring above a certain level on an end-of-year achievement test). Finally, the *GRS-S* can be used as part of a test battery in assessing giftedness. The *GRS-S* is designed to complement the WISC-IV in identifying intellectually and academically gifted students.

CASE STUDY OF LAQUISHA

The following case example illustrates the use of the *GRS-S* with the WISC-IV. The name of the student and some of the information has been changed to protect her confidentiality. Laquisha was recommended for the school's gifted program by her teacher. Laquisha is a well-behaved, easy going, and friendly 10 year-old described by her parents and teacher as a "born leader." She obtained the following scores as part of her gifted evaluation:

GRS-S (Mean = 50, SD = 10)

Domain	T-score	Classification
Intellectual ability	58	Moderate probability gifted
Academic ability	62	High probability gifted
Creativity	54	Low probability gifted
Artistic talent	54	Low probability gifted
Leadership	66	High probability
Motivation	62	Above average-to-high motivation

WISC-IV (Mean = 100, SD = 15)

Verbal Comprehension	121	Superior
Perceptual Reasoning	114	High average
Working Memory	124	Superior
Processing Speed Score	110	High average

Laquisha's *GRS-S* scores indicate that the teacher who completed the rating scale perceives this solid B student as having a moderate probability of being intellectually gifted and a high probability of being academically gifted. However, her scores on the WISC-IV (and a review of her classroom work and scores on the Wechsler Individual Achievement Test – WIAT II) do not provide corroborating evidence in support of an intellectually or academically gifted classification. Laquisha's academic and cognitive skills are higher than many other students of the same age and grade but not within the gifted range of ability. Although not necessarily a candidate for an academically accelerated gifted placement in her school, Laquisha might benefit from additional challenge in other ways such as after-school and weekend enrichment programs with enhanced opportunities for leadership development. Laquisha's situation highlights the use of the *GRS-S* in concert with the WISC-IV when making a diagnostic decision or gifted classification. A case example of how to use the gifted scales to measure change or growth in a student's profile of giftedness over time is described by Pfeiffer et al. (2006).

DISCUSSION

This chapter discusses the changes in content and structure from the WISC-III to the WISC-IV that may impact the identification of gifted children. In addition, as special education moves toward an "RtI" model of identification, we discuss the ways in which the WISC-IV continues to offer valuable information in identifying and responding to the needs of children who are gifted. The recent development of the extended norms tables for the WISC-IV is a further step in understanding those children who are extremely gifted. Finally, we have presented a recently developed rating scale for teachers (*GRS*) that can help in the process of identifying gifted students.

When deciding which tools to use in the identification of gifted students, many variables must be considered. The use of intelligence tests is a core tool, and justifiably so. In terms of reliability and validity, standardized intelligence tests are usually the most psychometrically sound instruments available. In addition, there is probably more consistency (reliability) among the many psychologists who administer these tests than any other tests developed for school-aged children and adolescents. Because the goal of our public schools is to provide mainly for the academic education of our youth, it is understandable that the type of test most predictive of an individual's academic achievement would be one of the most appropriate selections for use in identifying students who are gifted.

The WISC-IV for many reasons is one of the most appropriate IQ tests to be used for this purpose. It is the most widely used IQ test in schools today and was well-standardized. Issues of concern with the WISC-III are still evident in the WISC-IV, but probably to a lesser degree. Time bonuses have been cut back considerably, although ceiling effects are still an issue that are partially resolved by the introduction of extended norms, but continue to be problematic in the older age range. There is no data yet on cultural bias. The new structure with the deletion of VIQ and PIQ may make it more difficult for some children to qualify for gifted programs. However, the new four indices model and the use of the GAI score may make that less of an issue. Much depends on how states and school districts define "giftedness." At this time, some allow only an FSIQ at or above a certain point (e.g., 125 or 130). Others will accept VIQ or PIQ or GAI scores at this level. For the children in the WISC-IV standardization whom we categorized as gifted (IQ equal to or above of 130 on any index or FSIQ), the VC and PR were overwhelmingly the indexes where the gifted students scored at or above our required cutoff point, with the VC being the score most often elevated. Another problem with using the FSIQ is that now there are two Processing Speed subtests (relatively the weakest index for students who are gifted) included, which will have a tendency to lower the height of the FSIQ for students who are gifted.

Even on the strength of the many arguments in favor of using intelligence tests to identify gifted children, and even with all the appropriate cautions being taken into consideration, there are additional issues to consider when assessing potentially gifted children. Most often, intelligence testing is conducted with gifted children or children suspected of intellectual giftedness for purposes of educational planning and placement. The psychologist is charged with determining whether a given child is indeed academically gifted, and with making recommendations about educational programs that would best suit the child's needs. Of course, many schools have no special services for children who are gifted. In many schools, psychologists will administer the WISC-IV to a group of children and then classify them as "gifted" or "not gifted," solely on the basis of an arbitrary FSIQ, depending on local or state regulations and without regard to important issues regarding the interpretation of the score. Although this approach may be dictated by mandated regulations, the resulting placement decisions can relegate a child to an inappropriate educational setting indefinitely. It is our recommendation that from the WISC-IV, the VC, PR, or GAI be the scores used for determination of giftedness.

Finally, an IQ test alone should not be the sole criteria for classification of giftedness. Assessment with other instruments such as the *GRS*, academic achievement, review of academic work, and other factors, including creativity and leadership should be part of the comprehensive assessment of giftedness.

REFERENCES

Atkinson, G. (1991). Kolb's Learning Style Inventory: A practitioner's perspective. *Measurement and Evaluation in Counseling and Development,* 23, 149–161.

Barona, A., & Pfeiffer, S. I. (1992). Effects of test administration procedures and acculturation level on achievement test scores. *Journal of Psychoeducational Assessment,* 10, 124–132.

Baum, S., Cooper, c. R., & Neu, T. (2001). Duel differentiation: An approach for meeting the curricular needs of gifted students with learning disabilities. *Psychology in the Schools,* 38, 477–490.

Bianco, M. (2005). The effects of disability labels on special education and general education teachers' referrals for gifted programs. *Learning Disability Quarterly,* 28, 285–294.

Bracken, B. (1988). Ten psychometric reasons why similar produce dissimilar results. *Journal of School Psychology,* 26, 155–166.

Brody, L. E., & Mills, D. J. (1997). Gifted children with learning disabilities: A review of the issues. *Journal of Learning Disabilities,* 30, 282–286.

Cooper, C. R., Baum, S., & Neu, T. (2004). Developing scientific talent in students with special needs: An alternative model for identification, curriculum, and assessment. *The Journal of Secondary Gifted Education,* 15, 162–169.

Ferri, B., Gregg, N., & Heffoy, S. (1997). Profiles of college students demonstrating learning disabilities with and without giftedness. *Journal of Learning Disabilities,* 30, 552–559.

Fuchs, D., & Young, C. L. (2006). On the irrelevance of intelligence in predicting responsiveness to reading intervention. *Exceptional Children,* 73, 8–30.

Gagné, F. (1993). Constructs and models pertaining to exceptional human abilities. In K. A. Heller, F. J. Mönks, & A. H. Passow (Eds.), *International Handbook of Research and Development of Giftedness and Talent* (pp. 69–87). New York: Pergamon.

Gardner, H. (1983). *Frames of Mind: The Theory of Multiple Intelligences.* New York: Basic Books.

Harrington, R. G. (1982). Caution: Standardized testing may be hazardous to the educational programs of intellectually gifted children. *Education,* 103, 112–117.

Jarosewich, T., Pfeiffer, S. I., & Morris, J. (2002). Identifying gifted students using teacher rating scales: A review of existing instruments. *Journal of Psychoeducational Assessment,* 20, 322–336.

Johnston, R. S., & Morrison, M. (2007). Toward a resolution of inconsistencies in the phonological deficit theory of reading disorders. *Journal of Learning Disabilities,* 40, 66–79.

Kaufman, A. S. (1992). Evaluation of the WISC-III and WPPSI-R for gifted children. *Roeper Review,* 14, 154–158.

Kaufman, A. S. (1993). King WISC the Third assumes the throne. *Journal of School Psychology,* 31, 345–354.

Kaufman, A. S., & Kaufman, N. (1983). *Kaufman Assessment Battery for Children*. Circle Pines, MN: American Guidance Service.

Kaufman, A. S., & Harrison, P. L. (1986). Intelligence tests and gifted assessment: What are the positives? Special issue: The IQ controversy. *Roeper Review*, 8, 154–159.

Klausmeier, K., Mishra, S. P., & Maker, C. J. (1987). Identification of gifted learners: A national survey of assessment practices and training needs of school psychologists. *Gifted Child Quarterly*, 31, 135–137.

Lohman, D. F., & Hagen, E. (2001). *Cognitive Abilities Test (Form 6)*. Itasca, IL: Riverside Publishing.

Otis, A. S., & Lennon, R. T. (1997). *Otis-Lennon School Ability Test – Seventh Edition*. San Antonio, TX: The Psychological Corporation.

Pfeiffer, S. I. (2001). Professional psychology and the gifted: Emerging practice opportunities. *Professional Psychology: Research & Practice*, 32, 175–180.

Pfeiffer, S. I. (2002). Identifying gifted and talented students: Recurring issues and promising solutions. *Journal of Applied School Psychology*, 1, 31–50.

Pfeiffer, S. I. (2003). Challenges and opportunities for students who are gifted: What the experts say. *Gifted Child Quarterly*, 47, 161–169.

Pfeiffer, S. I. (2007). *Handbook of Giftedness in Children: Psychoeducational Theory, Research, and Best Practices*. New York: Springer Publishers.

Pfeiffer, S. I., & Jarosewich, T. (2003). *Gifted Rating Scales Manual*. San Antonio, TX: The Psychological Corporation.

Pfeiffer, S. I., & Jarosewich, T. (2007). The Gifted Rating Scales-School Form. An analysis of the standardization sample based on age, gender, race, and diagnostic efficiency. *Gifted Child Quarterly*, 51, 39–50.

Pfeiffer, S. I., Kumtepe, A., & Rosado, J. (2006). Gifted identification: Measuring change in a student's profile of abilities using the Gifted Rating Scales. *The School Psychologist*, 60, 106–111.

Raiford, S. E., Weiss, L. G., Rolfhus, E., & Coalson, D. (2005). General Ability Index (WISC-IV Technical Report No. 4). Retrieved February 25, 2008, from http://www.harcourtassessment.com/hai/images/pdf/wisciv/WISCIVTechReport4.pdf

Robinson, N. M., & Chamrad, D. L. (1986). Appropriate uses of intelligence tests with gifted children. Special issue: The IQ controversy. *Roeper Review*, 8, 160–163.

Sabatino, D. A., Spangler, R. S., & Vance, H. B. (1995). The relationship between the Wechsler Intelligence Scale for Children – Revised and the Wechsler Intelligence Scale for Children-III scales and subtests with gifted children. *Psychology in the Schools*, 32, 18–23.

Saklofske, D. H., Zhu, J., Raiford, S. E., Weiss, L. G., Rolfhus, E., & Coalson, D. (2005). General Ability Index: Canadian Norms (WISC-IV Technical Report No. 4.1). Retrieved February 25, 2008, from http://www.harcourtassessment.com/hai/images/pdf/wisciv/WISCIV_4.1_Rel.pdf

Seiver, R. C., Bain, S. K., & Hildman, L. K. (1994). Comparison of the WISC-R and WISC-III for gifted students. *Roeper Review*, 17, 39–42.

Shevitz, B., Weinfeld, T., Jeweler, S., & Barnes-Robinson, L. (2003). Mentoring empowers gifted/learning disabled students to soar. *Roeper Review*, 26, 37–40.

Sparrow, S. S., & Gurland, S. T. (1998). Assessment of gifted children with the WISC-III. In A. Prifitera, & D. H. Saklofske (Eds.), *WISC-III: Clinical Use and Interpretation* (pp. 59–72). New York: Academic Press.

Stephens, K. R., & Karnes, F. A. (2000). State definitions for the gifted and talented revisited. *Exceptional Children*, 66, 219–238.

Sternberg, R. J. (1982). Lies we live by: Misapplication of tests in identifying the gifted. *Gifted Child Quarterly*, 26, 157–161.

Sternberg, R. J. (1997). The concept of intelligence and its role in lifelong learning and success. *American Psychologist*, 52, 1030–1037.

Swanson, H. L., & Jerman, O. (2006). The influence working memory on reading growth in subgroups of children with reading disabilities. *Journal of Experimental Child Psychology*, 96, 249–283.

Terman, L. M. (1925). *Mental and Physical Traits of a Thousand Gifted Children*. Stanford, CA: Stanford University Press.

Thorndike, R. L., Hagen, E. P., & Sattler, J. M. (1986). *The Stanford-Binet Intelligence Scale* (4th ed.). Chicago, IL: Riverside Publishing.

Tyerman, M. J. (1986). Gifted children and their identification: Learning ability not intelligence. *Gifted Education International*, 4, 81–84.

Watkins, M. W., Greenawalt, C. G., & Marcell, C. M. (2002). Factor structure of the Wechsler Intelligence Scale for Children – Third Edition among gifted students. *Educational and Psychological Measurement*, 62, 164–172.

Wechsler, D. (1991). *Wechsler Intelligence Scale for Children – Third Edition*. San Antonio, TX: The Psychological Corporation (Wechsler, 1991).

Wechsler, D. (2003). *Wechsler Intelligence Scale for Children – Fourth Edition: Technical and Interpretative Manual*. San Antonio, TX: The Psychological Corporation.

Woodcock, R. W., & Johnson, M. B. (1989). *Woodcock Johnson Psycho-Educational Battery – Revised*. Allen, TX: DLM Teaching Resources.

Woodcock, R. W., McGrew, K. S., & Mather, N. (2001). *Woodcock-Johnson III*. Itasca, IL: Riverside Publishing.

Zigler, A., & Heller, K. (2000). Conceptions of giftedness from a meta-theoretical perspective. In K. A. Heller, F. J. Mönks, R. J. Sternberg, & R. F. Subotnik (Eds.), *International Handbook of Giftedness and Talent – 2nd Edition* (pp. 3–21). Amsterdam: Elsevier.

Zhu, J., Cayton, T., Weiss, L., & Gabal, A. (2008). *WISC-IV Extended Norms (WISC-IV Technical Report No. 7)*. San Antonio, TX: Harcourt Assessment, Inc.

APPENDIX A

WISC-IV EXTENDED NORMS FOR GIFTED STUDENTS

TABLE A.1(A)   Scaled Score Equivalents of Total Raw Scores for Subtest, By Age Group (Age 6)

Standard score	BD	SI	DS	PCn	CD	VC	LN	MR	CO	SS	PCm	CA	IN	AR	WR
Ages 6:0–6:3															
18	46–48	23–24	18	19	64	32–33	18	21	23–24	40–42	25	91–95	17	21–22	15
19	49–51	25–26	19	20	65	34–35	19	22	25	43–44	26	96–100	18	23	16
20	52–53	27–28	20	21	–	36–37	20	23	26	45	27	101–105	19	24	17
21	54–55	29–30	21	22	–	38–39	21	24	27	–	28	106–109	20	25–26	18
22	56–57	31–32	22	23	–	40–41	22	25	28	–	29	110–113	21	27	19
23	58–59	33–34	23	24	–	42–43	23	26	29	–	30	114–117	22	28	20
24	60–61	35–36	24	25	–	44–45	24	27	30	–	31	118–121	23	29	21
25	62–63	37–38	25	26	–	46–47	25	28	31	–	32	122–125	24	30	22
26	64–65	39–40	26	27	–	48–49	26	29	32	–	33	126–129	25	31	23
27	66–67	41–42	27	28	–	50–51	27	30	33	–	34	130–133	26	32	–
28	68	43–44	28–32	–	–	52–68	28–30	31–35	34–42	–	35–38	134–136	27–33	33–34	24

(continues)

TABLE A.1(A) (continued)

Standard score	BD	SI	DS	PCn	CD	VC	LN	MR	CO	SS	PCm	CA	IN	AR	WR
							Ages 6:4–6:7								
18	46–48	24–25	19	20	64	33–34	19	22	25	41–42	26	93–97	18	22–23	16
19	49–51	26–27	20	21	65	35–36	20	23	26	43–44	27	98–102	19	24	17
20	52–53	28–29	21	22	–	37–38	21	24	27	45	28	103–107	20	25	18
21	54–55	30–31	22	23	–	39–40	22	25	28	–	29	108–111	21	26–27	19
22	56–57	32–33	23	24	–	41–42	23	26	29	–	30	112–115	22	28	20
23	58–59	34–35	24	25	–	43–44	24	27	30	–	31	116–119	23	29	21
24	60–61	36–37	25	26	–	45–46	25	28	31	–	32	120–123	24	30	22
25	62–63	38–39	26	27	–	47–48	26	29	32	–	33	124–127	25	31	23
26	64–65	40–41	27	28	–	49–50	27	30	33	–	34	128–131	26	32	–
27	66–67	42–43	28	–	–	51–52	28	31	34	–	35	132–135	27	33	24
28	68	44	29–32	–	–	53–68	29–30	32–35	35–42	–	36–38	136	28–33	34	–
							Ages 6:8–6:11								
18	46–48	26–27	20	21	64	35–36	20	23	26	41–42	27	95–99	19	23–24	17
19	49–51	28–29	21	22	65	37–38	21	24	27	43–44	28	100–104	20	25	18
20	52–53	30–31	22	23	–	39–40	22	25	28	45	29	105–109	21	26	19
21	54–55	32–33	23	24	–	41–42	23	26	29	–	30	110–113	22	27–28	20
22	56–57	34–35	24	25	–	43–44	24	27	30	–	31	114–117	23	29	21
23	58–59	36–37	25	26	–	45–46	25	28	31	–	32	118–121	24	30	22
24	60–61	38–39	26	27	–	47–48	26	29	32	–	33	122–125	25	31	23
25	62–63	40–41	27	28	–	49–50	27	30	33	–	34	126–129	26	32	–
26	64–65	42–43	28	–	–	51–52	28	31	34	–	35	130–133	27	33	24
27	66–67	44	29	–	–	53–54	29	32	35	–	36	134–136	28	34	–
28	68	–	30–32	–	–	55–68	30	33–35	36–42	–	37–38	–	29–33	–	–

TABLE A.1(B)   Scaled Score Equivalents of Total Raw Scores for Subtest, By Age Group (Age 7)

Standard score	BD	SI	DS	PCn	CD	VC	LN	MR	CO	SS	PCm	CA	IN	AR	WR
Ages 7:0–7:3															
18	51–53	26–27	20	21	64	37–38	20	24	26–27	43–44	28	98–102	19	24–25	17
19	54–56	28–29	21	22	65	39–40	21	25	28	45	29	103–107	20	26	18
20	57–58	30–31	22	23	–	41–42	22	26	29	–	30	108–112	21	27	19
21	59–60	32–33	23	24	–	43–44	23	27	30	–	31	113–116	22	28–29	20
22	61–62	34–35	24	25	–	45–46	24	28	31	–	32	117–120	23	30	21
23	63–64	36–37	25	26	–	47–48	25	29	32	–	33	121–124	24	31	22
24	65–66	38–39	26	27	–	49–50	26	30	33	–	34	125–128	25	32	23
25	67–68	40–41	27	28	–	51–52	27	31	34	–	35	129–132	26	33	–
26	–	42–43	28	–	–	53–54	28	32	35	–	36	133–136	27	34	24
27	–	44	29	–	–	55–56	29	33	36	–	37	–	28	–	–
28	–	–	30–32	–	–	57–68	30	34–35	37–42	–	38	–	29–33	–	–
Ages 7:4–7:7															
18	51–53	27–28	21	22	64	39–40	21	25	27	43–44	30	100–104	20	25	18
19	54–56	29–30	22	23	65	41–42	22	26	28	45	31	105–109	21	26–27	19
20	57–58	31–32	23	24	–	43–44	23	27	29	–	32	110–114	22	28	20
21	59–60	33–34	24	25	–	45–46	24	28	30	–	33	115–118	23	29	21
22	61–62	35–36	25	26	–	47–48	25	29	31	–	34	119–122	24	30	22
23	63–64	37–38	26	27	–	49–50	26	30	32	–	35	123–126	25	31–32	23

(continues)

TABLE A.1(B) (continued)

Standard score	BD	SI	DS	PCn	CD	VC	LN	MR	CO	SS	PCm	CA	IN	AR	WR
24	65–66	39–40	27	28	–	51–52	27	31	33	–	36	127–130	26	33	–
25	67–68	41–42	28	–	–	53–54	28	32	34	–	37	131–134	27	34	24
26	–	43–44	29	–	–	55–56	29	33	35	–	–	135–136	28	–	–
27	–	–	30	–	–	57–58	30	34	36	–	38	–	29	–	–
28	–	–	31–32	–	–	59–68	–	35	37–42	–	–	–	30–33	–	–
Ages 7:8–7:11															
18	51–53	29–30	21	23	64	41–42	22	26	28	43–44	31	103–107	21	26–27	19
19	54–56	31–32	22	24	65	43–44	23	27	29	45	32	108–112	22	28	20
20	57–58	33–34	23	25	–	45–46	24	28	30	–	33	113–117	23	29	21
21	59–60	35–36	24	26	–	47–48	25	29	31	–	34	118–121	24	30	22
22	61–62	37–38	25	27	–	49–50	26	30	32	–	35	122–125	25	31–32	23
23	63–64	39–40	26	28	–	51–52	27	31	33	–	36	126–129	26	33	–
24	65–66	41–42	27	–	–	53–54	28	32	34	–	37	130–133	27	34	24
25	67–68	43–44	28	–	–	55–56	29	33	35	–	–	134–136	28	–	–
26	–	–	29	–	–	57–58	30	34	36	–	38	–	29	–	–
27	–	–	30	–	–	59–60	–	–	37	–	–	–	30	–	–
28	–	–	31–32	–	–	61–68	–	35	38–42	–	–	–	31–33	–	–

TABLE A.1(C)   Scaled Score Equivalents of Total Raw Scores for Subtest, By Age Group (Age 8)

Standard score	BD	SI	DS	PCn	CD	VC	LN	MR	CO	SS	PCm	CA	IN	AR	WR
							Ages 8:0–8:3								
18	56–58	29–30	22	23	54–56	42–43	22	27	28–29	31–32	31	106–110	21	26–27	20
19	59–61	31–32	23	24	57–59	44–45	23	28	30	33–34	32	111–115	22	28	21
20	62–63	33–34	24	25	60–62	46–47	24	29	31	35–36	33	116–120	23	29	22
21	64–65	35–36	25	26	63–65	48–49	25	30	32	37–38	34	121–124	24	30	23
22	66–67	37–38	26	27	66–68	50–51	26	31	33	39–40	35	125–128	25	31–32	–
23	68	39–40	27	28	69–71	52–53	27	32	34	41–42	36	129–132	26	33	24
24	–	41–42	28	–	72–74	54–55	28	33	35	43–44	37	133–136	27	34	–
25	–	43–44	29	–	75–77	56–57	29	34	36	45–46	–	–	28	–	–
26	–	–	30	–	78–80	58–59	30	–	37	47–48	38	–	29	–	–
27	–	–	31	–	81–83	60–61	–	35	38	49–50	–	–	30	–	–
28	–	–	32	–	84–119	62–68	–	–	39–42	51–60	–	–	31–33	–	–
							Ages 8:4–8:7								
18	56–58	31–32	22	24	57–59	44–45	23	28	29	33–34	32	108–112	23	27–28	20
19	59–61	33–34	23	25	60–62	46–47	24	29	30	35–36	33	113–117	24	29	21
20	62–63	35–36	24	26	63–65	48–49	25	30	31	37–38	34	118–122	25	30	22
21	64–65	37–38	25	27	66–68	50–51	26	31	32	39–40	35	123–126	26	31	23
22	66–67	39–40	26	28	69–71	52–53	27	32	33	41–42	36	127–130	27	32–33	–
23	68	41–42	27	–	72–74	54–55	28	33	34	43–44	37	131–134	28	34	24

(continues)

TABLE A.1(C) (continued)

Standard score	BD	SI	DS	PCn	CD	VC	LN	MR	CO	SS	PCm	CA	IN	AR	WR
24	–	43–44	28	–	75–77	56–57	29	34	35	45–46	–	135–136	29	–	–
25	–	–	29	–	78–80	58–59	30	–	36	47–48	38	–	30	–	–
26	–	–	30	–	81–83	60–61	–	35	37	49–50	–	–	31	–	–
27	–	–	31	–	84–86	62–63	–	–	38	51–52	–	–	32	–	–
28	–	–	32	–	87–119	64–68	–	–	39–42	53–60	–	–	33	–	–
Ages 8:8–8:11															
18	56–58	32–33	23	25	59–61	46–47	24	29	30–31	35–36	33	110–114	23	28–29	21
19	59–61	34–35	24	26	62–64	48–49	25	30	32	37–38	34	115–119	24	30	22
20	62–63	36–37	25	27	65–67	50–51	26	31	33	39–40	35	120–124	25	31	23
21	64–65	38–39	26	28	68–70	52–53	27	32	34	41–42	36	125–128	26	32	–
22	66–67	40–41	27	–	71–73	54–55	28	33	35	43–44	37	129–132	27	33	24
23	68	42–43	28	–	74–76	56–57	29	34	36	45–46	–	133–136	28	34	–
24	–	44	29	–	77–79	58–59	30	–	37	47–48	38	–	29	–	–
25	–	–	30	–	80–82	60–61	–	35	38	49–50	–	–	30	–	–
26	–	–	31	–	83–85	62–63	–	–	39	51–52	–	–	31	–	–
27	–	–	32	–	86–88	64–65	–	–	40	53–54	–	–	32	–	–
28	–	–	–	–	89–119	66–68	–	–	41–42	55–60	–	–	33	–	–

TABLE A.1 (D) Scaled Score Equivalents of Total Raw Scores for Subtest, By Age Group (Age 9)

Standard score	BD	SI	DS	PCn	CD	VC	LN	MR	CO	SS	PCm	CA	IN	AR	WR
Ages 9:0–9:3															
18	58–60	33–34	23	25–26	61–63	47–48	24	29	31–32	36–37	33	112–116	24	29–30	22
19	61–63	35–36	24	27	64–66	49–50	25	30	33	38–39	34	117–121	25	31	23
20	64–65	37–38	25	28	67–69	51–52	26	31	34	40–41	35	122–126	26	32	–
21	66–67	39–40	26	–	70–72	53–54	27	32	35	42–43	36	127–130	27	33	24
22	68	41–42	27	–	73–75	55–56	28	33	36	44–45	37	131–134	28	34	–
23	–	43–44	28	–	76–78	57–58	29	34	37	46–47	–	135–136	29	–	–
24	–	–	29	–	79–81	59–60	30	–	38	48–49	38	–	30	–	–
25	–	–	30	–	82–84	61–62	–	35	39	50–51	–	–	31	–	–
26	–	–	31	–	85–87	63–64	–	–	40	52–53	–	–	32	–	–
27	–	–	32	–	88–90	65–66	–	–	41	54–55	–	–	–	–	–
28	–	–	–	–	91–119	67–68	–	–	42	56–60	–	–	33	–	–
Ages 9:4–9:7															
18	58–60	34–35	24	26	64–66	49–50	25	30	32	37–38	34	114–118	24	30	22
19	61–63	36–37	25	27	67–69	51–52	26	31	33	39–40	35	119–123	25	31	23
20	64–65	38–39	26	28	70–72	53–54	27	32	34	41–42	36	124–128	26	32	–
21	66–67	40–41	27	–	73–75	55–56	28	33	35	43–44	37	129–132	27	33	24
22	68	42–43	28	–	76–78	57–58	29	34	36	45–46	–	133–136	28	34	–
23	–	44	29	–	79–81	59–60	30	–	37	47–48	38	–	29	–	–

(continues)

TABLE A.1(D)   (continued)

Standard score	BD	SI	DS	PCn	CD	VC	LN	MR	CO	SS	PCm	CA	IN	AR	WR
Ages 9:4–9:7															
24	–	–	30	–	82–84	61–62	–	35	38	49–50	–	–	30	–	–
25	–	–	31	–	85–87	63–64	–	–	39	51–52	–	–	31	–	–
26	–	–	32	–	88–90	65–66	–	–	40	53–54	–	–	32	–	–
27	–	–	–	–	91–93	67–68	–	–	41	55–56	–	–	–	–	–
28	–	–	–	–	94–119	–	–	–	42	57–60	–	–	33	–	–
Ages 9:8–9:11															
18	58–60	34–35	24	26	66–68	51–52	25	30	33	38–39	34	116–120	25	30–31	22
19	61–63	36–37	25	27	69–71	53–54	26	31	34	40–41	35	121–125	26	32	23
20	64–65	38–39	26	28	72–74	55–56	27	32	35	42–43	36	126–130	27	33	–
21	66–67	40–41	27	–	75–77	57–58	28	33	36	44–45	37	131–134	28	34	24
22	68	42–43	28	–	78–80	59–60	29	34	37	46–47	–	135–136	29	–	–
23	–	44	29	–	81–83	61–62	30	–	38	48–49	38	–	30	–	–
24	–	–	30	–	84–86	63–64	–	35	39	50–51	–	–	31	–	–
25	–	–	31	–	87–89	65–66	–	–	40	52–53	–	–	32	–	–
26	–	–	32	–	90–92	67–68	–	–	41	54–55	–	–	–	–	–
27	–	–	–	–	93–95	–	–	–	–	56–57	–	–	33	–	–
28	–	–	–	–	96–119	–	–	–	42	58–60	–	–	–	–	–

TABLE A.1(E)   Scaled Score Equivalents of Total Raw Scores for Subtest, By Age Group (Age 10)

Standard score	BD	SI	DS	PCn	CD	VC	LN	MR	CO	SS	PCm	CA	IN	AR	WR
							Ages 10:0–10:3								
18	60–61	36–37	24	26	68–70	51–52	25	31	33–34	39–40	35	118–122	25	31	23
19	62–63	38–39	25	27	71–73	53–54	26	32	35	41–42	36	123–127	26	32	–
20	64–65	40–41	26	28	74–76	55–56	27	33	36	43–44	37	128–132	27	33	24
21	66–67	42–43	27	–	77–79	57–58	28	34	37	45–46	–	133–135	28	34	–
22	68	44	28	–	80–82	59–60	29	–	38	47–48	38	136	29	–	–
23	–	–	29	–	83–85	61–62	30	35	39	49–50	–	–	30	–	–
24	–	–	30	–	86–88	63–64	–	–	40	51–52	–	–	31	–	–
25	–	–	31	–	89–91	65–66	–	–	41	53–54	–	–	32	–	–
26	–	–	32	–	92–94	67–68	–	–	–	55–56	–	–	–	–	–
27	–	–	–	–	95–97	–	–	–	42	57–58	–	–	33	–	–
28	–	–	–	–	98–119	–	–	–	–	59–60	–	–	–	–	–
							Ages 10:4–10:7								
18	60–61	36–37	24	26	70–72	53–54	25	31	34	40–41	35	120–124	26	31	23
19	62–63	38–39	25	27	73–75	55–56	26	32	35	42–43	36	125–129	27	32	–
20	64–65	40–41	26	28	76–78	57–58	27	33	36	44–45	37	130–134	28	33	24
21	66–67	42–43	27	–	79–81	59–60	28	34	37	46–47	–	135–136	29	34	–
22	68	44	28	–	82–84	61–62	29	–	38	48–49	38	–	30	–	–
23	–	–	29	–	85–87	63–64	30	35	39	50–51	–	–	31	–	–

(continues)

TABLE A.1(E) (continued)

Standard score	BD	SI	DS	PCn	CD	VC	LN	MR	CO	SS	PCm	CA	IN	AR	WR
Ages 10:4–10:7															
24	–	–	30	–	88–90	65–66	–	–	40	52–53	–	–	32	–	–
25	–	–	31	–	91–93	67–68	–	–	41	54–55	–	–	–	–	–
26	–	–	32	–	94–96	–	–	–	–	56–57	–	–	33	–	–
27	–	–	–	–	97–99	–	–	–	42	58–59	–	–	–	–	–
28	–	–	–	–	100–119	–	–	–	–	60	–	–	–	–	–
Ages 10:8–10:11															
18	61–62	36–37	24	26	72–74	54–55	25	31	34	40–41	35	122–126	26	31	23
19	63–64	38–39	25	27	75–77	56–57	26	32	35	42–43	36	127–130	27	32	–
20	65	40–41	26	28	78–80	58–59	27	33	36	44–45	37	131–134	28	33	24
21	66–67	42–43	27	–	81–83	60–61	28	34	37	46–47	–	135–136	29	34	–
22	68	44	28	–	84–86	62–63	29	–	38	48–49	38	–	30	–	–
23	–	–	29	–	87–89	64–65	30	35	39	50–51	–	–	31	–	–
24	–	–	30	–	90–92	66–67	–	–	40	52–53	–	–	32	–	–
25	–	–	31	–	93–95	68	–	–	41	54–55	–	–	–	–	–
26	–	–	32	–	96–98	–	–	–	–	56–57	–	–	33	–	–
27	–	–	–	–	99–101	–	–	–	42	58–59	–	–	–	–	–
28	–	–	–	–	102–119	–	–	–	–	60	–	–	–	–	–

TABLE A.1 (F)   Scaled Score Equivalents of Total Raw Scores for Subtest, By Age Group (Age 11)

Standard score	BD	SI	DS	PCn	CD	VC	LN	MR	CO	SS	PCm	CA	IN	AR	WR
Ages 11:0–11:3															
18	62	37–38	25	27	74–76	55–56	26	32	35	42–43	36	124–127	27	32	23
19	63–64	39–40	26	28	77–79	57–58	27	33	36	44–45	37	128–131	28	33	–
20	65	41–42	27	–	80–82	59–60	28	34	37	46–47	–	132–135	29	34	24
21	66–67	43–44	28	–	83–85	61–62	29	–	38	48–49	38	136	30	–	–
22	68	–	29	–	86–88	63–64	30	35	39	50–51	–	–	31	–	–
23	–	–	30	–	89–91	65–66	–	–	40	52–53	–	–	32	–	–
24	–	–	31	–	92–94	67–68	–	–	41	54–55	–	–	–	–	–
25	–	–	32	–	95–97	–	–	–	–	56–57	–	–	33	–	–
26	–	–	–	–	98–100	–	–	–	42	58–59	–	–	–	–	–
27	–	–	–	–	101–103	–	–	–	–	60	–	–	–	–	–
28	–	–	–	–	104–119	–	–	–	–	–	–	–	–	–	–
Ages 11:4–11:7															
18	62	37–38	25	27	76–78	56–57	26	32	35	42–43	36	125–128	28	32	23
19	63–64	39–40	26	28	79–81	58–59	27	33	36	44–45	37	129–132	29	33	–
20	65	41–42	27	–	82–84	60–61	28	34	37	46–47	–	133–136	30	34	24
21	66–67	43–44	28	–	85–87	62–63	29	–	38	48–49	38	–	31	–	–
22	68	–	29	–	88–90	64–65	30	35	39	50–51	–	–	32	–	–
23	–	–	30	–	91–93	66–67	–	–	40	52–53	–	–	–	–	–

(continues)

TABLE A.1(F) *(continued)*

Standard score	BD	SI	DS	PCn	CD	VC	LN	MR	CO	SS	PCm	CA	IN	AR	WR
Ages 11:4–11:7															
24	—	—	31	—	94–96	68	—	—	41	54–55	—	—	33	—	—
25	—	—	32	—	97–99	—	—	—	—	56–57	—	—	—	—	—
26	—	—	—	—	100–102	—	—	—	42	58–59	—	—	—	—	—
27	—	—	—	—	103–105	—	—	—	—	60	—	—	—	—	—
28	—	—	—	—	106–119	—	—	—	—	—	—	—	—	—	—
Ages 11:8–11:11															
18	62	37–38	25	27	78–80	56–57	26	32	36	42–43	36	126–129	28	32	23
19	63–64	39–40	26	28	81–83	58–59	27	33	37	44–45	37	130–133	29	33	—
20	65	41–42	27	—	84–86	60–61	28	34	38	46–47	—	134–136	30	34	24
21	66–67	43–44	28	—	87–89	62–63	29	—	39	48–49	38	—	31	—	—
22	68	—	29	—	90–92	64–65	30	35	40	50–51	—	—	32	—	—
23	—	—	30	—	93–95	66–67	—	—	41	52–53	—	—	—	—	—
24	—	—	31	—	96–98	68	—	—	—	54–55	—	—	33	—	—
25	—	—	32	—	99–101	—	—	—	42	56–57	—	—	—	—	—
26	—	—	—	—	102–104	—	—	—	—	58–59	—	—	—	—	—
27	—	—	—	—	105–107	—	—	—	—	60	—	—	—	—	—
28	—	—	—	—	108–119	—	—	—	—	—	—	—	—	—	—

TABLE A.1(G) Scaled Score Equivalents of Total Raw Scores for Subtest, By Age Group (Age 12)

Standard score	BD	SI	DS	PCn	CD	VC	LN	MR	CO	SS	PCm	CA	IN	AR	WR
Ages 12:0–12:3															
18	63–64	39–40	26	27	80–82	58–59	26	33	36	44–45	37	127–130	29	33	23
19	65	41–42	27	28	83–85	60–61	27	34	37	46–47	–	131–134	30	34	–
20	66–67	43–44	28	–	86–88	62–63	28	–	38	48–49	38	135–136	31	–	24
21	68	–	29	–	89–91	64–65	29	35	39	50–51	–	–	32	–	–
22	–	–	30	–	92–94	66–67	30	–	40	52–53	–	–	33	–	–
23	–	–	31	–	95–97	68	–	–	41	54–55	–	–	–	–	–
24	–	–	32	–	98–100	–	–	–	–	56–57	–	–	–	–	–
25	–	–	–	–	101–103	–	–	–	42	58–59	–	–	–	–	–
26	–	–	–	–	104–106	–	–	–	–	60	–	–	–	–	–
27	–	–	–	–	107–109	–	–	–	–	–	–	–	–	–	–
28	–	–	–	–	110–119	–	–	–	–	–	–	–	–	–	–
Ages 12:4–12:7															
18	63–64	40–41	26	27	82–84	58–59	26	33	37	44–45	37	128–131	29	33	23
19	65	42–43	27	28	85–87	60–61	27	34	38	46–47	–	132–135	30	34	–
20	66–67	44	28	–	88–90	62–63	28	–	39	48–49	38	136	31	–	24
21	68	–	29	–	91–93	64–65	29	35	40	50–51	–	–	32	–	–
22	–	–	30	–	94–96	66–67	30	–	41	52–53	–	–	–	–	–
23	–	–	31	–	97–99	68	–	–	–	54–55	–	–	33	–	–

(continues)

TABLE A.1(G)　(continued)

Standard score	BD	SI	DS	PCn	CD	VC	LN	MR	CO	SS	PCm	CA	IN	AR	WR
Ages 12:4–12:7															
24	–	–	32	–	100–102	–	–	–	42	56–57	–	–	–	–	–
25	–	–	–	–	103–105	–	–	–	–	58–59	–	–	–	–	–
26	–	–	–	–	106–108	–	–	–	–	60	–	–	–	–	–
27	–	–	–	–	109–111	–	–	–	–	–	–	–	–	–	–
28	–	–	–	–	112–119	–	–	–	–	–	–	–	–	–	–
Ages 12:8–12:11															
18	63–64	40–41	26	27	84–86	58–59	26	33	37	44–45	37	129–132	29	33	23
19	65	42–43	27	28	87–89	60–61	27	34	38	46–47	–	133–135	30	34	–
20	66–67	44	28	–	90–92	62–63	28	–	39	48–49	38	136	31	–	24
21	68	–	29	–	93–95	64–65	29	35	40	50–51	–	–	32	–	–
22	–	–	30	–	96–98	66–67	30	–	41	52–53	–	–	–	–	–
23	–	–	31	–	99–101	68	–	–	–	54–55	–	–	33	–	–
24	–	–	32	–	102–104	–	–	–	42	56–57	–	–	–	–	–
25	–	–	–	–	105–107	–	–	–	–	58–59	–	–	–	–	–
26	–	–	–	–	108–110	–	–	–	–	60	–	–	–	–	–
27	–	–	–	–	111–113	–	–	–	–	–	–	–	–	–	–
28	–	–	–	–	114–119	–	–	–	–	–	–	–	–	–	–

TABLE A.1(H) Scaled Score Equivalents of Total Raw Scores for Subtest, By Age Group (Age 13)

Standard score	BD	SI	DS	PCn	CD	VC	LN	MR	CO	SS	PCm	CA	IN	AR	WR
Ages 13:0–13:3															
18	65	41–42	27	27	86–88	60–61	26	34	38	46–47	37	131–133	30	33	—
19	66	43	28	28	89–91	62–63	27	—	39	48–49	—	134–136	31	34	24
20	67	44	29	—	92–94	64–65	28	35	40	50–51	38	—	32	—	—
21	68	—	30	—	95–97	66–67	29	—	41	52–53	—	—	—	—	—
22	—	—	31	—	98–100	68	30	—	—	54–55	—	—	33	—	—
23	—	—	32	—	101–103	—	—	—	42	56–57	—	—	—	—	—
24	—	—	—	—	104–106	—	—	—	—	58–59	—	—	—	—	—
25	—	—	—	—	107–109	—	—	—	—	60	—	—	—	—	—
26	—	—	—	—	110–112	—	—	—	—	—	—	—	—	—	—
27	—	—	—	—	113–115	—	—	—	—	—	—	—	—	—	—
28	—	—	—	—	116–119	—	—	—	—	—	—	—	—	—	—
Ages 13:4–13:7															
18	65	41–42	27	27	88–90	61–62	26	34	38	46–47	37	132–133	30	33	—
19	66	43	28	28	91–93	63–64	27	—	39	48–49	—	134–136	31	34	24
20	67	44	29	—	94–96	65–66	28	35	40	50–51	38	—	32	—	—
21	68	—	30	—	97–99	67–68	29	—	41	52–53	—	—	—	—	—
22	—	—	31	—	100–102	—	30	—	—	54–55	—	—	33	—	—
23	—	—	32	—	103–105	—	—	—	42	56–57	—	—	—	—	—

(continues)

TABLE A.1(H) *(continued)*

Standard score	BD	SI	DS	PCn	CD	VC	LN	MR	CO	SS	PCm	CA	IN	AR	WR
Ages 13:4–13:7															
24	–	–	–	–	106–108	–	–	–	–	58–59	–	–	–	–	–
25	–	–	–	–	109–111	–	–	–	–	60	–	–	–	–	–
26	–	–	–	–	112–114	–	–	–	–	–	–	–	–	–	–
27	–	–	–	–	115–117	–	–	–	–	–	–	–	–	–	–
28	–	–	–	–	118–119	–	–	–	–	–	–	–	–	–	–
Ages 13:8–13:11															
18	65	41–42	27	27	89–91	61–62	26	34	38	46–47	37	132–133	30	33	–
19	66–67	43	28	28	92–94	63–64	27	–	39	48–49	–	134–136	31	34	24
20	68	44	29	–	95–97	65–66	28	35	40	50–51	38	–	32	–	–
21	–	–	30	–	98–100	67–68	29	–	41	52–53	–	–	–	–	–
22	–	–	31	–	101–103	–	30	–	–	54–55	–	–	33	–	–
23	–	–	32	–	104–106	–	–	–	42	56–57	–	–	–	–	–
24	–	–	–	–	107–109	–	–	–	–	58–59	–	–	–	–	–
25	–	–	–	–	110–112	–	–	–	–	60	–	–	–	–	–
26	–	–	–	–	113–115	–	–	–	–	–	–	–	–	–	–
27	–	–	–	–	116–118	–	–	–	–	–	–	–	–	–	–
28	–	–	–	–	119	–	–	–	–	–	–	–	–	–	–

TABLE A.1 (I)   Scaled Score Equivalents of Total Raw Scores for Subtest, By Age Group (Age 14)

Standard score	BD	SI	DS	PCn	CD	VC	LN	MR	CO	SS	PCm	CA	IN	AR	WR
						Ages 14:0–14:3									
18	65	42–43	28	27	91–93	63–64	27	34	39	48–49	–	133–134	31	33	24
19	66–67	44	29	28	94–96	65–66	28	–	40	50–51	38	135–136	32	34	–
20	68	–	30	–	97–99	67–68	29	35	41	52–53	–	–	–	–	–
21	–	–	31	–	100–102	–	30	–	–	54–55	–	–	33	–	–
22	–	–	32	–	103–105	–	–	–	42	56–57	–	–	–	–	–
23	–	–	–	–	106–108	–	–	–	–	58–59	–	–	–	–	–
24	–	–	–	–	109–111	–	–	–	–	60	–	–	–	–	–
25	–	–	–	–	112–114	–	–	–	–	–	–	–	–	–	–
26	–	–	–	–	115–117	–	–	–	–	–	–	–	–	–	–
27	–	–	–	–	118–119	–	–	–	–	–	–	–	–	–	–
28	–	–	–	–	–	–	–	–	–	–	–	–	–	–	–
						Ages 14:4–14:7									
18	66	42–43	28	27	93–95	63–64	27	34	39	48–49	–	133–134	31	33	24
19	67	44	29	28	96–98	65–66	28	–	40	50–51	38	135–136	32	34	–
20	68	–	30	–	99–101	67–68	29	35	41	52–53	–	–	–	–	–
21	–	–	31	–	102–104	–	30	–	–	54–55	–	–	33	–	–
22	–	–	32	–	105–107	–	–	–	42	56–57	–	–	–	–	–
23	–	–	–	–	108–110	–	–	–	–	58–59	–	–	–	–	–

(continues)

TABLE A.1(1) *(continued)*

Standard score	BD	SI	DS	PCn	CD	VC	LN	MR	CO	SS	PCm	CA	IN	AR	WR
						Ages 14:4–14:7									
24	–	–	–	–	111–113	–	–	–	–	60	–	–	–	–	–
25	–	–	–	–	114–116	–	–	–	–	–	–	–	–	–	–
26	–	–	–	–	117–119	–	–	–	–	–	–	–	–	–	–
27	–	–	–	–	–	–	–	–	–	–	–	–	–	–	–
28	–	–	–	–	–	–	–	–	–	–	–	–	–	–	–
						Ages 14:8–14:11									
18	66	42–43	28	27	95–97	64–65	27	34	39–40	48–49	–	133–134	31	33	24
19	67	44	29	28	98–100	66–67	28	–	41	50–51	38	135–136	32	34	–
20	68	–	30	–	101–103	68	29	35	–	52–53	–	–	–	–	–
21	–	–	31	–	104–106	–	30	–	42	54–55	–	–	33	–	–
22	–	–	32	–	107–109	–	–	–	–	56–57	–	–	–	–	–
23	–	–	–	–	110–112	–	–	–	–	58–59	–	–	–	–	–
24	–	–	–	–	113–115	–	–	–	–	60	–	–	–	–	–
25	–	–	–	–	116–118	–	–	–	–	–	–	–	–	–	–
26	–	–	–	–	119	–	–	–	–	–	–	–	–	–	–
27	–	–	–	–	–	–	–	–	–	–	–	–	–	–	–
28	–	–	–	–	–	–	–	–	–	–	–	–	–	–	–

TABLE A.1 (J)   Scaled Score Equivalents of Total Raw Scores for Subtest, By Age Group (Age 15)

Standard score	BD	SI	DS	PCn	CD	VC	LN	MR	CO	SS	PCm	CA	IN	AR	WR
Ages 15:0–15:3															
18	66	43	29	27	97–99	65–66	27	34	40	50–51	–	134–135	32	–	24
19	67	44	30	28	100–102	67–68	28	–	41	52–53	38	136	–	34	–
20	68	–	31	–	103–105	–	29	35	42	54–55	–	–	33	–	–
21	–	–	32	–	106–108	–	30	–	–	56–57	–	–	–	–	–
22	–	–	–	–	109–111	–	–	–	–	58–59	–	–	–	–	–
23	–	–	–	–	112–114	–	–	–	–	60	–	–	–	–	–
24	–	–	–	–	115–117	–	–	–	–	–	–	–	–	–	–
25	–	–	–	–	118–119	–	–	–	–	–	–	–	–	–	–
26	–	–	–	–	–	–	–	–	–	–	–	–	–	–	–
27	–	–	–	–	–	–	–	–	–	–	–	–	–	–	–
28	–	–	–	–	–	–	–	–	–	–	–	–	–	–	–
Ages 15:4–15:7															
18	66	43	29	27	99–101	66–67	27	34	41	51–52	–	134–135	32	–	24
19	67	44	30	28	102–104	68	28	–	42	53–54	38	136	–	34	–
20	68	–	31	–	105–107	–	29	35	–	55–56	–	–	33	–	–
21	–	–	32	–	108–110	–	30	–	–	57–58	–	–	–	–	–
22	–	–	–	–	111–113	–	–	–	–	59–60	–	–	–	–	–
23	–	–	–	–	114–116	–	–	–	–	–	–	–	–	–	–

(continues)

TABLE A.1(J) *(continued)*

Standard score	BD	SI	DS	PCn	CD	VC	LN	MR	CO	SS	PCm	CA	IN	AR	WR
Ages 15:4–15:7															
24	–	–	–	–	117–119	–	–	–	–	–	–	–	–	–	–
25	–	–	–	–	–	–	–	–	–	–	–	–	–	–	–
26	–	–	–	–	–	–	–	–	–	–	–	–	–	–	–
27	–	–	–	–	–	–	–	–	–	–	–	–	–	–	–
28	–	–	–	–	–	–	–	–	–	–	–	–	–	–	–
Ages 15:8–15:11															
18	66	43	29	27	100–102	66–67	27	34	41	51–52	–	134–135	32	–	24
19	67	44	30	28	103–105	68	28	–	42	53–54	38	136	–	34	–
20	68	–	31	–	106–108	–	29	35	–	55–56	–	–	33	–	–
21	–	–	32	–	109–111	–	30	–	–	57–58	–	–	–	–	–
22	–	–	–	–	112–114	–	–	–	–	59–60	–	–	–	–	–
23	–	–	–	–	115–117	–	–	–	–	–	–	–	–	–	–
24	–	–	–	–	118–119	–	–	–	–	–	–	–	–	–	–
25	–	–	–	–	–	–	–	–	–	–	–	–	–	–	–
26	–	–	–	–	–	–	–	–	–	–	–	–	–	–	–
27	–	–	–	–	–	–	–	–	–	–	–	–	–	–	–
28	–	–	–	–	–	–	–	–	–	–	–	–	–	–	–

TABLE A.1 (K)   Scaled Score Equivalents of Total Raw Scores for Subtest, By Age Group (Age 16)

Standard score	BD	SI	DS	PCn	CD	VC	LN	MR	CO	SS	PCm	CA	IN	AR	WR
Ages 16:0–16:3															
18	67	43	29	27	102–104	67	28	–	41	52–53	–	135	–	–	–
19	68	44	30	28	105–107	68	29	35	42	54–55	38	136	33	34	–
20	–	–	31	–	108–110	–	30	–	–	56–57	–	–	–	–	–
21	–	–	32	–	111–113	–	–	–	–	58–59	–	–	–	–	–
22	–	–	–	–	114–116	–	–	–	–	60	–	–	–	–	–
23	–	–	–	–	117–119	–	–	–	–	–	–	–	–	–	–
24	–	–	–	–	–	–	–	–	–	–	–	–	–	–	–
25	–	–	–	–	–	–	–	–	–	–	–	–	–	–	–
26	–	–	–	–	–	–	–	–	–	–	–	–	–	–	–
27	–	–	–	–	–	–	–	–	–	–	–	–	–	–	–
28	–	–	–	–	–	–	–	–	–	–	–	–	–	–	–
Ages 16:4–16:7															
18	67	43	29	27	102–104	67	28	–	41	52–53	–	135	–	–	–
19	68	44	30	28	105–107	68	29	35	42	54–55	38	136	33	34	–
20	–	–	31	–	108–110	–	30	–	–	56–57	–	–	–	–	–
21	–	–	32	–	111–113	–	–	–	–	58–59	–	–	–	–	–
22	–	–	–	–	114–116	–	–	–	–	60	–	–	–	–	–
23	–	–	–	–	117–119	–	–	–	–	–	–	–	–	–	–

(continues)

TABLE A.1(K)   (continued)

Standard score	BD	SI	DS	PCn	CD	VC	LN	MR	CO	SS	PCm	CA	IN	AR	WR
Ages 16:4–16:7															
24	–	–	–	–	–	–	–	–	–	–	–	–	–	–	–
25	–	–	–	–	–	–	–	–	–	–	–	–	–	–	–
26	–	–	–	–	–	–	–	–	–	–	–	–	–	–	–
27	–	–	–	–	–	–	–	–	–	–	–	–	–	–	–
28	–	–	–	–	–	–	–	–	–	–	–	–	–	–	–
Ages 16:8–16:11															
18	67	43	29	27	102–104	67	–	–	41	52–53	–	135	–	–	–
19	68	44	30	28	105–107	68	29	35	42	54–55	38	136	33	34	–
20	–	–	31	–	108–110	–	30	–	–	56–57	–	–	–	–	–
21	–	–	32	–	111–113	–	–	–	–	58–59	–	–	–	–	–
22	–	–	–	–	114–116	–	–	–	–	60	–	–	–	–	–
23	–	–	–	–	117–119	–	–	–	–	–	–	–	–	–	–
24	–	–	–	–	–	–	–	–	–	–	–	–	–	–	–
25	–	–	–	–	–	–	–	–	–	–	–	–	–	–	–
26	–	–	–	–	–	–	–	–	–	–	–	–	–	–	–
27	–	–	–	–	–	–	–	–	–	–	–	–	–	–	–
28	–	–	–	–	–	–	–	–	–	–	–	–	–	–	–

TABLE A.2   WISC4 Extended Norms FSIQ Equivalents of Sum of Scaled Scores

Fiqsum	FSIQ	90% CI	95% CI	Percentile
167	150	144–153	144–153	>99.9
168	150	144–153	144–153	>99.9
169	151	145–154	145–154	>99.9
170	151	145–154	145–154	>99.9
171	152	146–155	146–155	>99.9
172	153	147–156	146–156	>99.9
173	154	148–157	147–157	>99.9
174	154	148–157	147–157	>99.9
175	155	149–157	148–158	>99.9
176	156	150–158	149–159	>99.9
177	157	151–159	150–160	>99.9
178	157	151–159	150–160	>99.9
179	158	152–160	151–161	>99.9
180	159	153–161	152–162	>99.9
181	160	154–162	153–163	>99.9
182	160	154–162	153–163	>99.9
183	161	155–163	154–164	>99.9
184	162	156–164	155–165	>99.9
185	163	157–165	156–166	>99.9
186	164	158–166	157–167	>99.9
187	164	158–166	157–167	>99.9
188	165	159–167	158–168	>99.9
189	166	160–168	159–169	>99.9
190	167	161–169	160–170	>99.9
191	168	162–170	161–171	>99.9
192	169	163–171	162–172	>99.9
193	169	163–171	162–172	>99.9
194	170	164–172	163–173	>99.9
195	171	165–173	164–174	>99.9
196	172	166–174	165–175	>99.9
197	172	166–174	165–175	>99.9
198	173	167–175	166–176	>99.9
199	174	168–176	167–177	>99.9
200	175	169–177	168–178	>99.9

(*continues*)

TABLE A.2 *(continued)*

Fiqsum	FSIQ	90% CI	95% CI	Percentile
201	175	169–177	168–178	>99.9
202	176	170–178	169–179	>99.9
203	177	171–179	170–180	>99.9
204	178	172–180	171–181	>99.9
205	178	172–180	171–181	>99.9
206	179	172–181	172–182	>99.9
207	180	173–182	173–183	>99.9
208	181	174–183	174–184	>99.9
209	181	174–183	174–184	>99.9
210	182	175–184	175–184	>99.9
211	183	176–185	176–185	>99.9
212	184	177–186	177–186	>99.9
213	184	177–186	177–186	>99.9
214	185	178–187	178–187	>99.9
215	186	179–188	178–188	>99.9
216	187	180–189	179–189	>99.9
217	187	180–189	179–189	>99.9
218	188	181–190	180–190	>99.9
219	189	182–190	181–191	>99.9
220	190	183–191	182–192	>99.9
221	190	183–191	182–192	>99.9
222	191	184–192	183–193	>99.9
223	192	185–193	184–194	>99.9
224	193	186–194	185–195	>99.9
225	193	186–194	185–195	>99.9
226	194	187–195	186–196	>99.9
227	195	188–196	187–197	>99.9
228	196	189–197	188–198	>99.9
229	196	189–197	188–198	>99.9
230	197	190–198	189–199	>99.9
231	198	191–199	190–200	>99.9
232	199	192–200	191–201	>99.9
233	199	192–200	191–201	>99.9
234	200	193–201	192–202	>99.9

(continues)

TABLE A.2 (*continued*)

Fiqsum	FSIQ	90% CI	95% CI	Percentile
235	201	194–202	193–203	>99.9
236	202	195–203	194–204	>99.9
237	202	195–203	194–204	>99.9
238	203	196–204	195–205	>99.9
239	204	197–205	196–206	>99.9
240	205	198–206	197–207	>99.9
241	205	198–206	197–207	>99.9
242	206	199–207	198–208	>99.9
243	207	200–208	199–209	>99.9
244	208	201–209	200–210	>99.9
245	208	201–209	200–210	>99.9
246	209	202–210	201–211	>99.9
247–280	210	203–211	202–212	>99.9

TABLE A.3 WISC4 Extended Norms GAI Equivalents of Sum of Scaled Scores

Gaisum	GAI	90% CI	95% CI	Percentile
100	150	143–153	142–154	>99.9
101	151	144–154	143–155	>99.9
102	152	145–155	144–156	>99.9
103	153	146–156	145–157	>99.9
104	155	148–158	147–158	>99.9
105	156	149–158	148–159	>99.9
106	157	150–159	149–160	>99.9
107	158	151–160	150–161	>99.9
108	160	153–162	152–163	>99.9
109	161	154–163	153–164	>99.9
110	162	155–164	154–165	>99.9
111	163	156–165	155–166	>99.9
112	165	158–167	157–168	>99.9
113	166	159–168	158–169	>99.9
114	167	160–169	159–170	>99.9
115	168	161–170	160–171	>99.9

(*continues*)

TABLE A.3 *(continued)*

Gaisum	GAI	90% CI	95% CI	Percentile
116	170	162–172	162–173	>99.9
117	171	163–173	163–174	>99.9
118	173	165–175	164–176	>99.9
119	174	166–176	165–177	>99.9
120	175	167–177	166–178	>99.9
121	176	168–178	167–179	>99.9
122	178	170–180	169–181	>99.9
123	179	171–181	170–181	>99.9
124	180	172–182	171–182	>99.9
125	181	173–182	172–183	>99.9
126	183	175–184	174–185	>99.9
127	184	176–185	175–186	>99.9
128	185	177–186	176–187	>99.9
129	186	178–187	177–188	>99.9
130	188	180–189	179–190	>99.9
131	189	181–190	180–191	>99.9
132	190	182–191	181–192	>99.9
133	191	183–192	182–193	>99.9
134	193	185–194	184–195	>99.9
135	194	186–195	185–196	>99.9
136	195	186–196	186–197	>99.9
137	196	187–197	187–198	>99.9
138	198	189–199	188–200	>99.9
139	199	190–200	189–201	>99.9
140	200	191–201	190–202	>99.9
141	201	192–202	191–203	>99.9
142	203	194–204	193–205	>99.9
143	204	195–205	194–205	>99.9
144	205	196–206	195–206	>99.9
145	206	197–206	196–207	>99.9
146	208	199–208	198–209	>99.9
147	209	200–209	199–210	>99.9
148–168	210	201–210	200–211	>99.9

TABLE A.4   WISC4 Extended Norms – VCI Equivalents of Sum of Scaled Scores

Sum of SS	VCI	90% CI	95% CI	Percentile
55	150	141–153	140–154	>99.9
56	152	143–155	142–156	>99.9
57	155	146–157	145–158	>99.9
58	158	149–160	148–161	>99.9
59	160	151–162	150–163	>99.9
60	162	153–164	152–165	>99.9
61	164	154–166	153–167	>99.9
62	166	156–168	155–169	>99.9
63	168	158–170	157–171	>99.9
64	170	160–171	159–173	>99.9
65	172	162–173	161–174	>99.9
66	174	164–175	163–176	>99.9
67	176	166–177	165–178	>99.9
68	178	168–179	167–180	>99.9
69	180	170–181	168–182	>99.9
70	182	171–183	170–184	>99.9
71	184	173–185	172–186	>99.9
72	186	175–187	174–188	>99.9
73	188	177–188	176–189	>99.9
74	190	179–190	178–191	>99.9
75	192	181–192	180–193	>99.9
76	194	183–194	182–195	>99.9
77	196	185–196	183–197	>99.9
78	198	186–198	185–199	>99.9
79	200	188–200	187–201	>99.9
80	202	190–202	189–203	>99.9
81	204	192–203	191–205	>99.9
82	206	194–205	193–206	>99.9
83	208	196–207	195–208	>99.9
84	210	198–209	197–210	>99.9

TABLE A.5   WISC4 Extended Norms – PRI Equivalents of Sum of Scaled Scores

Sum of SS	PRI	90% CI	95% CI	Percentile
55	151	140–153	139–155	>99.9
56	153	142–155	141–156	>99.9
57	155	144–157	143–158	>99.9
58	157	146–159	145–160	>99.9
59	159	148–161	147–162	>99.9
60	161	150–163	148–164	>99.9
61	163	152–164	150–166	>99.9
62	165	153–166	152–167	>99.9
63	167	155–168	154–169	>99.9
64	169	157–170	156–171	>99.9
65	171	159–172	158–173	>99.9
66	173	161–174	160–175	>99.9
67	175	163–175	161–177	>99.9
68	177	164–177	163–178	>99.9
69	179	166–179	165–180	>99.9
70	181	168–181	167–182	>99.9
71	183	170–183	169–184	>99.9
72	185	172–185	171–186	>99.9
73	187	174–186	172–188	>99.9
74	189	175–188	174–190	>99.9
75	191	177–190	176–191	>99.9
76	193	179–192	178–193	>99.9
77	195	181–194	180–195	>99.9
78	197	183–196	182–197	>99.9
79	199	185–198	183–199	>99.9
80	201	186–199	185–201	>99.9
81	203	188–201	187–202	>99.9
82	205	190–203	189–204	>99.9
83	207	192–205	191–206	>99.9
84	210	195–208	194–209	>99.9

TABLE A.6   WISC4 Extended Norms – WMI Equivalents of Sum of Scaled Scores

Sum of SS	WMI	90% CI	95% CI	Percentile
37	150	140–152	138–154	>99.9
38	152	141–154	140–155	>99.9
39	155	144–157	143–158	>99.9
40	158	147–160	146–161	>99.9
41	161	150–163	148–164	>99.9
42	165	153–166	152–167	>99.9
43	168	156–169	155–170	>99.9
44	171	159–172	158–173	>99.9
45	174	162–175	160–176	>99.9
46	177	164–177	163–178	>99.9
47	180	167–180	166–181	>99.9
48	184	171–184	170–185	>99.9
49	187	174–186	172–188	>99.9
50	190	176–189	175–190	>99.9
51	194	180–193	179–194	>99.9
52	197	183–196	182–197	>99.9
53	200	186–198	184–200	>99.9
54	204	189–202	188–203	>99.9
55	207	192–205	191–206	>99.9
56	210	195–208	194–209	>99.9

TABLE A.7   WISC4 Extended Norms – PSI Equivalents of Sum of Scaled Scores

Sum of SS	PSI	90% CI	95% Cl	Percentile
38	150	136–152	135–153	>99.9
39	154	140–155	139–156	>99.9
40	157	143–158	141–159	>99.9
41	160	145–160	144–162	>99.9
42	164	149–164	147–165	>99.9
43	167	151–166	150–168	>99.9
44	170	154–169	153–171	>99.9
45	174	158–173	156–174	>99.9
46	177	160–175	159–177	>99.9
47	180	163–178	161–179	>99.9
48	184	166–181	165–183	>99.9
49	187	169–184	168–186	>99.9
50	190	172–187	170–188	>99.9
51	194	175–190	174–192	>99.9
52	197	178–193	176–194	>99.9
53	200	180–196	179–197	>99.9
54	204	184–199	183–200	>99.9
55	207	187–202	185–203	>99.9
56	210	189–204	188–206	>99.9

7

ASSESSMENT OF MENTAL RETARDATION/ INTELLECTUAL DISABILITY WITH THE WISC-IV

JEAN SPRUILL[1] AND PATTI L. HARRISON[2]

[1]*Department of Psychology, The University of Alabama, Tuscaloosa, AL, USA*

[2]*Department of Educational Studies in Psychology, Research Methodology and Counseling, The University of Alabama, Tuscaloosa, AL, USA*

Increasingly, the term *intellectual disability* is being used instead of *mental retardation*. This change in terminology is exemplified by changes in organization names (e.g., the American Association on Intellectual and Developmental Disabilities, International Association for the Scientific Study of Intellectual Disabilities, President's Committee for People with Intellectual Disabilities), journal titles (e.g., *Intellectual and Developmental Disabilities*), book titles (e.g., Herr et al., 2003; Lakin & Turnbull, 2005), and published research (e.g., Stainton, 2001; Schroeder et al., 2002; Parmenter, 2004).

For the purposes of this chapter, the authors will continue to use the term mental retardation for a variety of reasons: the term is more familiar to mental health professionals; national and state regulations for special education services use the term; and current diagnostic criteria for mental retardation (discussed below) continue to use the term. It is expected that, in the future, the term "intellectual disability" will replace the term "mental retardation."

The initial assessment of a child that leads to a diagnosis of mental retardation is "the single most important diagnostic intervention during the entire course of providing services to the individual and family" (Mulick & Hale, 1996, p. 259). A diagnosis of mental retardation can determine the types of publicly supported services received by an individual. In many states, for children below age 3 who are diagnosed with mental retardation or who are at risk, early intervention services are available to maximize the child's potential and prepare him or her for appropriate educational services once they reach school age. For children aged 3 and above, special education and related services are made available through the school system. For older children, academic training is often supplemented by job training skills. A diagnosis of mental retardation also influences the manner in which individuals are viewed by society and eligibility for a variety of social programs, entitlements, and protections. Thus, considerable care must be displayed by professionals when assessing mental retardation.

Measures of intelligence, along with assessment of adaptive behavior, are the most important parts of an assessment for diagnosis of mental retardation and eligibility for services and play an important role in the diagnosis of many other developmental and acquired conditions that may have impairments in intelligence and everyday competence as a component. However, in all cases, an IQ score is only one component of the diagnosis and should never be the only component. As discussed below, mental retardation is characterized by significantly subaverage intellectual functioning accompanied by deficits in the skills needed to live independently, usually referred to as adaptive behavior. Thus adequate assessment of mental retardation requires the careful review and interpretation of information that describes various behavioral traits displayed in different settings during the person's life. The information should be acquired from multiple sources through the use of multiple assessment methods. Furthermore, to accurately diagnose and make recommendations for interventions, the professional must know the legal and professional definitions of mental retardation as well as possible etiologies and behavioral concomitants. Thus, assessment of mental retardation involves more than the use of standardized measures of intelligence and adaptive functioning.

This chapter provides a brief overview of definitions, prevalence, etiology, economic costs, and behavioral aspects of mental retardation and then focuses on the use of the *Wechsler Intelligence Scale for Children* – Fourth Edition (WISC-IV) as part of a comprehensive evaluation of a child with mental retardation.

DEFINITIONS OF MENTAL RETARDATION

Definitions and classifications used to describe individuals with mental retardation differ with respect to behavior, degree of impairment, and etiology. Prior to the use of standardized measures of intelligence, mental retardation was defined by deficits in social and vocational functioning. The definitions of mental retardation provided by the American Association on Mental Retardation/ American Association on Intellectual and Developmental Disabilities, the Individuals with Disabilities Education Act of 2004, and the American Psychiatric Association, the three most commonly used definitions for children and youth, are summarized below.

AMERICAN ASSOCIATION ON MENTAL RETARDATION/
AMERICAN ASSOCIATION ON INTELLECTUAL AND
DEVELOPMENTAL DISABILITIES

Effective since 2007, the American Association on Mental Retardation (AAMR) has changed its name to the American Association on Intellectual and Developmental Disabilities (AAIDD). The website (www.aaidd.com) continues to utilize the AAMR definition of mental retardation as "... a disability characterized by significant limitations both in intellectual functioning and in adaptive behavior as expressed in conceptual, social, and practical adaptive skills. This disability originates before age 18" (AAMR, 2002, p. 8). The AAMR/AAIDD provides several recommendations for cutoff scores on standardized instruments for a diagnosis of mental retardation. With regard to the intellectual criterion, a diagnosis of mental retardation is associated with an IQ test score of approximately 2 SDs below the mean, considering the standard error of measurement, or a score of 70 or below. Because the standard error of measurement for most IQ tests is approximately 5, the ceiling may go up to 75 in assessment of some individuals. The 2002 edition was the first AAMR manual to provide specific adaptive behavior criterion scores for a classification of mental retardation: scores that are at least 2 SDs below the mean on either (a) one of the following three types of adaptive behavior: conceptual, social, or practical, or (b) an overall score on a standardized measure of conceptual, social, and practical skills.

INDIVIDUALS WITH DISABILITIES EDUCATION
IMPROVEMENT ACT

The final regulations of IDEA-2004 (Individuals with Disabilities Education Improvement Act, 2006) define mental retardation as "significantly subaverage general intellectual functioning, existing concurrently with deficits in adaptive behavior and manifested during the developmental period, that adversely affects a child's educational performance." The IDEA definition does not provide specific criteria for subaverage intellectual functioning and adaptive behavior deficits. State regulations that implement IDEA may include specific criteria.

AMERICAN PSYCHIATRIC ASSOCIATION

The American Psychiatric Association's (2000) *Diagnostic and Statistical Manual of Mental Disorders* – Fourth Edition, text revision (DSM-IV-TR) defines mental retardation as "... significantly subaverage general intellectual functioning (Criterion A) that is accompanied by significant limitations in adaptive functioning in at least two of the following areas: communication, self-care, home living, social/interpersonal skills, use of community resources, self-direction, functional academic skills, work, leisure, health, and safety (Criterion B). The onset must occur before age 18 years" (p. 41). Like the AAMR/AAIDD definition, the criteria for significantly subaverage intellectual functioning generally is considered an

IQ that is 2 or more SDs below the population mean, usually an IQ of 70 or below. However, an IQ of 75 or below may constitute the criterion in some settings.

LEVELS OF MENTAL RETARDATION

The AAMR/AAIDD and IDEA do not specify different levels of severity of mental retardation. However, the DSM-TR-IV distinguishes four categories of mental retardation: mild, moderate, severe, and profound mental retardation. The descriptions below represent a compilation of information from several sources (Weiss & Weisz, 1986; American Psychiatric Association, 2000; Sattler, 2001; Kamphaus, 2002). Whereas the IQ scores given are those specified by the deviations below the population mean, the DSM-TR-IV specifies that the standard error of measurement be considered in a diagnosis of mental retardation. Thus a range of scores at either end of the classification is most appropriate. The cut-off scores for each category may vary among various state and federal agencies, school systems, etc., and the professional must be aware of the criteria required by the various agencies and/or states in which he or she works. Adaptive behavior (discussed later) consistent with the level of mental retardation also is important in the classification of the individual.

MILD MENTAL RETARDATION

Mild mental retardation is characterized by IQs between 55 and 69 for the WISC-IV (2–3 SDs below the population mean) and limitations in adaptive behavior. Although the development of motor, speech, social, cognitive, and other abilities of individuals who display mild mental retardation shows some delay, often the extent of their intellectual deficits is not identified as reaching the level of mental retardation until they enter school. Individuals who display mild mental retardation (particularly at the higher end of the spectrum) usually learn to read and write, often to about the sixth grade level, by late adolescence. They are capable of gainful employment, may become self-supporting, and may marry and raise a family. Once out of school, many of these individuals often blend into general society and may require assistance only during periods of severe personal or economic stress. Individuals in this category comprise approximately 85% of the individuals with a diagnosis of mental retardation.

MODERATE MENTAL RETARDATION

Moderate mental retardation is characterized by IQs between 40 and 54 (3–4 SDs below the mean) and limitations in adaptive behavior. Individuals with moderate mental retardation usually are identified as having mental retardation during infancy or early childhood. They often display significant delays in attaining one or more developmental milestones in motor, speech, social, or cognitive development. With appropriate educational services, individuals classified as having moderate mental retardation may eventually acquire academic skills similar to a third or fourth grade student. Individuals with moderate mental retardation typically require assistance and/or supervision in almost all aspects of daily living. With proper training, some may work at unskilled or semiskilled jobs. Individuals in this category comprise approximately 10% of the individuals with a diagnosis of mental retardation.

SEVERE MENTAL RETARDATION

Severe mental retardation is classified by IQs between 25 and 39 (4–5 SDs below the mean) and accompanying limitations in adaptive behavior. Because of their significant delays in acquiring motor and language skills, children with severe mental retardation are identified in infancy. They frequently display physical abnormalities. Although they may acquire some self-help skills, they are unable to function independently and will require close supervision throughout their life. Individuals in this category comprise approximately 3–4% of the individuals with a diagnosis of mental retardation.

PROFOUND MENTAL RETARDATION

Profound mental retardation is characterized by an IQ score below 25 (greater than 5 SDs below the population mean) and accompanying limitations in adaptive behavior (American Psychiatric Association, 2000). Individuals with profound mental retardation often are identified at birth or shortly thereafter in light of their physical abnormalities. Delays in the development of skills during infancy and early childhood will be apparent. Physical abnormalities may preclude their being able to walk or talk. They are unable to assume responsibility for activities of daily living or care for their own needs, requiring lifelong care. Individuals in this category comprise approximately 1–2% of the individuals with a diagnosis of mental retardation.

INCIDENCE OF MENTAL RETARDATION

Mental retardation is the most common developmental disorder. As many as 3 out of every 100 people in the country have mental retardation. According to a recent study by Scullin (2006), the percentage of enrolled children aged 6–17 who were classified as having mental retardation in the 1999–2000 school year was 1.19%. The percentage of children classified as having mental retardation varies from state to state, from a low of 0.33% in New Jersey to a high of 3.04% in Kentucky (Scullin, 2006).

Why the disparity in estimates of the number of individuals with mental retardation? Perhaps the major reason is the difference in standards for a diagnosis of mental retardation among the various agencies and states. In a survey of state agencies, Denning et al. (2000) found that approximately 25% of the states did not specify an IQ score required for a diagnosis of mental retardation and about 72% of the states did not list specific criterion scores for deficits in adaptive behavior. Differences in IQ and adaptive behavior deficits required for a classification of mental retardation can lead to disparities in diagnoses among the states and even in different agencies within a state. Thus, in practice, standardized measures and clinical judgment are used in diagnosing mental retardation (Sattler, 2001; Kamphaus, 2002).

ECONOMIC IMPACT OF MENTAL RETARDATION

It is estimated that nearly 2 million students are tested for special education services each year and each child qualifying for special education services must undergo periodic reevaluations, usually every 3 years, to determine if he or she remains eligible for continued services (Kanaya et al., 2003). The cost incurred by the assessment of mental retardation is substantial, but is only the beginning of the total cost. The special education services needed by children with mental retardation cost more than education in the regular classroom. As adults, individuals with mental retardation usually have less income and play less in taxes, and thus do not contribute to society economically in the same way that others contribute. Individuals with mental retardation are more likely to need long-term services or care. According to a report by the Centers for Disease Control and Prevention (2004), the average lifetime cost for one person born in 2000 with retardation is estimated to be $1,014,000 (in 2003 dollars). This represents costs over and above those experienced by a person who does not have a disability. The actual economic costs of mental retardation are even higher than what is reported in this study. And, this is only the financial cost; it says nothing about the emotional and personal cost to the individual and his or her family. This is even another reason for great care by the professional in making a diagnosis of mental retardation.

ETIOLOGY OF MENTAL RETARDATION

The causes of mental retardation are typically grouped into two broad categories: those with familial etiologies and those with organic etiologies. Only about 20–25% of the cases of mental retardation have a known or organic etiology (Jacobson & Mulick, 1996). Some examples of known etiologies for mental retardation are trauma before or after birth (e.g., head injury), infections present at birth or occurring after birth (e.g., congenital rubella, encephalitis, meningitis), chromosomal abnormalities (e.g., Down's Syndrome, Fragile X Syndrome,

Prader-Willi Syndrome), metabolic disorders (e.g., Reye's Syndrome, Rett Syndrome, Hunter Syndrome), toxic (e.g., lead poisoning, intrauterine exposure to alcohol, cocaine, amphetamines, and other drugs), and nutritional (e.g., malnutrition). For example, see Chapter 10 for a discussion of the relationship between systemic illness and cognitive impairment. The unexplained causes are often referred as "familial" and represent approximately 75–80% of the cases (Grossman, 1983; MedlinePlus Encyclopedia, 2007).

There is some overlap of intellectual abilities between the familial and organic categories; however, those with familial forms of mental retardation generally have IQs above 50. These individuals typically are from low socioeconomic groups; often have one or more family members who display diminished functioning, particularly in school settings; and seldom have neurological or obvious physical abnormalities. Most are diagnosed as having mental retardation during their elementary school years (Grossman, 1983). Those with organic forms of mental retardation typically have IQ scores below 50, do not have other family members with mental retardation, often have physical abnormalities, are usually diagnosed prior to school age; the socioeconomic status of their families is varied (Grossman, 1983; Jacobson & Mulick, 1996).

ADAPTIVE BEHAVIOR

The diagnosis of mental retardation requires documentation that an individual displays subaverage intelligence as well as significant deficits in adaptive behavior. Adaptive behavior generally refers to a person's ability to meet the standards of personal behavior and independence expected for their age peers within their culture. Measures of adaptive behavior typically ask respondents who know the person well to indicate whether the person displays important daily behaviors associated with a variety of adaptive skills.

The DSM-IV-TR (American Psychiatric Association, 2000) identifies 10 specific skill areas that comprise adaptive behavior: communication, self-care, home living, social/interpersonal skills, use of community resources, self-direction, functional academic skills, work, health and safety, and leisure. The AAMR/AAIDD (AAMR, 2002) identifies three broad domains of adaptive behavior that include specific skill areas: conceptual (e.g., communication, functional academics, self-direction, health and safety), social (e.g., social skills, leisure), and practical (e.g., self-care, home living, community use, health and safety, and work).

Several standardized measures of adaptive behavior are available, including the *Adaptive Behavior Assessment System* – Second Edition (Harrison & Oakland, 2003); *Vineland Adaptive Behavior Scales* – Second Edition (Sparrow et al., 2005); *AAMR Adaptive Behavior Scale-School* – Second Edition (Nihira et al., 1993a); *AAMR Adaptive Behavior Scale-Residential and Community* – Second Edition (Nihira et al., 1993b); and the *Scales of Independent Behavior-Revised* (Bruininks et al., 1996).

Individuals with mental retardation differ in their adaptive skill strengths and deficits and, except for those with severe and profound levels, are unlikely to show significant deficits in all areas of adaptive functioning. Typically, measures of adaptive functioning and intelligence correlate moderately, typically between 0.20 and 0.60 (e.g., Platt et al., 1991; Kamphaus, 2002), although there is evidence to suggest that correlations may vary for different domains of adaptive behavior and are higher for individuals with more severe disabilities (Reschly et al., 2002). Thus, the constructs of intelligence and adaptive behavior overlap statistically yet differ sufficiently to warrant their joint use when assessing mental retardation.

ASSESSING MENTAL RETARDATION USING THE WISC-IV

Unlike the WISC-III, which used the term "intellectually deficient" for IQs of 69 or below (Wechsler, 1991), the WISC-IV (Wechsler, 2003b) uses the term "extremely low" to avoid the implication that a low IQ score is sufficient for a diagnosis of mental retardation. Because the lowest IQ obtainable on the WISC-IV is 40, the WISC-IV cannot be used to assess children whose intellectual ability falls below that score. (Psychometric scaling to lower extremes of an IQ range on norm-referenced measures of intelligence, such as the WISC-IV, generally is not recommended, because few individuals at these IQ levels can be included in representative standardization samples for the instruments.) See comments above for information about the WISC-IV IQ range for mild and moderate levels of mental retardation. The WISC-IV has been shown to distinguish between the two levels of mental retardation (Wechsler, 2003c) and data for both levels of severity are generally consistent with previous reports by Atkinson (1992) and Spruill (1991) with adults and Wechsler (1991, 2003c) for children.

FACTOR STRUCTURE OF THE WISC-IV

The *WISC-IV Technical and Interpretative Manual* (Wechsler, 2003c) presented exploratory and confirmatory factor analyses to investigate the factor structure of the WISC-IV. Instead of the Verbal and Performance IQ of the previous editions of the WISC, four factors referred to as indexes were identified. The Verbal Comprehension Index (VCI) measures the child's verbal concept formation, verbal reasoning and knowledge acquired from one's environment. The VCI is thought to be "a more refined, purer measure of verbal reasoning and conceptualization than the WISC-III VIQ" (Wechsler, 2003c, p. 103). The Perceptual Reasoning Index (PRI) is a measure of perceptual and fluid reasoning, spatial processing, and visual–motor integration. The subtests of the PRI have a greater emphasis on fluid reasoning than was true of the Performance IQ in the WISC-III. The Working Memory Index (WMI) is a measure of a child's working memory abilities, primarily the child's attention, concentration, mental control, and reasoning. Working memory is considered an essential part of higher-order cognitive processes. The Processing Speed Index (PSI) provides a measure of the child's ability to quickly and correctly scan, sequence, or discriminate simple visual information and is also a measure of short-term visual memory, attention, and visual–motor coordination.

To date only one study has been published investigating the factor structure of the WISC-IV with a clinical population. Watkins et al. (2006) used a sample of 432 students referred for evaluation for special education services to determine the factor structure of the WISC-IV with this group. Using confirmatory factor analysis, their findings supported the four-factor model found in the standardization sample. The authors reported that "When transformed to an orthogonalized higher order model, the general factor accounted for the greatest amount of common (75.7%) and total (46.7%) variance. In contrast, the largest contribution by a first-order factor (Verbal Comprehension) was 6.5% of total variance. It was recommended that the interpretation of the WISC-IV not discount the strong general factor (p. 975)." It should be noted that only 5% of the children in this study were diagnosed as having mental retardation; thus the factor structure of the WISC-IV for children with mental retardation is yet to be determined. However, given that the four factors of the WISC-III (Verbal Comprehension, Perceptual Organization, Processing Speed, and, to a lesser extent, Freedom from Distractibility) have been shown to be robust across various clinical samples (e.g., Dickinson et al., 2002), we expect that the four factors of the WISC-IV also will be robust for clinical groups.

WISC-IV VERSUS WISC-III

During the standardization of the WISC-IV, 244 children were administered the WISC-IV and the WISC-III in a counter-balanced order with mean retest interval of 28 days. The mean WISC-IV scores were slightly lower than the corresponding scores for the WISC-III and the correlations between scores from the WISC-IV and WISC-III range from a high of 0.89 (FSIQ) to a low of 0.62 (Comprehension). According to the information in the *Technical and Interpretative Manual* (Wechsler, 2003c), the comparisons among the WISC-III and WISC-IV scores were statistically significant, with the WISC-IV scores being lower. This study was conducted for a non-clinical sample; there are not yet any published studies comparing scores of children with mental retardation who were tested with both the WISC-III and WISC-IV.

Over the last century, average IQ scores have been steadily increasing. This phenomenon, known as the Flynn effect, was first documented by James Flynn (1984) and is one reason that IQ tests are renormed periodically. As time passes and the test norms grow older, individuals obtain higher normative scores on the test and the mean IQ score increases. Currently, data indicate that for the population in general, the average increase is approximately 3 points per decade or about 0.3 points per year. Studies comparing scores on the WISC-R and WISC-III (e.g., Bolen et al., 1995; Slate & Saarino, 1995; Vance et al., 1996; Sanborn et al., 2003) and WAIS-R and WAIS-III (The Psychological Corporation, 1997) have shown that the Flynn effect exists for children and adults diagnosed as having mental retardation. In a recent publication Flynn analyzed data from large sample of children at all levels of intelligence (Flynn, 2006). He compared the predicted increase in scores (i.e., 0.3 points per year) with the actual scores for children tested on the WISC and WISC-R, the WISC-R and WISC-III, and the WISC-III and WISC-IV. He found that the Flynn effect did occur; stating that the WISC tests "behave with remarkable consistency. The data sets are large and at every IQ level from 55 to 100; the predicted and actual values are very close" (p. 8).

However, Zhou et al. (2007) compared Performance/Perceptual Reasoning IQs/ indexes of the WPPSI-R and WPPSI-III, WISC-III and WISC-IV, and WAIS-R and WAIS-III. The performance IQs were investigated because previous research has shown them to be more sensitive to the Flynn effect. The researchers compared scores of the older and new versions of the tests and found that a Flynn effect was found at the average ability level. The average IQ difference at higher ability levels demonstrated a reverse Flynn effect and, at lower ability levels, a much larger Flynn effect was found. Importantly, the researchers found that substantial within-group variability was evident across ability levels, suggested that a Flynn effect may be interpretable only as an aggregated phenomenon, and cautioned that applying a standard formula to account for a Flynn effect for *individuals* is invalid.

WISC-IV AND WAIS-III FOR ADOLESCENTS WITH MENTAL RETARDATION

Comparisons between the WISC-IV and WAIS-III for children aged 16 (the only age overlap) with mental retardation are not yet available in the research literature. The reader is referred to the *WISC-IV Technical and Interpretative Manual* (Wechsler, 2003c) for information about the comparisons of the WAIS-III and WISC-IV scores for children aged 16.

Because the WAIS-III and WISC-IV only overlap at age 16, it is not likely that children first tested on the WAIS-III would be retested on the WISC-IV; however, the reverse is highly likely. When the examiner is assessing a 16-year-old, which test should be used – the WISC-IV or the WAIS-III? Because the WISC-IV has a lower floor than the WAIS-III, we would recommend that the WISC-IV be used so that the individual's strengths and weaknesses may be better identified. Also, since the WISC-IV scores for 16 year olds generally were lower than those on the WAIS-III, individuals whose WISC-IV IQs are toward the high end of the range of mental retardation (i.e., approaching 70) might score higher on the WAIS-III and be classified as in the Borderline range and therefore no longer qualifying for special education services. Indeed such effects have been found for test–retest data for the WISC-R to WISC-III (Kanaya et al., 2003). As Kanaya et al. (2003) reported, the times "… to be particularly cautious are when a test is either at the beginning or at the end of its norming cycle" (p. 789).

WISC-IV AND WPPSI-III FOR CHILDREN WITH MENTAL RETARDATION

The WISC-IV (Wechsler, 2003b) and the WPPSI-III (Wechsler, 2003a) were normed at approximately the same time. During the standardization, 182 children ages 6 and 7 year olds tested with both tests. The scores were nearly identical, with less than 1 point difference between the corresponding index and Full Scale IQs. The reader is referred to the *WISC-IV Technical and Interpretative Manual* (Wechsler, 2003c) for detailed information about the WISC-IV and WPPSI-III data for the sample.

It is highly unlikely that anyone first diagnosed as having mental retardation using the WISC-IV would be retested on the WPPSI-III; however, the reverse is highly likely. Given the high correlations between the tests and the similar mean scores, children whose scores classified them as having mental retardation on the WPPSI-III probably would be classified as having mental retardation on the WISC-IV.

When assessing a child between the ages of 6 and 7 and with possible mental retardation, which test should be used? We recommend that the WPPSI-III be used because of the lower floor. The WPPSI-III will have more items for the child to answer than the WISC-IV and is more likely to provide a better estimate of the child's strengths and weaknesses.

WISC-IV AND ABAS-II

Correlations between measures of intelligence and adaptive behavior generally are in the 0.20–0.60 range (Kamphaus, 2002). Some research suggests that correlations between IQs and measures of adaptive behavior are somewhat higher for teacher ratings than for parent ratings. Scores from the WISC-IV were compared with those from the *Adaptive Behavior Assessment System – Second Edition* (ABAS-II; Harrison & Oakland, 2003) for both the Parent Form ($N = 121$) and the Teacher Form ($N = 145$) using two separate non-clinical samples of children ages 6 through 16. Results are reported in the ABAS-II manual. For the study with the ABAS-II Parent Form, the mean scores were 99.4 and 99.7 on the ABAS-II Parent Form General Adaptive Composite and the WISC-IV Full Scale IQ, respectively. The correlation between scores from the two measures were 0.41 for the General Adaptive Composite and WISC-IV Full Scale IQ; correlations between the ABAS-II Parent Form adaptive skill areas and the WISC-IV FSIQ ranged from 0.16 (self-care adaptive skill area) to 0.54 (communication adaptive skill area). For ABAS-II Teacher Form, the mean General Adaptive Composite was 104.8 and the mean WISC-IV FSIQ was 100.5. Compared to the ABAS-II Parent Form correlations, somewhat higher correlations were observed between the ABAS-II Teacher Forms and the WISC-IV. The correlation between the ABAS-II Teacher Form General Adaptive Composite and WISC-IV Full Scale was 0.58; correlations between the ABAS-II Teacher Form adaptive skill areas and the WISC-IV FSIQ ranged from 0.37 (leisure adaptive skill area) to 0.57 (functional academics and self-direction adaptive skill areas). There are not yet any published studies comparing scores of children with mental retardation who were assessed with both the ABAS-II and WISC-IV. The correlations between scores from the ABAS-II and WISC-IV are consistent with those found in previous research, and suggest that adaptive behavior and intelligence are distinct, but related constructs, thus supporting use of measures of both intelligence and adaptive behavior in the assessment of individuals with mental retardation.

DIAGNOSTIC AND CLINICAL ISSUES

UNUSUAL DIFFERENCES AMONG WISC-IV INDEX SCORES

The Full Scale IQ is the most reliable score obtained on the WISC-IV and is usually the first score to be considered when interpreting a child's score profile. However, unusual variability among the index scores that comprise the Full Scale IQ suggests the Full Scale IQ does not summarize the child's intellectual abilities accurately. The term *unusual differences* refers to differences that are both statistically significant and that occur rarely in a population. A difference is determined to be *unusual* by examining the frequency of differences occurring in the standardization sample (Tables B.2 and B.6, Wechsler, 2003b). These differences are called base rates. As a rule of thumb, differences that are both statistically significant and that occur in 10% or less of the standardization sample are considered unusual (Sattler, 2001). Table B.2 in the *WISC-IV Technical and Interpretative Manual* provides base rates for differences among index scores for the standardization group as a whole and for various levels of IQ. The base rates for children with IQs ≤ 79 differ from those from a normal population. It is recommended that the base rates for IQs ≤ 79 should be used for children with mental retardation. When unusual differences exist among the index scores, the validity of the Full Scale IQ as the best indicator of a child's intellectual abilities may be questionable. Thus, when an unusual amount of scatter exists among the index scores, it is possible that WISC-IV interpretations should rely heavily on the index scores instead of the Full Scale IQ. However, a number of researchers question the clinical utility and predictive validity of de-emphasizing the WISC-IV Full Scale IQ and emphasizing index scores or subtest patterns (e.g., Glutting et al., 2006).

Interpretation of the Full Scale IQ and index scores depends on a number of factors. The first consideration should be the classification of the various index scores. For example, if the PSI is in the Low Average or Borderline range and all other index scores are in the Extremely Low range, the child's intellectual ability is probably best represented by a classification of mental retardation. However, if for example, the VCI is 89 (Low Average), the PRI is 75 (Borderline), and the WMI and PSI are 62 and 65, respectively, a diagnosis of mental retardation is less defensible as attention problems could account for lower scores on Processing Speed and Working Memory. For further guidance, the reader is directed to Sattler (2003).

DIFFERENCES BETWEEN TEST–RETEST DATA

Regulations and policies promulgated by most state departments of education and other regulatory agencies policies that govern diagnostic or eligibility decisions do not consider changes in tests scores resulting from the renorming of tests or use of instruments that differ in reliability and validity. Therefore, when retesting a child over a period of time, with the new edition of a previously administered test (e.g., WISC-IV instead of the WISC-III), with a different test (e.g., WAIS-III instead of WISC-IV), or even the same test (e.g., WISC-IV), clinicians need to be prepared to explain any differences in the test scores and to justify selecting a particular score as being the best measure of the child's intellectual functioning and therefore a part of the basis for their diagnostic decisions.

The decision as to which score, the one from the previously administered test or the current test, reflects the child's ability level more accurately may be assisted through the use of other information. Certainly one issue to be considered is the Flynn effect. As discussed earlier the Flynn effect has been documented to be about 3 points per decade for groups of examinees. A Flynn effect for a particular individual is less certain and Zhou et al. (2007) stressed that routine application or interpretation of a Flynn effect for individuals is not supported. Clearly individual scores must demonstrate changes for the group to show changes; however, one individual's score may show an increase from Time A to Time B whereas another individual's score from Time A to Time B could show a decrease or no change. The examiner has no way of knowing whether the change in test scores is due to the Flynn effect or some other factor. It is recommended that the examiner consider additional hypotheses about differences in an examinee's test scores over time (e.g., classical measurement error, administration and setting factors).

A number of other factors should be considered to explain differences in IQ scores across test administrations. For example, if the child's IQ has changed from a previous administration of WISC-III to a current administration of the WISC-IV and this change is accompanied by corresponding changes in adaptive functioning, achievement test scores, and grades, then the score from the WISC-IV may be more accurate. If, on the other hand, *all other assessment measures* are essentially the same as on the earlier assessment, then further assessment of the child's cognitive functioning may be warranted.

Differences in scores on tests that purport to measure the same construct occur for various reasons, including personal variables (e.g., motivation, rapport, health, distractions); other reasons are psychometric. Bracken (1988) provided an excellent discussion of the 10 most common psychometric reasons for discrepancies between test scores. Two of the most common psychometric reasons are: (1) the differences in standardization or publication dates, an issue discussed previously and (2) regression to the mean.

REGRESSION TO THE MEAN

Another issue to consider in the diagnosis of mental retardation is the effect of regression to the mean on test scores. Over time, group mean scores for persons with mental retardation have been shown to move toward the normative mean (i.e., regression toward the mean). For example, Spitz (1983) found the mean WISC-R Full Scale IQ for a group of children with mental retardation to be 55 at age 13 and 58 at age 15. Thus, when a clinician is evaluating a child with mental retardation using the WISC-IV and finds a current score somewhat higher (and outside the usual range of mental retardation) than the child's previous WISC-IV score, should a continued classification of mental retardation be considered? Consider an example where the current Full Scale IQ score is 71 and the previous Full Scale IQ score was 65. Is this an example of regression to the mean or something else? There is no easy answer to this question.

At present, except for the test–retest study reported in the WISC-IV manual, there are no studies comparing changes in WISC-IV IQs over time. The mean test–retest Full Scale IQs for children tested 23 days apart were 101.0 and 106.6, respectively. However, research by Kanaya et al. (2003) has shown that WISC-R and WISC-III scores have been remarkably stable over the typical 3-year retest interval. In addition, small differences in test scores for an individual over time may be well within the standard error of measurement for a test.

However, knowledge of average expected changes for *groups* over time is not much help in determining the causes of an *individual's* different scores over time. Knowing that regression to the mean does occur may alert the examiner to possible reasons for an individual's changes in IQs over time. Above all, professionals in school districts and other agencies that make decisions using test scores, especially decisions about special education placement that can change the course of children's lives, must take into account a variety of evaluation data and other factors. A child's need for and expected benefit from special services, not just test scores, as well as numerous child, context, and instruction factors should guide decisions. Professional judgments of the individuals making decisions are the primary factors in effective and valid decision-making.

TESTING FOR MAXIMUM PERFORMANCE: CONSIDERATIONS WHEN TESTING CHILDREN WITH MENTAL RETARDATION

The testing process is guided by whether its goal is to describe a child's behaviors at their best or as they occur typically. When assessing achievement, intelligence, and perceptual qualities, clinicians generally attempt to create conditions that elicit children's best effort and work. Thus, professionals measure the child's *maximum* abilities and capabilities, not their typical performance. In contrast, when assessing adaptive behavior, personality, and social qualities, clinicians generally attempt to create conditions that provide an understanding of a child's *typical* performance. The administration of tests of maximum performance, such as the WISC-IV, attempts to elicit a child's very best behaviors (Oakland & Glutting, 1998). The *Guide to the Assessment of Test Session Behavior* (GATSB; Glutting & Oakland, 1993) provides a nationally standardized norm-referenced measure of test-taking ability and is very useful in assessing the child's cooperativeness and readiness for testing. Children who display deficit test-taking behavior generally obtain Full Scale IQs 7–10 points lower than those obtained by children with more suitable test-taking behaviors.

CONCLUSIONS

Mental retardation is a disability about which we are still learning. Mental retardation may exist concurrently with other developmental disabilities, mental and/or neurological disorders. A diagnosis of mental retardation can be made only after careful interpretation of the entire clinical data set: background information; history; intellectual, and adaptive behavior measures; behavioral observations; academic achievement; and various other factors relevant to a particular individual.

CASE STUDY: PSYCHOLOGICAL EVALUATION

REASON FOR REFERRAL

John, a 7-year, 0-month year old, was referred for an evaluation by his kindergarten teacher, Ms. Powers, for concerns regarding difficulties with reading and writing. Specifically, John guesses when he is reading rather than sounding out letters and words and he cannot copy material from the board. John repeated kindergarten and has been provisionally promoted to the first grade in the fall.

BACKGROUND INFORMATION

Kristy Jones, John's mother, reported that she was 16 and unmarried when she gave birth to John. No problems were noted with the birth or delivery, and his mother stated that John was "born in excellent condition." In 2003, Ms. Jones married Steven Jones and they have twin girls, age 3 years. John lives with them and frequently spends time with his maternal grandparents. When not in school, the twins and John are cared for by their grandparents when Mr. and Ms. Jones are working. Ms. Jones reports that John's father "abandoned" him at birth and only sees John a few times a year. However, John does visit his paternal grandparents. Ms. Jones encourages these visits in the hope that John's father will spend more time with him.

Although Ms. Jones was unable to remember specific dates, she said she initially believed that John was developing normally and did not notice any particular problems. She does remember that John's same age cousin started talking before John. As her twins have gotten older she now believes that John may have demonstrated mild delays in meeting his developmental milestones. No significant medical history was reported for John with the exception of frequent headaches and chronic sinus problems.

Regarding family medical and mental health history, Ms. Jones reported that her mother has bipolar disorder and a sister has a history of learning problems similar to John's. No other significant mental or physical problems were noted.

Ms. Jones reported that John is behind in school and has particular difficulties with learning to read and write. He repeated kindergarten in part because of these academic problems but also because he seemed very immature, as reported by teachers. She reports that John "never caught on" to reading. Ms. Powers, John's last teacher, reported that John was inattentive in class, often drawing when he should have been working. She said that without one-on-one instruction, John was rarely capable of keeping up with the rest of the class. She was reluctant to promote John to the first grade, but because he had spent 2 years in kindergarten she agreed to a provisional promotion. She also believes that John is immature socially and needs to learn to handle frustration and teasing more appropriately.

Ms. Jones says John complains that the schoolwork is too hard, that the teacher picks on him, and that other kids tease him, calling him names such as "crybaby," "dummy," and "fatso." John is slightly overweight and frequently uses complaints of stomach or headaches to get out of schoolwork and household chores, according to Ms. Jones. Ms. Jones says she tells John that if his head hurts or his stomach aches, then he has to rest in his bed without any TV or other distractions. Once she started doing this, the frequency of those complaints was reduced. However, he is increasingly frustrated with academic tasks; his mother notes that he cries and whines a lot, saying "This is too hard," "I can't do it," etc. Ms. Jones reports that she first soothes John and then assists him with his schoolwork when he becomes overly frustrated.

PREVIOUS TESTING

In January 2005, when he was 4 1/2 years old, John was administered the *Wechsler Preschool and Primary Scales of Intelligence* – Third Edition (WPPSI-III) and obtained a Full Scale IQ of 77, a Verbal IQ of 78, and a Performance IQ of 82. Based on these scores, John did not qualify for any special services.

CLINICAL OBSERVATIONS

John, a 7-year-old male, appeared to be of average height and slightly overweight. He was casually but neatly dressed for the evaluation. John and his mother and stepfather arrived on time for the morning appointment. John seemed tired and his mother says it is hard to get him "going" in the mornings. John readily accompanied the examiner to the testing room and rapport was easily established. Testing was spread out over 2 days and frequent breaks were taken to keep John motivated. Occasionally he yawned and put his head down on the table. John was given frequent reminders that he was supposed to do his best but that he is not supposed to know all the answers to the questions. This information plus frequent praise for "working hard" appeared to keep John motivated and attentive during testing.

During testing, John attempted to sound out reading words, but did not do so successfully. He was able to state all letters of the alphabet and numbers up to 20. No visual, motor, speech, or auditory problems were noted. Although John occasionally seemed frustrated, he appeared to put forth good effort. His test behaviors were assessed using the GATSB. His attentiveness, cooperation, and other responses to tests were in the average range on this measure (51st percentile). Thus, the test data reported here are likely to be a valid reflection of his current functioning.

INTERPRETATION OF INTELLECTUAL ASSESSMENT

The WISC-IV is an individually administered measure of cognitive functioning. On the WISC-IV, John achieved a VCI of 69, a PRI of 71, a WMI of 74, and a PSI of 73. John's Full Scale IQ of 65 is classified as Extremely Low and is ranked at the 2nd percentile. The probability is 95% that John's true Full Scale IQ falls between 61 and 71. There is little variability among John's index scores, and his Full Scale IQ is considered the best estimate of his overall intellectual ability. Extremely low general mental ability, such as that displayed by John is one of two criteria needed to make a diagnosis of mental retardation. Table 7.1 contains a summary of the WISC-IV scores.

Verbal Comprehension is a measure of verbal concept formation, verbal reasoning, and knowledge acquired from one's environment. John's VCI of 69 is classified as Extremely Low and falls at the 2nd percentile. John's VCI subtest scores ranged from 3 to 6 (10 is average). The difference between John's Similarities scaled score of 3 and his Vocabulary scaled score of 6 is statistically significant but not unusually so. Individuals with mental retardation often score much lower on the Similarities subtest, which requires some level of abstract thinking ability, than on the Vocabulary subset, which requires identifying picture items and

TABLE 7.1   WISC-IV Scores for John, Age 7 Years

	Standard scores	Percentile rank	Confidence interval	Classification
VCI	69	2	64–78	Extremely Low
PRI	71	3	66–81	Borderline
WMI	74	4	68–84	Borderline
PSI	73	4	67–85	Borderline
Full Scale IQ	65	2	64–74	Extremely Low

Note: A standard score of 100 is average, with most children scoring between 85 and 115.

Subtest	Scaled score	Subtest	Scaled score
Verbal Comprehension		Working Memory	
Similarities	3	Digit Span	6
Vocabulary	6	Letter–Number Sequence	5
Comprehension	3		
Perceptual Reasoning		Processing Speed	
Block Design	6	Coding	4
Picture Concepts	4	Symbol Search	6
Matrix Reasoning	6		

Note: A scaled score of 10 is average with most children scoring between 7 and 13.

defining words. At the lower age range of the test, the Vocabulary subtest words are fairly simple (e.g., hat, clock, cow).

The PRI assesses skills such as the ability to think in terms of visual images and to manipulate them with fluency, flexibility, and relative speed. John's PRI of 71 is descriptively classified as borderline, falling at the 3rd percentile. His subtest scores ranged from 4 to 6 indicating relatively even abilities in this area.

The WMI measures the ability to attend to verbally presented information, to process that information in memory, and then to manipulate it to formulate a response. John's WMI of 74 is classified as borderline and falls at the 4th percentile. His subtest scores ranged from 5 to 6, indicating relatively even abilities in this area.

The PSI is a measure of an individual's ability to process simple or routine visual information efficiently and to quickly perform tasks based on that information. John's PSI of 73 is descriptively classified as borderline and falls at the 4th percentile. Subtest scores ranged from 4 to 6.

Thus, John's ability to comprehend verbally presented information is within the Extremely Low range, while his ability to think in terms of visual images, to remember information and manipulate it in memory, and to quickly perform visual tasks are at the low end of the borderline range of intellectual functioning. His overall ability is in the extremely low range which probably accounts for much of his academic difficulties. His teacher mentioned that John is often inattentive in class. When children have difficulty understanding the material they often are inattentive. It is most likely that John's inattention is due to his difficulty in understanding the material rather than an underlying attention disorder. He is reported to appropriately attend to other activities such as TV programs, music, and coloring.

ACHIEVEMENT

Reading

The *Wechsler Individual Achievement Test* – Second Edition (WIAT-II) was used to assess John's achievement. Because John repeated kindergarten, both age- and grade-based scores are reported in Table 7.2. The grade-based norms used were those for children in the beginning of the first grade. John's skills in reading fall in the borderline to extremely low range. His Reading Composite score of 70 is descriptively classified as borderline. However, it should be noted that his score is inflated by the standard score of 84 on the Pseudoword Decoding task. John earned a raw score of 0 on this task; it is a statistical artifact that a raw score of 0 receives a standard score of 84. He was not able to read much, but what he did read he understood. Because he repeated kindergarten and was promoted to the first grade, his age-based scores are generally lower than the grade-based scores.

Mathematics

John's grade-based scores were all within the low borderline range, reflecting his repetition of kindergarten. He did best on tasks requiring basic number concepts (e.g., counting objects, determines which group of objects was the largest) John's age-based scores in Mathematics fall in the borderline to extremely low range; the composite score is classified as extremely low and at the 2nd percentile.

Written Language

With respect to writing, John's age- and grade-based scores fall in the borderline to low average range. His mother reports that she has been working with John, teaching him to write his name and telephone number. She also has been helping him write simple thank you letters for his recent birthday gifts. As a result, John has learned to write his name and telephone number, most letters of the alphabet, and some very simple words. He was not able to do this at the end of kindergarten.

TABLE 7.2   WIAT-II Scores for John, Age 7 years

WIAT-II subtests	Standard score (age)	Percentile	Standard score (grade)	Percentile
Reading				
Word Reading	60		60	
Reading Comprehension	74		82	
Pseudoword Decoding	84*		83*	
Composite Score	70±3	2	73±4	4
Mathematics				
Numerical Operations	73		76	
Math Reasoning	66		71	
Composite Score	66±9	1	71±10	3
Written Language				
Spelling	71		74	
Written Expression	79		83	
Composite Score	73±9	4	77±7	6
Oral Language				
Listening Comprehension	76		79	
Oral Expression	70		77	
Composite Score	69±9	2	75±9	5
Total Composite Score	70±4	2	73±4	4

Note: A standard score of 100 is average with most children scoring between 85 and 115.
*John was unable to complete any of the Pseudoword Decoding items, earning a raw score of 0.

Oral Language

John's age-based Composite Oral Language score of 69 falls at the 2nd percentile and is descriptively classified as extremely low. However, his listening Comprehension and Oral Expression scores are all in the borderline range for both age- and grade-based scores. During the Oral Expression subtest, John appeared to be reluctant to talk and when prompted to "tell me more" he rarely elaborated. Thus, this subtest may be a minimum estimate of his verbal skills. When outside of the testing situation, John's verbal expression was generally appropriate and consistent with a child with possible mild language delays. John's grade-based Oral Language scores were within the borderline range.

Overall, John's Achievement Composite scores (both age and grade) are descriptively classified as borderline. There is considerable variability among the various subtests with his Wording Reading score being the lowest. This is consistent with his performance in class and his mother's statement "John has never caught on to reading." It is likely that as John progresses through school, he will lag further behind his age group in academic achievement.

ADAPTIVE BEHAVIOR

John's adaptive behavior and skills were assessed using the *Adaptive Behavior Assessment System* – Second Edition (ABAS-II) Parent and Teacher Forms; John's ABAS-II scores are summarized in Table 7.3. Ms. Jones' responses on the ABAS-II Parent Form indicate that John displays deficits in adaptive behavior. His overall General Adaptive Composite of 65 on the Parent Form is in the extremely low range (1st percentile) compared to other children in his age group.

Abilities related to his Conceptual, Social, and Practical Composites are comparable and also classified as extremely low. According to his mother's ratings on the ABAS-II, John's adaptive skills on the individual adaptive skill areas all fall within the low borderline to extremely low range.

Responses from John's teacher, Ms. Powers, on the ABAS-II Teacher Form also indicate several deficits in adaptive behavior, although the teacher's scores demonstrate a great deal more variability than the mother's scores. Abilities related to John's General Adaptive Composite of 73 on the Teacher Form are in the borderline range (4th percentile). Abilities related to the Practical and Conceptual Composites are classified as extremely low. Teacher scores in the Social Composite are in the below average range (17.5th percentile) and represent a significant and personal strength for John, compared to his other composite scores. In the ABAS-II individual adaptive skills areas, his adaptive skills on the ABAS-II Teacher Form generally are in the extremely low and borderline range. However, his specific adaptive skills in the leisure and health and safety domains are in the average to below average range. The results suggest that John's teacher views his classroom adaptive behaviors in these areas to be stronger than in other areas.

Thus, both John's mother and teacher identified a number of deficits in adaptive behavior. However, an important finding is that John's teacher rated some of John's adaptive skills as being in the average to below average range, which is higher than his scores in other adaptive skill areas rated by the teacher and higher than scores in any of the adaptive skill areas rated by the parent. Subsequent interviews with John's mother and teacher suggest that the reasons for these discrepancies appear to be John's response to high structure in the classroom, his differing responses to frustration and teasing in the classroom versus at home, and differing responses from teacher and mother when John whines or complains. For example, John's teacher, Ms. Powers, reported that she runs a "tight ship" in the classroom in which complaining and whining are discouraged or ignored; his teacher says that she systematically requires all students to replace comments of "I can't do it" with "I can try" and then reinforces students for their attempts and efforts. His teacher reports that, over his year in the classroom with this teacher, John's responses to frustration and teasing have become somewhat milder and

TABLE 7.3   ABAS-II Scores for John, Age 7 Years

Composite scores	Parent standard score	Percentile rank	Confidence interval	Teacher standard score	Percentile rank	Confidence interval
General Adaptive Composite	65	1.0	61–69	73	3.6	70–76
Conceptual Composite	70	2.3	64–76	63	0.7	58–68
Social Composite	70	2.3	63–77	86	17.5	80–92
Practical Composite	68	1.6	63–77	70	2.3	64–76

Note: A standard score of 100 is average, with most children scoring between 85 and 115.

Adaptive skill areas	Parent	Teacher
Conceptual Composite		
Communication	2	5
Functional academics	5	2
Self-direction	5	2
Social Composite		
Leisure	4	8
Social	4	6
Practical Composite		
Home/school living	5	4
Community use	4	5
Health and safety	3	7
Self-care	5	2

Note: A scaled score of 10 is average, with most children scoring between 7 and 13.

classmates are teasing him less as a result. However, John's mother reports that he whines, complains, and says "I can't do this" frequently at home and that she finds it difficult to ignore his behaviors.

SUMMARY

On the WISC-IV John's Full Scale IQ of 65 is classified as Extremely Low and classifies his intellectual deficits in the mild range of mental retardation, according to the DSM-IV-TR. In addition, according to Ms. Jones and

Ms. Powers, John's overall adaptive functioning on the ABAS-II is classified as borderline to extremely low. These two factors meet criteria for a diagnosis of mental retardation. John's achievement scores, age- and grade-based, range from extremely low to borderline on the WIAT-II. His achievement scores are consistent with John's reported academic problems and suggest that John will need more intensive academic services to succeed in school. It is recommended that John be considered for special education services for academic content.

John's immature behaviors such as whining and crying at home may become less of a problem when he receives instruction and academic goals that are more appropriate for his ability levels. Also, it is recommended that John's teacher and mother work together to develop appropriate intervention plans that are consistent between home and school. His teacher's use of structure and ignoring frustration and whining in the classroom may be a good example of interventions that also could be implemented at home.

DIAGNOSTIC IMPRESSIONS

DSM-IV 317.0 Mild Mental Retardation.

REFERENCES

American Association on Mental Retardation (2002). *Mental Retardation: Definition, Classification, and Systems of Supports* (10th ed.). Washington, DC: American Association on Mental Retardation.

American Psychiatric Association (2000). *Diagnostic and Statistical Manual of Mental Disorders: Text Revision (DSM-IV-TR)* (4th ed.). Washington, DC: American Association on Mental Retardation.

Atkinson, L. (1992). Mental retardation and WAIS-R scatter analysis. *Journal of Intellectual Disability Research*, 36, 443–448.

Bolen, L. M., Aichinger, K. S., Hall, C. W., & Webster, R. E. (1995). A comparison of the performance of cognitively disabled children on the WISC-R and WISC-III. *Journal of Clinical Psychology*, 51, 89–94.

Bracken, B. (1988). Ten psychometric reasons why similar tests produce dissimilar results. *Journal of School Psychology*, 26, 155–166.

Bruininks, R. H., Woodcock, R. W., Weatherman, R. F., & Hill, B. K. (1996). *Scales of Independent Behavior-Revised*. Chicago, IL: Riverside.

Centers for Disease Control and Prevention (2004). Economic costs associated with mental retardation, cerebral palsy, hearing loss, and vision impairment – United States, 2003. *MMWR*, 53, 57–59.

Denning, C. B., Chamberlain, J. A., & Polloway, E. A. (2000). An evaluation of state guidelines for mental retardation: Focus on definition and classification. *Education and Training in Mental Retardation and Developmental Disabilities*, 35, 226–232.

Dickinson, D., Iannone, V. N., & Gold, J. M. (2002). Factor structure of the *Wechsler Adult Intelligence Scale-III* in schizophrenia. *Assessment*, 9, 171–180.

Flynn, J. R. (1984). Then mean IQ of Americans: Massive gains 1932 to 1978. *Psychological Bulletin*, 95, 29–51.

Flynn, J. R. (2006). Tethering the elephant: Capital cases, IQ, and the Flynn effect. *Psychology, Public Policy, and Law*, 12, 170–189.

Glutting, J. J., & Oakland, T. (1993). *Guide to the Assessment of Test Session Behaviors for the WISC-III and WIAT*. San Antonio, TX: The Psychological Corporation.

Glutting, J. J., Watkins, M. W., & Konold, T. R. (2006). Distinctions without a difference: The utility of observed versus latent factors from the WISC-IV in estimating reading and math achievement on the WIAT-II. *The Journal of Special Education*, 40, 103–114.

Grossman, H. J. (1983). *Classification in Mental Retardation*. Washington, DC: American Association on Mental Deficiency.

Harrison, P. L., & Oakland, T. (2003). *Adaptive Behavior Assessment System* (2nd ed). San Antonio, TX: Psychological Corporation.

Herr, S. S., Gostin, L. O., & Hoh, H. H. (Eds.) (2003). *The Human Rights of Persons with Intellectual Disabilities: Different but Equal*. Oxford, UK: University Press.

Individuals with Disabilities Education Act, 71, Fed. Reg. 46539–46845 (August 14, 2006). www.ed.gov/legislation/FedRegister/finrule/2006-3/0814069.html

Jacobson, J. W., & Mulick, J. A. (1996). *Manual of Diagnosis and Professional Practice in Mental Retardation*. Washington, DC: American Psychological Association.

Kamphaus, R. W. (2002). *Clinical Assessment of Children's Intelligence* (2nd ed.). Boston, MA: Allyn and Bacon.

Kanaya, T., Scullin, M. H., & Ceci, S. J. (2003). The Flynn effect and US policies: The impact of rising IQ scores on American society via mental retardation diagnoses. *American Psychologist*, 58, 778–790.

Lakin, K. C., & Turnbull, A. (Eds.) (2005). *National Goals and Research for People with Intellectual and Developmental Disabilities*. Washington, DC: American Association on Mental Retardation.

MedlinePlus Encyclopedia (2007). http://www.nlm.nih.gov/medlineplus/ency/article/001523.htm

Mulick, J. A., & Hale, J. B. (1996). Communicating assessment results in mental retardation. In: J. W. Jacobson, & J. A. Mulick (Eds.), *Manual of Diagnosis and Professional Practice in Mental Retardation* (pp. 257–263). Washington, DC: APA.

Nihira, K., Leland, H., & Lambert, N. (1993a). *AAMR Adaptive Behavior Scale-Residential and Community* (2nd ed.). Austin, TX: Pro-Ed.

Nihira, K., Leland, H., & Lambert, N. (1993b). *AAMR Adaptive Behavior Scale-School* (2nd ed.). Austin, TX: Pro-Ed.

Oakland, T., & Glutting, J. (1998). Assessment of test behaviors with the WISC-III. In: A. Prifitera, & D. Salofske (Eds.), *WISC-III: A Scientist–Practitioner Perspective*. New York: Academic Press.

Parmenter, T. R. (2004). Contributions of IASSID to the scientific study of intellectual disability: The past, the present, and the future. *Journal of Policy and Practice in Intellectual Disabilities*, 1, 71–78.

Platt, L. O., Kamphaus, R. W., Cole, R. W., & Smith, C. L. (1991). Relationship between adaptive behavior and intelligence: Additional evidence. *Psychological Reports*, 68, 139–145.

Reschly, D. J., Myers, T. G., & Hartel, C. R. (Eds.) (2002). *Disability Determination for Mental Retardation*. Washington, DC: National Academy Press.

Sanborn, K. J., Truscott, S. D., Phelps, L., & McDougal, J. L. (2003). Does the Flynn effect differ by IQ level in samples of students classified as learning disabled? *Journal of Psychoeducational Assessment*, 21, 145–159.

Sattler, J. M. (2001). *Assessment of Children: Cognitive Applications* (4th ed.). San Diego, CA: Jerome M. Sattler, Publisher.

Sattler, J. M. (2003). *Assessment of Children: Behavioral and Clinical Applications* (4th ed.). San Diego, CA: Jerome M. Sattler, Publisher.

Schroeder, S. R., Gertz, G., & Velazquez, F. (2002). *Final Project Report: Usage of the Term "Mental Retardation": Language, Image and Public Education*. Lawrence: University of Kansas, Center on Developmental Disabilities.

Scullin, M. H. (2006). Large state-level fluctuations in mental retardation classifications related to introduction of Renormed Intelligence Test. *American Journal on Mental Retardation*, 111(5), 322–335.

Slate, J., & Saarnio, D. A. (1995). Differences between WISC-III and WISC-R IQS: A preliminary investigation. *Journal of Psychoeducational Assessment*, 13, 340–346.

Sparrow, S. S., Balla, D. A., & Cicchetti, D. V. (2005). *Vineland Adaptive Behavior Scales* (2nd ed.). Circle Pines, MN: America Guidance Service.

Spitz, H. (1983). Intratest and intertest reliability and stability of the WISC, WISC-R and WAIS full scale IQs in a mentally retarded population. *Journal of Special Education*, 17, 69–80.

Spruill, J. (1991). A comparison of the *Wechsler Adult Intelligence Scale-Revised* with the *Stanford-Binet Intelligence Scale* (4th edition) for mentally retarded adults. *Psychological Assessment*, 3, 133–135.

Stainton, T. (2001). Reason and value: The thoughts of Plato and Aristotle and the construction of intellectual disability. *Mental Retardation*, 39, 452–460.

The Psychological Corporation (1997). *WAIS-III–WMS-III Technical Manual*. San Antonio, TX: The Psychological Corporation.

Vance, H., Maddux, C. D., Fuller, G. B., & Awadh, A. M. (1996). A longitudinal comparison of WISC-III and WISC-R scores of special education students. *Psychology in the Schools*, 33, 113–118.

Watkins, M. W., Wilson, S. M., Kotz, K. M., Carone, M. C., & Babula, T. (2006). Factor structure of the *Wechsler Intelligence Scale for Children* – Fourth Edition among referred students. *Educational and Psychological Measurement*, 66, 975–983.

Wechsler, D. (1991). *Wechsler Intelligence Scale for Children-III: Manual*. San Antonio, TX: The Psychological Corporation.

Wechsler, D. (2003a). *Wechsler Preschool and Primary Scales of Intelligence-III: Manual*. San Antonio, TX: The Psychological Corporation.

Wechsler, D. (2003b). *Wechsler Intelligence Scale for Children-IV: Manual*. San Antonio, TX: The Psychological Corporation.

Wechsler, D. (2003c). *Wechsler Intelligence Scale for Children-IV: Technical and Interpretive Manual*. San Antonio, TX: The Psychological Corporation.

Weiss, B., & Weisz, J. R. (1986). General cognitive deficits: Mental retardation. In: R. T. Brown, & C. R. Reynolds (Eds.), *Psychological Perspectives on Childhood Exceptionality* (pp. 344–390). New York: Wiley.

Zhou, X., Zhu, J., & Weiss, L. G. (2007). Peeking inside the "blackbox" of Flynn effect: Evidence from three Wechsler instruments. Paper presented at *The Annual Meeting of the American Psychological Association*, San Francisco, CA.

8

AUTISM SPECTRUM DISORDERS: WISC-IV APPLICATIONS FOR CLINICAL ASSESSMENT AND INTERVENTION

JANINE M. MONTGOMERY[1], DANIELLE I. DYKE[2]
AND VICKI L. SCHWEAN[2]

[1]Department of Psychology, University of Manitoba, Winnipeg, Manitoba, Canada
[2]Division of Applied Psychology, University of Calgary, Calgary, Alberta, Canada

CHAPTER RATIONALE AND PURPOSE

The overarching purpose of this chapter is to illustrate how a clinician might use the *Wechsler Intelligence Scale for Children – 4th Edition* (WISV-IV) to guide and inform assessment and intervention for individuals diagnosed with, or suspected of having, an Autism Spectrum Disorder (ASD). A brief overview of the contemporary literature in ASD, including diagnostic considerations and conceptual frameworks is provided, along with an abbreviated discussion of findings regarding proposed WISC intellectual profiles among ASDs and related clinical populations. Further, a case study is integrated to illustrate the process a clinician may utilize to conduct assessment and intervention with an individual who is suspected of having, or has been diagnosed with, an ASD. Finally, suggestions for intervention, stemming from the case study findings, are highlighted.

PERVASIVE DEVELOPMENTAL DISORDERS

In contemporary understanding, the term ASD most commonly refers to diagnoses within the Pervasive Developmental Disorders (PDDs) diagnostic category. The term PDDs describes a continuum of related clinical diagnoses characterized by profound difficulties with social interaction, communication, and language (Wing, 1981a). In the *Diagnostic and Statistical Manual of Mental Disorders –* Fourth Edition, Text Revision (DSM-IV-TR; American Psychiatric Association, 2000), five PDDs are described and include Autistic Disorder (AD), PDD not otherwise specified (PDD-NOS), Asperger Disorder/Asperger Syndrome (AS), Rett's Disorder, and Childhood Disintegrative Disorder (CDD). Although the *International Statistical Classification of Diseases and Related Health Problems –* Tenth Edition (ICD-10) includes additional diagnostic categories, for the purposes of this chapter and in light of the North American context, the DSM-IV categories will be the focus. Further, current research considers the features of Rett's Disorder to be distinct from other forms of PDDs; it has been characterized as "a phenotypically distinct, progressive X-linked dominant neurodevelopmental disorder that almost exclusively affects females" (Van Acker et al., 2005, p. 126). Indeed, some researchers argue for the reclassification of Rett's Disorder as a degenerative neurological disorder rather than a mental disorder (Tsai, 1992). Likewise, CDD has very specific onset criteria and a unique developmental course that differentiates it from other PDDs. As Rett's Disorder and CDD can typically be distinguished from other PDDs by course and physical symptoms, this chapter will highlight those PDDs or ASDs that are most closely related.

To demonstrate the utility of the WISC-IV to inform assessment and interventions for ASD, primary attention will be directed toward three related diagnoses, often conceptualized as being "high-functioning" ASD: AD (more specifically high-functioning autism; HFA), AS, and PDD-NOS. Classical AD (i.e., Kanner's autism) is excluded from discussions, as co-morbid conditions (e.g., mental retardation; MR) necessitate a different approach to assessment and intervention.

DIAGNOSTIC CONSIDERATIONS

Diagnosis of AD, AS and PDD-NOS requires complex formal assessment and clinical judgment as there is great diversity not only between individuals with the aforementioned diagnoses, but also within individuals who share the same diagnosis. AD, AS, and PDD-NOS are primarily characterized by severe and pervasive impairments in the areas of: reciprocal social interaction and communication, as well as the presence of stereotyped behaviors, interests, and activities. Further, the severity of these impairments is required to be qualitatively different from that of typically developing peers (American Psychiatric Association, 2000). Given the complexity and diversity of the needs of individuals with ASD, it is essential that the clinician employ a multimodal, multimethod assessment battery. Further, many clinicians, researchers, and advocacy groups suggest that multidisciplinary assessment teams trained in assessment of and intervention with PDDs, and who possess a thorough understanding of child and adolescent development, are essential to providing assessment and intervention services to children and adolescents with PDDs (Klin et al., 1997; Klin & Volkmar, 2003; Ozonoff et al., 2003).

Diagnostic Categories

Differentiating between subtypes of PDDs and related clinical diagnoses and syndromes is a complex and sometimes controversial process. For instance, when distinguishing between AD and AS, some argue that language development is the differentiating feature, while others assert that AS may simply be AD accompanied by average or above average intellectual abilities (Miller & Ozonoff, 2000). More specifically, many researchers contend that there is very little difference between AS and HFA (e.g., Manjiviona & Prior, 1999; Ozonoff & Griffith, 2000), a clinical term commonly used to describe individuals with average or above average intellectual abilities who also meet the criteria for AD. Others note that PDD-NOS serves as a "catch-all" diagnostic category for individuals who display subthreshold symptomatology or whose difficulties are viewed as "milder" than those present among others on the autism spectrum (Allen et al., 2001; Towbin, 2005). Moreover, there is some evidence to suggest that the numerous PDD diagnostic categories simply represent differences in severity of symptomatology along a "hypothetical spectrum or continuum" (Towbin, 2005, p. 166). Cleary, there is little consensus on how to reliably differentiate between PDDs, as distinctions between diagnostic categories continue to be somewhat unclear (Volkmar & Klin, 2005). Consequently, skilled clinicians familiar with the PDD literature are an essential element of good professional practice.

AUTISTIC DISORDER

Leo Kanner (1943) wrote of a syndrome he termed "early infantile autism", which described a group of children who lacked communicative speech, displayed language development delays, engaged in echolalia and pronoun reversal, had difficulty understanding abstract concepts, demonstrated "disturbed" behavior including stereotypical mannerisms or lack of imaginative play, and most significantly, did not interact with other people ("autistic aloneness"). Some have noted that the children described by Kanner were often preoccupied with parts of objects or spinning objects in a manner that severely and negatively impacted daily functioning (Janzen, 2003). In Kanner's description, these children displayed atypical cognitive and emotional development from infancy, despite seemingly typical physical development. This clinical disorder, now known as AD, was first included in the DSM in the third edition (1980) and the ninth edition of the ICD (Volkmar et al., 1994).

Traditionally, prevalence research asserted that 50 to 75 percent of children with AD also met the diagnostic criteria for MR; however, recent epidemiological studies utilizing broader inclusion criteria have suggested lower prevalence rates of MR in this population, with estimates ranging from approximately 25 to 50 percent (Chakrabarti & Fombonne, 2001). Some investigators argue that this shift in the demographics of AD is the result of early language intervention in those with "classical" autism and increasing awareness and more frequent diagnosis of "higher-functioning" ASD, such as HFA, AS, and PDD-NOS (Fombonne & Tidmarsh, 2003).

HIGH-FUNCTIONING AUTISM

HFA is not a formal diagnostic category in any version of the DSM; however, it is frequently used in clinical practice to describe individuals who meet the diagnostic criteria for AD, yet have typically developing (and sometimes above average) intellectual abilities. While some researchers contend that HFA and AS are simply two different terms that describe the same clinical disorder (see Schopler et al., 1998 for an extensive review), the diagnostic criteria in the DSM-IV-TR requires that AD be considered before an examination of the appropriateness of an AS diagnosis (i.e., the precedence rule). However, because the DSM-IV-TR definition of AD identifies a delay or absence of language development as one of the potential, but not essential, diagnostic criteria that could be met, many researchers and clinicians have interpreted this as meaning that the absence of language or significantly impaired language makes the diagnosis of AD most appropriate. As such, many clinicians view delayed or absent language development as the crucial criteria that differentiates between AD and AS (Szatmari, 2000, 2005). Indeed, the statement in the diagnostic criteria for AS that there should be no significant delay in language appears to support the language-based differentiation between AD and AS; however, the existence of the "precedence rule" adds further confusion. It is clear from the nature of the preceding discussion that this is an area of controversy for both researchers and practitioners in the field. Although it is not the purpose of this chapter to provide comprehensive coverage of all diagnostic arguments, it is important to be aware that diagnostic discussions remain controversial, thereby necessitating in-depth knowledge of the contemporary literature, as well as clinical judgment and skill, to ensure well-informed decision-making.

ASPERGER DISORDER/ASPERGER SYNDROME

AS is described as a "severe and chronic developmental disorder closely related to AD and pervasive developmental disorder-not otherwise specified" (Klin et al., 2005a, p. 88). Although Hans Asperger and Leo Kanner wrote of similar groups, they were initially unaware of each other's work (Wing, 1998 as cited in Schopler et al., 1998). Both authors profiled children with compromised social functioning; however, Kanner described a population with impaired cognitive and language skills, while Asperger reported on individuals with average to above average intelligence and typical, if not precocious, language skills. Moreover, highly specialized skills and circumscribed interests have often been attributed to those with AS, while those with HFA are frequently described as more likely to be preoccupied with objects or parts of objects (Wing, 1981a). Further, some investigators assert that unique learning styles (Tsatsanis, 2004) and cognitive profiles (Klin et al., 1995; Lincoln et al., 1995; Ehlers et al., 1997; Lincoln et al., 1998; Ghaziuddin et al., 2004) provide critical differentiation between the two clinical groups. Although the distinction between HFA and AS is controversial, there is consensus that these individuals experience "early-onset social disability that impairs their capacity for meeting the demands of everyday life" (Klin et al., 2005a, p. 88) and that "subtle differences in presentation" (Meyer & Minshew, 2002, p. 53) are important for distinguishing between ASD subtypes, as well as for planning interventions.

Although Asperger initially described the syndrome in 1944, it was not until 1981 that Lorna Wing's seminal work introduced AS to the western hemisphere of the world. Subsequently, a myriad of research on the topic has been conducted (Klin et al., 2000). Since the inclusion of tentative diagnostic criteria for Asperger disorder in the fourth edition of the DSM (American Psychiatric Association, 1994) and the tenth edition of ICD (World Health Organization, 1992), there has been a reported increase in the clinical incidence of AS (Wing & Potter, 2002; Fombonne & Tidmarsh, 2003). Recent estimates of prevalence vary, with conservative estimates ranging from 2.5 per 10,000 children (Fombonne & Tidmarsh, 2003) to 36 per 10,000 children (Ehlers & Gillberg, 1993). Regardless of the variability in reported prevalence rates, it appears that identification of individuals who meet the diagnostic criteria for AS is increasing, likely as a result of increased awareness (Fombonne & Tidmarsh, 2003; Fombonne, 2005). Finally, given the relatively recent introduction of this diagnostic category, efforts to validate AS as a unique diagnostic entity are still in their infancy (Volkmar, 1996; Prior et al., 1998; Ozonoff & Griffith, 2000; Klin & Volkmar, 2003; Szatmari, 2005), further complicating diagnostic discussions.

PERVASIVE DEVELOPMENTAL DISORDER – NOT OTHERWISE SPECIFIED

PDD-NOS (which includes atypical autism) is a diagnosis that is given when an individual manifests severe and pervasive impairments in reciprocal social functioning that are associated with (1) pervasive difficulties with verbal or nonverbal communication skills or (2) stereotypic behaviors, interests, and activities (DSM-IV-TR, American Psychiatric Association, 2000). The PDD-NOS classification is less precise than those of other PDDs and may rely more heavily on clinical judgment in its application (Zwaigenbaum & Szatmari, 1999). The PDD-NOS diagnostic category seems to serve as a "catch-all" classification for individuals whose symptomatology is consistent with PDDs; however, late age of onset of symptoms, atypical symptomatology, and/or subthreshold symptomatology (DSM-IV-TR, American Psychiatric Association, 2000) make other PDD diagnoses inappropriate. In clinical practice, a diagnosis of PDD-NOS is often made when clinically significant social difficulties consistent with PDDs are evident; however, the individual does not meet all of the diagnostic criteria for AD or AS (Towbin, 2005). Until recently, there has been little research comparing PDD-NOS and other PDDs. Interestingly, while it is listed as a distinct category in the DSM-IV TR, it retains the same numerical code (299.80) as Asperger Disorder (Towbin, 2005). Concerns about the validity of PDD-NOS as a unique disorder are similar to those surrounding AS, and investigation is required to further examine the diagnostic validity of PDD-NOS.

RELATED CLINICAL DISORDERS AND SYNDROMES

ASDs have been associated with genetic disorders such as fragile X syndrome, phenylketonuria, tuberous sclerosis, and neurofibromatosis (Lotspeich & Ciaranello, 1995). Further, partial trisomy 15, a long Y chromosome, trisomy 21, and XYY are chromosomal abnormalities that have also been related to ASD. Although less frequently reported, non-genetic conditions associated with ASD include infectious illnesses such as congenital rubella, acute encephalopathy, and cytomegalovirus.

In addition to the complexity in differentiating between PDDs outlined in the DSM-IV-TR, a substantial body of research has documented the existence of disorders with characteristics similar to those observed in individuals with ASD, including Obsessive Compulsive Disorder (OCD), Developmental Coordination Disorder (DCD), Non-Verbal Learning Disabilities (NLD) and Semantic-Pragmatic Language Disorder (Kanner, 1943; Johnson & Myklebust, 1971; Denkla, 1983; Rapin & Allen, 1983; Rourke, 1989; Melillo & Leisman, 2004). Although discussion of all related conditions is beyond the scope of this chapter, a review of the aforementioned clinical disorders and syndromes is strongly encouraged prior to engaging in assessment and intervention supports for individuals with ASDs.

NON-VERBAL LEARNING DISABILITIES

Byron Rourke's (1995, 2005) research has focused primarily on the neuropsychological profile of individuals with NLD. Utilizing a framework that outlines primary, secondary, and tertiary difficulties, he suggests that individuals with NLD manifest a pattern of neuropsychological strengths and weaknesses characterized by primary difficulties in tactile perception, visual perception, complex psychomotor activities, and the ability to process novel material. Secondary difficulties in areas such as tactile attention and visual attention are also reported, along with tertiary challenges that impact tactile memory, visual memory, concept formation, and problem-solving abilities. According to Rourke (1995), social-emotional and adaptive difficulties also manifest as a result of the aforementioned difficulties. Individuals with NLD have been further described as having significant difficulties processing novel or complex social information, which leads to an over-reliance on repetitive behaviors inconsistent with the adaptability required for appropriate social interactions in dynamic settings. Further, their social interaction with others has been described as stereotypical and lacking in reciprocity (Rourke & Tsatsanis, 2000).

Individuals with NLD also possess a numerous areas of competence. Primary assets are often noted in auditory perception, rote memory, and simple motor skills. Secondary strengths have been reported in the area of auditory and verbal attention, along with tertiary assets with verbally and auditory memory. Finally, well-developed verbal skills have been proposed to represent a hallmark feature of this group (Rourke & Tsatsanis, 2000). These strengths are believed to translate into highly related academic competencies (particularly in areas requiring strong verbal or rote memory), and are thought to provide compensatory opportunities in intervention efforts (Rourke & Tsatsanis, 2000; Tsatsanis, 2005). Intellectual profiles have also been proposed for individuals with NLD (Drummond et al., 2005) using the Wechsler scales. Recent findings suggest a Verbal Intelligence Quotient (VIQ) that is greater than the Perceptual Intelligence Quotient (PIQ) by 10 standard scores or more. Further, 80% of these individuals obtained their highest standard scores on the Information, Similarities, or Vocabulary subtests from the VIQ domain, and 90% displayed their lowest standard scores on the Block Design, Object Assembly, or Coding subtests from the PIQ domain. While limited information is available directly comparing those with AS to NLD on WISC subtests, significant differences have been noted in the differential between VIQ and PIQ in both groups, but not for an HFA group (Klin et al., 1995).

The neuropsychological profile of individuals with NLD shares many characteristics with the profile observed in ASD. Indeed, Klin et al. (1995) assert that AD is one of several pathways (including hydrocephalus, acquired brain injury, and Williams Syndrome) to the manifestation of the NLD profile. Further, preliminary evidence suggests that the NLD profile is present in many individuals with AS; however, as mentioned previously, it is not evident in those classified as HFA (Klin et al., 1995). Although NLD has not been recognized by the DSM-IV-TR as a diagnostic entity, it is a classification used by some practitioners in their clinical practice. Further, neurodevelopmental comparisons have been made between NLD and AS, with some investigators proposing that the NLD profile is "an adequate model of neuropsychological assets and deficits encountered in individuals with AS" (Klin et al., 1995, p. 1133). Similarly, many researchers and clinicians believe that the cognitive, affective, and behavioral profile, and associated interventions for NLD, demonstrate utility for further understanding many individuals with AS (Marans et al., 2005; Tsatsanis, 2005). Despite evidence that supports an emerging neuropsychological profile of NLD, and significant overlap between characteristics observed in AS and NLD (e.g. Klin et al., 1995), further study is needed to more clearly delineate the relationship between them.

DIFFERENTIAL DIAGNOSIS

ASPERGER SYNDROME AND AUTISTIC DISORDER

While the validity of AS as a separate diagnostic category from AD has been controversial, studies exploring the convergence and divergence of AS and AD have generated evidence of shared characteristics (validating the broader category of ASD), as well as evidence to support the differentiation of these two diagnostic categories. The field trials for AS in the DSM-IV revealed that individuals with AS were less likely to have language or communication delays and more likely to exhibit motor delays than individuals with AD. Further, they demonstrated different patterns of intellectual abilities, and were more likely to exhibit atypical preoccupations and interests than did the AD group (Volkmar et al., 1994). It is this evidence that led to the inclusion of AS as a separate category from AD in the DSM-IV and ICD-10 classification systems (Volkmar, 1996). Further, the broader diagnostic category of PDD has been retained, illustrating commonalities between diagnostic subtypes (Klin et al., 2005b); however, ongoing research attempts to ascertain differences between ASDs in etiology, familial patterns, neuropsychological and genetic profiles, as well as adaptive and behavioral outcomes.

PERVASIVE DEVELOPMENTAL DISORDER – NOT OTHERWISE SPECIFIED

Walker and colleagues (2004) compared individuals with PDD-NOS, AS, and AD on measures of communication, daily living, social and intellectual skills, and language acquisition, and found that individuals with PDD-NOS experienced fewer difficulties within these domains and displayed less stereotypical behaviors than individuals with AS and AD. In contrast, when clinicians were trained to classify individuals with an ASD without knowledge of their diagnosis, findings revealed poor agreement regarding the application of a PDD-NOS diagnosis (Mahoney et al., 1998). Consequently, some researchers argue that the terms atypical autism (as per ICD-10) and PDD-NOS be avoided whenever possible to provide more meaningful clinical information to parents and individuals (e.g., Zwaigenbaum & Szatmari, 1999). Others advocate the use of the PDD-NOS diagnosis when significant impairment in reciprocal social functioning is evident; however, all the key elements of ASD are not present, and the diagnostic criteria for other PDDs are not met (Towbin, 2005). As is the case with AS, a lack of consensus regarding the operational definition of PDD-NOS confounds research and complicates clinical practice. The development of diagnostic algorithms to clarify the conditions under which a PDD-NOS diagnosis is warranted is ongoing (Buitelaar, 1998; Walker et al., 2004).

DeBruin et al. (2006) compared the intellectual profiles of individuals with PDD-NOS with those with AS and AD. Findings revealed a pattern of strengths and weaknesses that, although not diagnostic, may be helpful in understanding PDD-NOS. One hundred children between the ages of 6 and 12 years (76 diagnosed with PDD-NOS, 13 with AD, and 11 with AS) completed the WISC-R. The PDD-NOS group displayed relative strengths on the Information, Similarities, Picture Arrangement and Mazes subtests, and relative weaknesses in performance on the Comprehension, Digit Span and Coding subtests. These findings differ from previous investigations that identified strengths on Digit Span and Block Design, and poor performance on the Picture Arrangement subtest (Happe, 1994; Lincoln et al., 1995; Siegel et al., 1996; Ehlers et al., 1997). "In PDD-NOS, however, this particular strength on Block Design did not appear, and more remarkable, Digit Span was a significant weakness and Picture Arrangement a significant strength" (deBruin et al., 2006, p. 269). The authors suggest that this profile may reflect a high level of factual knowledge combined with theoretical insight that enables sequencing of social situations in individuals with PDD-NOS; despite their struggles to understand social interactions in real-life situations (Klin et al., 1995).

Further examination of the WISC-R index scores revealed that the PDD-NOS group scored lower on the Freedom from Distractibility factor than on the Verbal Comprehension and Perceptual Organization factors. The authors concluded that children with PDD-NOS appear to have a VIQ–PIQ profile similar to children with AD (i.e., no significant difference between VIQ and PIQ). In contrast, individuals with AS in this study demonstrated a significant difference between VIQ and PIQ performance, with stronger performance exhibited on the VIQ. At the subtest level, however, those with PDD-NOS performed similarly to the broader ASD group. Moreover, it was not possible to distinguish PDD-NOS from AD or AS with the WISC-R.

CONTEMPORARY CONCEPTUAL FRAMEWORKS IN ASD

Theory of Mind

Theory of Mind (ToM), sometimes referred to as "mind-reading" (Baron-Cohen, 1995) or "mentalizing", is defined as the ability to recognize that others have thoughts, feelings, beliefs, and perceptions different from our own (Astington et al., 1988; Baron-Cohen, 1995; Baron-Cohen et al., 1999). There is evidence to suggest that individuals with AS display difficulties with ToM abilities, although much of the research on ToM has been conducted with individuals with AD, or has failed to draw distinctions between various ASD subtypes, instead treating them as a single entity. Consequently, the characteristics unique to each ASD subtype have not been adequately explored (see Baron-Cohen et al., 1985; Leslie & Frith, 1987; Happe et al., 1996). Conflicting data suggest that in contrast to individuals with AD (including those with HFA), individuals with AS often display more subtle ToM difficulties and in fact, some researchers have reported developmentally appropriate ToM skills (Ozonoff et al., 1991a;

Bowler, 1992; Ziatas et al., 1998). The application of these skills in real-life social situations, however, remains problematic for individuals with AS, as they are believed to experience difficulties intuitively processing ToM information and tend to process this type of information more slowly than their age-matched peers in real-life interactions (Kaland et al., 2002; Dissanayake & Macintosh, 2003). Some investigators have suggested that, in comparison to other ASDs, the relative strengths that individuals with AS display in intellectual and language abilities, as well as their ability to apply logical inferences, mediates their performance on ToM measures in the research setting and may account for higher rates of success on ToM measures (Ozonoff et al., 1991a; Tager-Flusberg & Sullivan, 1994).

Emotional Intelligence and Neural Substrates

Investigation into the neural substrates of emotional intelligence holds promise for further delineating the types of social-emotional challenges experienced by individuals with ASD. Bar-On and colleagues found that competencies most affected by damage to the neural circuitry associated with affective regulation involved the ability to be aware of oneself and one's emotions, express oneself and one's feelings, manage and control emotions, adapt flexibly to change and solve problems of a personal nature, and motivate oneself to mobilize positive effect (Bar-On et al., 2003). Recent research exploring the neural substrates of cognitive versus emotional intelligence has found that while the dorsolateral prefrontal cortex is thought to govern key aspects of cognitive function (Duncan, 2001), the neural systems that support trait-based emotional intelligence overlap with neural systems subserving affective decision-making (i.e., ventromedial prefrontal cortex, amygdala, and insular regions; Bar-On et al., 2003). Various neural networks within the cerebellum, the prefrontal cortex, the medial temporal lobe, and related limbic system structures are associated with functions related to emotion regulation, emotional hyperreactivity, low frustration tolerance, and lack of concern for others or empathy (Rolls et al., 1994; Courchesne et al., 1995), as well as with aspects of emotional intelligence. Montgomery et al. (2008) found that the competencies associated with emotional intelligence show strong relationships with various resiliency factors in young adults with AS. Future research may investigate whether these relationships also exist for individuals with other ASDs.

ASSESSMENT OF AUTISM SPECTRUM DISORDER

CASE STUDY: AN INTRODUCTION

Reason for Referral

Michael is a 15-year-old English-speaking male. Michael's parents expressed significant concerns with his ongoing social difficulties, prompting the referral for assessment. Difficulties initiating and maintaining peer relationships, as well as "artificial and stilted" language were reported. As an example, repetition of contextually inappropriate verbal phrases (learned from television programming) frequently occurred in his conversations with others. Further, Michael reportedly asks very specific and personal questions of new acquaintances. For example, he often inquires about dates of birth, middle names, phone numbers and home addresses; these personal inquiries have upset some individuals, and Michael has great difficulty understanding why. In addition, Michael's parents indicate that he seems to struggle to understand non-literal forms of language such as figures of speech and idioms. Issuing a phrase to Michael, such as "hold your horses", is undoubtedly met with a puzzled expression. Michael's parents have also noticed that recently, he seems to be increasingly affected by his poor social experiences, frequently withdrawing from opportunities to socialize.

In contrast to his difficulties with socialization, Michael's parents reported that he displays unique strengths for learning verbal information, particularly when it is related to an area that holds interest for him. Michael's mother reported that since early childhood, he has demonstrated an extraordinary memory for facts, and these memory skills appear to help him remember voluminous amounts of information in particular topics. For example, Michael often surprises people by recalling personal information that was relayed to him many months earlier. In spite of his strengths, Michael's parents expressed concern about how to support him in establishing and maintaining peer relationships, as well as how best to prepare him for the transition into adulthood.

Family Medical and Psychological History

A review of immediate and extended familial medical and psychological history revealed a paternal grandmother who may have had mental health concerns (i.e., reported social-emotional difficulties due to "nerves"), as well as a diagnosis of AD in one of Michael's maternal first cousins. Michael's father noted that with these exceptions, the familial medical and psychological history was unremarkable. A review of Michael's physical health records revealed no history of, or present medical concerns. Further, recent eye and ear examinations indicated no vision or hearing difficulties.

Developmental History and Present Behaviors

Michael's mother reported no significant prenatal or perinatal difficulties and no delays in the acquisition of developmental milestones during Michael's first 3 years. She indicated that in retrospect, there likely were some atypical behaviors present in subsequent years; however, they did not concern her at the time. As an example, Michael reportedly had an "obsessive" focus on vacuum cleaners that began at 4 years of age and persisted for at least a year. A subsequent and intense interest in trains followed his preoccupation with vacuums and thereafter, Michael became interested in the mechanics of various types of motors. Michael's parents both reported that he often appeared capable of tremendous depth in his learning about objects that were of particular interest to him. Specifically, Michael's father stated that Michael knew more about motors by the time he was 7 years old than Michael's father understood as an adult. More recently, Michael took an interest in astronomy and chemistry, acquiring great depth in his knowledge of these topics, often at the exclusion of obtaining knowledge in other academic areas. Further, his verbosity regarding these topics often inhibits him from engaging in reciprocal conversation. Similarly, his frequent attempts to shift conversations to topics of great interest to him, does not facilitate reciprocal communication.

When queried regarding behaviors characteristic of ASD (i.e., items regarding the presence of stereotypical and routinized behaviors, language, communicative and social difficulties), Michael's parents reported the following: literal, concrete, inflexible and at times, contextually inappropriate use of language (e.g., difficulties with comprehension and use of abstract, non-literal language such as idioms); difficulties with change and transition both within and between environments such as school, home, and community; clothing preferences associated with reported tactile sensitivities (i.e., prefers soft clothing that is not restrictive); and hand wringing behaviors, particularly when encountering stressful situations (such as a change in travel routes).

Educational History

Michael's mother recalled some difficulties in Michael's early schooling, noting that many teachers "hinted" at academic difficulties; however, they were never clearly articulated. References to difficulties attending, as well as a high level of distractibility, were made by several teachers, particularly during elementary school. Moreover, peer bullying and social exclusion were frequently observed by Michael's teachers throughout his schooling. Presently, Michael displays academic performance in the average to above average range. No concerns were reported regarding the quality of Michael's current teachers or school environment.

GENERAL AS.SESSMENT CONSIDERATIONS

The assessment of individuals with ASD is a complex and multifaceted process that necessitates multi-disciplinary and multimodal, multimethod evaluative practices. Ideally, an assessment team consists of experts from various disciplines, including psychology, child and adolescent psychiatry, education, pediatrics, neuropsychology, neurology, speech-language, and occupational therapy (see Volkmar et al., 2005). Further, the range of phenotypic expression within ASDs necessitates the identification of intrapersonal strengths and areas of difficulty, not only to facilitate a better understanding of the abilities of the individual undergoing assessment, but also to support appropriate intervention planning.

This diversity amongst individuals with ASD requires that the assessor have expertise in various assessment instruments and administrative methods, in addition to diverse knowledge in normative development, as well as developmental psychopathology (Volkmar et al., 2005). Further, clinical skills necessary for establishing rapport with individuals with exceptionalities, understanding unique strengths and needs, and framing direct assessment, observational, and interview data within their larger contextual framework are required. Moreover, comprehensive and individualized assessment should be cognizant of the genetic, neurodevelopmental, and maturational influences that contribute to the variability in phenotypic expression in ASD.

Individualized assessment often involves a range of observational and standardized data from a variety of interview, questionnaire, and direct assessment formats which sample the psychological, communicative, and behavioral characteristics of interest across numerous settings, such as the home, community, and school. This type of multimodal, multimethod data should be obtained from various practitioners, parents and other caregivers who are highly familiar with the individual undergoing assessment. Information about early development including prenatal and medical history, early childhood milestones, and early behaviors and familial characteristics are an essential part of a thorough examination of ASD. Further, it is important to examine the types of difficulties encountered in school, home, and community settings, as critical information needed for intervention planning is gleaned from these contexts. Moreover, it is necessary to determine if the behaviors of interest are context-specific or not, as this will also inform conceptualizations of the individual's areas of strength and need, as well as interventions to support their needs and build on their strengths. In addition, rich descriptions of unique characteristics of the individual within multiple contexts enable the clinician to gain insight that provides a context from which to interpret assessment performance and make recommendations for intervention.

Special Considerations

Children and adolescents with ASDs present unique challenges in the assessment process. This clinical population is characterized by enormous developmental variability in many domains typically assessed, such as intellectual and language abilities, which necessitates both the understanding and capacity to evaluate across the child and adolescent developmental continuum. Additionally, an appreciation of behaviors characteristic of autism spectrum that may interfere with the validity and reliability of the assessment instruments used, is important to ensure true sampling of abilities. Further, poor performance on assessment instruments may be attributed to confounding factors such as difficulties comprehending instructions, poor cooperation, impulsive behavior, variable attention, or a combination of any of these factors, among others (Lincoln et al., 2007). It is therefore critically important that the assessor be knowledgeable about how these behavioral factors might affect performance and how the assessment process might be appropriately adapted to ensure desired sampling of abilities and not confounding, behavioral factors.

Behavioral characteristics typically associated with ASD, including repetitive, perseverative, and self-stimulatory behaviors, as well as difficulties with novel tasks, settings, and individuals may impact the assessment process (Lincoln et al., 2007). Consequently, assessors require breadth and depth in their understanding of the assessment instruments so they are prepared to adjust the format and/or setting (without compromising standardized administration), to elicit motivation, cooperation, and valid responses from the individual undergoing assessment.

Domains typically assessed with individuals diagnosed with, or suspected of having, an ASD include, but are not limited to: global intellectual level and specific verbal and performance abilities; social competence; language (including expressive, receptive, and pragmatic forms); and adaptive skills (including self-care and activities of daily living). Further, assessment of learning, memory, and neuropsychological processes can provide insight that informs interventions. In addition to assessment in the aforementioned domains, consideration of assessment observations, developmental history, and current contextual framework (including familial, and broader cultural and communal factors), will facilitate a more refined understanding of the individual, and provide the data necessary to develop individualized interventions.

CASE STUDY: ASSESSMENT OBSERVATIONS

Michael exhibited a highly verbose and perseverative manner of speech, as evidenced by repetition of words and phrases and a high rate of speech, accompanied by poor topic maintenance and inappropriate topic shifts. Michael also exhibited imprecise articulation and made tangential remarks that did not promote fluidity in conversation. Michael acknowledged his verboseness and perseverative style of communication, stating that he has been told by others that he talks too much sometimes and tends to over-analyze things. As such, Michael displays difficulty with reciprocal, pragmatic language, and communication. He stated that it was "hard to start a conversation" as he tended to be "more serious than others" and was often interested in "things that other people don't care much about". Michael demonstrated great difficulty engaging in behavior consistent with commonly accepted social conventions, such as greeting the assessor or other individuals.

In addition, repetitive movements were noted to occur in several timed situations or when material became increasingly complex. Michael was also observed to wring his hands when formulating responses to more difficult questions. While Michael's response style was atypical and circuitous, he appeared to understand the questions asked of him and he displayed diligence and determination throughout the assessment process, often reluctant to "give up" on items he found challenging. Consequently, the results of the assessment are considered an accurate estimate of Michael's knowledge and skills in the areas assessed.

AUTISM SPECTRUM DISORDER AND INTELLIGENCE

EVALUATIVE CONSIDERATIONS

An evaluation of the intellectual abilities of individuals with ASD requires an appreciation of the broad base of literature regarding the typical organization of these abilities within this population. Although the diagnosis of AD with a co-morbid diagnosis of MR is beyond the scope of this chapter, it is critical that assessors possess the skills and knowledge necessary for determining an MR diagnosis. These assessment protocols require formal, individualized, and direct assessment of both intellectual and adaptive abilities. Consequently, an evaluation of these same competencies in individuals diagnosed with, or suspected of having an ASD, is a crucial component of the assessment process. It is important to note that an AD diagnosis is not synonymous with a co-morbid diagnosis of MR; an AD diagnosis can be made in an individual of any intellectual level (Baron-Cohen et al., 2005). In contrast, current diagnostic criteria for AS states that there must be no clinically significant delay in cognitive development, thereby further validating the critical importance of evaluation of intellectual abilities in ASD.

Although an assessment of cognitive abilities can be used to determine intellectual level, experienced clinicians are aware that much more than just IQ can be learned from using an intellectual assessment instrument such as the WISC-IV. Specifically, perceptual, attentional, learning, working memory, visuospatial, and abstract reasoning processes are critical to successful performance on the WISC-IV, and are also integral to successful performance in highly associated domains such as academics and adaptive functioning. Information regarding various intellectual abilities that have a pervasive influence on multiple domains of functioning and subsequent interventions can be gleaned from the results of a WISC-IV assessment.

WISC-IV INTELLECTUAL PROFILES IN ASD

Although methodological issues, primarily stemming from the heterogeneous and small samples evident in ASD research, have had an influential and inhibiting impact on attempts to identify cognitive performance patterns in ASD, there is some evidence to support the notion that differing intellectual abilities may exist among ASD subtypes.

Verbal and Non-verbal Skills

Studies examining the cognitive profiles of individuals with AS and HFA indicate atypical patterns of cognitive development (Lincoln et al., 2007), as well as distinctive patterns of cognitive strengths and areas of need. Some investigators report that individuals with HFA demonstrate less developed verbal intellectual skills and more advanced non-verbal intellectual skills than those with AS (Klin et al., 1995; Ehlers et al., 1997; Lincoln et al., 1995, 1998; Ghaziuddin & Mountain-Kimchi, 2004) and the opposite pattern has been cited in individuals with AD (Allen et al., 1991; Ozonoff et al., 1991b; Klin et al., 1995; Ehlers et al., 1997; Miller & Ozonoff, 2000; Klin & Volkmar, 2003; Ghaziuddin & Mountain-Kimchi, 2004). These findings, however, are not universal, as there is also evidence to support no modality differentiation (Szatmari et al., 1990; Manjiviona & Prior, 1999; Ozonoff et al., 2000). Further, the opposite trend (i.e., more advanced non-verbal abilities and less well-developed verbal abilities) has also been found in individuals with AS (Asarnow et al., 1987; Lincoln et al., 1988; Ameli et al., 1998).

Subtest Strengths and Weaknesses

In contrast to inconsistencies in verbal and non-verbal performance patterns among individuals with ASD, there is fairly robust evidence to support ASD group strengths on the Block Design subtest (e.g. Barnhill et al., 2000) and consistent difficulties with the Comprehension and Picture Arrangement subtests (Klin et al., 2005c). These findings suggest relative strengths with visuospatial reasoning skills and difficulties with measures that rely heavily on social judgment, requiring the individual to verbally reason with conventional social knowledge. Further, Comprehension and Picture Arrangement subtest discrepancies have been interpreted to reflect a modality processing preference, given the auditory and visual nature of the Comprehension and Picture Arrangement subtests, respectively. Modality preferences have important instructional implications, as learning novel information is most likely if it is delivered in the preferred modality (auditory versus visual). Furthermore, Lichtenberger (2004) reported that individuals with AD and those with AS display their poorest performance on the processing speed domain; the Symbol Search and Coding subtests prove particularly problematic (see Table 8.1.). Despite limited research examining the intellectual abilities of individuals with ASD, as assessed by the WISC-IV, information gathered from the WISC-IV standardization studies revealed some preliminarily information (summarized in Table 8.1).

TABLE 8.1 Reported Relative Strengths and Weakness in the WISC-IV Standardization Sample for Individuals with ASD

Group	Relative strength	Mean scaled score	Relative weakness	Mean scaled score
AD (n = 19)	Block Design	5.3	Comprehension	7.9
	Matrix Reasoning	5.2	Symbol Search	7.7
	Picture Concepts	4.0	Coding	7.4
AS (n = 27)	Similarities	12.1	Symbol Search	8.2
	Information	12.0	Cancellation	8.0
	Picture Completion	11.5	Coding	6.7

* Modified from Hebben (2004, p. 184).

As an understanding of unique intellectual profiles is critical in delineating perceptual, attentional, learning, memory, visuospatial, and abstract reasoning abilities, the WISC-IV provides insight into these intellectual abilities critical to successful performance across various settings. Assessing cognitive abilities critical to academic and adaptive functioning, the WISC-IV may be viewed as providing a framework from which to further probe specific cognitive functions. In this way, the WISC-IV can be used to confirm and/or refute preliminary hypotheses and guide further assessment of other skills and abilities, which may include academic, language, adaptive, and social-emotional competencies.

It is important to note that much of the literature investigating intellectual profiles on the Wechsler scales was conducted prior to the inclusion of AS as a diagnostic classification. Consequently, the application of the aforementioned typical intellectual profiles to individuals with AS is controversial. Furthermore, although there is preliminary evidence to suggest that individuals with AS demonstrate strengths in VIQ when compared to PIQ, and that the opposite pattern may reflect intellectual abilities in individuals with HFA, the heterogeneous nature of ASD requires that individualized assessment be conducted to determine the individual's unique intellectual strengths and areas of need. In sum, intellectual research with individuals within the ASD classification is in its infancy. At this time, no intellectual profile can be considered diagnostic; however, typical intellectual profiles identified within the contemporary literature may guide clinical decision-making and ultimately inform both assessment and intervention.

MULTIMODAL, MULTISOURCE ASSESSMENT BATTERY

The critical importance of utilizing multimodal, multisource information to inform the assessment process means that the WISC-IV is but one valuable tool used to obtain a better understanding of the strengths and areas of need of the individual. As such, an example of the types of assessment instruments that might inform a multimodal and multisource assessment is provided for the reader. The intent of this assessment battery illustration is not to endorse specific assessment instruments, but rather to provide an example of the types of domains that should be considered in a formal assessment process where cognitive assessment is implicated. It is important to note that the following assessment battery represents but one of many constellations of assessment instruments that might be used to assess individuals diagnosed with, or suspected of having, an ASD. Indeed, some instruments, like the *Autism Diagnostic Interview-Revised* (ADI-R; Rutter et al., 2003) and *Autism Diagnostic Observation Schedule* (ADOS; Lord et al., 1999), are available to primarily document and diagnose ASD. The ADI-R requires parental retrospective recall and is administered in an interview format, while the ADOS is an observation system well suited for young children. As such, the applicability of these instruments to assessment with adolescents and adults may be somewhat questionable. Furthermore, a lack of sensitivity for differentiating between PDD subtypes has been reported amongst these diagnostic instruments (Yirmiya et al., 1994; Cox et al., 1999).

Clinical decisions regarding the battery of assessment instruments used with individuals diagnosed with, or suspected of having, an ASD should be selected based on the referral questions and preliminary assessment outcomes. In addition to intellectual assessment, a typical assessment battery employed to evaluate the possibility of an ASD includes measures of communicative, affective, and adaptive abilities, as well as instruments designed to specifically assess the presence of ASD symptomatology. Where appropriate, assessment of academic, learning, memory, somatosensory, and motor abilities provides a more comprehensive understanding of the unique individual undergoing assessment (Klin et al., 2005b). Further, a comprehensive assessment of executive functions (e.g., self-regulatory, goal-directed skills such as organizational, inhibitory, and planning abilities) is often beneficial in designing interventions for an individual with an ASD. Thus, multidisciplinary assessment is regarded as best practice (Klin et al., 1997; Klin & Volkmar, 2003; Ozonoff et al., 2003).

The following section demonstrates how information gathered from interviews with parents, educators, and other caregivers, combined with information regarding performance on the WISC-IV, can be used to direct the assessment process. Importantly, the sample provided portrays the type of assessment battery that a psychologist may employ; however, it is not meant to be exhaustive, given that multidisciplinary teams are considered best practice for ASD.

CASE STUDY: ASSESSMENT OUTCOMES

Michael was administered a battery of assessment instruments believed to provide information regarding his intellectual, academic, visuospatial, adaptive, and language abilities, as well as his personality and behaviors. A summary of the assessment instruments is provided in Table 8.2. While it is acknowledged

TABLE 8.2   Sample Assessment Battery for Investigation of ASDs

Domain	Assessment instrument
Background Information	Semi-structured interview with parents and teacher
	Interview with the child
Cognitive Skills	*Wechsler Intelligence Scale for Children* – 4th edition
	Children's Memory Scale
Academic Achievement	*Woodcock Johnson Tests of Achievement* – 3rd edition
Language	*Test of Pragmatic Language* – 2nd edition
Psychological Well-being and Behavior	*Behavior Assessment System for Children* – 2nd edition
	Million Adolescent Clinical Inventory
	Test of Social Insight
	Beck Anxiety Inventory
Pervasive Developmental Disorders	*Beck Depression Inventory*
	Gilliam Autism Rating Scale – 2nd edition
	The Krug Asperger's Disorder Index
	Asperger Syndrome Diagnostic Scale

* This assessment battery is not exhausive and is intended as a sample only.

that this battery is more comprehensive than is often possible in educational or clinical settings, it is provided as an example of the process one might use to clarify various issues using commonly available assessment instruments. Further, interpretive considerations are provided to give the clinicians some practical insight.

CASE STUDY: ASSESSMENT FINDINGS

COGNITIVE ABILITIES

Summary of Michael's Performance on the WISC-IV (Canadian Norms)
Standard Scale/Index Scores

Scale/index	IQ score	95% Confidence interval	Percentile rank	Classification
Full Scale Intellectual Quotient (FSIQ)*	96	91–101	39	Average
Verbal Comprehension Index (VCI)	108	101–114	70	Average
Perceptual Reasoning Index (PRI)	84	78–93	14	Low average
Working Memory Index (WMI)	110	102–117	75	High average
Processing Speed Index (PSI)	97	88–106	42	Average

Subtest Standard Scores (SS)

Subtest	SS	Subtest	SS	Subtest	SS	Subtest	SS
VCI		PRI		WMI		PSI	
Vocabulary	14	Block Design	7	Digit Span	11	Coding	7
Similarities	13	Picture Concepts	7	Letter–Number Sequencing	13	Symbol Search	7
Comprehension	8	Matrix Reasoning	8	Arithmetic	11	Cancellation	8
Information	13	Picture Completion	7				

Note: FSIQ score is uninterpretable, given the variability in Michael's four index scores.

Results of performance on the WISC-IV revealed significant variability amongst index and subtest scores; as such, a composite descriptor (i.e., the FSIQ score) does not convey meaningful information. The following section provides a discussion of specific strengths and areas of need that will instead provide an understanding of Michael's unique cognitive skills.

Working Memory Index

Michael demonstrated his strongest performance on measures assessing the ability to attend to verbally presented information, process that information in memory, and then formulate a response; average attainments were achieved on the composite score for this Working Memory Index (WMI). Within the WMI, Michael demonstrated uniform skills that fell within the average to high average range. Overall, working memory skills may be viewed as an area of relative strength for Michael and because working memory abilities are critical for learning, Michael's typically-developed working memory abilities will indeed promote his learning.

Processing Speed Index

Michael displayed scores in the low average range on the index assessing speed of mental and graphomotor processing. More specifically, this index is believed to measure the speed of mental operations requiring visual–motor coordination and discrimination, as well as short-term visual memory. Michael's performances on subtests in this index indicate relatively uniform abilities; however, his low average performance within this index has important implications for efficient learning. Specifically, this suggests that Michael may process visual information at a rate that is slower than many of his peers and if so, this finding represents a key cognitive and individual difference variable (Weiss et al., 2006). Further, the rapidity with which an individual processes simple or routine information without making errors of omission or commission has important implications for various tasks that require these skills (e.g., reading). Additionally, the comprehension of novel information may also be limited by the rate at which an individual processes routine visual information. Importantly, however, factors that interfere with performance on this index, such as visual–motor coordination and motor planning difficulties, should be examined prior to determining that this index provides insight into the speed of cognitive processing.

Verbal Comprehension Index

The Verbal Comprehension Index (VCI) assesses verbal comprehension, reasoning and expression. Michael's overall score for this index fell in the high average range. Although it appears that Michael has a relative strength in verbal skills, significant variability within this index warrants further investigation. Within this index, Michael demonstrated high average to superior skills on a subtest of general, "common" knowledge regarding people, places, and things (Information subtest), and on a subtest believe to assess general knowledge and expression of word meanings (Vocabulary subtest), as well as on a subtest of verbal concept formation, or how words, and the entities they represent, relate to one another (Similarities subtest). In contrast, Michael performed in the average range on a subtest of verbal expression, as well as increasingly abstract understanding of social conventions (Comprehension subtest). The Comprehension subtest is also thought to index novel problem-solving and decision-making processes regarding "real-life" challenges. Michael's performance on the Comprehension subtest was consistent with his parents' reports of difficulties with comprehension of and flexibility with socially mediated information, as well as previously mentioned research evidence that suggests that performance on the Comprehension subtest is compromised in individuals with ASD. Consideration of the relative challenges Michael experienced on this subtest, together with a developmental history outlining persistent and pervasive social-emotional difficulties, suggests it is important to explore these competencies in greater depth. Consequently, an examination of how Michael communicates in social settings (i.e., pragmatic language) and behaves in social contexts (i.e., social skills) is warranted.

In concert, the verbal competencies measured by the VCI provide foundational skills critical for academic and "real-life" learning, for the development of social adjustment and conventionality, and for successful social interactions. Verbal abilities are also thought to be a good predictor of scholastic success and Michael's average attainments on many subtests in this index suggest some typically developed verbal skills; however, his difficulties with socially mediated comprehension and abstract, non-literal reasoning reflect an area of relative difficulty. Consequently, interventions designed to enhance Michael's socially mediated verbal skills may be beneficial.

Perceptual Reasoning Index

Relatively uniform, but weaker skills were evident on the Perceptual Reasoning Index (PRI) domain, which assesses abstract, visually mediated reasoning and the ability to draw inferences with novel visual information. The measures in this domain assess the capacity to generate rules for problem-solving with novel, visually presented information. The measures are essentially non-verbal and required Michael to interpret and/or organize visual information, as well as identify visual patterns and visuospatial relationships. Michael's composite score on the PRI fell in the low average range. Further, the significant difference Michael displayed between verbal and perceptual abilities is not commonly observed, and thus should be considered as a marker for a potentially atypical intellectual profile. In activities of daily living, it is likely that Michael will have difficulty reasoning with visual information. Instructionally, this means that Michael would benefit from verbally delivered instruction whenever possible. Further, it may be helpful to assist Michael to link verbal labels and verbally mediated information with novel visual information that needs to be learned and reasoned with.

Summary of Performance on WISC-IV

While Michael generally displayed intellectual skills within the average range, there was significant variability amongst these skills and consequently, an examination of his abilities at the index level is warranted. Michael's abilities to reason with visual information were significantly weaker than expected, given his generally strong verbal skills. This discrepancy is likely to cause Michael difficulty across settings, particularly where visual and/or spatial skills are required. As a result, a comprehensive and targeted examination of Michael's academic achievement, as well as his specific learning and memory abilities, will not only enhance our understanding of Michael's unique cognitive abilities, but also assist with the individualization of his intervention planning.

Furthermore a number of factors indicate that assessment specific to ASD symptomatology is appropriate. These factors include parental request to assess for an ASD, parent and teacher interview information and developmental history that suggests the possibility of an ASD, as well as assessment observations and the intellectual profile demonstrated on the WISC-IV. Finally, direct assessment of Michael's psychological well-being and behavior is also necessary to assess for related co-morbid clinical conditions and to clearly understand his unique strengths and areas of need.

USING THE WISC-IV TO GUIDE ASSESSMENT

For the case presented, the WISC-IV provided the anchor for a more comprehensive assessment. While convergent and divergent evidence was obtained from performance on the WISC-IV that supported initial clinical impressions of an ASD, it is clear that the WISC-IV alone does not generate sufficient information to confirm any assessment hypothesis. In line with models of cognitive-hypothesis testing (see Hale & Fiorello, 2004), intellectual assessment is one of the preliminary aspects of case formulation. Along with interview and observational information, as well as data regarding previous assessment and intervention, intellectual assessment provides an opportunity to obtain converging and diverging lines of evidence while generating questions for further investigation. As an example, in addition to ASD-specific assessment, questions about Michael's pragmatic language, visual–spatial skills, academic achievement, and memory arose from the background information and IQ assessment. Just as the results from WISC-IV assessment should be viewed as converging or diverging lines of evidence pertaining to specific hypotheses, findings from further assessment should be viewed in light of intellectual abilities, developmental history, contextual factors and observational data, to strengthen the decisions made and provide a comprehensive, holistic view of the child or adolescent.

LEARNING AND MEMORY

To understand how Michael learns and remembers information, he was administered the *Children's Memory Scale* (CMS). This instrument assesses various dimensions of learning and memory including: attention and concentration; ability to learn and retain new auditory and visual material; retention of information; and retrieval of information. It also assesses free recall and recognition memory. Recognition memory occurs when a cue is provided, such as in a multiple choice exam where one response amongst multiple responses is correct, whereas recall memory uses no such cue.

Attention and Working Memory

The Attention/Concentration Index of the CMS measures attentional and working memory abilities. Commensurate with his performance on the WISC-IV, Michael's strongest scores on the CMS were in this index, where he displayed uniformly average abilities. This finding provides further evidence of Michael's relative strength in working memory abilities.

Learning

Learning refers to the ability to encode and store new information. Michael's ability to recall new information immediately after initial presentation varied significantly. Within this domain, Michael achieved relatively discrepant scores (ranging from a subtest standard score of 3 to 9). Analysis of subtest scores reveals an intrapersonal strength for remembering de-contextualized verbal information over contextualized visual information. In other words, Michael appears to experience more success with lists of unrelated words or concepts rather than information that is imbedded in socially meaningful stories. This finding appears consistent with rote memory skill strengths and socially mediated information processing difficulties frequently observed in individuals with ASD.

Further, a preference for learning and recalling verbally presented material was also evident; these findings are consistent with those observed on verbally mediated subtests of the WISC-IV and parental reports.

Memory

Michael's performance was inconsistent on measures of recall after a delay (of approximately 30 minutes). He demonstrated a relative strength in freely recalling verbally presented material after a delay; however, he experienced great difficulty on measures of delayed recall of visually presented information, with performance that fell within the well below average range. Michael's discrepant performance on measures associated with primarily verbal or visual modalities again suggests that Michael appears to learn and remember verbally mediated information better than visual information. Instructionally, this means that Michael would likely benefit from having material presented verbally whenever possible. In addition, his performance on measures of recognition memory suggest that he is likely to benefit from cues or prompts to assist his recall of newly learned information.

ACADEMIC ACHIEVEMENT

To assess academic knowledge and skills, the *Woodcock Johnson Tests of Academic Achievement* – 3rd edition (WJ-III-Ach) was administered. Comparisons of Michael's scores on various measures of academic skills with his attained scores on the VCI of the WISC-IV revealed similar results. For the most part, Michael's average scores on the achievement measure are commensurate with his average scores on the cognitive measures. Importantly, however, Michael's scores on the oral language domain, while within the expected range, were slightly lower than scores in other academic areas on the WJ-III-Ach. These relative weaknesses were demonstrated on measures of linguistic competency, listening ability, and comprehension. Moreover, both measures with which Michael had difficulty required him to listen and respond to detailed and complex verbal information.

Given Michael's strong performance on most of the verbal measures on the WISC-IV and his well-developed working memory skills, this finding suggests difficulties with more complex verbal reasoning skills (as compared to those involving more simplistic, language abilities that place great emphasis on rote memory abilities); these findings are consistent with current literature regarding verbal abilities in AS (Flanagan & Kaufman, 2004). Further, Michael's difficulties with narrative memory measures on the WJ-III-Ach and the CMS indicate difficulties learning and recalling contextual and socially mediated information. Additionally, it is possible that his attention to details within the story may be impeding has ability to comprehend the "big picture", including story context and themes. If this is the case, it is consistent with literature that describes an inability to omprehend the "gestalt" because of inappropriate attention to detail, that is characteristic of many individuals with ASD (e.g., Frith, 1989).

PRAGMATIC LANGUAGE

Parent-reported social difficulties, combined with poor performance on the Comprehension subtest from the WISC-IV, prompted an assessment of Michael's pragmatic language skills using the *Test of Pragmatic Language –* 2nd edition (TOPL-2). Pragmatic language can be described as social language used to achieve goals, involving not only what is said, but why and for what purpose. It includes recognition of the subcomponents of socially appropriate language: consideration of physical setting, audience, topic, purpose, visual–gestural cues and abstraction.

On the pragmatic language scale, Michael's score fell in the impaired range relative to a comparison group of individuals his age. Item analysis revealed that Michael had the most difficulty on items requiring multi-part or detailed responses. On some items, he appeared to fixate on small visual details and was unable to formulate a response. This is consistent with the hypothesis that attention to detail seems to impair his ability to understand the broader context. Michael's consistent difficulties with pragmatic language necessitate consideration of specific interventions to assist him with socially laden communication.

PSYCHOLOGICAL WELL-BEING AND BEHAVIOR

In an effort to obtain information regarding Michael's psychological well-being, parent and self-reported ratings of Michael's behavior were obtained. The *Behaviour Assessment System for Children –* 2nd edition (BASC-2) was administered to assess a range of adaptive and maladaptive behaviors, across the home, school and community settings. On this instrument, any score in the clinically significant range suggests a high level of maladjustment. A score in the at-risk range indicates the presence of significant difficulties that, while requiring intervention, may not be severe enough to warrant formal diagnosis. However, scores in the at-risk range may signify developing difficulties that should be monitored carefully.

Self-report

Results of Michael's self-ratings suggest that he experiences some characteristics consistent with those observed in individuals with anxiety, depression, and social stress, with overall ratings that fell in the at-risk range. Concerns surrounding anxiety and social stress should be viewed within the context of interview information provided by Michael's father who indicated that new social situations create distress for Michael. Pervasive and long-standing feelings of tension, pressure, and a lack of coping resources (particularly outlets through close friends and social contact) are tapped by the Social Stress subscale. When queried further, Michael indicated that his depressive affect was related to his socially mediated anxiety. While self-reported difficulties in the domains of anxiety and depression did not reveal clinically significant symptomatology, these are critically important areas to monitor on an ongoing basis, and they highlight the need for proactive and preventative interventions.

Parent Report

Parental reports revealed clinical-significant concerns in the area of withdrawal and when queried further regarding these ratings, Michael's parents spoke of his limited opportunities for social engagement, preference for sameness, routine and spending time alone, as well as his difficulties understanding socially mediated information. Further, parental ratings in the at-risk range on the Adaptive and Social Skills subscales were primarily related to social inflexibilities and routinized behaviors, which pervasively and negatively impact his activities of daily living. Given these elevated parental ratings, a more comprehensive assessment of adaptive abilities is strongly recommended, as a more detailed understanding of adaptability is of critical importance in ensuring positive inter- and intrapersonal experiences. Furthermore, supports to foster Michael's social and adaptive skills will be fundamentally important to providing effective and appropriate intervention supports.

Anxiety

Michael's atypical communicative patterns (i.e., his highly verbose and perseverative manner of speech), as well as his hand-wringing behaviors, are characteristic of individuals with ASD, as well as those experiencing anxiety. As such, the *Beck Anxiety Inventory* (BAI) was administered to provide a brief screening for anxiety-related symptomatology. Results suggest that Michael is experiencing moderate levels of anxiety that are predominantly socially mediated and stem from his difficulties developing and maintaining friendships.

Depression

Parental and self-reports of social difficulties and withdrawal, prompted an assessment of depression-related symptomatology using the *Beck Depression Inventory* (BDI). Results indicate that Michael is reporting moderate levels of depression, which is primarily related to self-reported difficulties developing and maintaining peer relationships.

Social Insight

Individuals with ASD often have difficulty understanding socially mediated information and interacting in social contexts. To assess knowledge of and skills related to social understandings, a measure of perception for social situations, the Test of Social Insight, was administered. Michael's self-ratings reflect a passive or conforming response style (i.e., ignore; don't listen, do nothing; move away, or do what the others are doing), even when faced with somewhat unpleasant consequences. Further, his "rule bound" response reflects social conformity, which is often observed in individuals with ASD.

Personality Characteristics and Clinical Syndromes

To further evaluate Michael's psychological well-being, he completed the *Million Adolescent Clinical Inventory* (MACI), which assesses adolescent personality characteristics and clinical syndromes. Results of the MACI were unremarkable, indicating no personality-related concerns. The MACI did, however, provide qualitative information that was of interest, as Michael's response style and comments indicated a tendency to interpret situations literally.

Autism Scale

To probe the possibility that Michael displayed characteristics consistent with those observed in individuals with ASD, Michael's mother completed the *Gilliam Autism Scale* – 2nd edition (GARS-2). The GARS-2 is a measure of the severity of autism spectrum symptomatology that provides a general or overall score, as well as scores for three subscales related to DSM-IV criteria: Communication, Stereotypical Behaviors, and Social Interaction. Consistent with previous parental reports, Michael's mother rated his motor, adaptive, and language development as typical; however, some atypical behavior was reportedly present from a very young age (i.e., before 3 years), namely repetitive behaviors and restricted interests.

The GARS-2 provides ratings of the likelihood that the individual's severity of symptomatology is consistent with what is typically reported by parents of individuals with AD. Michael's overall score fell within the possible range, suggesting that the severity of autism-like symptomatology reported by Michael is likely consistent with symptomatology experienced by individuals with ASD. Specifically, Michael's Social Interaction, Communication and Stereotyped behaviors uniformly fell within the possible range. These findings provide some evidence to suggest that Michael experiences symptomatology severity characteristic of ASD.

Asperger Screening

Cumulative evidence suggests that Michael's behaviors might be consistent with AS. Specifically, suspicion of autism spectrum symptomatology, combined with typical early language development, generally average intellectual abilities, and pervasive pragmatic language and socially mediated difficulties, prompted the administration of an AS assessment instrument, the *Asperger Syndrome Diagnostic Scale* (ASDS), which was completed by Michael's parents. Parental ratings resulted in an overall score in the very likely range. These findings strongly suggest that Michael's behaviors are comparable to those observed in individuals with AS. Due to the range of phenotypic expression amongst individuals with AS, it is important to closely examine skills in several domains including language development, social-emotional and intellectual abilities, adaptability, and sensorimotor skills, to promote individualization of the assessment process and subsequent intervention planning.

Finally, one additional screen for AS was administered to provide further validation of the working hypothesis that Michael may have AS. The *Krug Asperger Disorder Index* (KADI) was also completed by Michael's parents and findings supported results from the GARS-2 and ASDS, with ratings that fell in the "highly likely range". In conjunction, results on the GARS-2, ASDS, and KADI, combined with interview, direct assessment, and observational data, provide converging lines of evidence to retain the working hypothesis of an ASD, and more specifically AS.

BRIEF SUMMARY

Michael's performance on cognitive, academic, and pragmatic language instruments, combined with parental and self-ratings on personality, psychological well-being and behavioral measures, as well as interview and observational data, suggest that Michael may have AS. Further, instruments sensitive to ASD symptomatology appear to provide further validation for this working hypothesis. Additional insight regarding Michael's sensorimotor, gross and fine motor, speech–language and neuropsychological development, as well as specialized ASD diagnostic assessment would be needed to confirm the validity of this hypothesis. Additionally, neuropsychological assessment may be helpful to determine if the NLD profile captures his pattern of strengths and weaknesses. The results of the current assessment, however, indicate that Michael would benefit from diverse supports with his cognitive, academic, and social-emotional abilities and across home, school and community contexts.

RECOMMENDATIONS FOR INTERVENTION

GENERAL CONSIDERATIONS

Specific interventions should be conceived and implemented in a thoughtful, consistent, and individualized manner (Klin et al., 2000). More importantly, specific recommendations should be data-based (i.e., based on an evaluation of events observed, documented, or charted), and continually monitored, with useful strategies being maintained and unhelpful ones discarded so as to promote a constant adjustment of the intervention to the specific needs of the individual.

Outcomes for individuals with ASD can be enhanced with timely and appropriate interventions. Interventions should always be linked to assessment information gathered from a variety of sources, using a variety of methods. As outlined previously, individualized assessment should generate information about areas of competence as well as areas of difficulty. This is one of the ways in which assessment can be concretely linked to plans for intervention. For instance, in Michael's case, results indicated that he performs more effectively when information is presented verbally. Thus, presenting information in verbal form or pairing verbal with visual information may allow him to compensate for his weakness in the latter area. This is also consistent with ASD literature asserting that interventions designed to reflect modality-based strengths provide opportunities to improve performance (Marans et al., 2005). Further, verbally based interventions are widely accepted as "best practice" for those with AS (Klin et al., 2000; Tsatsanis, 2004).

Timing and Intensity

There are some key factors that should be included in all approaches to intervention with individuals with ASD. First, it is important to begin intervention as early as possible. Early intervention has been shown to be essential for individuals with ASD (Smith et al., 2000; Landa & Holman, 2005) as the central nervous system is highly susceptible to neural changes early in development (Dawson et al., 2000). Another key factor for intervention is intensity; research indicates that intensity is related to intervention efficacy (Smith et al., 2000). Furthermore, it is important that interactive experiences and repetition in both familiar and novel environments is incorporated into interventions, as this increases flexibility and generalization of knowledge and skills (Landa, 2007).

Supporting Implementation

While comprehensive intervention plans may appear to be the best approach to addressing the complex challenges experienced by individuals with ASD, too many recommendations for intervention often inhibits their implementation. Too often, a clinician generates pages of interventions in an attempt to meet all of the individual's needs without priorizing the most critical supports. As a result, those who are asked to carry out the interventions may be overwhelmed, have difficulty deciding where to begin, and be less likely to implement the suggestions. Alternatively, interventionists may attend to treatment recommendations that are more peripheral to the primary areas of need and consequently, the intervention programming may not be as effective as expected. As such, it is essential that clinicians be selective in choosing intervention targets. This does not preclude follow-up assessment and intervention plans which may address less pressing, yet still important issues at a later date. Instead, it increases the likelihood of intervention success if interventionists are better informed regarding not only the types of supports needed, but the manner in which to deliver them. However, for the purposes of introducing the reader to a variety of recommendations for intervention, the examples provided in this chapter may be more comprehensive than those provided in actual professional practice. Due to space limitations, suggestions for recommendations in a variety of domains illuded to in this chapter, will unfortunately not be discussed further. However, the suggestions provided are intended to address some of Michael's primary areas of need.

In an attempt to increase the likelihood that recommendations for interventions will be appropriately implemented, some clinicians have found it useful to apply SMART goals, a commonly used approach to educational planning, to the recommendations they propose. While there are several interpretations of the SMART acronym, essentially, it refers to goals that are:

- S – Specific: clear and detailed descriptions of concrete intervention plans.
- M – Measurable and Meaningful: can be measured by observation, data collection, or some other method; and they are important to improving the school, home, and community experiences of the individual.
- A – Attainable: specified in a manner which demonstrates the feasibility for the individual; this may include specific steps and subskills that need to be addressed.
- R – Realistic: the team has the resources to carry out the intervention, and the procedures, time frame, and responsibilities are acceptable to all those involved.
- T – Timely: a plan for when the interventions will be implemented and when follow-up intervention will occur is incorporated.

In addition to increasing the likelihood that interventions are delivered in a manner that promotes implementation, recommendations created with SMART goals translate easily to Individualized Educational Programs (IEPs) or Individualized Program Plans (IPPs), which are required by most school division/districts for students who are receiving funding for specialized educational supports. Consequently, the use of this approach enables educational teams to use the information generated by clinicians to plan educational programs for their students.

The following is a sample of interventions appropriate for Michael in light of information gathered from the WISC-IV and other aspects of the assessment battery. In the interest of space, the following interventions only include some aspects of SMART goals; however, sample recommendations are given to provide the clinician with some insight into how assessment outcomes translate to recommendations for intervention.

CASE STUDY: INTERVENTION PLANNING

General Recommendations

The following recommendations for intervention are designed to address strengths and areas of need identified in Michael's assessment, with a focus on intellectual competencies, as assessed by the WISC-IV, as well as other cognitive abilities indexed by performance on other instruments such as the CMS and WJ-III-Ach. Further, specific recommendations based on WISC-IV performance are provided to illustrate how one might specifically link WISC-IV findings to interventions.

Learning and Memory

The results of Michael's assessment of cognitive abilities indicate that he may benefit from the following recommendations:

- Prompts and cues to assist in his retrieval of information would be best provided in verbal form (e.g., presented in lists or key words delivered verbally, rather than in pictorial form).
- Present material repeatedly to enhance likelihood of recall. Rote learning will help to establish material in Michael's memory.
- Break information into its component parts, ensure unimportant details are minimized, and present essential details repeatedly.
- Explain how parts relate to the whole. This may assist Michael in understanding the "gestalt" of situations, which is problematic for him when he attends only to details without attempting to make sense of their context.
- Given Michael's difficulty remembering socially-mediated, and visually presented information, it will be important to avoid this type of information and format of presentation whenever possible.
- Link learning to Michael's areas of interest whenever possible.
- Give Michael time to process information, as he is more likely to perform better when given time to consolidate information.
- Explicitly informing Michael that he will need to recall information later may increase his retention of information. Further, if using this strategy, it will be important to check for comprehension at a later time.
- Provide verbal reminders (via lists or verbal prompts) of instructions for a task, or a model of a completed project for Michael to refer to as he works. Providing visual supports which include written verbal aspects may increase independence, and allow for memory resources to be committed to the measure at hand (see Marans et al., 2005 for a review of studies pertaining to this approach).

Speed of Visual Processing

To enhance Michael's visual processing speed, it is important that all other cognitive demands be minimized. Suggestions include: (a) allowing Michael to tape record classroom instructions and other pertinent discussions, (b) providing teacher outlines of course material, or (c) giving him a note-taker. Additional suggestions to increase Michael's processing speed include:

- Providing Michael with extra time, without penalty, for completion of assignments and examinations.

- Emphasis should be placed on the quality of Michael's work and not the quantity. Allowing Michael to demonstrate proficiency on a few measures will be better than overwhelming him with more than he is able to handle within a reasonable time frame.
- The speed at which Michael processes simple and complex material will be enhanced as knowledge becomes automatized. Automatization occurs with repeated exposure and practice. As a result, direct instruction and repeated opportunities to practice a skill will be important in teaching Michael.

Visual and Spatial Abilities

It is imperative that recognition be given to Michael's assets (i.e., relative strengths in verbal abilities) and that intervention efforts build upon these strengths to ensure positive outcomes. At the same time, Michael's relatively weaker visual–spatial abilities must be recognized and compensatory strategies to address these weaknesses should be identified. Suggested strategies include:

- Work toward integrating verbal and non-verbal processes. For example, use Michael's verbal strengths to analyze and mediate information and self-talk to provide direction for completing tasks (e.g., by sequencing the steps to a task and saying each step to oneself; Foss, 2002).
- Michael will likely respond positively to direct instruction and guided practice designed to enhance his visual perception of spatial relationships. Direct instruction should incorporate the following underlying principles: (a) be clear and direct in addressing the difficulty; (b) begin the work with what is most familiar and simple; (c) rely heavily on the student's verbal and analytic strengths; (d) model verbal mediation of non-verbal information while teaching Michael how to use this strength; (e) provide specific sequenced verbal instruction, teaching Michael to verbally self-direct and eventually to internalize this process; (f) provide instruction to directly associate and integrate verbal labels and description with concrete objects, actions, and experiences; (g) encourage Michael to use multi-sensory integration, both receptively and expressively; (h) teach in a sequential, step-by-step fashion; and (i) identify opportunities to generalize newly learned skills to other contexts (see Foss, 2002).

Social Communication & Interpersonal Skills

Michael's difficulties with insight and self-reflection may create challenges with his adaptability to social and interpersonal demands. A focus on pragmatic communication, in addition to social and adaptive skills, would prepare Michael to cope with dynamic interpersonal expectations, thus enhancing his social insight and associated self-regulatory behavior, and subsequently promoting increased opportunities to develop and maintain relationships. The following are suggestions intended to foster socially insightful and adaptive behaviors (Klin & Volkmar, 1995):

- Provide explicit verbal instructions on how to interpret others' social behavior, taught, and exercised in a rote fashion. The meaning of non-verbal behaviors such as eye contact, gaze, various inflections as well as tone of voice, facial and hand gestures, non-literal communications such as humor, figurative language, irony, sarcasm, and metaphor should be made verbally explicit and repeatedly practiced. The same principles should guide further development of Michael's expressive skills: concrete knowledge and skills should be taught and practiced in the intervention setting, and subsequently generalized to naturally occurring situations across a variety of contexts.
- Use direct instruction and support in real-life contexts to develop Michael's interaction skills with peers, including conversation topic management, diversity and depth of a variety of topics initiated by others, and increasing comfortability with a range of topics that are typically discussed by same-age peers.
- Michael's pragmatic communication skills should be fostered. Recognition and use of a variety verbal methods to interact, mediate, negotiate, persuade, discuss, and disagree will be critically important to further developing his pragmatic language. In light of information gathered in the interview with Michael's parents, it will be important to provide supports for the formal properties of language. Specifically, Michael may benefit from supports to explicitly teach idiomatic language and enable practice identifying this type of language in both text and conversation. Additionally, given pragmatic language assessment findings, it will be important to help Michael to develop the ability to make inferences, to predict, to explain motivation, and to anticipate multiple outcomes so as to increase the flexibility with which he both thinks about and uses language with other people.

CONCLUSION

The nature of the relationship between intellectual abilities and ASD symptomatology remains unclear (Joseph et al., 2002). Although many individuals with ASD display below average intellectual abilities, ASD symptomatology can occur with equal severity across the developmental spectrum of intellectual abilities. Evidence from behavioral genetic investigations (Bolton et al., 1994; Fein et al., 1999; Szatmari et al., 2000) suggest that "IQ broadly defined (e.g., high versus low Verbal or Full Scale IQ) may index etiological heterogeneity and provide a basis for subtyping in autism" (Joseph et al., 2002, p. 807). In addition to ongoing attempts to elucidate the complex relationship between intellectual abilities and ASD symptomatology (Bailey et al., 1996), there has also been interest in understanding the cognitive profiles of individuals with ASD.

Verbal and Performance IQ discrepancies have played a prominent role in efforts to define AS as distinct from AD (e.g., see Klin et al., 1995). However, considerable debate remains regarding the ability to differentiate AS from AD on the basis of intellectual abilities and Wechsler IQ profiles (Manjiviona & Prior, 1999; Ozonoff et al., 2000). The inconsistency in the contemporary literature regarding Verbal and Performance IQ discrepancies among ASDs may stem from variability in diagnostic classification practices and eligibility requirements for research participation, which promote heterogeneity within research samples and makes cross-study comparisons difficult. Further, the emphasis on identifying a prototypical cognitive profile that distinguishes between ASD subtypes has occurred at the expense of considering individual differences and the possibility that numerous cognitive profiles might exist within ASD (Joseph et al., 2002).

At a conceptual level, recent advances in genetics and neurophysiology have provided insight into the heterogeneous nature of cognitive and behavioral phenotypes in ASD. As a result of this heterogeneity, the assessment of ASD is a complex process that is dependent on multidisciplinary, multimodal and multimethod practices. The WISC-IV is integral to gaining a comprehensive understanding of children or adolescents suspected of having or diagnosed with an ASD, as the findings can be used to inform further assessment decisions. Further, cognitive profiles captured by the WISC-IV, while not diagnostic, can be used to inform intervention planning. Although research exploring the cognitive profiles of children with ASD remains in its infancy, when used in conjunction with standardized information from cognitive, academic, social, language and behavioral assessment measures, as well as observational and interview data, the practice can contribute to differential diagnosis, to understanding of individual strengths and challenges, and to the identification of appropriate interventions.

REFERENCES

Allen, D., Steinberg, M., Dunn, M., Fein, D., Feinstein, C., Waterhouse, L., et al. (2001). AD versus other pervasive developmental disorders: Same or different? European Child and Adolescent Psychiatry, 10(1), 67–78.

Allen, H., Lincoln, A., & Kaufman, A. (1991). Sequential and simultaneous processing abilities of high-functioning autistic and language impaired. Journal of Autism and Developmental Disorders, 21(4), 483–502.

Ameli, R., Courchesne, E., Lincoln, A., Kaufman, A., & Grillon, C. (1988). Visual memory processes in high-functioning individuals with autism. Journal of Autism and Developmental Disorders, 18(4), 601–615.

American Psychiatric Association (1994). Diagnostic and Statistical Manual of Mental Disorders: DSM-IV (4th ed.). Washington, DC: American Psychiatric Association.

American Psychiatric Association (2000). *Diagnostic and Statistical Manual of Mental Disorders, Fourth Edition, Text Revision (DSM-IV-TR)*. Washington, DC: American Psychiatric Association.

Asarnow, R. F., Tanguay, P. E., Bott, L., & Freeman, B. J. (1987). Patterns of I.Q. in nonretarded autistic and schizophrenic children. *Journal of Child Psychology and Psychiatry*, 28, 273–280.

Astington, J. W., Harris, P. L., & Olson, D. R. (1988). *Developing Theories of Mind*. New York: Cambridge University Press.

Bailey, A., Phillips, W., & Rutter, M. (1996). Autism: Towards an integration of clinical, genetic, neuropsychological, and neurobiological perspectives. *Journal of Child Psychology and Psychiatry*, 37, 89–126.

Barnhill, G., Hagiwara, R., Myles, B. S., & Simpson, R. L. (2000). Asperger syndrome: A study of the cognitive profiles of 37 children and adolescents. *Focus on Autism and Other Developmental Disabilities*, 15, 146–153.

Bar-On, R., Tranel, D., Denburg, N. L., & Bechara, A. (2003). Exploring the neurological substrate of emotional and social intelligence. *Brain*, 126, 1790–1800.

Baron-Cohen, S. (1995). *Mindblindness: An essay on autism and theory of mind*. Cambridge, MA: MIT Press.

Baron-Cohen, S., Leslie, A. M., & Frith, U. (1985). Does the autistic child have a "theory of mind"? *Cognition*, 21(1), 37–46.

Baron-Cohen, S., O'Riordan, M., Stone, V., Jones, R., & Plaisted, K. (1999). Recognition of faux pas by normally developing children and children with Asperger syndrome or high-functioning autism. *Journal of Autism and Developmental Disorders*, 29(5), 407–418.

Baron-Cohen, S., Wheelwright, S., Robinson, J., & Woodbury-Smith, M. (2005). The Adult Asperger Assessment (AAA): A Diagnostic Method. *Journal of Autism and Developmental Disorders*, 6, 1–13.

Bolton, P., Macdonald, H., Pickles, A., Rios, P., Goode, S., Crowson, M., Bailey, A., & Rutter, M. A. (1994). Case-control family history study of autism. *Journal of Child Psychology and Psychiatry*, 35, 877–900.

Bowler, D. M. (1992). Theory of mind in Asperger's syndrome. *Journal of Child Psychology and Psychiatry and Allied Disciplines*, 33(5), 877–893.

Bryson, S. E., Rogers, S. J., & Fombonne, E. (2003). Autism spectrum disorders: Early detection, intervention, education, and psychopharmacological management. *Canadian Journal of Psychiatry*, 48, 506–516.

Buitelaar, J. K. (1998). Diagnostic rules for children with PDD-NOS and multiple complex developmental disorder. *Journal of Child Psychology and Psychiatry and Allied Disciplines*, 39(6), 911–919.

Chakrabarti, S., & Fombonne, E. (2001). Pervasive developmental disorders in preschool children. *Journal of the American Medical Association*, 285, 3093–3099.

Cox, A., Klein, K., Charman, T., Baird, D., Baron-Cohen, S., & Swettenham, J. (1999). Autism disorders at 20 and 43 months of age: Stability of clinical and ADI-R diagnosis. *Journal of Child Psychology and Psychiatry*, 40.

Courchesne, E., Townsend, J. P., & Chase, C. (1995). Neurodevelopmental principles guide research on developmental psychopathologies. In: D. Cicchetti, & D. Cohen (Eds.), *Developmental psychopathology: Vol 1. Theories and Methods* (pp. 195–226). New York: Wiley.

Dawson, G., Ashman, S., & Carver, L. (2000). The role of early experience in shaping behavioral and brain development and its implications for social policy. *Development and Psychopathology*, 12, 695–712.

deBruin, E. I., Verheij, F., & Ferdinand, R. (2006). WISC-R subtest but no overall VIQ–PIQ difference in Dutch children with PDD-NOS. *Journal of Abnormal Child Psychology*, 34(2).

Denkla, M. B. (1983). The neuro-psychology of social-emotional learning disabilities. *Archives of Neurology*, 40, 461–462.

Dissanayake, C., & Macintosh, K. (2003). Mind reading and social functioning in children with AD and Asperger's disorder. In: B. Repacholi, & V. Slaughter (Eds.), *Individual differences in theory of mind: Implications for typical and atypical development*. New York: Psychology Press.

Drummond, C. R., Ahmad, S. A., & Rourke, B. P. (2005). Rules for the classification of younger children with nonverbal learning disabilities and basic phonological processing disabilities. *Archives of Clinical Neuropsychology*, 20, 171–182.

Duncan, J. (2001). An adaptive coding model of neural function in prefrontal cortex. *Nature Reviews Neuroscience*, 2, 820–829.

Ehlers, S., & Gillberg, C. (1993). The epidemiology of Asperger syndrome: A total population study. *Journal of Child Psychology and Psychiatry*, 34(8), 1327–1350.

Ehlers, S., Nyden, A., Gillberg, C. L., Sandberg, A. D., Dahlgren, S. O., Hjelmquist, E., *et al.* (1997). Asperger syndrome, autism and attention disorders: A comparative study of the cognitive profiles of 120 children. *Journal of Child Psychology and Psychiatry and Allied Disciplines*, 38(2), 207–217.

Fein, D., Stevens, M., Dunn, M., Waterhouse, L., Allen, D., Rapin, I., & Feinstein, C. (1999). Subtypes of pervasive developmental disorder: Clinical characteristics. *Child Neuropsychology*, 5, 1–23.

Flanagan, D. P., & Kaufman, A.S. (2004). *Essentials of WISC-IV Assessment.* Wiley: Indianapolis, IN.

Fombonne, E. (2005). The changing epidemiology of autism. *Journal of Applied Research in Intellectual Disabilities*, 18(4).

Fombonne, E., & Tidmarsh, L. (2003). Epidemiologic data on Asperger disorder. *Child and Adolescent Psychiatry Clinics of North America*, 12(1), 15–21. v–vi.

Foss, J. M. (2002). Nonverbal learning disability: How to recognize it and minimize its effects. *ERIC Digest* .

Frith, U. (1989). *Autism: Explaining the enigma.* Oxford, England: Blackwell.

Ghaziuddin, M., & Mountain-Kimchi, K. (2004). Defining the intellectual profile of Asperger syndrome: Comparison with high-functioning autism. *Journal of Autism and Developmental Disorders*, 34(3), 279–284.

Hale, J. B., & Fiorello, C. A. (2004). *School neuropsychology: A practitioner's manual.* New York: Guilford Press.

Happe, F. (1994). Wechsler IQ profile and theory of mind in autism: A research note. *Journal of Child Psychology and Psychiatry*, 35, 1461–1471.

Happe, F., Ehlers, S., Fletcher, P., Frith, U., Johansson, M., Gillberg, C., *et al.* (1996). "Theory of mind" in the brain. Evidence from a PET scan study of Asperger syndrome. *Neuroreport*, 8(1), 197–201.

Hebben (2004). A review of special group studies with the WISC-IV and assessment of low-incidence populations. In: D. P. Flanagan, & A. S. Kaufman (Eds.), *Essentials of WISC-IV assessment* (pp. 183–199). New York: John Wiley.

Hebben, N., Milberg, W., & Janzen, J. (2003). *Understanding the Nature of Autism, Second Edition.* San Antonio, TX: Psychorp.

Janzen, J. E. (2003). *Understanding the nature of Autism: A guide to autism spectrum disorders, Second Edition.* San Antonio, TX: PsychCorp.

Johnson, D. J., & Myklebust, H. R. (1971). *Learning Disabilities.* New York: Grune & Stratton.

Joseph, R. M., Tager-Flusberg, H., & Lord, C. (2002). Cognitive profiles and social-communicative functioning in children with autism spectrum disorder. *Journal of Child Psychology and Psychiatry*, 43(6), 807–821.

Kaland, N., Moller-Nielsen, A., Callesen, K., Mortensen, E. L., Gottlieb, D., & Smith, L. (2002). A new "advanced" test of theory of mind: Evidence from children and adolescents with Asperger syndrome. *Journal of Child Psychiatry*, 43(4), 517–528.

Kanner, L. (1943). Autistic disturbances of affective contact. *Nervous Child*, 2, 217–253.

Klin, A., & Volkmar, F. R. (1995). Asperger's Syndrome: Guidelines for Treatment and Intervention. Washington, DC: Learning Disabilities Association of America.

Klin, A., & Volkmar, F. R. (2003). Asperger syndrome: Diagnosis and external validity. *Journal of Child and Adolescent Psychiatry*, 12(1), 1–13, v.

Klin, A., Volkmar, F. R., Sparrow, S. S., Cicchetti, D. V., & Rourke, B. P. (1995). Validity and neuropsychological characterization of Asperger syndrome: Convergence with nonverbal learning disabilities syndrome. *Journal of Child Psychology and Psychiatry*, 36(7), 1127–1140.

Klin, A., Carter, A., & Sparrow, S. S. (1997). Psychological assessment of children with autism. In: D. J. Cohen, & F. Volkmar (Eds.), *Handbook of Autism and Pervasive Developmental Disorders*. New York: Wiley.

Klin, A., Volkmar, F. R., & Sparrow, S. S. (Eds.), *Asperger syndrome*. (2000). New York: Guilford Press.

Klin, A., McPartland, J., & Volkmar, F. R. (2005a). Asperger syndrome. In: D. J. Cohen, & F. Volkmar (Eds.), *Handbook of Autism and Pervasive Developmental Disorders*. New York: Wiley.

Klin, A., Pauls, D., Schultz, R., & Volkmar, F. R. (2005b). Three diagnostic approaches to Asperger syndrome: Implications for research. *Journal of Autism and Developmental Disorders*, 35(2), 221–234.

Klin, A., Saulnier, C., Tsatsanis, K., & Volkmar, F. R. (2005c). Clinical evaluation in autism spectrum disorders: Psychological assessment within a transdisciplinary framework. In: F. R. Volkmar, R. Paul, A. Klin, & D. Cohen (Eds.), *Handbook of Autism and Pervasive Developmental Disorders* (3rd ed., pp. 772–798). Hoboken, NJ: John C. Wiley & Sons, Inc.

Landa, R. (2007). Early communication development and intervention for children with autism. *Mental Retardation and Developmental Disabilities Research Reviews*, 13(1), 16–25.

Landa, R., & Holman, K. C. (2005). The effects of targeting interpersonal synchrony on social and communication development in toddlers with autism. Presented at *Annual Collaborative Programs Excellence in Autism/Studies to Advance Autism Research and Treatment Meeting*, November 9, 2005, Washington, DC.

Leslie, A. M., & Frith, U. (1987). Metarepresentation and autism: How not to lose one's marbles. *Cognition*, 27(3), 291–294.

Lichtenberger, E. A. (2004). Autistic-spectrum disorders. In: D. P. Flanagan, & A. S. Kaufman (Eds.), *Essentials of WISC-IV assessment* (pp. 183–199). New York: John Wiley.

Lincoln, A. J., Courchesne, E., Kilman, A., Elmasian, R., & Allen, M. H. (1988). A study of intellectual abilities in high-functioning people with autism. *Journal of Autism and Developmental Disorders*, 18(4), 505–524.

Lincoln, A. J., Allen, M. H., & Kilman, A. (1995). The assessment and interpretation of intellectual abilities in people with autism. In: E. Schopler, & G. B. Meisibov (Eds.), *Learning and Cognition in Autism: Current Issues in Autism*. New York: Plenum Press.

Lincoln, A. J., Courchesne, E., Allen, M. H., Hanson, E., & Ene, M. (1998). Neurobiology of Asperger syndrome: Seven case studies and quantitative magnetic resonance imaging findings. In: E. Schopler, & G. B. Meisibov (Eds.), *Asperger syndrome or high-functioning autism? Current issues in autism*. New York: Plenum Press.

Lincoln, A., Hanzel, E., & Quirmbach, L. (2007). Assessing intellectual abilities of children and adolescents with autism and related disorders. In: R. Stevens, & L. Smith (Eds.), *The Clinical Assessment of Children and Adolescents: A Practitioner's Handbook* (pp. 527–544). Mahwah, NJ: Laurence Erlbaum Associates.

Lord, C., Rutter, M., DiLavore, P. C., & Risi, S. (1999). *Autism Diagnostic Observation Schedule*. Los Angeles, CA: Western Psychological Services.

Lotspeich, L. J., & Ciaranello, R. D. (1995). The neurobiology of early infantile autism. *Neuroscientist*, 1, 361–367.

Mahoney, W. J., Szatmari, P., MacLean, J. E., Bryson, S. E., Bartolucci, G., Walter, S. D., et al. (1998). Reliability and accuracy of differentiating pervasive developmental disorder subtypes. *Journal of the American Academy of Child and Adolescent Psychiatry*, 37(3).

Manjiviona, J., & Prior, M. (1999). Neuropsychological profiles of children with Asperger syndrome and autism. *Autism*, 3(4), 327–356.

Marans, W. D., Rubin, E., & Laurent, A. (2005). Addressing social communication skills in individuals with high functioning autism and Asperger syndrome: Critical priorities in educational programming. In: F. Volkmar, R. Paul, A. Klin, & D. Cohen (Eds.), *Handbook of Autism and Pervasive Developmental Disorders, V. 2*. NJ: John Wiley and Sons.

Melillo, R., & Leisman, G. (2004). *Neurobehavioural disorders of childhood: An evolutionary perspective*. New York: Springer Science & Business Media Inc.

Meyer, J. A., & Minshew, N. J. (2002). An update on neuro-cognitive profiles in Asperger syndrome and high-functioning autism. *Focus on Autism and Other Developmental Disabilities*, 17(3), 152–160.

Miller, J., & Ozonoff, S. (2000). The external validity of Asperger disorder: Lack of evidence from the domain of neuropsychology. *Journal of Abnormal Psychology*, 109(2), 227–238.

Montgomery, J. M., Schwean, V. L., Burt, J. G., Dyke, D. I., Thorne, K. J., Hindes, Y. L., McCrimmon, A. W., & Kohut, C. S. (2008). Emotional intelligence and resiliency in young adults with Asperger's disorder: Challenges and opportunities. *Canadian Journal of School Psychology*, 23(1), 70–93.

Ozonoff, S., & Griffith, E. (2000). Neuropsychological function and the external validity of Asperger syndrome. In: A. Klin, F. Volkmar, & S. S. Sparrow (Eds.), *Asperger Syndrome*. New York: Guilford Press.

Ozonoff, S., Pennington, B. F., & Rogers, S. J. (1991a). Executive function deficits in high-functioning autistic individuals: Relationship to theory of mind. *Journal of Child Psychology and Psychiatry*, 32(7), 1081–1105.

Ozonoff, S., Rogers, S., & Pennington, B. (1991b). Asperger's syndrome: Evidence of an empirical distinction from high-functioning autism. *Journal of Child Psychology and Psychiatry*, 32(7), 1107–1122.

Ozonoff, S., Rogers, S. J., & Hendren, R. L. (2003). *Autism Spectrum Disorders: A Research Review*. Arlington, VA: American Psychiatric Publishing, Inc.

Ozonoff, S., South, M., & Miller, J. (2000). DSM-IV-defined Asperger syndrome: Cognitive, behavioral and early history differentiation from high-functioning autism. *Autism*, 4(1), 29–46.

Prior, M., Eisenmajer, R., Leekam, S., Wing, L., Gould, J., Ong, B., et al. (1998). Are there subgroups within the autistic spectrum? A cluster analysis of a group of children with autistic spectrum disorders. *Journal of Child Psychology and Psychiatry*, 39(6), 893–902.

Rapin, I., & Allen, D. (1983). Developmental language disorders. In: U. Kirk (Ed.), *Neuropsychology of Language, Reading, and Spelling*. New York: Academic Press.

Rolls, E. T., Hornak, J., Wade, D., & McGrath, J. (1994). Emotion-related learning in patients with social and emotional changes associated with frontal lobe damage. *Journal of Neurology, Neurosurgery, and Psychiatry*, 57, 1518–1524.

Rourke, B. P. (1989). *Nonverbal Learning Disabilities: The Syndrome and the Model*. New York: Guilford Press.

Rourke, B. (1995). *Syndrome of Nonverbal Learning Disabilities: Neurodevelopmental Manifestations* (Ed.), New York: The Guilford Press.

Rourke, B. P. (2005). Neuropsychology of learning disabilities: Past and future. *Learning Disabilities Quarterly*, 28, 111–114.

Rourke, B. P., & Tsatsanis, K. D. (2000). Nonverbal learning disabilities and Asperger syndrome. In: A. Klin, F. Volkmar, & S. Sparrow (Eds.), *Asperger syndrome* (pp. 231–253). New York: The Guilford Press.

Rutter, M., Le Couteur, A., & Lord, C. (2003). *ADI-R: The Autism Diagnostic Interview-Revised*. Los Angeles, CA: Western Psychological Services.

Schopler, E., Mesibov, G. B., & Kunce, L. J. (1998). *Asperger Syndrome or High-Functioning Autism?* New York: Plenum Press.

Siegel, D. J., Minshew, N. J., & Goldstein, G. (1996). Wechsler IQ profiles in diagnosis of high-functioning autism. *Journal of Autism and Developmental Disorders*, 26, 389–406.

Smith, T., Groen, A. D., & Wynn, J. W. (2000). Randomized trial of intensive early intervention for children with pervasive developmental disorders. *American Journal on Mental Retardation*, 105(4), 269–288.

Szatmari, P. (2000). The classification of autism, Asperger's syndrome, and pervasive developmental disorder. *Canadian Journal of Psychiatry*, 45(8), 731–738.

Szatmari, P. (2005). Developing a research agenda in Asperger syndrome. In: K. P. Stoddart (Ed.), *Children, individuals, and adults with Asperger syndrome: Integrating multiple perspectives*. London, UK: Jessica Kingsley Publishers.

Szatmari, P., Tuff, L., Finlayson, M., & Bartolucci, G. (1990). Asperger's syndrome and autism: Neurocognitive aspects. *Journal of the American Academy of Child and Adolescent Psychiatry*, 29(1), 130–136.

Szatmari, P., MacLean, J. E., Jones, M. B., Bryson, S. E., Zwaigenbaum, L., Bartolucci, G., Mahoney, W. J., & Tuff, L. (2000). The familial aggregation of the lesser variant in biological and nonbiological relative of PDD probands: A family history study. *Journal of Child Psychology and Psychiatry*, 41, 579–586.

Tager-Flusberg, H., & Sullivan, K. (1994). Predicting and explaining behavior: A comparison of autistic, mentally retarded and normal children. *Journal of Child Psychology and Psychiatry*, 35(6), 1059–1075.

Towbin, K. E. (2005). Pervasive developmental disorder – not otherwise specified. In: F. R. Volkmar, R. Paul, A. Klin, & D. J. Cohen (Eds.), *Handbook of Autism and Pervasive Developmental Disorders*. Hoboken, NJ: John Wiley & Sons.

Tsai, L. Y. (1992). Is Rett syndrome a subtype of pervasive developmental disorders? *Journal of Autism and Developmental Disorders*, 22(4), 551–561.

Tsatsanis, K. D. (2004). Heterogeneity in learning style in Asperger syndrome and high-functioning autism. *Topics in Language Disorders*, 24(4), 260–270.

Tsatsanis, K. D. (2005). Neuropsychological characteristics in autism and related conditions. In: F. R. Volkmar, R. Paul, A. Klin, & D. J. Cohen (Eds.), *Handbook of Autism and Pervasive Developmental Disorders*. Hoboken, NJ: John Wiley & Sons.

Van Acker, R., Loncola, J. A., & Van Acker, E. Y. (2005). Rett's syndrome: A pervasive developmental disorder. In: F. R. Volkmar, R. Paul, A. Klin, & D. Cohen (Eds.), *Handbook of Autism and Pervasive Developmental Disorders* (3rd ed., pp. 126–164). Hoboken, NJ: Wiley.

Volkmar, F. R. (1996). Brief report: Diagnostic issues in autism: Results of the DSM-IV field trial. *Journal of Autism and Developmental Disorders*, 26(2), 155–157.

Volkmar, F. R., & Klin, A. (2005). Issues in the classification of autism and related conditions. In: F. R. Volkmar, R. Paul, A. Klin, & D. Cohen (Eds.), *Handbook of Autism and Pervasive Developmental Disorders* (3rd ed., pp. 42–69). Hoboken, NJ: Wiley.

Volkmar, F. R., Klin, A., Siegel, B., Szatmari, P., Lord, C., Campbell, M., et al. (1994). Field trial for AD in DSM-IV. *American Journal of Psychiatry*, 151(9), 1361–1367.

Volkmar, F. R., Paul, R., Klin, A., & Cohen, D. (Eds.) (2005). *Handbook of Autism and Pervasive Developmental Disorders* (3rd ed). Hoboken, NJ: Wiley.

Walker, D. R., Thompson, A., Zwaigenbaum, L., Goldberg, J., Bryson, S. E., Mahoney, W. J., et al. (2004). Specifying PDD-NOS: A comparison of PDD-NOS, Asperger syndrome, and autism. *Journal of American Academy of Child and Adolescent Psychiatry*, 43(2), 172–180.

Weiss, L. G., Prifitera, A., & Saklofske, D. H. (2006). Interpreting the WISC-IV index scores. In: A. P. Prifitera, D. H. Saklofske, & L. G. Weiss (Eds.), *WISC-IV clinical use and interpretation: Scientist–practitioner perspectives*. San Diego, CA: Elsevier Academic Press.

Wing, L. (1981a). Asperger's syndrome: A clinical account. *Psychological Medicine*, 11(1), 115–129.

Wing, L., & Potter, D. (2002). The epidemiology of autistic spectrum disorders: Is the prevalence rising? *Mental Retardation and Developmental Disabilities Review*, 8(3), 151–161.

World Health Organization (1992). *ICD-10: International Statistical Classification of Diseases and Related Health Problems, tenth revision*. Geneva: World Health Organization.

Yirmiya, N., Sigman, M., & Freeman, B. J. (1994). Comparison between diagnostic instruments for identifying high-functioning children with autism. *Journal of Autism and Developmental Disorders*, 24(281–291).

Ziatas, K., Durkin, K., & Pratt, C. (1998). Belief term development in children with autism, Asperger syndrome, specific language impairment, and normal development: Links to theory of mind development. *Journal of Child Psychology and Psychiatry*, 39(5), 755–763.

Zwaigenbaum, L., & Szatmari, P. (1999). Psychosocial characteristics of children with pervasive developmental disorders. In: V. L. Schwean, & D. H. Saklofske (Eds.), *Handbook of psychosocial characteristics of exceptional children*. New York: Plenum Publishers.

9

ASSESSMENT OF CHILDREN WITH EMOTIONAL DISTURBANCE USING THE WISC-IV

LINDA C. CATERINO[1], AMANDA L. SULLIVAN[1]
AND SEAN C. MCDEVITT[2]

[1]*Arizona State University, Tempe, AZ, USA*

[2]*Behavioral-Developmental Initiatives, Phoenix, AZ, USA*

INTRODUCTION

It is currently estimated that up to 20% of school-age children have a diagnosable psychiatric disorder; others have suggested that even higher numbers of children require mental health services (Gresham, 2005). In 1999, the US Surgeon General estimated that 5% of children have "extreme" impairment due to mental illness, while an additional 11% have "significant" impairment (US Department of Health and Human Services, 1999). In contrast, US Department of Education has estimated a much lower prevalence rate for students requiring special education services under the category of emotional disturbance at 2%. Even more surprisingly the Department of Education reported that less than 1% of children and youth are currently served in this special education category (Gresham, 2005). As of 2004, there were nearly one-half million children identified as emotionally disturbed under the Individuals with Disabilities Education Act (IDEA) (Wagner Kutash, Duchnowski, Epstein, & Sumi, 2005). Many have noted the disparity between those who are estimated to be in need of services and the number of students actually receiving special education services for emotional disturbance in schools.

These children and adolescents include those with internalizing disorders such as Depression and Anxiety, externalizing disorders such as Attention

Deficit/Hyperactivity Disorder (ADHD) combined type, Conduct Disorder, and Oppositional Defiant Disorder, and others such as Schizophrenia. Internalizing disorders are often typified by characteristics such as social withdrawal, depression, immaturity, somatic complains, anxiety, and obsessive-compulsive behavior, while externalizing disorders are often characterized by hyperactivity, aggression, and delinquency (Topping & Flynn, 2004).

Children with emotional disorders (ED) are at risk for a number of educational consequences including higher rates of suspension/expulsion and retention and less access to general education than students with other disabilities (Wagner et al., 2005). Among all students with disabilities, only about one-third will live independently, less than half will attain full-time employment, and few will attend post-secondary institutions. Students with ED perform even more poorly on post-school outcomes (Ackerman, 2006) as they are even less likely to be employed or continue their educations (Zigmond, 2006). Throughout their lives individuals with mental illness are likely to experience hospitalization, involvement in the criminal justice system, and homelessness (Alexander, 1996). Given the host of problems associated with childhood ED, it is essential that assessment leads to effective diagnosis and intervention in order to maximize positive outcomes for these children.

The *Wechsler Intelligence Scale for Children* – Fourth Edition (WISC-IV) (Wechsler, 2003) as a measure of intellectual ability is standardized on a school-age population. While children may be tested in hospital and clinic settings for reasons of medical necessity, the vast majority of cognitive ability tests are administered in the public school setting. Therefore, consideration of the use of the WISC-IV in relation to behavioral and emotional issues must include its use in the educational sphere, as well as clinical practice. This chapter will examine the dual components of clinical and educational usefulness of the WISC-IV. It begins by defining emotional disturbance. The components of a comprehensive psychoeducational assessment of emotional disturbance are then outlined, followed by a discussion of the use of the WISC-IV with children with ED. Finally, a case study is presented to illustrate the use of the WISC-IV, other evidence, and clinical interpretation in the comprehensive assessment and treatment planning of a child with an ED.

IDEA DEFINITION OF EMOTIONAL DISTURBANCE

The IDEA (2004) sets forth the definition of emotional disturbance or emotional disability used in schools to determine eligibility and need for special education and related services. IDEA defines emotional disturbance by the following:

(i) The term means a condition exhibiting one or more of the following: characteristics over a long period of time and to a marked degree that adversely affects a child's educational performance:

   (a) An inability to learn that cannot be explained by intellectual, sensory, or health factors.
   (b) An inability to build or maintain satisfactory interpersonal relationships with peers and teachers.

    (c) Inappropriate types of behavior or feelings under normal
    circumstances.
    (d) A general pervasive mood of unhappiness or depression.
    (e) A tendency to develop physical symptoms or fears associated with
    personal or school problems.
  (ii) The term includes schizophrenia. The term does not apply to children
who are socially maladjusted, unless it is determined that they have an emotional disturbance (34 C. F. R. 300.8).

Most states have adopted this definition of ED, although some may omit the schizophrenia clause and/or the social maladjustment (SM) clause (Kidder-Ashley, Deni, Azar, & Anderton, 2000).

There are a range of students served under this category, including those with (1) anxiety disorders including Generalized Anxiety Disorder, Obsessive-Compulsive Disorder (OCD), etc., (2) mood disorders such as Depression and Bipolar Disorder, (3) conduct problems, (4) Pervasive Developmental Disorders, and (5) psychosis. Children with ADHD are sometimes serviced under the category of Other Health Impairment and sometimes under the category of ED depending on state and district policies. One study found that over 60% of children with ED also have a diagnosis of ADHD and nearly one-third also receive services for learning disabilities (Wagner et al., 2005). In general, students classified as ED are rated as having poorer social skills than their non-disabled peers, especially in the areas of self-control and cooperation, and many are also regarded as having communication problems (Wagner et al., 2005). On average, children with ED begin receiving services just before age 8, which is nearly a year later than children with all other disabilities (Wagner et al., 2005).

While the *Diagnostic and Statistical Manual for Mental Disorders*, Fourth Edition, Text Revision (DSM-IV TR) (American Psychiatric Association, 2000) diagnoses look to several areas of impairment, IDEA is only concerned with impaired educational performance. Thus, it is conceivable that a child with a DSM-IV TR (American Psychiatric Association, 2000) diagnosis such as generalized anxiety who is performing well at school would be excluded from special education services, even though he or she is experiencing significant distress and impairment in non-academic areas. Multidisciplinary educational teams in school districts may not authorize special education placements for children with emotional disturbances who are not performing below grade level in an academic subject. For example, a youngster who has difficulty falling asleep at night and has frequent nightmares may qualify for an anxiety diagnosis but may be able to perform well at school during the day.

Some researchers have argued that the notion of "educational performance" should be expanded to include social, affective, and vocational domains in addition to the traditional focus of academic performance (Gresham, 2005). This differentiation sometimes causes conflict between school psychologists who are following the IDEA (2004) procedures and independent psychologists who are evaluating the presence of a clinical disorder and may be seeking a special education placement as a therapeutic intervention for their school-aged client.

DIFFERENTIATING ED FROM SM

The IDEA definition of ED requires the rule out of SM when determining a child's eligibility for special education services. The law does allow a child to qualify for special education services if they meet the criteria for *both* ED and SM; however, the law does not allow those students with just SM to qualify for an ED placement. However, IDEA does not explicitly define SM. The requirement, however, is based on the assumption that children with SM are in control of their behavior and are thus responsible for the choices they make, whereas children and youth with an emotional disability are not. As such, many believe that children with SM should not be protected by the procedural safeguards reserved for children with "true" disabilities. Despite this requirement, many educational agencies ignore this exclusionary clause and identify children with SM as ED (Merrell & Walker, 2004). Some argue that because of the potentially negative outcomes for these children, they are just as in need of services as those who are considered to have a "true" disability (Olympia, Farley, Christiansen, Petersson, Jenson, & Clark, 2004). Olympia et al. (2004) point out a number of common misconceptions about SM, including the notion that SM is equivalent to the DSM-IV TR (APA, 2000) diagnoses of conduct disorder and oppositional defiant disorder, or externalizing disorders in general. Others state that these disorders are often co-morbid with other psychiatric disorders and that the majority of children served in the ED category (upwards of 80%) do indeed have externalizing disorders (Olympia et al., 2004).

Gacono and Hughes (2004) suggest that assessing psychopathy presents a useful method of differentiating children in these two groups. Children with psychopathic traits tend to prey upon others and are generally unaffected or worsened by psychological treatment, with the exception of behavior management strategies. Gacono and Hughes (2004) also distinguish between ED as encompassing DSM-IV Axis I psychiatric disorders and syndromes, while psychopathy (and SM by extension) is viewed as a personality disorder. In reviewing the definitions of Conduct Disorder and Oppositional Defiant Disorder as described in the DSM-IV TR (APA, 2000) it is also evident that these disorders are distinct from psychopathy, which is characterized by an absence of irrational thinking, shallow affect, lack of remorse, low levels of physiological arousal, and various other interpersonal and affective traits (Gacono & Hughes, 2004). Differentiating between ED and SM is seen as an issue of assessing emotional regulation, since it is emotional dysregulation that is the hallmark of an emotional disability and those students with SM alone will not experience dysregulation.

INTEGRATING IDEA'S DEFINITION OF ED AND
DSM-IV DIAGNOSES

The most extensive and widely used classification system of emotional and behavioral problems can be found in the DSM-IV TR (APA, 2000). The DSM-IV TR is a multiaxial, clinically derived system that includes 10 categories of major disorders that are first diagnosed in infancy, childhood, or adolescence. The childhood emotional and behavioral disorders presented in the DSM-IV TR include ADHD, Conduct Disorder, Oppositional Defiant Disorder, Separation Anxiety, Enuresis, and Encopresis. Youth may also present with several other disorders described in the *DSM-IV TR* (APA, 2000) including Anorexia and Bulimia, Bipolar Disorder, Depression, Generalized Anxiety Disorder, Obsessive-Compulsive Disorder, Panic Disorder, Post-Traumatic Stress Disorder, Schizophrenia, and specific phobias. Common disorders such as Depression and OCD are often observed in children with some deviations from the symptomology usually exhibited by adults. In order to receive a diagnosis, a disorder must generally result in significant impairment of education, social, or daily functioning. While the DSM-IV TR (American Psychiatric Association, 2000) is employed in private practice, hospital and agency settings, it may not typically be used in the educational environment since special education funding is tied to educational diagnoses based on the IDEA. In addition, many school psychologists who are certified by the state departments of education may not feel as comfortable making psychiatric diagnoses as individuals who are licensed psychologists.

However, it is advisable to provide a DSM-IV TR (American Psychiatric Association, 2000) diagnosis when making an ED determination whenever possible. A DSM-IV TR (American Psychiatric Association, 2000) diagnosis is much more likely to inform appropriate intervention than the broad IDEA label of ED since the children served under the ED category are a heterogeneous group and encompass children who may be exhibiting psychiatric disorders. When a specific DSM-IV TR diagnosis is made, the most appropriate evidence-based treatment method can be used in the intervention process. A child with depression may need cognitive behavioral therapy to deal with overwhelming sadness, but a youngster labeled "emotionally handicapped" may not even be depressed. Additionally, offering a differential diagnosis, as opposed to only the ED eligibility, can be much more informative and helpful to parents, as the ED label is somewhat ambiguous. A DSM-IV TR (APA, 2000) diagnosis contributes much more to helping parents understand their troubled children than the vague label of "emotional disability." It can aid in their search for additional services and support. With the child being the hub of an ecological system, comprised of the family, school, and community, it is obvious that a child with emotional and behavioral difficulties will come into contact with professionals from various disciplines: educational, psychological, psychiatric, medical, correctional, etc. In order to facilitate communication and services between the school and community professionals and agencies, it is important for school psychologists to employ both educational and DSM-IV TR (American Psychiatric Association, 2000) diagnoses.

USE OF THE WISC-IV FOR CHILDREN WITH EMOTIONAL DISTURBANCE

The WISC-IV provides a valid and reliable measure of cognitive functioning, which is useful in ruling out mental retardation or learning disabilities as the source of students' emotional and behavioral difficulties in school. The information provided by the WISC-IV is also essential in treatment planning, as cognitive functioning can affect the selection of interventions. A child's responses to test items can provide insight into their thought processes, which can be useful in identifying the maladaptive cognitions that may be present. Testing also allows the examiner to observe how the child copes with novel situations and frustrations, and any other idiosyncratic behaviors that may be presented.

RELATIONSHIP OF IQ TO ED

In general, past research examining the relationship between intelligence and emotional/behavioral difficulties has been somewhat ambiguous as there is considerable variability across studies. Early researchers reported ED samples with IQ scores nearly one standard deviation below average (Paget, 1982; Vance Fuller & Ellis, 1983). Glutting, McDermott, Prifitera, and McGrath (1994) found a low negative correlation between IQ and behavior problems at home and in school. Other studies have shown that the Full Scale IQ scores of students with Conduct Disorder or ADHD are particularly low (Weiss & Hechtman, 1986; Teeter & Smith, 1993). Still others reported that children with borderline intelligence were more likely to have conduct or personality problems (Stone, 1981) and that children with cognitive functioning in the mentally retarded range were at increased risk for several psychiatric disorders (Scott, 1994) including depression (Lefkowitz & Tesiny, 1985). More recent research by Goodman and colleagues (Goodman, Dimonoff, & Stevenson, 1995) have found that lower IQ was related to increased behavioral problems, supporting the notion that low IQ may be a cause or marker of ED. In contrast, Zimet, Farley, Shapiro-Adler, and Zimmerman (1994) found that only a small percentage of children with severe ED (9.4%) have below average intelligence. Using WISC-III scores, McHale Obrzut, and Sabers (2003) found that aggressive students with ED generally had lower IQ scores. These researchers also found that there was a significant decrease in Full Scale IQ from an initial evaluation to a later evaluation for students with ED, suggesting that the child's emotional impairment may impact the child's cognitive development. Preiss and Franova (2006) in a Czech study also found a relationship between self-reported depressive symptoms as noted by boys on the Children's Depression Inventory (CDI) and scores on the WISC with lower full scale and verbal IQ being significantly related to depression. Lower IQ has also been found to be correlated with problematic performance on behavior rating scales. For example, Reynolds, Girling, Coker, and Eastwood (2006) found that both parent and teacher ratings on a behavior rating screening instrument, the *Strengths and Difficulties Questionnaire* (Goodman, Ford, Simmons, Gatward, & Meltzer, 2000), were significantly and positively related to IQ, with children with higher IQs on the *Wechsler Abbreviated Scales of Intelligence* (Wechsler, 1999) exhibiting less problematic behaviors than those with lower scores.

FACTOR STRUCTURE

In analyzing the WISC-III factors with a sample of child psychiatric inpatients, the four-factor structure of the WISC was found to be the best fit for this population, just as it is in the general population (Tupa, Wright, & Fristad, 1997). Analysis of WISC-IV factor structure for students referred to special education also confirmed the four-factor structure (Watkins, Wilson, Kotz, Carbone, & Babula, 2006).

Most of the research has centered on one factor, the Processing Speed Index (PSI) which appears to be implicated in several psychiatric diagnostic categories. In an adult study using the WAIS-III, Depression was found to be significantly associated with poorer performance on the PSI (Gorlyn, Keilp, Oquendo, Burke, Sackeim, & Mann, 2000). Using the WISC-III, Calhoun and Mayes (2005) found that children with Bipolar Disorder, Depression, and ADHD, as well as those with Autism and learning disorders, performed poorly on the PSI. In addition, the clinical sample of children with ADHD discussed in the *WISC-IV Technical Manual* shows depressed performance on this index (The Psychological Corporation, 2003). More recent research by Mayes and Calhoun (2007) found that all of the children in their study ($n = 92$) who had ADHD scored lowest on the Working Memory Index or the Processing Speed Index.

SUBTEST SCORES

A few researchers have found that specific disorders are correlated with Wechsler subtest patterns. For example, Saigh and his colleagues (Saigh, Yasik, Oberfield, Halamandaris, & Bremner, 2006) found that children with Post-Traumatic Stress Disorder (PTSD) scored lower on verbal subtests than a comparison group without PTSD. In contrast, Mayes and Calhoun (2004) noted that children with brain injuries scored more poorly on non-verbal subtests than on verbal subtests. Sweitzer's (2007) research revealed that scores on the Beck Youth Inventories of Social and Emotional Impairment (BYI-D) were significantly related to the Digit Span score. Children who reported higher levels of depressive symptomatology on the BYI-D scored lower on the Digit Span subtest of the WISC-IV.

However, Brown (2000) noted that it is difficult to find a definite pattern of subtest scores on the Wechsler scales that is clearly indicative of ADHD. For example, while Performance IQ scores are typically lower than Verbal IQ scores for individuals with ADHD, sometimes this pattern is reversed, particularly for those individuals with highly developed technical skills. Moreover, he stated that specific subtest scores may not always be helpful in diagnosing ADHD. For example, while Digit Span, which involves maintaining attention and focus, is typically lower than the other Verbal subtests for most individuals with ADHD, there is sometimes a false positive pattern where patients are "able to focus on the neutral material of Digit Span and remember numbers adequately" (p. 474), especially for a short time period where limited information is presented. (This result was evident in our case study subject.) Brown also found Arithmetic to be lower than the other verbal subtests on the WISC-III, but on the WISC-IV this subtest is optional and may not always be administered. Arithmetic scores may also be depressed due to other factors such as mathematical learning disabilities, anxiety, poor instruction, etc. According to Brown (2000), Coding is one of the most sensitive subtests for neurological impairment since it involves the coordination of many different skills including visual, spatial, motor, and sequencing abilities, and interestingly, this subtest was severely compromised in our subject.

Hebben (2004) described data from the Technical Manual of the Wechsler Intelligence Scale for Children – IV (The Psychological Corporation, 2003) regarding children with Attention Deficit Hyperactivity alone. For this group, the mean Full Scale IQ score on the WISC-IV was in the average range (97.6) with the four highest subtest scores being Picture Concepts (10.5), Picture Completion (10.4), Word Reasoning (10.1), and Similarities (10.1) and the three lowest subtests being Cancellation (9.1), Arithmetic (8.7), and Coding (8.3) (p. 188), Scores, however, were quite different for those children who were diagnosed with both ADHD and learning disabilities. Thus, Hebben (2004) indicated the need for caution in generalizing from specific studies with special populations since there are several methodological considerations that must be taken into consideration. For example, diagnostic criteria may vary, subjects in these studies are not randomly selected, most of the reported studies had only a small number of subjects, test administration procedures may vary and moreover group data may not represent an entire diagnostic class. She stated that patterns of cognitive performance alone should not be used to make differential diagnoses, and that many different variables should be considered in the assessment process.

In summary, Mayes and Calhoun (2004) conclude that while studies tend to show that children with ED score lower on cognitive assessments, no consistent pattern of performance can be found and there does not appear to be a typical subtest profile for students with specific emotional or behavioral disorders. While cognitive assessment using the WISC-IV cannot be used to determine the presence or absence of an ED, the data provided by the assessment is necessary for determining information processing deficits that may otherwise account for symptoms and the qualitative information gained during testing can provide evidence that is useful in making a particular diagnosis as well as informing best course for treatment planning.

COMPREHENSIVE ASSESSMENT FOR CHILDREN WITH SUSPECTED ED

Given the complexity of ED, it is important that a diagnosis or special education determination be based on a comprehensive psychoeducational evaluation. There are numerous components of an ED evaluation including: cognitive assessment, achievement tests, a general clinical interview and/or structured diagnostic interview, behavior rating scales, self-report checklists, observations, and projective tests. Surveys of school psychologists have found that most include interviews, observations, behavior rating scales, and projective measures in their assessments for ED (Stinnett et al., 1994; Shapiro & Heick, 2004). While the use of projective measures can be quite controversial, they can provide a wealth of idiographic, qualitative data to an evaluation.

Cognitive assessment is necessary to rule out intellectual factors in a student's education impairment under the IDEA definition of ED and is particularly useful in treatment planning for children with ED. Cognitive–behavioral therapy which has been suggested in the treatment of anxiety and depression may be best suited for children with well-developed intellectual abilities. Reynolds, Girling, Coker, and Eastwood (2006) found that children with higher IQ scores as measured by the Wechsler Abbreviated Scales of Intelligence (WASI) (Wechsler, 1999) performed better on a task measuring basic cognitive–behavioral therapy skills (i.e., the ability to discriminate between thoughts, feelings, and behaviors). Similar research with learning disabled adults has also found a relationship between WASI IQ scores and the ability to discriminate between feelings and behaviors (Sams, Collins, & Reynolds, 2006).

CAPTURING QUALITATIVE INDICATORS DURING COGNITIVE ASSESSMENT

Clinically, testing children with the WISC-IV is frequently initiated to determine overall cognitive functioning level, to rule out learning difficulties, or identify giftedness as a component of the child's profile of adjustment. These purposes focus on the overall IQ score, or the relationship between IQ and achievement. But evaluators who are also working to determine a diagnostic category, either an educational or a clinical syndrome, may find that testing with the WISC-IV provides useful data for developing convergent evidence of symptoms or behavioral patterns that inform the diagnostic process. In effect, we propose that psychologists may develop an informal "norm" after evaluating a number of students. While the test observations are not empirically based, they are derived from the accumulation of clinical knowledge developed by experienced psychologists. For example, two of the authors of this chapter have more than 30 years of assessment experience in both schools and private practice and through this process they individually developed a set of "qualitative indicators". Qualitative indicators are signs or observations that are not found in an IQ or subtest score, but rather emerge from the process of administering the WISC-IV with numerous clients. Interestingly, while both authors developed these observations independently, they were found to be remarkably congruent. These qualitative indicators are similar to test behaviors shown by others to be related to overall test performance (Glutting & Oakland, 1993;

Oakland, Glutting, & Watkins, 2005), but are used in the context of clinical assessment to provide behavioral evidence of symptoms that relate to clinical or educational diagnosis. Since cognitive assessment provides a significant sample of behavioral responses, it generates a professionally derived inventory of response tendencies that may converge with parent, teacher, or self-ratings of behavior to signify the presence of emotional or behavioral problems. There are at least three sources of qualitative indicators: (1) observations of potentially symptomatic behavior demonstrated by the client during testing, (2) unusual content of responses to the items presented, and (3) unusual problem solving strategies that are selected to respond to the items. Although there is currently no standardized method of rating these indicators for the WISC-IV, development of a scheme to do so may be of value in working with a clinical population. In the meantime clinicians rely on these observations to improve their understanding of the youngster's personality and behavior.

Because there are many different educational and clinical diagnostic categories, qualitative indicators for emotional, social, and behavioral disorders may be quite varied, and some may not be limited to just the WISC-IV instrument itself. It may be that qualitative indicators tend to carry more weight in working with younger children and adolescents who may be unable or unwilling to express their feelings or report symptoms directly in the way that adults are able to do. The discussion below is meant to review some of the ones identified in the professional experience of the authors, but cannot be considered exhaustive. It should be noted that while there is general agreement among clinicians that these signs are important, there is little research evidence validating any of these signs; therefore their scientific status lies somewhere between accepted clinical tradition and personal hypotheses. Given the infrequency of the specific signs and lack of empirical methods for coding them, it is likely that qualitative indicators will continue to be useful, but not validated sources of evidence used by psychologists in their assessments of children. The sections below will review qualitative indicators that may be observed in children with selected areas of dysfunction. It should be noted that some signs overlap between disorders (e.g., difficulty regulating attention) and may be listed more than once in differing contexts.

DEPRESSION

According to the DSM-IV TR (American Psychiatric Association, 2000), The primary features of depression in children are sadness, irritability, and flat affect, which may be accompanied by feelings of hopelessness, helplessness, and worthlessness. Qualitative indicators of depression tend to reflect these characteristics. Depressed children tend to be easily discouraged and their performance on the WISC-IV may reflect their withdrawal and pessimism. These children may be reluctant to respond, showing little energy or eye contact with the examiner. Responses may be limited to one word and when questioned for a better response, the child may not answer or give just one additional word. Timed tests may be problematic in that the child may show no effort or enthusiasm in speeding up responses to gain additional credit. Given their characteristically slow rate of response, items that the child would pass if given sufficient time may be failed due to time limits.

ANXIETY

Children with generalized anxiety and OCD tend to show extreme inhibition and fearfulness and preoccupation with potential dangers. Their performance on IQ testing may reflect a reluctance to respond to items for fear of making a mistake. Frequently there is a repeated concern about time limits on subtests and the youngster may make frequent queries of the examiner regarding the correctness of their answers. Answers may be offered tentatively followed by, "Is that right?" Or there may be two or more answers offered without wanting to commit to one of them. At times the subject may seem more interested in what the examiner is writing, than in doing the test itself. On written subtests, there may be multiple erasures or responding may be stopped to look back at the accuracy of previous responses. Motor grip on the pencil may be very tight and severely anxious children may show tremor. On verbal subtests anxious children may ask that the item be repeated or request that the question be clarified before responding. On the Similarities subtest, OCD children may become very focused on minute aspects or irrelevant dimensions of similarity and never identify the general conceptual link between the disparate items.

ASPERGER'S SYNDROME

Ghaziuddin (2008) found that children with Asperger's Syndrome have average intellectual ability (104.8), as well as average Verbal (107.8) and Performance (100.2) IQ scores. Lichtenberger's (2004) report of data from the WISC-IV Technical Manual (2003) on children with Asperger's Syndrome revealed a similar profile of average Verbal Comprehension (105.6), Perceptual Reasoning (101.2), Working Memory (95.4) and Full Scale IQ scores (99.2) with low average performance on the Processing Speed Scale (86.5). However, this data was based on only 27 children. In general, children with Asperger's Syndrome exhibit some atypical behaviors. The key features of Asperger's Syndrome are preoccupation with a "specialty" area which the child or adolescent knows well and makes the focal point of interaction with others. These youngsters have almost no social awareness; they have a need for sameness and have difficulty comprehending the needs and motives of other individuals (Barnhill, Hagiwara, Myles, & Simpson, 2000). Specific behaviors seen during testing may include intrusive thoughts or discussion about their area of "expertise," an odd or pedantic manner of speaking, unusual verbalizations in response to comprehension questions, or lowered scores in the Comprehension subtest.

ATTENTION DEFICIT HYPERACTIVITY DISORDER

Inattention and impulsivity are two of the primary characteristics of ADHD combined type, in addition to hyperactivity. Children with ADHD commonly exhibit an inability to sustain attention during testing, impulsive responding, carelessness or failure to monitor responses, loss of focus during responding, frequent requests for repetition of directions or test items, excessive talking, excessive touching of materials, and excessive movement. One pattern of performance exhibited by individuals with ADHD noted by Brown (2000) includes

> rapid and efficient completion of low-level items, occasional impulsive errors as the items become more complex and then difficulty with the higher-level items marked by frequent requests for repetition of the question and inability to complete problems when the solution requires remembering the result of intermediate calculations, a function that clearly involves working memory at higher levels of difficulty (p. 472).

However, these indicators cannot be used as a definitive diagnosis for ADHD since such attention problems may also be present in children with a variety of other disorders such as Depression and Bipolar Disorder.

OTHER DISORDERS

Additionally, children with Bipolar Disorder may exhibit pressured speech, disorganized speech, and violent or bizarre verbal responses (Papalos & Papalos, 1999). Those with childhood schizophrenia may display a flat affect, difficulty interacting with the examiner and the presence of unusual verbal responses, or may even report such atypical behaviors as auditory or visual hallucinations. Children and adolescents with conduct problems or oppositional behavior may be observed to respond especially negatively to correction and may refuse to engage in tasks. They may fail to follow directions or fail to respond to items.

CASE STUDY

This case study is presented to show how the use of the WISC-IV can lend itself to an ED evaluation and how nomothetic and idiographic information can be extracted to aid in diagnosis and treatment planning. The importance of clinical judgment is highlighted.

Adrian Nickson is a Caucasian male almost 14 years of age (13 years, 10 months). He was referred by his mother, Elaine, due to his "unhappiness." Mrs. Nickson is a teacher, and his father is a small business owner. Adrian has one brother, Owen, 18, and a half-brother, Dean, 25, who both live at home. Owen has been previously treated for ADHD, bipolar disorder, and social anxiety. He was in special education placements at school for Emotionally Disturbed and Gifted students and has just graduated from a public high school. He will attend community college in the fall. Dean has experienced some depression in the past, but is doing better at present and is working for his stepfather. There is a family history of unipolar and bipolar depression on the maternal side.

Mrs. Nickson reported that her pregnancy with Adrian was uneventful and his birth history was normal. He appeared to reach his developmental milestones at appropriate ages. He began walking at 12 months of age and his verbal milestones were a bit precocious since he was reported to understand his first words by 6 months of age, spoke in single words by 10 months and in sentences by 16 months. Adrian has not experienced any serious accidents, although he did have mononucleosis at age 7. He also has hay fever and migraine headaches.

Adrian frequently complains about muscle aches and stomachaches, particularly when he is required to attend school. He also seems to have difficulty falling asleep and has a poor appetite. Recently, he has lost weight. About 3 years ago, Adrian appeared rather depressed and seemed to have difficulty making new friends at school. His mother had him evaluated by a child psychiatrist who prescribed an anti-depressant, Zoloft, and a stimulant, Adderall XR. After taking this medication for the past 3 years, Adrian's pediatrician recently discontinued the Zoloft and prescribed Seroquel, and his depressive symptoms and weight loss have increased.

Mrs. Nickson described Adrian's temperament as more difficult than average. She noted that he tends to withdraw from new situations, generally has a negative mood, is irritable, and easily distractible. He usually withholds affection, and does not easily share his feelings. She felt that he is unhappy most of the time and that he seems especially uncomfortable in new situations. He also seems to have concentration problems and a short attention span and usually has difficulty completing his schoolwork. Mrs. Nickson described Adrian as having many fears including a fear of making mistakes, fear of the dark, fear of getting hurt, etc. She described Adrian as shy and noted that he is "picked on" by other students. While he has one friend from early childhood, he has not made any new friends in the last few years and is alone most of the time. If he does socialize, it is with his female cousin. Typically, he spends most of his time on the computer.

Mrs. Nickson reported that Adrian was a happy baby and toddler. However, he began to show some symptoms of separation anxiety when he started pre-school. He then had some negative experiences in kindergarten and since then, Mrs. Nickson feels that he has been significantly apprehensive about school. He did seem to be somewhat positive about his early school years in first through fourth grades, but by fifth grade he was struggling with work completion and since then has become more and more negative about school. By the end of middle school, Adrian's grades were failing and he was increasingly resistant to attending school.

Adrian attended a private pre-school program and a charter elementary school. In sixth grade, his parents decided to transfer him to a public middle school so that he could meet more of the neighborhood youth. However, Adrian reported that he did not make any friends during middle school. He is unsure what high school he wishes to attend in the fall. He has never been in special education, nor has he participated in individual or family counseling until now.

Mrs. Nickson reports that Adrian is generally obedient, and not much discipline is needed. However, he is not assigned any household chores and there are few demands made on him. Typically his affect is rather flat, although Adrian can anger easily when asked to stop playing video games. His typical punishment is grounding from the computer.

Mrs. Nickson referred Adrian for counseling and also requested a cognitive evaluation to determine his academic capabilities. She noted that in his early school years his academic testing was significantly above average, but during the last few years it has declined and he did not qualify for the district's gifted program.

Throughout his contacts with the psychologist, Adrian was extremely quiet and taciturn. He did not willingly participate in the counseling sessions, but on one occasion he did express some concern about his relationship with his brother and became quite tearful. He noted that he does not interact with his father or half-brother, but is closer to his mother. Mrs. Nickson said that while Adrian may talk with her on a very limited basis, he does not show any affection. Adrian stated that he is closest to his brother, Owen, but that Owen can be very critical of him, making "mean comments." It was after this revelation that Adrian seemed to become more resistant to sharing his feelings in therapy. Goals for counseling were to increase Adrian's understanding and expression of feelings, to increase his socialization, to improve family relations, and to find an appropriate educational setting for high school.

Adrian is an attractive, slender teen with blonde hair and blue eyes who appeared much younger than his stated age. While he was appropriately dressed, his hair was uncombed and he presented a rather disheveled appearance. Adrian had some difficulty separating from his mother during the assessment sessions. On one occasion he stated that he was too tired and that he did not want to participate in the assessment session and his mother acquiesced. On a second occasion, he again attempted to resist the assessment procedure, but this time his mother (at the suggestion of the psychologist) intervened and encouraged him to participate with the promise of a reward of a new computer game.

Throughout the assessment process Adrian appeared to be somewhat disengaged. He did not make eye contact and frequently kept his head down, at times even putting his head on the desk and covering his eyes. He gave brief responses and refused to elaborate on any of the verbal items. His voice was of appropriate volume for most of the testing, but on occasion it was soft enough to require the psychologist to ask for repetition, which he did, rather begrudgingly. Adrian's use of language and his vocabulary skills were good. He was able to maintain attention throughout each subtest, but between subtests, he would ask when the assessment session would be over, how much more, etc. and in general, he needed a great deal of encouragement to continue. Toward the end of the assessment session he appeared fatigued and declined to complete the optional Arithmetic subtest, stating that he didn't like math. He also refused to complete the Sentence Completion form and was very slow in completing the Millon Adolescent Clinical Inventory (MACI), requiring more than one session to complete it. Adrian was taking stimulant medication (Adderall XR) during the assessment procedure.

TEST SCORES

Wechsler Intelligence Scale for Children – Fourth Edition (WISC-IV)

Subtest	Scale scores
Block Design	8
Similarities	13
Digit Span	11
Picture Concepts	10
Coding	5
Vocabulary	15
Letter–Number Sequence	12
Matrix Reasoning	9
Comprehension	11
Symbol Search	9
Cancellation	4
Information	14
Arithmetic	Refused
Word Reasoning	Not given

Index	Scores	Percentile	95% confidence interval
VC	116	86	108–122
PR	94	34	87–102
WM	107	68	99–114
PS	83	13	76–94
FS	102	55	97–107

Conners Parent Rating Scale, Revised (S)

	Mother	Father
Oppositional	58	61
Cognitive Problems	51	75
Hyperactivity	63	63
Conners ADHD Index	69	69

Conners Teacher Rating Scale	Ms. X	Mr. Y
Oppositional	45	66
Cognitive Problems/Inattentive	55	59
Hyperactivity	44	47
Anxious–Shy	75	75
Perfectionism	47	46
Social Problems	46	46
ADHD Index	65	57
Restless Impulsive	58	50
Emotional Lability	51	51
Global Index Total	56	51
DSM-IV Inattentive	64	62
DSM-IV Hyperactive-Impulsive	52	43
DSM-IV Total	58	54

Child Behavior Checklist (CBCL)

Competence Scales	T-scores	
	Mother	Father
Activities	25	24
Social	28	27
School	40	43

Syndrome Scales

Anxious–Depressed	77	75
Withdrawn–Depressed	95	87
Somatic Complaints	78	70
Social Problems	70	70
Thought Problems	60	55
Attention Problems	75	70
Rule Breaking Behavior	50	50
Aggressive Behavior	50	51

Teacher Report Form (TRF)

	Mrs. X (English)	Mr. Y (Math)
Anxious–Depressed	70	76
Withdrawn–Depressed	72	77
Somatic Complaints	62	65
Social Problems	58	70
Thought Problems	50	50
Attention Problems	66	65
Rule Breaking Behavior	50	50
Aggressive Behavior	50	50

Youth Self-Report (YSR)

	T-score
Anxious–Depressed	72
Withdrawn–Depressed	70
Somatic Complaints	75
Social Problems	70
Thought Problems	50
Attention Problems	65
Rule Breaking Behavior	55
Aggressive Behavior	55

Millon Adolescent Clinical Inventory (MACI)

	BR
Disclosure	62
Desirability	60
Debasement	60
Introversive	107

BR

Inhibited	89
Doleful	86
Submissive	70
Dramatizing	73
Egotistic	42
Unruly	59
Forceful	50
Conforming	60
Oppositional	62
Self-demeaning	76
Borderline Tendency	44
Identity Diffusion	66
Self-devaluation	68
Body Disapproval	58
Sexual Discomfort	50
Peer Insecurity	109
Social Insensitivity	63
Family Discord	68
Childhood Abuse	36
Eating Dysfunction	58
Substance Abuse Proneness	56
Delinquent Predisposition	53
Impulsivity Propensity	48
Anxious Feelings	82
Depressive Affect	72
Suicidal Tendency	48

Wechsler Individual Achievement Test-II

Written Expression	90
Spelling	94
Pseudoword Decoding	109
Word Reading	111
Reading Comprehension	113
Numerical Operations	96
Mathematics Reasoning	92

Behavior Assessment Scale for Children-2

Clinical scales	*Teacher T-score*	*Parent T-score*
Hyperactivity	65	75
Aggression	60	52
Conduct Problems	51	56
Anxiety	82	59
Depression	82	53
Somatization	107	98
Atypicality	52	61
Withdrawal	83	56
Attention Problems	54	64
Learning Problems	66	

Clinical scales	Teacher T-score	Parent T-score
Adaptive Scales		
Adaptability	28	48
Social Skills	47	39
Leadership	40	36
Activities of Daily Living		42
Study Skills	51	
Functional Communication	40	30
Composites		
Externalizing	59	62
Internalizing	103	75
Adaptive Skills	40	37
Behavior Symptom Index	74	72

Adrian's human figure drawing was a small male figure in the center of the page. It was quickly executed, with little detail. Adrian was reluctant to verbally discuss the drawing and gave brief, non-committal answers to the psychologist's questions regarding the drawing. In his Kinetic Family Drawing, Adrian drew five stick figures representing each of his family members in separate sections on the page. Again, he did not verbally describe the picture, but did state that one of the family's three wishes was to "get along." Adrian did not wish to complete the Sentence Completion Form either by writing or giving oral responses. In addition, he declined to complete the BASC-2 or the Conners-Wells Self-Report scales. It was also determined that due to his lack of cooperation and limited verbalizations, Adrian would not be a good candidate for a projective test such as the Thematic Apperception Test, so it was not attempted.

Adrian's full scale score on the WISC-IV was in the average range. He scored in the high average range on the Verbal Comprehension Index and in the average range on the Perceptual Reasoning and Working Memory Indices. Interestingly, Adrian's WISC-IV profile reveals a low PSI score (83) which is consistent with research conducted by Mayes and Calhoun (2007) describing the link between ADHD and Processing Speed, as well as the research conducted by Preiss and Franova (2006) where a poor Processing Speed performance is correlated with depressive symptomatology. Adrian also scored poorly on the Coding subtest, not completing many items and making one error. His performance on this subtest is consistent with Brown's (2000) work suggesting a relationship between Coding and ADHD. Adrian also worked slowly on the Cancellation subtest and mentioned that he had more difficulty with the random task, which was also evident in his scores.

Adrian's verbal skills are good; especially his vocabulary knowledge and his conceptual reasoning skills, and he demonstrated average ability on working memory and attentional tasks.

While Adrian's report card grades are low, especially in writing, and to a lesser extent, math, none of his academic achievement scores as measured by the *Wechsler Individual Achievement Test – Second Edition* (WIAT-II) is significantly weak. His reading skills, both in decoding and comprehension, do appear to be better developed than his math or written language skills. This is in contrast to his failing report card scores in eighth grade.

The rating scales administered to Adrian's parents and his teachers, as well as his self-report results reveal problems in anxiety, depression, social relations, and somatic complaints and to a lesser extent, attentional problems. However, he has been on medication to control his ADHD symptomatology so these scores may have been affected. Adrian's parent rating scales reveal difficulty in attention with both parents' scores being in the moderately atypical range for the Conners ADHD Index. The parents' responses to the Child Behavior Checklist revealed significant clinical elevations on the Anxious–Depressed, Withdrawn–Depressed, Somatic Complaints, and Social Problems scales, as well as the Attention Problems scale.

Adrian's teacher ratings were from both his English (Mrs. X) and his math teachers (Mr. Y). As is frequently the case, the teachers' subtest scores are discrepant on several scales. Both teachers' responses, however, yielded a score in the markedly atypical range on the Anxious–Shy scale, with the math teacher's score on the Social Problems and Oppositional Scales being in the moderately atypical range. The English teacher's responses yielded a Conners' ADHD Index score in the mildly atypical range, with the math teacher's score being in the slightly atypical range. On the Teacher's Report Form, a similar pattern of a borderline elevation on the attention scale was noted for both teachers and significant elevations were noted on the Anxious–Depressed and Withdrawn–Depressed scales for both. Borderline elevations were noted on the Somatic complaints scale for Adrian's English teacher, and a significant elevation was noted on the Social Problems Scale for the math teacher.

Adrian's own responses on the Youth Self-Report Form revealed significant clinical elevations on the Anxious–Depressed, Withdrawn–Depressed, Somatic Complaints, and Social Problems scales, with a borderline elevation noted on the Attention Scale. Adrian's scores on the MACI appeared to be valid. He demonstrated anxiety and mistrust of others, as well as a self-deprecating style. He seems to have chosen a path of social withdrawal and isolation as way of protecting himself from negative social interactions. He appears to be concerned about his attractiveness, adequacy at school, and his poor relationship with peers.

DIAGNOSIS

Adrian's primary diagnoses appear to be Generalized Anxiety Disorder and Major Depression. Social anxiety should also be considered. Although depression and anxiety can both affect attention and cognitive focus, it appears that ADHD, predominantly inattentive, should be considered as a separate diagnosis, particularly due to his lack of work completion and the diagnosed presence of this disorder prior to his present depressive incident. Unfortunately, a school observation was not able to be made due to the summer schedule, but this should be undertaken in the fall.

Adrian should continue in individual therapy; however, he may be resistant, seeing therapy as too revealing. Treatment efforts should be directed toward countering his withdrawal tendencies so as to prevent him from becoming even more socially isolated. However, these efforts to enhance Adrian's social interest must be made in a slow, well-thought-out manner, so that he is not overwhelmed. Cognitive–behavioral techniques may be used to examine his thoughts regarding his own self-worth and his acceptance by peers. For example, he may need to identify and examine his cognitive distortions regarding peers' opinions of him and the consequences of such thought patterns. Adrian's cognitive abilities and his high average verbal skills as measured by the WISC-IV suggest that he would be able to learn the principles of cognitive–behavioral therapy. He should be able to differentiate feelings, thoughts, and behaviors, and to conceptualize their interrelationship and by doing so learn to utilize more appropriate cognitions.

Adrian may also benefit from family counseling. His father and eldest brother do not appear to be active in his life and Adrian reports that he never talks with them. It does appear, however, that Adrian would like to have a closer relationship with his middle brother, Owen, but that Owen is attempting to assert his independence from the family, leaving Adrian without any close relationships to family members. Mrs. Nickson, as the family member with whom he appears to have the best relationship, should attempt to lessen his isolation, initially by spending more structured individual time with him. This behavior would be a change from her current role of allowing Adrian to spend all of his time at home alone and may require more assertiveness on her part.

Adrian will continue to need medication for his depression, but he appeared to do better on the anti-depressant Zoloft, than he did on Seroquel. It seems that he might have been placed on this medication due to the family history of Bipolar Disorder, without a careful analysis of his unique symptoms. A suggestion to Adrian's doctor that he consider a return to Zoloft as his primary medication for depression and anxiety was made, and after his medication was changed, his mood appeared to improve and he was less tearful. While his attempts to initiate socialization did not increase, his was more open to responding positively to socialization attempts made by his best friend. Adrian's physician should also assess his response to his stimulant medication (Adderall XR) to determine if he would benefit from a change in dosage or medication

EDUCATIONAL IMPLICATIONS

While Adrian was referred by his parents and not school personnel, his educational needs still need to be considered. A learning disability placement was rejected, since Adrian is not performing significantly below grade level or his ability level on standardized academic testing (WIAT-II). However, a placement for Emotionally Disturbance is strongly considered. According to IDEA,

(i) Adrian needs to demonstrate "one or more of the following: characteristics over a long period of time and to a marked degree that adversely affects a child's educational performance."

    (1) "An inability to learn that cannot be explained by intellectual, sensory, or health factors." While Adrian's report card grades are low, his achievement testing is not significantly weak. It appears that he may indeed be learning, but not demonstrating his academic skills within the classroom setting, due to lack of work completion. However, the term "educational performance" does include academic performance within the classroom setting and Adrian is not meeting his school's academic requirements.

    (2) "An inability to build or maintain satisfactory interpersonal relationships with peers and teachers." Adrian clearly meets this criterion. He has not maintained satisfactory relationships with peers, with the exception of one childhood friend and he only seemed to relate on a superficial level to one of his two eighth grade teachers.

    (3) "Inappropriate types of behavior or feelings under normal circumstances." Adrian does not appear to demonstrate behaviors consistent with this criterion.

    (4) "A general pervasive mood of unhappiness or depression." Adrian does clearly display depressive symptomatology, pervasive unhappy mood, difficulties in sleeping and eating, poor socialization, and meets the DSM-IV criteria for a diagnosis of major depression.

    (5) "A tendency to develop physical symptoms or fears associated with personal or school problems." Adrian has a history of headaches, stomach aches, and other somatic complaints, typically associated with school attendance.

(ii) "The term includes Schizophrenia. The term does not apply to children who are socially maladjusted, unless it is determined that they have an emotional disturbance" (34 C. F. R. 300.8). Adrian does not display any hallucinations or other behavior consistent with a diagnosis of Schizophrenia. His behavior is not considered to be socially maladjusted.

According to IDEA criteria, even though the psychologist has identified the presence of psychological difficulties relating to Major Depression, Generalized Anxiety, and ADHD, the school multidisciplinary committee is ultimately responsible in determining whether Adrian qualifies for a special education placement as an Emotionally Disturbed student. The parent, however, must concur in an initial placement. The possibility of a 504 accommodations was brought up to Mrs. Nickerson, which she is still considering. If a 504 plan is implemented, specific accommodations for Adrian could include an individualized academic program designed to minimize written work and homework assignments, with the use of computers when possible. Shortened assignments, as well as additional time for assignment completion, should be considered.

Adrian would also benefit from working with an assigned buddy on group projects, preferably a student with good social skills who could serve as a model and support for him. Adrian should also be encouraged to broaden his activities at school by participating in at least one extracurricular activity. Finally, school personnel should work closely with both the home and Adrian's private psychologist and psychiatrist to coordinate his care. According to state law, all charter schools must provide psychological and special education services for their pupils. If Adrian does not make progress with the accommodations provided, a special education ED placement should be reconsidered at the charter school or Adrian could be transferred to such a program at the public school.

Adrian's clinical diagnosis, viewed by the private psychologist and psychiatrist, would be as follows:

DSM-IV Diagnosis

Axis I	296.20 Major depression, moderate
	314.00 Attention Deficit/Hyperactivity Disorder, predominantly Inattentive Type
	300.02 Generalized anxiety disorder
Axis II	V71.09 No diagnosis
Axis III	Migraine headaches; allergies
Axis IV	Problems related to family environment
	Educational problems
Avis V	Global Assessment of Functioning (GAF) = 60

Clinical treatment should focus on the provision of ongoing psychotherapy, including individual cognitive–behavioral therapy, and family therapy to decrease anxiety and improve Adrian's mood at home, in the classroom and with peers. Cognitive–behavioral therapy should focus on feelings of hopelessness, helplessness, and worthlessness. The restructuring approach would likely be less threatening than dynamic therapy. Social skills training would probably be effective in improving peer relationships; a social skills therapy group, if available would be most beneficial in overcoming Adrian's social anxiety. Additionally, medications should be assessed for efficacy with Adrian to improve his range of emotional response and decrease vegetative symptoms. Due to his ADHD, consideration should be given for the establishment of 504 accommodations, especially increased time to complete tests, due to his weakness in processing speed, and collaboration between parent and teachers to monitor his completion of assignments.

CONCLUSION

The WISC-IV provides a valid and reliable measure of cognitive functioning, which is essential for ruling out cognitive deficits as a source of students' impairment. The information provided by the WISC-IV is also essential in treatment planning, as cognitive functioning influences the clinician's selection of interventions. In addition, intellectual assessment provides a standardized sample of behavioral responses which clinicians can interpret as reflective of emotional and social functioning. A child's responses to test items provide insight into his or her thought processes and may reveal maladaptive cognitions indicative of an ED. Testing also allows the examiner to observe how the child handles novel situations and frustrations, and any other idiosyncratic behaviors that may be presented. Given the complexity of ED, it is important that a diagnosis or special education determination be based on a comprehensive psychoeducational evaluation, which should routinely include a measure of cognitive assessment. The WISC-IV has an extensive clinical base and has been validated with clinical populations, making it a valuable component of a comprehensive evaluation.

REFERENCES

Ackerman, B. (2006). Learning self-determination: Lessons from the literature for work with children and youth with emotional and behavioral disabilities. *Child Youth Care Forum*, 35, 327–337.

Alexander, R. (1996). The quality of life of persons with severe emotional disability: A review of empirical studies. *Journal of Health and Social Policy*, 7, 9–23.

American Psychiatric Association (APA) (2000). *Diagnostic and Statistical Manual of Mental Disorders* (4th ed., text revision). Washington, DC: American Psychiatric Association.

Barnhill, G., Hagiwara, T., Myles, B. S., & Simpson, R. L. (2000). Asperger syndrome: A study of 37 children and adolescents. *Focus on Autism and Other Developmental Disabilities*, 15, 146–153.

Brown, T. E. (Ed.) (2000). *Attention-Deficit Disorders and C-morbidities in Children, Adolescents and Adults*. Washington, DC: American Psychiatric Press.

Calhoun, S. L., & Mayes, S. D. (2005). Processing speed in children with clinical disorders. *Psychology in the Schools*, 42, 333–343.

Gacono, B., & Hughes, T. (2004). Differentiating emotional disturbance from social maladjustment: Assessing psychopathy in aggressive youth. *Psychology in the Schools*, 41, 849–860.

Ghaziuddin, M. (2008). A family history study of Asperger syndrome. *Journal of Autism and Developmental Disorders*, 38, 138–142.

Glutting, J., & Oakland, T. (1993). *Guide to the assessment of test session behavior for the WISC-III and the WIAT*. San Antonio, TX: The Psychological Corporation.

Glutting, J. J., McDermott, P. A., Prifitera, A., & McGrath, E. A. (1994). Core profile types for the WISC-III and the WIAT: Their development and application in identifying multivariate IQ achievement discrepancies. *School Psychology Review*, 23, 619–639.

Goodman, R., Dimonoff, E., & Stevenson, J. (1995). The impact of child IQ, parent IQ and sibling IQ on child behavioral deviance scores. *Journal of Child Psychology and Psychiatry*, 36, 409–425.

Goodman, R., Ford, T., Simmons, H., Gatward, R., & Meltzer, H. (2000). Using the Strengths and Difficulties Questionnaire (SDQ) to screen for child psychiatric disorders in a community sample. *British Journal of Psychiatry*, 177, 534–539.

Gorlyn, M., Keilp, J. G., Oquendo, M. A., Burke, A. K., Sackeim, H. A., & Mann, J. J. (2000). The WAIS-III and major depression: Absence of VIQ/PIQ differences. *Journal of Clinical and Experimental Neuropsychology*, 28, 1145–1157.

Gresham, F. R. (2005). Response to intervention: An alternative means for identifying students as emotionally disturbed. *Education and Treatment of Children*, 28, 328–344.

Hebben, N. (2004). Review of special group studies and utility of the process approach with the WISC-IV. In: D. Flanagan, & A. Kaufman (Eds.), *Essentials of WISC-IV Assessment*. New York: Wiley & Sons.

Individuals with Disabilities Education Act (2004). PL108-446, 20 U. S. C. 1400-87.

Kidder-Ashley, P., Deni, J. R., Azar, K. R., & Anderton, J. B. (2000). Comparison of 40 States' procedures for identifying students with serious educational problems. *Education*, 120, 558–568.

Lefkowitz, M. M., & Tesiny, E. (1985). Depression in children: Prevalence and correlates. *Journal of Consulting and Clinical Psychology*, 53, 647–656.

Lichtenberger (2004). Autistic-spectrum disorders. In: D. Flanagan, & A. Kaufman (Eds.), *Essentials of WISC-IV Assessment*. New York: Wiley & Sons (pp. 199–208).

Mayes, S. D., & Calhoun, S. L. (2004). Similarities and differences in *Wechsler Intelligence Scale for Children* – Third Edition (WISC-III) profiles: Support for subtest analysis in clinical referrals. *The Clinical Neuropsychologist*, 18, 559–572.

Mayes, S. D., & Calhoun, S. L. (2007). *Wechsler Intelligence Scale for Children* – Third Edition and fourth edition predictors of academic achievement in children with attention-deficit/hyperactivity disorder. *School Psychology Quarterly*, 22, 234–249.

McHale, B. G., Obrzut, J. E., & Sabers, D. L. (2003). Relationship of cognitive functioning and aggressive behavior with emotionally disabled and specific learning disabled students. *Journal of Developmental and Physical Disabilities*, 15, 123–140.

Merrell, K., & Walker, H. (2004). Deconstructing a definition: Social maladjustment versus emotional disturbance and moving the EBD field forward. *Psychology in the Schools*, 41, 899–910.

Oakland, T., Glutting, J., & Watkins, M. (2005). Assessment of test behaviors with the WISC-IV. In: A. Prifitera, D. Saklofske, & L. Weiss (Eds.), *WISC-IV Clinical Use and Interpretation: Scientist–Practitioner Perspectives*. New York: Academic Press (pp. 435–463).

Olympia, D., Farley, M., Christiansen, E., Petersson, H., Jenson, W., & Clark, E. (2004). Social maladjustment and students with behavioral and emotional disorders: Revisiting basic assumptions and assessment issues. *Psychology in the Schools*, 41, 835–847.

Paget, K. D. (1982). Intellectual patterns of conduct problems on the WISC-R. *Psychology in the Schools*, 19, 439–445.

Papalos, D., & Papalos, J. (1999). *The Bipolar Child: The Definitive and Reassuring Guide to Childhood's Most Misunderstood Disorder*. New York: Random House.

Preiss, M., & Franova, L. (2006). Depressive symptoms, academic achievement, and intelligence. *Studia Psychologica*, 48, 57–67.

The Psychological Corporation (2003). *WISC-IV Technical and Interpretive Manual*. San Antonio, TX: The Psychological Corporation.

Reynolds, S., Girling, E., Coker, S., & Eastwood, L. (2006). The effect of mental health problems on children's ability to discriminate amongst thoughts, feelings and behaviours. *Cognitive Therapy Research*, 30, 599–607.

Saigh, P. A., Yasik, A. E., Oberfield, R. A., Halamandaris, P. V., & Bremner, J. D. (2006). The intellectual performance of traumatized children and adolescents with or without posttraumatic stress disorder. *Journal of Abnormal Psychology*, 115, 332–340.

Sams, K., Collins, S., & Reynolds, S. (2006). Cognitive therapy abilities in people with learning disabilities. *Journal of Applied Research in Intellectual Disabilities*, 19, 25–33.

Scott, S. (1994). Mental handicap. In: M. Rutter, E. Taylor, & L. Hersov (Eds.), *Child and Adolescent Psychiatry* (3rd Ed.). Oxford: Blackwells (pp. 616–646).

Shapiro, E. & Heick, P. (2004). School psychologist assessment practices in the evaluation of students referred for social/behavioral/emotional problems. *Psychology in the Schools*, 41, 551–561.

Stinnett, T. A., Havey, J. M., & Oehler-Stinnett, J. (1994). Current test usage by practicing school psychologists: A national survey. *Journal of Psychoeducational Assessment*, 12, 331–350.

Stone, F. B. (1981). Behavior problems of elementary-school children. *Journal of Abnormal Child Psychology*, 9, 407–418.

Sweitzer, S. T. (2007). Cognitive deficits associated with childhood depression: Patterns of performance on the *Wechsler Intelligence Scale for Children*: Fourth Edition. Unpublished dissertation. Dissertation Abstracts International: Section B: The Sciences and Engineering, 68.

Teeter, P. A., & Smith, P. L. (1993). WISC-III and WISC-R: Predictive and Discriminant validity for students with severe emotional disturbances. *Journal of Assessment: Advances in Psychoeducational Assessment: WISC-III Monograph* Cordova–Psychoeducational Co. (pp. 114–124).

Topping, K. J., & Flynn, B. (2004). Treating seriously emotionally disturbed adolescents: The views and working practice of school psychologists. *The Behavior Analyst Today*, 5, 39–90.

Tupa, D. J., Wright, M. O., & Fristad, M. A. (1997). Confirmatory factor analysis of the WISC-II with child psychiatric inpatients. *Psychological Assessment*, 9, 302–306.

US Department of Health and Human Services. (1999). *Mental Health: A Report of the Surgeon General*. Rockville, MD: US Department of Health and Human Services, Substance Abuse and Mental Health Services Administration, Center for Mental Health Services, National Institutes of Health, National Institute of Mental Health.

Vance, H. B., Fuller, G. B., & Ellis, R. (1983). Discriminant function analysis of LD/BD scores on the WISC-R. *Journal of Clinical Psychology*, 39, 749–753.

Wagner, M., Kutash, K., Duchnowski, A. J., Epstein, M. H., & Sumi, W. C. (2005). The children and youth we serve: A national picture of the characteristics of students with emotional disturbances receiving special education. *Journal of Emotional and Behavioral Disorders*, 13, 79–96.

Watkins, M. W., Wilson, S. M., Kotz, K. M., Carbone, M. C., & Babula, T. (2006). Factor structure of the *Wechsler Intelligence Scale for Children* – Fourth Edition among referred students. *Education and Psychological Measurement*, 66, 975–983.

Wechsler, D. (1999). *Wechsler Abbreviated Scale of Intelligence (WASI)*. London: The Psychological Corporation.

Wechsler, D. (2003). Wechsler Intelligence for Children – Fourth Edition Technical Manual. San Antonio, TX: Psychological Corporation.

Weiss, R., & Hechtman, L. (1986). *Hyperactive Children Grown Up*. New York: Guilford Press.

Zigmond, N. (2006). Twenty-four months after high school: Paths taken by youth diagnosed with severe emotional and behavioral disorders. *Journal of Emotional and Behavioral Disorders*, 14, 99–107.

Zimet, S. G., Farley, G. K., Shapiro-Adler, S., & Zimmerman, T. (1994). Intellectual competence of children who are beginning inpatient and day psychiatric treatment. *Journal of Clinical Psychology*, 50, 866–877.

10

THE COGNITIVE IMPACT

OF SYSTEMIC ILLNESS

IN CHILDHOOD AND

ADOLESCENCE

R. GRANT STEEN[1] AND FRANCES CAMPBELL[2]

[1]*Department of Psychiatry, University of North Carolina at Chapel Hill, Chapel Hill, NC, USA*

[2]*Frank Porter Graham Child Development Institute, University of North Carolina at Chapel Hill, Chapel Hill, NC, USA*

ABSTRACT

To what extent is the developing brain vulnerable to insults that arise in the context of systemic illness? We review the cognitive consequences of systemic illness, insofar as such consequences can be assessed by standardized cognitive tests. We used PubMed to search the literature for data on cognitive impairment (CI) as a function of specific disease entities, limiting the search to children and adolescents (age 6–18 years). We excluded from consideration any mental retardation unrelated to systemic illness, any CI resulting from direct injury or a disease that has a direct effect on the brain, and any CI associated with developmental syndromes that primarily affect the brain. Nevertheless, illness is broadly defined to include any systemic condition that interferes with brain maturation, including malnutrition and poverty.

Many systemic illnesses are associated with mild-to-moderate CI. The degree of decrement in tests of Full-Scale Intelligence Quotient (FSIQ) is usually ≤ 10 points, but some illnesses can be associated with larger deficits in FSIQ. Most systemic illnesses that result in CI produce an effect by disrupting delivery of some critical substrate needed for brain metabolism. For example, mild chronic hypoxia is associated with significant CI. Chronic hypoxia can occur in acute lymphoblastic leukemia (ALL), sickle cell disease (SCD), pulmonary disease, very low birth weight (VLBW), and sleep-disordered breathing (SDB). Similarly, chronic hypoglycemia may be damaging in patients with diabetes and perhaps malnutrition. Acute exposure to toxins, whether given in treatment of illness or resulting from the pathophysiology of illness, is responsible for CI in ALL and lead poisoning.

White matter in the brain is apparently more vulnerable to injury than is gray matter. Both radiation and drug therapy have an effect specifically on white matter, in the case of treatment-induced neurotoxicity in ALL patients. It is a tenable hypothesis that most CI is mediated by white matter changes. Conceptually, CI is due to any of several etiologies: treatment-related neurotoxicity (e.g., chemotherapy in ALL); treatment-related systemic effects; illness-associated neurotoxicity (e.g., hypoxia in sickle cell); or illness-associated systemic effects.

SUMMARY OF BEST-PRACTICE RECOMMENDATIONS

1. Undiagnosed acute or chronic illness can depress a child's performance on cognitive tests, so clinicians should be aware of the general state of health when testing a child.

2. It may be beneficial to test children for cognitive impairment (CI) as soon as possible after a chronic illness is diagnosed, to provide a benchmark for later evaluations.

3. Specific deficits in attention can potentially explain CI, so care should be taken to characterize attention in patients with systemic illness.

4. Children with unexplained CI, particularly on tests of mathematical reasoning, should be evaluated for anemia, sleep disorder, or other causes of chronic hypoxia.

5. In many children, growth impairment and CI are linked by a common etiology, so children who are growth-impaired should receive cognitive testing.

6. Up to 25% of children in the United States live in housing with lead-based paint and so are at risk for CI, hence Medicaid-eligible children be screened for lead exposure at 1 and 2 years of age.

7. Poverty is implicated as a cause of CI, and roughly 13% of children in the United States live in poverty. Medicaid-eligible children should be tested for CI, so that intervention can begin before academic failure develops.

8. Motivation is a key element of any child's success on cognitive tests, and clinicians must be aware of motivational deficits as a potential pitfall to peak performance.

INTRODUCTION

Children surviving acute lymphoblastic leukemia (ALL) often suffer long-term cognitive sequelae. Meta-analysis suggests that the deficit in Full-Scale Intelligence Quotient (FSIQ) after childhood ALL averages about 11 points ($p < 0.001$) with 8 years of follow-up (Campbell et al., 2007). It has been assumed that this cognitive deficit arises from aggressive methods that are typically used to treat ALL, though it is possible that long-term CI is associated with critical illness itself (Hopkins & Brett, 2005). This uncertainty raises a larger question; To what extent is the developing brain vulnerable to insults that arise in the context of systemic illness?

We undertook a systematic PubMed literature search on the relationship between CI and specific childhood illnesses. We used a search strategy of the key words "cognitive impairment and X", where X is any of the listed diseases (Table 10.1). The search was limited to children and adolescents (age 6–18 years), using the "limits" feature of PubMed; our focus is not on early childhood due to the limitations of testing young subjects. We specifically excluded from consideration mental retardation unrelated to systemic illness. We also excluded CI resulting from direct injury (e.g., traumatic brain injury, stroke) or from disease that has a primary effect on the brain (e.g., brain tumor, Parkinsons disease, multiple sclerosis, schizophrenia, epilepsy, eating disorder), since our focus is on the cognitive effects of systemic illness. Finally, we excluded genetic and developmental syndromes with a primary effect on the brain (e.g., Downs syndrome, fragile X, phenylketonuria, neurofibromatosis, autism, cortical dysplasia, velocardiofacial syndrome, Turners syndrome, Williams syndrome). However, illness was broadly defined to include any systemic condition that potentially interferes with brain maturation, including malnutrition and poverty.

We are aware that PubMed searches alone (unsupplemented by manual searches) offer roughly 82% (Steen et al., 2006) to 89% (Steen et al., 2005c) yield of the relevant literature. But PubMed searches tend to have a high yield of the most recent literature, which is our focus here. Nevertheless, we supplemented PubMed searches with systematic manual searches, and many of the references reviewed here were not identified in the original PubMed search (Table 10.1).

TREATMENT OF PATIENTS WITH ALL

When the modern era of combination chemotherapy for childhood ALL began, roughly 50 years ago, the 5-year event-free survival rate for ALL was just 4% (Rivera et al., 1993). Recognition that leukemic relapse in the brain afflicted about 44% of patients, and that prophylactic treatment was required to reduce such therapeutic failures, was crucial to progress in ALL treatment. At first, prophylactic therapy for meningeal relapse included both cranial radiation therapy (RT) and systemic chemotherapy, and there was a gratifying increase in the cure rate.

TABLE 10.1   PubMed Search Results for Cognitive Impairment as a Function of Disease Entity, in Children and Adolescents (6–18 years)

Illness	Total PubMed references	PubMed references since 2001	Notes (Search date December, 2006)
All cancers	108	—	Not discussed in text, except for leukemias
Brain tumor	58	—	Not discussed, since effect on brain is direct
Tumor syndromes (NF-1)	16	—	Not discussed, since effect on brain is direct
Mixed/other cancer	8	—	Not discussed, as references are too scarce
Leukemia	26	8	Discussed, chemo/RT conflated in most early studies
Heart disease	33	18	Most references on Downs, Williams, or 22q11.2 syndrome
Muscular dystrophy	30	9	Discussed
Diabetes	26	7	Discussed
Severe anemia	23	1	Discussed
Very low birth weight	20	12	Discussed
Malnutrition/nutrient deficiency	16	8	Discussed
Pulmonary disease	15	3	Discussed
Sickle cell disease	14	4	Discussed
Lead poisoning	12	8	Discussed
Sleep-disordered breathing	11	6	Discussed
Asphyxia	11	5	Not discussed
Carbon monoxide poisoning	9	3	Not discussed
Malaria	8	6	Not discussed
Asthma	7	2	Not discussed
Chronic anemia	7	5	Discussed
Otitis media	7	3	Not discussed
Arthritis	6	2	Not discussed
Tuberculosis	5	2	Not discussed
Iron deficiency anemia	4	2	Discussed
Cystic fibrosis	4	0	Not discussed
Poverty	4	2	Discussed
Hepatitis	3	1	Not discussed
Diarrhea	2	1	Discussed
Infectious disease	2	1	Not discussed
Renal failure	2	2	Not discussed
Total references =	307	121	

Many relevant references used in the text are not included here because this table includes only PubMed results, not manual search results, some of which were used in writing the text.

Within 20 years, the 5-year event-free survival rate had increased from 4% to 53%, and the rate of meningeal relapse fell to 13% (Rivera et al., 1993). Now, after 20 additional years of progress, 89% of ALL patients are expected to be free of leukemic relapse 10 years after diagnosis (Pui et al., 2005).

Yet this dramatic increase in therapeutic success came at a cost. Reports began to surface in the late 1970s and early 1980s that surviving ALL patients often had severe CI and endocrinologic sequelae (Duffner, 2004). The adverse impact of RT on the pediatric brain was not recognized initially, perhaps because few children survived and the follow-up interval among surviving children tended to be short. For example, a study compared 34 children with ALL, all of whom got 2,400 cGy of prophylactic cranial RT, to 27 children with other forms of cancer who got no cranial RT (Soni et al., 1975). No evidence of CI was found for children who received cranial RT, using the Wechsler Intelligence Scale for Children (WISC), but prospective follow-up of patients was just 18 months. When larger patient samples were evaluated, and especially when longer follow-up intervals were used, a clear trend was demonstrated for higher ALL cure rates to be associated with greater CI (Duffner, 2004).

Strong evidence suggests that children who get aggressive therapy for ALL are likely to experience more academic difficulties than are children who get less aggressive therapy (Duffner, 2004). Learning is impaired in roughly half of all long-term survivors of infant leukemia, who typically are treated with aggressive therapy (Leung et al., 2000). Yet it has not been proven that treatment-related neurotoxicity is the only factor that is responsible for CI in children with ALL. Is it possible that patients at high risk of relapse suffer some type of illness-associated CI, compared to children at lower risk of relapse? This uncertainty is compounded in other systemic illnesses, which can be associated with CI, but which have been studied to a lesser extent than ALL (Table 10.1).

There is often a poor understanding of the etiology of CI in children with systemic illness. In principle, CI associated with systemic illness could be due to any combination of several etiologies: treatment-related (direct) neurotoxicity; treatment-related systemic effects; illness-associated neurotoxicity; and illness-associated systemic effects. Each of these effects will be discussed in greater depth in relation to ALL.

TREATMENT-RELATED NEUROTOXICITY IN ALL

Treatment-related neurotoxicity is damage directly to the brain due to the effects of treatment for a systemic illness such as ALL. Children whose cranial prophylaxis includes RT have a significantly lower FSIQ (Rowland et al., 1984). Leukemic children who were randomized to receive either intrathecal (IT) methotrexate alone or IT methotrexate plus 2,400 cGy cranial RT differ in their neuropsychological performance. The wide ranging achievement test (WRAT), which measures academic ability, showed that children who get cranial RT are at risk of mild global intellectual impairment (Rowland et al., 1984). Such impairment is greater when methotrexate is combined with RT than when methotrexate is given alone, and combined therapy is associated with deficits in attention, concentration, sequencing, and visual processing (Langer et al., 2002). There is often an RT-associated deficit specifically in verbal learning (Precourt et al., 2002), as well as in working memory and Processing Speed (Schatz et al., 2000).

Lower radiation doses may spare cognitive function, so there has been an impetus to reduce radiation exposure even for children at relatively high risk of relapse (Waber et al., 2001). Among 201 children given prophylatic cranial RT at 1,800 cGy for high-risk ALL, the 5-year event-free survival was 75%, and both FSIQ and memory were within the mean range expected for age. Nevertheless, performance on a complex figure-drawing task was impaired, and children irradiated at less than 3 years of age showed significant verbal deficits (Waber et al., 2001). Follow-up of 369 children treated with 1,800 cGy for high-risk ALL showed that 8-year event-free survival was 80%, and average academic achievement, visuospatial reasoning, and verbal learning were within the normal range. Yet some studies did not find any benefit from reducing prophylactic cranial RT from 2,400 to 1,800 cGy (Rodgers et al., 1991) and children given 1,800 cGy may still have some degree of CI, compared to children who are not irradiated (Anderson et al., 2000).

The weight of evidence clearly shows that radiation can be harmful to the brain. Prophylactic cranial RT for childhood ALL is associated with a 28-fold increase in the standardized incidence of secondary brain tumor (Pui et al., 2003). White matter is more vulnerable to RT-related injury than is gray matter (Schultheiss et al., 1995). The first clinical dose–response relationship for damage to irradiated pediatric brain found that white matter structural alteration can occur at a radiation dose of just 2,000–3,000 cGy, with RT-associated changes in white matter becoming significant in as little as 6 months (Steen et al., 2001). In contrast, there was no evidence of RT-related gray matter injury, even at 6,000 cGy. A new magnetic resonance imaging (MRI) method called diffusion-tensor imaging suggests that white matter structure is actually altered by cranial RT (Khong et al., 2006). The mechanism of RT-related white matter injury is poorly understood, but functional magnetic resonance imaging (fMRI) suggests that blood perfusion of white matter is reduced by irradiation (Zou et al., 2005). This is consistent with the finding that glucose metabolism is lower in the white matter of long-term ALL survivors who got cranial RT (Phillips et al., 1991; Taki et al., 2002), though this finding is somewhat controversial (Kahkonen et al., 2000).

The hypothesis that systemic chemotherapy can also have a harmful effect on the brain in children with ALL was not well supported, until recently. Most children who received prophylaxis for meningeal relapse in earlier treatment eras got chemotherapy and cranial RT together, so treatment effects were conflated and could have been synergistic. It is only since cranial RT was phased out of most ALL treatment protocols that evidence began to emerge showing that chemotherapy can also cause CI. Another complication is that it is hard to determine what a child's intelligence might have been in the absence of illness; by the time a child has completed ALL treatment, he may have been critically ill for months and under treatment for years. Some researchers have advocated using the WISC within 2 weeks of diagnosis, to characterize the impact of treatment on cognition (Jansen et al., 2004). Another option is to compare patients to their siblings, since this may help to control for the heritability of intelligence and the impact of socioeconomic factors.

The main chemotherapeutic agent identified as a problem so far is methotrexate, one of the first chemotherapies used for ALL, and one which is still in wide use (Hill et al., 2004). Clear evidence has emerged that methotrexate can be associated with brain pathology, including cortical atrophy and mineralizing microangiopathy (Moleski, 2000). Among 132 ALL patients treated with methotrexate – but not cranial RT – there was strong evidence of CI in certain patient sub-groups (von der Weid et al., 2003). Children treated with methotrexate at less than 6 years of age showed deficits in FSIQ, Verbal IQ, Performance IQ, Comprehension, Block Design, Object Assembly, and Similarities, relative to children treated at an older age. For unknown reasons, girls treated with methotrexate were more likely to be impaired than boys, on virtually every cognitive test (von der Weid et al., 2003). A recent protocol that used IT methotrexate alone found that patients suffered an average decrement of 13 points in Verbal IQ and 15 points in Performance IQ, relative to healthy children, with higher methotrexate doses associated with more CI (Montour-Proulx et al., 2005). Wechsler Intelligence Scale for Children-Revised (WISC-R) factor scores were lower in children treated with methotrexate with significant deficits in Verbal Comprehension, Perceptual Organization, and Freedom from Distractability (Raymond-Speden et al., 2000). Visuomotor reaction time was increased by methotrexate treatment, especially in girls or in children treated at a young age (Buizer et al., 2005). School performance was impaired with respect to same-age peers, probably because of attentional deficits (Buizer et al., 2006), although there is also evidence that patients can have specific information processing difficulties (Mennes et al., 2005).

Some recent studies report that methotrexate prophylaxis is associated with little or no CI, even when used in combination with other chemotherapies (Kingma et al., 2002; Rodgers et al., 2003). However, studies which report no CI in treated patients tend to be small, meaning that they may simply lack the power to detect differences that are nonetheless present. It is also possible that new treatment protocols have reduced the rate of neurotoxicity, although this has not been established. Reduced neurotoxicity could be related to methotrexate dose-reduction, to increased skill in supporting patients through the period of greatest risk for brain injury, or to a greater willingness to accept a slightly higher risk of relapse in exchange for a lower risk of cognitive morbidity.

Methotrexate can have an effect specifically on white matter in the brain. Transient changes in white matter, as visualized by MRI (Figure 10.1), can occur soon after methotrexate is given, and young children are more likely to show such

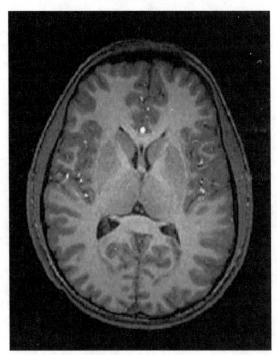

FIGURE 10.1   Magnetic resonance imaging (MRI) can be used to generate exquisitely detailed images of the brain. Such images can be used to characterize abnormalities that may be associated with cognitive impairment (CI), to diagnose tumors or other brain diseases, to plan surgery, or to document sequelae of treatment. This is an image of a healthy female, which clearly shows the visual difference between white matter and gray matter. In general, white matter is the "wiring" of the brain, comprised of long cell processes – known as axons – that link neurons together. Axons are covered by a fatty insulating layer of myelin, and it is the myelin covering that makes white matter look white. Gray matter is comprised of densely packed neurons and other cells that lack a fatty myelin layer, and gray matter more nearly represents the "computing power" of the brain. MRI suggests that white matter is more prone to damage by radiation, and white matter volume can be reduced in patients treated for ALL.

changes (Paakko et al., 2000). White matter MRI abnormalities were associated with impaired visuomotor integration, and white matter calcifications seen by computed tomography (CT) were associated with low FSIQ and Performance IQ, as well as impaired attention (Iuvone et al., 2002). A sophisticated analysis of brain volume, as measured by MRI, has shown that white matter volume is significantly and substantially reduced in patients treated for ALL (Reddick et al., 2006). Among 112 long-term ALL survivors, most of whom were treated with methotrexate alone, the greatest effect of treatment was on attention. Patient white matter volume correlated directly and significantly with estimated IQ, and with measures of academic achievement such as math reasoning, math composite, numerical operations, reading composite, reading comprehension, and spelling (Reddick et al., 2006). A conceptual model has been developed which suggests that attentional abilities, but not memory, could explain the relationship between white matter volume and FSIQ in brain tumor patients (Reddick et al., 2003). In patients with ALL, it has been proposed that specific deficits in attention – which includes elements such as focus, sustain, and shift – could potentially explain a more generalized finding of CI (Rodgers et al., 2003). This proposal is consistent with results of a double-blind, placebo-controlled trial of methylphenidate (Ritalin) among ALL survivors, which showed that methylphenidate could temporarily reduce attentional deficits that had a negative impact on cognitive ability (Mulhern et al., 2004). Although a great deal of work remains to be done in this field, it is clear that ALL patients suffer some degree of treatment-related neurotoxicity.

TREATMENT-RELATED SYSTEMIC
EFFECTS IN ALL

Treatment-related systemic effects include damage done indirectly to the brain because of the effects of treatment for a systemic illness. There is, as yet, little or no evidence that treatment of ALL can be associated with systemic effects that have an indirect impact on cognitive ability. Yet there is strong evidence of systemic effects in treatment of other childhood diseases, so it is reasonable to examine the evidence that systemic effects might also exist in ALL.

Chemotherapy for ALL induces functional dysregulation within bone marrow stromal cells that can cause chronic post-chemotherapy anemia (Corazza et al., 2004). In well children, there is a dose–response relationship between hemoglobin concentration and cognitive function (Sungthong et al., 2002). There is a strong adverse impact of chronic or intermittent hypoxia on cognition and academic achievement in children with illness (Bass et al., 2004). Of controlled studies in a systematic review, 84% reported an adverse effect of hypoxia, even at mild levels of oxygen desaturation. In children with sickle cell disease (SCD), who typically receive neither radiation nor chemotherapy, chronic anemia is linked to CI, and FSIQ is significantly and substantially lower in children with a hematocrit less than 27 (Steen et al., 2003). Chronic anemia is associated with significant deficits in Verbal IQ, Verbal Comprehension, and Freedom From Distractability. The correlation between FSIQ and hematocrit is significant ($p < 0.005$), explaining roughly 23% of the variance in FSIQ (Steen et al., 2003).

It is a reasonable hypothesis that there is a link between anemia and CI in children with ALL. Children with ALL show induction of the hypoxia-inducible factor 1 (HIF-1) gene in leukemic bone marrow cells (Wellmann et al., 2004), so there is at least some hypoxia in the marrow, though it is not clear to what extent hypoxia is an issue in the brain. If chronic anemia was a problem in children treated for ALL, one would expect fatigue to be reported frequently by long-term survivors. While the prevalence of fatigue is very high during treatment, the prevalence of fatigue among survivors 14 years post-therapy is 30%, which is not higher than the general population prevalence of 11–45% (Meeske et al., 2005). This suggests that chronic fatigue is probably not a long-term problem for most ALL survivors. Nevertheless, ALL survivors with fatigue were 2.6-fold more likely to have CI, and roughly 56% of patients with fatigue also had clinical depression.

ILLNESS-ASSOCIATED NEUROTOXICITY IN ALL

Illness-associated neurotoxicity is damage directly to the brain as a result of systemic illness. There is no known illness-associated neurotoxicity in patients with ALL. Yet there is evidence that newly diagnosed ALL is associated with physiological states that could potentially have an impact on cognition. In a small group of children with ALL, zinc deficiency was present at diagnosis (Sahin et al., 2000), and zinc deficiency is linked to CI and psychomotor retardation in infants (Ashworth et al., 1998). Extreme hypercalcemia can also be a presenting feature of ALL (Mathur et al., 2003), and chronic hypercalcemia is associated with CI in adults (Duque et al., 2005). Finally, in children with ALL, homocysteine levels can be abnormal at diagnosis (Refsum et al., 1991), and serum homocysteine can predict CI (Krajinovic et al., 2005).

The relationship between plasma homocysteine levels and CI is complex and only partially understood. Serum homocysteine is inversely associated with serum folate, and homocysteine may be elevated in ALL patients because of folate deficiency and an increased burden of proliferating leukemic cells (Refsum et al., 1991). Certain gene polymorphisms that affect folate metabolism and serum homocysteine may be risk factors for development of ALL (Krajinovic et al., 2004). Methotrexate-related folate depletion or homocysteinemia could play a role in methotrexate-related neurotoxicity, and polymorphisms that control serum homocysteine predict changes in FSIQ following ALL treatment (Krajinovic et al., 2005). These findings suggest that genotyping for variants that control homocysteine levels might identify ALL patients at risk of CI after treatment (Krajinovic et al., 2005).

It may also be noteworthy that cells bearing neuronal antigens can be generated in vivo from bone marrow cells; this is the widely publicized capacity for stem cells to "turn blood into brain," at least under experimental circumstances (Mezey et al., 2000). Stem cells in experimental animals appear able to cross-differentiate between blood and brain; if a neural stem cell is transplanted into sub-lethally irradiated mice, clones of hematopoietic cells appear after 5–6 months, and form B- and T-cell lineages (Moore, 1999). Conversely, mice injected with labeled bone marrow cells can form microglia, fibrous astrocytes of the subcortical white matter, and astrocytes of the neocortex from donor cells (Moore, 1999). If such a relationship exists between neural stem cells and hematopoietic stem cells in humans, this could potentially explain why ALL patients are prone to relapse in the brain. Thus, the question of whether there is potentially an illness-associated neurotoxicity in ALL patients has not been adequately addressed.

ILLNESS-ASSOCIATED SYSTEMIC EFFECTS IN ALL

Illness-associated systemic effects include damage indirectly to the brain because of the effects of a systemic illness. A chief presenting sign of ALL is severe anemia (Redaelli et al., 2005), and even mild anemia can be associated with chronic brain hypoxia (Bass et al., 2004). Hypoxia could thus potentially be both an illness-associated systemic effect (before treatment) and a treatment-related systemic effect. In fact, there may be little point in determining whether systemic effects are related to illness or to treatment in the case of ALL, although this determination is easier in other illnesses.

Very mild hypoxemia can affect cognition and academic performance in children (Urschitz et al., 2005). In a community-based study of 995 German third-graders, the nocturnal nadir of arterial oxygen saturation, measured by pulse oximetry, predicted impaired academic performance in mathematics. Children with mild noctural hypoxemia (nocturnal saturation nadir of 91–93%) were 1.7-fold more likely to perform poorly in mathematics, even after exclusion of children with a history of heart disease or habitual snoring. Mild nocturnal hypoxemia may be rather common in children, as the prevalence was 10% in a large sample. Among children with mild hypoxemia, the prevalence of impaired mathematics performance was 20.4% (Urschitz et al., 2005). Such findings imply that children with unexpectedly poor performance on tests of mathematical reasoning should perhaps be tested for sleep disorder.

The weight of evidence strongly favors the conclusion that there is an adverse impact of even intermittent mild hypoxemia on development, behavior, and academic achievement in otherwise-healthy children (Bass et al., 2004). Children with chronic illness are physiologically stressed in other ways as well, so anemia may be particularly damaging. Anemia is very common in the pediatric cancer patient and is often related to cognitive dysfunction (Cunningham, 2003). Anemia-related cerebral hypoxia causes symptoms such as headache, vertigo, tinnitus, and dizziness, and these symptoms could directly cause or indirectly exacerbate CI (Cunningham, 2003).

Children with ALL suffer chronic illness, and they may show illness-associated systemic effects. There is good evidence that children with ALL have more school absences, are more restricted from the active aspects of learning, and tire more easily than healthy children (Raymond-Speden et al., 2000). Children with ALL who get cranial RT and systemic chemotherapy spend an average of 47.5 nights in hospital, whereas children with ALL who get chemotherapy alone spend 38.6 nights in hospital. In contrast, children with an unrelated severe chronic illness (asthma) spent 16.9 nights in hospital, while healthy children typically spend no time at all in hospital (Raymond-Speden et al., 2000). In an academic year that may have only 180 days, ALL patients thus can miss 20% of the school days in a year, which would be expected to affect the pace of learning and the risk of grade retention. There is also a risk that school absence will be associated with social isolation and clinical depression, and this could have an additional impact on CI in children.

HEART DISEASE AND CI

There are fewer references that relate heart disease to CI than expected, as many references listed (Table 10.1) describe the impact of heart disease on cognition in the context of a neurodevelopmental disorder that has a direct effect on brain function (e.g., Downs, Williams, CHARGE (Coloboma of the eye, Heart defects, Atresia, Retardation of growth, Genital abnormalities, Ear abnormalities), and velocardiofacial syndromes). If the PubMed search is done instead with a disease category of "congenital heart disease," only seven references are found.

An early report on the cognitive consequences of congenital heart disease found few long-term sequelae of severe infantile cyanosis (DeMaso et al., 1990). This study compared three groups of children, all of whom were diagnosed with congenital heart disease at under 1 year of age. One group of 63 children had transposition of the great arteries, a congenital condition in which the pulmonary artery and aorta are reversed in position; this can mean that blood is inadequately oxygenated. A second group of 77 children had tetralogy of Fallot, a congenital heart malformation characterized by pulmonary stenosis, ventricular septal defect, and an aorta that draws blood from both ventricles; this also means that blood is poorly oxygenated. Both malformations are fatal if not surgically corrected. Children with cardiac malformations were compared to 36 children who were diagnosed with congenital heart disease, but whose condition spontaneously cleared. At age 6, both groups with cardiac malformation had more CI than the group of "control" children. This study was flawed by the absence of a true control group; children who spontaneously recover from congenital heart disease may still have CI, compared to healthy children (DeMaso et al., 1990). These results are therefore not compelling, as roughly half of adult survivors of cardiac arrest experience anoxic brain damage and CI (Pusswald et al., 2000), and the infant brain would likely be more at risk from cyanosis than the adult brain.

Recent work on children born with transposition of the great arteries is consistent in finding cognitive sequelae of cardiac malformation (Hovels-Gurich et al., 2002). Among 60 children tested at 10 years of age, 55% had some level of impairment, with the most common disability relating to speech production (40% of patients). There was also commonly impairment of motor function and other abilities, and deficits were correlated with the severity of preoperative acidosis and hypoxia and with the duration of time spent on a cardiac bypass machine (Hovels-Gurich et al., 2002). Children who underwent surgery to correct transposition of the great arteries had a Performance IQ score (94.9) significantly lower ($p < 0.001$) than their Verbal IQ score (99.8), although both scores were within the normal range (Bellinger et al., 2003). Overall, children were somewhat impaired in academic achievement, fine motor function, visual–spatial skills, working memory, sustained attention, and higher-order language skills. When two methods of doing arterial switch surgery (low-flow cardiopulmonary bypass versus total circulatory arrest) were compared, children randomly assigned to total circulatory arrest were more impaired on tests of manual dexterity, speech apraxia, visual–motor tracking, and phonologic awareness. The duration of circulatory arrest predicted neurodevelopmental outcome, suggesting that hypoxia has a cumulative effect (Wypij et al., 2003). Poor outcome of surgery was associated with a 7-point lower FSIQ (Newburger et al., 2003).

There is strong additional evidence that children with severe heart disease suffer illness-associated systemic effects. Children with congenital heart disease who have "cyanotic lesions" show CI in comparison with children having "acyanotic lesions" prior to surgical correction of the heart defect (Wray & Sensky, 2001), although these lesions were not defined. Post-operatively, children with cyanotic lesions showed a progressive deterioration in performance and achieved significantly lower cognitive test scores than did children with acyanotic lesions. Successful cardiac surgery does not normalize cognitive function, which may be permanently impaired by the degree of hypoxia characteristic of children with congenital heart defects (Wray & Sensky, 2001). Among children awaiting heart or heart–lung transplantation, mean developmental scores are mostly in the normal range, but scores are lower in aggregate than in a healthy control group (Wray & Radley-Smith, 2004). Young children with congenital heart disease have low scores specifically in locomotor ability, speech, hearing, hand–eye coordination, and performance. Such deficits have been characterized as a developmental delay (Wray & Radley-Smith, 2004), although this label implies that deficits are temporary, which may not be the case. Longitudinal assessment of children who received heart or heart–lung transplants documented enduring and progressive behavioral deficits (Wray & Radley-Smith, 2006). About 10% of well children have behavioral problems at school, whereas 33% of transplant patients had such problems 1 year after surgery. By the third year after surgery, roughly 75% of the children with congenital heart disease had behavioral problems at school.

Children with heart disease who develop CI are a particularly clear example of illness-associated systemic effects. There is no reason to suspect that congenital heart disease is associated with a genetic mutation that could have an effect on the brain in most cases, so illness-associated neurotoxicity can generally be ruled out. Treatment is usually surgical, so treatment-related neurotoxicity or systemic effects are also likely to be minimal. Yet there is evidence that cardiac surgery itself can be associated with CI, especially if circulatory arrest is used intra-operatively (Wypij et al., 2003), or if extracorporeal membrane oxygenation (ECMO) – essentially an artificial lung external to the body – is required for blood oxygenation post-operatively (Golej & Trittenwein, 1999). Yet both of these measures are short term and probably less harmful than the chronic state of illness-associated hypoxia in congenital heart disease.

MUSCULAR DYSTROPHY AND CI

Muscular dystrophy (MD) is a family of diseases in which genetic mutation leads to a gradual but irreversible muscular deterioration that ends in premature death, often due to respiratory failure. In early reports, patients with Duchenne MD had intelligence test scores roughly one standard deviation below the norm, with better scores on Performance IQ than Verbal IQ (Leibowitz & Dubowitz, 1981). The hypothesis was that CI arose through a mechanism of intermittent or chronic hypoxia, such as during sleep apnea (Finnimore et al., 1994). Nevertheless, though many MD patients have fragmented nocturnal sleep or apnea, no correlation was found between the severity of sleep apnea and the degree of CI (Broughton et al., 1990).

Early reports suggested that a third of all MD patients have FSIQ < 75 (Bresolin et al., 1994). Yet early studies probably failed to include mild MD cases, since genetic testing was not available and patients were diagnosed clinically; thus mild cases were probably under-diagnosed (Rubinsztein et al., 1997). If mild clinical cases are examined, such patients are found not to be impaired in general intelligence relative to normal (Rubinsztein et al., 1997). Nevertheless, a meta-analysis confirms that children with Duchenne MD show deficits in verbal reasoning and verbal processing, with no illness-related deficits in FSIQ or Performance IQ (Cotton et al., 2005). It may be noteworthy that cognitive deficits appear to decrease with age, as adolescents and adults are less impaired than children.

The presentation of MD is clinically quite variable, and there may be a distinction between adolescent-onset MD, which is typically associated with mild CI, and congenital MD, which is associated with severe CI (Perini et al., 1999). The severity of symptoms is apparently determined by the degree of disruption of the protein dystrophin, which is present in many tissues, most notably in skeletal muscle and certain neurons in the brain (Anderson et al., 2002). Although dystrophin disruption is associated with pathology of the skeletal muscle, which is ultimately fatal, there may also be a direct effect of dystrophin in the brain. Brain architecture can be disordered, with dendritic abnormality and loss of axons, and there are neuronal conduction velocity abnormalities that can be detected by electroencephalography (Anderson et al., 2002).

Brain abnormality in MD patients was recently documented by magnetic resonance imaging (MRI). Up to 84% of young patients have small lesions in white matter that are apparent on T2-weighted (water-sensitive) imaging (Censori et al., 1994). Yet this type of lesion does not prove that MD has a direct effect on the brain, since T2 hyperintensity is common in hypertensive patients (Benedetti et al., 2006). Measurement of brain volume by MRI has shown a generalized atrophy of brain tissue in MD patients with myotonic dystrophy (DM1) or proximal myotonic myopathy (DM2), with atrophy generally more severe in DM1 patients (Kassubek et al., 2003). Brain atrophy is consistent with a hypothesis that MD has a direct effect on the brain (Spencer et al., 2005). Regional brain glucose metabolism is also lower than normal in MD patients, especially in brain regions where the dystrophin gene is expressed (Lee et al., 2002), consistent with MD having a direct effect on the brain. Finally, there appears to be an association between the extent of disruption of the dystrophin gene and the severity of CI (Felisari et al., 2000). Thus, the most recent findings argue that MD may have a direct effect on the brain, and that it may not be appropriate to regard MD as having only a systemic (indirect) effect on the brain.

DIABETES AND CI

Diabetes is a metabolic disorder in which tissues become glucose-starved because insulin – which stimulates glucose uptake – does not have the normal physiologic effect in the diabetic patient. Evidence of illness-associated systemic effects is unequivocal for diabetes; the human brain accounts for 20% of the metabolic cost of the entire body and it uses glucose exclusively as a fuel (Deary & Frier, 1996). Consequently, if the brain is starved of glucose even briefly, cognitive processes are impaired and a tense, tired mood state ensues. This effect is very common, as many non-diabetics also experience mood shifts when they become hungry.

A systematic review of the literature confirms that diabetes is associated with impaired academic achievement in children (Taras & Potts-Datema, 2005). Children with type I (childhood-onset) diabetes are impaired specifically on the Performance IQ sub-test of the WISC-R, which could be due to slowed responses on timed tasks (Holmes & Richman, 1985). Although FSIQ scores tend to fall within the normal range, children with early-onset or long-duration diabetes score lower on most cognitive tests (Holmes & Richman, 1985). Six years after disease onset, children with type I diabetes are impaired on measures of intelligence, attention, Processing Speed, long-term memory, and executive skills (Northam et al., 2001). Onset of disease at less than age 7 is associated with greater impairment on Performance IQ and greater delay in Information Processing, and may also be associated with mild brain atrophy (Ferguson et al., 2005). Children with a history of severe hypoglycemia have more CI, more learning difficulties reported by parents, and more need for special educational services, suggesting that severe hypoglycemia is a risk factor for CI (Hannonen et al., 2003).

Some studies have failed to document that type I diabetes is associated with CI, even though children with poor diabetic control have weaker academic performance (McCarthy et al., 2002). Yet cross-sectional "prevalence" studies are less convincing than are the experimental studies that have been done in diabetic children and adults. Experimental studies clearly show that even mild hypoglycemia is associated with acute loss of mental efficiency, according to an insulin-clamp technique that has been used to maintain a state of hypoglycemia (Ryan et al., 1990). During a hypoglycemic plateau, children perform poorly on the trails-making test (a measure of cognitive flexibility), and on various measures that require planning, decision-making, attention to detail, and rapid response. Recovery from hypoglycemia was not associated with an immediate recovery of cognitive function (Ryan et al., 1990). We note that studies which rely on teacher reports of classroom performance (McCarthy et al., 2002) may be insensitive to transient CI associated with intermittent hypoglycemia if a child's diabetes is usually well controlled.

Experimental studies leave little doubt that hypoglycemia is associated with short-term CI (Ryan et al., 1990). Hypoglycemia causes a significant deterioration of visual and auditory selective attention, attentional flexibility deteriorates, and the speed of information processing slows (McAulay et al., 2006). Acute hypoglycemia can even impair visual information processing in non-diabetic subjects, and diabetic subjects can show a sharp decline in Processing Speed while visual acuity is unaffected (Ewing et al., 1998). Even in healthy adults who experience hypoglycemia during an insulin-clamp experiment, memory can be impaired (Benedict et al., 2006). Frequent or severe hypoglycemia is associated with impaired cognition, and the chronic shortage of glucose in the brain could account for cognitive deficits (Northam et al., 2001).

Patients who suffer frequent episodes of hypoglycemia tend to have poorly controlled disease, so it is possible that such patients may also have frequent episodes of hyperglycemia. It has been suggested that CI in diabetes is actually associated with chronic hyperglycemia, rather than with intermittent hypoglycemia (Ferguson et al., 2003). Consistent with this hypothesis is the finding that hyperglycemia is associated with deficits in Performance IQ during an experimental insulin-clamp study (Davis et al., 1996), for reasons that remain poorly understood.

Children with type I diabetes tend to have more lesions visible by T2-weighted MRI, as well as a slight reduction in brain volume consistent with atrophy (Ferguson et al., 2005). Central brain structures in particular are reduced in volume among children with early-onset illness. Mild hypoglycemia is associated with an increase in cerebral blood flow rate, as would be expected if hyperemia is compensatory for a reduced ability to absorb glucose (Jarjour et al., 1995). Children with diabetes suffer at least mild CI, although it remains controversial whether this impairment is related to hypo- or hyperglycemia. Thus, CI in diabetes is the result of illness-associated effects, rather than treatment-related effects. Illness-associated effects probably relate to the scarcity or overabundance of glucose, rather than to the presence of a neurotoxin, so such effects would fall under the rubric of illness-associated systemic effects.

SCD, OTHER ANEMIAS AND CI

SCD is due to a mutation of the hemoglobin protein in red blood cells. As a consequence of this mutation, patients can become severely anemic, their blood has a reduced oxygen-carrying capacity, and red blood cells are prone to "sickle" and obstruct capillary blood flow. Early evidence suggested that SCD leads to a rather profound decrease in FSIQ (Swift et al., 1989), but this study included relatively few patients, and the patients may have had severe disease. A recent meta-analysis concluded that there is just a 4-point depression in FSIQ overall, comparing patients to well-matched controls (Schatz et al., 2002a).

Yet the degree of CI associated with SCD remains controversial (Taras & Potts-Datema, 2005). Some groups have reported average FSIQ decrements substantially larger than 4 points in SCD patients; one study of 150 children free of a clinical history of stroke concluded that FSIQ was 90.0 (Armstrong et al., 1996), while another large study reported an FSIQ of 84.8 in children normal by MRI (Wang et al., 2001). This would seem to be a 10- to 15-point deficit in FSIQ, compared to healthy controls. Yet the comparison between normative controls and African-American children suffering from the effects of chronic illness, as well as from the effects of poverty, discrimination, and inadequate schooling is essentially meaningless (Steen et al., 2005b). If healthy African-American subjects are randomly selected from the normative database used to construct the WISC-III, the average FSIQ is 90.8, suggesting that the deficit between SCD patients and well-matched controls is at least 4 points (Steen et al., 2005b), as reported (Schatz et al., 2002a). However, some studies have reported average FSIQ values for SCD patients that are lower than 85 points (Swift et al., 1989; Steen et al., 1998b; Brown et al., 2000; Steen et al., 2005b). This could be a function of disease severity, small sample size, quality of schooling, relative poverty, or other socioeconomic factors. Nevertheless, there is a consensus that SCD is associated with significant and substantial CI impairment (Hogan et al., 2006).

The etiology of CI in patients with SCD is perhaps even more controversial than the degree of CI. Many early studies of cognitive ability in children with SCD probably included a substantial number of patients who had experienced a clinically silent stroke, so it has been hypothesized that stroke accounts for all CI in SCD patients (White & DeBaun, 1998; Nabors & Freymouth, 2002). There is a clear relationship between lesion burden and the degree of FSIQ decrement, suggesting that the progressive accumulation of small lesions causes CI (Schatz et al., 2002b). Nevertheless, patients who are entirely free of brain lesions visible by MRI can still be cognitively impaired (Steen et al., 2005b). When a cohort of 54 SCD patients was screened by MRI, to exclude 24 patients with any evidence of silent stroke, the remaining 30 patients had significant deficits in FSIQ, Verbal IQ, Performance IQ, Perceptual Organization, and Processing Speed, even though they were normal by MRI. The FSIQ was 12 points less than in healthy children matched by age, race, and gender, who were randomly selected from the Wechsler normative database (Steen et al., 2005b). These findings are consistent with a hypothesis that brain injury in SCD can occur through a mechanism of chronic hypoxia (Steen et al., 1999).

There is growing evidence for the importance of chronic hypoxia in causing brain injury in children with SCD (Hogan et al., 2006). Oxygen saturation of blood in SCD patients is often abnormally low, especially in children with severe disease (Homi et al., 1997). Daytime oxyhemoglobin saturation is correlated with FSIQ and inversely correlated with cerebral blood flow velocity (CBFV). Analysis suggests that increased blood flow velocity is compensatory for poor oxygen delivery, but that increased blood flow may not be able to fully compensate for impaired oxygen-carrying capacity (Hogan et al., 2006). This is consistent with an earlier study that found an inverse relationship between hematocrit and arterial volume in the brain (Steen et al., 1998a). Interestingly, there is a relationship between CBFV and Verbal IQ, but not between CBVF and Performance IQ (Hogan et al., 2006). Low overnight oxygen saturation is associated with an increased risk of stroke and with higher blood flow velocity (Kirkham et al., 2001). In summary, these results suggest that reduced FSIQ is a function of chronically poor oxygen delivery to the brain (Steen et al., 1998a; Hogan et al., 2006) and that chronic hypoxia is part of the pathophysiology of SCD (Steen et al., 2003). This could explain why CI is often seen in children who are free of stroke injury (Wang et al., 2001; Steen et al., 2005b).

Even very young SCD patients manifest cognitive problems that may be related to chronic hypoxia (Hogan et al., 2005). There is increased reaction time and decreased auditory event-related potential at an early age, and these deficits may be responsible for impairment of attentiveness, performance, and cognitive ability (Hamon, Seri, & Sangare, 1990). Brain volume is lower in children with SCD, specifically in the central gray matter, and volumetric growth of the brain may be delayed (Steen et al., 2005a). The volume of the corpus callosum is reduced in children with SCD, and this independently predicts deficits in sustained attention, speed of production, and working memory (Schatz & Buzan, 2006). Children with SCD show short-term memory deficits, specifically in digit-span backwards, which may be related to an auditory processing deficit (Schatz & Roberts, 2005). An auditory processing deficit was also noted in a study using a local test of school-readiness given to children entering kindergarten in Memphis (Steen et al., 2002). At age 5, children with SCD scored lower than matched controls on a test of auditory discrimination and there was also a trend to lower scores in language.

Academic attainment is reduced in children with SCD, and this could be related to the number of illness-related school absences (Schatz, 2004). School absence is generally well correlated with various health measures – including the number of clinic visits, physician rating of activity limitations, and specific health conditions – among children with chronic health conditions (Fowler et al., 1985). Yet, in patients with SCD, school absence did not predict scores on a national achievement test, even though children scored poorly. This suggests that it is SCD itself, rather than the absences that SCD causes, that is responsible for cognitive decline. Nevertheless, SCD was associated with a mean of 23 days absence per year, compared to an average of only 7 days among healthy children (Fowler et al., 1985).

There is less evidence that other forms of severe childhood anemia beyond SCD are associated with CI, although there is a growing consensus that chronic or intermittent hypoxia is likely to have an effect on cognition (Bass et al., 2004). Further research is needed to determine the cognitive impact of illnesses such as β-thalassemia, Fanconi anemia, Diamond–Blackfan Syndrome, aplastic anemia, iron-deficiency anemia, Jakschs anemia, hemolytic anemia, and so on, all of which may be associated with some degree of acute or chronic hypoxia.

PULMONARY DISEASE AND CI

Pulmonary disease in childhood primarily takes two forms: Respiratory Distress Syndrome (RDS), which is usually associated with a deficiency of lung surfactant; and Bronchopulmonary Dysplasia (BPD), which is usually associated with mechanical lung ventilation. RDS is a syndrome of severe respiratory failure associated with premature birth or very low birth weight (VLBW), and characterized by grave hypoxemia, often with bilateral fluid infiltrates seen on chest X-ray. RDS results in poor matching of ventilation and perfusion in the lung and mortality in children may be as high as 60% if RDS onset is acute (Davis & Sargent, 2006). As the survival rate has increased for infantile RDS and VLBW, more survivors have shown symptoms of BPD. Ventilator-related lung injury may cause BPD, which has emerged as the leading cause of chronic lung disease of childhood in the United States (Short et al., 2003).

In the past, infants with respiratory failure were treated with ECMO and follow-up of such children found that CI is common (Schumacher et al., 1991). Among 118 infants treated with ECMO, survival was 87%, but roughly a third of the patients were rehospitalized within a year with recurrence of respiratory illness. Abnormal growth, which may be a sensitive surrogate measure for chronic hypoxia, was present in 26% of infants, and roughly 16% of patients exhibited moderate-to-severe neurologic abnormalities. Cognitive delay can be hard to measure in infants, because the tests are relatively insensitive, but at least 8% of these children had moderate-to-severe cognitive delay. Overall, about 20% of children showed at least mild CI. Though ECMO was not associated with improved cognitive outcome, relative to children who got conventional therapy, at least it was not associated with reduced cognition, even though children who received ECMO may have had more severe illness (Schumacher et al., 1991). Nevertheless, 10-year follow-up of a small cohort of infants who received ECMO found that average FSIQ was 9 points lower than normal, with high-frequency sensorineural hearing loss and chronic lung disease common in these patients (Hofkosh et al., 1991).

Infants with severe respiratory failure are now treated with surfactant therapy. Early results suggest that many such children recover completely and have normal neurodevelopmental outcome (Auten et al., 2000), but relatively few infants have been studied to date. Infants treated with lung ventilation for neonatal RDS can have height, Verbal IQ, and motor development that is appropriate for age, and surfactant replacement with ventilation ameliorates the acute lung injury that is common in RDS (Gerstmann et al., 2001). Nevertheless, we note that acute hypoxia in infants may result in different cognitive sequelae than chronic hypoxia in older children, since infants seem rather tolerant of even severe hypoxia (Parer, 1998). In older children with RDS, the overall hypoxic burden appears to predict CI (Hopkins & Brett, 2005).

Preterm infant lungs are highly prone to injury because they can be structurally immature, deficient in natural surfactant, filled with fluid infiltrate, and unsupported by a stiff chest wall (Clark et al., 2001). The main cause of BPD may be use of mechanical ventilation in children with either RDS or VLBW. Children with BPD frequently have VLBW, so it can be difficult to deconvolve what may be separate effects. However, a recent study did an excellent job of separating out children with different diagnoses (Short et al., 2003). Infants were defined as having BPD if birth weight was less than 1,500 g, if supplemental oxygen was required for more than 28 days, and if there was radiographic evidence of lung disease; such infants thus had VLBW as well as BPD. Infants were defined as having VLBW if birth weight was less than 1,500 g, and if supplemental oxygen was required for less than 14 days, so none of these infants had BPD. Finally, infants were defined as healthy controls if there were no illnesses or birth abnormalities, if birth weight was greater than 2,500 g, and if birth age was >36 weeks gestation. Using these criteria, 98 BPD infants, 75 VLBW infants, and 99 healthy control infants were enrolled, making this a very large study, with groups demographically well matched at study enrollment.

When cognitive testing was done at an average age of 8 years, children with BPD were impaired with respect to children with VLBW (Short et al., 2003). Relative to children with VLBW, BPD children showed a 9-point deficit in FSIQ, an 8-point deficit in Verbal IQ, and a 9-point deficit in Performance IQ, with all differences statistically significant ($p < 0.001$). Compared to completely healthy children, children with BPD had a 19-point deficit in FSIQ, a 15-point deficit in Verbal IQ, and a 20-point deficit in Performance IQ ($p < 0.001$). BPD children also showed deficits compared with VLBW children in reading, mathematics, and gross motor skills, as well as in use of special education services. Roughly 20% of BPD children had mild mental retardation (FSIQ < 70), whereas only 11% of VLBW and 3% of healthy children had FSIQ < 70. In children with BPD, the duration of oxygen supplementation predicted Performance IQ, FSIQ, and most achievement test scores. These findings are corroborated by other smaller and less-definitive studies (Giacoia et al., 1997; Hughes et al., 1999; Seeman et al., 2001; Lewis et al., 2002; Gray et al., 2004). In short, BPD has illness-associated systemic effects that are highly significant and strongly linked to chronic hypoxia.

VERY LOW BIRTH WEIGHT AND CI

VLBW, often defined as a birth weight less than 1,500 g (3.3 lbs), is a major public health problem in the United States. The creation of hospital neonatal intensive care units in the 1960s led to a substantial increase in survival rate of infants born prematurely or at very low weight. Infant mortality rates fell from 100 deaths per 1,000 births (10%) in 1900, to 7.2 deaths per 1,000 births (0.7%) in 1997 (Hamvas, 2000). Collectively, VLBW and RDS are second only to congenital abnormality as a contributor to infant mortality. Pulmonary function is the main limiting factor in the survival of VLBW infants and VLBW children are at risk for pulmonary disorder. Such disorder could be due to a deficiency of lung surfactant in premature infants (Hintz et al., 2005), though CI is also common in VLBW infants treated with artificial lung surfactant (D'Angio et al., 2002).

Children with VLBW – even if they are free of BPD – tend to show CI relative to full-term or normal birth weight children (Short et al., 2003). Compared to controls, VLBW children show a 10-point deficit in FSIQ, a 7-point deficit in Verbal IQ, and a 12-point deficit in Performance IQ, with all differences statistically significant ($p < 0.001$). There are also significant deficits in achievement in mathematics, in gross motor skills, and in use of educational services. These are very compelling findings since a rigorous (radiographic) effort was made to exclude children with BPD, and since these results confirm earlier studies (Horwood et al., 1998; Hack et al., 2002). Even 20 years after birth, problems persist for adults who were born at VLBW, and many VLBW adults fail to graduate from high school or go on to college (Hack et al., 2002).

Head size in infancy may be a good predictor of CI among VLBW infants (Hack et al., 1991). Deficits in FSIQ at age 8 years are largely limited to those children with an abnormally small head as infants. Infants with sub-normal head size at 8 months had an FSIQ of 84 at 8 years, whereas infants with a normal head size at 8 months had an FSIQ of 98 at 8 years (Hack et al., 1991). Another study reported that the best predictor of CI in boys was short stature together with small head size, whereas the best predictor in girls was head size alone (Cooke & Foulder-Hughes, 2003). These results may mean that growth impairment and CI are linked by a common etiology.

Infants with extremely low birth weight ($<1,000$ g or 2.2 lbs) generally suffer worse long-term sequelae than children with VLBW (Taylor et al., 2000). When small birth weight infants were split into two groups (<750 g and 750–1,499 g) and compared to term infants at middle-school age, there was a significant trend for Wechsler Individual Achievement Test (WIAT) scores to increase with increasing weight at birth ($p < 0.01$). Small VLBW infants had a Reading Comprehension score of 87.7, while larger VLBW infants had a reading score of 96.4 and term infants had a reading score of 102.4. Similar weight-related trends were seen for the Woodcock–Johnson tests of word identification and broad math, and for measures of attention, academic performance, and adaptive behavior (Taylor et al., 2000). In another study, the rate of mental retardation (FSIQ < 70) at school age varied from 21% in the lightest VLBW infants (<750 g) to 8% in the heavier group (750–1,499 g), and 2% in normal-term children tested at school age (Hack et al., 1994). Among extremely low birth weight infants tested at age 2 years, there was global impairment rather than specific deficits in executive domains (Anderson et al., 2004). Extremely low birth weight infants report lower scholastic performance, lower athletic ability, less job competence, and less romantic confidence as teenagers (Grunau et al., 2004). Yet test scales that are often used in infants with VLBW have poor predictive validity at age 8, so it is not yet possible to target intervention to those children who are most likely to have CI (Hack et al., 2005).

We hypothesize that CI in VLBW infants is an illness-associated systemic effect resulting from chronic hypoxia. Some CI could also result from oxygen toxicity or over-distension of the lung during mechanical ventilation (Clark et al., 2001), in which case CI could also result from treatment-related systemic effects.

MALNUTRITION, TRACE NUTRIENT DEFICIENCY, AND CI

Roughly 130 million children – 5% of all children living in developing countries worldwide – have impairments that relate to severe malnutrition in the first year of life (Olness, 2003). The United Nations has estimated that 35–40% of children suffer moderate malnutrition, and that 10% of children suffer a period of severe malnutrition during the crucial period between the second trimester of pregnancy and age 2 years. Malnutrition may be more prevalent in the United States than we would care to admit, given that prenatal and newborn care for many infants is poor, drug- or alcohol-addicted pregnant women are themselves often malnourished, and there is little in the way of a safety net for at-risk infants.

It can be hard to objectively assess the degree of malnutrition that an infant has suffered. Nutritionists generally agree that anthropometric measurements (height for age, weight for age, weight for height, skinfold thickness, arm circumference, etc.) provide the best measure of malnutrition (Galler & Barrett, 2001), but some children would be small even without malnutrition. The natural variability in body size can make it very hard to study malnutrition, except in regions where the condition is rather common.

Malnourishment takes many forms. Mild malnutrition can lead to children being stunted in growth, whereas severe malnutrition is associated with specific symptoms. Severe protein deficiency – usually called kwashiorkor – can occur when children between the ages of 1 and 3 years are switched from breast milk to a diet of starchy solids (Galler & Barrett, 2001). Children with kwashiorkor show growth failure, muscle wasting, severe depletion of blood proteins, liver hypertrophy, behavioral apathy, and edema, the latter of which produces the most distinctive symptom; a grossly protuberant belly. Severe caloric deficiency – usually called marasmus – often occurs in children under 1 year of age and accompanies early weaning. Children with marasmus show marked growth failure (the child is often <60% of normal weight for age), with muscle wasting, behavioral irritability, loss of subcutaneous fat, and an emaciated appearance, but without the swollen belly of kwashiorkor. Both kwashiorkor and marasmus often co-occur with severe diarrhea, parasitic infection, and anemia, which aggravate the general wasting of malnourishment. Deficiencies of specific nutrients like iron or iodine can also produce a form of malnutrition. Eating disorders – though they can result in severe malnutrition – are specifically excluded from consideration here as they are psychiatric disorders and therefore have a direct impact on the brain.

Children with early malnutrition typically develop CI and learning disability in later years (Galler et al., 1984). A cohort of 129 children in Barbados was identified soon after suffering moderate-to-severe protein-energy malnutrition, and these children have been followed for 30 years; nearly every Barbadan child born from 1967 to 1972 who suffered even a single episode of malnutrition is included in this study. When children were aged 5–11 years, school performance was impaired with respect to healthy children, with deficits in language, mathematics, general science, social science, reading, religion, and arts and crafts. Poor school performance was largely accounted for by inattention in class and, to a lesser extent, by a reduction in Full-Scale IQ. Follow-up of this cohort of children at age 11 to 18 showed that both kwashiorkor and marasmus reduce academic performance to about the same degree (Galler et al., 1987). At age 11, Barbadan children take a national examination that is used to assign each child to an academic or vocational track (Galler et al., 1990). Because every child takes the same exam, this provides a well-standardized benchmark. Children with malnutrition in the first year of life scored significantly worse on this "11-plus examination." Low scores correlated with teacher reports of classroom inattention, documented when children were as young as 5–8 years of age. Infantile stunting at 3 and 6 months also predicted poor performance on the exam (Galler et al., 2004). Stunted children tend to catch up in physical size in later years, but CI resulting from severe malnutrition may be irreversible (Galler & Barrett, 2001). Malnourished children show a loss of roughly 10–13 points in Full-Scale IQ, and have short attention span, poor memory, and are more easily distracted, less cooperative, and more restless than healthy children. Up to 60% of previously malnourished children suffer from Attention-Deficit Disorder (ADD), whereas only 15% of healthy children show signs of ADD. Deficits persist at least 18 years, as malnutrition is associated with dropping out of school and poor job performance. These findings have been confirmed in Jamaica (Powell et al., 1995), the Philippines (Mendez & Adair, 1999), and Peru (Berkman et al., 2002), where stunted children scored 10 points lower on the WISC-R than healthy children.

Severe childhood diarrhea – which may cause nutrient deficiency and is a leading cause of childhood mortality worldwide – also predicts impaired school performance (Berkman et al., 2002). In Peru, 239 children were prospectively studied from birth to age 2 and then were evaluated for CI at age 9. Children with severe diarrhea resulting from infestation with the gut parasite *Giardia* scored 4 points lower than normal on the WISC-R. Early childhood diarrhea was associated with greater impairment of semantic than phonetic fluency (Patrick et al., 2005). Victims of severe childhood diarrhea are often delayed in starting school and impaired while in school (Lorntz et al., 2006).

Trace nutrient deficiency – especially of iron and iodine – is also associated with CI. More than 30% of pregnant women in developing countries have iron deficiency anemia, and infants born with iron deficiency show delayed brain maturation (Olness, 2003). Iodine deficiency is also a preventable cause of retardation; in Tuscany, where the cumulative prevalence of school-age goiter is 52%, children from an area of endemic goiter scored significantly lower on cognitive tests than did children from an area free of goiter (Fenzi et al., 1990). In summary, malnutrition – whether of calories, protein, or essential micronutrients – forms an illness-associated systemic cause of CI.

LEAD POISONING AND CI

Lead poisoning is an ancient problem; lead's sweet flavor was used to counteract the astringency of tannin in wine, and a Greek physician from the 2nd century BC described the colic and paralysis that can follow ingestion of large quantities of lead (Needleman, 2004). However, the realization that even small amounts of lead could cause CI was a long time in coming.

Until the 1970s, the main sources of lead poisoning in the United States were air and soil pollution from burning of leaded gasoline, weathering and chipping of leaded house paint, and various occupational exposures (Needleman, 2004). Leaded gasoline was phased-out beginning in 1976, and leaded paint was banned in 1971, but 320,000 American workers were occupationally exposed to lead in 1998, and indirect exposure of children to occupational lead remains a problem. Furthermore, inner-city children – who often live in poorly maintained structures built before the lead paint ban in 1971 – can still encounter high levels of lead contamination in their own home. House dust accounts for about half of a young child's total lead intake, and children who live in homes with lead paint can achieve blood lead levels of $20 \mu g/dL$ without eating paint chips. Children are more sensitive to lead than are adults for several reasons; they are more likely to accumulate high levels of lead through ingestion of particles; their gut absorbs lead more readily than the adult gut; and the developing brain is more vulnerable to toxicants than is the mature brain.

The decrease in prevalence of lead poisoning over the past 30 years may be the greatest public health success in the United States during the 20th century. In the 1960s, a large-scale screening on the East Coast found that up to 20% of inner-city children had more than $40 \mu g/dL$ of lead in their bloodstream (Needleman, 2004). From 1976 to 1980, before regulations banning lead had taken full effect, American children aged 1–5 years had a median blood lead level of $15 \mu g/dL$; from 1988 to 1991 the median fell to $3.6 \mu g/dL$; in 1999, the median was just $1.9 \mu g/dL$ (Rogan et al., 2005). Yet blood lead levels are a poor measure of total exposure, because blood lead has a half-life that is only about 35 days. If a child has had high levels of lead exposure, evidence of that exposure cannot be detected if a blood sample is drawn more than a few months afterward.

A ground-breaking study in 1979 overcame the problem of blood lead being a poor surrogate for total lead exposure using a very ingenious method (Needleman et al., 1979). Parents and teachers in two towns in Massachusetts were asked to collect deciduous teeth, as the children lost them, the idea being that lead is locked away in the bone, forming a relatively permanent marker of lead exposure. Deciduous teeth were collected from 2,146 children, and those children with the highest lead exposure were compared with those having the lowest exposure. Children with high lead exposure had lower Full-scale and Verbal IQ, lower scores on tests of Auditory Processing and Attention, and more behavioral problems than did children at the lowest level of exposure. These results were particularly noteworthy because the study was conducted among relatively well-to-do children, so few children had the high levels of lead exposure often noted in the inner city. This study was the first hint that blood lead levels below $10\,\mu g/dL$ might be a problem.

There is now a great deal of evidence that blood lead levels less than $10\,\mu g/dL$ predispose a child to CI. A 12-year follow-up of the cohort of children who had donated teeth showed that small elevations of dentine lead are associated with an increased risk of school failure, reading disability, poor class standing in high school, and problems in fine motor control (Needleman et al., 1990). Each $10\,\mu g/dL$ increase in blood lead at 24 months of age is associated with a 5.8-point decline in Full-Scale IQ at school age (Bellinger et al., 1992). Full-Scale IQ declines by about 7.4 points as the lifetime average blood lead increases from 1 to $10\,\mu g/dL$ (Canfield et al., 2003). These results have been confirmed in a group of lead-exposed children in Ecuador, who were exposed to high levels of lead because their parents were pottery-glazers (Counter et al., 2005). Pre-industrial humans may have had a level of lead exposure 100- to 1,000-fold lower than people of today, and there may be no threshold below which lead is non-toxic (Koller et al., 2004).

Disturbingly, in a sample of 780 young children with blood lead levels of 20–44 $\mu g/dL$, chelation therapy to reduce blood lead levels did not improve cognition, behavior, or psychological function (Rogan et al., 2001). This may mean that brain injury from lead is irreversible, even though blood lead levels declined strikingly within 6 months. This is troubling because it has been estimated that up to 25% of children in the United States live in housing with deteriorated lead-based paint, and so are at risk for CI (Rogan et al., 2005). It has been recommended that all Medicaid-eligible children be screened for lead exposure at 1 and again at 2 years of age (Rogan et al., 2005). Although lead toxicity is poorly understood, trace quantities can interfere with the function of cellular enzymes and have directly neurotoxic effects, showing an illness-associated neurotoxicity of plumbism.

SLEEP-DISORDERED BREATHING AND CI

The prevalence of habitual snoring among otherwise-healthy children varies geographically, perhaps as a function of regional allergens, but snoring has a prevalence of 6–27% nationwide (Montgomery-Downs et al., 2005). Snoring is the chief symptom of sleep-disordered breathing (SDB), a class of illness that includes obstructive sleep apnea and upper airway resistance syndrome. SDB is present in up to 3% of children, and it is associated with sleep fragmentation, oxygen exchange problems, and potentially severe intermittent hypoxia.

A cross-sectional study of 835 children in Cleveland found that African-American children are more likely than other children to have SDB (Emancipator et al., 2006). Children with SDB are also more likely to have been born prematurely or at VLBW. There is a well-recognized association between obesity and SDB; the body-mass index (BMI) of children with SDB is roughly 8% higher than in children free of SDB. When children with SDB were compared to children free of SDB, poor sleep was associated with a significant reduction in cognitive ability, even when age, sex, and birth weight were statistically controlled. Children with SDB tend to show deficits in academic ability, language comprehension, and organizational skills. Children who habitually snore also score lower on the Peabody Picture Vocabulary test and on the Kaufman Assessment Battery for Children, even after every other known risk factor for CI is statistically controlled (Emancipator et al., 2006).

Acute sleep restriction leads to CI in children who otherwise sleep well, and verbal creativity and abstract thinking are impaired after a single night of sleep starvation (Randazzo et al., 1998). Children with recurrent snoring or SDB may be chronically sleep-starved, and academic performance may be poor (Mitchell & Kelly, 2006). Children with SDB can have an impairment of memory, immediate recall, visual–spatial function, attention, vigilance, mental flexibility, and intelligence. SDB is also associated with behavioral problems including depression, anxiety, hyperactivity, aggression, irritability, and emotional dysregulation. Overall, the quality of life in children with SDB is reduced as much as in children with chronic asthma or rheumatoid arthritis (Mitchell & Kelly, 2006). Even children who snore, but who do not have severe obstructive sleep apnea, show mild CI (Blunden et al., 2000). Children with high intelligence may be protected from the effects of SDB by an increased cognitive reserve (Alchanatis et al., 2005).

If adenotonsillectomy is done at a young age, surgery is associated with improved cognition, behavior, and quality of life (Montgomery-Downs et al., 2005). An elegant study compared 19 children with SDB to 19 matched controls with normal sleep, with the patients evaluated before and an average of 4 months after corrective surgery. Patients spent a night in the sleep lab, so that sleep architecture could be characterized both before and after surgery, and controls likewise were studied. Prior to surgery, a compelling difference between patients and controls was seen in the nadir of the nighttime percent arterial oxygen saturation. Healthy control children had a nadir value of 94% O_2 saturation, while pre-surgery patients had a nadir of only 82% saturation; after surgery the nadir value in patients increased to 92%. Cognitive scores were abnormally low in patients prior to surgery, and the differential ability scale (DAS) score was 11 points lower than the controls. After surgery, the DAS score increased by

5 points in 4 months, and measures of sleep architecture normalized. Cognitive ability of patients improved so much that there was no longer a significant difference from controls, confirming an earlier study that found an acute improvement in cognitive scores following corrective surgery (Friedman et al., 2003).

One must wonder whether the seemingly mild and intermittent hypoxia of SDB is sufficient to cause long-term cognitive sequelae, or whether reported findings are perhaps an artifact of small sample sizes and a referral bias. However, a community-based study of 995 German third-graders found that the nadir of the nocturnal arterial O_2 saturation was a very good predictor of academic performance, especially in mathematics (Urschitz et al., 2005). In this large and presumably representative sample of children, the most hypoxic children had a nocturnal O_2 saturation <90%, and this was associated with a 2.3-fold increase in the risk of mathematics impairment (Urschitz et al., 2005). In a small sample of children with SDB, the average nadir of nocturnal O_2 saturation was 82% (Montgomery-Downs et al., 2005), which is dramatically less than normal. Robust evidence suggests that such levels of hypoxia, even if intermittent, are a risk factor for CI (Bass et al., 2004). A recent clinical trial found that oral anti-inflammatory therapy and intranasal steroids significantly attenuated the residual effects of SDB in patients who got tonsillectomy (Kheirandish et al., 2006). That CI in SDB children can be alleviated by surgery to open the airway suggests that CI in SDB is an illness-associated systemic effect related to chronic hypoxia.

POVERTY AND CI

In a recent web-based report on the status of children in the United States, the National Center for Children in Poverty (2006) reported that 39% or 28.4 million children live in low-income families. Of these, 12.8 million live in families below the federal poverty level. Almost two-thirds (61%) of children in Hispanic or African-American families live in poverty, in contrast to about a quarter of children from Asian or white families. Research has shown that children of Hispanic and African-American origin tend to achieve lower scores on tests of cognitive ability than children of Asian or white families. Other research indicates, however, that when factors related to poverty, such as low levels of parental education and the quality of the home environment are taken into account, racial and ethnic differences in cognitive test performance between children of color and other children are much reduced (Brooks-Gunn et al., 1996). This implicates poverty itself in the etiology of CI.

We review studies in which the effect of socioeconomic status (SES) on cognitive scores was assessed while taking into account factors that could relate to poverty. We note that there has been a recent redesign of Wechsler tests, to minimize SES-related differences in test performance, so some of these findings may not be relevant to current tests. Furthermore, some research involves children below age 5, which is below the age cut-off used in the rest of this review, because a great deal of the research on poverty and cognitive development has been done with preschool children. Nevertheless, even if poverty has its most potent effect on cognitive development in very young children, such effects will likely persist into adulthood.

Whether actual CI is involved in the lower test performance of poor children has not been convincingly shown to date. The effects of poverty on cognition are virtually impossible to disentangle from the effects of other correlated factors that poverty entails. Lead poisoning, poor nutrition, and increased exposure to upper respiratory-tract disease have all been implicated as a potential cause of CI in impoverished children. Additional characteristics of poor families that may also impact cognitive development include poor parental education, parents who are unable to support their child's early learning, and homes where appropriate learning materials are lacking.

Another mechanism by which poverty might impair cognitive development is through heightened stress in parents and children. Living in an unsafe neighborhood, economic pressure from unstable or low-level employment of parents, and family discord causing anxiety in children could all create family stress. Chronic stress can lead to brain changes because of increased glucocorticoid levels (Lupie et al., 2001); low-SES children (aged 6–10 years) had significantly higher levels of salivary cortisol than did children from a high-SES background. Nevertheless, the only difference in cognitive function that relates to elevated cortisol was on tests of selective attention.

The effect of the degree and timing of family poverty on IQ, verbal ability, and academic ability was assessed in two large longitudinal samples (NLSY and IHDP) of children (Smith et al., 1997). Even if the effects of parental education and quality of the home environment were statistically controlled, low income reduced IQ scores by up to 6 points. Both the timing and duration of poverty mattered, and the worst-case scenario involved children who were poor continuously from early childhood. Analysis suggested that the home environment was more strongly correlated with maternal education than with poverty itself. This implies that well-educated mothers can provide a home environment that is supportive of childhood learning despite conditions of poverty.

Research conducted with first-graders in Turkey showed that an index of family poverty that characterized parental education and whether a home was heated by a stove (which could cause carbon monoxide poisoning) predicted the risk of scoring poorly on the WISC (Ozmert et al., 2005). In addition, early hearing loss, uncorrected poor vision, and parental smoking also predicted low cognitive test scores.

One factor that confounds the relationship between poverty and IQ is the strong correlation between parent and child IQ. Low-IQ parents have low-IQ children and both are more likely to live in poverty (Feldman & Walton-Allen, 1997). Many previous studies have investigated the role of genes in determining a child's IQ (e.g., Scarr & Weinberg, 1976). A recent study examining the interaction of SES with genotype, with shared environment, and with non-shared environment found that the degree to which IQ is predicted by genes and environment varies according to SES level. In poor families, 60% of the variance in child IQ at age 7 was accounted for by shared environment, with genotype contributing little (Turkheimer et al., 2003). Yet the situation was reversed in affluent families, where genotype accounted for nearly 80% of the variance in IQ, and shared environment accounted for little. Thus, the role of genes is exaggerated in favorable environments, whereas environmental factors may overwhelm the genes in poor families. Nevertheless, it is not possible to separate genes from environment in an individual child (Turkheimer et al., 2003).

Recently, an attempt was made to "establish a neurocognitive profile of childhood poverty" through studies comparing poor kindergartners, first graders, and middle school students to well-off students matched for age, gender, and ethnicity (Farah et al., 2005). By comparing the performance of low- and middle-SES children on various cognitive tasks, significant SES-related differences in function were found for language, memory, and executive function. Scientists concluded that children growing up in low-SES environments often perform poorly on tests that tax these specific systems. Poor performance could arise from inadequate nutrition, early exposure to environmental toxins, maternal substance abuse, lead poisoning, or other factors.

Another aspect of poverty that can impact a child's intellectual test performance has to do with test-taking skills and motivation. In an early study (Kieffer & Goh, 1981) the test-taking situation for low- and middle-SES children was varied by allowing children to choose either social or tangible rewards before taking the WISC-R. The scores of low-SES children increased by 11 points under conditions of social reward and by 7 points in the tangible reward situation, compared to the mean for low-SES controls. In contrast, the scores of middle-SES children did not change as a function of the offered rewards. Such findings should give pause in an era when high-stakes academic testing is the centerpiece of educational reform (Waber et al., 2006). Though these findings have apparently not been corroborated, lack of motivation to succeed on cognitive tests could potentially play a role in the lower IQ scores that are often earned by children of poverty.

A key component of the effect of poverty on CI may be mediated by the kinds of early childhood stimulation that are provided by parents. If poverty is associated with poor parental education, a lack of understanding of developmentally appropriate ways to support early childhood learning, and low-paying jobs that require long work hours, then less time can be spent with children, and available time may be spent in ways that are less supportive of the child's development. Young children reared in poverty are thus likely to be deprived not only of materials that foster learning, but also of parental stimulation.

The importance of early childhood stimulation is supported by long-term results from the Abecedarian study, which strongly argue that enrichment of the early childhood environment enables children to develop their cognitive potential more fully (Gottleib & Blair, 2004). Intellectual development of study participants, measured by the Wechsler scales from age 5–21, shows a strong treatment effect in the early years. There is a gradual attentuation of this treatment effect over time, but the effect size at age 21 was still significant and substantial, especially so many years after early childhood treatment ended (Campbell et al., 2001).

The strongest evidence for a mechanism by which poverty impacts CI is probably through deprivation of high-quality nutrients for the developing brain, which may be compounded by chronic stress or environmental toxins. It is also possible that impoverished social interactions take a toll; lack of adequate learning materials, poor cognitive stimulation during interactions with adults, and lack of motivation could all interact to depress the test performance of poor children.

CHRONIC HYPOXIA AS A COMMON ETIOLOGY OF CI

Most systemic illnesses that result in CI produce an effect by disrupting delivery of some critical substrate needed for a healthy brain. Among the 10 systemic illnesses that we have examined in detail, perhaps as many as 6 are associated with some degree of hypoxia (i.e., ALL, heart disease, SCD, pulmonary disease, VLBW, SDB), and hypoxia could also play a role in CI from poverty through a mechanism of chronic anemia. Chronic hypoxia could also be associated with additional systemic illnesses (Table 10.1) that we have not reviewed (e.g., asphyxia, asthma, carbon monoxide poisoning, chronic anemia, tuberculosis, iron-deficiency anemia, cystic fibrosis, infectious disease). A recent meta-analysis suggests that chronic hypoxia, of even a mild form, is associated with significant and substantial CI (Bass et al., 2004). Research in animal models confirms that mild-to-moderate hypoxia can be associated with impaired performance on various tests (Bass et al., 2004), though there is not yet a clear way to use animal data to predict impairment in humans. Nevertheless, because hypoxia may be a common etiology of CI in humans and because animal models of this condition already exist, it will be important to refine these models, so that the clinical effects of mild-to-moderate hypoxia can be understood.

Most clinical conditions that cause chronic hypoxia are treatable. Erythropoietin is already used as supportive therapy during treatment of many types of cancer, and a recent systematic review concluded that erythropoietin reduces the risk of severe anemia by at least 50%, especially if treatment is given early (Lyman & Glaspy, 2006). Even if chemotherapy-related anemia is excluded from consideration, anemia is present in 30–90% of all cancer patients (Knight et al., 2004). Patients with anemia have poor survival overall and a reduced quality of life, and treatment of anemia has a beneficial impact on survival and quality of life in most studies. If anemia can have such a dramatic effect in the context of an acute illness like cancer, it may be that treatment of anemia would also improve the quality of life for children with other systemic illnesses. Whether treatment of anemia could moderate CI in children with systemic illness remains an open question, but one that is easily addressed in clinical trials.

IS CI IN CHILDHOOD PREVENTABLE?

There are public health measures that could substantially reduce the prevalence and severity of CI in children. For example, lead poisoning causes a substantial amount of CI in children. Because lead has already been removed from gasoline, the major remaining source of lead for most children is leaded paint in older dwellings. About 80% of the houses built before 1950, which may include 23 million dwellings, contain leaded paint (Needleman, 2004). A cost–benefit analysis, done in 1991 by the Public Health Service, estimated that the cost of lead abatement in homes would total $33.7 billion dollars. The cost savings from lead abatement, in terms of reduced medical costs and increased income due to higher intelligence, could be as high as $61.7 billion. This indicates a strong net cost savings from lead abatement. Yet these figures may be out of date, because many of the homes present in 1991 have been torn down, and because the costs of lead abatement have probably increased.

A recent estimate suggests that there are actually 4 million lead-contaminated houses (Rogan et al., 2005). Adjusted for inflation, the cost of lead abatement in these houses would have been about $28 billion in 2002. Removing lead paint from these houses would be cost-effective if it prevented just two-thirds of the lead exposure likely to be encountered by a single-year cohort of 2-year-olds. In this estimate, all succeeding cohorts would benefit at no additional cost, so this is a small price to pay indeed.

Another recent estimate calculated the economic gain that could result from a reduction in childhood exposure to lead (Grosse et al., 2002). From 1976 to 1999, the average blood lead level in children less than 5 years old fell by 15.1 µg/dL. This decrease in lead exposure was associated with an expected average increase in Full-Scale IQ of about 2.2–4.7 points. Each 1 point increase in Full-Scale IQ increases worker productivity by 1.8–2.4%. With discounted lifetime earnings of $723,300 for each 2-year old (in year 2000 dollars), this would amount to a savings of $110 billion to $319 billion, relative to what these people would have earned had they been exposed to the lead levels of 1975 (Grosse et al., 2002). This calculation averages across the entire cohort of 3.8 million 2-year olds in the United States in the year 2000 (Grosse et al., 2002). A second estimate, done in the same year, concluded that lead poisoning cost the American taxpayer about $43.4 billion, even discounting the cost of late complications such as CI (Landrigan et al., 2002). A third estimate concluded that the loss of 5 Full-Scale IQ points from lead exposure would cost the United States $275 billion to $326 billion per year (Muir & Zegarac, 2001). Clearly, these estimates are just estimates, and some of them may be unreliable. Yet it is also clear that failure to abate lead in older buildings has a human cost, as well as an economic cost;

while it is possible to weight the numbers to justify virtually any social policy, including one of benign neglect, the human cost of inaction will remain high.

The prevalence of mild mental retardation (FSIQ <70) in 10-year old children in the United States is about 12 per 1,000 children (Murphy et al., 1995). The prevalence of mild mental retardation is somewhat higher in black children than in white children, which may reflect race-related differences in poverty and other SES factors. Low income, minority status, and lower educational attainment in the head of household are independently associated with poor performance on cognitive tests at age 10 (Kramer et al., 1995). To a lesser degree, cognitive performance is influenced by a child's health status, history of birth complications, and gender. Thus, if we are to prevent CI, all of these issues must be confronted.

Racial differences in Full-Scale IQ can be explained largely by economic status, maternal age, maternal education, and a child's birth order and gender (Yeargin-Allsopp et al., 1995). Together, these 5 factors explain roughly half of the excess prevalence of mild mental retardation in black children. Thus, poverty is a major risk factor for CI and mild mental retardation (Farah et al., 2006). To whatever extent the effects of poverty can be ameliorated by schooling – and recent results suggest that schooling can have a major impact on poverty (Campbell et al., 2001) – Americans owe their own children a first-class education.

Ironically, if everyone were instantly to become 20 IQ points smarter than they are now, wars might cease, the economy might grow to a point where wealth is distributed more equitably, and energy production might even be freed of reliance on oil, but there would still be people disadvantaged by their relative impairment. As long as traits follow a normal distribution, there will be some people hurt by their position in that distribution (Steen, 1996). But the best that our society can become is intimately and irrevocably tied to the best that others can become; as a society, we are not so rich in talent that we can afford to waste any of it.

ACKNOWLEDGMENTS

Dr. Steen was supported by the National Alliance for Research on Schizophrenia and Depression (NARSAD) as a Hofmann Trust Investigator. Dr. Campbell's work on the Abecedarian Project has been supported by grants from the Maternal and Child Health Bureau, the National Institutes of Health, the Office of Educational Research and Improvement, and the David and Lucile Packard Foundation.

REFERENCES

Alchanatis, M., Zias, N., Deligiorgis, N., Amfilochiou, A., Dionellis, G., & Orphanidou, D. (2005). Sleep apnea-related cognitive deficits and intelligence: An implication of cognitive reserve theory. *Journal of Sleep Research*, 14, 69–75.

Anderson, J. L., Head, S. I., Rae, C., & Morley, J. W. (2002). Brain function in Duchenne muscular dystrophy. *Brain*, 125, 4–13.

Anderson, P. J., Doyle, L. W., & Group, V. I. C. S. (2004). Executive functioning in school-aged children who were born very preterm or with extremely low birth weight in the 1990s. *Pediatrics*, 114, 50–57.

Anderson, V. A., Godber, T., Smibert, E., Weiskop, S., & Ekert, H. (2000). Cognitive and academic outcome following cranial irradiation and chemotherapy in children: a longitudinal study. *British Journal of Cancer*, 82, 255–262.

Armstrong, F. D., Thompson, R. J., Wang, W., Zimmerman, R., Pegelow, C. H., Miller, S., *et al.* (1996). Cognitive functioning and brain magnetic resonance imaging in children with sickle cell disease. *Pediatrics*, 97, 864–870.

Ashworth, A., Morris, S. S., Lira, P. I., & Grantham-McGregor, S. M. (1998). Zinc supplementation, mental development and behaviours in low birth weight term infants in northeast Brazil. *European Journal of Clinical Nutrition*, 52, 223–227.

Auten, R. L., Merzbach, J., Myers, G., Goldstein, R. F., & Palumbo, D. (2000). Neurodevelopmental and health outcomes in term infants treated with surfactant for severe respiratory failure. *Journal of Perinatology*, 20, 291–294.

Bass, J. L., Corwin, M., Gozal, D., Moore, C., Nishida, H., Parker, S., et al. (2004). The effect of chronic or intermittent hypoxia on cognition in childhood: A review of the evidence. *Pediatrics*, 114, 805–816.

Bellinger, D. C., Stiles, K. M., & Needleman, H. L. (1992). Low-level lead exposure, intelligence and academic achievement: A long-term follow-up study. *Pediatrics*, 90, 855–861.

Bellinger, D. C., Wypij, D., duPlessis, A. J., Rappaport, L. A., Jonas, R. A., Wernovsky, G., *et al.* (2003). Neurodevelopmental status at eight years in children with dextro-transposition of the great arteries: The Boston Circulatory Arrest Trial. *Journal of Thoracic Cardiovascular Surgery*, 126, 1385–1396.

Benedetti, B., Charil, A., Rovaris, M., Judica, E., Valsasina, P., Dormani, M. P., et al. (2006). Influence of aging on brain gray and white matter changes assessed by conventional, MT, and DT MRI. *Neurology*, 66, 535–539.

Benedict, L., Nelson, C. A., Schunk, E., Sullwold, K., & Seaquist, E. R. (2006). Effect of insulin on the brain activity obtained during visual and memory tasks in healthy human subjects. *Neuroendocrinology*, 83, 20–26.

Berkman, D. S., Lescano, A. G., Gilman, R. H., Lopez, S. L., & Black, M. M. (2002). Effects of stunting, diarrhoeal disease, and parasitic infection during infancy on cognition in late childhood: A follow-up study. *Lancet*, 359, 564–571.

Blunden, S., Lushington, K., Kennedy, D. N., Martin, J. B., & Dawson, D. (2000). Behavior and neurocognitive performance in children aged 5–10 years who snore compared to controls. *Journal of Clinical and Experimental Neuropsychology*, 22, 554–568.

Bresolin, N., Castelli, E., Comi, G. P., Felisari, G., Bardoni, A., Perani, D., et al. (1994). Cognitive impairment in Duchenne muscular dystrophy. *Neuromuscular Disorders*, 4, 359–369.

Brooks-Gunn, J., Klebanov, P. K., & Duncan, G. J. (1996). Ethnic differences in children's intelligence test scores: Role of economic deprivation, home environment, and maternal characteristics. *Child Development*, 67, 396–408.

Broughton, R., Stuss, D., Kates, M., Roberts, J., & Dunham, W. (1990). Neuropsychological deficits and sleep in myotonic dystrophy. *Canadian Journal of Neurological Sciences*, 17, 410–415.

Brown, R. T., Davis, P. C., Lambert, R., Hsu, L., Hopkins, K., & Eckman, J. (2000). Neurocognitive functioning and magnetic resonance imaging in children with sickle cell disease. *Journal of Pediatric Psychology*, 25, 503–513.

Buizer, A., de Sonneville, L. M. J., van den Heuvel-Eibrink, M. M., Njiokiktjien, C., & Veerman, A. J. P. (2005). Visuomotor control in survivors of childhood acute lymphoblastic leukemia treated with chemotherapy only. *Journal of International Neuropsychological Society*, 11, 554–565.

398

2. CLINICAL APPLICATIONS

Buizer, A., de Sonneville, L. M. J., van den Heuvel-Eibrink, M. M., & Veerman, A. J. P. (2006). Behavioral and educational limitations after chemotherapy for childhood acute lymphoblastic leukemia or Wilms tumor. *Cancer*, 106, 2067–2075.

Campbell, F. A., Pungello, E. P., Miller-Johnson, S., Burchinal, M., & Ramey, C. T. (2001). The development of cognitive and academic abilities: Growth curves from an early childhood educational experiment. *Developmental Psychology*, 37, 231–242.

Campbell, L. K., Scaduto, M., Sharp, W. S., Dufton, L., Van Slyke, D., Whitlock, J. A., et al. (2007). A meta-analysis of the neurocognitive sequelae of treatment for childhood acute lymphoblastic leukemia. *Pediatric Blood Cancer*, 49, 65–73.

Canfield, R. L., Henderson, C. R., Cory-Slechta, D. A., Cox, C., Jusko, T. A., & Lanphear, B. P. (2003). Intellectual impairment in children with blood lead concentrations below 10 ug per deciliter. *New England Journal of Medicine*, 348, 1517–1526.

Censori, B., Provinciali, L., Danni, M., Chiaramoni, L., Maricotti, M., Foschi, N., et al. (1994). Brain involvement in myotonic dystrophy: MRI features and their relationship to clinical and cognitive conditions. *Acta Neurologica Scandinavica*, 90, 211–217.

Clark, R. H., Gerstmann, D. R., Jobe, A. H., Moffitt, S. T., Slutsky, A. S., & Yoder, B. A. (2001). Lung injury in neonates: Causes, strategies for prevention, and long-term consequences. *Journal of Pediatrics*, 139, 478–486.

Cooke, R. W. I., & Foulder-Hughes, L. (2003). Growth impairment in the very preterm and cognitive and motor performance at 7 years. *Archives of Disease in Childhood*, 88, 482–487.

Corazza, F., Hermans, C., Ferster, A., Fondu, P., Demulder, A., & Sariban, E. (2004). Bone marrow stroma damage induced by chemotherapy for acute lymphoblastic leukemia in children. *Pediatric Research*, 55, 152–158.

Cotton, S. M., Voudouris, N. J., & Greenwood, K. M. (2005). Association between intellectual functioning and age in children and young adults with Duchenne muscular dystrophy: Further results from a meta-analysis. *Developmental Medicine and Child Neurology*, 47, 257–265.

Counter, S. A., Buchanan, L. H., & Ortega, F. (2005). Neurocognitive impairment in lead-exposed children of Andean lad-glazing workers. *Journal of Occupational and Environmental Medicine*, 47, 306–312.

Cunningham, R. S. (2003). Anemia in the oncology patient: Cognitive function and cancer. *Cancer Nursing*, 26, 38S–42S.

D'Angio, C. T., Sinkin, R. A., Stevens, T. P., Landfish, N. K., Merzbach, J. L., Ryan, R. M., et al. (2002). Longitudinal, 15-year follow-up of children born at less than 29 weeks' gestation after introduction of surfactant therapy into a region: Neurologic, cognitive, and educational outcomes. *Pediatrics*, 110, 1094–1102.

Davis, E. A., Soong, S. A., Byrne, G. C., & Jones, T. W. (1996). Acute hyperglycaemia impairs cognitive function in children with IDDm. *Journal of Pediatric Endocrinology and Metabolism*, 9, 455–461.

Davies, M. W., & Sargent, P. H. (2006). Partial liquid ventilation for the prevention of mortality and morbidity in paediatric acute lung injury and acute respiratory distress syndrome. *Cochrane Database of Systematic Reviews*, 2004, Issue 4, Art. no. CD003845.

Deary, I. J., & Frier, B. M. (1996). Severe hypoglycaemia and cognitive impairment in diabetes. *British Medical Journal*, 313, 767–768.

DeMaso, D. R., Beardslee, W. R., Silbert, A. R., & Fyler, D. C. (1990). Psychological functioning in children with cyanotic heart defects. *Journal of Developmental and Behavioral Pediatrics*, 11, 289–294.

Duffner, P. K. (2004). Long-term effects of radiation therapy on cognitive and endocrine function in children with leukemia and brain tumors. *The Neurologist*, 10, 293–310.

Duque, G., Segal, R., & Bianco, J. (2005). Chronic hypercalcemia as a reversible cause of cognitive impairment: Improvement after a single administration of pamidronate. *Journal of the American Geriatrics Society*, 53, 1633–1634.

Emancipator, J. L., Storfer-Isser, A., Taylor, H. G., Rosen, C. L., Kirchner, H. L., Johnson, N. L., et al. (2006). Variation of cognition and achievement with sleep-disordered breathing in full-term and preterm children. *Archives of Pediatrics and Adolescent Medicine*, 160, 203–210.

Ewing, F. M. E., Deary, I. J., McCrimmon, R. J., Strachan, M. W. J., & Frier, B. M. (1998). Effect of acute hypoglycemia on visual information processing in adults with Type I diabetes mellitus. *Physiology and Behavior*, 64, 653–660.

Farah, M. J., Noble, K. G., & Hurt, H. (2005). Poverty, privilege, and brain development: Empirical findings and ethical implications. In: J. Illes (Ed.), *Neuroethics in the 21st Century* (pp. 277–289). New York: Oxford University Press.

Farah, M. J., Shera, D. M., Savage, J. H., Betancourt, L., Giannetta, J. M., Brodsky, N. L., et al. (2006). Childhood poverty: specific associations with neurocognitive development. *Brain Research*, 1110, 166–174.

Feldman, M. A., & Walton-Allen, N. (1997). Effects of maternal mental retardation and poverty on intellectual, academic, and behavioral status of school-age children. *American Journal of Mental Retardation*, 101, 352–364.

Felisari, G., Martinelli-Boneschi, F., Bardoni, A., Sironi, M., Comi, G. P., Robotti, M., et al. (2000). Loss of Dp140 dystrophin isoform and intellectual impairment in Duchenne dystrophy. *Neurology*, 55, 559–564.

Fenzi, G. F., Giusti, L. F., Aghini-Lombardi, F., Bartalena, L., Marcocci, C., Santini, F., et al. (1990). Neuropsychological assessment in schoolchildren from an area of moderate iodine deficiency. *Journal of Endocrinology Investment*, 13, 427–431.

Ferguson, S. C., Blane, A., Perros, P., McCrimmon, R. J., Best, J. J. K., Wardlaw, J., et al. (2003). Cognitive ability and brain structure in Type 1 diabetes: Relation to microangiopathy and preceding severe hypoglycemia. *Diabetes*, 52, 149–156.

Ferguson, S. C., Blane, A., Wardlaw, J., Frier, B. M., Perros, P., McCrimmon, R. J., et al. (2005). Influence of early-onset age of Type I diabetes on cerebral structure and cognitive function. *Diabetes Care*, 28, 1431–1437.

Finnimore, A. J., Jackson, R. V., Morton, A., & Lynch, E. (1994). Sleep hypoxia in myotonic dystrophy and its correlation with awake respiratory function. *Thorax*, 49, 66–70.

Fowler, M. G., Johnson, M. P., & Atkinson, S. S. (1985). School achievement and absence in children with chronic health conditions. *Journal of Pediatrics*, 106, 683–687.

Friedman, B. C., Hendeles-Amitai, A., Kozminsky, E., Leiberman, A., Friger, M., Tarasiuk, A., et al. (2003). Adenotonsillectomy improves neurocognitive function in children with obstructive sleep apnea syndrome. *Sleep*, 26, 999–1005.

Galler, J. R., & Barrett, L. R. (2001). Children and famine: long-term impact on development. *Ambulatory Child Health*, 7, 85–95.

Galler, J. R., Ramsey, F., & Solimano, G. (1984). The influence of early malnutrition on subsequent behavioral development. III. Learning disabilities as a sequel to malnutrition. *Pediatric Research*, 18, 309–313.

Galler, J. R., Ramsey, F. C., Forde, V., Salt, P., & Archer, E. (1987). Long-term effects of early kwashiorkor compared with marasmus. II. Intellectual performance. *Journal of Pediatric Gastroenterology and Nutrition*, 6, 847–854.

Galler, J. R., Ramsey, F. C., Morley, D. S., Archer, E., & Salt, P. (1990). The long-term effects of early kwashiorkor compared with marasmus. IV. Performance on the national high school entrance examination. *Pediatric Research*, 28, 235–239.

Galler, J. R., Ramsey, F., Harrison, R. H., Taylor, J. P., Cumberbatch, G., & Forde, V. (2004). Postpartum maternal moods and infant size predict performance on a national high school entrance examination. *Journal of Child Psychology and Psychiatry*, 45, 1064–1075.

Gerstmann, D. R., Wood, K., Miller, A., Steffen, M., Ogden, B., Stoddard, R. A., et al. (2001). Childhood outcome after early high-frequency oscillatory ventilation for neonatal respiratory distress syndrome. *Pediatrics*, 108, 617–623.

Giacoia, G. P., Venkataraman, P. S., EWest-Wilson, K. I., & Faulkner, M. J. (1997). Follow-up of school-age children with bronchopulmonary dysplasia. *Journal of Pediatrics*, 130, 400–408.

Golej, J., & Trittenwein, G. (1999). Early detection of neurologic injury and issues of rehabilitation after pediatric cardiac extracorporeal membrane oxygenation. *Artificial Organs*, 23, 1020–1025.

Gottleib, G., & Blair, D. (2004). How early experience matters in intellectual development in the case of poverty. *Preventive Science*, 5, 245–252.

Gray, P. H., O'Callaghan, M. J., & Rogers, Y. M. (2004). Psychoeducational outcome at school age of preterm infants with bronchopulmonary dysplasia. *Journal of Paediatric and Childhood Health*, 40, 114–120.

Grosse, S. D., Matte, T. D., Schwartz, J. E., & Jackson, R. J. (2002). Economic gains resulting from the reduction in children's exposure to lead in the United States. *Environmental Health Perspective*, 110, 563–569.

Grunau, R. E., Whitfield, M. F., & Fay, T. B. (2004). Psychosocial and academic characteristics of extremely low birth weight (<800 g) adolescents who are free of major impairment compared with term-born control subjects. *Pediatrics*, 114, e725–e732.

Hack, M., Breslau, N., Weissman, B., Aram, D., Klein, N., & Borawski, E. (1991). Effect of very low birth weight and subnormal head size on cognitive abilities at school age. *New England Journal of Medicine*, 325, 231–237.

Hack, M., Taylor, H. G., Klein, N., Eiben, R., Schatschneider, C., & Mercuri-Minich, N. (1994). School-age outcomes in children with birth weights under 750 g. *New England Journal of Medicine*, 331, 753–759.

Hack, M., Flannery, D. J., Schluchter, M., Cartar, L., Borawski, E., & Klein, N. (2002). Outcomes in young adulthood for very-low-birth-weight infants. *New England Journal of Medicine*, 346, 149–157.

Hack, M., Taylor, G. H., Drotar, D., Schluchter, M., Cartar, L., Wilson-Costello, D., et al. (2005). Poor predictive validity of the Bayley Scales of infant Development for cognitive function of extremely low birth weight children at school age. *Pediatrics*, 116, 333–341.

Hamon, J. F., Seri, B., & Sangare, A. (1990). Auditory event-related potentials and reaction times during simple sensory-motor tasks in subjects with sickle cell disease and related hemoglobinopathies. *Italian Journal of Neurological Sciences*, 11, 251–258.

Hamvas, A. (2000). Disparate outcomes for very low birth weight infants: Genetics, environment, or both? *Journal of Pediatrics*, 136, 427–428.

Hannonen, R., Tupola, S., Ahonen, T., & Riikonen, R. (2003). Neurocognitive functioning in children with type-1 diabetes with and without episodes of severe hypoglycaemia. *Developmental Medicine and Child Neurology*, 45, 262–268.

Hill, F. G., Richards, S. S., Gibson, B., Hann, I., Lilleyman, J., LKinsey, S., et al. (2004). Successful treatment without cranial radiotherapy of children receiving intensified chemotherapy for acute lymphoblastic leukaemia: Results of the risk-stratified randomized central nervous system treatment trial MRC UKALL XI. *British Journal of Haematology*, 124, 33–46.

Hintz, S. R., Kendrick, D. E., Vohr, B. R., Poole, W. K., & Higgins, R. D. (2005). Changes in neurodevelopmental outcomes at 18 to 22 months corrected age among infants of less than 25 weeks gestational age born in 1993–1999. *Pediatrics*, 115, 1645–1651.

Hofkosh, D., Thompson, A. E., Nozza, R. J., Kemp, S. S., Bowen, A., & Feldman, H. M. (1991). Ten years of extracorporeal membrane oxygenation: Neurodevelopmental outcome. *Pediatrics*, 87, 549–555.

Hogan, A. M., Kirkham, F. J., Prengler, M., Telfer, P., Lane, R., Vargha-Khadem, F., et al. (2005). An exploratory study of physiological correlates of neurodevelopmental delay in infants with sickle cell anaemia. *British Journal of Haematology*, 132, 99–107.

Hogan, A. M., Pit-ten Cate, I. M., Vargha-Khadem, F., Prengler, M., & Kirkham, F. J. (2006). Physiological correlates of intellectual function in children with sickle cell disease: Hypoxaemia, hyperaemia and brain infarction. *Developmental Science*, 9, 379–387.

Holmes, C. S., & Richman, L. C. (1985). Cognitive profiles of children with insulin-dependent diabetes. *Journal of Developmental and Behavioral Pediatrics*, 6, 323–326.

Homi, J., Levee, L., Higgs, D., Thomas, P., & Serjeant, G. (1997). Pulse oximetry in a cohort study of sickle cell disease. *Clinical and Laboratory Haematology*, 19(1), 17–22.

Hopkins, R. O., & Brett, S. (2005). Chronic neurocognitive effects of critical illness. *Current Opinion in Critical Care*, 11, 369–375.

Horwood, L. J., Mogridge, N., & Darlow, B. A. (1998). Cognitive, educational, and behavioural outcomes at 7 to 8 years in a national very low birthweight cohort. *Archives of Disease in Childhood – Fetal and Neonatal Edition*, 79, F12–fF20.

Hovels-Gurich, H. H., Seghaye, M.-C., Schnitker, R., Wiesner, M., Huber, W., Minkenberg, R., et al. (2002). Long-term neurodevelopmental outcomes in school-aged children after neonatal arterial switch operation. *Journal of Thoracic Cardiovascular Surgery*, 124, 448–458.

Hughes, C. A., O'Gorman, L. A., Shyr, Y., Schork, M. A., Bozynski, M. E., & McCormick, M. C. (1999). Cognitive performance at school age of very low birth weight infants with bronchopulmonary dysplasia. *Journal of Developmental and Behavioral Pediatrics*, 20, 1–8.

Iuvone, L., Mariotti, P., Colosimo, C., Guzzetta, F., Ruggiero, A., & Riccardi, R. (2002). Long-term cognitive outcome, brain computed tomography scan, and magnetic resonance imaging in children cured for acute lymphoblastic leukemia. *Cancer*, 95, 2562–2570.

Jansen, N. C., Kingma, A., Tellegen, P., van Dommelen, R. I., Bouma, A., Veerman, A. J. P., et al. (2004). Feasibility of neuropsychological assessment in leukaemia patients shortly after diagnosis: Directions for future prospective research. *Archives of Disease in Childhood*, 90, 301–304.

Jarjour, I. T., Ryan, C. M., & Becker, D. J. (1995). Regional cerebral blood flow during hypoglycaemia in children with IDDM. *Diabetologia*, 38, 1090–1095.

Kahkonen, M., Metsahonkala, L., Minn, H., Utriainen, T., Korhonen, T., Norvasuo-Heila, M.-K., et al. (2000). Cerebral glucose metabolism in survivors of childhood acute lymphoblastic leukemia. *Cancer*, 88, 693–700.

Kassubek, J., Juengling, F. D., Hoffman, S., Rosenbohm, A., Kurt, A., Jurkat-Rott, K., et al. (2003). Quantification of brain atrophy in patients with myotonic dystrophy and proximal myotonic myopathy: A controlled 3-dimensional magnetic resonance imaging study. *Neuroscience Letters*, 348, 73–76.

Kheirandish, L., Goldbart, A. D., & Gozal, D. (2006). Intranasal steroids and oral leukotriene modifier therapy in residual sleep-disordered breathing after tonsillectomy and adenoidectomy in children. *Pediatrics*, 117, e61–e66.

Khong, P.-L., Leung, L. H. T., Fung, A. S. M., Fong, D. Y. T., Qiu, D., Kwong, D. L. W., et al. (2006). White matter anisotropy in post-treatment childhood cancer survivors: Preliminary evidence of association with neurocognitive function. *Journal of Clinical Oncology*, 24, 884–890.

Kieffer, D. A., & Goh, D. S. (1981). The effect of individually contracted incentives on intelligence test performance of middle-and lower-SES children. *Journal of Clinical Psychology*, 37, 175–179.

Kingma, A., van Dommelen, R. I., Mooyaart, E. L., Wilmink, J. T., Deelman, B. G., & Kamps, W. A. (2002). No major cognitive impairment in young children with acute lymphoblastic leukemia using chemotherapy only: a prospective longitudinal study. *Journal of Pediatric Hematology/Oncology*, 24, 106–114.

Kirkham, F. J., Hewes, D. K. M., Prengler, M., Wade, A., Lane, R., & Evans, J. P. M. (2001). Nocturnal hypoxaemia and central nervous system events in sickle cell disease. *Lancet*, 357, 1656–1659.

Knight, K., Wade, S., & Balducci, L. (2004). Prevalence and outcomes of anemia in cancer: A systematic review of the literature. *American Journal of Medicine*, 116(Suppl 7A), 11S–26S.

Koller, K., Brown, T., Spurgeon, A., & Levy, L. (2004). Recent developments in low-level lead exposure and intellectual impairment in children. *Environmental Health Perspective*, 112, 987–994.

Krajinovic, M., Lamothe, S., Labuda, D., Lemieux-Blanchard, E., Theoret, Y., Moghrabi, A., et al. (2004). Role of MTHFR genetic polymorphisms in the susceptibility to childhood acute lymphoblastic leukemia. *Blood*, 103, 252–257.

Krajinovic, M., Robaey, P., Chiasson, S., Lemieux-Blanchard, E., Rouillard, M., Primeau, M., et al. (2005). Polymorphisms of genes controlling homocysteine levels and IQ score following the treatment for childhood ALL. *Pharmacogenomics*, 6, 293–302.

Kramer, R. A., Allen, L., & Gergen, P. J. (1995). Health and social characteristics and children's cognitive functioning: Results from a national cohort. *American Journal of Public Health*, 85, 312–318.

Landrigan, P. J., Schechter, C. B., Lipton, J. M., Fahs, M. C., & Schwartz, J. E. (2002). Environmental pollutants and disease in American children: Estimates of morbidity, mortality, and costs for lead poisoning, asthma, cancer, and developmental disabilities. *Environmental Health Perspective*, 110, 721–728.

Langer, T., Martus, P., Ottensmeier, H., Hertzberg, H., Beck, J. D., & Meier, W. (2002). CNS late-effects after ALL therapy in childhood. Part III. Neuropsychological performance in long-term survivors of childhood ALL: impairments of concentration, attention, and memory. *Medical and Pediatric Oncology*, 38, 320–328.

Lee, J. S., Pfund, Z., Juhasz, C., Behen, M. E., Muzik, O., Chugani, D. C., et al. (2002). Altered regional brain glucose metabolism in Duchenne muscular dystrophy: A PET study. *Muscle and Nerve*, 26, 506–512.

Leibowitz, D., & Dubowitz, V. (1981). Intellect and behavior in Duchenne muscular dystrophy. *Developmental Medicine and Child Neurology*, 23, 577–590.

Leung, W., Hudson, M., Zhu, Y., Rivera, G. K., Ribeiro, R. C., Sandlund, J. T., et al. (2000). Late effects in survivors of infant leukemia. *Leukemia*, 14, 1185–1190.

Lewis, B. A., Singer, L. T., Fulton, S., Salvator, A., Short, E. J., Klein, N., et al. (2002). Speech and language outcomes of children with bronchopulmonary dysplasia. *Journal of Communication Disorders*, 35, 393–406.

Lorntz, B., Soares, A. M., Moore, S. R., Pinkerton, R. C., Gansneder, B., Bovbjerg, V. E., et al. (2006). Early childhood diarrhea predicts impaired school performance. *Pediatric Infectious Disease*, 25, 513–520.

Lupie, S. J., King, S., Meaney, M. J. & McEwen, B. S. (2001). Can poverty get under your skin? Basal cortisol levels and cognitive function in children from low and high socioeconomic status. *Development and Psychopathology*, 13, 653–676.

Lyman, G. H., & Glaspy, J. (2006). Are there clinical benefits with early erythropoietic intervention for chemotherapy-induced anemia? A systematic review. *Cancer*, 106, 223–233.

Mathur, M., Sykes, J. A., Saxena, V. R., Rao, S. P., & Goldman, G. M. (2003). Treatment of acute lymphoblastic leukemia-induced extreme hypercalcemia with pamidronate and calcitonin. *Pediatric Critical Care Medicine*, 4, 252–255.

McAulay, V., Deary, I. J., Sommerfield, A. J., & Frier, B. M. (2006). Attentional functioning is impaired during acute hypoglycemia in people with Type I diabetes. *Diabetic Medicine*, 23, 26–31.

McCarthy, A. M., Lindgren, S., Mengeling, M. A., Tsalikian, E., & Engvall, J. C. (2002). Effects of diabetes on learning in children. *Pediatrics*, 109, E9–E19.

Meeske, K. A., Siegel, S. E., Globe, D. R., Mack, W. J., & Bernstein, L. (2005). Prevalence and correlates of fatigue in long-term survivors of childhood leukemia. *Journal of Clinical Oncology*, 24, 5501–5510.

Mendez, M. A., & Adair, L. S. (1999). Severity and timing of stunting in the first two years of life affect performance on cognitive tests in late childhood. *Journal of Nutrition*, 129, 1555–1562.

Mennes, M., Stiers, P., Vandenbussche, E., Vercruysse, G., Uyttebroeck, A., De Meyer, G., et al. (2005). Attention and information processing in survivors of childhood acute lymphoblastic leukemia treated with chemotherapy only. *Pediatric Blood Cancer*, 44, 478–486.

Mezey, E., Chandross, K. J., Harta, G., Maki, R. A., & McKercher, S. R. (2000). Turning blood into brain: Cells bearing neuronal antigens generated in vivo from bone marrow. *Science*, 290, 1779–1782.

Mitchell, R. B., & Kelly, J. P. (2006). Behavior, neurocognition and quality-of-life in children with sleep-disordered breathing. *International Journal of Pediatric Otorhinolaryngology*, 70, 395–406.

Moleski, M. (2000). Neuropsychological, neuroanatomical, and neurophysiological consequences of CNS chemotherapy for acute lymphoblastic leukemia. *Archives of Clinical Neuropsychology*, 15, 603–630.

Montgomery-Downs, H. E., Crabtree, V. M., & Gozal, D. (2005). Cognition, sleep and respiration in at-risk children treated for obstructive sleep apnoea. *European Respiratory Journal*, 25, 336–342.

Montour-Proulx, I., Kuehn, S. M., Keene, D. L., Barrowman, N. J., Hsu, E., Matzinger, M.-A., et al. (2005). Cognitive changes in children treated for acute lymphoblastic leukemia with chemotherapy only according to the Pediatric Oncology Group 9605 Protocol. *Journal of Child Neurology*, 20, 129–133.

Moore, M. A. S. (1999). Turning brain into blood-clinical applications of stem-cell research in neurobiology and hematology. *New England Journal of Medicine*, 341, 605–607.

Muir, T., & Zegarac, M. (2001). Societal costs of exposure to toxic substances: Economic and health costs of four case studies that are candidates for environmental causation. *Environmental Health Perspective*, 109(Suppl. 6), 885–903.

Mulhern, R. K., Khan, R. B., Kaplan, S., Helton, S., Christensen, R., Bonner, M. J., et al. (2004). Short-term efficacy of methylphenidate: A randomized, double-blind, placebo-controlled trial among survivors of childhood cancer. *Journal of Clinical Oncology*, 22, 4795–4803.

Murphy, C. C., Yeargin-Allsopp, M., Decoufle, P., & Drews, C. D. (1995). The administrative prevalence of mental retardation in 10-year-old children in metropolitan Atlanta, 1985 through 1987. *American Journal of Public Health*, 85, 319–323.

Nabors, N. A., & Freymouth, A. K. (2002). Attention deficits in children with sickle cell disease. *Perceptual and Motor Skills*, 95, 57–67.

Needleman, H. (2004). Lead poisoning. *Annual Review of Medicine*, 55, 209–222.

Needleman, H. L., Gunnoe, C., Leviton, A., Reed, R., Peresie, H., Maher, C., et al. (1979). Deficits in psychologic and classroom performance of children with elevated dentine lead levels. *New England Journal of Medicine*, 300, 689–695.

Needleman, H. L., Shell, A., Bellinger, D., Leviton, A., & Allred, E. N. (1990). The long-term effects of exposure to low doses of lead in childhood: An 11-year follow-up report. *New England Journal of Medicine*, 311, 83–88.

Newburger, J. W., Wypij, D., Bellinger, D. C., duPlessis, A. J., Kuban, K. C. K., Rappaport, L. A., et al. (2003). Length of stay after infant heart surgery is related to cognitive outcome at age 8 years. *Journal of Pediatrics*, 143, 67–73.

Northam, E. A., Anderson, P. J., Jacobs, R., Hughes, M., Warne, G. L., & Werther, G. A. (2001). Neuropsychological profiles of children with Type I diabetes 6 years after disease onset. *Diabetes Care*, 24, 1541–1546.

Olness, K. (2003). Effects on brain development leading to cognitive impairment: A worldwide epidemic. *Developmental and Behavioral Pediatrics*, 24, 120–130.

Ozmert, E. N., Yurdakok, K., Soysal, S., Kulak-Kayikci, M. E., Belgin, E., Ozmert, E., et al. (2005). Relationship between physical, environmental and sociodemographic factors and school performance in primary schoolchildren. *Journal of Tropical Pediatrics*, 51, 25–32.

Paakko, E., Harila-Saari, A., Vanionpaa, L., Himanen, S., Pyhtinen, J., & Lanning, M. (2000). White matter changes on MRI during treatment in children with acute lymphoblastic leukemia: correlation with neuropsychological findings. *Medical and Pediatric Oncology*, 35, 456–461.

Parer, J. T. (1998). Effects of fetal asphyxia on brain cell structure and function: Limits of tolerance. *Comparative Biochemistry and Physiology*, 119A, 711–716.

Patrick, P. D., Oria, R. B., Madhavan, V., Pinkerton, R. C., Lorntz, B., Lima, A. A., et al. (2005). Limitations in verbal fluency following heavy burdens of early childhood diarrhea in Brazilian shantytown children. *Child Neuropsychology*, 11, 233–244.

Perini, G. I., Menegazzo, E., Ermani, M., Zara, M., Gemma, A., Ferruzza, E., et al. (1999). Cognitive impairment and (CTG)n expansion in myotonic dystrophy patients. *Biological Psychiatry*, 46, 425–431.

Phillips, P. C., Moeller, J. R., Sidtis, J. J., Dhawan, V., Steinherz, P. G., Strother, S. C., et al. (1991). Abnormal cerebral glucose metabolism in long-term survivors of childhood acute lymphocytic leukemia. *Annals of Neurology*, 29, 263–271.

Powell, C. A., Walker, S. P., Himes, J. H., Fletcher, P. D., & Grantham-McGregor, S. M. (1995). Relationships between physical growth, mental development and nutritional supplementation in stunted children: the Jamaica study. *Acta Paediatrica.*, 84, 22–29.

Precourt, S., Robaey, P., Lamothe, I., Lassonde, M., Sauerwein, H. C., & Moghrabi, A. (2002). Verbal cognitive functioning and learning in girls treated for acute lymphoblastic leukemia by chemotherapy with or without cranial irradiation. *Developmental Neuropsychology*, 21, 173–195.

Pui, C.-H., Cheng, C., Leung, W., Rai, S. N., Rivera, G. K., Sandlund, J. T., et al. (2003). Extended follow-up of long-term survivors of childhood acute lymphoblastic leukemia. *New England Journal of Medicine*, 349, 640–649.

Pui, C.-H., Pei, D., Sandlund, J. T., Campana, D., Ribeiro, R. C., Razzouk, B. I., et al. (2005). Risk of adverse events after completion of therapy for childhood acute lymphoblastic leukemia. *Journal of Clinical Oncology*, 23, 7936–7941.

Pusswald, G., Fertl, E., Faltl, M., & Auff, E. (2000). Neurological rehabilitation of severely disable cardiac arrest survivors. Part II. Life situation of patients and families after treatment. *Resuscitation*, 47, 241–248.

Randazzo, A. C., Muehlbach, M. J., Schweitzer, P. K., & Walsh, J. K. (1998). Cognitive function following acute sleep restriction in children ages 10–14. *Sleep*, 21, 861–868.

Raymond-Speden, E., Tripp, G., Lawrence, B., & Holdaway, D. (2000). Intellectual, neuropsychological, and academic functioning in long-term survivors of leukemia. *Journal of Pediatric Psychology*, 25, 59–68.

Redaelli, A., Laskin, B. L., Stephens, J. M., Botteman, M. F., & Pashos, C. L. (2005). A systematic litearture review of the clinical and epidemiological burden of acute lymphoblastic leukaemia (ALL). *European Journal of Cancer Care*, 14, 53–62.

Reddick, W. E., White, H. A., Glass, J. O., Wheeler, G. C., Thompson, S. J., Gajjar, A., et al. (2003). Developmental model relating white matter volume to neurocognitive deficits in pediatric brain tumor survivors. *Cancer*, 97, 2512–2519.

Reddick, W. E., Shan, Z. Y., Glass, J. O., Helton, S., Xiong, X., Wu, S., et al. (2006). Smaller white-matter volumes are associated with larger deficits in attention and learning among long-term survivors of acute lymphoblastic leukemia. *Cancer*, 106, 941–949.

Refsum, H., Wesenberg, F., & Ueland, P. M. (1991). Plasma homocysteine in children with acute lymphoblastic leukemia: Changes during a chemotherapeutic regimen including methotrexate. *Cancer Research*, 51, 828–835.

Rivera, G. K., Pinkel, D., Simone, J. V., Hancock, M. L., & Crist, W. M. (1993). Treatment of acute lymphoblastic leukemia: 30 years' experience at St. Jude Children's Research Hospital. *New England Journal of Medicine*, 329, 1289–1295.

Rodgers, J., Britton, P. G., Kernahan, J., & Craft, A. W. (1991). Cognitive function after two doses of cranial irradiation for acute lymphoblastic leukaemia. *Archives of Disease in Childhood*, 66, 1245–1246.

Rodgers, J., Marckus, R., Kearns, P., & Windebank, K. (2003). Attentional ability among survivors of leukaemia treated with cranial irradiation. *Archives of Disease in Childhood*, 88, 147–150.

Rogan, W. J., Dietrich, K. N., Ware, J. H., Dockery, D. W., Salganik, M., Radcliffe, J., et al. (2001). The effect of chelation therapy with succimer on neuropsychological development in children exposed to lead. *New England Journal of Medicine*, 344, 1421–1426.

Rogan, W. J., Shannon, M. W., Best, D., Binns, H. J., Kim, J. J., Mazur, L. J., et al. (2005). Lead exposure in children: Prevention, detection, and management. *Pediatrics*, 116, 1036–1046.

Rowland, J. H., Glidewell, O. J., Sibley, R. F., Holland, J. C., Tull, R., Berman, A., et al. (1984). Effects of different forms of central nervous system prophylaxis on neuropsychologic function in childhood leukemia. *Journal of Clinical Oncology*, 2, 1327–1335.

Rubinsztein, J. S., Rubinsztein, D. C., McKenna, P. J., Goodburn, S., & Holland, A. J. (1997). Mild myotonic dystrophy is associated with memory impairment in the context of normal general intelligence. *Journal of Medical Genetics*, 34, 229–233.

Ryan, C. M., Atchison, J., Puczynski, S., Puczynski, M., Arslanian, S., & Becker, D. (1990). Mild hypoglycemia associated with deterioration of mental efficiency in children with insulin-dependent diabetes mellitus. *Journal of Pediatrics*, 117, 32–38.

Sahin, G., Ertem, U., Duru, F., Birgen, D., & Yuksek, N. (2000). High prevalence of chronic magnesium deficiency in T cell lymphoblastic leukemia and chronic zinc deficiency in children with acute lymphoblastic leukemia and malignant lymphoma. *Leukmia and Lymphoma*, 39, 555–562.

Scarr, S., & Weinberg, R. A. (1976). IQ test performance of black children adopted by white families. *American Psychology*, 31, 726–739.

Schatz, J. (2004). Academic attainment in children with sickle cell disease. *Journal of Pediatric Psychology*, 29, 627–633.

Schatz, J., & Buzan, R. (2006). Decreased corpus callosum size in sickle cell disease: Relationship with cerebral infracts and cognitive functioning. *Journal of International Neuropsychological Society*, 12, 24–33.

Schatz, J., & Roberts, C. W. (2005). Short-term memory in children with sickle cell disease: Executive versus modality-specific processing deficits. *Archives of Clinical Neuropsychology*, 20, 1073–1085.

Schatz, J., Finke, R. L., Kellett, J. M., & Kramer, J. H. (2002). Cognitive functioning in children with sickle cell disease: A meta-analysis. *Journal of Pediatric Psychology*, 27, 739–748.

Schatz, J., Kramer, J. H., Ablin, A., & Matthay, K. K. (2000). Processing speed, working memory, and IQ: A developmental model of cognitive deficits following cranial radiation therapy. *Neuropsychology*, 14, 189–200.

Schatz, J., White, D. A., Moinuddin, A., Armstrong, M., & DeBauno, M. R. (2002). Lesion burden and cognitive morbidity in children with sickle cell disease. *Journal of Child Neurology*, 17, 891–895.

Schultheiss, T. E., Kun, L. E., Ang, K. K., & Stephens, L. C. (1995). Radiation response of the central nervous system. *International Journal of Radiation Oncology, Biology, Physics*, 31, 1093–1112.

Schumacher, R. E., Palmer, T. W., Roloff, D. W., LaClaire, P. A., & Bartlett, R. H. (1991). Follow-up of infants treated with extracorporeal membrane oxygenation for newborn respiratory failure. *Pediatrics*, 87, 451–457.

Seeman, T. E., McEwen, B. S., Rowe, J. W., & Singer, B. H. (2001). Allostatic load as a marker of cumulative biological risk: MacArthur studies of successful aging. *Proceedings of National Academy of Sciences USA*, 98, 4770–4775.

Short, E. J., Klein, N. K., Lewis, B. A., Fulton, S., Eisengart, S., Kercsmar, C., et al. (2003). Cognitive and academic consequences of bronchopulmonary dysplasia and very low birth weight: 8-year-old outcomes. *Pediatrics*, 112, e359–e366.

Smith, J. R., Brooks-Gunn, J., & Klebanov, P. K. (1997). Consequences of living in poverty for young children's cognitive and verbal ability and early school achievement. In G. J. Duncan, & J. Brooks-Gunn (Eds.), *Consequences of Growing Up Poor* (pp. 132–189). New York: Russell Sage Foundation.

Soni, S. S., Marten, G. W., Pitner, S. E., Duenas, D. A., & Powazek, M. (1975). Effects of central nervous system irradiation on neuropsychologic functioning of children with acute lymphoblastic leukemia. *New England Journal of Medicine*, 293, 113–118.

Spencer, M. D., Gibson, R. J., Moorhead, T. W. J., Keston, P. M., Hoare, P., Best, J. J. K., et al. (2005). Qualitative assessment of brain anomalies in adolescents with mental retardation. *American Journal of Neuroradiology*, 26, 2691–2697.

Steen, R. G. (1996). *DNA & Destiny: Nature and Nurture in Human Behavior*. New York: Plenum Press.

Steen, R. G., Langston, J. W., Ogg, R. J., Manci, E., Mulhern, R. K., & Wang, W. (1998a). Ectasia of the basilar artery in children with sickle cell disease: Relationship to hematocrit and psychometric measures. *Journal of Stroke Cerebrovascular Disease*, 7, 32–43.

Steen, R. G., Reddick, W. E., Mulhern, R., Langston, J. W., Ogg, R., Bierberich, A., et al. (1998b). Quantitative MRI of the brain in children with sickle cell disease reveals abnormalities unseen by conventional MRI:. *JMRI*, 8, 535–543.

Steen, R. G., Langston, J. W., Ogg, R. J., Xiong, X., Ye, Z., & Wang, W. C. (1999). Diffuse T1 reduction in gray matter of sickle cell disease patients: Evidence of selective vulnerability to damage? *Magnetic Resonance Imaging*, 17, 503–515.

Steen, R. G., Spence, D., Wu, S., Xiong, X., Kun, L. E., & Merchant, T. (2001). Effect of therapeutic ionizing radiation on the human brain. *Annals of Neurology*, 50, 787–795.

Steen, R. G., Hu, J., Elliott, V. E., Miles, M. A., Jones, S., & Wang, W. C. (2002). Kindergarten readiness skills in children with sickle cell disease: Evidence of early neurocognitive damage? *Journal of Child Neurology*, 17, 111–116.

Steen, R. G., Miles, M., Helton, K., Strawn, S., Wang, W. C., Xiong, X., et al. (2003). Cognitive impairment in children with hemoglobin SS sickle cell disease: Relationship to MR imaging findings and hematocrit. *AJNR*, 24, 382–389.

Steen, R. G., Emudianughe, T., Hunte, M., Glass, J., Wu, S., Xiong, X., et al. (2005a). Brain volume in pediatric patients with sickle cell disease: Evidence of volumetric growth delay? *American Journal of Neuroradiology*, 26, 455–462.

Steen, R. G., Fineberg-Buchner, C., Hankins, G., Weiss, L., Prifitera, A., & Mulhern, R. K. (2005b). Cognitive deficits in children with sickle cell disease. *Journal of Child Neurology*, 20, 102–107.

Steen, R. G., Hamer, R. M., & Lieberman, J. A. (2005c). Measurement of brain metabolites by 1H magnetic resonance spectroscopy in patients with schizophrenia: A systematic review and meta-analysis. *Neuropsychopharmacology*, 30, 1949–1962.

Steen, R. G., Mull, C., McClure, R., Hamer, R., & Lieberman, J. A. (2006). Brain volume in first-episode schizophrenia: Systematic review and meta-analysis of magnetic resonance imaging studies. *British Journal of Psychiatry*, 188, 510–518.

Sungthong, R., Mosuwan, L., & Chongsuvivatwong, N. (2002). Effects of haemoglobin and serum ferritin on cognitive function in school children. *Asia Pacific Journal of Clinical Nutrition*, 11, 117–122.

Swift, A. V., Cohen, M. J., Hynd, G. W., Wisenbacker, J. M., McKie, K. M., Makari, G., et al. (1989). Neuropsychologic impairment in children with sickle cell anemia. *Pediatrics*, 84, 1077–1085.

Taki, S., Higashi, K., Oguchi, M., Tamamura, H., Tsuji, S., Ohta, K., et al. (2002). Changes in regional cerebral blood flow in irradiated regions and normal brain after stereotactic radiosurgery. *Annals of Nuclear Medicine*, 16, 273–277.

Taras, H., & Potts-Datema, W. (2005). Chronic health conditions and student performance at school. *Journal of School Health*, 75, 255–266.

Taylor, H. G., Klein, N., Minich, N. M., & Hack, M. (2000). Middle-school-age outcomes in children with very low birth weight. *Child Development*, 71, 1495–1511.

Turkheimer, E., Haley, A., Waldron, M., D'Onofrio, B., & Gottesman, I. I. (2003). Socioeconomic status modifies heritability of IQ in young children. *Psychological Science*, 14, 623–628.

Urschitz, M. S., Wolff, J., Sokollik, C., Eggebrecht, E., Urshitz-Duprat, P. M., Schlaud, M., et al. (2005). Nocturnal arterial oxygen saturation and academic performance in a community sample of children. *Pediatrics*, 115, e204–e209.

von der Weid, N., Mosimann, I., Hirt, A., Wacker, P., Beck, M. N., Imbach, P., et al. (2003). Intellectual outcome in children and adolescents with acute lymphoblastic leukemia treated with chemotherapy alone: Age- and sex-related differences. *European Journal of Cancer*, 39, 359–365.

Waber, D. P., Gerber, E. B., Turcios, V. Y., Wagner, E. R., & Forbes, P. W. (2006). Executive functions and performance on high-stakes testing in children from urban schools. *Developmetnal Neuropsychology*, 29, 459–477.

Waber, D. P., Shapiro, B. L., Carpentieri, S. C., Gelber, R. D., Zou, G., Dufresne, A., et al. (2001). Excellent therapeutic efficacy and minimal late neurotoxicity in children treated with 18 Grays of cranial radiation therapy for high-risk acute lymphoblastic leukemia: A 7-year follow-up study of the Dana-Farber Cancer Institution Consortium Protocol 87-01. *Cancer*, 92, 15–22.

Wang, W., Enos, L., Gallagher, D., Thompson, R., Guarini, L., Vichinsky, E., et al. (2001). Neuropsychologic performance in school-aged children with sickle cell disease: A report from the Cooperative Study of Sickle Cell Disease. *Journal of Pediatrics*, 139, 391–397.

Wellmann, S., Guschmann, M., Griethe, W., Eckert, C., von Stackelberg, A., Lottaz, C., et al. (2004). Activation of HIF pathway in childhood ALL; prognostic implications of VEGF. *Leukemia*, 18, 926–933.

White, D. A., & DeBaun, M. (1998). Cognitive and behavioral function in children with sickle cell disease: A review and discussion of methodological issues. *Journal of Pediatric Hematology/Oncology.*, 20, 458–462.

Wray, J., & Radley-Smith, R. (2004). Developmental and behavioral status of infants and young children awaiting heart or heart-lung transplantation. *Pediatrics*, 113, 488–495.

Wray, J., & Radley-Smith, R. (2006). Longitudinal assessment of psychological functioning in children after heart or heart-lung transplantation. *Journal of Heart Lung Transplantation*, 25, 345–352.

Wray, J., & Sensky, T. (2001). Congenital heart disease and cardiac surgery in childhood: Effects on cognitive function and academic ability. *Heart*, 85, 687–691.

Wypij, D., Newburger, J. W., Rappaport, L. A., duPlessis, A. J., Jonas, R. A., Wernovsky, G., et al. (2003). The effect of duration of deep hypothermic circulatory arrest in infant heart surgery on late neurodevelopment: The Boston Circulatory Arrest Trial. *Journal of Thoracic Cardiovascular Surgery*, 126, 1397–1403.

Yeargin-Allsopp, M., Drews, C. D., Decoufle, P., & Murphy, C. C. (1995). Mild mental retardation in black and white children in metropolitan Atlanta: A case-control study. *American Journal of Public Health*, 85, 324–328.

Zou, P., Mulhern, R. K., Butler, R. W., Li, C.-S., Langston, J. W., & Ogg, R. (2005). BOLD responses to visual stimulation in survivors of childhood cancer. *NeuroImage*, 24, 61–69.

11

CONSIDERATIONS IN USING THE WISC-IV WITH HISPANIC CHILDREN

JOSETTE G. HARRIS[1], MARÍA R. MUÑOZ[2] AND ANTOLIN M. LLORENTE[3]

[1]Departments of Psychiatry and Neurology, University of Colorado School of Medicine, Denver, CO, USA

[2]Pearson, San Antonio, TX, USA

[3]Department of Pediatrics, University of Maryland School of Medicine, Baltimore, MD, USA

Topics concerned with cross-cultural assessment of cognition and intelligence were once primarily associated with research methodologies comparing groups of individuals residing within different countries. Over time, however, within an increasingly mobile world, and with sophistication in conceptualizing the facets of diversity existing within regional and national boundaries, cross-cultural topics are appropriately now seen to additionally encompass "cultures" within broader cultures, such as a single country. In our efforts to understand the relationship between culture and certain psychological variables, such as intelligence, it is necessary to carefully characterize those cultures and to define the measurement of intelligence. Efforts to do so, however, sometimes oversimplify the constructs and obscure the interpretation of both group and individual performances.

The intellectual assessment of "minority" children is an example of such constructs of convenience. Describing children as "minority" says little about the cultural, linguistic, educational, and socioeconomic issues that may differentially impact these children and their performances on tests of intelligence. Further distinctions by racial or ethnic grouping may be similarly limited in value because of the heterogeneity within such groups. This chapter focuses on this topic of heterogeneity as a means to inform our thinking about individual and group differences in performance. While many of the issues described in this chapter, such as language proficiency, are applicable to individuals from a variety of backgrounds and ethnicities, we have chosen to focus primarily on the "Hispanic" population, because it represents a particularly large segment of the world's population; that is, there are numerous Spanish-speaking countries around the world, including the United States. Ultimately the goal of this chapter is to raise issues and examples that will foster individualized assessment practices with all schoolchildren who are evaluated with the *Wechsler Intelligence Scale for Children* – Fourth Edition (WISC-IV) (Wechsler, 2003).

HETEROGENEITY IN ETHNIC MINORITY POPULATIONS

While an argument can be made that any ethnic group residing within a society or country may be rather heterogeneous, the Hispanic population provides a particularly salient example. The term Hispanic is a broad term encompassing Spanish speakers of Latin American origin (i.e., Latinos) as well as individuals from any of a number of other Spanish-speaking countries outside of Latin America (e.g., Spaniards). Hispanic individuals living within a given country share many societal institutional structures such as the political, economic, and general educational systems. Yet, groups of individuals representing different Hispanic cultures vary greatly with regard to country of origin, educational attainment, religion, use of language(s), and other important variables. The panethnic label Hispanic fails to capture these unique attributes, and in reality is a term of convenience with little descriptive specificity to any given Hispanic individual.

The term Hispanic has often been used as a racial category, creating significant confusion. Its distinction by some as a separate race stems from a historical blending of races. The conquest of Mesoamerica by the Spaniards in the 16th century, for example, led to the intermingling of the European Spaniards with the indigenous Indians, producing offspring referred to as mestizo (mixed). Many Mexican–Americans (some favoring the additional distinction of "Chicano" to represent certain political perspectives, as well as a shared ethnic identity) consider themselves to be descendents of this "new race" of mestizos that migrated northward to the United States. The term Hispanic is, in actuality, an umbrella term for a number of cultural and ethnic groupings. Hispanic individuals can claim any racial origin(s), as well as any ethnicity or culture. Table 11.1 presents the most recent census estimates for the US Hispanic population, according to country of origin (United States Census Bureau, 2006).

Even within a specific category, such as the largest group, Mexican, there are additional variables to consider. For example, the label Mexican encompasses

TABLE 11.1   Census Estimates for the Hispanic Population Living in the United States According to Country of Origin

Hispanic or Latino by type of origin: 2006	Population	Percent of Hispanic population
Hispanic or Latino	44,252,278	100.0
Mexican	25,339,354	64.0
Puerto Rican	3,987,947	9.0
Cuban	1,520,276	3.4
Dominican	1,271,225	2.8
Central American	3,372,090	7.6
Costa Rican	104,793	.2
Guatemalan	874,799	2.0
Honduran	490,317	1.1
Nicaraguan	295,059	.7
Panamanian	123,631	.3
Salvadoran	1,371,666	3.1
South American	2,421,297	5.5
Argentinean	183,427	0.4
Bolivian	82,322	0.2
Chilean	104,861	0.2
Colombian	801,363	1.8
Ecuadorian	498,705	1.1
Peruvian	435,368	1.0
Venezuelan	177,866	0.4
Spaniard	377,140	0.9
All other Hispanic or Latino	3,016,949	6.8

Source: U.S. Census Bureau, 2006 American Community Survey, Selected Population Profiles and Detailed Tables, S0201.

both Mexican immigrants and US born descendents of Mexican ancestry. Those emigrating from Mexico may identify with any of at least 50 indigenous ethnic groups that reside in the home country (Vázquez, 1994). In addition to the traditional Spanish language of Mexico, there are 27 distinct indigenous languages recognized by the Mexican government for the publication of the "Bill of Labor Rights and Responsibilities" (Carta de Derechos y Obligaciones Laborales), including Náhuatl, Maya, Mixteco, Zapoteco, Tarhaumara, and Huichol (México & Gobierno de La República, 2004). There are reportedly in excess of 200 additional living languages spoken by indigenous peoples throughout Mexico (Grimes & Grimes, 2004). Hispanic children within the United States may consequently be of any race(s), any ethnicity, or a combination of ethnicities (e.g., parents with Puerto Rican and Colombian nationalities), and may be monolingual Spanish speakers, monolingual English speakers, bilingual (e.g., Spanish–Mayan), or multilingual (e.g., Tarhaumara–Spanish–English), even if English is not yet a proficient language. At one end of the continuum Hispanic children may represent recently immigrated monolingual Spanish-speaking children, and at the other end of the continuum they may represent children whose ancestors have been living in the United States for multiple generations and whose parents may not share the same ethnicity (Hispanic or other), and may not even speak the Spanish language.

Similar diversity exists for other racial and ethnic groupings, such as Black, African American, North American Native, Aboriginal, and Alaskan Native. In Canada, where English and French are predominantly spoken, approximately 32,000 individuals reported they could carry on a conversation in Inuktitut, the second most common Aboriginal language, according to reliable governmental surveys (Canadian Heritage, 2002). For individuals belonging to any of these groups, the assimilation of a specific language as primary or secondary varies according to such factors as age of language exposure and acquisition, degree of acculturation to "mainstream" society, regional location within a country, and support for maintenance of the native language and culture.

This discussion begins to provide a glimpse into the complexities of psychological assessment with diverse individuals. It underscores the need for appropriate psychological and cognitive instruments to assess such diverse populations, as well as the need for methods to understand individual performance and the meaning of both individual and group differences.

ETHNIC DIFFERENCES IN WECHSLER SCALE PERFORMANCE

The original *Wechsler Intelligence Scale for Children* (Wechsler, 1949) has undergone three revisions since its publication in 1949. The resulting publications are the WISC-R (Wechsler, 1974), the WISC-III (Wechsler, 1991), and the WISC-IV (Wechsler, 2003). Most recently, an adaptation and translation of the WISC-IV into Spanish was published for use with Spanish-speaking children in the United States and Puerto Rico (Wechsler, 2005). These versions have each reflected concomitant advances in theoretical models of intelligence, cognitive theory, information processing paradigms, test construction, and professional practice and assessment guidelines. For example, the most recent WISC-IV (English) manual specifically addresses the application of the WISC-IV to diverse individuals, including English-language learners and recent immigrants, reflecting standards and guidelines developed by the American Educational Research Association (American Educational Research Association, American Psychological Association, & National Council on Measurement in Education, 1999) and by the American Psychological Association (APA 1990, 2002).

With each English-language revision, however, a rather stable scientific finding has persisted concerning the lower performance, relative to nonminority examinees, of African American and Hispanic children in the standardization sample (Kaufman & Doppelt, 1976; Prifitera et al., 1998; Prifitera, Saklofske, Weiss, & Rolfhus, 2005; Sattler, 1992; Weiss et al., 2006; Weiss, Prifitera & Roid, 1993). This disparity in cognitive performance is neither unique to the WISC nor to the other Wechsler scales. There has been considerable scientific and public debate concerning the explanations for these findings (Hernstein & Murray, 1994; Neisser et al., 1996), including for example, concerns that cognitive measures lack cultural equivalence and that there are inherent problems with bias in the measures (Helms, 1992). In evaluating the Wechsler scales for various types of bias, it has been noted that impressions of bias most often reflect personal reactions to test content and misinterpretations about the consequences of test use, rather than specific findings resulting from bias analyses (Reynolds, 2000; Reynolds & Kaiser, 2003; Weiss et al., 2006).

CONCEPTUAL EQUIVALENCE OF INTELLIGENCE AND WISC-IV MODERATOR VARIABLES

It is certainly not contested that intelligence can be represented differently within specific cultures, but it can also be represented similarly when individuals share salient aspects of their cultural and educational backgrounds.

Studies concerning the cultural equivalence of the WISC in cross-national studies support the notion of universal cognitive processes across cultures (Georgas, Weiss, Van de Vijver, & Saklofske, 2003). There is remarkable consistency in the factor structure of the WISC, when adapted and translated into other languages in other countries (Georgas et al., 2003). When mean score differences have been identified among cross-national samples, these findings have been thought to be attributable to education-related or economic factors (Georgas, Van de Vijver, Weiss, & Saklofske, 2003). Variations in IQ scores across countries have, for example, been found to be related to the pupil–teacher ratio for preprimary, primary, and secondary education and duration of each education level, according to these authors. These investigators also suggested that affluence-related factors, such as the physical quality of the child's living environment, may explain cross-cultural score differences, although education and affluence are also noted to be highly and positively correlated.

The factor structure for specific racial and ethnic groups within the United States (i.e., white, African American, and Hispanic) is also generally consistent, although

TABLE 11.2 Mean WISC-IV Scores of Hispanic and White Non-Hispanic Children from the Standardization Sample

IQ or index score	Hispanic	White non-Hispanic
FSIQ	93.1	103.2
VCI	91.5	102.9
PRI	95.7	102.8
WMI	94.2	101.3
PSI	97.7	101.4

n = 2080 *Source: Wechsler Intelligence Scale for Children* – Fourth Edition, 2003. Reprinted with permission by Harcourt Assessment.

TABLE 11.3 Standardization Mean WISC-IV Scores of Hispanic and White Non-Hispanic Children Equated for Age, Gender, Number of Parents Living in the Household, Parental Education Level, and US Region

IQ or index score	Hispanic	White non-Hispanic
FSIQ	95.2	100.0
VCI	93.7	99.7
PRI	97.7	100.3
WMI	95.7	98.7
PSI	97.9	99.6

n = 161.

there may be some differences in factor loadings in the lower age ranges within groups due to developmental differences in the acquisition of specific cognitive abilities, such as working memory skills (Wechsler, 2003). In score comparisons among ethnic groups within a given country, socioeconomic factors have been found to partially account for variability in performance (Prifitera et al., 1998). In group comparisons of WISC-IV performance, the typical pattern of reduced performances in the Hispanic group emerges, with a difference of 10 points evident on the Full Scale IQ (FSIQ) and a similar depressed score exhibited on the Verbal Comprehension Index (VCI) compared with white non-Hispanic children (Table 11.2). However, when subjects are matched on age, gender, region of the country, parental education level (a proxy for socioeconomic status (SES), and number of parents living in the household, differences are reduced with the largest differences of approximately 5 and 6 points found on FSIQ and VCI, respectively (Table 11.3) (Prifitera, Saklofske, Weiss, & Rolfhus, 2005).

For some members of ethnic minority groups, the interplay of education and economics is particularly complex. While educational attainment to a large degree dictates and certainly facilitates income potential, it is also the case that socioeconomic advancement facilitates educational attainment. For example, immigrant high school graduates who do not have legal residency status but who wish to attend college, are ineligible for in-state tuition rates in most jurisdictions in the United States (National Conference of State Legislatures, 2003, 2004). Parental income of these children is often constrained by the lack of legal residency. Language constraints may further limit parental educational and income opportunities. Data on the number of undocumented students who graduate high school and are unable to enroll in college are not readily available. It is estimated, however, that there are 1.6 million children under the age of 18 living without legal residency status in the United States (Passel et al., 2004). These circumstances certainly contribute to the low percentage of Hispanics graduating college in the United States. Table 11.4 presents the profile of educational attainment for Hispanics within the United States (United States Census Bureau, 2003a). Across all Hispanic groups, 28.2% graduate high school. In contrast, in the white non-Hispanic population, 33.7% graduate high school, 27.3% achieve a minimum of a bachelor's degree, and 4.8% have attained less than 9 years of education. It is noteworthy that the dropout rate for Hispanic students for grades 10 through 12 in 2002 was 5.3% (male = 6.2%; female = 4.4%), higher than any other ethnic group (United States Census Bureau, 2004). As course content demands increase in school, the need for linguistic competence increases. Those children who immigrate at later ages and who are denied support for their emerging second language skills are clearly most at risk to fail and to remove themselves from the school environment.

These realities conspire to depress the SES for the group of Hispanics as a whole. As a given minority group gains an economic foothold, educational and other opportunities tend to increase. For example, Portes and Rumbaut (1990) noted that Koreans surpassed other ethnic minority groups that have historically immigrated to the United States in their rapid rate of success, measured from an economic standpoint. The authors attributed part of this rapid rise to the group's higher average SES before immigrating to the United States, which serves to facilitate additional gains. However, with limitations in the accessibility of education and employment to some immigrant groups, it is obvious that the initial economic foothold may be very difficult if not impossible to achieve. While 17.1% of all children live below the poverty level in the United States, 30.4% of all Hispanic children live below the poverty level (United States Census Bureau, 2003b), a testimony to this economic disparity and challenge.

There are significant implications of these disparities for normative studies. Test publishers typically stratify SES (using parental education) within racial and ethnic groupings to reflect the characteristics of the country's population. When IQ scores are compared across ethnic groups, the overall reference group, which is overwhelmingly represented by the nonminority cases, will tend to have higher mean SES and parental education than the subgroups that are the focus of the comparison (Prifitera et al., 1998; Weiss et al., 2006). The lower

TABLE 11.4   Educational Attainment of US Hispanics 25+ Years Old by Country of Origin

Educational attainment	Mexican (%)	Central/South American (%)	Puerto Rican (%)	Cuban (%)	Other Hispanic (%)	Non-Hispanic (%)
Less than 9th grade	31.7	22.1	16.7	17.3	14.6	4.8
9th–12th grade (no diploma)	16.9	13.3	18.5	9.0	13.3	8.3
High school graduate	26.6	29.5	29.8	33.3	32.0	33.7
Some college/ associate degree	17.7	17.8	22.1	17.2	25.4	26.0
Bachelor's degree	5.2	11.7	8.5	13.9	9.1	18.1
Advanced degree	1.8	5.5	4.4	9.3	5.6	9.2

Source: US Census Bureau, Current Population Survey, March 2000. Educational Supplement, Internet Release date: June 18, 2003. US Hispanics include native and foreign born.

performances of individuals from ethnic minority groups reflects both the correlation between SES and IQ as well as the composition of the normative sample.

IMMIGRATION PATTERNS AND THE REPRESENTATIVENESS OF NORMS

There are additional variables that impact the composition of a normative sample, with implications for group and individual comparisons of performance. Patterns of immigration to the United States are one such consideration and provide often overlooked data that should be considered in the norming process of psychoeducational and neuropsychological instruments (Llorente et al., 2000). Migration is not the result of chance processes but rather the result of selective factors associated with both the sending and host countries (Hamilton & Chinchilla, 1990; Portes and Borocsz, 1989; Portes & Rumbaut, 1990; United States Immigration and Naturalization Service, 1991). For example, favorable US policies toward specific countries have contributed to increased immigration of individuals from those countries. Those policies may be dictated by humanitarian concerns, manpower needs, or other international policies and political agendas.

The proportion of "Hispanic" immigrants from specific countries may vary substantially over time for different ethnic groups relative to their representation

TABLE 11.5   Immigration Trends for Fiscal Years 1995–2002

Region and country of birth	1995	1996	1997	1998	1999	2000	2001	2002
Mexico	89,932	163,572	146,865	131,575	147,573	173,919	206,426	219,380
South America	45,666	61,769	52,877	45,394	41,585	56,074	68,888	74,506
Central America	31,814	44,289	43,676	35,679	43,216	66,443	75,914	68,979
Cuba	17,937	26,466	33,587	17,375	14,132	20,831	27,703	28,272
Spain	1,321	1,659	1,241	1,043	874	1,264	1,726	1,376
Uruguay	414	540	429	368	271	430	545	549
Puerto Rico	1	2	1	2	3	3	4	2

Source: United States Department of Homeland Security (2003). 2002 Year book of Immigration Statistics.

in the US population. Migrations to the United States from some countries (e.g., Uruguay) have remained relatively constant and small in magnitude over time relative to migrations from other countries (e.g., Mexico), which have exhibited profound increases (Table 11.5). The US Department of Homeland Security (United States Department of Homeland Security, 2003) reported that 20.5% of all legally admitted immigrants came from Mexico in 2000. Patterns of immigration have implications for the inclusion of specific Hispanic ethnicities in normative samples. For example, while Cubans represented 3.5% of the total US Hispanic population in 2002, a higher target of Cuban children was established for the standardization of the WISC-IV Spanish (Wechsler, 2005), in order to adequately represent Cubans in the standardization sample and to perform supplemental data analyses. Additional criteria for all examinees in the standardization sample included a limit of no more than five consecutive years attendance in a US school and the requirement that children speak and/or understand Spanish better than English or be adept in both languages. These criteria were established to target those children most likely to benefit from assessment in Spanish. Given that Cubans represent the smallest numbers immigrating in recent years, however, it was difficult to access Cuban children that met all the standardization requirements and the stratification of parental education. This strained the data collection process, although the target was eventually met.

Ultimately, while a normative reference group reflects overall population statistics, the norms may not reflect the specific demographic characteristics of an individual from a given ethnic group. Gravitations toward certain occupations exist for specific groups of immigrants. Related to these occupational affiliations, Hispanic ethnic groups tend to differentially exhibit geographic affinity for certain areas within the United States. What this means, for example, is that there is a concentration of lower educated immigrants from Mexico in the Southwest and California, while segments of the East Coast and Florida may reflect a broader socioeconomic spectrum of Cuban and Central and South American immigrants, who have migrated for both economic and humanitarian reasons. These geographical predilections may confound the acquisition of data utilized in establishing standardization norms. For example, the underrepresentation of the WISC IV Spanish reliability sample in the Midwest region of the United States and its overrepresentation in the South and West Regions was noted by Braden & Iribarren (2007) in their review of the WISC IV Spanish. However, in order to reach target numbers of specific Hispanic subgroups, such as Hispanic children from Caribbean countries, some regions were overrepresented (e.g., South) due to the diminished likelihood of finding sufficient numbers of children in other regions (e.g., Caribbean children in the West). In spite of this, minimum numbers of examinees within each region were established and successfully met. Other aspects of so-called "cultural validity" are also deemed important in evaluating test adaptations and their application outside of the English-speaking populations for which they were originally developed (Clinton, 2007).

Further, the geographic concentrations of various ethnic groups have implications for the degree of assimilation of American culture and use of languages by its group members. So, for example, in Miami, Florida, it is quite possible to function well within the community as a monolingual Spanish speaker without the need to use English and possible to retain many of the traditions of the country of origin. Ultimately, these issues impact the utility of the norms used for interpretation of individual test performance and are variables that test users, regardless of purpose (research or clinical), should consider in evaluating the appropriateness of specific test norms.

As a case in point, Rey et al. (1999) found differences in psychological test performance among Cuban and Mexican normative groups living in Dade County, Florida. Close scrutiny of demographic variables associated with the two samples of Spanish speakers revealed that selection biases associated with lower levels of education in the Mexican group were responsible for the differences observed in test performance. The limited representation of Mexican nationality examinees in Dade County compared with Cuban examinees had limited the range of education of participants accessible to the researchers. When Cuban and Mexican subjects were matched on age, gender, and education, the observed discrepancies in performance between the two groups of participants vanished.

Such results underscore the potential confounds associated with both traditional (education) and nontraditional (geographic locale) demographic characteristics. These variables must be carefully scrutinized to avoid the introduction of systematic error into the normative data acquisition and interpretation processes. Certainly, comparing the WISC-IV scores of a young Cuban immigrant to the general population of US schoolchildren will yield important information about the child's ability to "compete" among his or her broadly defined peer group. However, possessing additional knowledge about the US Cuban population, the specific child's background, parental education, and the representativeness of the reference group being used for comparison will enable the examiner to hone his or her interpretation of and inferences regarding test performance. The child of migrant parents seeking economic opportunities in a new country likely differs substantially from the background of a child whose parents are escaping political persecution in another country. Clearly, all these factors have the potential to impact the acquisition of normative data and the inferences derived from the use of psychological instruments, including the WISC-IV. Other potential confounds, such as age of immigration, acculturation (Marin & Marin, 1991), and proficiency in a second language may be difficult to measure accurately but may synergistically interact with demographic variables known to influence test performance (cf., Heaton et al., 1986). Careful consideration of these factors by test users is necessary to avoid individual misdiagnosis, misattribution of differences in cognitive and neuropsychological performance among ethnic groups, and between nonminority and various ethnic groups. Ultimately, practitioners must design "child driven" as opposed to "score driven" interventions based upon the contextually informed interpretation of population-based cognitive ability scores in context with salient demographic and environmental variables (Weiss et al., 2006).

LANGUAGE PROFICIENCY AND COGNITIVE PERFORMANCE

The relationship of language proficiency and bilingualism to cognitive performance has long been a sensitive topic but one that has direct bearing on the performance discrepancies observed for some ethnic minority (e.g., Hispanic) versus nonminority groups on the WISC-IV. Early studies concluded that bilingualism was a cognitive and academic learning liability. This was later identified as in part a reflection of flawed research methodologies, such as failure to control for socioeconomic and other confounding variables, the heterogeneity in the samples designated as "bilingual," and failure to measure abilities in both the stronger and the weaker languages (Hakuta, 1986; Hamers & Blanc, 1989; Romaine, 1995). The social and political context of bilingualism and acceptance of the acquisition of two languages is also a critical factor in the perceived advantages or disadvantages of speaking two languages. In other words, social expectations and support for bilingualism are essential to the acquisition and development of proficiency in a second language as much as other factors, such as individual differences in ability to learn a second language (Ardila, 1998, 2002; Centeno & Obler, 2001). Support may not exist until a language has been officially sanctioned by governmental policies (e.g., Canada's Official Language Act of 1968–1969 and similar European laws) (Centeno & Obler, 2001) or when the norm for bilingualism is otherwise ingrained in the societal and educational structure of a nation. Unfortunately, in the United States preserving the native language has always been viewed as incompatible with learning the English language and indeed bilingual education has a controversial and poorly understood history.

IMPLICATIONS OF LANGUAGE PROFICIENCY
FOR WISC-IV PERFORMANCE

This discussion exposes a rather unique constellation of considerations in examinees who may fall anywhere along a continuum of limited English proficient on one extreme to balanced bilingual (i.e., equal proficiency in the two languages) on the other extreme. Children who make up a specific ethnic group or culture may vary considerably in their English-language proficiency. To place this in the proper context, 2000–2001 survey data of school-age children indicated that 18.4% of the population ages 5–17 years spoke a non-English language at home (United States Census Bureau, 2003c). Nationwide, in the 2000–2001 school year, it was estimated that more than 4.5 million English-language learners or limited English-proficient students were enrolled in public schools. In a survey conducted for this period, more than 400 languages spoken by English language learners (ELL) nationwide were identified, with the majority of ELL students speaking Spanish (79%) as their native language, followed by Vietnamese (2.0%), Hmong (1.6%), Cantonese (1.0%), Korean (1.0%), Haitian Creole (.9%), Arabic (.9%), and other (15.4) (Kindler, 2002). In some states, such as Colorado, the growth has been particularly evident, with the number of residents who speak a language other than English growing by 88.4% to 604,019 in 2000 alone (United States Census Bureau, 2003d).

In developing norms for a measure such as the WISC or WAIS, it is common practice to exclude individuals from the standardization sample who are not proficient in the English language, although those who speak English as a second language may be included. These children indeed represent a proportion of US schoolchildren who are ELLs. Realistically, however, little is known about the language abilities of these learners and the degree to which they are bilingual. It is uncommon to find children screened or otherwise assessed to verify reported linguistic proficiency or competency before inclusion in standardization. Even in settings where children are assessed for their fluency or language competencies before testing, such as in clinical or school settings, there is little consistency in method, measure, or specific criteria for a determination of "fluent" or "proficient." Establishing proficiency in English presents considerable challenges, a problem encountered by all clinicians. Often examiners are dependent on the report of the child, parents, or teacher for an estimate of linguistic ability.

Those investigating second language acquisition have noted that academic English proficiency takes years longer to acquire than the simple ability to use English for social purposes, a fact that presents additional complexities. Cummins (1979, 1989) was one of the first to write of the dangers in interpreting control over the surface structures of a language as indicative of sufficiently developed academic language skills. He initially distinguished between "surface fluency" (basic interpersonal communication skills or BICS) and more cognitively and academically related aspects of language proficiency (CALP). In an effort to move away from the oversimplification of his theory into "communicative" versus "cognitive" proficiency, he later attempted to couch his theory in terms of con-textualized language and decontextualized language experiences, and cognitive demand. He argued that in face-to-face verbal communication, the meaning of the communication is supported by contextual cues (e.g., facial expression, gestures, and intonation), where this is rarely the case in academic uses of a language (e.g., reading a text). He described intellectual test situations as context reduced, cognitively demanding circumstances, requiring significant language proficiency in excess of that utilized in basic social communication. In general, those tests that show fewer group differences may be less "culturally biased" in the sense that they are less cognitively demanding and more context independent, or embedded.

Cummins' (1981a, 1981b) work and that of others demonstrated that it is not until the later grades of elementary school that students acquiring English approach grade norms of native English speakers. In his studies in both the United States and Canada, he found that those arriving after the age of 6 years needed 5–7 years on average to approach grade norms in academic-related aspects of English proficiency. These findings were echoed by Ramirez et al. (1991), who studied three different bilingual programs (immersion strategy, early-exit, and late-exit), which varied only on the amount of L1 (first language) instruction. While after 2 years of education (K–1) students appeared to be doing equally well in the three programs, differences began to emerge by the end of grade 3. Students in the immersion programs who received no L1 instruction were declining in performance (normal curve equivalents, NCE). In early exit programs, where children received limited L1 support in grades K through 2, slight gains in NCEs relative to the norm in English reading and slight declines in English math were observed (Ramirez et al., 1991). Most striking were the findings that students in the late exit programs who received L1 support for grades K through 6 were, by sixth grade, at the 51st NCE in English math and at the 45th NCE in English reading. In a review of other studies of long-term language-minority student data on academic achievement, Collier (1992) concluded that the investigations repeatedly demonstrated "... the greater the amount of L1 instructional support for language-minority students, combined with balanced L2 support, the higher they are able to achieve academically in L2 in each succeeding academic year, in comparison to matched groups being schooled monolingually in L2" (p. 205).

It seems logical, then, to conclude that children acquiring skills in English may not possess sufficient proficiency to effectively perform on the more demanding, context-reduced IQ tests. But what about examinees who appear to be fluent and proficient? A study of non-native English-speaking adults who participated in the WAIS-III standardization illustrates the concerns and challenges of determining when an examinee possesses sufficient proficiency for English language intellectual assessment.

A sample of 151 adult examinees was selected for study inclusion, all of whom reported that they were born outside of the United States. In addition, all individuals reported that they were fluent in English, a criterion corroborated by the standardization test examiner based on observation of the examinees' conversation before and during the testing session. The individuals represented 37 countries of origin, with Mexico and Cuba representing two-thirds of the sample. Three variables, obtained from a demographic questionnaire completed by all study participants, served as proxies for acculturation: (1) a "language preference" variable, derived by weighting reported language preference for speaking, thinking, reading, and writing in English and in the additional spoken language; (2) a variable "US experience," calculated by dividing the number of years residing in the United States by the total age of the examinee, and (3) a variable "US education," calculated by dividing the number of years educated in the United States by the total number of years of education attained by the examinee. For additional detail, see Harris et al. (2003). The relationship of these variables to performance on the Wechsler Adult Intelligence Scale III and Wechsler Memory Scale III factor scores was analyzed. All of the variables were significant predictors of performance on the various factor scores, with the variable "language preference" predicting performance on the Verbal Comprehension, Perceptual Organization, Processing Speed, and Visual Memory (using the Visual Reproduction subtest) indices. While language preference is not synonymous with language proficiency, clearly the examinee's self-reported preferred language is a key variable for planning assessment strategies and for other decision making, such as inclusion in normative studies.

Children who are ELLs, even if well on their way to becoming expressive bilinguals, do not necessarily have the foundational skills for academic success in spite of possessing the necessary oral and auditory skills for social communicative competence. Furthermore, it has been noted that children who are ELLs have limited access to courses such as science and mathematics compared with other English-speaking students (Minicucci & Olsen, 1992) and may be placed into curricula that have less challenging course content (Oakes, 1990). What are the implications of this for demonstrating academic knowledge as assessed by standardized academic or intelligence tests? At least for some proportion of Hispanic children, they are lagging in learning as a function of their status as ELLs and the fact that they may not be learning the same academic content as their peers.

Presumably, an adequate level of linguistic competence and proficiency has been achieved by all the ELLs included in a standardization sample. As already noted, however, the degree of proficiency can vary widely among individuals with minority group status, which is not the case for the vast majority of nonminority white examinees. In a sample of standardization participants who agreed to complete the "WISC-IV Home Environment Questionnaire," 6% of children were identified as speaking a native language other than English. Of the Hispanic standardization participants who responded to the survey, 34% indicated that English was not the child's native language and nearly all endorsed Spanish as the native tongue. Within various ethnic groups represented in the standardization sample, not only is there heterogeneity of English receptive and expressive abilities, but the very concept of bilingualism signifies more than a simple characterization of two languages for these children.

To further examine the possible influence of English-language acquisition on performance, we studied a group of WISC-IV standardization participants, matched on age, parental education level, and gender. However, the examinees selected for study differed along one important language variable, gleaned from a comprehensive family survey administered to WISC-IV examinees. One group, the white non-Hispanic sample was composed of monolingual English speakers. A second group of Hispanic children were selected who indicated that they spoke English as their native language. A third group of Hispanic children indicated that they spoke Spanish as their native language. Table 11.6 illustrates the impact of controlling for language when comparing index score performances across the three groups.

The "typical" finding of reduced performance, particularly in verbal indices, for Hispanic examinees is now evident only in the group of Hispanic children who speak Spanish as their native language. In fact, although the sample is small, the native English-speaking Hispanic children surpass the nonminority examinees in their PSI. Such findings are a powerful illustration of the impact of socioeconomic and linguistic variables on performance. What initially appeared to be a large gap between Hispanic and non-Hispanic white students now appears to be a minimal difference. This finding is not to be construed in any way as indicative of liabilities associated with retaining the native language, but rather indicative of the challenges test developers and clinicians must address in determining when a suitable level of proficiency has been reached for testing in English. Indeed, scientifically rigorous studies of bilingualism conducted in the later half of the 20th century in adults and children suggest that bilingualism is associated with a number of advantages in cognition (Bialystok, 1988; Bialystok & Cummins, 1991; Galloway, 1982; Mohanty 1990; Ricciardelli, 1992a, 1992b). These advantages may persist into adulthood and old age. A recent study concluded that the lifelong experience of managing two languages attenuates the typical age-related decline in the efficiency of inhibitory processing, and reduced "working memory costs" in bilingual adults (Bialystok, Craik, Klein, & Viswanathan, 2004).

TABLE 11.6   Matched Sample Mean WISC-IV Scores of Spanish Versus English-Speaking Hispanic and White Non-Hispanic English-Speaking Children (Equated for Age, Gender, and Parental Education Level)

IQ/index score	Hispanic–Spanish	Hispanic–English	Non-Hispanic white
FSIQ	93.00 (10.95)	96.58 (12.87)	94.12 (15.58)
VCI	92.31 (9.74)	96.19 (13.02)	94.31 (12.06)
PRI	94.50 (12.24)	97.92 (11.54)	96.69 (15.73)
WMI	93.65 (13.07)	96.27 (15.20)	97.42 (15.04)
PSI	98.31 (11.47)	98.27 (13.84)	91.58 (14.23)

$n = 78$.

WISC-IV SPANISH

A review of the assessment considerations with Hispanic children would be incomplete without mention of the WISC-IV Spanish.

The WISC-IV Spanish is a translation and adaptation of the WISC–IV for use with Spanish-speaking children ages 6 years 0 months through 16 years 11 months. The test was developed to meet the needs of Spanish-speaking children learning English as a second language, many of whom are recent immigrants and in the process of acculturating to the United States The structure and content of the WISC-IV Spanish parallels the WISC-IV and reflects the advances in theory and practice of cognitive assessment in children that were incorporated into the WISC IV. Like the WISC IV, the Spanish version yields five composite scores, FSIQ, VCI, PRI, WMI, and PSI. The WISC-IV Spanish is comprised of core and supplemental subtests but does not contain the Word Reasoning subtest found in the WISC IV due to difficulties with item translation. One optional subtest, Coding Copy is included for use as a process score in conjunction with coding (Form B) to provide additional information concerning the contribution of graphomotor speed to coding performance.

Stimuli for the Perceptual Reasoning and Processing Speed subtests were maintained from WISC IV. Verbal subtests were modified and new items created based upon expert reviewer recommendations and bias analyses. Some verbal items are presented with two equivalent words to address variability within the Spanish language (e.g., "Umbrella" was translated as "Sombrilla/Paraguas"). Other modifications were made to Working Memory subtests. For example, because some letters (e.g., "v" have different names in various Spanish-speaking cultures, the sequences were modified to avoid use of those letters. Modifications were made to objects in the Arithmetic subtest due to the lack of appropriate translation equivalents for some words and also to make the subtest more culture-appropriate (e.g., including proper names in Spanish). Item order within some subtests was changed based on item difficulty analyses. While stimulus items are administered in Spanish, the examinee may respond and receive credit for answers in either language. Further, additional queries have been introduced in WISC-IV Spanish (e.g., Si sabes la respuesta en inglés, dímela [If you know the answer in English, say it to me.]) to provide the child the maximal opportunity to demonstrate his or her knowledge. For example, a child who is learning English as a second language may know the correct response in English but may be unable to respond in Spanish.

A noted strength of the Spanish WISC-IV is the standard score equivalence of the English and Spanish versions (Braden & Iribarren, 2007). This approach provides continuity in measurement tools, particularly for repeat assessment when a child initially assessed in Spanish might later be more appropriately assessed with the English version after acquiring cognitive language proficiency. US population percentile ranks are provided, which help characterize performance relative to the WISC-IV US standardization sample and represent the child's performance in relation to children who are fluent in English. In addition, adjusted percentile ranks are provided to enable comparison of the child to other

Spanish-speaking children in the US who are similar in terms of educational experience in the US and parental education level.

To illustrate the ways in which WISC-IV Spanish might guide intervention, the following brief case is presented.

The following two cases illustrate the ways in which WISC IV Spanish (Case 1) and WISC IV (Case 2) might guide intervention.

CASE 1

RV is a 10.5-year-old Spanish-speaking child, who arrived in the United States from Sonora, Mexico 3 months prior to referral. She had completed 5 years of education in a public school in Mexico, and was described as an average student by her parents, both of whom had completed high school. RV was referred for assessment due to concerns that she was not participating in class and appeared to have difficulty following directions and instructions. She was attending a transitional bilingual program, although her parents reported that her experiences with the English language had been minimal prior to immigration to the United States. She appeared to be developing friends among both English-speaking and Spanish-speaking peers. Table 11.7 summaries RV's scores.

TABLE 11.7   WISC IV Spanish Scores and Percentile Ranks.

Scale	Sum of scaled scores	Composite scores	95% Confidence interval	Percentile rank US population	Percentile rank method A
Verbal Comprehension	29	VCI 98	91–105	45	68
Perceptual Reasoning	27	PRI 94	87–102	34	61
Working Memory	14	WMI 83	77–93	13	19
Processing Speed	19	PSI 97	87–108	42	69
Full Scale	89	FSIQ 91	86–96	27	57

RV's composite scores were converted to US population percentile ranks. With the exception of the Working Memory percentile of 13, all of the index scores and the FSIQ fall within one standard deviation of the mean. The percentile rank of 13 is one that raised some initial concern on the part of the examiner. In this case, the examiner proceeded to utilize the adjusted percentile ranks to more closely examine the child's performance in relation to other Spanish speaking children of similar background and experience. The adjusted percentiles were derived by using the parent education levels (PEL) of the two parents (high school for each parent = PEL 3) and US educational experience of the child (0 years completed in the United States = A) which yielded a classification category of II (see Chapter 2, Wechsler, 2005). By using the Adjusted Percentile Rank tables in Appendix C of the WISC-IV Spanish Manual, the classification category of II yielded an adjusted percentile rank of 19 for WMI. While overall, the examinee appears to be doing relatively well for a child who is new to the US educational system and who has high school educated parents, the WM score is one that stands apart from the other scores. Performances on WMI subtests were as follows: Digit Span = 8, Letter-Number Sequencing = 6, and Arithmetic (supplemental) = 6.

A deeper review of RV's adjusted percentile ranks indicates that she is performing at a higher level when compared to peers who are similar in background than when compared to US peers of the same age. However, this difference is almost negligible in the Working Memory domain (13 US percentile rank compared to 19 adjusted). These results suggest that RV's deficits in this area may be a "true" disability and not one related to language acquisition, proficiency, or other cultural factors (Table 11.8).

Discrepancy analysis provided additional information for evaluating this child's Working Memory performance. The lower WMI compared to VCI occurred in only 6.0% of the overall reliability sample and in only 4.9% of the students with similar background and experience as RV (Classification category II) (Table 11.8).

TABLE 11.8

Index pair	SS 1	SS 2	Difference	Critical value (.05)	Significant Difference	Overall base rate	Adjusted base rate
VCI–PRI	98	94	4	10.17	N		
VCI–WMI	98	83	15	10.60	Y	6.0	4.9
VCI–PSI	98	97	1	14.09	N		
PRI–WMI	94	83	11	10.60	Y	17	16
PRI–PSI	94	97	−3	14.09	N		
WMI–PSI	83	97	−14	14.40	N		

As a result of these findings, the examiner referred this child for additional assessment of Working Memory and sought to evaluate her academic performance in reading and math. Indeed, RV performed well below grade level in reading comprehension (67 in the Basic Reading Skills cluster of the Batería III), although she fared slightly better in math (79 in Math Calculation). Given these findings, the following interventions were initiated in her school programming, based in part on the recommendations provided by Yates and Ortiz (2004).

Place RV in a bilingual program at a nearby school
Review key words and concepts in Spanish (RV's native language) prior to each lesson
Break down instructions and give them one by one
Repeat instructions and ask RV to say them back to the teacher
Provide visual cues and present information in a variety of sensory modalities

Peer tutoring
Pursue and facilitate continued parent involvement
Ensure RV's teachers have been trained on issues related to cultural
    differences and second language acquisition processes, and provide
    additional modifications based on RV's individual needs

CASE 2

The use of the WISC-IV is illustrated within the context of a neuropsychological evaluation of a Hispanic child. The use of the WISC-IV in this context permits the elucidation of a broad array of issues, such as longitudinal assessment, and recommendations for educational programming and rehabilitation.

Reason for Referral

Jamie is a 12-year-old, right-handed, first-generation, bilingual (Spanish-English), Mexican-American male with a history of a right temporal lobe astrocytoma, which was partially resected 26 months prior to the evaluation. He was referred by his neuro-oncologist to assess his current level of functioning, to identify areas of cognitive strengths and weaknesses, and to assist with therapeutic and educational programming.

Jamie was first seen for medical evaluation following a seizure which occurred seven months prior to surgery. At that time, he was taken to a local hospital where he had a computed tomography (CT) scan, followed by magnetic resonance imaging (MRI), which revealed a 1.5 cm by 1.5 cm right temporal lobe tumor. He was placed immediately on oxcarbazepine (Trileptal) with a plan to acquire serial MRIs to monitor what was thought to be a slow growing tumor. However, some months later, Jamie had another seizure and increasingly experienced episodes of vomiting. At that time, an MRI was obtained that showed the tumor had increased in size and involved the insula, external capsule, caudate, thalamus, subcallosum, anterior temporal lobe, and hippocampus. He then underwent surgery for resection of the tumor, followed by radiation and chemotherapy.

Background information

The mother reported that her pregnancy with Jamie was medically uneventful and she received consistent prenatal care. Jamie was born at 38 weeks gestation and weighed 8 pounds, 7 ounces. He achieved all developmental milestones and did not have any history of significant illnesses, head injury, or loss of consciousness.

Before entering elementary school, Jamie was a monolingual Spanish speaker. He conversed with his mother, grandparents, and bilingual father in Spanish. Upon entering school and for the subsequent two years, he received 4 hours of English as a second language (ESL) instruction per day with regular educational instruction in math. Although Jamie continued to speak primarily Spanish with his mother and grandparents, he spoke both Spanish and English with his father, and most of his peers were English speakers. His parents reported that he rapidly gained expressive language competencies in English, and at the time of assessment, they considered him to be bilingual.

At the time Jamie's tumor was diagnosed, he was attending an eminent private middle school. He repeated the sixth grade as a result of school absences associated with his medical condition, but his teachers indicated that his academic progress was not a major concern. Before his illness, he obtained excellent grades (A-Bs). Following surgery and treatment, he received home schooling and then returned to school. At the time of the evaluation he was attending sixth grade in public school. He was unlabeled and receiving regular education services with after-school assistance and minor laboratory support, and receiving Bs without any curriculum modifications. Jamie reported that he had many friends (bilingual and monolingual English speakers) and was involved in Boy Scouts. Jamie reported that his mood was typically happy, and that while he had normal appetite, he continued to occasionally experience mild nausea. His mother acknowledged that he was coping well with his medical condition and maintained a positive outlook.

Prior assessments

Jamie underwent two psychological evaluations prior to the current assessment. He was administered the WISC-III before his enrollment in the private middle school. That evaluation revealed an overall performance in the very superior range across all IQ and Index scores (IQ = 132–139). He was administered the WISC-III again 3 months after his surgery (approximately 3 years from the initial WISC III evaluation) where he obtained IQ and index scores in the low average range (80s), with the exception of Freedom from Distractibility and Processing Speed indices on which he obtained scores in the borderline (70s) and deficient (60s) range, respectively.

Behavioral observations

For the current evaluation, Jamie was evaluated over two sessions. He was appropriately dressed and groomed during both assessment sessions. He demonstrated a broad range of affect. He interacted well with the examiner and rapport was easily established. He was mildly active and somewhat fidgety throughout the evaluation, although he responded well to redirection. He informed the examiner that he preferred English for "schoolwork and tests," but acknowledged that he spoke Spanish daily, particularly with his mother, and that he was comfortable with both languages. His speech was fluent in both languages. He appeared to put forth excellent effort on all tests administered, and results were considered valid.

CURRENT ASSESSMENT

INTELLECT

A summary of test data is shown in Table 11.9. His scores, as assessed by the *Wechsler Intelligence Scale for Children – Fourth Edition* (WISC-IV), were within the low average to very superior range. Jamie obtained an FSIQ score of 121, which placed his performance within the superior range (92nd percentile). With a 95% confidence interval, his score would fall between 116 and 125. His VCI score of 136 fell in the very superior range (99th percentile) and his PRI of 125 (95th percentile) fell in the superior range. In contrast, the WMI score (107) (68th percentile) and PSI score (85) (16th percentile) were in the average and low average range, respectively. The discrepancy between these two index scores and his VCI score and PRI score was clinically significant. An examination of base rates indicated that such discrepancies occurred only in a small percentage of the children comprising the WISC-IV standardization sample. Thus, his verbal comprehension and perceptual reasoning skills appear to represent relative strengths when compared to his working memory and his processing speed skills. He appears to have made significant gains since his evaluation 3 months after the surgery, and a select number of his scores have either returned to or are near baseline levels when compared to his scores from the examination conducted before entering middle school. Although it is not possible to directly compare WISC-III and WISC-IV performances due to changes in the composition of the subtests, the WISC-IV scores appear to reflect improvements in function associated with resolution of Jamie's illness and any treatment side effects.

TABLE 11.9   Case Study: Neuropsychological Test Scores

Wechsler Intelligence Scale for Children – Fourth Edition (WISC IV)

	Index and IQ score
Verbal Comprehension Index (VCI)	136
Perceptual Reasoning Index (PRI)	125
Working Memory Index (WMI)	107
Processing Speed Index (PSI)	85
Full Scale Intelligence Quotient (FSIQ)	121 (116–125)
VCI	**Scaled score**
Similarities	16
Vocabulary	17
Comprehension	15
PRI	
Block Design	16
Picture Concepts	15
Matrix Reasoning	11
WMI	
Digit Span	12
Letter–Number Sequence	11

(*continues*)

TABLE 11.9 *(continued)*

PSI	Scaled score
Coding	7
Symbol Search	8

California Verbal Learning Test – Children's Version (CVLT-C)

	Raw	*T*-score
List A 1–5 Trials Free Recall	52	53
		Standard score
List A Trial 1 Free Recall	6	−0.5
List A Trial 5 Free Recall	13	0.5
List B Free Recall	5	−0.5
List A Short Delay Free Recall	10	0.0
List A Short Delay Cued Recall	11	0.0
List A Long Delay Free Recall	11	0.0
List A Long Delay Cued Recall	12	0.5
Recognition Hits	14	0.0
Discriminability	97.78	0.5
False positives	0	−0.5

Children's Memory Scale (CMS)

	Scaled score
Faces – Immediate	3
Faces – Delayed	7
Stories – Immediate	11
Stories – Delayed	11
Stories – Recognition	11

Rey-Osterrieth Complex Figure Test (RCFT)

	Raw score	Percentile	*Z*-score
Delay	14	8	−1.44
Copy	34	69	0.57

Wechsler Individual Achievement Test – Second Edition (WIAT-II)

	Standard score
Word Reading	123
Numerical Operations	124
Spelling	115

Clinical Evaluation of Language Fundamentals – Fourth Edition (CELF-4)

	Standard score
Concepts and Directions	13
Recalling Sentences	12

(continues)

TABLE 11.9 (*continued*)

Boston Naming Test (BNT)	Raw score	Z-score
Total	55	1.63
Grooved Pegboard Test (GPT)	**Raw score**	**Z-score**
Dominant	**62**	**0.66**
Non-Dominant	**117**	**−1.01**
Finger Tapping Test (FTT)	**Raw score**	**Z-score**
Dominant	42.2	0.19
Non-Dominant	30.8	−1.13

Reitan-Kløve Sensory–Perceptual Examination

	Errors
Finger Recognition	0
Finger-Tip Number Writing	0

Test of Visual–Perceptual Skills (nonmotor) (TVPS)

	Scaled score
Visual Memory	14
Visual Sequential Memory	10

Developmental Test of Visual–Motor Integration (VMI)

	Standard score
Total	128

Judgment of Line Orientation Test (JLO)

	Raw score	Z-score
Total	28	0.87

Delis-Kaplan Executive Function System (D-KEFS)

	Scaled score
Trails – scan	7
Trails – number	11
Trails – letter	13
Trails – switch	12
Trails – motor	13
Verbal fluency – letter	14
Verbal fluency – category	11
Verbal fluency – switch	15

(*continues*)

TABLE 11.9   (*continued*)

Wisconsin Card Sorting Test (WCST)

	Raw score	*T*-score
Total Error	15	61
% Error	18	59
Perseverative Responses	6	65
% Perseverative Responses	7	65
Perseverative Errors	6	65
% Perseverative Errors	7	64
Nonperseverative Errors	9	56
% Nonperseverative Errors	11	53
% Conceptual Level Responses	79	60

	Raw score	Percentile
Categories Completed	6	>16
Trials to complete Ist Category	11	>16
Set Failure	0	>16
Learning to Learn	0	>16

Behavior Rating Inventory of Executive Function (BRIEF)

(Parent)	*T*-score
Inhibit	50
Shift	42
Emotional Control	48
Initiate	44
Working Memory	47
Plan/Organize	53
Organization of materials	55
Monitor	60
BRI	50
MI	52
GEC	51

Behavioral Assessment Scale for Children (BASC)

(Parent)	*T*-score
Hyperactivity	46
Aggression	45
Conduct	47
Anxiety	56
Depression	50
Somatization	58
Atypicality	45

(*continues*)

TABLE 11.9 *(continued)*

	T-score
Withdrawal	51
Attention	43
Social Skills	57
Leadership	58
Externalizing Problems	45
Internalizing Problems	56
BSI	47
Adaptive	58

BASC (self)

	T-score
Attitude to School	52
Attitude to Teachers	40
Sensation Seeking	49
Atypicality	47
Locus of Control	56
Somatization	65
Social Stress	52
Anxiety	57
Depression	49
Sense of Inadequacy	45
Parent Relations	57
Interpersonal Problems	51
Self-Esteem	46
Self-Reliance	52
School Maladjustment	46
Clinical Maladjustment	57
Personal adjustment	52
ESI	51

Children's Depression Inventory (CDI)

	T-score
Total	52

With regard to specific subtests, his scores varied from the very superior range on measures of word knowledge (Vocabulary), verbal abstraction (Similarities), and "conventional standards of behavior" (Comprehension) to the low average range on subtests assessing attention, speed of information processing, and visual–motor skills (e.g., Coding, Symbol Search). From a qualitative stand-point, his scores on the latter measures were observed to be the result of a slow processing posture without errors. All other subtests fell in the high average to average range.

Memory and Learning

Memory assessment consisted of measures of verbal and visual memory, evaluating both rote and contextual components of this domain. On a measure of rote verbal memory (California Verbal Learning Test – Children's Version; CVLT – C), Jamie was able to remember detailed new information even after a delay with interspersed distracting information. Repeated exposure to the information assisted his recall. His score on a test of contextual verbal memory (Children's Memory Scale, Stories; CMS), requiring recall and recognition of stories, revealed performance within normal limits on the immediate and delayed recall portions of the test. Recognition memory on this task also fell within normal limits. In contrast, his performance on measures of visual memory revealed moderate variability. For instance, his visual sequential memory and visual memory on the Test of Visual–Perceptual Skills (TVPS) fell in the average and above average range, respectively. However, he experienced much more difficulty while recalling a complex geometric figure (Rey-Osterrieth Complex Figure Test; RCFT) and remembering pictures of faces on the CMS (Faces) in which his scores fell in the borderline range of functioning. The latter performance appeared to be a problem with encoding as his delayed recall was better than immediate recall. The CMS and RCFT are different than the TVPS in that they require the individual to encode larger and more complex amounts of information before recalling the information. In addition, far more data organization is required in the two procedures relative to the TVPS.

Language Functions

Jamie did not exhibit speech difficulties in any area of functioning informally assessed. Likewise, formal language assessment revealed normal functioning in receptive and expressive language skills. On a measure of emergent confrontation object naming (Boston Naming Test; BNT) he scored within normal limits (above average). Similarly, his scores on subtests assessing the ability to follow increasingly complex directions (Clinical Evaluation of Language Fundamentals – Fourth Edition; CELF-4, Concepts and Directions), sentence repetition (CELF-4, Recalling Sentences), and controlled word generation (Delis-Kaplan Executive Function System; DKEFS, Verbal Fluency) were all within normal limits.

Visual Processing and Visual–Motor Skills

On measures assessing visual processing and visual–motor skills, all scores fell within the expected range. He scored within the upper end of the average range on a measure assessing his ability to copy a complex geometric design (RCFT). On a simpler visual–motor task requiring that he copy geometric designs of increasing complexity, he scored in the superior range (Developmental Test of

Visual–Motor Integration; VMI). He obtained a score within normal limits on a measure assessing visual processing without a motor component which required that he determine the angular distance between pairs of lines (Judgment of Line Orientation Test; JLO).

Sensory–Perceptual and Motor Skills

Bilateral sensory–perceptual and dominant (right) hand fine motor skills were within normal limits. An area where subtle weaknesses were found on the evaluation was fine motor speed in the nondominant (left) hand (Grooved Pegboard Test, GPT; Finger Tapping Test, FTT). On both fine motor measures administered, his scores fell within the borderline range with his nondominant hand. More important, a significant raw score lateralizing difference emerged between his dominant and nondominant hand.

Executive Skills

Procedures assessing executive functions (D-KEFS) revealed a subtle weakness confined to visual scanning difficulties, which may very well represent fluctuations in attention. Inspection of the other test results in this domain revealed scores within the expected range. For example, Jamie was able to effectively develop and implement problem-solving strategies on the Wisconsin Card Sorting Test (WCST). He was also able to adequately plan, organize, and integrate complex visual information (RCFT, Copy). Evaluation of executive functioning skills in daily life based on parental report was measured using the Behavior Rating Inventory of Executive Function (BRIEF). No problems were identified with regard to behavioral regulation or metacognitive awareness.

Academic Achievement Screening

Academic achievement was briefly screened in the areas of reading, mathematics, and spelling skills using the *Wechsler Individual Achievement Test – Second Edition* (WIAT-II). His word reading and mathematical computational skills were in the superior range, whereas his spelling skills fell in the high-average range. His academic scores were commensurate with his chronological age, current grade placement, and overall intellectual scores. Close scrutiny of his spelling score revealed that the majority of his difficulties were associated with simple misspellings, most likely the result of inattention. Screening in Spanish using the Woodcock-Johnson Pruebas de Aprovechamiento-Revisada revealed performance in the average range. These scores suggested proficiency in Spanish consistent with his spoken abilities and parental report regarding competency in the language.

Behavioral and Emotional Functioning

With regard to behavioral and emotional indicators, Jamie was asked to complete the Behavior Assessment System for Children-Self Report (BASC) to assess his coping, adjustment, and behavior. He produced a valid and consistent profile, with only mild elevation on the somatization scale, which is consistent with his medical presentation. His mother also completed the BASC and did not report any concerns or problems. On the Children's Depression Inventory (CDI), Jamie obtained a score well within normal limits.

Summary, Conclusions, and Recommendations

Jamie was diagnosed with a right temporal lobe anaplastic astrocytoma and underwent partial resection of the tumor with significant success. Jamie and his mother did not report acute changes in his behavior, cognition, or personality. He was repeating the sixth grade at the time of assessment but had not received formal (e.g., individualized education plan (IEP)) special education.

Results of the neuropsychological evaluation revealed that the majority of Jamie's cognitive skills fell in the average to superior range. The only relative weaknesses that were identified in the evaluation included difficulties related to remembering complex visual information, visual scanning, and fine motor speed in the nondominant (left) hand. These subtle inefficiencies or weaknesses are consistent with the typology and nature of his medical condition (excised tumor from the right temporal lobe). Aside from the possible effects of his current medication on memory functions, his relatively lower scores on indices of Processing Speed and Working Memory could be partially attributed to effects of his tumor, the subsequent chemotherapy and radiation therapy, and their impact on overall processing speed. A similar conclusion may be reached related to his circumscribed delays in fine motor skills of his nondominant (left) hand. Possible mild side effects of his antiseizure medication regimen may also partially explain his relative weaknesses in processing speed.

Jamie's academic curriculum appears to be appropriate with some accommodations, and he has been making suitable progress despite his complex medical and academic history and the rigorous nature of his educational programming in a highly demanding public school. However, given his medical condition and treatment, including radiation, chemotherapy, and the use of antiseizure medication, he is at risk for possible cognitive difficulties in the future, particularly as demands in school increase. Typically, the impact of radiation on cognitive functioning is not identified until 12–24 months after treatment. Therefore, it will be important to continue to monitor Jamie's academic progress, as well as cognitive and emotional functioning.

With regard to specific school recommendations, given the subtle and overt findings that emerged during the course of this evaluation, it is important to keep in mind several factors when working with Jamie, all of which were discussed with school officials. For instance, his relative weaknesses in information processing led to structural classroom recommendations, including seating arrangement (i.e., in front of the classroom next to his teacher), work environment (e.g., smaller work groups, smaller teacher-to-student ratio, use of a teacher's aid), and adjusting the quantity of work (e.g., use of criterion-based learning with reduction in quantity of work). School officials also were reminded of the importance of providing him with extra time (or untimed) to complete hands-on tasks or demanding academic tasks which require significant sustained attention and fine motor skills. It was also noted that visual information will need to be kept clear and organized so as to avoid a lot of visual scanning, which may be difficult for him. His scores on learning and memory were used to underscore the importance of repeated exposure to new information, in particular visual information. It was also recommended that previous lessons be reviewed before exposing the child to new material. In addition, the use of memorization strategies, including verbal and visual mnemonics, were recommended for this child. Other school recommendations included requesting the school to label the child under the Other Health Impaired label as a result of his medical condition, which was accomplished through attendance at his IEP meeting. The results from the WISC-IV index scores were used in that meeting to substantiate claims that the child would benefit from programming accommodations as a result of his relative weaknesses in information processing speed and working memory. Ongoing involvement in structured age-appropriate social activities was noted to be important, including continued extracurricular activities in school and in the home.

CASE SUMMARY

This case underscores several important practice issues. First and foremost, the approach taken with this patient is consistent with ethical standards and practice guidelines set forth by the APA (APA 1990; 2002) and the Standards for Educational and Psychological Testing (AERA et al., 1999). The language and choice of assessment measures were guided by both the examinee's language preference and the examinee's educational history as a non-native English speaker. Although this child is "Hispanic," he is unique with respect to acculturation, language, immigration, and SES. In fact, he does not "fit" the panethnic "Hispanic" or the ethnocultural label "Mexican–American," illustrating the lack of specificity and inadequacy of such constructs. The child has maintained his native language and culture, but has also assimilated US culture. It appears that this child is truly bilingual beyond surface fluency. His competencies in both languages were observed, screened, and corroborated by his parents. While he may have been effectively assessed in either language, he is most appropriate for evaluation in English as a result of his formal educational experiences and bicultural background. Had there been concerns about either his established level of English proficiency or a possible language impairment, additional testing in Spanish (e.g., WISC-IV Spanish, CELF-3 Spanish) would be recommended. Because this child never immigrated, a number of potential acute or chronic stressors associated with the process of immigration that would be capable of influencing test performance are not applicable to this child (e.g., anxiety, depression, posttraumatic stress disorder). Clearly all these factors could have had significant implications for test selection and the validity of the inferences derived from the WISC-IV and other tests. Finally, the educational and socioeconomic background of the parents varies from average Census and other governmental survey statistics for individuals of Mexican origin. The standardization sample from the WISC-IV is appropriately representative of the child's current demographic background and is suitable for score interpretation.

CONCLUSION

When one considers the multitude of variables masked by ethnic umbrella terms, and particularly the variability of cultures and language competencies among diverse individuals, it is actually surprising that WISC score differences and discrepancies traditionally identified among and within groups are not more dramatic. Index score differences in the WISC-IV between Hispanic and white non-Hispanic children were seen to narrow substantially when children were matched on relevant demographic or contextual variables. Score differences altogether disappeared when the native languages of Hispanic children were controlled in our small study.

Taking into consideration the issues addressed in this chapter, it is critical that examiners understand the background and environmental context of each individual, and not simply rely on general group membership to determine test selection, interpretation, and intervention practices (Harris et al., 2001; Weiss et al., 2006). Practitioners must fully appreciate the composition of the normative sample used for comparison and appreciate the potential inherent limitations of the nomothetic approach for interpretation of individual performance. For those children who are relative newcomers to a country, such as those who have 5 years or less experience within the educational system of the new host country, there is a good likelihood that linguistic competencies necessary to optimally demonstrate intellectual abilities are not fully developed. In such cases, it may still be informative to assess the child in English with the caveat that the test may be measuring language skills as much as, or more so, than cognitive abilities, rendering the scores a crude approximation. True abilities may consequently be underestimated. For those children assessed in English, reevaluation should proceed on a more frequent basis to capture cognitive gains associated with the rapid development of English-language competencies. Whenever possible, children should, at the very least, have the opportunity to respond to test stimuli in either the primary or secondary language, unless specific English-language abilities must be quantified and described.

The WISC-IV Spanish (Wechsler, 2005) may be a more suitable alternative in many cases where a child speaks English as a second language. Even with the availability of the WISC-IV Spanish, criteria or models for selecting the "right" language version for assessment are just beginning to be explored. It may indeed be best practice to utilize both language versions of the WISC-IV for VC and WM subtests. "Testing the limits" by administering missed or partial credit items in the second language after completing standard testing in the preferred language may be one such approach. However, the potential alteration of item difficulty as a result of translation, variability in item length as a function of specific language properties, lack of standardized equivalent items, and the potential for practice effects or for fatigue all may introduce error and all may weaken the conclusions derived from such a practice.

Even for standardization samples that include Hispanics or other ethnic groups representative of the US population, it is important to consider the proportion of cases within that sample. Because individuals who originate from Mexico account for 52.8% of the US Hispanic population, they likely represent the largest proportion of Hispanics in most standardization samples. Given the lower average educational attainment for individuals of Mexican nationality residing within the United States, the average obtained scores of "Hispanics" in a given normative sample may consequently be depressed. For tests that publish norms specific to ethnic groups or broad ethnodemographic (e.g., African American or Hispanic) adjustments, supplemental tables may be necessary to sufficiently understand the performance of a child from a specific background and to avoid errors in test interpretation.

The rich diversity of the highly mobile and migratory world of the 21st century is difficult to capture in psychological measures designed to assess the intellectual and cognitive abilities of individuals. Ethnic umbrella categories, such as "white" or "Hispanic" are typically used as a matter of convenience to organize test data both for test developers and test users. Unfortunately, these broad terms are often viewed as representing homogeneities and consistencies among individuals that will somehow ensure the integrity of data collection, interpretation, and subsequent interventions. Failure to appreciate the true variability within ethnic groupings may constrain not only the ability to appropriately select and utilize measures, but also interfere with the practitioner's own success in diagnostic decision making and the development of appropriate treatment interventions. For generations, the Wechsler scales and their adaptations have been reliable and valid tools for the assessment of intellectual abilities. Each revision has reflected the most current advances in cognitive and neuropsychological assessment and has validated its utility. The continued success of the WISC-IV with culturally diverse children will depend on the combined efforts of both its developers and users to incorporate the advances in society's own evolution to understand and embrace the diversity among the population of schoolchildren for whom the measure was developed.

ACKNOWLEDGMENTS

The authors extend their gratitude to Alejandrina Guzmán Bonilla, Susan Kongs, and Diana Allensworth for their assistance with manuscript preparation and for their helpful comments on earlier drafts of this chapter. The authors also wish to thank Eric Rolfhus for assistance with data analyses.

REFERENCES

American Educational Research Association, American Psychological Association, & National Council on Measurement in Education (1999). *The Standards for Educational and Psychological Testing*. Washington, DC: American Psychological Association.

American Psychological Association (1990). *Guidelines for Providers of Services to Ethnic, Linguistic, and Culturally Diverse Populations*. Washington, DC: American Psychological Association.

American Psychological Association (2002). Ethical principles of psychologists and code of conduct. *American Psychologist*, 57, 1060–1073.

Ardila, A. (1998). Bilingualism: A neglected and chaotic area. *Aphasiology*, 12, 131–134.

Ardila, A. (2002). Spanish–English bilingualism in the United States of America. In: F. Fabbro (Ed.), *Advances of Neurolinguistics of Bilingualism. Essays in Honor of Michael Paradis* (pp. 49–67). Udine (Italy): Forum.

Braden, J. P. & Iribarren, J.A. (2007). Wechsler Intelligence Scale for Children – Fourth Edition Spanish. San Antonio, TX: Psychological Corporation. *Journal of Psychoeducational Assessment*, 25, 292–299.

Bialystok, E. (1988). Levels of bilingualism and levels of linguistic awareness. *Developmental Psychology*, 24, 560–567.

Bialystok, E., Craik, F. I. M., Klein, R., & Viswanathan, M. (2004). Bilingualism, aging, and cognitive control: Evidence from the Simon task. *Psychology and Aging*, 19, 290–303.

Bialystok, E., & Cummins, J. (1991). Language, cognition, and education of bilingual children. In: B. Ellen (Ed.), *Language Processing in Bilingual Children* (pp. 222–232). Cambridge, UK: Cambridge University Press.

Canadian Heritage (2002). *Canadian heritage: Annual report. Official languages 2000–2001*. Ottawa: Public Works and Government Services.

Centeno, J. G., & Obler, L. K. (2001). Principles of bilingualism. In: M. O. Ponto'n, J. Leo'n, & Carrio'n (Eds.), *Neuropsychology and the Hispanic patient: A Clinical Handbook* (pp. 75–86). Mahwah, NJ: Lawrence Erlbaum Associates, Publishers.

Clinton, A. (2007). Test Review: Wechsler, D. (2005). Wechsler Intelligence Scale for Children – Fourth Edition Spanish. San Antonio, TX: Psychological Corporation. Journal of Psychoeducational Assessment, 25, 285–292.

Collier, V. P. (1992). A synthesis of studies examining long-term language minority student data on academic achievement. *Bilingual Education Research Journal*, 16(1/2), 187–221.

Cummins, J. (1979). Linguistic interdependence and the educational development of bilingual children. *Review of Educational Research*, 49(2), 222–251.

Cummins, J. (1981a). Age on arrival and immigrant second language learning in Canada: A reassessment. *Applied Linguistics*, 2(2), 132–149.

Cummins, J. (1981b). *The Role of Primary Language Development in Promoting Educational Success for Language Minority Students. In California State Department of Education, Schooling and Language Minority Students: A Theoretical Framework*. Los Angeles: Evaluation, Dissemination and Assessment Center.

Cummins, J. (1989). *Empowering Language Minority Students*. Sacramento, CA: California Association for Bilingual Education.

Galloway, L. M. (1982). Bilingualism: Neuropsychological considerations. *Journal of Research and Development in Education*, 15(3), 12–28.

Georgas, J., Van de Vijver, F. J. R., Weiss, L. G., & Saklofske, D. H. (2003a). A cross-cultural analysis of the WISC-III. In: J. Georgas, L. G. Weiss, F. J. R. Van de Vijver, & D. H. Saklofske (Eds.), *Culture and Children's Intelligence: Cross-Cultural Analysis of the WISC-III* (pp. 277–313). San Diego, CA: Academic Press.

Georgas, J., Weiss, L.G., Van de Vijver, F.J.R., Saklofske, D.H. (2003b). Culture and Children's intelligence: Cross-Cultural Analysis of the WISC-III . San Diego: Academic Press.

Grimes, B. F., & Grimes, J. E. (2004). *Ethnologue: Languages of the World* (14th ed.). Dallas, TX: SIL International.

Hakuta, K. (1986). *Mirror of Language*. New York: Basic Books.

Hamers, J. F., & Blanc, M. H. A. (1989). *Bilinguality and Bilingualism*. Cambridge, England: Cambridge University Press.

Hamilton, N., & Chinchilla, N. S. (1990). Central American migration: A framework for analysis. *Latin American Research Review*, 25, 75–110.

Harris, J. G., Echemendi'a, R., Ardila, A., & Rosselli, M. (2001). Cross-cultural cognitive and neuropsychological assessment. In: J. W. Andrews, H. Janzen, & D. Saklofske (Eds.), *Handbook of Psychoeducational Assessment: Ability, Achievement, and Behavior in Children*. San Diego: Academic Press.

Harris, J. G., Tulsky, D. S., & Schultheis, M. T., et al. (Eds.) (2003). Assessment of the non-native English speaker: Assimilating history and research findings to guide clinical practice. In: D. S. Tulsky, D. H. Saklofske, G. J. Chelune, R. J. Heaton, R. J. Ivnik, R. Bornstein, *Clinical Interpretation of the WAIS-III and WMS-III* (pp. 343–390). San Diego: Academic Press.

Heaton, R. K., Grant, I., & Matthews, C. G. (1986). Differences in neuropsychological test performance associated with age, education, and sex. In: I. Grant, & K. M. Adams (Eds.), *Neuropsychological Assessment of Neuropsychiatric Disorders* (pp. 100–120). New York: Oxford University Press.

Helms, J. (1992). Why is there no study of cultural equivalence in standardized cognitive ability testing? *American Psychologist*, 47, 1083–1101.

Hernstein, R. J., & Murray, C. (1994). *The Bell Curve: Intelligence and Class Structure in American Life*. New York: Free Press.

Kaufman, A. S., & Doppelt, J. E. (1976). Analysis of WISC-R standardization data in terms of stratification variables. *Child Development*, 74, 165–171.

Kindler, A. (2002). What are the most common language groups for LEP students? Retrieved June 23, 2004 from http://www.ncela.gwu.edu/pubs/reports/state-data/2000/usa.pdf.

Llorente, A. M., Taussig, I. M., Perez, L., & Satz, P. (2000). Trends in American immigration: Influences on neuropsychological assessment and inferences with ethnic-minority populations. In: E. Fletcher-Janzen, T. Strickland, & C. R. Reynolds (Eds.), *Handbook of Cross-Cultural Neuropsychology* (pp. 345–359). New York: Kluwer Academic/Plenum Publishers.

Marin, G., & Marin, B. V. (1991). *Research with Hispanic Populations*. Newbury Park, CA: Sage.

México, Gobierno de La República. *Carta de derechos y obligaciones laborales en lenguas indígenas*. Retrieved June 20, 2004 from http://www.gob.mx/wb2/egobierno/egob_Derechos_y_ Obligaciones_Laborales.

Minicucci, C., & Olsen, L. (1992, Spring). Programs for secondary limited English proficient students: A California study. (Occasional Papers in Bilingual Education, No. 5.) Washington, DC: National Clearinghouse for Bilingual Education.

Mohanty, A. K. (1990). Psychological consequences of mother-tongue maintenance and the language of literacy for linguistic minorities in India. *Psychology and Developing Societies*, 2, 31–51.

National Conference of State Legislatures (2003). Tuition and unauthorized immigrant students. Issued: August 14, 2003. Retrieved July 1, 2004 from http://www.ncsl.org/programs/immig/tuition2003.htm.

National Conference of State Legislatures (2004). In-state tuition and unauthorized immigrant students. Issued: April 29, 2003. Retrieved July 1, 2004 from http://www.ncsl.org/programs/immig/ TuitionApril04.htm.

Neisser, U., Boooo, G., Bouchard, T. J., Boykin, A. W., Brody, N., Ceci, S. J., Halpern, D. F., Loehlin, J. C., Perloff, R., Sternberg, R. J., & Urbina, S. (1996). Intelligence: Knowns and unknowns. *American Psychologist*, 51, 77–101.

Oakes, J. (1990). *Multiplying inequalities: The effects of race social class, and tracking on opportunities to learn mathematics and science*. Santa Monica, CA: RAND.

Passel, J. S., Capps, R., & Fix, M. (2004). Undocumented immigrants: Facts and figures. http:// www.urban.org/UploadedPDF/1000587_undoc_immigrants_facts.pdf.

Portes, A., & Borocsz, J. (1989). Contemporary immigration: Theoretical perspectives on determinants and modes of incorporation. *International Migration Review*, 23, 606–630.

Portes, A., & Rumbaut, R. G. (1990). *Immigrant America: A Portrait*. Los Angeles: University of California Press.

Prifitera, A., Saklofske, D. H., Weiss, L. G., & Rolfhus, E. (2005). WISC-IV: Foundations of Clinical Interpretation. In: A. Prifitera, D. H. Saklofske, & L. G. Weiss (Eds.), *WISC-IV Clinical Use and Interpretation*. San Diego, Elsevier.

Prifitera, A., Weiss, L. G., & Saklofske, D. H. (1998). The WISC-III in context. In: A. Prifitera, & D. H. Saklofske (Eds.), *WISC-III Clinical Use and Interpretation: Scientist–Practitioner Perspectives* (pp. 1–38). San Diego, CA: Academic Press.

Ramirez, J., Pasta, D., Yuen, S., Ramey, D., & Billings, D. (1991). Final report: longitudinal study of structured English immersion strategy, early-exit and late-exit bilingual education programs for language-minority children. (Vols. I, II) (No. 300–87–0156). San Mateo, CA: Aguirre International.

Rey, G. J., Feldman, E., Rivas-Vasquez, R., Levin, B. E., & Benton, A. (1999). Neuropsychological test development for Hispanics. *Archives of Clinical Neuropsychology*, 14, 593–601.

Reynolds, C. R. (2000). Methods for detecting and evaluating cultural bias in neuropsychological tests. In: E. Fletcher-Janzen, T. Strickland, & C. R. Reynolds (Eds.), *Handbook of Cross-Cultural Neuropsychology* (pp. 249–285). New York: Kluwer Academic/Plenum Publishers.

Reynolds, C. R., & Kaiser, S. M. (2003). Bias in the assessment of aptitude. In: C. R. Reynolds, & R. W. Kamphaus (Eds.), *Handbook of Psychological and Educational Assessment of Children* (2nd ed., pp. 519–562). New York: Wiley.

Ricciardelli, L. A. (1992a). Creativity and bilingualism. *Journal of Creative Behavior*, 26, 246–254.

Ricciardelli, L. A. (1992b). Bilingualism and cognitive development in relation to threshold theory. *Journal of Psycholinguistic Research*, 21, 301–316.

Romaine, S. (1995). *Bilingualism* (2nd ed.). Oxford, England: Blackwell.

Sattler, J. M. (1992). Assessment of Children (Revised and updated, 3rd ed.). San Diego: Author.

United States Census Bureau (2003a). Educational attainment of the population 25 years and over by age, sex, race, and Hispanic or Latino origin type: March 2000. Internet release date: June 18, 2003. Retrieved June 23, 2004, from http://www.census.gov/prod/2003pubs/c2kbr24.pdf.

United States Census Bureau (2003b). Poverty status of the population in 1999 by sex, age, Hispanic orgin, and race: March 2000. Internet release date: June 18, 2003. Retrieved June 23, 2004, from http://www.census.gov/populations/socdemo/hispanic/ppl-171/tabl4-1.pdf.

United States Census Bureau (2003c). Language use, English ability, and linguistic isolation for the population 5 to 17 years by state: 2000. Internet release date: February 25, 2003. Retrieved June 23, 2004, from http://www/census.gov/population/cen2000/phc-t20/tab02.pdf.

United States Census Bureau. (2003d). Language use and English speaking ability: 2000. Issued October, 2003. Retrieved October 9, 2003 from http://www.census.gov/prod/2003pubs/c2kbr-29.pdf.

United States Census Bureau (2004). Annual high school dropout rates by sex, race, grade, and Hispanic origin: October 1967–2002. Internet release date: January 9, 2004. Retrieved June 23, 2004, from http://www.census.gov/population/socdemo/school/tabA-4.pdf.

United States Census Bureau (2006). American Community Survey, Selected Population Profiles and Detailed Tables, S0201.

United States Department of Homeland Security (2003). *2002 Yearbook of Immigration Statistics*. Washington, DC: U.S. Government Printing Office. (Formerly entitled Statistical Yearbook of the Immigration and Naturalization Service.)

United States Immigration and Naturalization Service (1991). *1990 Statistical Yearbook of the Immigration and Naturalization Service*. Washington, DC: U.S. Government Printing Office.

Vázquez, J. Z. (1994). *Una Historia de Mexico. [A History of Mexico]*. Mexico City: L Editorial Patria.

Wechsler, D. (1949). *Manual for the Wechsler Intelligence Scale for Children*. New York: The Psychological Corporation.

Wechsler, D. (1974). *Manual for the Wechsler Intelligence Scale for Children – Revised*. San Antonio, TX: The Psychological Corporation.

Wechsler, D. (1991). *Manual for the Wechsler Intelligence Scale for Children* (3rd ed.). San Antonio, TX: The Psychological Corporation.

Wechsler, D. (2003). *Manual for the Wechsler Intelligence Scale for Children* (4th ed.). San Antonio, TX: The Psychological Corporation.

Wechsler, D. (2005). *Wechsler Intelligence Scale for Children – Fourth Edition Spanish Manual*. San Antonio, TX: Harcourt Assessment.

Weiss, L., Harris, J. G., Prifitera, A., Courville, T., Rolfhus, E., Saklofske, D. H., & Holdnack, J. A. (2006). Beyond the basics: Contextual interpretation of WISC-IV indices. In: L. G. Weiss, D. H. Saklofske, A. Prifitera, & J. A. Holdnack (Eds.), *WISC IV Advanced Clinical Interpretation* (pp. 1–52). San Diego: Elsevier Science.

Weiss, L. G., Prifitera, A., & Roid, G. H. (1993). The WISC-III and fairness of predicting achievement across ethnic and gender groups. Advances in psychological assessment: Wechsler Intelligence Scale for Children – Third Edition. *Journal for Psychoeducational Assessment monograph series*, pp.35–42.

Yates, J. R. & Ortiz, A. A. (2004). Developing individualized education programs for exceptional language minority students. In: L. M. Baca, & H. T. Cervantes (Eds.), The bilingual special education interface (4th ed.; pp. 204–229). Upper Saddle River, N. J: Pearson/Merrill Prentice Hall.

PART 3

INTERFACING WISC-IV ASSESSMENT AND INTERVENTION: SOME FURTHER CONSIDERATIONS

12

NEUROPSYCHOLOGICAL APPLICATIONS OF THE WISC-IV AND WISC-IV INTEGRATED

DANIEL C. MILLER[1] AND JAMES B. HALE[2]

[1]*Texas Woman's University, Denton, TX, USA*
[2]*Philadelphia College of Osteopathic Medicine, Philadelphia, PA, USA*

INTELLECTUAL ASSESSMENT IN NEUROPSYCHOLOGICAL PRACTICE

Standardized intellectual measures are psychometrically some of the best tools available to practitioners, and often serve as a foundation for interpreting pediatric and school neuropsychological test results. As actuarial and clinical decision-making should be based on measures with known reliability and validity (Anastasi & Urbina, 1997), incorporating well-standardized measures such as the *Wechsler Intelligence Scale for Children – Fourth Edition* (WISC-IV; Wechsler, 2003) into a neuropsychological test battery is arguably an essential assessment practice. Although individual consultation regarding a student's learning or behavior problem may not require intellectual assessment or neuropsychological evaluation, it is clear that some children will not respond to our standard intervention efforts (e.g., Hale, Kaufman, Naglieri, & Kavale, 2006; Miller, 2004, 2007). For children who do not respond to intervention, a comprehensive evaluation of intellectual, cognitive, neuropsychological, academic, and/or socioemotional functioning may be necessary. Driven by cognitive and neuropsychological theory and research, this comprehensive evaluation can provide critical information regarding individual strengths and needs, and serve as a foundation for collaborative development of individualized interventions that are subsequently monitored using single subject designs to ensure they have ecological and treatment validity (Hale & Fiorello, 2004).

Despite their widespread use in comprehensive evaluation of children, fierce debates regarding intelligence test interpretation have raged for some time, with evidence presented that supports idiographic (Hale, Fiorello, Kavanagh, Holdnack, & Aloe, 2007) or nomothetic (Watkins, Glutting, & Lei, 2007) interpretation of the intelligence test results. Even some neuropsychologists argue that intelligence test results are only useful for determining a global intelligence quotient (IQ) or factor scores because profile analysis appears to be unreliable (Livingston, Jennings, Reynolds, & Gray, 2003), while others suggest use of such global scores is misinformed at best, and can be highly misleading (e.g., Kaplan, 1988; Lezak, 1988; Luria, 1980). Some academics even suggest intellectual tests should not be administered because they are not useful for diagnostic or intervention purposes (e.g., Reschly, 2005), especially given their limited utility in determining global IQ–achievement discrepancy for specific learning disability classification (e.g., Fletcher et al., 2002). Although concerns over administration and interpretation of intellectual measures may seem valid, it seems both illogical and implausible that practitioners avoid administering these well-standardized measures because they have not been used effectively in the past (e.g., Scruggs & Mastropieri, 2002). Instead, renewed interest in effective interpretive strategies should fuel empirical investigations that demonstrate the idiographic utility of intellectual assessment in clinical practice (Hale et al., 2007).

Putting interpretive issues momentarily aside, it is important to recognize that good psychological assessment tools are necessary for good psychological evaluations, and the Wechsler scales are some of the most technically sound and well-researched measures for the purpose of intellectual and cognitive assessment (Flanagan & Kaufman, 2004). Without an understanding of a child's level *and* pattern of intellectual performance, it is difficult to establish critical baseline information regarding a child's current psychological and neuropsychological status (e.g., Groth-Marnat, Gallagher, Hale, & Kaplan, 2000). This intellectual foundation helps practitioners identify how individual differences in cognition, academic, and socioemotional functioning are displayed on other measures, and how results can translate into meaningful academic and behavioral interventions that have ecological and treatment validity. Whether the practitioner interprets intellectual test results from a nomothetic or idiographic perspective, it makes good clinical sense to evaluate a child's intellectual status if previous attempts at standard or problem-solving interventions have been unsuccessful (Hale, 2006).

Perhaps the greatest limitation of prior research linking putative factor or subtest profiles with meaningful outcomes is the over-reliance on data from large-scale normative populations instead of examination of clinical samples. As has been demonstrated elsewhere (Fiorello, Hale, McGrath, Ryan, & Quinn, 2001; Fiorello et al., 2007; Fiorello, Hale, & Snyder, 2006; Hale, Fiorello, Kavanagh, Hoeppner, & Gaither, 2001; Hale, Hoeppner, & Fiorello, 2002; Hale, Fiorello, Kavanagh, Holdnack, & Aloe, 2007), the results found for normative and clinical samples are not always consistent, with greater support found for idiographic interpretation in the latter group, especially given that global IQ can be biased in the prediction of academic achievement for clinical populations (e.g., Hale et al., 2007). As profile analysis of subcomponent scores is common practice among psychologists working with clinical populations (e.g., Pfeiffer, Reddy, Kletzel, Schmelzer, & Boyer, 2000), more objective methods for idiographic interpretation of profiles should be developed and validated instead of ignoring the practice altogether, as some have suggested (McDermott, Fantuzzo, & Glutting, 1990).

One of the requisites for idiographic interpretation is that measures have specificity for individual interpretation, and in clinical populations, factor score specificity is ample for idiographic interpretation (Hale et al., 2007). Given this requisite specificity, it should not be surprising that differences among the WISC-IV factors between clinical groups (Calhoun & Mayes, 2005; Mayes & Calhoun, 2006) and factor prediction of reading and math achievement for children with learning disabilities (Hale et al., 2007) have begun to emerge. While psychometric information is essential for idiographic interpretation of intellectual assessment results, moving away from interpretive strategies based solely on psychometric representation of data may hold the key to developing hypotheses about child strengths and needs, especially when these hypotheses are evaluated with additional cognitive and neuropsychological measures, with individualized interventions developed and evaluated to establish their ecological and treatment validity (Hale & Fiorello, 2004).

Acknowledging that intellectual subcomponent scores are neither diagnostic nor predictive without additional evidence, Hale and Fiorello (2004) developed the Cognitive Hypothesis Testing (CHT) model for establishing the utility of intellectual and neuropsychological test results for diagnostic and intervention purposes (Figure 12.1). In the CHT model, hypotheses derived from history, prior intervention attempts, observations, ratings, and intellectual assessment data are developed

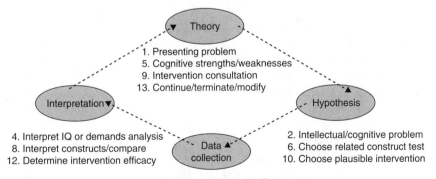

FIGURE 12.1   CHT model. Adapted from Hale & Fiorello (2004).

and tested using additional cognitive and/or neuropsychological measures to verify or refute initial findings, which is similar to a quantitative process approach in neuropsychology (Poreh, 2006). Using an intellectual measure such as the WISC-IV as a *screening tool*, this model has been used to validate individual profile results, and develop individualized interventions that are subsequently monitored using single subject methodology to establish treatment validity (e.g., Hale et al., 2006). Profile variability is not sufficient for these purposes, as it is too common in both clinical and typical populations (Fiorello et al. 2007; Hale et al., 2007). Instead, variable intellectual, academic, and behavioral results establish a need for further individual evaluation of hypotheses, and establish critical ecological and treatment validity data. It is this premise which serves as the foundation for our analysis of WISC-IV and WISC-IV Integrated (Wechsler, 2004) measures in this chapter.

It is critical for readers to avoid using the following sections in a "cookbook" approach, because similar scores may mean different things for different children (Hale & Fiorello, 2004). Nomothetic representations of data serve as a foundation for idiographic interpretation, but they are not sufficient to account for the performance of all children, especially those with disabilities (Fiorello et al., 2007). After nomothetic explanations have been explored and exhausted, further fine-grain analysis of data requires idiographic examination of a child's performance, with any hypothesis derived systematically evaluated to ensure ecological and treatment validity (Hale & Fiorello, 2004). Global IQ yields little information regarding a child's specific strengths and needs, which should be the primary focus of intellectual and cognitive assessment (Woodcock, 1997). Moving beyond global IQ scores requires both clinical acumen and thorough detective work, as understanding the underlying psychological processes of test performance is more important than any summative score that hides individual differences in brain functioning (e.g., Luria, 1980). This is unfortunate, as we can easily identify the type of input (i.e., visual, auditory) and output (i.e., motor, verbal) required on a particular test, but accurate differential diagnosis and individualized interventions require *inferences* about underlying (neuro)psychological processes (Hale et al., 2006), and these inferences are more likely to represent interpretive error than reality if we are not careful and thorough in our approach. As we explore the WISC-IV and WISC-IV Integrated in the following sections, it is important to realize that subcomponent scores are clinically valuable, but only if we verify or refute our CHT hypotheses derived from them using additional data sources.

NEUROPSYCHOLOGICAL INTERPRETATION OF WISC-IV AND WISC-IV INTEGRATED SUBTESTS

In Table 12.1, the WISC-IV/WISC-IV Integrated subtests are conceptually grouped according to the School Neuropsychological Model developed

TABLE 12.1   WISC-IV and WISC-IV Integrated Subtests Related to a School Neuropsychological Conceptual Model (Miller, 2007)

	Sensory–motor	Attention	Visual–spatial	Language/crystallized	Memory	Executive/fluid	Processing speed
Core subtests							
• Block Design	S		P			S	S
• No Time Bonus	S		P			S	S↓
• Multiple Choice			P↑			S	S
• Multiple Choice – No Time Bonus			P↑			S	S↓
• Design Process Approach	S		P↑			S	
• Similarities				P	S		
• Multiple Choice					P↓	S↑	S
• Digit Span		S			P		
• Forward		S			P		
• Backward		S			P		
• Visual Digit Span		S	S↑		P		
• Spatial Span		S	S↑		P		
• Forward		S	S↑		P		
• Backward		S	S↑		P		
• Letter Span		S		S	P		
• Rhyming		S		S	P		
• Non-rhyming		S		S	P		
• Picture Concepts				S		P	
• Coding	S	S	S		S		P
• Coding Recall	S	S	S		P		S
• Coding Copy	P	S	S				S
• Vocabulary				S	P	S	
• Multiple Choice				P↓	S↑		
• Picture Vocabulary Multiple Choice				P↓	S↓		
• Letter–Number Sequencing		S	S	S	P		S
• Letter–Number Sequencing Process Approach		S	S		P↓		S

(continues)

TABLE 12.1 (*continued*)

	Sensory–motor	Attention	Visual–spatial	Language/crystallized	Memory	Executive/fluid	Processing speed
• Matrix Reasoning			S			P	
• Comprehension				P	S	S	
• Multiple Choice				P↓	S↑		P
• Symbol Search	S	S	S		S	S	P
Supplemental subtests							
• Picture Completion	S	S	P	S	S		
• Cancellation	S	S	S				P
• Information				S	P		
• Multiple Choice				S↓	P↓	S	
• Arithmetic		S		S	P	S	
• With Time Bonus		S↓	S↑	S	P↓	S	S↑
• Process Approach: Part A (orally and visually)		S↓	S↑	S	P↓	S	
• Process Approach: Part A with Time Bonus		S↓	S↑	S	P↓	S	S↑
• Process Approach: Part B (orally and visually with paper and pencil)	S↑	S↓	S↑	S	P↓	S	
• Process Approach: Part B with Time Bonus	S↑	S↓	S↑	S	P↓	S	S↑
• Written Arithmetic		S↓	S↑	S↓	P↓	S	
• Word Reasoning				P		S	
• Elithorn Mazes	S		S			P	S
• No Time Bonus	S		S			P	S↓

Note: The subtests that appear shaded are from the WISC-IV Integrated. The non-shaded subtests are from the WISC-IV. P – Primary neurocognitive construct measured. S – Secondary neurocognitive construct measured. ↓ – Decreased emphasis on the neurocognitive construct as compared to the standard administration format. ↑ – Increased emphasis on the neurocognitive construct as compared to the standard administration format.

by Miller (2007). The rationale for this classification of primary and secondary neurocognitive constructs related to each of the WISC-IV subtests comes from a variety of sources, including Flanagan and Kaufman's (2004) interpretive approach, the factor analytic study conducted by Keith et al. (2006), the neuropsychological profile approach by Groth-Marnat et al. (2000), numerous studies using the WISC-III/WISC-IV, and the authors' clinical judgment.

PRIMARY VERSUS SECONDARY MEASURES

Most measures on cognitive abilities test are not factorially pure because they sample a wide range of behavior and require multiple brain structures and functions for successful performance. Test publishers strive for measures where the primary neurocognitive construct being measured accounts for the majority of the test variance. However, most samples of behavior involve a primary neurocognitive construct measured in addition to one or more secondary neurocognitive constructs. Although a child's performance on a particular measure could reflect the status of the primary neurocognitive construct tapped by that measure, there are other possible explanations for a particular outcome and these must be entertained for accurate interpretation. For instance, the WISC-IV Working Memory subtests require auditory–verbal skills, even though these are not the primary constructs tapped by these measures. Additionally, all samples of behavior on a test have some portion of error variance (e.g., administration error, situational factors) that must be factored into the interpretation. One of the most difficult realities we face in idiographic interpretation is the reality that not every subtest measures the same thing for every child (Hale & Fiorello, 2004). Although greater confidence can be placed in interpreting primary neurocognitive constructs for a task, these constructs might become more or less important in determining a child's ultimate performance depending on how the child approaches the task.

For example, the primary neurocognitive construct assessed by the WISC-IV Block Design subtest is Perceptual Reasoning according to the factor structure reported in the standardization manual (Wechsler, 2003). According to a Cattell–Horn–Carroll (CHC) classification scheme (Flanagan & Kaufman, 2004; Keith et al., 2006), Block Design primarily requires visual–spatial thinking not perceptual reasoning or fluid ability. The Block Design subtest has several other secondary neurocognitive constructs that are required for successful completion of the task including aspects of executive functioning such as non-verbal reasoning and problem-solving, perceptual analysis and synthesis, and visual–motor coordination. Neuropsychological interpretation of the measure requires even further analysis, including the type of visual processing required (visual–spatial or visual-detail), motor planning and control, and visual–motor integration. For instance, Kaplan's (1988) process approach to Block Design showed that left hemispheric dysfunction leads to directional errors (e.g., the diagonal goes the wrong direction, or errors in the visual details) but right hemispheric dysfunction leads to configuration errors (e.g., too many blocks for a part of the stimulus or errors in the visual gestalt or signs of neglect of the left side of the designs). For a fine motor coordination problem, it is important to determine if the problem is motor (possibly cortical or subcortical), or one due to poor visual or somatosensory feedback to the motor system. Finally, any error variance that contributed to the child's overall performance must be considered in the test interpretation, some of which is related to the measurement properties of the subtest and some related to situational factors. For example, if the child was unmotivated during administration of the Block Design subtest, a low test score would not reflect poor visual–spatial–directional thinking, perceptual reasoning, or visual–motor coordination. Rather the examinee variable of poor motivation could be the primary variable being measured by this sample of behavior.

Accurate interpretation requires determination of the neurocognitive factors that contribute to a child's successful or poor performance on a particular task, and then consider those findings within the context of other measures and data sources. Given the multifactorial nature of intelligence subtests, and the number of plausible explanations for any given performance, it is extremely difficult to make absolute determinations of a child's neurocognitive strengths and weaknesses based on the results of one subtest. In neuropsychology, practitioners look for pathognomonic or telltale signs of brain dysfunction, but the multifactorial nature of intelligence tests makes it unlikely that conclusions about the integrity of the brain or any particular neuropsychological function can be made. Although some claim this renders subtest profile analysis meaningless (e.g., Dana & Dawes, 2007), it is important to consider plausible causes of variable intellectual performance rather than just dismissing it outright (e.g., Hale et al., 2007). Instead, it is imperative that the examiner generates hypotheses about the causality of successful or poor performance on a task and use other samples of behavior, both informal and formal, to confirm or reject those hypotheses. This interpretive model is consistent with the CHT model (Hale & Fiorello, 2004) previously discussed. With these caveats in mind, we now discuss the various constructs in the Miller (2007) model, with several sources serving to support our conceptual model described below, including works by Groth-Marnat et al. (2000), Flanagan and Kaufman (2004), Keith et al. (2006), and Sattler and Dumont (2004).

SENSORY–MOTOR FUNCTIONS

The WISC-IV was not designed to directly measure sensory–motor functions. However, visual–motor coordination is a required skill for successful performance of several WISC-IV subtests including Block Design, Coding, Symbol Search, and Cancellation. Specifically, Block Design involves coordinated manipulation of the blocks. Neuropathological indictors such as hand tremors, motor awkwardness, and dropped or grossly misaligned blocks should be noted on this test and followed up with an occupational or physical therapy evaluation as warranted. The Coding, Symbol Search, and Cancellation subtests require minimal motor output (e.g., marking a stimulus item with a pencil or writing a symbol), but differences among these may be worth further examination. For instance, Coding may be lower than the other two subtests, because only Coding requires more constructional praxis or graphomotor skills than Symbol Search or Cancellation, suggesting difficulty with the primary or secondary motor (i.e., supplementary motor/premotor) cortex, the motor executive circuit (including the basal ganglia and thalamus) or cerebellum. However, if Symbol Search is lower than Coding, quick efficient decision-making may be an issue, which would reflect cingulate circuit dysfunction. If confirmed with other measures of sensory–motor function, this could have direct implications for intervention, not only for whether occupational or physical therapy is needed, but also for classroom instruction as well.

There are several WISC-IV Integrated subtests that also require visual–motor coordination including: Block Design Process Approach, Coding Recall, Coding Copy, and Elithorn Mazes (see Table 12.1). The Block Design Process Approach and Coding Recall only require visual–motor coordination secondarily. The Block Design Process Approach is still a primary measure of visual–spatial thinking and the Coding Recall primarily requires immediate recall memory. The Coding Copy was designed to primarily measure visual–motor coordination. On this process subtest, which is a variation of the WISC-IV Coding subtest, the immediate memory requirements of the test are removed. The child does not have to copy symbols that are associated with numbers, rather the child is asked to just copy directly symbols one at a time. Poor performance on the WISC-IV Integrated Coding Copying will be more indicative of visual–motor coordination weakness. But even if graphomotor skills appear to be deficient, further fine-grained analysis is necessary. The examiner must explore possible causes for the problem, which include visual and somatosensory feedback to the motor system, the type of motor dysfunction displayed, and whether integration of sensory and motor systems is the primary cause of the deficit.

The primary neurocognitive demands of the WISC-IV Integrated Elithorn Mazes subtest include executive functions of planning and the ability to inhibit impulsive responses. Secondarily, the Elithorn Mazes requires the child to have good motor execution skills, motor sequential processing skills, and graphomotor control. The Elithorn Mazes subtest has some additional process scores that may assist the examiner in explaining poor performance on the test. For example, a base rate is calculated for the number of times the child's upward path touches a diamond or edge of the maze. This type of error is called motor imprecision and may be reflective of poor graphomotor control (Wechsler et al., 2004). In a more pragmatic approach, close examination of the child's handwriting samples can yield useful information regarding the types of interventions needed.

When the WISC-IV/WISC-IV Integrated is administered to a child and sensory–motor functions are suspected to be a contributing cause of a child's current educational difficulties, it is suggested that the examiner further explores those potential deficits by administering additional tests. For example, the sensorimotor subtests from the NEPSY/NEPSY-II (Korkman, Kirk, & Kemp, 1998, 2007) may be useful for school age children, and the Dean–Woodcock Neuropsychological Battery (Dean & Woodcock, 2003) was designed to attempt to parse out these causes of constructional apraxia. Another commonly used measure is the *Developmental Test of Visual–Motor Integration – Fifth Edition* (Beery, Buktenica, & Beery, 2004), which allows for comparisons of visual, motor, and visual–motor integration performance.

ATTENTIONAL PROCESSES

Attention is a multifaceted construct, with many brain systems and functions contributing to adequate attentional functioning (e.g., Mirsky, 1987, 1996). The WISC-IV was not designed to directly measure attentional processes. However, attentional skills are considered prerequisites for higher order cognitive processing. For example, if a child is not paying attention to the task demands of the WISC-IV Picture Concepts subtest, the resulting poor performance is not indicative of the child's perceptual reasoning skills, but rather the poor attentional skills. Children with attentional processing disorders are commonly classified as having Attention-Deficit/Hyperactivity Disorder (ADHD). The *Diagnostic and Statistical Manual of Mental Disorders, Fourth Edition* (DSM-IV) (American Psychiatric Association, 1994) classifies ADHD within four subtypes: 314.00 ADHD, Predominantly Inattentive Type; 314.01 ADHD, Predominantly Hyperactive-Impulsive Type; 314.01 ADHD, Combined Type; and 314.9 is ADHD Not Otherwise Specified (NOS). Unfortunately, these four DSM-IV ADHD diagnoses do not adequately address the neuropsychological subtypes of attention problems that have been documented in the literature (Hale, Fiorello, & Brown, 2005; Miller, 2007). In fact, attention is unlikely to be the primary deficit in ADHD, rather it is frontal–subcortical circuit *control* of attention that is the cause of ADHD (Hale et al., 2005). In other words, ADHD could be called an *intention*-deficit disorder (Denckla, 1996). With this distinction in mind, many types of attention problems are related to the five (dorsolateral, orbital, cingulate, occulomotor, and motor) frontal–subcortical circuits and their executive control over attentional resources (see Hale & Fiorello, 2004; Lichter & Cummings, 2001).

Mirsky et al. (1987, 1996) conducted a comprehensive factor analysis of neuropsychological data, including several Wechsler subtests. Each of the neuropsychological measures was thought to measure some aspect of attention. Mirsky and his colleagues identified a taxonomy of attention functions including: *focus/execute, sustain* and *stabilize, shift,* and *encode.* The *focus/execute, sustain,* and *shift* subcomponents have endured in the neuropsychological literature, albeit with different names (Baron, 2004). Miller (2007) included two additional attention components for consideration within a school neuropsychological assessment model that are consistent with extant neuropsychological literature. These constructs include divided attention and attentional capacity.

Selective/Focused Attention

Selective attention is defined as "the ability to maintain a cognitive set in the presence of background 'noise' or distraction" (Baron, 2004, p. 222). The child is asked to copy symbols that are paired with simple geometric shapes or numbers. Although sometimes derided as a simple clerical task, the Coding subtest is cognitively complex, meaning it measures several neurocognitive processes, including selective and sustained attention. Within the WISC-IV factor structure, the Coding subtest primarily measures processing speed, yet it also requires the neurocognitive processes of selective and sustained attention, visual perception of abstract visual stimuli, very short-term (visual sensory) memory, associative learning, visual–motor coordination, visual-scanning ability, cognitive flexibility, motivation (cortical tone), and graphomotor skills. The WISC-IV Symbol Search subtest also requires the child to scan a search group and indicate whether the target symbol or symbols match any of the symbols in the search group. The attention to detail and matching the target stimuli on this task also require selective attention, although Symbol Search primarily measures processing speed. In terms of attentional processes, the WISC-IV Cancellation subtest requires aspects of both selective/focused attention and sustained attention. The child has to pick out or match target stimuli from an array of pictures, which requires selective attention. Finally, Arithmetic is a primary measure of math skills as well as working memory and fluid reasoning, but the child must also selectively attend to the essential elements of the verbally presented arithmetic problem in order to successfully complete the task items.

When the WISC-IV/WISC-IV Integrated is administered to a child and selective/focused attentional processing deficits are suspected to be a contributing cause of a child's current educational difficulties, it is suggested that the examiner further explores those potential deficits by administering additional measures and rating scales. The NEPSY's Auditory Attention and Response Set subtest (NEPSY: ages 5–12 years/NEPSY-II: ages 5–16 years) and the Visual Attention subtest (NEPSY: ages 3–12 years) require selective attention for portions of these tests (Korkman et al., 1998, 2007). The Test of Everyday Attention (TEA-CH; Manly, Robertson, Anderson, & Nimmo-Smith, 1999) is a battery of nine subtests designed to assess different components of attention in children and adolescents ages 6–16 years. Two of the TEA-CH subtests were designed to measure selective attention: Map Mission and Sky Search. Finally, the Delis–Kaplan Executive Systems' (D-KEFS) Color–Word Interference Test (Delis, Kaplan, & Kramer, 2001) is a Stroop-like test. While all of the subtest conditions of the Color–Word Interference Test require sustained visual attention, the third condition of the test requires the student to name the ink color of the printed word rather than name the color word (e.g., red). This task requires selective/focused attention as well as inhibition of a competing response, and is especially sensitive to anterior cingulate function (e.g., Hale & Fiorello, 2004).

Sustained Attention

Sustained attention is the ability to stay on task in a vigilant manner for a prolonged period of time (Mirsky, 1996). Continuous Performance Tests (CPT) are classic examples of tests which require sustained attention (see Riccio, Reynolds, & Lowe, 2001 for a comprehensive review). On the WISC-IV, the Cancellation subtest is a supplemental and primary measure of processing speed. On the subtest, the child is asked to scan either a random or structured array of pictures and mark pictures that match a target stimulus. Although it is clearly a processing speed measure, the Cancellation subtest secondarily requires the neurocognitive processes of visual selective attention, visual scanning/search, and visual sustained attention or vigilance.

Difficulties with sustained attention or vigilance are often hallmark features of ADHD. If an ADHD diagnosis is suspected and the WISC-IV is the principle cognitive abilities measure administered, it is suggested that some supplemental measures of sustained attention be added to the test battery. For example, The Auditory Attention and Response Set subtest (NEPSY: ages 5–12 years/NEPSY-II: ages 5–16 years) and the Visual Attention subtest (NEPSY: ages 3–12 years) on the NEPSY or NEPSY-II (Korkman et al., 1998, 2007) require sustained attention in addition to selective attention. As previously mentioned, CPT (e.g., Auditory Continuous Performance Test (ACPT); Keith, 1994) directly measure sustained attention and help supplement the WISC-IV. Two of the TEA-CH subtests (Manly et al., 1999) were also designed to measure sustained attention: Score!, Score DT, Walk Don't Run, and Code Transmission. The Conners' CPT-II (Conners, 2004) is also a commonly used measure of sustained attention and vigilance, and has been found to be sensitive to stimulant medication treatment in children with ADHD (Hale et al., 2005, 2006, 2007). The Cognitive Assessment System (Naglieri & Das, 1997) and Woodcock Johnson-III Tests of Cognitive Abilities (Woodcock et al., 2001) include useful cancellation tasks for hypothesis testing of sustained attention and processing speed.

Shifting Attention

Requiring the executive function of mental flexibility, shifting attention is the ability to consciously reallocate attentional resources from one activity to another (Mirsky, 1996). The WISC-IV and WISC-IV Integrated do not have subtests designed to directly or indirectly measure shifting attention, but Digits Backward requires executive control and mental flexibility to shift from forward to backward sequence (Hale, Hoeppner, & Fiorello, 2002). The shifting element of the Digits Span subtest is very nominal because the child is only asked to shift to recalling digits backward once and after practicing first.

Difficulties with shifting attention is a hallmark feature of executive dysfunction found in clinical population such as ADHD. Children who have difficulty shifting from one activity to another are labeled as perseverating. Perseverative responses can sometimes be observed across subtest items on the WISC-IV such as on Block Design (visual–motor preservations) or Similarities (verbal preservations). When the WISC-IV/WISC-IV Integrated is administered to a child and shifting attention deficits are suspected to be a contributing cause of a child's current educational difficulties, it is suggested that the examiner further explores those potential deficits by administering additional tests.

There are several good tasks for measurement of mental flexibility/shifting attention on the D-KEFS (Delis et al., 2001), including the Trail Making Test, Verbal Fluency, Color–Word Interference Test, and Design Fluency. Each of the tests has a condition that requires the child to shift from one stimulus response to another. The Part B of the Auditory Attention and Response Set on the NEPSY and NEPSY-II requires the child to shift their response set contrary to a more typical way of responding. For example, the child is asked to put a red chip in the box when the examiner says the word "yellow" and put a yellow chip in the box when the examiner says the word "red." Two of the TEA-Ch subtests (Manly et al., 1999) were also designed to measure shifting attention: Creature Counting and Opposite Worlds. However, card sorting tasks such as the Wisconsin Card Sorting Test (Heaton et al., 1993) also tap concept formation, inductive reasoning, hypothesis testing, mental flexibility and perseverative behavior, and sustained and shifting attention are needed for successful performance on this task as well.

Divided Attention

"Divided attention refers to the ability to respond to more than one task or event simultaneously" (Baron, 2004, p. 222). Some tests that measure divided attention also require working memory. For example, within the WISC-IV factor structure, the Letter–Number Sequencing is a core Working Memory subtest. However, neurocognitive processes such as *divided attention*, sequential processing, mental manipulation skills, short-term auditory memory, and visuospatial imaging (for some children), and processing speed are all secondarily being measured by this task. On the Letter–Number Sequencing subtest, the child is asked to listen to a sequence of numbers and letters read aloud by the examiner. The child is then asked to recall the numbers in ascending order first, followed by the letters in alphabetical order. The ability to respond to more than one stimulus simultaneously, in this case the numbers and letters, requires divided attention. The WISC-IV Integrated has a subtest called the Letter–Number Sequencing Process Approach. This subtest is a variation of the Letter–Number Sequencing subtest; however, this version of the test has words embedded in the presented sequences of letters and numbers. Ideally, the embedded words serve as an added verbal cue and can aid in the recall of the letter strings. If an examiner wants to supplement the WISC-IV/WISC-IV Integrated testing with another measure of divided attention, the TEA-Ch could be added to the battery. The TEA-Ch (Manly et al., 1999) has one subtest designed to measure divided attention: Sky Search DT.

Attentional Capacity

Attentional capacity is related to short-term (sensory) capacity, so its measurement is related to the type of stimulus input required. Although part of the Working Memory factor, the Digit Span subtest is a measure of attentional capacity because the child is asked to recall digit sequences of increasing length (Miller, 2007). The Digits Forward task in particular is sensitive to attentional capacity as it is a measure of auditory memory (Hale et al., 2002). When measuring attentional capacity, tasks often increase in length, but these tasks differ in complexity. For instance, if the stimuli are words in isolation, this requires primarily attentional capacity, but if words are presented in sentences or stories, lexical-semantic information load increases and attentional capacity may lessen, because the child can use comprehension skills to facilitate encoding and retrieval of the stimuli. Although Digits Backward also requires attentional capacity, it also requires working memory, mental flexibility, and shifting cognitive set (Hale et al., 2002).

The WISC-IV Integrated includes several span subtests that are designed to vary the presentation modality of the stimuli (e.g., visual versus auditory), or vary the characteristics of the span stimuli (e.g., letters versus numbers), or vary the response output (e.g., motor response rather than verbal response). The WISC-IV Integrated Visual Digit Span subtest is similar to the WISC-IV Digit Span subtest, in that digits are still presented in increasing lengths to the child for recall, but the digits are presented visually rather than read by the examiner. Differences in Digit Span versus Visual Digit Span performance may be due to the differences in auditory sensory/short-term memory and visual sensory/short-term memory being measured, respectively. The WISC-IV Integrated also includes a subtest called Spatial Span. A board with raised blocks is shown to the child. The blocks are numbers on the examiner's side for ease of administration. The examiner touches the blocks one at a time in a sequence of increasing length, then the child is instructed to touch the same blocks in the same sequence. Like the WISC-IV Digit Span subtest, the Spatial Span subtest includes forward and backward portions of the test. The child's performance on the Digit Span Forward can be compared to the Spatial Span Forward score. A similar comparison can be made between the Digit Span Backward and the Spatial Span Backward scores. Finally, the WISC-IV Integrated includes a Letter Span subtest. The subtest has four trials with the first two containing letters that rhyme (e.g., Z-D) and the last two trials containing letters that do not rhyme (e.g., T-H). When this subtest is used in conjunction with the WISC-IV Digit Span subtest, differences between auditory encoding skills and auditory processing of letters versus numbers can be examined (Wechsler et al., 2004). The WISC-IV/WISC-IV Integrated authors have constructed a comprehensive assessment of attentional capacity, so there is no need to administer any additional assessments in this area. However, while there are good measures of auditory and visual attentional capacity, there are no tasks currently available that directly tap somatosensory attention, rather these must be inferred on the basis of tasks that examine somatosensory perception (e.g., Process Assessment of the Learner and Halstead-Reitan Neuropsychological Test Battery sensory–perceptual tests). Considering performance on these measures may be important, because one of the characteristics of parietal lobe (particularly right parietal) dysfunction is poor attention to self and the environment, but this type of attention problem does not respond well to medication (Hale et al., 2005, 2006).

VISUAL–SPATIAL PROCESSES

Visual–spatial processing is difficult to measure because it is often associated with other neurocognitive processes which could be the source or result of low scores on these measures (Miller, 2007). For example, within the sensory–motor area, visual–motor coordination is often measured, but as noted earlier, difficulties in this area could be due to visual, motor, or integration requirements (Hale & Fiorello, 2004). Within the memory domain, visual immediate or delayed memory may be assessed, and results could vary depending on whether visual stimuli are abstract or meaningful. Visual processing is often required on executive tasks, so deficits could be related to perceptual or executive problems. Miller (2007) suggested that the neurocognitive processes most related to visual–spatial functions would be visual perception (with a motor response), visual perception (motor-free), visual-perceptual planning and organization, visual scanning and/or tracking, and visual–motor integration. These processes require multiple brain structures, including the occipital–parietal (dorsal stream), occipital–temporal (ventral stream), supplementary/premotor and motor cortices, the motor and occulomotor circuits (including the thalamus, basal ganglia, and cerebellum), and other subcortical structures (e.g., M and P pathways) for efficient performance.

Another difficulty with interpretation of visual–spatial processing measure results has to do with confusion over the lateralization of spatial perception (Hale & Fiorello, 2004). Although visual processes in general were once attributed to the right hemisphere, it is now clear that spatial/global processing is accomplished by the right hemisphere, whereas visual detail/local processing is performed by the left hemisphere (Delis, Robertson, & Efron, 1986; Fink, Marshall, Halligan, & Dolan, 1999; Hale & Fiorello, 2004; Kaplan, 1988; Moses et al., 2002). In addition, while abstract visual stimuli (e.g., spatial shapes) are processed by the dorsal stream (i.e., the "where" pathway), meaningful visual stimuli (e.g., object recognition) are processed by the ventral stream (i.e., the "what" pathway) (Milner & Goodale, 1995), with a degree of exposure/familiarity determining whether it is processed by the right (e.g., novel faces) or left (e.g., familiar faces) hemispheres (Hale & Fiorello, 2004). Regardless, these performance measures tend to be impaired in children who have experienced a traumatic brain injury (Mayes & Calhoun, 2006), and there is a strong association between attention, executive function, and performance type measures (Denckla, 1996).

Block Design

The WISC-IV has several subtests that were primarily designed to measure visual–spatial processing, including subtests from the Perceptual Reasoning and Processing Speed factors. As previously mentioned, Block Design primarily requires visual perception (with a motor response) and visual-perceptual organization. Block Design subtest may also secondarily measure other neurocognitive processes such as non-verbal concept formation, simultaneous/holistic processing, visual–motor coordination, learning, and processing speed. For successful performance, one must separate figure and ground within a visual stimulus for perceptual analysis and synthesis, which leads to comparisons of global/holistic (right parietal) versus local/detail (left parietal) comparisons (see Kaplan, 1988; Moses et al., 2002; Schatz, Ballantyne, & Trauner, 2000). The WISC-IV does include a supplemental measure for Block Design (Block Design – No Time Bonus) in which the contribution of processing speed is minimized – but not eliminated – because 0 points are still awarded if the design is not completed within the time limit. A discrepancy comparison can be made between the Block Design subtest and Block Design – No Time Bonus scaled scores to evaluate the potential contribution that processing speed made to the overall performance on the test.

Several subtests on the WISC-IV Integrated were designed to systematically decrease the motor planning and motor output demands of the Block Design subtest (Wechsler et al., 2004). On the Block Design Multiple Choice subtest, the child does not physically construct the block designs, but rather matches the correct constructed design from four possible pictured alternatives. If performance increases on the Block Design Multiple Choice compared to the Block Design subtest, the change in performance could be caused by the change in the motor output demand differences between the two versions of the task, but be aware that multiple choice formats may be difficult for children with decision-making difficulties. The Block Design Process Approach subtest was constructed to help the examiner understands the nature of a child's poor performance on the WISC-IV Block Design subtest. There are two parts to the Block Design Process Approach subtest. Part A uses 12 red-and-white clocks to construct designs within a specified time period, which eliminates the directional confusion (i.e., left hemisphere local/detail problems) sometimes seen on the traditional Block Design subtest. On Part B, the child is re-administered those items from Part A that were scored as a 0, but this time a grid overlay is used to assist the child's block construction, which decreases the spatial/holistic (i.e., global/holistic) requirements of the task. Further fine-grained analysis following Kaplan's (1988) Process Approach is provided for to allow for analysis of error patterns made during the performance of the test, even if the final product is ultimately correct. Base rates are provided regarding en route configuration, rotation, or directional errors during the construction, and whether these are subsequently self-corrected in the final product.

Picture Completion

Picture Completion is a supplemental subtest designed to primarily measure visual–spatial processing, but again part–whole/figure–ground relationships become important considerations for interpretation because the child must identify missing elements in meaningful pictures. Picture Completion specifically measures visual perception with or without a motor response depending upon the child's mode of response (verbal or pointing). Although verbal or gestural motor demands are minimal, the choice of naming the missing object versus pointing to it may be indicative of a preferred response style. If the child correctly points on several items without any verbal response, or responds with an incorrect but semantically similar word, this finding could suggest difficulty with word retrieval. The subtest secondarily measures the neurocognitive constructs of visual scanning, concentration, and visual recognition (memory) of essential details of objects, making it in part of measure of ventral stream functioning. Given that it taps long-term visual memory of objects, this measure is related to crystallized abilities and memory, tapping both left and right hemisphere temporal lobe functions.

Matrix Reasoning

Matrix Reasoning is a core Perceptual Reasoning subtest, yet based on a CHC factor analytic study (Keith et al., 2006; as cited in Flanagan & Kaufman, 2004); the subtest may principally load on non-verbal reasoning or problem-solving within the executive functions domain and secondarily load on visual–spatial processing. Matrix Reasoning certainly has a visual perceptual requirement, but the essential neurocognitive process required is good nonverbal problem-solving skills. Matrix analogy types of tasks have long been recognized as good measures of fluid reasoning (Flanagan & Harrison, 2005). Careful examination of item responses could reveal visual processing differences in abstract-spatial items and those of meaningful, known objects, consistent with right and left hemisphere visual processes respectively.

Picture Concepts

According to the WISC-IV factor structure, Picture Concepts is a core Perceptual Reasoning subtest. On this subtest, the child is shown pictures spread across several rows and is instructed to choose a picture from each row that shares a common characteristic (e.g., all vehicles). Picture Concepts, similar to the Matrix Reasoning subtest, was designed to measure abstract, categorical reasoning ability. Based on the CHC factor analytic study conducted by Keith et al. (2006), Picture Concepts is a very solid measure of fluid reasoning. Certainly, one must explore multiple possible relationships among the items, which makes it a measure of right hemisphere discordant/divergent processing, but because it includes perception of meaningful pictures and convergent/concordant thought to produce a categorical response, it in part taps left hemisphere functions as well (e.g., Bryan & Hale, 2001).

Coding and Symbol Search

The Coding and Symbol Search subtests are primary measures of processing speed. Secondarily, these subtests require visual scanning with a certain degree of visual discrimination and perception of abstract stimuli, with a motor response. As a result, secondary visual–spatial processing requirements should be considered as one plausible explanation for performance on these measures.

Elithorn Mazes

The Elithorn Mazes subtest is part of the WISC-IV Integrated test. According to the WISC-IV factor structure, Elithorn Mazes primarily loads with the other measures of perceptual reasoning. In the area of visual–spatial processing, the test measures visual scanning, and visual and motor sequential processing (Archibald, 1978).

Tasks with Increased Visual–Spatial Demands

Several of the WISC-IV Integrated subtests modify the presentation modality of the stimuli (e.g., visual versus auditory) to determine if the child's performance will be enhanced or adversely affected by these changes. On the WISC-IV Digit Span subtest, the string of numbers to be recalled by the child are all presented verbally by the examiner. The WISC-IV Integrated includes the Visual Digit Span and the Spatial Span subtests which use visual stimuli to measure short-term sensory memory and/or attentional capacity. Similarly, the Picture Vocabulary Multiple Choice subtest on the WISC-IV Integrated decreases the demands for verbal expression and memory retrieval by using the multiple-choice format while maintaining the requirement for word knowledge and verbal concept formation (Wechsler et al., 2004). Finally the WISC-IV Integrated includes two subtests designed to provide the examiner with insight into the potential causes of poor performance of the WISC-IV Arithmetic subtest. The WISC-IV Integrated Arithmetic Process Approach and the Written Arithmetic subtests change the presentation modality of the arithmetic problems by adding more visual cues or allowing the child to use paper and pencil to solve the problems.

Visual–Spatial Processing Summary

The WISC-IV administered in combination with the WISC-IV Integrated provides a good assessment of a child's visual–spatial processes. Supplemental tests for measuring visual perception (with a motor response) include subtests from the NEPSY-II: Geometric Puzzles (ages 3–6 years), Picture Puzzles (ages 7–16 years), and Recognition of Reversals (ages 5–16 years) (Korkman et al., 2007). Supplemental tests for measuring visual perception (motor-free) include the NEPSY-II's Arrows subtest (Korkman et al., 2007). Supplemental tests for measuring visual scanning and/or tracking include the NEPSY's Visual

Attention subtest (Korkman et al., 1998; ages 3–12 years). There are several additional measures that can be used for hypothesis testing of visual processes, including many visual memory tasks found on the Children's Memory Scale (CMS; Cohen, 1997), Test of Memory and Learning –Second Edition (TOMAL-2; Reynolds & Voress, 2007), or Wide Range Assessment of Memory and Learning-2 (WRAML-2; Sheslow & Adams, 2003). In addition to these tasks and those reported earlier in the sensory–motor section, see Miller (2007) for a comprehensive list of tests that measure the visual–spatial constructs.

LANGUAGE/CRYSTALLIZED PROCESSES

Miller (2007) categorizes language processes within three basic domains: phonological processing, receptive language, and expressive language. In terms of examining brain structure and function, it is important to note that these measures are in part related to language and in part related to crystallized abilities or achievement due to prior exposure and learning, making them primarily left hemisphere tasks (Hale & Fiorello, 2004), yet some right hemisphere language processing may also be required (e.g., Bryan & Hale, 2001). As a result, these crystallized measures are strong predictors of achievement in typical and learning disability populations (Hale et al., 2001, 2007). The WISC-IV and WISC-IV Integrated do not include a subtest or subtests designed to directly measure phonological processing, but children with deficits in this area may perform poorly on Digit Span (especially Digits Forward) and Letter–Number Sequencing. Qualitative signs of phonological processing problems may also result in poor performance on Verbal Comprehension tasks, such as the child requesting repetition of items or directions.

The WISC-IV Verbal Comprehension subtests that measure receptive and expressive language include the Similarities, Vocabulary, Comprehension, Information, and Word Reasoning subtests. These tasks also measure other neurocognitive processes such as memory retrieval, concept formation, reasoning, and concordant/convergent thought to a greater or lesser degree depending on the task. Within the school neuropsychological conceptual model (Miller, 2007), all of the aforementioned subtests, except Information, could be categorized under the language functions domain. The Information subtest is a measure of crystallized intelligence and long-term memory processes (Wechsler et al., 2004) including attention/executive function for efficient retrieval (Hale & Fiorello, 2004). Because of its high memory/executive demands, the Information subtest will be reviewed in the memory processes section of this chapter.

WISC-IV Verbal Comprehension Subtests

Similarities

The Similarities subtest is a core Verbal Comprehension measure. The test was designed to measure verbal reasoning and concept formation. The Similarities subtest primarily measures language skills that involve auditory comprehension, distinction between non-essential and essential features, and oral expression. The Similarities subtest also requires long-term retrieval of verbal concepts (crystallized and memory processes of the left hemisphere) and verbal reasoning skills (left hemisphere frontal executive functions) to engage in concordant (recognizing how the two words are similar) and convergent (the word that best represents both stimulus words) thought. Both receptive and expressive language demands are typically low, as the child only needs to recognize the words presented and often responds using a simple categorical response, but retrieval issues could be present if the child produces a similar concept, but an inexact word. For instance, a child may produce a concrete similarity (e.g., have roots), resulting in a one-point response, as opposed to the more abstract term (e.g., both are vegetables). The most typical explanation for this pattern is the child is less intellectually advanced, and that is why the concrete as opposed to the abstract response was given. But if this pattern is inconsistent (i.e., concrete on some items, abstract on others), there could be difficulty with efficient long-term memory retrieval, and further hypothesis testing is necessary.

Vocabulary

The Vocabulary subtest is a core Verbal Comprehension measure, and is one of the most crystallized tasks on the WISC-IV. As a result, it is less likely than other WISC-IV measures to be significantly impaired by brain damage, and can be used as an indicator of premorbid intelligence, although this practice has been challenged (Crawford, Parker, & Besson, 1988). The test is primarily designed to measure language skills including auditory perception, receptive language, word knowledge, verbal concept formation, and expressive language skills. As compared to the Similarities test, the importance of frontal executive control and Broca's area for word retrieval, language formulation, and grammar are greater on this task and the Comprehension subtest. Careful documentation of the child's oral response is therefore critical for evaluation of expressive language skills.

Comprehension

The Comprehension subtest is a core Verbal Comprehension measure. The test is primarily designed to measure verbal reasoning, receptive and expressive language skills, prior experience and learning, and common sense problem-solving. Because there is an element of novelty and ambiguity in some items, Comprehension is likely related to both left hemisphere concordant/convergent and right hemisphere discordant/divergent language functions (e.g., Bryan & Hale, 2001). Although the socially laden content has been reduced in each version of the Wechsler scales, it is still evident on some items. The combination of the novel problem-solving required and socially laden nature of some items could account for Comprehension's sensitivity to at least some forms of childhood psychopathology (e.g., Hale, Rosenberg, Hoeppner, & Gaither, 1997; Lipsitz, Dworkin, & Erlenmeyer-Kimling, 1993; Mayes & Calhoun, 2004), yet interpreting it as a measure of social intelligence or competence may be of questionable merit (Beebe, Pfiffner, & McBurnett, 2000).

Word Reasoning

Word Reasoning is a supplemental measure of Verbal Comprehension on the WISC-IV. On this test, the child is provided with a series of verbal clues by the examiner and asked to identify the common concept. The subtest was designed to measure a variety of cognitive processes including receptive and expression language skills, reasoning ability, and verbal abstraction (Ackerman, Beier, & Bowen, 2000; Delis et al., 2001). Although this would appear to be a stronger measure of discordant/divergent language processes, correlations with non-verbal reasoning/fluid ability measures are not as high as might be expected, possibly because of the construction of the task (hierarchical cues and single correct responses). However, differences can be seen based on how quickly the child recognizes the correct response as opposed to the amount of structure/cueing needed to solve the problem. Since this task is supplemental, the examiner could ask the child to generate as many possible solutions after each cue, which would be more indicative of discordant/divergent language skills, but the results of this non-standardized format should not be reported for quantitative purposes.

WISC-IV Integrated Verbal Comprehension Subtests

The WISC-IV Integrated included four subtests designed to test the limits of some of the traditionally administered WISC-IV Verbal Comprehension subtests. The WISC-IV Integrated includes the Similarities Multiple Choice, Vocabulary Multiple Choice, Picture Vocabulary Multiple Choice, and Comprehension Multiple Choice. On each of these subtests, the contents of the respective WISC-IV and WISC-IV Integrated subtests are essentially the same, except the presentation and response formats are different. The multiple-choice format used by the WISC-IV Integrated subtests places a decreased emphasis on the oral expressive (Glosser & Friedman, 1995; Goldstein & Green, 1995) and memory retrieval (Groth-Marnat, 1997; Joy, Fein, Kaplan, & Freedman, 1999; Lezak, 1995; Milberg, Hebben, & Kaplan, 1986) demands of the task.

Secondary Measures of Language Processing

The Letter Span subtest on the WISC-IV Integrated is a primary measure of visual immediate memory; however, it secondarily measures both receptive and expressive language. As previously mentioned at the start of this section, the WISC-IV Information subtest is probably best classified as a measure of crystallized intelligence and involves more long-term memory skills. However, Information secondarily requires both receptive and expressive language skills. Poor performance on the Information subtest may be caused by poor receptive language skills, difficulty with memory retrieval, or limited expressive language skills. Further hypothesis testing is needed to determine if the problem is receptive, expressive, or executive in nature, and/or how much of the deficit is related to a processing problem or due to limited experience and education or crystallized abilities.

Language Processes Summary

As previously mentioned, the WISC-IV and WISC-IV Integrated do not include a subtest specifically designed to measure phonological processing. If a referral question is related to a suspected phonological processing deficit, and the WISC-IV/WISC-IV Integrated are used as the primary cognitive measure, the examiner will need to supplement the assessment battery with a direct measure of phonological processing. An example of a phonological measure would be the Phonological Processing subtest from the NEPSY-II (Korkman et al., 2007) or the WJ-III Incomplete Words and Sound Blending subtests (Woodcock et al., 2001). The Comprehensive Test of Phonological Processing (CTOPP; Wagner, Torgesen, & Rashotte, 1999) and the *Process Assessment of the Learner –* Second Edition (PALS-II; Berninger, 2007) also have excellent measures for examining phonological awareness, analysis, and assembly.

The WISC-IV Similarities, Vocabulary, Comprehension, and Word Reasoning subtests all measure aspects of language processing; however, frequently the contributions of receptive versus expressive language processes are difficult to separate. Also these subtests are cognitively complex and measure other higher order cognitive functions in addition to language, such as memory retrieval, verbal concept formation, reasoning, and concordant/convergent thought.

If the referral question is related to a suspected receptive and/or expressive language deficit, and the WISC-IV/WISC-IV Integrated is used as the primary cognitive measure, the examiner will need to supplement the assessment battery with direct measures of receptive and expressive language. As an example, the Listening Comprehension subtest on the WIAT-II (Wechsler, 2001) could be added to an assessment battery because it contains both receptive and expressive language measures. The NESPY/NEPSY-II (Korkman et al., 1998, 2007) contains several measures of expressive language including: Body Part Naming (and Identification) (ages 3–4 years), Oromotor Sequences (ages 3–12 years), Repetition of Nonsense Words (ages 5–12 years), Speeded Naming (NEPSY: ages 5–12 years/NEPSY-II: ages 3–16 years), and Verbal Fluency (NEPSY: ages 3–12 years/NEPSY-II: ages 3–16 years). It would be appropriate to elicit the aid of a speech and language pathologist, when the quality of a child's receptive or expressive language skills are questioned. Speech and language pathologists often administer tests that specifically measure the phonological, receptive, and expressive aspects of language. An example would be the *Clinical Evaluation of Language Fundamentals –* Fourth Edition (CELF-4; Semel, Wiig, Secord, 2003) for children ages 5–21 years. Finally, as noted earlier, the CMS (Cohen, 1997), TOMAL-2 (Reynolds & Voress, 2007), and WRAML-2 (Sheslow & Adams, 2003) tests all have measures that require acquisition, storage, and retrieval of verbal information.

MEMORY AND LEARNING PROCESSES

As part of a school neuropsychological model, Miller (2007) classified memory and learning into seven broad categories: verbal immediate (short-term) memory, visual immediate (short-term) memory, verbal (delayed) long-term memory, visual (delayed) long-term memory, verbal–visual associative learning and memory, working memory (ability to perform complex mental operations on material placed in immediate memory), and semantic memory (knowledge of basic facts). The WISC-IV used in combination with the WISC-IV Integrated provides a fairly good assessment of memory functions across the broad categories, but it is not as specific to memory as the CMS (Cohen, 1997), the TOMAL-2 (Reynolds & Voress, 2007), or the WRAML-2 (Sheslow & Adams, 2003).

Before reviewing Miller's (2007) model, it is important to recognize that memory is an elusive construct that has been studied at the cortical, subcortical, and neurocellular levels. Although conceptualizing memory from a verbal–visual perspective makes sense given the WISC-IV and other measures available, it is important to note that a more complex neuropsychological analysis of memory may be in order, given that hemispheric functions change as one learns a task (Goldberg, 2001). Short-term memory has been replaced in some models with the notion of immediate sensory and/or motor memory; that is, the auditory, visual, somatosensory, and motor cortices each perform immediate memory demands, whether that is initial registration of stimuli or the process of carrying out an act. Beyond immediate memory, frontal executive and hemispheric processing differences begin to emerge. Novel tasks or those requiring new learning require more frontal and right hemisphere activity because executive and working memory demands are quite high, but as information is encoded into long-term memory (mediated by the frontal circuits and the hippocampus), the more the left hemisphere systems that eventually process the learned information or perform the known actions become involved (Hale & Fiorello, 2004). For instance, the long-term memory for a motor action and the long-term memory for language expression are likely stored in the left hemisphere supplementary motor region and Broca's area respectively, which could account for the high comorbidity between apraxia and aphasia (e.g., Beland & Ska, 1992; Joshi, Roy, Black, & Barbour, 2003; Kaplan, Gallagher, & Glosser, 1998). In addition, during the encoding of information into long-term memory, bilateral hemisphere functions are required, with the left frontal regions important for concordant/convergent thought to relate the new information to old information; whereas right frontal discordant/divergent thought is required for memory retrieval as one explores multiple possible words to respond to the task at hand (see Bryan & Hale, 2001; Tulving & Markowitsch, 1997).

Verbal Immediate (Short-Term) Memory

Digit Span Forward

The Digit Span subtest is classified on the WISC-IV as a core Working Memory measure, but there are differences between Digit Span Forward and Digit Span Backward. The Digit Span Backward is actually a measure of working memory because it meets the test of actively manipulating material placed in immediate memory. The Digit Span Forward portion of the subtest would be classified as a verbal immediate memory measure (Hale & Fiorello, 2004; Miller, 2007). The Digit Span subtest measures attentional capacity, verbal immediate memory, sequential processing, and sustained attention/concentration, but the backward component requires additional executive control for mental flexibility and working memory to produce the sequence in reverse order, suggesting these tasks should be interpreted separately (Hale et al., 2002).

Letter Span

The WISC-IV Integrated includes the Letter Span subtest that is similar to the WISC-IV Digit Span Forward subtest except that the stimuli have been changed from numbers to letters. The Letter Span subtest has embedded rhyming and non-rhyming words which places different demands on linguistic memory and encoding (Wechsler et al., 2004). Similar to the Digit Span subtest, the Letter Span subtest was designed to measure attentional capacity, verbal immediate memory, sequential processing, and sustained attention/concentration (Miller, 2007; Reynolds, 1997). Statistical and clinical comparisons can be made between the verbal immediate memory for numbers (Digit Span) and letters (Letter Span), which could reflect facility with one stimuli over another, which could be due to prior experience/competence in numbers and/or letters, but all are related to superior temporal lobe functioning.

Visual Immediate (Short-Term) Memory

Visual Digit Span

The WISC-IV Integrated Visual Digit Span is similar to the WISC-IV Digit Span subtest; however, the stimuli are digits presented visually to the child rather than verbally. The test is designed to measure attentional capacity, visual sensory memory, sequential processing, and sustained attention/concentration (Elwood, 2001; Miller, 2007). Statistical and clinical comparisons can be made between the Digit Span, Letter Span, and Visual Digit Span subtests.

Spatial Span Forward

The WISC-IV Integrated Spatial Span subtest includes Spatial Span Forward and Spatial Span Backward components. On this test, the examiner taps increasingly long sequences on raised blocks and then asks the child to tap the same sequence, either in forward or backward sequence. The Spatial Span Backward portion of the test measures working memory and will be discussed later in this section. The Spatial Span Forward was designed to measure rote learning and visual memory, sustained and selective attention, encoding, and spatial and sequential processing (Miller, 2007; Smyth & Scholey, 1992). Sequencing of the motor response is required; therefore, it is important to consider praxis as influencing Spatial Span performance. Children with apraxia could have difficulty not because of deficits in rote visual memory or spatial skills, but instead have difficulty carrying out a series of sequential motor responses.

When comparing these immediate visual memory measures, it is important to note that while both Visual Digit Span and Spatial Span Forward measure rote visual memory for assessment of the integrity of the occipital–striate memory processes (e.g., Brodman's Areas 17/18 or V1/V2), the occipital–parietal dorsal stream is likely involved in both, with the Visual Digit Span tapping the left dorsal stream, and the spatial span tapping the right dorsal stream. However, as is the case with the auditory–verbal span tasks, the frontal–subcortical circuits play a minor role in sequencing, especially on more difficult items.

Secondary Measures of Visual Immediate (Short-Term) Memory

The WISC-IV Coding and Symbol Search subtests are primary measures of processing speed; however, they both secondarily measure visual short-term memory. It is important to examine Coding performance throughout the task, and the WISC-IV Integrated Coding measures described earlier, to determine if memory processes are involved in overall performance. For instance, if a child repeatedly looks to the template before responding, this suggests the child has not made the symbol-shape or symbol-number association, and this can be further evaluated with additional measures of short-term visual memory. Although memory is not required for Symbol Search, the task does require rapid visual comparison/contrast of the targets and distracters. Therefore, the child may complete fewer overall items because of poor stimuli encoding in visual immediate memory.

Working Memory

Letter–Number Sequencing

The Letter–Number Sequencing subtest is a core Working Memory measure. The examiner reads a sequence of letters and numbers and then asks the child to recall the numbers first in ascending order, then the letters in alphabetically order. Verbal (and possibly visual) working memory is required for this task because the child must actively manipulate the information stored in immediate verbal memory. The task measures sequential processing, auditory working memory, selective and sustained attention, verbal immediate memory, and processing speed (Crowe, 2000; Miller, 2007; Sattler & Dumont, 2004). However, it is important to note that some young children may not use working memory on this task and still receive enough credit to obtain an average score. They do this by using immediate auditory sensory memory only, and repeat the stimuli as presented, which does result in credit on several initial items.

Letter–Number Sequencing Process Approach

The WISC-IV Integrated Letter–Number Sequencing Process Approach subtest is similar to the WISC-IV version of the test except that the Integrated version has embedded words in two of the three trials, making it more of a lexical-semantic task, which aids memory encoding and/or retrieval. The embedded words may alter the child's performance on the task because it may provide a memory cue and thereby reducing the demands on auditory working memory. This test measures sequential processing, auditory and visual working memory, selective and sustained attention, verbal immediate memory, and processing speed (Crowe, 2000; Miller, 2007; Sattler & Dumont, 2004).

Digit Span Backward

The Backward portion of the Digit Span subtest is a core Working Memory measure. The task measures mental flexibility and auditory–verbal working memory and for some children, possibly visuospatial imaging (Groth-Marnat, 1997; Hale et al., 2002; Kaufman, 1994; Reynolds, 1997; Sattler, 2001; Sattler & Dumont, 2004).

Arithmetic

Arithmetic is a supplemental subtest for the Working Memory scale. The Arithmetic subtest requires multiple cognitive processes including: verbal working memory, concentration, selective and sustained attention, short- and long-term memory, and mathematical reasoning ability (Groth-Marnat, 1997; Kaufman, 1994; Sattler, 2001; Sattler & Dumont, 2004), but a recent study found that it measures fluid reasoning as well (Keith et al., 2006), likely because it requires problem-solving and translating verbal to numeric information.

WISC-IV Integrated Arithmetic Subtests

The Arithmetic Process Approach subtest is also on the WISC-IV Integrated. On this adaptation of the Arithmetic subtest, the child is asked to solve math problems presented in multiple formats in a specified time period. On Part A of the test, the child is asked to solve a math problem that is read aloud by the examiner and simultaneously presented in a stimulus booklet. On Part B of the test, the child is given a pencil and paper to assist with the calculations of those items missed in Part A. The Arithmetic Process Approach is similar to the Arithmetic subtest in terms of what it is measuring; however, the visual presentation of items and the allowance of paper and pencil to assist with performance decrease the attentional and auditory working memory demands (Lezak, 1995; Milberg et al., 1986; Sattler, 2001; Sattler & Dumont, 2004). The WISC-IV Integrated Written Arithmetic subtest allows for comparison to WISC-IV Arithmetic performance, thereby reducing auditory–verbal working memory requirements, and allows for direct analysis of procedural math knowledge and skill. Compared to the Arithmetic subtest, the Written Arithmetic subtest increases visual demands, and reduces the attentional, working memory, and oral expressive demands (Lezak, 1995; Sattler, 2001; Sattler & Dumont, 2004).

Spatial Span Backward

Spatial Span is a subtest on the WISC-IV Integrated. The Backward condition measures visual working memory (Smyth & Sholey, 1997), selective and sustained attention (Lezak, 1995), and attentional capacity (Miller, 2007). Performance on the Spatial Span Backward can be compared to performance on the Digit Span Backward to look for differences based on modality presentation, thereby allowing for comparisons of right and left dorsal streams, respectively, and how these influence prefrontal executive/working memory demands.

Semantic Memory

Semantic memory is our knowledge of basic facts. On the WISC-IV, the Comprehension, Information, and Vocabulary subtests all require retrieval of acquired knowledge such as social judgment or common sense solutions to problems (Comprehension), general facts (Information), or definitions of words (Vocabulary). Semantic memory is referred to as comprehension/knowledge in the CHC vernacular (Flanagan & Kaufman, 2004) or a crystallized ability (Wechsler et al., 2004).

Information

The Information subtest is a measure of crystallized intelligence and involves more long-term retrieval skills (Wechsler et al., 2004). Secondarily, the Information subtest is a measure of language skills such as receptive and expressive language (Cooper, 1995; Groth-Marnat, 1997; Horn, 1985; Kaufman, 1994; Sattler, 2001; Sattler & Dumont, 2004).

Comprehension

The Comprehension subtest principally measures language skills such as verbal reasoning and conceptualization. The subtest does secondarily require knowledge and retrieval of conventional standards of behavior (Bannatyne, 1974; Groth-Marnat, 1997; Kaufman, 1994; Sattler, 2001; Sattler & Dumont, 2004).

Vocabulary

The Vocabulary subtest is also a primary measure of language skills such as word knowledge and verbal concept formation. Vocabulary secondarily requires the retrieval from the fund of knowledge (Bannatyne, 1974; Groth-Marnat, 1997; Kaufman, 1994; Sattler, 2001; Sattler & Dumont, 2004).

The WISC-IV Integrated includes multiple-choice versions of the Vocabulary, Comprehension, and Information subtests. The addition of the multiple-choice format reduces the demands on for verbal expression and memory retrieval (Comprehension and Information) or word retrieval (Vocabulary) (Glosser & Friedman, 1995; Goldstein & Green, 1995; Groth-Marnat, 1997; Joy et al., 1999; Milberg et al., 1986).

Memory Areas Not Assessed by the WISC-IV or WISC-IV Integrated

The WISC-IV and WISC-IV Integrated do not contain subtests that directly measure verbal or visual long-term memory, or verbal–visual associate memory and learning. In terms of memory assessment, the Wechsler Scales have a narrow focus on assessing immediate and working memory. If long-term memory or verbal–visual associative memory and learning deficits are suspected, it is recommended that the CMS (Cohen, 1997), TOMAL-2 (Reynolds & Voress, 2007), or WRAML-2 (Sheslow & Adams, 2003) be added to the assessment battery.

Summary of the Assessment of Memory and Learning by the WISC-IV and WISC-IV Integrated

The WISC-IV used in combination with the WISC-IV Integrated provides a fairly good assessment of memory functions across the broad categories of memory and learning identified by Miller (2007). It is unfortunate that the WISC-IV and WISC-IV Integrated authors chose to use the label "working memory" to describe only a few of the subtests that measure memory on these scales. In actuality, there are several measures that are either primary or secondary measures of memory, including auditory immediate memory, visual immediate memory, and semantic memory, in addition to working memory. Regardless, working memory measures have been found to be deficient in a number of disorders, including learning disabilities, ADHD, and autism (Calhoun & Mayes, 2005; Fiorello et al., 2006; Hale et al., 2001; Mayes & Calhoun, 2006). The WISC-IV and WISC-IV Integrated test results specific to memory assessment should be viewed as the first step in generating hypotheses about the presence or absence of memory dysfunctions. If a memory dysfunction is suspected in any one of the subcategories of memory and learning, it is suggested that the examiner administers a full battery of memory and learning tests such as the CMS (Cohen, 1997), TOMAL-2 (Reynolds & Voress, 2007), or WRAML-2 (Sheslow & Adams, 2003), and/or the memory measures on the NEPSY-II (Korkman et al., 2007).

EXECUTIVE FUNCTIONS/FLUID REASONING ABILITIES

Within the school neuropsychological assessment model (Miller, 2007), measures of executive functions were categorized into groups labeled as: concept generation, inhibition, motor programming, and planning, reasoning, and problem-solving. As there is a strong relationship between executive functioning and the cognitive construct of fluid ability or reasoning assessed by novel problem-solving tasks (Decker, Hill, & Dean, 2007; Hale & Fiorello, 2004; Prabhakaran, Smith, Desmond, Glover, & Gabrieli, 1997; Saggino, Perfetti, Spitoni, & Galati, 2006), these measures are addressed here. Other cognitive processes such as set shifting, sustained attention, and working memory all have components of executive functioning but have been covered in other portions of the chapter.

Although these processes are difficult to attribute to any one brain region, they are most likely related to one of the frontal–subcortical circuits (see Lichter & Cummings, 2001). These circuits or loops connect five different frontal–prefrontal regions to the basal ganglia and thalamus to govern executive function.

The five circuits have been labeled the occulomotor, motor, dorsolateral, orbital, and cingulate circuits. According to Hale and Fiorello (2004) (also see Hale et al., 2005), the occulomotor circuit is involved in visual attention and tracking; the motor circuit is involved in motor coordination and control; the dorsolateral circuit is involved in traditional executive functions such as planning, organization, flexibility, monitoring, and evaluation; the orbital circuit is responsible for self-regulation and emotion control; and the cingulate circuit is involved in processing speed and efficiency, as well as effective decision-making. The WISC-IV and WISC-IV Integrated include several measures that require perceptual reasoning skills including Picture Concepts and Matrix Reasoning, and as a result, these are in part measures of executive functions (Decker et al., 2007).

Picture Concepts

Picture Concepts is a core Perceptual Reasoning measure. The child is presented several rows of pictures and is asked to choose one picture from each row to form a group that shares a common property (e.g., all pieces of furniture). The subtest was designed to measure abstract, categorical reasoning ability (Flavell, 1985; Deak & Maratsos, 1998; Shulman et al., 1995). As a result, multiple possible relationships among pictured items must be considered (i.e., right hemisphere discordant/divergent processes), but then a correct response requires noting the relationship among two of the stimuli (i.e., left hemisphere convergent/concordant processes) (e.g., Bryan & Hale, 2001). This could account for the factorial complexity of this task, with correlations noted for both the Verbal Comprehension and Perceptual Reasoning factors (Wechsler, 2003).

Matrix Reasoning

Matrix Reasoning is a core Perceptual Reasoning measure. For every item, the child is shown an incomplete visual matrix and asked to choose the missing piece. Matrix Reasoning is an overall measure of fluid intelligence and specifically measures processes such as visual discrimination and perceptual reasoning (Wechsler et al., 2004). Although executive demands are evident to engage in the deductive problem-solving required, it is important to note whether there is intrasubtest scatter between items that require analogies using meaningful (left ventral stream) versus abstract (right ventral stream) visual stimuli.

Elithorn Mazes

Elithorn Mazes is categorized as a Perceptual Reasoning domain subtest on the WISC-IV Integrated; however, it draws heavily from executive processes such as planning, organization, motor execution, processing speed, and response inhibition (Archibald, 1978). Elithorn Mazes also requires aspects of visual scanning, and visual–motor sequential motor execution (Wechsler et al., 2004). The task requires the child to draw a path through a specified number of dots from the bottom to the top of the page within a prescribed time limit. The time spent in motor planning and latency time can be calculated for the test, both of which are designed to be more direct measures of executive functions (Wechsler et al., 2004). Base rates for errors such as rule violations, motor imprecision, and backward and across responses can also be reported.

Elithorn Mazes – No Time Bonus

The WISC-IV Integrated also includes a measure of the performance on the Elithorn Mazes subtest without consideration of the time factor. Comparisons can be made between the scaled scores for Elithorn Mazes with and without the time bonus factored into the score. Children with poor processing speed are often penalized for the subtests that require performance under time constraints.

Secondary Measures

There are several measures on the WISC-IV and WISC-IV Integrated that secondarily measure reasoning and problem-solving skills including: Block Design (all variations), Comprehension, Comprehension Multiple Choice, Symbol Search, Arithmetic, Written Arithmetic, Arithmetic Process Approach, and Word Reasoning. The executive processes of reasoning and problem-solving must be taken into account when interpreting a child's performance on these tests. A child's poor performance on Block Design may not be related to any visual–spatial, or visuoconstructional difficulties, but rather a deficit in perceptual reasoning.

Summary of the Assessment of Executive Functions by the WISC-IV and WISC-IV Integrated

Several of the subtests from the WISC-IV and WISC-IV Integrated require either reasoning or problem-solving skills, or planning and organizational skills. If the referral questions suggest executive dysfunctions, it is recommended that the examiner expands the assessment battery to include subtests from the NEPSY/NEPSY-II (Korkman et al., 1998, 2007) or the D-KEFS (Delis et al., 2001).

PROCESSING SPEED

Schrank and Flanagan (2003, pp. 28–29) defined processing speed as "the speed with which an individual performs simple cognitive tasks." Processing Speed tasks typically require multiple cognitive processes including: motor speed and number facility (see Feldman, Kelly, & Diehl, 2004 for a review). Teasing out processing speed from visual–motor integration is a challenge, as suggested earlier in this chapter. The WISC-IV Processing Speed Index is composed of the Coding, Symbol Search, and Cancellation subtests, all of which rely on some element of visual–motor processes in addition to processing speed proper. Graphomotor or visual motor coordination processes are not as involved on the Symbol Search and Cancellation subtests as they are on the Coding subtest. As the integrity of multiple cortical structures is necessary to perform these tests quickly and efficiently, these measures have a long history of being sensitive to brain trauma (Donders, Tulski, &

Zhu, 2001; Ewing-Cobbs, Fletcher, & Levin, 1998) and are likely indicative of the cingulate function (see Hale & Fiorello, 2004; Lichter & Cummings, 2001), which may be impaired in children with ADHD (Hale et al., 2005). However, Mayes and Calhoun (2004) found that children with traumatic brain injury were likely to have WISC-III Performance scores without low Coding performance.

Coding

The Coding subtest is a core Processing Speed measure. The child is shown a legend that pairs a geometric shape or number with a symbol. In the space below, the child is asked to copy as quickly as possible the symbol that corresponds to each of the geometric shapes or numbers in the legend above. The Coding subtest is cognitively complex as it measures processing speed, visual short-term memory, learning, visual perception with a motor response, visual–motor coordination, visual-scanning ability, visual sequential processing, selective and sustained attention, cognitive flexibility, and motivation (Cooper, 1995; Groth-Marnat, 1997; Kaufman, 1994; Miller, 2007; Sattler, 2001; Sattler & Dumont, 2004). This subtest has been found to be impaired in children with learning disabilities, autism, ADHD, and TBI (Ewing-Cobbs et al., 1998; Fiorello et al., 2006; Hale et al., 2001; Mayes & Calhoun, 2004).

Symbol Search

The Symbol Search subtest is a core Processing Speed measure. On the task, the child scans a visual array of objects and indicates whether the target symbol(s) match(es) any of the symbols in the search group. Symbol Search measures processing speed, visual short-term memory, visual–motor coordination, flexibility in thinking, visual discrimination, planning and organization, and learning (Kaufman, 1994; Sattler, 2001; Sattler & Dumont, 2004).

Cancellation

The Cancellation subtest is a supplemental Processing Speed measure. On this task, the child scans a random or structured array of pictures and marks target pictures within a designated time period. Cancellation measures processing speed, visual selective attention, and sustained attention (Bate, Mathias, & Crawford, 2001; Gauthier, Dehaut, & Joanette, 1989; Geldmacher, 1996; Halligan, Marshall, & Wade, 1989; Wojciulik, Husain, Clarke, & Driver, 2001).

Secondary Measures of Processing Speed

Processing speed is involved anytime a test has time constraints that may affect the overall performance. Examples of secondary measures of processing speed include: Block Design, Block Design Multiple Choice, Coding Recall, Coding Copy, and Elithorn Mazes. The influence of processing speed must be considered in the interpretation of these test results.

CASE STUDY ILLUSTRATION

Demographics

John was 7 years, 11 months olds at the time of the school neuropsychological assessment. He was placed in a regular second grade classroom with some supplemental instructional support in reading. English was the only language spoken by John.

Reasons for Referral

Despite supplemental reading instruction, John was not making adequate progress in reading. The school neuropsychological evaluation was requested to determine if John qualified for special education services under the category of specific learning disabled for his reading difficulties, to identify his current profile of cognitive strengths and weaknesses, and to tailor an intervention plan that maximizes his cognitive strengths and help to strengthen his cognitive weaknesses.

Birth and Developmental History

John's birth history was unremarkable. Most developmental milestones were reached within normal limits, except language, which was delayed. John was toilet trained at age 3 but still occasionally wets his bed. John is considered overweight for his age and is dieting under the care of a physician.

Medical History

When John was 1 year old, he had several febrile seizures. As a toddler, he cut several tendons on his right hand on an open food can. Although he had surgery to repair the tendons, John's flexibility is limited and impacts his ability to hold a pencil. John is generally a healthy child with only occasional colds and ear infections. He wears glasses for reading. He passed recent vision and hearing screenings at school.

Educational History

John attended preschool for 2 years and he received speech and language therapy due to poor articulation. In the first grade, an early intervention team determined that John was not making adequate progress in reading and supplemental reading instruction was started.

Assessment Validity

John displayed frequent articulation errors during the course of the evaluations, but his speech was understood by the examiner. He often demonstrated impulsivity and required extra prompts to complete longer tasks. John was right-handed and demonstrated a functional grip; however, he curled his wrist over the top of his writing. The current assessment results were considered to be a valid estimate of his current levels of functioning.

SENSORY–MOTOR FUNCTIONS

Remember, the WISC-IV and WISC-IV Integrated were not designed to measure sensory–motor functions in isolation. If you are going to use the WISC-IV or WISC-IV Integrated as a core assessment, it is recommended to supplement your battery with a test of sensory–motor functioning.

Scales	Where Derived?	Standard/(Scaled) Score	Percentile
Sensory Motor Functions			
Primary Measures			
• Coding Copy	WISC-IV Integ.	(10)	50
• Design Copying	NEPSY	(11)	26–75
• Fingertip Tapping	NEPSY	(9)	26–75
• Visuomotor Precision	NEPSY	(6)	11–25
• Car – Time	NEPSY	–	3–10
• Car – Errors	NEPSY	–	26–75
• Motorcycle – Time	NEPSY	–	3–10
• Motorcycle – Errors	NEPSY		26–75
Secondary Measures to Consider			
• Block Design	WISC-IV	(12)	74
• Block Design No Time Bonus	WISC-IV	(12)	74
• Block Design Process Approach	WISC-IV Integ.	(9)	36
• Coding	WISC-IV	(7)	16
• Symbol Search	WISC-IV	(9)	36
• Cancellation	WISC-IV	(9)	36
• Elithorn Mazes	WISC-IV Integ.	(8)	26
• No Time Bonus	WISC-IV Integ.	(8)	26

In this case study example, John was administered the WISC-IV/WISC-IV Integrated along with the sensorimotor subtests from the NEPSY. John's sensorimotor skills are within the average or at-expected range of functioning for his given age group. The low score on the NEPSY's Visuomotor Precision subtest was caused by an impulsive response style, as reflected by the below expected level scores on the Car – Time and Motorcycle – Time supplemental scores.

ATTENTIONAL PROCESSES

In addition to the WISC-IV/WISC-IV Integrated, John was administered the subtests from the NEPSY that measure attention, and four subtests from the D-KEFS that measure shifting attention. The WRAML-2 subtests and the NEPSY Narrative Memory subtest were administered to evaluate John's attentional capacity and subcomponents of memory (discussed later).

Selective/Focused Attention

John's visual selective/focused attention is at the expected or above expected level for his age as evidenced by his excellent performance on the NEPSY's

Visual Attention subtest. Auditorily, John appears to be able to selectively attend to details at a slightly below expected level for his age.

Sustained Attention

Sustained attention is indirectly measured on the WISC-IV Cancellation test and partially by the NEPSY Auditory Attention and Response Set subtest. John's sustained attention appears to fall within the expected level for his given age group. If a more direct measure of sustained attention needed to be administered a continuous performance task or the sustained attention tasks from the TEA-Ch would be recommended.

Shifting Attention

Set shifting appears to be a significant area of weakness for John. On the NEPSY Auditory Attention and Response Set subtest, John achieved a scaled score of 8 which was at the expected level for the first part of the task that requires selective/focused attention and to a lesser degree sustained attention. However, on the second part of the subtest, John was required to shift his cognitive set (e.g., put yellow chips in the box when the word red was spoken and vice versa). On the four subtests from the D-KEFS that require shifting attention or cognitive set, John performed in the below average to well below average range for his age group. The shifting attentional difficulties were not attributable to other processing deficits (e.g., visual scanning, number or letter sequencing, or motor speed deficits on the Trail Making Test, or any difference between verbal retrieval of words that start with a particular letter as compared to words that fit into a particular semantic category).

Divided Attention

John's divided attention is at the expected or above expected level for his age.

Attentional Capacity

John has a clear pattern of performance in the area of attentional capacity. John does not perform well on tasks that require learning or attending to isolated chunks of information (e.g., number strings, letter strings). John learns best when the contextual cues increase. For example, John performs poorly on learning strings of numbers or letters; however, his performance improves when he is asked to recall sentences of increasing lengths, and he performs very well on recalling stories (which maximize semantic cues).

VISUAL–SPATIAL PROCESSES

Visual Perception with a Motor Response

John's visual perception skills when combined with a motor response are at the expected level for his age group.

Visual Perception (Motor-Free)

John continues to perform at the expected level for his age group when the motor output demands are lessened on visual perceptual tasks.

Scales	Where Derived?	Standard/(Scaled) Score	Percentile
Attentional Processes			
Selective/Focused Attention (Primary Measures)			
• Auditory Attention & Response Set Part A – Attention Task	NEPSY	(8)	11–25
• Visual Attention	NEPSY	(14)	76–99
Selective/Focused Attention (Secondary Measures to Consider)			
• Color-Word Interference Test – Cond 3	D-KEFS	(7)	16
• Coding	WISC-IV	(7)	16
• Cancellation	WISC-IV	(9)	36
• Symbol Search	WISC-IV	(9)	36
• Arithmetic	WISC-IV	(9)	36
Sustained Attention (Secondary Measures to Consider)			
• Cancellation	WISC-IV	(9)	36
• Auditory Attention & Response Set	NEPSY	(8)	11–25
• Part A – Attention Task	NEPSY	(8)	11-25
• Part B – Response Set	NEPSY	(3)	≤2
Shifting Attention (Primary Measures)			
• Auditory Attention & Response Set			
• Part B – Response Set	NEPSY	(3)	≤2
• Trail Making Test – Condition 4	D-KEFS	(6)	9
• Verbal Fluency – Condition 3	D-KEFS	(7)	16
• Color-Word Interference – Condition 4	D-KEFS	(4)	2
• Design Fluency – Condition 3	D-KEFS	(5)	5
Divided Attention (Secondary Measures to Consider)			
• Letter-Number Sequencing	WISC-IV	(11)	64
• Letter-Number Sequencing Process Approach	WISC-IV Integrated	(8)	26
Attentional Capacity (Secondary Measures to Consider)			
• Digit Span Forward	WISC-IV	(6)	9
• Visual Digit Span	WISC-IV Integ.	(5)	5
• Spatial Span Forward	WISC-IV Integ.	(9)	36
• Letter Span Rhyming	WISC-IV Integ.	(5)	5
• Letter Span Nonrhyming	WISC-IV Integ.	(8)	26
• Finger Windows	WRAML-2	(9)	36
• Number/Letter	WRAML-2	(6)	9
• Sentence Memory	WRAML-2	(8)	26
• Story Memory	WRAML-2	(13)	84
• Narrative Memory	NEPSY	(12)	26–75

Scales	Where Derived?	Standard/(Scaled) Score	Percentile
Visual-Spatial Processes			
Visual Perception with Motor Response (Primary Measures)			
• Block Design	WISC-IV	(12)	74
• No Time Bonus	WISC-IV	(12)	74
Visual Perception with Motor Response (Secondary Measures to Consider)			
• Matrix Reasoning	WISC-IV	(13)	84
Visual Perception Motor Free (Primary Measures)			
• Block Design			
• Multiple Choice	WISC-IV Integ.	(12)	74
• Multiple Choice – No Time Bonus		(12)	74
• Design Process Approach		(9)	36
• Picture Completion	WISC-IV	(13)	84
• Picture Concepts	WISC-IV	(9)	36
• Arrows	NEPSY	(9)	26–75
Visual Scanning/Tracking (Primary Measure)			
• Trail Making Test Condition 1	D-KEFS	(10)	50
Visual Scanning/Tracking (Secondary Measures to Consider)			
• Coding	WISC-IV	(7)	16
• Symbol Search	WISC-IV	(9)	36
• Visual Attention	NEPSY	(14)	76–99

Visual Scanning/Tracking

John has average visual scanning or tracking skills for his age. His performance becomes somewhat compromised when he is asked to transfer shapes within a confined space rapidly (e.g., Coding). The weaker Coding score appears to be a function of his slower processing speed and perhaps some fine motor controls using his right hand.

LANGUAGE PROCESSES

Phonological Processing

John achieved an average score of the NEPSY Phonological Processing subtest but he did show some difficulties with the rearranging of phonemes in words. John's performance on the WIAT-II Pseudoword Decoding subtest was within the low average range for his age group. He had difficulty applying phonetic decoding rules to nonsense words. His teacher and parents report that John has difficulty with remembering words without sounding them out each time and understanding what he has read. John has not learned to memorize whole words which will facilitate his reading fluency and comprehension.

Oral Expression

John's oral expression is well developed for his age; however, he still has some persistent misarticulations.

Receptive Language (Listening Comprehension)

John's receptive language (listening comprehension) skills are at the expected level compared to other children his age.

Scales	Where Derived?	Standard/(Scaled) Score	Percentile
Language Processes			
Phonological Processing (Primary Measures)			
• Phonological Processing	NEPSY	(9)	26–75
• Pseudoword Decoding	WIAT-II	85	8
Oral Expression (Primary Measures)			
• Similarities	WISC-IV	(15)	95
• Vocabulary	WISC-IV	(13)	84
• Comprehension	WISC-IV	(10)	50
• Word Reasoning	WISC-IV	(13)	84
• Speeded Naming	NEPSY	(10)	26–75
• Oral Expression	WIAT-2	109	73
Oral Expression (Secondary Measures to Consider)			
• Information	WISC-IV	(9)	36
Receptive Language (Primary Measures)			
• Similarities Multiple Choice	WISC-IV Integ.	(11)	64
• Vocabulary Multiple Choice	WISC-IV Integ.	(9)	36
• Picture Vocabulary Multiple Choice	WISC-IV Integ.	(11)	64
• Comprehension Multiple Choice	WISC-IV Integ.	(11)	64
• Comprehension of Instructions	NEPSY	(13)	84
• Listening Comprehension	WIAT-2	118	88

MEMORY AND LEARNING PROCESSES

Immediate Memory

Verbal Immediate Memory

John's immediate verbal memory varies based on the semantic loading of the task. John does not perform well on memory for isolated non-meaning information. His performance for memorizing sentences or stories falls within the average range. John's performance on the WRAML-2 Verbal Learning subtest indicates that he is capable of learning isolated words if he is given repeated trials for learning.

Visual Immediate Memory

A similar pattern of performance was observed on the visual immediate memory tasks as observed on the verbal immediate memory tasks. As the complexity of the visual stimuli increased, John's performance improved. The exception to this finding was his performance on the NEPSY Memory for Faces subtest, which was lower due to his distractibility on the task.

Verbal–Visual Associative Learning

John does not learn well when visual and verbal stimuli are paired together. His difficulty with pairing sounds with symbols or names is one of the reasons he having difficulties with reading. John is stuck in the process of sounding out everything that he reads because he has automated the sound-symbol associations. This inability to form the sound-symbol associates has adversely affected his reading fluency and reading comprehension.

Scales	Where Derived?	Standard/(Scaled) Score	Percentile
Memory and Learning Processes: Immediate Memory			
Verbal Immediate Memory (Primary Measures)			
• Digit Span: Forward	WISC-IV	(6)	9
• Letter Span: Rhyming	WISC-IV Integ.	(5)	5
• Letter Span: Nonrhyming	WISC-IV Integ.	(8)	26
• Number/Letter	WRAML-2	(6)	9
• Sentence Memory	WRAML-2	(8)	26
• Verbal Learning	WRAML-2	(10)	50
• Story Memory	WRAML-2	(13)	84
• Narrative Memory	NEPSY	(12)	74
Visual Immediate Memory (Primary Measures)			
• Visual Digit Span	WISC-IV Integ.	(5)	5
• Spatial Span: Forward	WISC-IV Integ.	(9)	36
• Finger Windows	WRAML-2	(9)	36
• Picture Memory	WRAML-2	(9)	36
• Design Memory	WRAML-2	(13)	84
• Memory for Faces: Immediate	NEPSY	(7)	16
Visual Immediate Memory (Secondary Measures to Consider)			
• Coding	WISC-IV	(7)	16
• Symbol Search	WISC-IV	(9)	36
Verbal-Visual Associative Learning (Primary Measures)			
• Sound-Symbol	WRAML-2	(6)	9
• Memory for Names: Learning	NEPSY	(5)	5

Long-Term (Delayed) Memory

Verbal Long-Term (Delayed) Memory

When the semantic content has been maximized or multiple trials of verbal learning have been offered to John, he retains the verbal information in his long-term memory and he is able to retrieve it later.

Visual Long-Term (Delayed) Memory

John's visual long-term memory is within the average range compared to other children his age.

Verbal–Visual Associative (Delayed) Memory

John does not encode verbal–visual associations well, and as a result, he is not able to recall those verbal–visual associations after a delayed period of time.

Working Memory

John's working memory generally falls within the average range compared to other children his age. As previously reported, John's memory skills are better developed when there is meaning attached to what needs to be manipulated within memory stores.

Scales	Where Derived?	Standard/(Scaled) Score	Percentile
Memory and Learning Processes: Long-Term (Delayed) Memory			
Verbal Long-Term (Delayed) Memory (Primary Measures)			
• Story Memory: Delayed Recall	WRAML-2	(12)	74
• Story Memory: Retention	WRAML-2	(11)	64
• Story Memory: Delayed Recognition	WRAML-2	(12)	74
• Verbal Learning: Delayed Recall	WRAML-2	(9)	36
• Verbal Learning: Recognition	WRAML-2	(10)	50
Visual Long-Term (Delayed) Memory (Primary Measures)			
• Coding Recall	WISC-IV Integ.	(8)	26
• Design Memory: Recognition	WRAML-2	(12)	74
• Picture Memory: Recognition	WRAML-2	(9)	36
• Memory for Faces: Delayed	NEPSY	(9)	36
Verbal-Visual Associative Delayed Memory (Primary Measure)			
• Sound-Symbol: Delayed Recall	WRAML-2	(7)	16
• Memory for Names: Delayed Recall	NEPSY	(7)	16

Scales	Where Derived?	Standard/(Scaled) Score	Percentile
Memory and Learning Processes: Working Memory			
(Primary Measures)			
• Letter-Number Sequencing	WISC-IV	(11)	64
• Letter-Number Sequencing Process Approach	WISC-IV Integ.	(8)	26
• Digit Span: Backward	WISC-IV	(7)	16
• Spatial Span: Backward	WISC-IV Integ.	(10)	50
• Arithmetic	WISC-IV	(9)	36
• With Time Bonus	WISC-IV Integ.	(9)	36
• Process Approach: Part A (orally & visually)	WISC-IV Integ.	(11)	64

Scales	Where Derived?	Standard/(Scaled) Score	Percentile
• Process Approach: Part A with Time Bonus	WISC-IV Integ.	(11)	64
• Process Approach: Part B (orally, visually, & with paper and pencil)	WISC-IV Integ.	(12)	74
• Process Approach: Part B with Time Bonus	WISC-IV Integ.	(12)	74
• Written Arithmetic	WISC-IV Integ.	(12)	74
• Verbal Working Memory	WRAML-2	(8)	26
• Symbolic Working Memory	WRAML-2	(10)	50

Semantic Memory

Despite some verbal–visual associative memory and learning challenges that John faces, he has a wealth of knowledge that falls within the average range for children compared to his age.

Scales	Where Derived?	Standard/(Scaled) Score	Percentile
Memory and Learning Processes: Semantic Memory (Primary Measures)			
• Information	WISC-IV	(9)	36
• Information Multiple Choice	WISC-IV Integ.	(10)	50
(Secondary Measures to Consider)			
• Comprehension	WISC-IV	(10)	50
• Comprehension Multiple Choice	WISC-IV Integ.	(11)	64
• Vocabulary	WISC-IV	(10)	50
• Vocabulary Multiple Choice	WISC-IV Integ.	(11)	64
• Picture Vocabulary Multiple Choice	WISC-IV Integ.	(12)	74

EXECUTIVE FUNCTIONS

John's planning, reasoning, and problem-solving skills all fall within the average range for his given age group. Within the executive functions domain, shifting attention and working memory can be considered as well. As previously reported, John has poor shifting attention skills, which interferes with his transitions from one activity to another. John's working memory is well developed for his age.

Scales	Where Derived?	Standard/(Scaled) Score	Percentile
Executive Functions			
Planning, Reasoning, & Problem Solving (Primary Measures)			
• Picture Concepts	WISC-IV	(9)	36
• Matrix Reasoning	WISC-IV	(13)	84
• Tower	NEPSY	(9)	36
Planning, Reasoning, & Problem Solving (Secondary Measures to Consider)			
• Similarities	WISC-IV	(15)	95
• Similarities Multiple Choice	WISC-IV Integ.	(11)	64
• Block Design	WISC-IV	(12)	74
• Comprehension	WISC-IV	(10)	50
• Comprehension Multiple Choice	WISC-IV Integ.	(11)	64
• Arithmetic (numerical reasoning)	WISC-IV	(9)	36
• Elithorn Mazes	WISC-IV Integ.	(8)	26
• Elithorn Mazes – No Time Bonus	WISC-IV Integ.	(8)	26

PROCESSING SPEED

John's processing speed generally falls within the average range or expected level compared to children his own age. John does demonstrate some impulsive behaviors in the classroom and he does have a tendency to rush through assignments, yet his accuracy does not seem to unduly suffer.

Scales	Where Derived?	Standard/(Scaled) Score	Percentile
Processing Speed			
(Primary Measures)			
• Coding	WISC-IV	(7)	16
• Symbol Search	WISC-IV	(9)	36
• Cancellation	WISC-IV	(9)	36
(Secondary Measures to Consider)			
• Speeded Naming: Completion Time	NEPSY	–	≤2
• Visuomotor Precision: Car Completion Time	NEPSY	–	26–75
• Visuomotor Precision: Motorcycle Completion Time	NEPSY	–	26–75
• Coding Recall	WISC-IV Integ.	(8)	26
• Coding Copy	WISC-IV Integ.	(10)	50
• Letter-Number Sequencing	WISC-IV	(11)	64
• Letter-Number Sequencing Process Approach	WISC-IV Integ.	(8)	26
• Elithorn Mazes	WISC-IV Integ.	(8)	26
• Elithorn Mazes – No Time Bonus	WISC-IV Integ.	(8)	26

OVERALL INTELLECTUAL FUNCTIONING

John's WISC-IV composite scores and his Full Scale IQ are presented in the following table. All of the scales fall within the average range of functioning for his given age group. If only the WISC-IV Composite Scores were reported in a report, many of John's strengths and weaknesses would be under-identified.

WISC-IV Composite Scores	Standard Score	Percentile
• Verbal Comprehension	108	70
• Perceptual Reasoning	108	70
• Working Memory	91	27
• Processing Speed	88	21
Full Scale	102	55

ACADEMIC ACHIEVEMENT

John was administered the *Wechsler Individual Achievement Test* – Second Edition (WIAT-II; Wechsler, 2001) and the second grade reading probes from the DIBELS Oral Reading Fluency Test (Shaw & Shaw, 2002). John's reading accuracy and reading comprehension fell within the below expected range for his given age. John made frequent phonological errors while reading (e.g., *bat* for *cat*) and he solely relied on phonologically decoding every word he attempted to read. His sight word vocabulary, even for small words, was limited.

Academic Area	Where Derived?	Standard/(Scaled) Score	Percentile
Reading			
• Word Reading	WIAT-2	83	5
• Reading Comprehension	WIAT-2	76	16
• Pseudoword Decoding	WIAT-2	85	8
• Oral Reading Fluency (2nd grade probes)	DIBELS	—	<16
Math			
• Numerical Operations	WIAT-2	87	19
• Math Reasoning	WIAT-2	94	34
• Written Arithmetic	WISC-IV Integ.	(10)	50
Written Language			
• Spelling	WIAT-2	91	27
• Written Expression	WIAT-2	83	13
Oral Language			
• Listening Comprehension	WIAT-2	118	88
Oral Expression			
• Oral Expression	WIAT-2	109	73

John's math calculation skills were within the low end of the average range. He performed best on written arithmetic from the WISC-IV Integrated which placed additional structure on the task. John's mathematical reasoning skills fell with the average range.

John's written language skills fell within the low average to below average for his given age comparison group. In writing samples, John made the same types of dysphonetic errors as he did in this reading. John's oral expression and listening comprehension fall within the at-expected or average range for his age comparison group.

SUMMARY OF STRENGTHS AND WEAKNESSES AND EDUCATIONAL IMPLICATIONS

John was referred for a school neuropsychological evaluation because he had been identified as having reading difficulties, and despite early remedial reading instruction he was not making adequate progress.

Strengths

John has some excellent cognitive and academic strengths which need to be capitalized upon to facilitate his learning. Despite his cut right tendon in his hand, John has developed some good compensatory sensorimotor functions. John has well-developed selective/focused attention, particularly in the visual modality. His sustained attention, divided attention, visual–spatial processes, expressive language, receptive language, attentional or memory capacity for semantically loaded material, executive functions, and processing speed are also well developed for his age. Specific educational recommendations that will utilize these cognitive processing strengths are presented in the table below.

Strengths	Educational Implications
• Sensorimotor Functions	• When John wears his glasses for reading and writing his skills are improved. • Despite John's medical history of a cut, then repaired, right hand tendon, he has developed some compensatory fine motor coordination skills.
• Selective/Focused Attention (visual selective attention better developed than auditory selective attention)	• Maximize visual cues to help engage John's attention.
• Sustained Attention	• John can pay attention to instruction over prolonged periods of time.
• Divided Attention	• John can manage competing demands for his attention.
• Visual-Spatial Processes	• John performs well on tasks that require visual perception and organization.

Strengths	Educational Implications
• Oral Expression / Listening Comprehension	• John should be able to engage in classroom assignments that require expressive and receptive language skills.
• Attentional/Memory Capacity for Semantically Loaded Information	• Maximize the contextual cues used in learning activities.
• Executive functions	• John has good reasoning, planning, and problem solving skills.
• Processing Speed	• John has an impulsive response style (e.g., he rushes through assignments) but his accuracy does not appear to suffer.

Weaknesses

As a toddler, John cut several tendons on his right hand. Although he had surgery to repair the tendons, John's flexibility is limited and impacts his ability to hold a pencil. John's physical limitations with his right-hand movements impact his ability to control his fine motor coordination (e.g., copying of symbols into small areas) and his writing fluency. Under IDEA, John could qualify for special education services under the category of Other Health Impaired. His tendon damage in his right-hand seems to be adversely impacting his educational achievement in the area of written expression. However, John's weak fine motor coordination does not explain his difficulties with reading.

John has a constellation of processing weaknesses that contribute to his poor progress in reading. Initially almost all children learn to read by phonetically sounding out words. Eventually, most children form sound-symbol associations with the words they read and they start to memorize the whole word as they see it. When children reach this whole word reading stage, their reading fluency and reading comprehension improve. The intermediate stage of forming sound-symbol associations is crucial to improve a child's automaticity of reading. John's reading acquisition is breaking down at that intermediate, sound–symbol association stage. He has a great deal of difficulty forming sound–symbol associations which forces him to sound out everything that he reads, thereby slowing his reading fluency and adversely affecting his reading comprehension.

In addition to John's weak sound–symbol association learning, he has difficult shifting his attention from one task to another and memorizing isolated bits of information that are not associated with meaning. Some educational recommendations associated with John's identified cognitive and academic weaknesses are presented in the table below.

Weaknesses	Educational Implications
• Shifting Attention	• John has difficulty shifting from one activity to another. Provide John with cues to upcoming transitions (e.g., moving from one assignment to another) and teach John self-monitoring techniques.

• Attentional/Memory Capacity for Isolated Information	• In order to maximize John's learning potential, increase the semantic associations required for tasks. Do not try to teach isolated facts, or require memorization of isolated facts, unless paired with multiple learning trials.
• Verbal-Visual Associative Learning	• Minimize the blending of verbal and visual information in learning activities. John will learn best using one of the two modalities in isolation.
• Over-reliance on phonetic decoding rather than memorizing the whole word to increase fluency and comprehension.	• Help John develop a sight word vocabulary using flash cards. Consider a reading intervention program such as Reading Recovery (http://www.readingrecovery.org/) or Read Naturally (http://www.readnaturally.com/).
• Misarticulations in Oral Speech	• Continued speech therapy is recommended.
• Reading Decoding and Reading Comprehension	• Help John form sound-symbol associations by using flash cards that pair the sounds with the visual representation of the word and have a sentence that uses the word in context or have a definition of the word. When reading with John, frequently stop and ask him questions about what he has just read.
• Written Expression	• Due to John's physical limitations with his motor control of his right hand, and since he is right-handed, extra time will need to be allocated to John for all of his writing assignments.

Under IDEA, John could also qualify for special education services under the category of Specific Learning Disability in the areas of basic reading skills and reading comprehension. Regardless of the qualification used to provide John special education services, he needs to receive targeted reading interventions designed to improve his sound–symbol associations which will improve his whole word approach to reading. Once his whole word approach to reading improves his reading fluency reading comprehension will also improve.

SUMMARY

The WISC-IV used in conjunction with the WISC-IV Integrated can be the basis for a core battery for a school neuropsychological evaluation. These tests can be useful in providing an understanding of a child's level and pattern of intellectual performance, which in turn can be used to develop meaningful academic and behavioral interventions that have ecological and treatment validity. The WISC-IV can serve as a foundation for a school neuropsychological assessment; however, if used in isolation, the test will not address many of the areas, which are typically addressed in a comprehensive school neuropsychological assessment. The WISC-IV Integrated is a useful supplement to the WISC-IV, as a means of clarifying the causal factors of low scores on WISC-IV subtests. For a comprehensive school neuropsychological evaluation, the WISC-IV and WISC-IV Integrated must be supplemented with other neuropsychological measures based on the referral question(s) and the pattern of performance on the baseline measures. Supplemental measures of sensorimotor functions, attentional processing, and memory and learning processes should be considered as warranted.

The case study presented in this chapter illustrated how the WISC-IV and WISC-IV Integrated subtests can fit within a school neuropsychological conceptual model (Miller, 2007). The case study also illustrates the fact that if the WISC-IV and WIAT-II were the only tests administered, the underlying reasons for John's reading difficulties would have not been discovered. It is recommended that any school neuropsychological evaluation follow a hypothesis testing model such as the Hale and Fiorello's CHT Model (2004).

An important point to reiterate is that the classification of the WISC-IV and WISC-IV Integrated subtests based on their underlying neurocognitive task demands is intended to serve as a tentative interpretative guide only. A child's performance on a particular test may be a result of multiple factors that relate to the manifestation of the child's neurocognitive strengths and weaknesses, or the reliability and validity of the test measure itself, or non-cognitive factors (e.g., motivational, cultural, social, or environmental). The "art form" of psychology, and the specialized areas of school psychology and school neuropsychology, lies in generating hypotheses about the causal factors of samples of behavior, testing and verifying those hypotheses with multiple sources of data (e.g., observations, direct samples of behavior, behavioral rating scales), and ultimately linking empirically based interventions to help remediate identified areas of weakness.

REFERENCES

Ackerman, P. L., Beier, M. E., & Bowen, K. R. (2000). Explorations of crystallized intelligence: Completion tests, cloze tests, and knowledge. *Learning and Individual Differences, 12*, 105–121.

American Psychiatric Association (1994). *Diagnostic and Statistical Manual of Mental Disorders* (4th ed.). Washington, DC: American Psychiatric Association.

Anastasi, A., & Urbina, S. (1997). *Psychological Testing* (7th ed.). Upper Saddle River, NJ: Prentice Hall.

Archibald, Y. M. (1978). Time as a variable in the performance of hemisphere-damaged patients on the Elithorn Perceptual Maze Test. *Cortex, 14*, 22–31.

Bannatyne, A. (1974). Diagnosis: A note on recategorization of the WISC scaled scores. *Journal of Learning Disabilities, 7*, 272–273.

Baron, I. S. (2004). *Neuropsychological Evaluation of the Child*. New York: Oxford University Press.

Bate, A. J., Mathias, J. L., & Crawford, J. R. (2001). Performance on the Test of Everyday Attention and standard tests of attention following severe traumatic brain injury. *The Clinical Neuropsychologist, 15*, 405–422.

Beebe, D. W., Pfiffner, L. J., & McBurnett, K. (2000). Evaluation of the validity of the *Wechsler Intelligence Scale for Children* – Third Edition comprehension and picture arrangement subtests as measures of social intelligence. *Psychological Assessment, 12*, 97–101.

Beery, K. E., Buktenica, N. A., & Beery, N. A. (2003). *Beery–Buktenica Developmental Test of Visual–Motor Integration* (5th ed.). Minneapolis, MN: Pearson Assessments.

Beland, R., & Ska, B. (1992). Interaction between verbal and gestural language in progressive aphasia: A longitudinal case study. *Brain and Language, 43*, 355–385.

Berninger, V. W. (2007). *Process Assessment for the Learner: Test Battery for Reading and Writing – Second Edition*. San Antonio, TX: Harcourt Assessment, Inc.

Bryan, K. L., & Hale, J. B. (2001). Differential effects of left and right cerebral vascular accidents on language competency. *Journal of International Neuropsychological Society, 7*, 655–664.

Calhoun, S. L., & Mayes, S. (2005). Processing speed in children with clinical disorders. *Psychology in the Schools, 42*, 333–343.

Cohen, M. J. (1997). *Children's Memory Scale*. San Antonio, TX: Harcourt Assessment, Inc.

Conners, C. K., & Multihealth Systems Staff (2004). *Conners' Continuous Performance Test II Version 5 for Windows (CPT II V.5)*. North Tonawanda, NY: Multihealth Systems, Inc.

Cooper, S. (1995). *The Clinical Use and Interpretation of the Wechsler Intelligence Scale for Children* (3rd ed.). Springfield, IL: Charles C. Thomas.

Crawford, J. R., Parker, D. M., & Besson, J. A. (1988). Estimation of premorbid intelligence in organic conditions. *British Journal of Psychiatry, 153*, 178–181.

Crowe, S. F. (2000). Does the letter number sequencing task measure anything more than digit span? *Assessment, 7*, 113–117.

Dana, J., & Dawes, R. (2007). Comment on Fiorello et al. "Interpreting intelligence test results for children with disabilities: Is global intelligence relevant?". *Neuropsychology, 14*, 21–25.

Deak, G. O., & Maratsos, M. (1998). On having complex relationships of things: Preschoolers use multiple words for objects and people. *Developmental Psychology, 34*, 224–240.

Dean, R. S., & Woodcock, R. W. (2003). *Dean–Woodcock Neuropsychological Battery*. Itasca, IL: Riverside Publishing.

Decker, S. L., Hill, S. K., & Dean, R. S. (2007). Evidence of the construct similarity in executive functions and fluid reasoning abilities. *International Journal of Neuroscience, 117*, 735–748.

Delis, D., Kaplan, E., & Kramer, J. H. (2001). *Delis–Kaplan Executive Function System Examiner's Manual*. San Antonio, TX: The Psychological Corporation.

Delis, D. C., Robertson, L. C., & Efron, R. (1986). Hemispheric specialization of memory for visual hierarchical stimuli. *Neuropsychologia, 24*, 205–214.

Denckla, M. B. (1996). Biological correlates of learning and attention: What is relevant to learning disability and attention deficit hyperactivity disorder? *Journal of Developmental and Behavioral Pediatrics, 17*, 114–119.

Donders, J., Tulski, D. S., & Zhu, J. (2001). Criterion validity of new WAIS-III subtest scores after traumatic brain injury. *Journal of International Neuropsychological Society, 7*, 892–898.

Elwood, R. W. (2001). MicroCog: Assessment of cognitive functioning. *Neuropsychology Review, 11*, 89–100.

Ewing-Cobbs, L., Fletcher, J. M., & Levin, H. S. (1998). Academic achievement and academic placement following traumatic brain injury in children and adolescents: A two-year longitudinal study. *Journal of Clinical and Experimental Neuropsychology, 20*, 769–781.

Flavell, J. H. (1985). *Cognitive Development* (2nd ed.). Englewood, NJ: Prentice-Hall.

Fink, G. R., Marshall, J. C., Halligan, P. W., & Dolan, R. J. (1999). Hemispheric asymmetries in global/local processing are modulated by perceptual salience. *Neuropsychologia, 37*, 31–40.

Feldman, G. M., Kelly, R. M., & Diehl, V. A. (2004). An interpretative analysis of five commonly used processing speed measures. *Journal of Psychoeducational Assessment, 22*, 151–165.

Fiorello, C. A., Hale, J. B., Holdnack, J. A., Kavanagh, J. A., Terrell, J., & Long, L. (2007). Interpreting intelligence test results for children with disabilities: Is global IQ relevant? *Applied Neuropsychology, 14*, 2–12.

Fiorello, C. A., Hale, J. B., McGrath, M., Ryan, K., & Quinn, S. (2001). IQ interpretation for children with flat and variable test profiles. *Learning and Individual Differences, 13*, 115–125.

Fiorello, C. A., Hale, J. B., & Snyder, L. E. (2006). Cognitive hypothesis testing and response to intervention for children with reading problems. *Psychology in the Schools, 43*, 835–853.

Flanagan, D. P., & Harrison, P. L. (2005). *Contemporary Intellectual Assessment: Theories, Tests, and Issues* (2nd ed.). New York: The Guilford Press.

Flanagan, D. P., & Kaufman, A. S. (2004). *Essentials of WISC-IV Assessment*. New York: John Wiley & Sons, Inc.

Fletcher, J. M., Lyon, G. R., & Barnes, M. (2002). Classification of learning disabilities: An evidence-based evaluation. In: R. Bradley, L. Danielson, & D. P. Hallahan (Eds.), *Identification of Learning Disabilities: Research to Practice* (pp. 185–250). Mahwah, NJ: Lawrence Erlbaum Associates Publishers.

Gauthier, L., Dehaut, F., & Joanette, Y. (1989). The bells test: A quantitative and qualitative test for visual neglect. *International Journal of Clinical Neuropsychology, 11*, 49–54.

Geldmacher, D. S. (1996). Effects of stimulus number and target-to-distractor ratio on the performance of random array letter cancellation tasks. *Brain and Cognition, 32*, 405–415.

Glosser, G., & Friedman, R. B. (1995). A cognitive neuropsychological framework for assessing reading disorders. In R. L. Mapou, & J. Spector (Eds.), *Clinical Neuropsychological Assessment: A Cognitive Approach* (pp. 115–136). New York: Plenum.

Goldberg, E. (2001). *The Executive Brain: Frontal Lobes and the Civilized Mind*. New York: Oxford University Press.

Goldstein, F. C., & Green, R. C. (1995). Assessment of problem solving and executive functions. In: R. L. Mapou, & J. Spector (Eds.), *Clinical Neuropsychological Assessment: A Cognitive Approach* (pp. 49–81). New York: Plenum.

Groth-Marnat, G. (1997). *Handbook of Psychological Assessment* (3rd ed.). New York: John Wiley & Sons.

Groth-Marnat, G., Gallagher, R. E., Hale, J. B., & Kaplan, E. (2000). The *Wechsler Intelligence Scales*. In: G. Groth-Marnat (Ed.), *Neuropsychological Assessment in Clinical Practice: A Guide to Test Interpretation and Integration* (pp. 129–194). Hoboken, NJ: John Wiley & Sons Inc.

Hale, J. B. (2006). Implementing IDEA with a three-tier model that includes response to intervention and cognitive assessment methods. *School Psychology Forum: Research and Practice, 1*, 16–27.

Hale, J. B., & Fiorello, C. A. (2004). *School Neuropsychology: A Practitioner's Handbook*. New York: The Guilford Press.

Hale, J. N., Fiorello, C. A., & Brown, L. L. (2005). Determining medication treatment effects using teacher ratings and classroom observations of children with ADHD: Does neuropsychological impairment matter? *Educational and Child Psychology, 22*, 39–61.

Hale, J. B., Fiorello, C. A., Kavanagh, J. A., Hoeppner, J. B., & Gaither, R. A. (2001). WISC-III predictors of academic achievement for children with learning disabilities: Are global and factor scores comparable? *School Psychology Quarterly, 16*, 31–55.

Hale, J. B., Fiorello, C. A., Kavanagh, J. A., Holdnack, J. A., & Aloe, A. M. (2007). Is the demise of IQ interpretation justified? A response to special issue authors. *Applied Neuropsychology, 14*, 37–51.

Hale, J. B., Hoeppner, J. B., & Fiorello, C. A. (2002). Analyzing digit span components for assessment of attention processes. *Journal of Psychoeducational Assessment, 20*, 128–143.

Hale, J. B., Kaufman, A., Naglieri, J. A., & Kavale, K. A. (2006). Implementation of IDEA: Integrating response to intervention and cognitive assessment methods. *Psychology in the schools, 43*, 753–770.

Hale, J. B., Rosenberg, D., Hoeppner, J. B., & Gaither, R. (1997, April). Cognitive predictors of behavior disorders in children with learning disabilities. Paper presented at the *Annual Convention of the National Association of School Psychologists*, Anaheim, CA.

Halligan, P. W., Marshall, J. C., & Wade, D. T. (1989). Visuospatial neglect: Underlying factors and test sensitivity. *Lancet*, October 14, 908–911.

Heaton, R. K., Chelune, G. J., Talley, J. L., Kay, G., & Curtiss, G. (1993). *Wisconsin Card Sorting Test Manual*. Odessa, FL: Psychological Assessment Resources.

Horn, J. L. (1985). Remodeling old models of intelligence. In: B. B. Wolman (Ed.), *Test Validity* (pp. 129–145). Hillsdale, NJ: Erlbaum.

Joshi, A., Roy, E. A., Black, S. E., & Barbour, K. (2003). Patterns of limb apraxia in progressive aphasia. *Brain and Cognition, 53*, 403–407.

Joy, S., Fein, D., Kaplan, E., & Freedman, M. (1999). Information multiple choice among healthy older adults: Characteristics, correlates, and clinical implications. *The Clinical Neuropsychologist, 13*, 48–53.

Kaplan, E. (1988). A process approach to neuropsychological assessment. In: T. Boll, & B. K. Bryant (Eds.), *Clinical Neuropsychology and Brain Function: Research, Measurement, and Practice* (pp. 125–167). Washington, DC: American Psychological Association.

Kaplan, E., Gallagher, R. E., & Glosser, G. (1998). Aphasia-related disorders. In: M. T. Sarno (Ed.), *Acquired Aphasia* (3rd ed., pp. 309–339). San Diego, CA: Academic Press.

Kaufman, A. S. (1994). *Intelligence Testing with the WISC-III.* New York: Wiley.

Keith, R. W. (1994). *Auditory Continuous Performance Test Examiner's Manual.* San Antonio, TX: Harcourt Assessment, Inc.

Keith, T. Z., Fine, J. G., Taub, G. E., Reynolds, M. R., & Kranzler, J. H. (2006). Hierarchical multi-sample, confirmatory factor analysis of the *Wechsler Intelligence Scale for Children* – Fourth Edition: What does it measure? *School Psychology Review, 35*, 108–127.

Korkman, M., Kirk, U., & Kemp, S. (1998). *NEPSY: A Developmental Neuropsychological Assessment.* San Antonio, TX: The Psychological Corporation.

Korkman, M., Kirk, U., & Kemp, S. (2007). *NEPSY-II: A Developmental Neuropsychological Assessment.* San Antonio, TX: The Psychological Corporation.

Lezak, M. D. (1988). IQ: R.I.P. *Journal of Clinical and Experimental Neuropsychology, 10*, 351–361.

Lezak, M. D. (1995). *Neuropsychological Assessment* (3rd ed.). New York: Oxford University Press.

Lichter, D. G., & Cummings, J. L. (2001). Introduction and overview. In: D. G. Lichter, & J. L. Cummings (Eds.), *Frontal–Subcortical Circuits in Psychiatric and Neurological Disorders* (pp. 1–43). New York: The Guilford Press.

Lipsitz, J. D., Dworkin, R. H., & Erlenmeyer-Kimling, L. (1993). Wechsler comprehension and picture arrangement subtests and social adjustment. *Psychological Assessment, 5*, 430–437.

Livingston, R. B., Jennings, E., Reynolds, C. R., & Gray, R. M. (2003). Mutlivariate analyses of the profile stability of intelligence tests: High for IQs, low to very low for subtest analyses. *Archives of Clinical Neuropsychology, 18*, 487–507.

Luria, A. R. (1980). *Higher Cortical Functions in Man* (2nd ed.). New York: Basic Books.

Manly, T., Robertson, I. H., Anderson, V., & Nimmo-Smith, I. (1999). *Test of Everyday Attention for Children (TEA-Ch) Manual.* San Antonio, TX: Harcourt Assessment, Inc.

Mayes, S. D., & Calhoun, S. L. (2006). Frequency of reading, math, and writing disabilities in children with clinical disorders. *Learning and Individual Differences, 16*, 145–157.

McDermott, P. A., Fantuzzo, J. W., & Glutting, J. J. (1990). Just say no to subtest analysis: A critique on Wechsler theory and practice. *Journal of Psychoeducational Assessment, 8*, 290–302.

Milberg, W. P., Hebben, N., & Kaplan, E. (1986). The Boston process approach to neuropsychological assessment. In: I. Grant, & K. M. Adams (Eds.), *Neuropsychological Assessment of Neuropsychiatric Disorders* (pp. 65–86). New York: Oxford University Press.

Miller, D. C. (2004). Neuropsychological assessment in the schools. In: C. Spielberger (Ed.), *Encyclopedia of Applied Psychology* (Vol. 2, pp. 657–664). San Diego, CA: Academic Press.

Miller, D. C. (2007). *Essentials of School Neuropsychological Assessment.* New York: Wiley.

Milner, A. D., & Goodale, M. A. (1995). *The Visual Brain in Action.* New York: Oxford University Press.

Mirsky, A. F. (1987). Behavioral and psychophysiological markers of disordered attention. *Environmental Health Perspectives, 74*, 191–199.

Mirsky, A. F. (1996). Disorders of attention: A neuropsychological perspective. In: G. R. Lyon, & N. A. Krasnegor (Eds.), *Attention, Memory and Executive Function* (pp. 71–95). Baltimore, MD: Paul H. Brookes Publishing Co.

Moses, P., Roe, K., Buxton, R. B., Wong, E. C., Frank, L. R., & Stiles, J. (2002). Functional MRI of global and local processing in children. *NeuroImage, 16*, 415–424.

Naglieri, J., & Das, J. P. (1997). *Das–Naglieri Cognitive Assessment System.* Itasca, IL: Riverside Publishing Company.

494   3. SOME FURTHER CONSIDERATIONS

Pfeiffer, S. I., Reddy, L. A., Kletzel, J. E., Schmelzer, E. R., & Boyer, L. M. (2000). *School Psychology Quarterly, 15*, 376–385.
Poreh, A. M. (Ed.) (2006). *The Quantified Process Approach to Neuropsychological Assessment*. New York, NY: Psychology Press.
Prabhakaran, V., Smith, J. A., Desmond, J. E., Glover, G. H., & Gabrieli, G. (1997). Neural substrates of fluid reasoning: An fMRI study of neocortical activation during performance of the Raven's Progressive Matrices Test. *Cognitive Psychology, 33*, 43–63.
Reschly, D. J. (2005). Learning disabilities identification: Primary intervention, secondary intervention, and then what? *Journal of Learning Disabilities, 38*, 510–515.
Reynolds, C. R. (1997). Forward and backward memory span should not be combined for clinical analysis. *Archives of Clinical Neuropsychology, 12*, 29–40.
Reynolds, C. R., & Voress, J. K. (2007). *Test of Memory and Learning – Second Edition*. Austin, TX: PRO-ED, Inc.
Riccio, C. A., Reynolds, C. R., & Lowe, P. A. (2001). *Clinical applications of Continuous Performance Tests: Measuring attention and impulsive responding in children and adolescents*. New York: John Wiley & Sons, Inc.
Saggino, A., Perfetti, B., Spitoni, G., & Galati, G. (2006). Fluid intelligence and executive functions: New perspectives. In: L. V. Wesley (Ed.), *Intelligence: New Research* (pp. 1–22). Hauppauge, NY: Nova Science Publishers.
Sattler, J. M. (2001). *Assessment of Children: Cognitive Applications* (4th ed.). La Mesa, CA: Jerome M. Sattler.
Sattler, J. M., & Dumont, R. (2004). *Assessment of Children: WISC-IV and WPPSI-III Supplement*. La Mesa, CA: Jerome M. Sattler.
Schatz, A. M., Ballantyne, A. O., & Trauner, D. A. (2000). A hierarchical analysis of Block Design errors in children with early focal brain damage. *Developmental Neuropsychology, 17*, 75–83.
Schrank, F. A., & Flanagan, D. P. (2003). *WJIII clinical use and interpretation: Scientist-Practitioner perspectives*. San Diego: Academic Press.
Schrank, F. A., Flanagan, D. P., Woodcock, R. W., & Mascolo, J. T. (2003). *Essentials of WJIII Cognitive Abilities Assessment*. New York: John Wiley & Sons, Inc.
Scruggs, T. E., & Mastropieri, M. A. (2002). On babies and bathwater: Addressing the problems of identification of learning disabilities. *Learning Disability Quarterly, 25*, 155–168.
Semel, E., Wiig, E. H., & Secord, W. A. (2003). *Clinical Evaluation of Language Fundamentals – Fourth Edition*. San Antonio, TX: Harcourt Assessment, Inc.
Shaw, R., & Shaw, D. (2002). *DIBELS Oral Reading Fluency-Based Indicators of Third Grade Reading Skills for Colorado State Assessment Program (CSAP)*. Eugene, OR: University of Oregon. (Technical Report)
Sheslow, D., & Adams, W. (2003). *Wide Range Assessment of Memory and Learning – Second Edition*. Wilmington, DE: Wide Range, Inc.
Shulman, C., Yirmiya, N., & Greenbaum, C. W. (1995). From categorization to classification: A comparison among individuals with autism, mental retardation, and normal development. *Journal of Abnormal Psychology, 104*, 601–609.
Smyth, M. M., & Scholey, K. A. (1992). Determining spatial span: The role of movement time and articulation rate. *Quarterly Journal of Experimental Psychology: Human Experimental Psychology, 45A*, 479–501.
Tulving, E., & Markowitsch, H. J. (1997). Memory beyond the hippocampus. *Current Opinion in Neurobiology, 7*, 209–216.
Wagner, R., Torgesen, J., & Rashotte, C. (1999). *Comprehensive Test of Phonological Processing*. Minneapolis, MN: Pearson Assessments.
Watkins, M. W., Glutting, J. J., & Lei, P. W. (2007). Validity of the full scale IQ when there is significant variability among WISC-III and WISC-IV factor scores. *Applied Neuropsychology, 14*, 13–20.
Wechsler, D. (2001). *Wechsler Individual Achievement Test – Second Edition*. San Antonio, TX: Harcourt Assessment, Inc.

Wechsler, D. (2003). *Wechsler Intelligence Scale for Children – Fourth Edition*. San Antonio, TX: Harcourt Assessment, Inc.

Wechsler, D. (2004). *WISC-IV Integrated*. San Antonio, TX: Harcourt Assessment, Inc.

Wechsler, D., Kaplan, E., Fein, D., Morris, E., Kramer, J. H., Maerlender, A., & Delis, D. C. (2004). *The Wechsler Intelligence Scale for Children – Fourth Edition Integrated Technical and Interpretative Manual*. San Antonio, TX: Harcourt Assessment, Inc.

Wojciulik, E., Hasain, M., Clarke, K., & Driver, J. (2001). Spatial working memory deficit in developmental dyslexias. *Journal of Educational Psychology, 91*, 415–438.

Woodcock, R. W. (1997). The Woodcock Johnson Tests of Cognitive Ability – Revised. In: D. O. Flanagan, J. L. Genshaft, & P. L. Harrison (Eds.), *Contemporary Intellectual Assessment: Theories, Tests, and Issues* (pp. 230–246). New York: Guilford Press.

Woodcock, R. W., McGrew, K. S., & Mather, N. (2001). *Woodcock–Johnson III Tests of Cognitive Abilities*. Itasca, IL: Riverside Publishing.

13

EXTENDING THE WISC-IV: EXECUTIVE FUNCTIONING

S. DUKE HAN[1,2,3], DEAN C. DELIS[4,5] AND JAMES A. HOLDNACK[6]

[1]Department of Psychology, Loyola University Chicago, Chicago, IL, USA

[2]Department of Neurology, Loyola University Medical Center, Maywood, IL, USA

[3]Neuroscience Institute, Loyola University Medical Center, Maywood, IL, USA

[4]Psychology Service, VA San Diego Healthcare System, San Diego, CA, USA

[5]Department of Psychiatry, UCSD School of Medicine, San Diego, CA, USA

[6]The Psychological Corporation, San Antonio, TX, USA

INTRODUCTION

The term "executive functions" (EFs) is used broadly to refer to a group of cognitive abilities usually associated with the prefrontal brain regions or the frontal–striatal–thalamic–cortical (FSTC) circuitry (Denckla, 1996). Interest in EF as a neurocognitive domain has enjoyed a renaissance due to the widening study of EF in more applied settings (e.g., Ardila et al., 2005), and the theorized evolutionary importance of EF development to achieving success in various significant intellectual and social environments (see Barkley, 2001, for a review). Because of this current interest, several newly developed questionnaires (e.g., Behavior Rating Inventory of Executive Function (BRIEF); Guy et al., 2004) and neuropsychological testing measures (e.g., Delis–Kaplan Executive Functions System (D-KEFS); Delis et al., 2001) designed to assess either EF skills directly (testing measures) or indirectly (questionnaires) have enjoyed recent publication and widespread use among the neuropsychology clinical and research community. However, despite this recent clinical and research interest in EF, the theoretical constructs underlying EF remain somewhat unclear and are often the subject of debate.

EXECUTIVE FUNCTIONS

Tranel et al. (1994) offered one of the first attempts to present a unified construct of EF. In addition to highlighting the seminal work by Goldman-Rakic (1987) and the necessary inclusion of working memory considerations in the construct, they define EF as "higher-order cognitive capacities." Moreover, the authors describe the cognitive abilities subsumed under the EF construct and the operations of the prefrontal region of the brain as having "an intimate relationship" (p. 126). Distilling through many then-contemporary published accounts and opinions of what should specifically constitute as an EF ability, Tranel et al. identified four common and prevailing themes: planning, decision-making, judgment, and self-perception (i.e., "self-monitoring, self-modulation").

Denckla (1996) advocates for a more narrowly construed view of the EF construct and a wider consideration of the neuroanatomical correlates involved with EF abilities. Again citing the importance of working memory considerations, she views EF abilities as "control processes" that involve "inhibition and delay of responding" (p. 265). More specifically, these control processes aid in the development of an anticipatory set, the goal-directed preparation to act, the ability to control the impact of interference, and the ability to sequence responses. Her argument for a more constricted view of the EF construct follows from a criticism of EF theorists as "reinventing the g of general intelligence." This criticism usually follows when a theorist speaks of EF as "supraordinate" or "higher order." Her argument for considering brain regions beyond the prefrontal areas to the circuit connections between prefrontal areas and subcortical regions follows from a keen understanding of the importance of frontal regions as coordinating center for multiple neurobehavioral systems. In addition to these valuable contributions to the development of the EF construct, Denckla highlights the importance of considering language abilities as having a mediating role in EF abilities.

Taking a somewhat opposite approach to the EF construct, Barkley (2001) advocates for a more generalized behavioral definition of EFs and the broadening application of the EF construct to evolutionary and social perspectives. He argues that the EF construct serves the singular purpose of self-regulation through behavioral inhibition (pp. 7–8) and describes four specific EFs: "sensing to the self" (non-verbal working memory), "speech to the self" (verbal working memory), "emotion/motivation to the self" (self-regulation of affect/motivation/arousal), and "play to the self" (flexibility, generativity). Barkley asserts that the development of EF abilities has a strong foundation in evolutionary principles, providing the substrate for learning and cultural value transmission.

Whereas theoretical models of EFs are still nascent, behavioral descriptions of the dysexecutive syndrome are well documented. Descriptions of cognitive and behavior impairments after damage to the frontal lobes or subcorticofrontal circuitry provide a strong basis on which measures of executive functioning have been developed. A common feature of frontal lobe injury is observable deficits in more unstructured daily living skills and specific components of cognition despite relatively intact intellectual functioning. A broad description of EFs is that they are higher-order cognitive skills associated with the ability to engage in independent, goal-directed behavior. The specific skill sets associated with executive functioning are quite varied, though some are inter-related. In general EF skills are those that enable or facilitate goal-directed behavior and ability to solve novel or complex problems. The ability to *inhibit* automatic responses (e.g., overlearned responses) or to avoid being "pulled" by the environment into making a response prior to reflecting upon the best response are critical self-regulatory behaviors. *Initiating* and *sustaining* (e.g., productivity) problem-solving behavior is important when long-term goals, projects, or complex problems must be completed. *Developing* the correct *cognitive set* and *maintaining* the set allow individuals to complete tasks within specific rules, restrictions, or specified parameters. *Self-monitoring* one's behavior is the process by which individuals are able to maintain set and maintain goal-directed behavior by monitoring for off-task, erroneous, or rule-violating behaviors. The ability to *plan* and *organize* facilitates both short- and long-term problem-solving. In many situations or when solving complex problems, initial efforts may not yield acceptable or desired results, in these situations it is essential that the individual is *flexible* in their problem-solving approach and can *switch* their behaviors to meet the demands of the task or environment. The capacity to think beyond the immediate concrete circumstances and stimuli and think about problems *abstractly* is a key element of executive functioning. The ability of the individual to express these diverse skills when facing novel or complex situations is the essence of the construct of executive functioning.

While there appears to be some discrepancy between researchers, theorists generally agree in the value and existence of EF as a useful neurocognitive construct and the importance of considering EF from a developmental perspective. We recently argued for the importance of considering EF assessments alongside standardized testing measurements in school-age children (Delis et al., 2007). Furthermore, EF dysfunction may be a fundamental underlying mechanism or symptom of certain pediatric disorders (e.g., Barkley, 1997).

BEHAVIORAL MANIFESTATIONS OF EF IMPAIRMENTS IN PEDIATRIC POPULATIONS

Deficits in executive functioning may result in obvious behavior disorder or subtle problems with behavioral regulation. Children with *inhibitory control* problems engage in frequent impulsive, poorly thought-out behaviors. They may react to environmental stimuli (e.g., grab items off shelves in a store, respond aggressively to mild provocation), fail to inhibit inappropriate behaviors (e.g., talk out of turn, leave their seat when they are not supposed to, say inappropriate things), and have difficulty coping with frustration (e.g., get angry when told "no", become emotionally over-reactive). Children who have poor *behavioral initiation* often fail to start chores, homework, or other tasks that are not of interest to them. An inability to *sustain behavior* results in incomplete or inadequate task performance such as partially completed homework or half-finished chores. Problems with *self-monitoring behavior* result in behaviors that interfere with accomplishing a goal: the child seems easily *distracted*, fails to pay attention to rules, has sloppy or haphazardly completed work or seems forgetful (e.g., losing track of what he or she is doing). *Organization deficits* may manifest in not having materials needed to complete a task (e.g., leaving needed books at school, unable to find the right type of marker for a task), having a cluttered, nonfunctional living/work space, and a general haphazard approach to solving problems and completing necessary tasks. *Planning* difficulties often co-exist with organizational problems as children react to their environment more than pausing to think about what needs to be accomplished and what is the best way to accomplish it. These symptoms are often associated with attention-deficit disorder.

The disorganized and impulsive child displays one type of EF impairment profile. In other instances, the child may have problems coping with changes in their environment and they may become very agitated and upset when something interferes with their routine. Problems with *cognitive flexibility* are observed in children that have difficulty coping with changes (i.e., planned or unplanned) in their environment: they may repeat behaviors even if they do not help them solve a problem or even when they have be told to not engage in that behavior. They may also have difficulty learning from experience because they often approach a task in the same manner each time regardless of a positive or negative outcome related to that behavior. Children with poor *abstract reasoning* abilities will respond to the immediate environment in a very concrete manner (e.g., not understand figurative language, not understand when others are making a joke). Additionally, this group of children may have an inability to understand that other people may have a different understanding or have different experiences than their own. Not being able to understand the perspective of others (e.g., theory of mind) leads to atypical social behaviors. Children with concrete thinking, limited cognitive flexibility, and poor theory of mind skills are at risk for significant psychosocial difficulties. These EF limitations have been associated with autistic spectrum disorders.

Some children have a mixture of executive functioning deficits that do not result in a specific behavioral syndrome but nonetheless affect their ability to function. In some instances, children with poor mental flexibility, poor frustration tolerance, and mild language problems will exhibit conduct related problems. Some children may have cognitive problems that are restricted to more academic tasks such as poor productivity for writing, or disorganization and poor planning for school subjects but not other tasks. Other behavior descriptors that might relate to EF deficits include: inefficiency (takes more steps to complete task than necessary); difficulty understanding consequences and cause–effect relationships; frequently violation of rules despite apparent knowledge of the rules; apathy (lacking motivation, does not set goals, engages in behavior only when prodded); difficulties accessing knowledge; poor frustration tolerance; emotional lability; poor judgment; and inefficacy (does not work up to ability level or performs inconsistently on tasks within his ability level). Since many EF behaviors are associated with personality style and motivation, it is essential to determine if cognitive factors underlie these behaviors so the child's problems are understood as not necessarily intentional (e.g., "lazy," "stubborn," "disobedient"), but rather a reflection of skill deficit.

EF IN PEDIATRIC DISORDERS

ADHD

Attention-Deficit Hyperactivity Disorder (ADHD) is a term used to describe a condition which usually manifests in problems of sustained attention, impulse inhibition, and motor control. The *Diagnostic and Statistical Manual of Mental Disorders*-IV-TR (DSM-IV-TR; American Psychiatric Association, 2000) identifies three subtypes of ADHD: (1) inattentive type, (2) hyperactive type, and (3) combined type. Symptoms must occur prior to age 7 and in more than one setting. Barkley (1997) identified ADHD as a fundamental deficit in behavioral inhibition, manifested most clearly in deficits of working memory, regulation of motivation, and motor control. Roth and Saykin (2004) add to this list by presenting examples of problems of cognitive flexibility, initiation, interference control, planning and organization, response inhibition, self-monitoring, and working memory. Roth and Saykin also review evidence for a disruption in the FSTC circuitry in ADHD. In addition to ADHD participants performing significantly lower on the *Wechsler Intelligence Scale for Children* – Third Edition (WISC-III) Full Scale IQ, Mahone et al. (2002) present evidence for ADHD participants rating lower on all five subscales of the BRIEF questionnaire (working memory, inhibition, metacognition, behavioral regulation, and global executive composite) compared to control subjects. In a well-constructed neuropsychological study, Oosterlaan et al. (2005) showed ADHD participants exhibited deficits in planning and working memory, but not verbal fluency. Using an EF battery of tests, Harris et al. (1995) showed that ADHD-only and ADHD + Tourette's children performed worse than Tourette's-only children. Geurts et al. (2005) presented results showing a difference between ADHD-combined types and control participants on measures of inhibition, but no other EF abilities. A large meta-analytic study found children with ADHD (i.e., clinical and community samples) perform significantly worse on measures of executive functioning than typically developing controls, with effect sizes ranging from 0.49 to 0.69 (Wilcutt et al., 2005). The results held even when controlling for the effects of general intellectual ability, academic skills, and comorbidities. The largest observed effects were on sustained attention (e.g., continuous performance tests, CPTs), inhibitory control (e.g., stop-signal and CPT commission errors), planning (e.g., tower tasks), and spatial working memory (Wilcutt et al., 2005).

While EF dysfunction appears to be a fundamental symptom of ADHD, it must be noted that some studies refute this association. Larry Seidman (2006) recently reaffirmed that not all persons with ADHD have EF dysfunction and some may have dysfunction in certain brain reward systems not associated with EF abilities. Marks et al. (2005) recently found no association between EF measures and ADHD symptoms in a group of 22 preschoolers at risk. Jonsdottir et al. (2006) also found no association between EF measures and ADHD, but did find an association between EF measures and comorbid depressive and autistic symptomatology.

While the behavioral manifestation of ADHD appears consistent with impairments in executive functioning, EF tests may not always differentiate children with ADHD from controls. Additionally, EF tests vary considerably in their sensitivity to ADHD such that studies with small samples using less sensitive EF tests may not find significant differences between groups.

TOURETTE SYNDROME

Tourette Syndrome (TS) is characterized by involuntary motor and vocal tics occurring continuously for more than 1 year (APA, 2000). TS is considered a neurodevelopmental disorder, and frontostriatal dysfunction is considered one of the main underlying mechanisms of TS. Because of the implication of frontostriatal circuitry in the syndrome, it is logical to assume that TS children would evidence EF dysfunction. However, many studies have been unable to support EF dysfunction as a symptom of TS. Testing inhibition, visual working memory, planning, cognitive flexibility, and verbal fluency, Verte et al. (2005) found that TS children performed at equivalent levels with control children. Using measures of flexibility, planning, and inhibition, Ozonoff and Jensen (1999) presented evidence again showing no difference between TS children and controls. While many studies have reported no deficits in EF in TS, other studies have reported that TS is associated with inhibitory control deficits (Channon et al., 2003; Crawford et al., 2005). In general, uncomplicated TS patients do not exhibit impairments in EF; however, some children with TS may have inhibitory control problems.

TRAUMATIC BRAIN INJURY

The cognitive sequelae following Traumatic Brain Injury (TBI) depends on a host of factors, including whether or not the injury was an open head injury or closed head injury, severity of head injury, length of loss of consciousness, and location of coup and contrecoup. Nevertheless, the frontal lobes and the FSTC circuit are often affected by moderate to severe TBI, and by extension, EF deficits are often observed (Wilde et al, 2005). Utilizing a large battery of EF measures, Brookshire et al. (2004) identified a four-factor model of EF differences between head-injured children and normally developing children. The authors termed the factors as EF discourse, problem-solving, processing speed, and declarative memory. Slomine et al. (2002) presented evidence showing TBI sustained at a younger age is associated with greater perseveration of response and worse word generation performance. Impairments on executive functioning tasks after pediatric TBI have been reported for Porteus Mazes (Levin et al., 2001); gambling tasks (Levine et al., 2005); Wisconsin Card Sort Test and Letter Fluency (Slomine et al., 2002); D-KEFS Design Fluency, Verbal Fluency, Card Sorting, Color–Word Interference Test, and Trail-Making Test (Holdnack et al., 2006a, b); and Theory of Mind (Snodgrass & Knott, 2006). Anderson and Catroppa (2005) report some EF deficits may persist 2 years after initial injury. Research indicates that EF deficits occur relatively frequently subsequent to moderate to severe pediatric TBI and are observed on a variety of EF measures, suggesting comprehensive assessment of these functions is warranted.

LEARNING DISABILITIES

Learning disabilities may manifest as a single deficit (or group of deficits) in a specific area of learning, or multiple deficits in multiple areas of learning. Because of the heterogeneity of known learning disorders, EF correlates may be unique depending on the particular learning disability. Increasingly, EFs and working memory functions are identified as important skills associated with reading disorders (Reiter et al., 2005). More specifically, children diagnosed with Dyslexia had significantly worse performance on working memory, complex inhibitory control, and verbal and design fluency (Reiter et al., 2005). Brosnan et al. (2002) presented evidence for deficits in inhibition of distracters and sequencing of events among children with dyslexia. Van der Schoot et al. (2000) found that EF deficits (e.g., inhibitory control, cognitive interference, and planning) in reading disorder were associated with children that would guess the correct decoding of a word rather than those that used a letter by letter spelling-out-the-word approach.

Children identified as having Writing Disorder were found to have lower scores on initiation and set shift tasks (Hooper et al., 2002). Altemeier et al. (2006) found executive functioning to be an important predictor of children's ability to read, take notes, and write a report from their notes. Additional work by this group supports the importance of understanding the impact of executive functioning skills in helping children with writing problems (Chenault et al. 2006).

Van der Sluis et al. (2004) reported children with arithmetic learning disabilities were impaired on specific tasks of inhibition and shifting, but children with reading disabilities were not. Seidman et al. (2001) also reported an association between arithmetic learning disability and worse performance on EF measures among ADHD children. Studies are emerging that illustrate the important role of EFs in the development of academic abilities and their relationship to the development of learning disorders. Children who are having academic struggles and are at risk for learning disabilities should be evaluated to determine the impact that poor EFs may play in their learning difficulties.

AUTISM

High-Functioning Autism (HFA) is characterized by three major symptoms: (1) impairment in social interaction, (2) impairment in communication, and (3) "restricted, repetitive, and stereotypic patterns of behaviors, interests, and activities" (Verte et al., 2006). In a study comparing HFA, ADHD, and control children, Geurts et al. (2004) showed that HFA children exhibited relatively lower performances in planning, cognitive flexibility, and verbal fluency when compared to controls, and worse performances in planning and cognitive flexibility when compared to ADHD children. Verte et al. (2005) compared HFA, TS, and control children, and found that HFA children exhibited lower EF performances across measures of inhibition, visual working memory, planning, cognitive flexibility, and verbal fluency when compared to controls, and lower performances on inhibition and cognitive flexibility when compared to TS children. In a study that bridges the findings of the previous two studies, Ozonoff and Jensen (1999) compared EF performances on tests of cognitive flexibility, planning, and response inhibition among HFA, ADHD, and TS children. The authors showed that HFA children exhibited lower performances on measures of cognitive flexibility and planning when compared to ADHD or TS children. Verte et al. (2006) extend these findings by providing evidence for shared or similar EF deficits among children with HFA, Asperger Syndrome (AS), or Pervasive Developmental Disorder Not Otherwise Specified (PDDNOS). Consistent are the findings of Kleinhans et al. (2005), who showed that adults and adolescents with HFA or AS display deficits in verbal cognitive switching and lexical retrieval initiation, and Lopez et al. (2005), who showed that working memory, cognitive flexibility, and inhibition of response were strongly associated with restrictive and repetitive behaviors of autism.

Despite a number of studies that identify EF deficits in HFA children, it must be noted that a few studies challenge the association of HFA with EF deficiencies. For example, Griffith et al. (1999) found no EF differences between HFA and control children at a young age (mean = 4.3 years) using eight EF measures. Liss et al. (2001) found that a difference in perseverative errors observed between HFA and developmental language disorder (DLD) children was no longer significant when the authors accounted for verbal IQ.

PHENYLKETONURIA

Phenylketonuria (PKU) is a metabolic disorder which leaves the child unable to appropriately metabolize phenylalanine (PHE), an amino acid. The result, if untreated, is an accumulation of PHE that is toxic to brain development and leads to mental retardation. Successful treatment usually involves a PHE-reduced or restricted diet begun as early in life as possible. However, despite successful intervention, children with PKU have been reported to have lower IQ and other cognitive deficits (see Smith et al., 2000). Welsh et al. (1990) hypothesize that these cognitive deficits arise from subtle prefrontal dysfunction due to mild dopamine depletion caused by elevated PHE levels. They present data showing overall EF impairment in PKU children on a battery of measures assessing set maintenance, planning, and organized speech. The authors also found a correlation between EF impairment and PHE levels in their participants at testing. In an elegant study, Antshel and Waisbren (2003) studied exposure to PHE prenatally (maternal PKU) and postnatally. They also found a dose-dependent correlation between higher exposure levels of PHE and worse performances on processing speed and executive functioning measures. Smith et al. (2000) showed that PKU students perform lower on problem-solving and verbal memory tasks compared to matched control children. Vanzutphen et al. (2007) found D-KEFS measures of executive functioning were sensitive to concept formation and reasoning deficits in children with PKU. Additionally, PHE levels were associated with performance on inhibitory control and cognitive flexibility tests (Vanzutphen et al., 2007).

EPILEPSY

Cognitive and interpersonal behavior problems vary in pediatric epilepsy cases and are dependent on a number of factors. Some of these factors include type of epilepsy (e.g., frontal lobe epilepsy, or FLE, versus temporal lobe epilepsy, or TLE), seizure severity and frequency, and resultant brain damage (see Riva et al., 2005). If the locus of seizure activity is in the frontal lobes, such as in the case of FLE, then it is logical to assume EF abilities would be impaired. Riva et al. (2005) presented evidence for impairments in verbal and design fluency and the ability to plan and execute complex sequential motor acts among children with FLE. Furthermore, these impairments occurred in the presence of global intellectual functioning in the normal range. Culhane-Shelburne et al. (2002) showed that children with FLE exhibited EF impairments in planning and behavioral inhibition when compared to children with TLE.

WISC-IV MEASUREMENT OF EF IN CHILDREN

The WISC-IV and the companion WISC-IV Integrated batteries were developed to include measurement of some EF constructs. In addition, some traditional subtests are more influenced by executive functioning abilities than others, even if they were not specifically designed as EF measures. In general, specific measures of EF have low to moderate correlations with IQ measures and dissociations between these skills are frequently observed (Delis et al., 2007). It should be considered that EF skills can come to bear on any test. Children with impulse control problems may do poorly on any type of test due to responding too quickly and failing to consider alternative responses. Additionally, measures of general cognitive functioning are designed to measure novel problem-solving as well as abstract reasoning. The capacity to solve novel problems (e.g., a problem that cannot be solved with retrieval of overlearned behavior or information) often requires the engagement of executive, strategic, problem-solving approaches. Finally, WISC-IV studies of children with known deficits in executive functioning provide evidence that the executive factors are differentially related to WISC-IV subtest performance.

The WISC-IV introduced a new subtest called Word Reasoning. This subtest was developed to assess deductive reasoning abilities. This WISC-IV subtest is a modified version of the Word Reasoning Task from the D-KEFS (Delis et al., 2001). The subtest provides children with clues about a word and the children have to deduce to which word the clues are referring. The child must search semantic and associative memory uncovering known or novel associations between the clue and target word. The test measures aspects of abstract reasoning, strategic and organized memory search, and semantic knowledge.

The WISC-IV Integrated provides clinicians with an established measure of executive functioning, Elithorn Mazes. This subtest requires children to plan a specific route through a maze following specific rules for completing each item. The items are designed to "pull" for impulsive behavior by presenting easily spotted solutions that appear at first glance to meet all the rules. However, once the child starts on that path they cannot possibly obtain a correct solution without violating a task rule. The subtest provides base rates for errors as a means of estimating impulsive response tendencies. The test provides clinicians with a method for measure planning skills in children.

The WISC-IV Integrated contains multiple-choice versions of all the standard verbal comprehension subtests (e.g., Vocabulary, Similarities, Comprehension, and Information). The multiple-choice versions provide the clinician with a means for measuring memory retrieval problems. Poor performance on the standard version of a verbal task may be due to a lack of knowledge or to difficulties in retrieving that knowledge from long-term memory. Problems accessing information may reflect disorganized search strategy or information storage, indicating difficulties with executive control of memory storage and retrieval functions. Additionally, the items are designed to "pull" for concrete or highly probable but incorrect responses. The clinician is able to gain a sense of the child's tendency to think concretely or to impulsively respond to obvious, but poorly considered answers. Weiss et al. (2006) reported that children with expressive and social/pragmatic language impairments benefited from the multiple-choice format while children who have sustained a TBI generally performed worse on the multiple choice compared to the standard version. The nature of the executive functioning deficit affects performance on these measures. The lowest verbal comprehension scores of children diagnosed with autism were on Comprehension and Comprehension Multiple Choice and Elithorn Mazes of the Perceptual Reasoning Tasks (Wechsler, 2004).

ADDITIONAL MEASURES OF EXECUTIVE FUNCTIONING

Executive functioning is a key concept that should routinely be assessed as part of psychoeducational, psychological, or neuropsychological assessment. The level of detail of the assessment of EF functions and type of interpretation (e.g., depending on the background, training of the examiner, and the specific referral question) will vary in these different reports. While the WISC-IV provides some insights into potential EF deficits and enables the examiner to hypothesize about the nature of those problems, specific tests of the construct in questions should be utilized.

MEASURES OF PLANNING

Immediate planning skills are typically measured using tower and maze procedures. Tower-based tasks require the child to move objects from one location to another from a start point to an end point using a set of rules that must be followed (e.g., a large one cannot be placed on a smaller one, only one can be moved at a time). The tower task items usually require the child to move away from the end goal in order to achieve the final solution. This requires planning in order to avoid making an incorrect move from which they will not be able to recover. Tower tests can be found on the NEPSY (Korkman et al., 1998) and D-KEFS (Delis et al., 2001). Each test provides base rate data for rule violations which is a good indicator of poor planning and impulsivity. As noted previously, the WISC-IV Integrated contains the Elithorn Mazes subtest which also measures short-term planning abilities.

MEASURES OF INHIBITORY CONTROL

Inhibitory control is measured by attention and interference tasks. On attention tasks, the child must attend to target stimuli and ignore non-targets. These tests may use an anticipatory cue that is paired with the target (e.g., the target is an "x" when it comes after an "a"). The anticipatory cue is followed by a target or non-target such that the child gets drawn into disinhibited responses. This type of task is found on continuous performance tasks such as the Gordon continuous performance task (Gordon & Mettleman, 1987) and Rosvold and Mirsky continuous performance test (Rosvold et al., 1956). Another paradigm requires the child to frequently respond to a target and occasionally inhibit a non-target. The Connors' Continuous Performance Test – Second Edition exemplifies this approach to measuring automatic, disinhibited responding.

Interference tasks use competing responses to draw children into disinhibited responding. The child sees a highly salient stimulus and must inhibit the automatic association to the stimulus and replace it with an alternate response. The Stroop paradigm is a classic example of a response inhibition test. The child inhibits the overlearned tendency to read a color word and must name the color of ink the word is printed in. The D-KEFS contains an interference task based on this paradigm. Another type of interference test requires the child to replace a highly automatic response with a novel response (e.g., child sees a square and must say circle). This task requires the inhibition of the learned association with a novel association. This type of inhibitory task is found on the NEPSY-II (Korkman et al., 2007). Each of these tests provides data regarding speed of performance as well as error rate. Speed of performance measures the degree to which interference effects require the child to slow their processing, and error rate is a good indicator of a failure to inhibit overlearned responses.

MEASURES OF COGNITIVE FLEXIBILITY AND BEHAVIORAL PRODUCTIVITY

The ability to change one's problem-solving behavior or to view novel or multiple solutions to a problem is an indicator of cognitive flexibility. Cognitive flexibility is measured by a variety of tasks that require either ideational switching (e.g., changing the way one thinks about a problem even though the stimuli do not change) or stimulus based switching (e.g., as the characteristic of the stimulus changes the examinees behavior also changes). Sorting and fluency tasks represent common forms of ideational cognitive flexibility tasks. There are two well-known sorting tasks that measuring different components of ideational flexibility, the Wisconsin Card Sorting Test (WCST) (Heaton et al., 1993), and the D-KEFS Sorting subtest (Delis et al., 2001). The WCST shows the child a set of four target cards that never change. The child must figure out what category to respond to and place additional cards based on the category. The child receives feedback on every trial and knows if they are sorting correctly or not. The category keeps switching after a pre-determined set of correct responses so the child must think about the problem from a different perspective and sort to a new category. The D-KEFS sorting tasks require the child to come up with different ways to sort a set of cards into different categories. They receive no feedback on the correctness of their response. The child must think of different ways to sort the cards based on the characteristics of the cards. Later, the examiner sorts the cards and determines if the child can infer the correct category. The NEPSY-II card sorting test is similar to the D-KEFS version except the D-KEFS asks the child to explain why they sorting the cards the way they did and the NEPSY-II does not ask them to explain their behavior. The WCST measures the child's ability to use feedback to change their problem-solving behavior based on changing response contingencies. The D-KEFS and NEPSY-II sorting tasks measure the child's ability to think of different solutions to a single problem.

Fluency tests are based on the premise of giving a child a specific stimulus to which the child has to come up with as many responses that meet the criteria of the stimulus and follow the task rules. On verbal tasks, the child may have to name as many animals as they can or to say as many words that start with a specific letter as they can. Visual fluency tasks ask the child to draw as many different designs as they can think of using a specified number of lines and following certain task rules. The ability to produce and sustain behavior is in part related to cognitive flexibility. Sustaining productivity on these tasks requires thinking about multiple solutions to the same problem. Both the D-KEFS and NEPSY-II have verbal and visual fluency tasks.

Stimulus-based cognitive flexibility tests are best exemplified by the Trail-Making Test and the switching conditions of interference tests. The Trail-Making Test requires the child to connect dots by switching back and forth from numeric to alphabetical order (e.g., 1-a-2-b-3-c). All the stimuli are in front of the child and they must remember and attend to the switching at the stimulus level. Some ideational flexibility can be invoked when the child has to think about which letter or number should come next, but the child is not really thinking about the problem in a different way or deriving a different solution. He or she is only trying to figure out what the single correct solution is. The switching conditions on interference tasks provide a cue (e.g., a box around the stimuli or a change in stimuli color) that informs the child to switch their behavior. These are not ideational switches as the child does not think about the problem in a different way, but instead the cue tells them to perform the one and only correct behavior (e.g., say the name of the object or read it). These tests capture the ability to change one's behavior when cued to do so, and they are influenced by attention and self-monitoring as much as behavioral flexibility. These tasks are found on the D-KEFS and NEPSY-II.

LINKING ASSESSMENT TO INTERVENTION

Evaluation of executive functioning is critical to understanding why some children have difficulty with behavioral control and learning. Understanding the nature of underlying cognitive deficits is essential to designing effective interventions. As stated previously, EFs are a diverse set of skills, and impairments in one type of EF skill versus another would lead to dramatically different conclusions about a child's behavior and learning problems. The child with poor planning skills but good cognitive flexibility will behave and learn differently from the child with severe problems with inhibitory control but adequate organizational skills. Therefore, the first step for developing interventions is to identify the core impairments in EFs and understand how the deficits relate to the behavior or learning problem.

POOR PLANNING

Children with significant planning deficits often initiate problem-solving or learning tasks without thinking about the best strategy. On larger projects, they will not take time to consider the materials required, how to obtain the materials, what additional information will be required, and how to accomplish all the necessary subcomponents of the project to complete within the specified timelines. Interventions for children with planning deficits need to consider several components.

- Devise strategies to help the child break down tasks into subcomponents.
- Devise strategies to help the child sequence tasks in a logical order.
- Devise strategies to help the child prioritize the relative importance of steps within the process.
- Instruct the child in planning procedures such as thinking prior to acting, planning the first step, staying on task, and keeping the end goal in mind.
- Help the child identify common derailment points when completing projects over time.

Some children do not improve in their planning skills despite intervention. In these situations, some accommodations may be helpful to enable the child to best show their abilities. These may include providing explicit steps in a checklist format when learning new tasks (e.g., steps for completing long division) and requiring the child to submit specific steps of longer projects (e.g., list of materials required, or notes for papers). The goal is not to relieve the child of the responsibility to plan their behavior but rather to provide prompts to cue them to engage in planful behavior.

IMPULSIVITY

Children displaying very impulsive behavior can be very difficult to manage in a traditional classroom environment. Often these children are placed in special educational classrooms that employ token economy interventions to help control their behavior in that setting. These children often have multiple cognitive difficulties and require more intensive intervention that focuses on behavioral and cognitive limitations. For children with less severe impulsivity problems, their difficulties will have a significant impact on the quality of their schoolwork and their capacity to attend during classroom activities. These children's schoolwork will often be riddled with careless errors, incomplete items, missing punctuation, and words left out of sentences. These children also may have problems with distractibility (e.g., they easily disrupted by other students or extraneous activity outside the classroom). Additionally, these children frequently break classroom rules even though they know and can state them when questioned. Most strategies are accommodative rather than remediative with impulsive children.

- Classroom seating near children that are not disruptive but can also tolerate the impulsive student.
- Classroom seating in front of the teacher away from windows and doors.
- Child earns privilege points for remaining seated, talking in turn, and attending during lectures.

- After the child hands in their assignment, requiring them to review it before handing it in.
- Setting time minimums for assignments (e.g., you must continue to work on your test for at least 30 minutes).
- Requiring homework be redone correctly before accepting (e.g., child stays in for recess to fix missing items or sloppy work).
- Teaching "stop and think" strategies to help reduce automatic responding.

The interventionist must balance training, rewards, and punitive contingencies to help improve the child's behavior. Providing only accommodations and rewards for good behavior will not instill a sense of personal responsibility that is needed to make training effective. Response contingencies that are too punitive will frequently result in an increase in negative behaviors. The child may become frustrated by their constant punishment and lack of rewards or incentives for cooperating with the programming.

COGNITIVE FLEXIBILITY

Children with significant weaknesses in cognitive flexibility do not change their behavior even when the behavior does not get them what they want or lead to a positive outcome. They are unable to think of other options and frequently rely on an overlearned behavioral repertoire (e.g., running away from the stressor, acting out with verbal abuse or aggression, hiding). Often, these responses are inconsistent with environmental demands resulting in frustration for the child and the teacher. In addition to behavioral problems, these children will have academic difficulties in that they will make the same mistakes repeatedly despite corrective feedback. These children have difficulty coping with change and become anxious when their routine is disrupted or when something changes in the environment (e.g., a new student joins the class or a substitute teacher takes the class). These children benefit from a combination of environmental management (e.g., identifying factors that disrupt the child's behavior, preparing the child in advance for changes in routine), intensive training in alternative behavioral responding (e.g., teaching and practicing different responses to known stressors), and errorless learning techniques.

- Inflexible child cannot think of alternative responses under stress so new appropriate behaviors have to be taught to them until they become automatic.
- Teaching children new information but not allowing them to learn an incorrect step (e.g., children will recall the behavior, not the correctness of the behavior, so they need errorless learning trials).
- Environmental factors can often be identified prior to the event occurring (e.g., a new child is joining the class, so helping the inflexible child reduce anxiety by discussing the issue and perhaps meeting the new student ahead of time).

- Identify children in the classroom that cause the inflexible child to have behavior problems (e.g., keep antagonists seated away from the child).
- If there is to be a routine change, warn the child in advance when possible and train alternative responses when feeling anxious about a new situation.
- Train staff working with the child in de-escalation techniques.

Most intervention programs will need to be tailored to the individual child's needs and the school environment. The ability to modify the child's environment to reduce problematic situations will help the entire classroom function more effectively. Using de-escalation techniques once the child becomes upset rather than worrying about reward or punishment can help the child to learn to de-escalate their own behavior. Most important is training in alternative responses since the child cannot think of new ways to act when they are upset. These children can be very demanding on classroom resources and often they require more intensive intervention than is available in traditional classroom settings.

SUMMARY

The EF construct is a topic of great interest in the current literature because of its implications for academic achievement, social adjustment, and professional success. Current assessment practices would benefit from consideration of EF in the administration of measures, behavioral observations, and interpretation of results. The WISC-IV provides some insight into the child's EFs; however, additional testing is required to fully evaluate these skills. There are a number of well-standardized measures of executive functioning for children. The clinician is able to select a subset of executive functioning skills to be assessed and chooses those measures that provide them with a direct assessment of that construct. Integrating these measures within a standardized assessment battery enables the clinician to understand the core cognitive deficits affecting learning and behavior as well as to help them design suitable intervention and accommodation plans.

REFERENCES

Altemeier, L., Jones, J., Abbott, R. D., & Berninger, V. W. (2006). Executive functions in becoming writing readers and reading writers: Note taking and report writing in third and fifth graders. *Developmental Neuropsychology*, 29(1), 161–173.

American Psychiatric Association (2000). *Diagnostic and Statistical Manual of Mental Disorders, Text Revision* (4th ed.). Washington, DC: American Psychiatric Association.

Anderson, V., & Catroppa, C. (2005). Recovery of executive skills following paediatric traumatic brain injury (TBI): A 2 year follow-up. *Brain Injury*, 19(6), 459–470.

Antshel, K. M., & Waisbren, S. E. (2003). Timing is everything: Executive functions in children exposed to elevated levels of phenylalanine. *Neuropsychology*, 17(3), 458–468.

Ardila, A., Rosselli, M., Matute, E., & Guajardo, S. (2005). The influence of the parents' educational level on the development of executive functions. *Developmental Neuropsychology*, 28(1), 539–560.

Barkley, R. A. (1997). Behavioral inhibition, sustained attention, and executive functions: Constructing a unifying theory of ADHD. *Psychological Bulletin*, 121(1), 65–94.

Barkley, R. A. (2001). The executive functions and self-regulation: An evolutionary neuropsychological perspective. *Neuropsychology Review*, 11(1), 1–29.

Brookshire, B., Levin, H. S., Song, J. X., & Zhang, L. (2004). Components of executive function in typically developing and head-injured children. *Developmental Neuropsychology*, 25(1–2), 61–83.

Brosnan, M., Demetre, J., Hamill, S., Robson, K., Shepherd, H., & Cody, G. (2002). Executive functioning adults and children with developmental dyslexia. *Neuropsychologia*, 40(12), 2144–2155.

Channon, S., Pratt, P., & Robertson, M. M. (2003). Executive function, memory, and learning in Tourette's syndrome. *Neuropsychology*, 17(2), 247–254.

Chenault, B., Thomson, J., Abbott, R. D., & Berninger, V. W. (2006). Effects of prior attention training on child dyslexics' response to composition instruction. *Developmental Neuropsychology*, 29(1), 243–260.

Crawford, S., Channon, S., & Robertson, M. M. (2005). Tourette's syndrome: Performance on tests of behavioural inhibition, working memory and gambling. *Journal of Child Psychology Psychiatry*, 46(12), 1327–1336.

Culhane-Shelburne, K., Chapieski, L., Hiscock, M., & Glaze, D. (2002). Executive functions in children with frontal and temporal lobe epilepsy. *Journal of the International Neuropsychological Society*, 8(5), 623–632.

Delis, D. C., Kaplan, E., & Kramer, J. H. (2001). *Delis–Kaplan Executive Function System*. San Antonio, TX: The Psychological Corporation.

Delis, D. C., Lansing, A., Houston, W. S., Wetter, S., Han, S. D., Jacobsen, M., Holdnack, J., & Kramer, J. (2007). Creativity lost: The importance of testing higher-level executive functions in school-aged children. *Journal of Psychoeducational Assessment*, 25, 29–40.

Denckla, M. B. (1996). A theory and model of executive function: A neuropsychological perspective. In: G. Reid Lyon, A. Norman, & A. Krasnegor (Eds.), *Attention, Memory, and Executive Function* (pp. 263–278). Baltimore, MD: Paul H. Brookes Publishing Co.

Geurts, H. M., Verte, S., Oosterlaan, J., Roeyers, H., & Sergeant, J. A. (2004). How specific are executive functioning deficits in attention deficit hyperactivity disorder and autism? *Journal of Child Psychology and Psychiatry*, 45(4), 836–854.

Geurts, H. M., Verte, S., Oosterlaan, J., Roeyers, H., & Sergeant, J. A. (2005). ADHD subtypes: Do they differ in their executive functioning profile? *Archives of Clinical Neuropsychology*, 20(4), 457–477.

Goldman-Rakic, P. S. (1987). Circuitry of primate prefrontal cortex and regulation of behavior by representational memory. In: F. Plum (Ed.), *Handbook of Physiology – the Nervous System: Higher Function of the Brain* (pp. 373–417). Bethesda, MD: American Physiology Association.

Gordon, M., & Mettleman, B. B. (1987). *Technical Guide to the Gordon Diagnostic System (GDS)*. DeWitt, NY: Gordon Systems.

Griffith, E. M., Pennington, B. F., Wehner, E. A., & Rogers, S. J. (1999). Executive functions in young children with autism. *Child Development*, 70(4), 817–832.

Guy, S. C., Isquith, P. K., & Gioia, G. A. (2004). *BRIEF-SR: Behavior Rating Inventory of Executive Function-Self Report Version: Professional Manual*. FL: Psychological Assessment Resources.

Harris, E. L., Schuerholz, L. J., Singer, H. S., Reader, M. J., Brown, J. E., Cox, C., Mohr, J., Chase, G. A., & Denckla, M. B. (1995). Executive function in children with Tourette syndrome and/or attention deficit hyperactivity disorder. *Journal of the International Neuropsychological Society*, 1(6), 511–516.

Heaton, R., et al. (1993). *Wisconsin Card Sorting Test Manual: Revised and Expanded*. Odessa, FL: Psychological Assessment Resources, Inc.

Holdnack, J. A., Drozdick, L. L., Sichi, M., Lane, A., & Chelune, G. (2006a). Sensitivity of D-KEFS sorting, trail-making test and color–word interference measures in pediatric TBI versus ability and demographically matched controls. Presented at the *26th Annual National Academy of Neuropsychology Conference*, San Antonio, TX.

Holdnack, J. A., Drozdick, L. L., Lane, A., Sichi, M., & Chelune, G. (2006b). Sensitivity of D-KEFS design and verbal fluency measures in pediatric TBI versus ability and demographically matched controls. Presented at the *26th Annual National Academy of Neuropsychology Conference*, San Antonio, TX.

Hooper, S. R., Swartz, C. W., Wakely, M. B., de Kruif, R. E., & Montgomery, J. W. (2002). Executive functions in elementary school children with and without problems in written expression. *Journal of Learning Disabilities*, 35(1), 57–68.

Jonsdottir, S., Bouma, A., Sergeant, J. A., & Scherder, E. J. A. (2006). Relationships between neuropsychological measures of executive function and behavioral measures of ADHD symptoms and comorbid behavior. *Archives of Clinical Neuropsychology*, 21(5), 383–394.

Kleinhans, N., Akshoomoff, N., & Delis, D. C. (2005). Executive functions in autism and Asperger's disorder: Flexibility, fluency, and inhibition. *Developmental Neuropsychology*, 27(3), 379–401.

Korkman, M., Kirk, U., & Kemp, S. (1998). *NEPSY – A Developmental Neuropsychological Assessment*. San Antonio, TX: The Psychological Corporation.

Levin, H. S., Song, J., Ewing-Cobbs, L., & Roberson, G. (2001). Porteus Maze performance following traumatic brain injury in children. *Neuropsychology*, 15(4), 557–567.

Levine, B., Black, S. E., Cheung, G., Campbell, A., O'Toole, C., & Schwartz, M. L. (2005). Gambling task performance in traumatic brain injury: Relationships to injury severity, atrophy, lesion location, and cognitive and psychosocial outcome. *Cognitive Behavioral Neurology*, 18(1), 45–54.

Liss, M., Fein, D., Allen, D., Dunn, M., Feinstein, C., Morris, R., Waterhouse, L., & Rapin, I. (2001). Executive functioning in high-functioning children with autism. *Journal of Child Psychology and Psychiatry*, 42(2), 261–270.

Lopez, B. R., Lincoln, A. J., Ozonoff, S., & Lai, Zona. (2005). Examining the relationship between executive functions and restricted, repetitive symptoms of autistic disorder. *Journal of Autism and Developmental Disorders*, 35(4), 445–460.

Mahone, E. M., Cirino, P. T., Cutting, L. E., Cerrone, P. M., Hagelthorn, K. M., Hiemenz, J. R., Singer, H. S., & Denckla, M. B. (2002). Validity of the Behavior Rating Inventory of Executive Function in children with ADHD and/or Tourette syndrome. *Archives of Clinical Neuropsychology*, 17(7), 643–662.

Marks, D. J., Berwid, O. G., Santra, A., Kera, E. C., Cyrulnik, S. E., & Halperin, J. M. (2005). Neuropsychological correlates of ADHD symptoms in preschoolers. *Neuropsychology*, 19(4), 446–455.

Oosterlaan, J., Scheres, A., & Sergeant, J. A. (2005). Which executive functioning deficits are associated with AD/HD, ODD/CD and comorbid AD/HD + ODD/CD? *Journal of Abnormal Child Psychology*, 33(1), 69–85.

Ozonoff, S., & Jensen, J. (1999). Specific executive function profiles in three neurodevelopmental disorders. *Journal of Autism and Developmental Disorders*, 29(2), 171–177.

Reiter, A., Tucha, O., & Lange, K. W. (2005). Executive functions in children with dyslexia. *Dyslexia*, 11(2), 116–131.

Riva, D., Avanzini, G., Franceschetti, S., Nichelli, F., Saletti, V., Vago, C., Pantaleoni, C., D'Arrigo, S., Andreucci, E., Aggio, F., Paruta, N., & Bulgheroni, S. (2005). Unilateral frontal lobe epilepsy affects executive functions in children. *Neurological Sciences*, 26(4), 263–270.

Rosvold, H. E., Mirsky, A. F., Sarason, I., Bronsome, E. D., & Beck, L. H. (1956). A continuous performance test of brain damage. *Journal of Consulting Psychology*, 20, 343–350.

Roth, R. M., & Saykin, A. J. (2004). Executive dysfunction in attention-deficit/hyperactivity disorder: Cognitive and neuroimaging findings. *Psychiatric Clinics of North America*, 27(1), 83–96.

Seidman, L. J. (2006). Neuropsychological functioning in people with ADHD across the lifespan. *Clinical Psychology Review*, 26, 466–485.

Seidman, L. J., Bierderman, J., Monuteaux, M. C., Doyle, A. E., & Faraone, S. V. (2001). Learning disabilities and executive dysfunction in boys with attention-deficit/hyperactivity disorder. *Neuropsychology*, 15(4), 544–556.

Slomine, B. S., Gerring, J. P., Grados, M. A., Vasa, R., Brady, K. D., Christensen, J. R., & Denckla, M. B. (2002). Performance on measures of "executive function" following pediatric traumatic brain injury. *Brain Injury*, 16(9), 759–772.

Slomine, B. S., Salorio, C. F., Grados, M. A., Vasa, R. A., Christensen, J. R., & Gerring, J. P. (2005). Differences in attention, executive functioning, and memory in children with and without ADHD after severe traumatic brain injury. *Journal of the International Neuropsychological Society*, 11(5), 645–653.

Smith, M. L., Klim, P., & Hanley, W. B. (2000). Executive function in school-aged children with phenylketonuria. *Journal of Developmental and Physical Disabilities*, 12(4), 317–332.

Snodgrass, C., & Knott, F. (2006). Theory of mind in children with traumatic brain injury. *Brain Injury*, 20(8), 825–833.

Tranel, D., Anderson, S. W., & Benton, A. (1994). Development of the concept of "executive function" and its relationship to the frontal lobes. In: F. Boller, & J. Grafman (Eds.), *Handbook of Neuropsychology* (Vol. 9, pp. 125–148). Amsterdam: Elsevier Science.

Van der Schoot, M., Licht, R., Sergeant, J. A., & Horsley, T. M. (2000). Inhibitory deficits in reading disability depend on sub-type: guessers but not spellers. *Child Neuropsychology*, 6, 4, 297–312.

van der Sluis, S., de Jong, P. F., & van der Leij, A. (2004). Inhibition and shifting in children with learning deficits in arithmetic and reading. *Journal of Experimental Child Psychology*, 87(3), 239–266.

Vanzutphen, K. H., Packman, W., Sporri, L., Needham, M., Morgan, C., Weisiger, K., & Packman, S. (2007). Executive functioning in children and adolescents with phenylketonuria. *Clinical Genetics*, 72(1), 13–18.

Verte, S., Geurts, H. M., Roeyers, H., Oosterlaan, J., & Sergeant, J. A. (2005). Executive functioning in children with autism and Tourette syndrome. *Development and Psychopathology*, 17(2), 415–445.

Verte, S., Geurts, H. M., Roeyers, H., Oosterlaan, J., & Sergeant, J. A. (2006). Executive functioning in children with an autism spectrum disorder: Can we differentiate within the spectrum? *Journal of Autism and Developmental Disorders*, 36(3), 351–372.

Wechsler, D. (2004). *WISC-IV Canadian manual*. Toronto: Harcourt Assessment.

Weiss, L., Prifitera, A., Saklofske, D., & Holdnack, J. (2006). *WISC-IV Advanced Clinical Interpretation*. San Diego, CA: Elsevier Science.

Welsh, M. C., Pennington, B. F., Ozonoff, S., Rouse, B., & McCabe, E. R. B. (1990). Neuropsychology of early-treated phenylketonuria: Specific executive function deficits. *Child Development*, 61(6), 1697–1713.

Wilde, E. A., Hunter, J. V., Newsome, M. R., Scheibel, R. S., Bigler, E. D., Johnson, J. L., Fearing, M. A., Cleavinger, H. B., Li, X., Swank, P. R., Pedroza, C., Roberson, G. S., Bachevalier, J., & Levin, H. S. (2005). Frontal and temporal morphometric findings on MRI in children after moderate to severe traumatic brain injury. *Journal of Neurotrauma*, 22(3), 333–344.

Wilcutt, E. G., Doyle, A. E., Nigg, J. T., Faraone, S. V., & Pennington, B. F. (2005). Validity of the executive function theory of attention-deficit/hyperactivity disorder: a meta-analytic review. *Biological Psychiatry*, 57, 1336–1346.

14

CULTURAL ISSUES IN CLINICAL USE OF THE WISC-IV

JACQUES GRÉGOIRE[1], JAMES GEORGAS[2],
DONALD H. SAKLOFSKE[3], FONS VAN DE VIJVER[4],
CLAUDINE WIERZBICKI[5], LAWRENCE G. WEISS[6]
AND JIANJUN ZHU[6]

[1]Catholic University of Louvain, Belgium

[2]University of Athens, Greece

[3]University of Calgary, Canada

[4]University of Tilburg, The Netherlands

[5]ECPA, Paris, France

[6]Pearson Assessment, San Antonio, USA

Cultural and linguistic diversity is an important consideration in test development and especially in the administration and interpretation of intelligence tests. These factors are among the very reasons that test scores cannot be viewed in isolation from the "world" of the child, and by themselves, can neither diagnose nor prescribe interventions. Culturally sensitive assessment requires an understanding of how children from different cultures typically approach and respond to standardized testing, a knowledge of the child's cultural background and how this can impact test scores and interpretation, and in many cases an examiner who is familiar with the child's language, dialect and culture.

It is well known that there are differences in mean IQ scores between socioeconomic and ethnic groups. Less well known is "why" these differences exist, and how much of the difference is explained by environment. In discussing differences in IQ test scores among socioeconomic groups more than three decades ago,

Wechsler stated, "The cause is elsewhere and the remedy is not in denigrating or banishing the IQ but in attacking and removing the social causes that impair it" (Wechsler, 1971). Despite this admonishment, early attempts to understand these socioeconomic and ethnic differences in IQ test scores focused mainly on identifying biased test items. Later research to examine differential prediction of achievement from IQ found none (Weiss et al., 1993; Weiss & Prifitera, 1995). Other efforts focused on describing culturally different approaches to the demands of the testing environment and the interaction between examiners and examinees. More recent studies have been directed at understanding those environmental and cultural factors that enhance or diminish cognitive potential during the child's developmental years.

The assessment of intelligence and cognitive processes of individuals from different ethnic, cultural and linguistic and even socio-economic backgrounds has been an area of controversy for psychologists following the introduction and widespread use of intelligence tests (see Tulsky et al., 2003). With the ever increasing immigration of ethnic groups to multicultural countries, the search for psychometrically sound strategies for accurately and meaningfully assessing and evaluating the cognitive skills of children from different backgrounds is imperative. However, the assessment of cognitive processes of ethnic children also requires knowledge about the relationships between these background factors and cognitive processes.

This chapter will present issues related to the culturally sensitive assessment of children from diverse cultures with particular focus on the *Wechsler Intelligence Scale for Children* – Fourth Edition (WISC-IV; Wechsler, 2003). The first section focuses on the various kinds of bias that must be considered by both test developers and users, followed by an overview of the various adaptations of the most recent Wechsler scales for children. A review is presented of the findings from a cross-cultural study of the WISC-III as well as a summary of findings of WISC-IV comparisons of the three largest ethnic groups in the United States. The chapter ends with suggestions that can guide the psychologist when assessing culturally diverse children using the WISC-IV.

CULTURAL BIAS IN INTELLIGENCE TESTING

Bias refers to the presence of nuisance factors that challenge the comparability of scores from intelligence and other tests and measures across cultural groups (van de Vijver & Leung, 1997). If scores are biased, their psychological meaning is culture/group dependent and group differences in assessment outcome are to be accounted for, at least to some extent, by auxiliary psychological constructs or measurement artifacts. Bias arises in the application of an instrument in at least two cultural groups and the ensuing comparison of scores, patterns or item values. The need for cross-cultural validation and verification should not be interpreted as blind empiricism. Nor should we simply concede that cultural differences make the comparison of such latent traits as intelligence impossible; rather we should use our psychometric skills and psychological knowledge to make every effort to minimize bias and maximize equivalence. On the contrary, not all instruments are equally susceptible to bias. For example, structured test administrations are less prone to bias influences. Analogously, comparisons of closely related groups will be less susceptible to bias than comparisons of groups with a widely different cultural background.

In order to detect and/or prevent bias, we need to recognize factors that can induce bias. Table 14.1 provides an overview of sources of bias, based on a classification by van de Vijver and Tanzer (2004) and van de Vijver and Poortinga (1997). Sources of bias are numerous, thus the overview is necessarily limited.

TABLE 14.1   Sources of Bias in Cross-Cultural Assessment (van de Vijver, 2003)

Type of bias	Source of bias
Construct bias	• Incomplete overlap (or complete non-overlap) in the definition of intelligence across cultures
	• Differential appropriateness of items associated with the construct (e.g., skills do not belong to the repertoire of one of the cultural groups)
	• Poor sampling of all relevant behaviors (e.g., short instruments)
	• Incomplete coverage of all relevant aspects/facets of the construct (e.g., not all relevant domains are sampled)
Method bias	• Sample bias
	• Incomparability of samples (e.g., caused by differences in educational background or motivation)
	• Administration bias
	• Differences in environmental administration conditions, such as ambient noise in the classroom
	• Ambiguous instructions for pupils and/or guidelines for administrators
	• Differential expertise of test administrators
	• Differential usage of norms/instructions Tester/interviewer/observer effects (e.g., halo effects)
	• Communication problems between respondent and pupil
	• Instrument bias
	• Differential familiarity with stimulus material
	• Differential familiarity with response procedures
	• Differential response styles (e.g., social desirability, extremity scoring, acquiescence)
Item bias (Differential item functioning)	• Poor translation and/or ambiguous items
	• Nuisance factors (e.g., item may invoke additional traits or abilities)
	• Cultural specifics (e.g., incidental differences in connotative meaning and/ or appropriateness of the item content)

CONSTRUCT BIAS

The first kind of bias, construct bias, is found when the construct measured is not identical across groups. Construct bias precludes the cross-cultural measurement of a construct with the same/identical measure. Construct bias can be a consequence of differential appropriateness of the behaviors associated with the construct in the different cultures. An example comes from studies on cross-cultural differences in everyday definitions of intelligence. Western intelligence tests tend to focus on reasoning and logical thinking (such as the Raven's Progressive Matrices) while tests of acquired knowledge have typically been added in large batteries (such as Vocabulary scales of the Wechsler scales). When Western individuals are asked which characteristics they associate with an intelligent person, skilled reasoning and knowing much are frequently mentioned. In addition, social aspects of intelligence are mentioned. The latter aspects are even more prominent in everyday conceptions of intelligence in non-Western groups. For, example, Kokwet mothers (Kenya) say that an intelligent child knows its place in the family and behaviors associated with it, like proper ways of addressing other people. Studies in various non-Western countries (Azuma & Kashiwagi, 1987; Serpell, 1993; Grigorenko et al., 2001) also show that descriptions of an intelligent person go beyond the school-oriented domain and involve social aspects and even obedience. Yan and Saklofske (2004) described the five basic human attributes found in ancient China: humility, loyalty, courtesy, intelligence and trustworthiness. Most Western psychologists would view these qualities as a mixture of intelligence, personality and conative characteristics. Until recently, the domain covered by most intelligence tests was usually restricted to scholastic intelligence but that has very much changed as reflected in the newest Wechsler scales. More recently Ackerman (2007) has called for a redefinintion of adult intelligence and proposed a four component model that includes intelligence-as-process, personality, interests and motivation, and intelligence-as-knowledge.

METHOD BIAS

The second kind of bias, called method bias, can result from such factors as sample incomparability, instrument differences, tester effects and administration mode. Method bias is used here as a label for all sources of bias emanating from factors often described in the methods section of empirical papers or study documentations. They range from differential stimulus familiarity in mental testing to differential social desirability in personality and survey research. Identification of method bias requires detailed and explicit documentation of all the procedural steps in a study. As an example of method bias, Deregowski and Serpell (1971) asked Scottish and Zambian children in one condition to sort miniature models of animals and motor vehicles and in another condition to sort photographs of these models. Although no cross-cultural differences were found for the actual models, the Scottish children obtained higher scores than the Zambian children when photographs were sorted.

Among the various types of method bias, sample bias is more likely to jeopardize cross-cultural comparisons when the cultures examined differ in more respects. Such a larger cultural distance will often increase the number of alternative explanations for cross-cultural differences to be considered. Recurrent rival explanations are cross-cultural differences in social desirability and stimulus familiarity (test-wiseness). The main problem with test-wiseness is their relationship with country affluence; more affluent countries can be expected to be more acquainted with psychological testing. Subject recruitment procedures are another source of sample bias in cognitive tests. For instance, the motivation to display one's attitudes or abilities may depend on the amount of previous exposure to psychological tests, the freedom to participate or not, and other sources that may show cross-cultural variation.

Administration method bias can be caused by differences in the procedures or mode used to administer an instrument. For example, when interviews are held in respondents homes, physical conditions (e.g., ambient noise, presence of others) are difficult to control. Respondents are more prepared to answer sensitive questions in self-completion contexts than in the shared discourse of an interview. Examples of social environmental conditions are individual (versus group) administration, the physical space between respondents (in group testing), or class size (in educational settings). Other sources of administration that can lead to method bias are ambiguity in the questionnaire instructions and/or guidelines or a differential application of these instructions (e.g., which answers to open questions are considered to be ambiguous and require follow-up questions). The effect of test administrator on measurement outcomes has been empirically studied; regrettably, various studies apply inadequate designs and do not cross the cultures of testers and pupils. The presence of the tester is usually not very obtrusive if the test administration takes place under standardized conditions (Jensen 1980). A final source of administration bias is constituted by communication problems between the pupil and the tester. The almost unavoidable obtrusiveness of interpreters is another example. Communication problems are not restricted to working with translators. Language problems may be a potent source of bias when an interview or test is administered in the second or third language of interviewers or respondents.

Instrument bias is a common source of bias in cognitive tests. A Raven-like figural inductive reasoning test was administered to high-school students in Austria, Nigeria and Togo (educated in Arabic) (Broer, 1996). The most striking findings were cross-cultural differences in item difficulties related to identifying and applying rules in a horizontal direction (i.e., left to right), which was interpreted by the authors as bias in terms of the different directions in writing Latin as opposed to Arabic.

The presence of method bias can be easily overlooked. When a single test is administered at a single occasion, it is not always easy to estimate the influence of method bias. Evidence on the presence of method bias can also be collected from applications of test–retest, training and intervention studies.

Nkaya et al. (1994) administered Raven's Standard Matrices three times to sixth-graders in France and Congo. Under untimed conditions score improvements were similar for both groups, but under timed conditions the Congolese pupils progressed more from the second to the third session than did the French pupils. Ombredane et al. (1956) have shown that in some groups repeated test administrations can also affect the relationship with external measures. The predictive validity of the Raven test increased after repeated administration in a group of illiterate, Congolese mine workers. It is likely that the results of both studies are due to learning processes that took place during the testing, such as a better task comprehension and more acquaintance with the test and the testing procedure. In this line of reasoning, the validity of the first test administration is challenged by sources of method bias.

ITEM BIAS (DIF)

The third type of bias distinguished here refers to anomalies at the item level and is called item bias or differential item functioning (DIF). According to a definition that is widely used in education and psychology, an item is biased if respondents with the same standing on the underlying construct (e.g., they are equally intelligent), but who come from different cultures, do not have the same mean score on the item. The score on the construct is usually derived from the total test score. Of all bias types, item bias has been the most extensively studied; various psychometric techniques are available to identify item bias (e.g., Holland & Wainer, 1993; Camilli & Shepard, 1994; van de Vijver & Leung, 1997).

Although item bias can arise in various ways, poor item translation, ambiguities in the original item, low familiarity/appropriateness of the item content in certain cultures, and the influence of cultural specifics such as nuisance factors or connotations associated with the item wording are the most common sources. For instance, if a geography test administered to pupils in Poland and Japan contains the item "*What is the capital of Poland?*", Polish pupils can be expected to show higher scores on the item than Japanese students, even if pupils with the same total test score were compared. The item is biased because it favors one cultural group across all test score levels.

Even translations which seem to be correct can produce problems. A good example is the test item "*Where is a bird with webbed feet most likely to live?*", which was part of a large international study of educational achievement (*cf.* Hambleton 1994). Compared to the overall pattern, the item turned out to be unexpectedly easy in Sweden. An inspection of the translation revealed why: the Swedish translation of the English was "bird with swimming feet" which gives a strong clue to the solution not present in the English original.

This brief discussion on bias reminds us that bias can affect all stages of the testing and assessment enterprise from the theories and models that in turn guide the development of the test itself, to the standardization features or the test (norms, administration and scoring) and finally to the actual clinical use and interpretation. Thus minimizing bias is not an exclusive concern of only test developers, but of all who use tests in both research and clinical practice. Since bias can challenge all stages of a project, ensuring quality is a matter of combining good theory, questionnaire design, administration and clinical interpretation.

WHAT DID WE LEARN FROM THE WISC ADAPTATIONS ACROSS CULTURES?

Following from the recognition that psychological tests may travel a "smooth or bumpy road" when they move from their place of origin to another country or culture, we now turn to a more focused discussion of how the Wechsler tests have addressed bias issues.

THE WISC ADAPTATIONS

The term "test adaptation" should be preferred to "test translation," the first one being broader and more reflective of what happens when a test is developed in a culture based on a test previously developed for use in another culture. "Test translation is only one of the steps in the process of test adaptation and even at this step, adaptation is often a more suitable term than translation to describe the actual process that takes place" (Hambleton, 2005, p.4). Often, the translation of an item or an instruction is not straightforward. The translator has to find words, concepts or expressions that are equivalent in the source and the target languages. Finding such equivalences goes far beyond a literal translation that could be misleading. For example, a literal translation of the French expression "*J'ai le cafard*" would be in English "*I have the cockroach*", while the best equivalence is "*I have the blues*". Similarly, a literal translation of the English expression "*I've got butterflies in the stomach*" would be meaningless in French, the correct equivalence being "*J'ai le trac*" *(I get nervous)*.

Test adaptation first includes the appraisal that the construct could be measured in a different culture. This is followed by the complex process of selecting the translators, decisions related to accommodating the directions, formats, contents and scoring rules to another culture and the assessment of the equivalence between the original or source measure and the adapted test. So, the whole process of test adaptation is most complex and time consuming. The psychometric qualities of the adapted test are closely related to the quality of this procedure. The International Test Commission has published a set of validated guidelines for test adaptation across languages and cultures (Hambleton, 1994, 2005). The 22 guidelines address all the facets of the test development procedure. They are currently used as a reference for test adaptation throughout the world.

The Wechsler scales are among the most adapted tests in the world. Despite the large number of these adaptations since the publication of the Wechsler–Bellevue in 1939, few comparative studies across languages and cultures have been conducted. Most of these studies were only comparisons between the factor structure of a single adapted version and the original test structure of the US version. The first broad study comparing simultaneously several adaptations of the Wechsler scales was published by Georgas et al. (2003). This study was based on the data of 12 adaptations of the WISC-III: (1) The United States, (2) Canada, (3) United Kingdom, (4) Austria, Germany and Switzerland (German adaptation), (5) France and French-Speaking Belgium, (6) The Netherlands and Flemish-Speaking Belgium, (7) Greece, (8) Sweden, (9) Slovenia, (10) Lithuania, (11) Japan, (12) South Korea and Taiwan.

Published in 2003 in the United States, the WISC-IV is currently adapted and standardized in Canada (both English and French versions), United Kingdom, Australia, Germany and France. Swedish and Chinese adaptations are pending. We can expect that a similar broad cross-cultural and cross-linguistic comparison, similar to the Georgas et al. (2003) study, will be possible in the near future. These comparisons are very useful because they help in identifying where are the most important cultural differences in the test and how large is their impact on the scores. In one of the following sections, the main observations done in Georgas et al. (2003) study will be discussed. But we will first discuss adaptations of the Wechsler verbal subtests as these are the most frequently modified of the WISC subtests across languages and cultures. In contrast, the performance subtests remain unmodified in the majority of WISC adaptations. Support for the robustness of the original performance subtests will be presented and discussed within the framework of cultural and country similarities in non-verbal tasks. Following this will be a summary of the empirical comparisons between the scores of the standardization samples of 12 adaptations of the WISC-III as presented by Georgas et al. (2003). The similarity of the test structure across the adaptations will be emphasized and the subtest scores differences between countries will be discussed.

ADAPTATION OF THE VERBAL SUBTESTS

The necessity to translate and, often, to adapt verbal subtests to each language/culture seems obvious. In the WISC-IV, these subtests are included in the Verbal Comprehension scale and the Working Memory scale. In the WISC-III, most of the verbal subtests (included in the verbal scale) required at least some modifications when adapted in another country (Georgas et al., 2003). The most frequent modifications were found in the Vocabulary subtest. In Slovenia, Korea and Lithuania only 23% of the vocabulary items were modified. But in Japan, 93% of these items were modified. In non-English-speaking countries, Information was the second most modified WISC-III subtests (from 10% of the items in Taiwan to 57% of the items in Japan), followed by Comprehension (0–56% of the items), Similarities (0–37% of the items) and Arithmetic (0–42%). Digit Span stayed unchanged across adaptations. It should be noted that, even in another English-speaking country, the United Kingdom, some items were modified in the Comprehension and the Information subtests. This example shows us that test adaptation is not only a linguistic issue, but a broader cultural one.

Some items cannot be retained in the adapted version because, when translated, the answer is included in the question itself. One of the most typical example is an information item: *"How many things make a dozen?"*. Literally translated, the English word *"dozen"* is *"douzaine"* in French, and the correct answer *"douze"* is essentially given in the question. Consequently, the original item, even correctly translated, could not be used in the French adaptation and had to be replaced by an equivalent one (i.e., an item having the same difficulty level).

Some items have to be modified because of scoring issues. For example, the information item *"Name two kinds of coins"* cannot be scored in the same way in Germany or Korea compared to the United States because these countries have different categories of coins. Another example is the comprehension item *"Why doctors take additional classes after practicing medicine for a while?"*. Such an item requires an adaptation of the scoring rules in all the countries where "additional classes" are not required by the state board for keeping the medical license.

The most difficult issue when adapting verbal items is to find questions having a similar difficulty level in the source and the target culture. An item correctly translated can have a very different difficulty level in the target language than in the source language. For example, the question *"What is the Koran?"* will be easy in a dominant Muslim country, as Turkey, but more difficult in a mainly Christian country, as the United States. Similarly, a word such as a noun can be more common in one language than in another one, and will consequently be easier in the first one than in the second one. For example, *"What is a cranberry?"* will be easier for an American than for a Belgian child because this kind of berry is scarce in Belgium, but very common in the United States. In this case, a correct translation is not the solution. An equivalent word, having the same difficulty level, has to be identified. Finding such an equivalent item is not easy, and a selection only based on a subjective judgment could be problematic (e.g., should we select "raspberry" or "blueberry" as equivalent to "cranberry"?). An empirical assessment of the difficulty level of the word is often required before taking a decision. For this reason, test translators tend to create more verbal items than needed, and to select the best ones after the empirical assessment of their difficulty level. Such an empirical procedure is very helpful to develop a scale having equivalent graduations (i.e., items ranked according to their difficulty levels) in the source and the target languages.

The adaptation of the arithmetic items raises specific problems. When questions refer to dollars or US measures, as miles or F°, a literal translation is often misleading. For example, a literal translation in Japanese of the following item would be inappropriate: *"If 5 bottles of water cost 6 dollars, what is the price of 25 bottles of water?"*. The price of a bottle of water could be US 1.20$, but certainly not 1.20 Japanese Yen (US $1.00 ≈ 120 Yen). If the price of the bottle of water is adapted to the Japanese currency (i.e., 148 Yen), the adapted item will be much more difficult than the original one. The best solution would be keeping the numbers and the calculation from the original item (i.e., (25/5) × 6), but adapting the verbal problem to these numbers and calculation. This will likely result in the greater probability of a match between the difficulty levels of the adapted item and the original one. Because of problems encountered in adapting some arithmetic items, the best suggestion would be to think of the potential adaptations when developing the original items, and avoiding the use of US currencies and measures in the arithmetic problems.

Among the verbal subtests, Digit Span and Letter–Number Sequencing are the only ones that were not modified in the adaptations of the WISC-III and the WISC-IV. These subtests are always literally translated. Since they are only composed of digits and/or letters, they look identical across languages and cultures. However, as we will see, this apparent similarity doesn't prevent cultural influences on the performances on these subtests.

ADAPTATION OF THE NON-VERBAL SUBTESTS

The non-verbal subtests (i.e., the subtests included in the Perceptual Reasoning and the Processing Speed scales), have the reputation to be less culturally loaded than the verbal ones. Most often, they are not modified or adapted in other countries and only the instructions are translated. The cross-cultural analysis of the WISC-III across 12 cultures/language showed that Japan was the only country where some non-verbal subtests (i.e., performance subtests) were modified. From this observation, we might conclude that these subtests are culture fair and represent universal measures of intelligence. Such a conclusion would be naïve. Understanding non-verbal stimuli and reasoning with these stimuli are also culturally influenced cognitive procedures. Non-verbal items do not measure "genuine" intelligence, independently of any cultural and educational influences. Cultural experiences are always the framework through which we perceive, analyze and process all the non-verbal stimuli. Even the capacity to analyze geometrical figures (orientation, number of components and angles...) presented in the Raven's matrices or in the matrices subtest of the WISC-IV is developed during the school education. Consequently, children with limited education will be less efficient in these tasks than children having a regular school experience.

With the exception of the Block Design Subtest, all the non-verbal subtests of the WISC-IV use pictures (Picture Concepts, Matrix Reasoning and Picture Completion) or symbols (Coding and Symbol Search). Like words, pictures are a relationship between a signifier (the perceived picture) and a signified (what this picture represent, i.e., its meaning). Some pictures represent rather a universal signified, what they represent being easily identified by most of the people across the world (e.g., a square or a car). But the signified can also be specific to some cultures and not be recognized in other cultures, even using the best pictures (e.g., some exotic fruits could not be recognized by Europeans, or some electronic devices could not be recognized in developing countries). Even when the signified is universally known, some pictures can be rather weak representations. For example, a "pick-up" would not be the best picture to represent the concept "car" or a figure would not be the most appropriate signifier of the concept "fruit."

A majority of the pictures presented in the WISC-IV do not require adaptation in most of the cultures where this test has been adapted, because these pictures are typical and unambiguous representations of realities well known in the target cultures. However, the familiarity with these realities and their representations should always be appraised rather than simply taken for granted. For example, pictures related to baseball (glove, ball, bat...) are very familiar to American children: they know the real objects and the pictures are very typical representations of these objects. Many French or Spanish children could recognize these pictures, because they may have seen these objects in American movies or television shows. But most of them have never seen the real object or played with them as baseball is not a popular or well-known sport in either France or Spain. In these countries, we could also expect that the familiarity with these pictures varies according to social class. Consequently, to keep unchanged the difficulty level of the items and to avoid potential bias related to social class, these pictures should be changed in the adapted version of the test. Equivalent characteristics to the original ones should be found in the target culture: the baseball glove could become a boxing glove, the baseball ball a tennis ball and the baseball player a soccer player. In both cultures, these characteristics and the associated pictures refer to popular games all the children are familiar with. Even when the problematic pictures are not part of the correct answer, they should be replaced with more familiar ones because children could be distracted with these unusual and even meaningless pictures.

The knowledge of the words corresponding to the pictures should also be assessed in each culture. These word–picture connections are essential for giving the correct answer. For example, Swedish and Australian children could easily recognize the picture of a kangaroo, but naming this picture (i.e., giving the correct word "kangaroo") could be easier for Australians because they are more familiar with this animal. Even when the use of the words corresponding to the pictures is not required to give the correct answer, these words can facilitate the cognitive processing of some problems. Some children verbalize (out loud or not) the pictures of the Picture Concepts and Matrix Reasoning subtests because they can more easily process the items in this way. If they do not know the words corresponding to some pictures, such verbal mediation will be more difficult or even impossible.

Sometimes, the reality represented by the picture is familiar in both the source and the target cultures, but its representation varies across cultures. There are fire hydrants in United States, France and Switzerland, but their appearance is different in each country. In this case, the US picture of a fire hydrant cannot be used in France and Switzerland and should be redrawn. Unfortunately, the fire hydrants are also different in France and Switzerland so the redrawn picture of the French adaptation of the WISC-IV is very familiar to the French children, but meaningless for the Swiss children (several Swiss children identified this picture as a ketchup bottle!). Mailboxes and ambulances raise a similar adaptation problem across countries, even culturally very close countries such as France and Switzerland. Thus when an original picture is retained in the adapted subtest, many details have to be changed to avoid distracting the children with inappropriate information. For example, the English texts appearing on the objects (newspaper, fire extinguisher, license plate...) have to be erased or modified.

INVARIANT STRUCTURE ACROSS CULTURES

The cross-cultural study of the WISC-III conducted by Georgas et al. (2003) provides important information about cultural differences on both the subtest scores and on the composite scores. Because the WISC-III and the WISC-IV share 11 subtests, the findings from this study can be very relevant to the clinical use of this latest version of the Wechsler scales. A strength of this study was that the analyses were based on representative samples of 6- to16-year-old children ($n = 15,999$) from 12 countries, in terms of geographical areas, parental education and occupation, gender, ethnic groups and other variables ($n = 15,999$) of relevance to describing the demographics of these countries. There are few examples in the literature on intelligence and cognitive processes with samples so carefully selected and representative of the social structural variables in each country.

The countries shared similar socioeconomic features. Except for Lithuania and Slovenia, they are among the most affluent countries in the world, with developed economies and educational systems. Their governments and their people place high value on the role of education for occupational success and a better life. All these countries have highly invested in information technology. However, these countries are from the northern hemisphere and are not representative of a wide range of cultures, economic levels and educational systems of the poor countries of Africa, South America or East and West Asia.

In each country, indigenous researchers adapted the items to avoid cultural bias. Although some degree of item bias due to cultural factors is still possible, children in all these countries were familiar with the tasks: verbal stimuli, pictures, blocks, puzzles, etc. Consequently, the different culturally adapted versions of the WISC-III reported here can be considered as conceptually very similar.

The main question in this cross-cultural study was the structural equivalence of the WISC-III across 12 countries. That is, are the same cognitive structures measured by the WISC-III found in each of these countries? If this structural equivalence is found, it would provide some support for the universality of the kind of intelligence measured by the WISC-III, and consequently also to a large extent, by the WISC-IV since the two tests are based on a similar model of intelligence and share similar tasks.

In order to assess the similarity of the intelligence construct measured by the WISC-III across the 12 countries, an analysis of the structural equivalence was conducted following van de Vijver and Leung (1997). The "one-to-one" procedure employed to determine structural equivalence consisted of determining the factorial agreement of all pairs of countries. The first step was to conduct an exploratory factor analysis of the standard scores of the 12 subtests, for each of the 12 data sets. Three and four factors were extracted. The second step was to compare the factor structure of each country with the data sets of all the other country. One country was arbitrarily designated as the target and the factor loadings of the second country were rotated so as to maximize their similarity with the target country. The similarity of the factor structures was assessed by comparing the factor loadings of all pairs of countries for each of the four factors with Tucker's phi, a factorial coefficient of agreement. This resulted in a country-by-country matrix of 66 (= (12 × 11)/2) Tucker's phi coefficients. A phi value ≥1 is considered as an indication that two factors are identical. All the coefficients were larger than 0.90 for the factors Verbal Comprehension, Perceptual Organization and Processing Speed, indicating factorial stability in the factor equivalence across all the 12 data sets on these factors. Many of the phi coefficients are at the level of 0.99.

However, this was not the case with the factor freedom from distractibility, some phi coefficients being below 0.90. A close inspection of the factor structure suggested that the Arithmetic subtest was the main source of distortion. In most countries, the loadings of Arithmetic are split between Verbal Comprehension and freedom from distractibility. In some countries, the higher loading of Arithmetic was on freedom from distractibility, while it was the reverse in other countries. This instability of the Arithmetic factor loadings across countries is one of the reasons why Arithmetic is no longer a regular subtest in the WISC-IV, where it is now replaced by Letter–Number Sequencing for the usual calculation of the Working Memory Index.

The main finding of Georgas et al. (2003) study was that there is clearly a structural equivalence across the 12 data sets of a three-factor structure. A four-factor solution was very stable for the first three factors, but less stable for the fourth one. The median value of the coefficient of factorial agreement for the fourth factor was 0.95, which is well above the minimum threshold value of 0.90. The conclusion is that there is a remarkable similarity of the structure across these countries underlying the WISC-III. This finding provided evidence of universal cognitive processes across these cultures and also indicated that the WISC-III can be validly administered with the same interpretations regarding its cognitive structure across these countries. A similar study will need to be conducted with the WISC-IV adaptations. Because of the overlap between the both versions of the WISC, we can expect that a robust factor structure across cultures will also be observed with the WISC-IV. For example, a recent study comparing the United States and the Canadian WAIS-III (Bowden et al., in press) showed that the measurement model, involving four latent variables reflecting VCI, PRI, WMI and PSI, satisfied the assumption of invariance across samples. The subtest scores also showed similar reliability in both samples, although slightly higher latent variable means were found in the Canadian normative sample.

CROSS-CULTURAL COMPARISONS OF SUBTEST AND COMPOSITE SCORES

An important question in Georgas et al. (2003) study concerned the comparative analysis of the WISC-III scores on the subtests, and the IQ scores. Do countries differ in level of intelligence, as measured with the WISC-III? These analyses were conducted with the raw scores from each country and not the scaled scores, nor the actual verbal, performance and Full-Scale IQs (FSIQs), because comparisons of means of scaled scores across countries would result in zero differences.

In order to test the potential cross-cultural differences in mean scores on the WISC-III, analyses of variance were conducted with the full-scale, verbal and performance IQ raw scores, and with the subtest raw scores, using country as the independent variable. Although, as described above, these analyses were conducted with the raw scores, in order for the results to be meaningful to the reader, the results are presented in Figure 14.1 as IQ scores (mean = 100 and SD = 15).

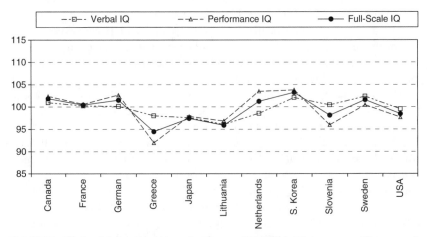

FIGURE 14.1   Means of verbal, performance, and Full-Scale IQ, by country (Georgas et al., 2003).

The main conclusion is that cross-cultural differences in composite scores (IQ scores) of the 12 data sets were very small (Figure 14.1). There were no major mean score differences on the WISC-III across the countries; neither the FSIQ, the verbal IQ or the performance IQ showed large cross-cultural score differences.

Because of the large sample ($n = 15,999$), the size of differences was not evaluated through the traditional level of statistical significance, but by the η^2 values, which estimate the proportion of variance accounted for by country in the explanation of the dependent variable and not by level of significance. The η^2 values were low, the mean value being 0.033 (range from 0.003 to 0.103). This means that the influence of the countries on the observed differences is low. For each difference between a country mean and the global mean, the effect size was calculated dividing each difference by the average standard deviation. According to Cohen (1988), an effect size of 0.20 is considered as small, 0.50 as medium and 0.80 as high. According to Cohen's criteria, all the effect sizes were small.

Table 14.2 shows the proportion of variance (η^2) accounted for by country in the differences observed on the six verbal scores. This proportion of variance is always low, with the exception of the Digit Span subtest where larger differences between countries were observed. The larger effect sizes were observed for Lithuania (-0.45) and South Korea (0.69). As the subtest was literally translated in both countries, without any modification, these differences cannot be explained by the non-equivalent difficulty level of modified items (as they could

TABLE 14.2   Effect Size for the Six Verbal Scores, by Country (Georgas et al., 2003)

	Inf.	Sim.	Ari.	Voc.	Com.	DS
Canada	−0.03	0.41	−0.21	−0.09	0.12	0.04
France	0.13	−0.18	0.12		0.23	−0.27
Germany	−0.10	−0.09	−0.05	0.34	0.16	−0.23
Greece	−0.01	−0.22	−0.16	0.02	0.08	−0.25
Japan	−0.23	−0.04	0.09		−0.59	0.26
Lithuania	−0.25	−0.25	−0.17	0.17	−0.04	−0.45
The Netherlands	0.00	0.18	0.12		−0.27	−0.37
South Korea	−0.03	−0.31	0.34	−0.18	0.01	0.69
Slovenia	0.02	−0.33	−0.04	0.22	0.07	0.16
Sweden	0.44	0.33	−0.04		0.10	−0.33
U.S.A.	−0.01	0.33	−0.23	−0.17	0.01	−0.07
η^2	0.006	0.034	0.017	0.022	0.024	0.091

Note: For Vocabulary, the information missing for several countries because too many items were modified and comparisons were therefore not possible.

for the high score on Information in Sweden or the low score in Comprehension in Japan).

The most plausible explanation is related to Baddeley's phonological loop hypothesis. According to Baddeley (1986), we can store more short words than long words in our short-term memory because speech-based information is held in memory through an articulatory control process based on inner speech. As various East Asian languages, such as South Korea, have short words for digits, people speaking these languages can store more digits in their short-term memory. On the other hand, Lithuanians have longer words for digits and, consequently, people speaking Lithuanian can store fewer digits in their short-term memory. This observation is very important for a culturally based interpretation of the Digit Span subtest. Thus, Lithuanians do not have a weaker short-term memory than the South Koreans; rather the observed difference between Korea and Lithuania can be explained by the specificity of each language. It is not a consequence of a poor test adaptation, and there is no psychometric procedure to erase this difference. Therefore, translating the Digit Span subtest to assess a child speaking a different language is not a magical solution to eliminate cultural bias.

Table 14.3 shows the proportion of variance (η^2) accounted for by country in the differences observed on the six performance scores. This proportion of variance is very low, with the exception of the Symbol Search subtest where larger differences between countries were observed. The larger effect sizes were

TABLE 14.3   Effect Size for the Six Performance Scores, by Country (Georgas et al., 2003)

	PC	CD	PA	BD	OA	SS
Canada	0.19	0.22	0.07	0.00	0.13	−0.05
France	−0.03	0.22	0.02	0.13	0.10	−0.29
Germany	0.00	0.03	0.07	0.09	0.46	−0.02
Greece	−0.40	0.06	−0.35	−0.10	−0.51	−0.52
Japan	0.41	−0.40	−0.04	−0.04	−0.10	−0.28
Lithuania	−0.22	−0.02	−0.21	0.07	−0.03	−0.29
The Netherlands	0.08	0.18	0.12	0.04	0.24	0.16
South Korea	−0.05		0.03	−0.07	−0.04	0.87
Slovenia	−0.02	−0.37	−0.15	0.09	−0.20	−0.24
Sweden	0.12	−0.15	0.14	0.03	0.10	−0.11
U.S.A.	−0.10	0.07	0.03	−0.10	−0.21	−0.20
η^2	0.014	0.021	0.011	0.009	0.034	0.103

Note: For Korea, the information was missing for the Coding subtest. PC = Picture Completion, CD = Coding, PA = Picture Arrangements, BD = Block Design, OA = Object Assembly and SS = Symbol Search.

observed for Greece (-0.52) and South Korea (0.87). Georgas et al. (2003) suggested that South Koreans' high score on Symbol Search may have reflected a strong motivation because other studies and international comparisons of educational achievement suggest that South Koreans often show high motivation in education-related matters. However, no suggestion was offered for explaining the lower score of children from Greece.

Another interpretation of the high score for South Korean children could be related to Korean writing. Korean is written using an alphabetic system (called Hangeul) and a system of characters close to the Chinese one (called Hanja). Learning to read and write using both systems could improve the ability to analyze and recognize symbols such as those presented in the Symbol Search subtest. If the mastery of the Korean writing system improves the performances on the Symbol Search subtest, it should also improve the performances on the Coding subtest since this subtest also requires children to analyze, memorize and write symbols. Unfortunately, this information was missing for Korea in the Georgas et al. (2003) research.

However, a study conducted by Chen and Zhu (2004) on Taiwanese children using Chinese letters provided a strong support to this hypothesis. These authors postulated that children who routinely read and write Chinese may perform faster on both the Coding and Symbol Search tasks than peers who primarily read and write English because the symbols used in the subtests are more similar to Chinese characters than to English alphabet. To test this hypothesis, a total of 1,003 cases from the normative sample data of the Taiwan WISC-III and the US WISC-III were matched by age, gender and parent educational level. To facilitate this comparison because Taiwan is a more homogeneous society than the United States, minority children of the US normative sample were excluded from the study. Except for the language difference, the items, instructions, administration procedures and scoring rules were the same for the Taiwan and the US editions of the non-verbal subtests. Mean raw total scores of the matched Taiwan and US samples on Block Design, Object Assembly, Picture Completion, Picture Arrangement, Mazes, Coding and Symbol Search subtests were compared directly. The effect sizes of the mean score difference were calculated using Cohen's d.

The results revealed that on the Picture Completion, Picture Arrangement and Object Assembly subtests, Taiwanese children had lower scores than their US peers. But the average effect sizes across the 11 age groups were rather small (-0.11, -0.26 and -0.09, for Picture Completion, Picture Arrangement and Object Assembly, respectively). However, Taiwanese children did significantly better than their US peers on Coding, Symbol Search, Block Design and Mazes subtests. The average effect sizes across the 11 age groups were 1.20, 0.89, 0.67 and 0.55, respectively. The effect sizes were particularly large for Coding and Symbol Search. These results supported the hypothesis that reading and writing Chinese on daily bases facilitates children's performance on processing speed tasks that utilize symbols. However, further research is needed before drawing a strong conclusion on this issue. This research should particularly address the relatively poor performances of Japan on the Coding subtest and of Greece on the Symbol Search subtest. These differences could be related to cultural specificity in early education, but this interpretation is not currently supported by empirical data.

WITHIN COUNTRY DIFFERENCES: THE US EXPERIENCE

Before examining the ways of managing the possible cultural bias in the administration, scoring and interpretation of the WISC-IV, it is important that users of this and all other intelligence tests understand some of the other causes of bias that may creep into our efforts to assess the cognitive abilities of children. In the cross-cultural research described above, IQ test scores in the 12 different countries were also examined as a function of national indicators of affluence and education (Georgas et al., 2003). The factors which influence mean IQ test scores between nations (i.e., gross national product and percent of gross national product spent on education) are essentially group level counterparts of the individual difference variables known to moderate IQ tests scores between ethnic groups within the United States (i.e., parent education and income).

More recently, data from the standardization studies of the WISC-IV have been used to explore the environmental factors that enhance or negatively impact cognitive potential during the child's developmental years (Prifitera et al., 2005; Weiss et al., 2006). While genetics is a significant determiner of intellectual ability, children are not borne with a genetically predetermined, fixed IQ score, but with a range of intellectual potential. Thus we are not contesting the large contribution of genetics to measured intelligence but rather reinforcing that intellectual potential may be fully or partially actualized depending on qualities of the environment during the critical developmental years. In brief, cognitively and linguistically stimulating environments enhance intellectual growth while cognitively and linguistically impoverished environments negatively impact intellectual potential – and much of this may be related to parental behaviors that occur within the home during the child's developmental years. The United States provides a natural laboratory for this research. It is comprised of African American, Hispanic and Caucasian majorities although these demographics are showing change with the influx of people from other countries. Further, in spite of the "melting pot" philosophy in the United States, there is also evidence that income, education and other critical social–economic factors differ across these major groups. Of course the WISC-IV was developed and carefully standardized in the United States such that data from all three groups could be analyzed in a comparative manner.

Weiss et al. (2006) reported that ethnicity explained 1.4% of the variability in IQ scores between Hispanic and White children, and that this difference was eliminated after controlling for the educational level and income of the parents. With respect to African American – White IQ score differences, Weiss et al. found that race accounted for 4.7% of the variance in IQ scores. After controlling for parental education and income, race explained only 1.6% of the remaining variance. It is not known why the African American – White difference was not completely eliminated by controlling for parent education and income as it was in the Hispanic – White analyses. However, Weiss et al. suggested that differences in quality of education and historical discrimination in employment practices among the generations that are now parents of children and adolescents may have resulted in these variables (parent education level and income) not having the same meaning and relevance for African Americans as Whites.

Next, the role of parent's expectations of children's academic success was examined. Parent expectations explained 30.7% of the variance in IQ scores across all children – far greater than that explained by race, ethnicity, parent education or income. Finally, parental expectations as a function of parent education and income was investigated, and after controlling for parent education and income, parental expectations continued to account for 15.9% of the variance in children's IQ test scores – still large. This means that parent expectations are not fully overlapping with socio-economic status. Weiss et al. conjectured that the expectations which parents hold for their children's academic success motivate parenting behaviors that enhance the intellectual development of their children toward the upper end of the range of their potential. The specific parental behaviors and the general characteristics of cognitively enriching home environments need to be better understood by researchers and clinicians alike, but may include an increased amount and variety of linguistic and motoric stimulation in the early developmental years followed by parental monitoring of homework and leisure activities during later childhood and adolescence. One of the most obvious take away points from this analysis is that culturally sensitive assessment practices should include understanding the unique aspects of each child's home environment without making generalizations based on race, ethnicity or socio-economic status.

HOW TO ADDRESS CULTURAL BIAS WHEN ASSESSING COGNITIVE ABILITY?

Clinicians frequently are requested to assess the intelligence of children with different cultural and linguistic backgrounds. In such situations, their main concern is to avoid bias and conduct a fair assessment. With this aim, they can act in different ways. Some of their actions can be efficient, but others could be inappropriate. The most common actions to overcome possible cultural bias in cognitive ability tests are reviewed in the next sections, and their advantages and limitations are pointed out.

ASSESSING ACCULTURATION

The first step when assessing a child with a different cultural and linguistic background is to assess his degree of acculturation to the culture in which he is tested and he is living. To what extent can the child be considered as being a member of the population in which the test was developed and standardized?

To answer to this question, several acculturation scales were developed. Acculturation is not a dichotomous phenomenon: being or not being member of a specific culture. It is continuous and often long process of incorporation of a different culture. Berry (1996) suggested appraising the degree of acculturation referring to two dimensions: the immersion in the culture of the native society and the immersion in the culture of the immigration society. Comparing the levels of immersion in each culture corresponds to four acculturation processes: assimilation (moving away from the native culture and immersing fully in the immigration culture), integration (equal immersion in both cultures), separation (complete immersion in the native culture and withdrawal from the immigration culture) and marginalization (lacking of meaningful immersion in both cultures).

The *Stephenson Multigroup Acculturation Scale* (Stephenson, 2000) is a good example of a scale assessing acculturation. It includes 32 items reflecting acculturation in the domains of language, interaction, media and food. For example, acculturation to the native culture is assessed with items such as: "I like to speak my native language" or "I regularly read magazines of my ethnic groups." Acculturation to the immigration culture is assessed with items as: "I like to eat American food" or "I speak English at home."

Acculturations scales can be useful if a test is appropriate for assessing a child with a different cultural background. However the results cannot be regarded alone or in isolation. They should take into account other relevant information regarding linguistic and school education. If the child's acculturation position in Berry's categories is assimilation or the integration, the test developed in the dominant culture may be used without major problem. On the other hand, if the child's acculturation position is segregation or marginalization, the regular test for the dominant culture cannot be used and another instrument or procedure should be identified.

DEVELOPING SPECIFIC NORMS

Most of the international languages include several dialects and variants across the countries where these languages are spoken. For example, different variations of French are spoken in France, Belgium, Switzerland and Canada. Differences between the standard language (usually spoken by the main group of the population or in the larger country where this language is spoken) and its local variants can be small, but sometimes important. Typically, when developing or adapting a test, only the standard language is taken into account. The test is then considered as the reference for all the variants of this language. But not taking variants and dialects into account when developing or adapting a test can lead to assessment bias and unfair decisions based on the scores in the adapted instrument.

One solution to this problem is to develop a local adaptation and norms. For example, the US WISC-IV is not the only English version. Norms were developed for the same test in Canada, United Kingdom and Australia. However, the content of the test was not modified, with minor exceptions. Why develop local norms if the test is similar to the original one? Why not use the US norms? In fact this is an empirical question that can best be addressed when sufficient data are available. While the United States and Canada share a common border and English is the majority language spoken, the question of how well the Wechsler scales travel from the United States, where the tests were developed, standardized and normed, to Canada has been addressed. It was first shown that with only a very few word changes, the items from these tests work very well in both countries (DIF analysis, subtest reliabilities, etc.) but in the case of the WISC-III and WAIS-III, there were some very noticeable differences in the raw scores and score distributions on particular subtests and index scores. For example, the PRI difference between the United States and Canada was about five-scaled score points thereby necessitating the development of Canadian norms. More recently with the addition of more "fluid" intelligence to the WISC-IV, it was observed that not only did the items fit very well but that the FSIQ difference between countries was only about two points. In the US, the Spanish version of the WISC-IV not only reflects item translation but also the generation of norms for specific use with Spanish-speaking children. This will be further discussed later (see Harris & Antolin, this book).

Developing local norms is not always possible because it is too expensive in small populations. For example, there is only one French version of the WISC-IV for France and French-speaking Belgium, and the standardization sample includes only children from France. While the same language is spoken in both countries, there are some dialectal differences (vocabulary, syntax, expressions...) that could create bias in the verbal items and, consequently, lead to unfair assessment for the Belgian children. However, before the standardization of the French adaptation of the WISC-IV, a try-out of all the verbal items was conducted simultaneously in France and Belgium with an analysis of DIF. Biased items, showing a differential functioning between the French and Belgium groups, were flagged and deleted. Although the norms for the French WISC-IV did not includ any Belgian children, the DIF analysis conducted during the item try-out helped to make possible a more fair measure for assessing these children. Unfortunately, DIF analysis conducted between linguistic subgroups of the population for which a test is being developed or adapted is uncommon. This methodology is well known in educational measurement (Holland & Wainer, 1993; Camilli & Shepard, 1994), but should be used more often for developing and adapting psychological tests across linguistic groups. Use of DIF would improve the fairness of the common linguistic version of a test.

SCORE ADJUSTMENT

Based on the idea that we can only compare what is comparable, some authors proposed to adjust the scaled scores according to the child's socio-cultural characteristics in order to "correct" their test performance bias.

In the United States, such a procedure was proposed by Mercer (1979) with her *"System of Multiculticultural and Pluralistic Assessment"* (SOMPA). Mercer considered that each child should be compared to individuals living in similar social and cultural conditions. Consequently, practitioners should always appraise the socio-cultural characteristics of the children they are testing including such variables as the size and structure of their family, the socio-economic status of their parents and their urban acculturation. This information should be quantified according to their ethnic group (White, African American and Hispanic). The child's "socio-cultural" score is used to adjust his/her IQ calculated with the regular norms, producing an estimated potential learning IQ (EPL IQ). The EPL IQ is supposed to be a more precise measure of the child's true learning potential. According to the multiple norms proposed by Mercer, the more a child is marginal regarding the dominant culture, the higher will be her/his EPL IQ compared to her/his regular IQ. The adjusted IQs are often higher than the traditional IQ score, resulting in a reduction in the number of children identified as disabled.

Mercer's score adjustment procedure was criticized from an empirical and an epistemological viewpoint. Johnson and Danley (1981) conducted research on the predictive validity of the EPL IQ. They compared two groups of children with similar IQs. The children of one group came from disadvantaged sections of the population, according to the SOMPA socio-cultural scales. Consequently, the EPL IQ of these children was higher than their regular IQ, while the EPL IQ of the children from the other group was equal to their regular IQ. The children of both groups received two learning tasks, selected as being less influenced by the dominant culture. Johnson and Danley observed that the EPL IQ and the regular IQ were both weak predictors of the learning performance. The correlations between both IQs and the learning tasks were moderate and very similar. Johnson and Danley concluded that EPL IQ is not a better predictor of learning outcomes than the regular IQ. Consequently, it should not be considered as a better estimate of the child's learning potential than the traditional IQ.

The other critique addressed to Mercer was epistemological and related to the status of knowledge underlying the SOMPA. Mercer considered the specific knowledge of all cultural groups as equal, defending therefore a relativistic view on knowledge. However, several authors emphasized that different educational environments do not develop equally efficient cognitive aptitudes. Some environments develop stronger aptitudes useful for adaptation in a broad society, while other environments develop only limited aptitudes useful in a very narrow society. Not recognizing these differences may lead to rejection of needed educational supports resulting in an increase in the cognitive differences between individuals living in the same society. Consequently, SOMPA seems to be a wrong answer to a good question. As Jirsa (1983, p.19) emphasized: "The statistical manipulation of current performance (WISC-R IQ) may succeed in eliminating certain children from special education programming, but that in no sense changes the child in terms of his or her current functioning." The goal of intellectual assessment is not to reflect the desired picture of oneself, but to collect useful information to help psychologists make the most appropriate and beneficial choices to help solve real-life problems. The messenger who carries bad news should not to be killed. On the contrary, their news should be taken into account to defining and addressing the issues at hand.

ADAPTING ADMINISTRATION RULES AND ITEMS

When the child's degree of acculturation is insufficient, some clinicians use to accommodate the testing procedures, believing they could eliminate some bias in this way. However, these modifications of the standard instructions and procedures entail negative consequences. The norms of a test were collected according to standard conditions: item format, material, instructions and scoring rules being similar for all the individuals. To compare a child's scaled score to the norms of the standardization sample, the testing should be conducted according to the standard application rules. If some conditions were modified during the testing (e.g., the wording of several questions or the demonstration of items), such a comparison may be no longer valid. In this case, using the standard norms could lead to an overestimation of the child's intelligence because the modification of the testing rules could have been too helpful for this child.

The best solution would be standardizing tests with item formats and instructions reducing the problems associated with cultural differences. For example, most of the WISC-IV subtests use demonstration items, limiting potential bias due to verbal instructions. Some subtests, such as Picture Concept and Matrix Reasoning, allow pointing at the correct answer instead of giving a verbal answer that could be more difficult to produce for a child with limited vocabulary. However, this last procedure has some limitations. For example, how could we test verbal memory without using a specific language, or even a selection of syllables and phonemes that are always specific to each language?

Translating instructions and items to the native language of the child could appear to be a good solution to avoid cultural bias. However, we have seen in the section devoted to the adaptations of the WISC that a literally translated item can be easier than the original one because translated words could give some clues to the correct answer. It can also be more difficult when the translated words are less common in the target language than in the source language. A translated item, even literally, is not *ipso facto* equivalent to the original item. We have seen, for example, that the length of the words representing the digits explained the huge difference between South Koreans' and Lithuanians' performances. Consequently, when a clinician has to assess a child who is not fluent with the language used in the WISC-IV, a literal translation of the instructions and the items in the native language of the child should not be seen as the best solution. There is always a risk of bias when using a modified testing procedure. Translated instructions should be used very cautiously and, when they are necessary, the practitioner should always document the nature of the adapted procedures used in the clinical report.

SELECTING SUBTESTS

When a child's acculturation and language knowledge are too weak to allow testing with the version of WISC-IV typically used in the country where he or she is being tested (i.e., the local version), the best option would be to use an adaptation of the test in the child's native language. However, this solution is not always an option when there is no test adaptation in the child's native language, or when the clinician is unable to use the existing adaptation because of a too limited knowledge of the child's native language. In this case, clinicians often chose to present the child with only the non-verbal subtests of the WISC-IV, usually the subtests of Perceptual Reasoning scale, and occasionally the subtests of Processing Speed scale. The Perceptual Reasoning Index (PRI) is then used as an estimate of the FSIQ. For several reasons, such a procedure should be used cautiously, and only when no other option is available.

First, the non-verbal subtests are not culture free. Removing the verbal component from testing doesn't mean there is no longer any cultural influence on test performance. As discussed above, the pictures and the geometrical figures presented in these subtests can be more or less familiar to children according to their cultural background. Moreover, modifications of the instructions are often needed for explaining the tasks to children with limited knowledge of the local language. These modifications could have an influence on the children's performances. The task is to assess cognitive ability and not some artifact that has been confounded because of language or cultural differences.

Another reason to be cautious is the imperfect correlation between the PRI and the FSIQ. The US manual reports a correlation of 0.82 (Wechsler, 2003), which is rather high, but only allows a rough estimation of the FSIQ on the basis of the PRI score. Moreover, index scores showed relatively important scatter in several WISC-IV standardization samples (Longman, 2005; Grégoire & Wierzbicki, 2007). For example, in the French standardization sample, 50% of the children showed a significant difference of 7 or more points between their PRI score and their average index score, and 25% showed a significant difference of 11 or more points. That means the PRI is not always representative of the child's general ability. Sometimes, it can underestimate this general ability, and sometimes, it can overestimate it.

The final reason to be cautious using the PRI to estimate the child's general ability is that the correlation between the PRI and measures of school achievement are lower than the correlations observed with the FSIQ, or with the verbal comprehension index (VCI). The US manual (Wechsler, 2003) reports the following correlations with the total achievement score on the WAIT-II: FSIQ = .87, VCI = .80 and PRI = .71. The PRI score is clearly a weaker predictor of school achievement than the FSIQ or the VCI. Therefore, it should be used cautiously as an indicator of the child's learning potential.

INTERPRETING THE SCORES

Even when an immigrant child's acculturation is sufficient to allow the use of the local version of the WISC-IV (i.e., the version adapted and normed in the country where the child is currently living and being tested), cultural bias should be controlled throughout the testing procedure. In a WISC-IV protocol, we commonly observe a very small number of biased items and children having no culturally related difficulties with most of the WISC-IV subtests. For example, some children from Morocco (Muslim country), but living in Belgium for a long time and being acculturate to this society, told us that the important part missing from the woman's face (Picture Completion subtest) was her veil, while the correct answer was her eyelashes. In this case, the item should be scored according to the rules used for the test standardization, and the children should receive no credit for this item. Some clinicians may consider such a decision as too strict and would advocate giving credit for this answer because it was meaningful. However, practitioners should stick to the scoring rules if they want to use the norms collected according to standard conditions. Any departure from the testing rules could invalidate the observed scores. Instead of modifying instructions or scoring rules, it seems more appropriate to always add an interpretation to the scaled scores in the psychological report. This interpretation should include clinical observations related to the impact of culture on the testing (misunderstanding of instructions, lack of knowledge of words or pictures, unusual answers...) that could moderate some scores or explain some differences between scores.

Isolated instances of culturally biased items in a WISC-IV protocol will usually have a limited impact on the subtest and the composite scaled scores. For example, one biased item in the Vocabulary subtest would only be 1/35 of the whole subtest, and much less of the whole test. However, when the number of biased items in a subtest is large, it could invalidate the subtest. When the proportion of inappropriate items in a subtest becomes too large, the best option is to invalidate the subtest and use an alternative subtest when possible. When no alternative subtest is available, the calculation of the composite scores should be prorated, i.e. multiplying the sum of the valid scaled scores per a fraction where the denominator is the regular number of scores (e.g., 5) and the numerator is the number of valid scores (e.g., 4).

CONCLUSION

There is no way to assess intelligence independently of any cultural influence. There is no culture free test and no culture fair test. Bruner (1974, p.364) emphasized that: "Culture free means intelligence free." Even if the roots of intelligence are in our genetic inheritance, our intellectual behaviors are always shaped by culture. We cannot think in a vacuum independently of any content. The contents are cultural knowledge, learned through education and experience.

It is simplistic to think that only verbal knowledge is influenced by culture. Non-verbal knowledge is equally influenced by culture.

As every intelligence test, the WISC-IV is a cultural product. Its items reflect the society in which it was developed. However, Georgas et al. (2003) study conducted on the standardization sample data of 12 adaptations of the WISC-III across the world showed that its factor structure was universal. Even if a lot of items were modified in these adaptations, their common factor structures allow cross-cultural and cross-linguistic comparisons. Such an international comparison has not yet been conducted with the WISC-IV. Because of the substantial content and structural overlap between the WISC-III factor based index scores and the WISC-IV, the observation of a similar universal factor structure can be expected.

When a clinician has to assess the intelligence of a child from a different cultural and linguistic background, their main concern is to avoid bias and conduct a fair assessment. Before applying the WISC-IV, clinician should assess the child's degree of acculturation to the local culture in which the test was developed. When the degree of acculturation is insufficient, the first option is to apply a version of the WISC-IV adapted to the child's native culture. When this option is not possible, the clinicians should avoid modifying the local version of the WISC-IV to fit the child's characteristics. However, some clinicians do personal adaptation of the testing rules. The most common modifications are: the translation of instructions or items, the non-standard demonstrations of the subtests and modifications of the scoring rules. The main consequence of these modifications of the testing rules is that the comparison of the child's performances to the local norms is no longer valid and thus score interpretation may be very unreliable and valid. A better option is to select the most appropriate subtests fitting the child's characteristics, usually the subtests of the PRI, and calculate an estimate of the FSIQ on the basis of this selection of subtests applied according to the standard rules. However, such a procedure should be used cautiously because it may under-represent the construct of intelligence as defined in the WISC-IV, and provides only a rough estimate of the FSIQ. Moreover the predictive validity for say, achievement of the estimated FSIQ is usually lower than the predictive validity of the traditional FSIQ.

When an immigrant child's degree of acculturation is high, the national or country version of the WISC-IV may be used. Minor biases may nevertheless be observed during the testing. These biases should not lead to any modification of the scoring rules. It is always appropriate, in fact necessary, to mention in the psychological report the possible impact of culture on the child's performance. This information should be used to moderate and guide the interpretation of scores and score differences.

REFERENCES

Ackerman, P. L. (2007, May). *Adult intellectual development: An integrated cognitive, affective and conative framework*. Paper presented at the 19th Annual convention of the Association for Psychological Science, Washington, DC.

Azuma, H., & Kashiwagi, K. (1987). Descriptors for an intelligent person: A Japanese study. *Japanese Psychological Research*, 29, 17–26.

Baddeley, A. (1986). *Working Memory*. Oxford: Oxford University Press.

Berry, J. W. (1996). Immigration, acculturation and adaptation. *Applied Psychology*, 46, 5–34.

Bowden, S. C., Lange, R. T., Weiss, L. G., & Saklofske, D. H. (in press). Invariance of the measurement model underlying the Wechsler Adult Intelligence Scale-III in the United States and Canada. *Educational and Psychological Measurement*.

Broer, M. (1996). Rasch-homogene Leistungstests (3DW, WMT) im Kulturvergleich Chile-Österreich. Erstellung einer spanischen Version einer Testbatterie und deren interkulturelle Validierung in Chile [Rasch-homogeneous performance tests in cross-cultural comparison Chile-Austria. Making a Spanish version of a test battery and its intercultural validation in Chile]. Unpublished thesis, University of Vienna, Austria.

Bruner, J. S. (1974). *Beyond the Information Given*. London: Allen & Unwin.

Camilli, G., & Shepard, L. A. (1994). *Methods for Identifying Biased Test Items*. Thousand Oaks, CA: Sage Publications.

Chen, H., & Zhu, J. (2004, August). *Developmental trend on children's digit symbol coding and symbol search abilities: U.S.A. and Taiwan WISC-III norms compared*. Paper presented at the 28th International Congress of Psychology, Beijing, China.

Cohen, J. (1988). *Statistical Power Analysis for Behavioral Sciences*. Hillsdale, NJ: Lawrence Erlbaum.

Deregowski, J. B., & Serpell, R. (1971). Performance on a sorting task: A cross-cultural experiment. *International Journal of Psychology*, 6, 273–281.

Georgas, J., Weiss, L. G., van de Vijver, F. J. R., & Saklofske, D. H. (Eds.) (2003). *Culture and Children's Intelligence: Cross-Cultural Analysis of the WISC-III*. San Diego, CA: Academic Press.

Grégoire, J., & Wierzbicki, C. (2007). Analyse de la dispersion des Indices du WISC-IV en utilisant l'écart significatif par rapport à la moyenne des quatre Indices [Analysis of the WISC-IV Index score scatter using the significant deviation from the mean of the four Index scores]. *Revue Européenne de Psychologie Appliquée*, 57, 101–106.

Grigorenko, E. L., Geissler, P. W., Prince, R., Okatcha, F., Nokes, C., Kenny, D. A., Bundy, D. A., & Sternberg, R. J. (2001). The organisation of Luo conceptions of intelligence: A study of implicit theories in a Kenyan village. *International Journal of Behavioral Development*, 25, 367–378.

Hambleton, R. K. (1994). Guidelines for adapting educational and psychological tests: A progress report. *European Journal of Psychological Assessment*, 10, 229–244.

Hambleton, R. K. (2005). Issues, designs, and technical guidelines for adapting tests into multiple languages and cultures. In: R. K. Hambleton, P. F. Merenda, & C. D. Spielberger (Eds.), *Adapting Educational and Psychological Tests for Cross-Cultural Assessment* (pp. 3–38). Mahwah, NJ: Lawrence Erlbaum.

Holland, P. W., & Wainer, H. (Eds.) (1993). *Differential Item Functioning*. Hillsdale, NJ: Erlbaum.

Jensen, A. R. (1980). *Bias in Mental Testing*. New York: Free Press.

Jirsa, J. E. (1983). The SOMPA: A brief examination of technical considerations, philosophical rationale, and implications for practice. *Journal of School Psychology*, 21, 13–21.

Johnson, D. L., & Danley, W. (1981). Validity: Comparison of WISC-R and SOMPA estimated learning potential scores. *Psychological Reports*, 49, 123–131.

Longman, R. S. (2005). Tables to compare WISC-IV index scores against overall means. In: A. Prifitera, D. H. Saklofske, & L. G. Weiss (Eds.), *WISC-IV. Clinical Use and Interpretation* (pp. 66–69). San Diego, CA: Elsevier Academic Press.

Mercer, J. R. (1979). *System of Multicultural Pluralistic Assessment. Technical manual*. San Diego: The Psychological Corporation.

Nkaya, H. N., Huteau, M., & Bonnet, J. (1994). Retest effect on cognitive performance on the Raven-38 Matrices in France and in the Congo. *Perceptual and Motor Skills*, 78, 503–510.

Ombredane, A., Robaye, F., & Plumail, H. (1956). Résultats d'une application répétée du matrix-couleur à une population de Noirs Congolais [Results of a repeated application of the colored matrices to a population of Black Congolese]. *Bulletin du Centre d'Etudes et Recherches Psychotechniques*, 6, 129–147.

Prifitera, A., Saklofske, D. H., & Weiss, L. G. (2005). *WISC-IV. Clinical Use and Interpretation*. San Diego, CA: Elsevier Academic Press.

Serpell, R. (1993). *The Significance of Schooling. Life-Journeys In an African Society*. Cambridge, UK: Cambridge University Press.

Stephenson, M. (2000). Development and validation of the Stephenson Multigroup Acculturation Scale (SMAS). *Psychological Assessment*, 12, 77–88.

Tulsky, D., Saklofske, D. H., Chelune, G. J., Heaton, R. K., Ivnik, R. J., Bornstein, R., Prifitera, A., & Ledbetter, M. F. (Eds.) (2003). *Clinical Interpretation of the WAIS-III and WMS-III*. San Diego, CA: Academic Press.

van de Vijver, F. J. R., & Leung, K. (1997). *Methods and Data Analysis for Cross-Cultural Research*. Newbury Park, CA: Sage.

van de Vijver, F. J. R., & Poortinga, Y. H. (1997). Towards an integrated analysis of bias in cross-cultural assessment. *European Journal of Psychological Assessment*, 13, 29–37.

van de Vijver, F. J. R., & Tanzer, N. K. (2004). Bias and equivalence in cross-cultural assessment: An overview. *European Review of Applied Psychology*, 54, 119–135.

van de Vijver, F. J. R. (2003). Test adaption/translation methods. In: R. Fernandez-Ballesteros (Ed.), *Encyclopedia of Psychological Assessment* (pp. 960–964). Thousand Oaks: Sage.

Wechsler, D. (1971). *Manual for the Wechsler Adult Intelligence Scale – Revised*. New York: Psychological Corporation.

Wechsler, D. (2003). *Wechsler Intelligence Scale for Children-IV*. San Antonio, TX: Psychological Corporation.

Weiss, L. G., & Prifitera, A. (1995). An evaluation of differential prediction of WAIT achievement scores from WISC-III FSIQ across ethnic and gender groups. *Journal of School Psychology*, 33, 297–304.

Weiss, L. G., Prifitera, A., & Roid, G. (1993). The WISC-III and the fairness of predicting achievement across ethnic and gender groups. *Journal of Psychoeducational Assessment, Monograph Series*, 15(2).

Weiss, L. G., Saklofske, D. H., Prifitera, A., & Holdnack, J. A. (2006). *WISC-IV Advanced Clinical Interpretation*. San Diego, CA: Academic Press.

Yan, G., & Saklofske, D. H. (2004, August). *Intelligence: Views of Chinese psychologists*. Paper presented at the 28th International Congress of Psychology, Beijing, China.

15

OF WHAT VALUE IS INTELLIGENCE?

LINDA S. GOTTFREDSON

School of Education, University of Delaware, Newark, DE, USA

First developed a century ago, intelligence tests remain the best known, best researched, and perhaps most frequently used of all psychological assessments. But why? After all, they have been dogged by public controversy since the beginning. The answer turns out to be simple, although hard-won in a century of research and debate among many hundreds of scholars. My aim here is to provide enough of that scientific account to put into broader social perspective what we know about intelligence and how we know it, as well as what intelligence tests reveal about fundamental human differences, how they do so, and why we care about them.

FROM WHAT VANTAGE POINTS – PERSON OR POPULATION – DO WE LOOK AT INTELLIGENCE?

The term "ability," like intelligence, is often used in two ways: first, to refer to a domain of tasks that might be performed well, especially as development proceeds (e.g., a child is better able to reason abstractly at age 15 than age 5), and second, to refer to differences among individuals in such capabilities (e.g., one 15 year old is more adept at abstract reasoning than another 15 year old). The distinction is between "*what* is done well" and "*who* has the edge in doing it well." "What" research focuses on typical trends in development (intraindividual change over time), and seeks to gauge competence against some external criterion. "Who" research focuses on population variation around the trend line at a given age, and it usually takes a norm-referenced approach to abilities, which involves comparing an individual to others in some reference group. In short, one approach studies the common human theme; the other, variations on it. Both are concerned, of course, with the same underlying phenomenon – some particular continuum of competence.

Tests of intelligence, personality, and the like remain mostly in the second tradition referred to as the study of individual differences or differential psychology. So, the key question in research on IQ tests has been "What do they tell us about human variation, and how is that information useful?" Tests can be useful for many purposes without our knowing what they measure. For example, colleges and employers both use ability tests to identify which applicants are most likely to succeed if selected (Campbell & Knapp, 2001). Like my car, a test can be a mysterious black box as long as it gets me where I want to go. Predictive or diagnostic utility was the aim of the first intelligence test, developed by Binet and Simon in 1906, because they wished to identify children who would not succeed in school without special assistance.

For other purposes, clinical, scientific, or political, we also have to understand what phenomenon intelligence tests measure, that is, their *construct validity*. Researchers who seek to understand the nature of intelligence itself must know, at a minimum, what latent constructs the tests measure and how they do so. Evidence about predictive validity is crucial but not sufficient. Knowing what construct a test measures is a long iterative process in which provisional answers to that question are used to generate additional testable predictions about the trait's stability and course of development, which kinds of tasks call it forth most strongly, which circumstances make it rise or fall, how well it predicts different kinds of life success, and so on.

Perhaps in no other applied setting is construct validity more important than for clinicians who are asked to diagnose individuals and intervene in their lives. Such is the case for school psychologists, for example, when they assess individual students who are having difficulties in the classroom in order to design interventions for ameliorating those difficulties. They must create a theory, so to speak, of that particular child based on a broad set of information gathered from tests, teachers, and often parents too. They need such a theory, a close-up ideographic portrait, to understand what is impeding that particular child's learning or adjustment and to develop strategies for eliminating or working around those impediments. Arguably, a battery of cognitive tests is the most important single tool in sketching that portrait. That is why the present book focuses on the richness of information that the WISC-IV index scores can provide about a child's profile of strengths and weaknesses, in addition to overall level of intellectual functioning reflected in the total IQ, in order to gain leverage in diagnosis and treatment.

The aim of the current chapter is to place that ideographic client-centered use of intelligence testing within the broader social context in which IQ tests are used and judged. To do that, I bring to the foreground what has been mostly background in this book's advice for painting complex cognitive portraits of individual children, namely the general intelligence factor, g, as gauged by the WISC-IV Full-Scale IQ (FSIQ). So, instead of examining the profile of highs and lows among different abilities within a single person, this chapter turns to examining differences in a single very important ability across many different people. Whatever one's views about the scientific validity of using tests to assess interindividual differences in intelligence, I suspect all would agree that ranking individuals by general intelligence generates the most public controversy (Williams, 2000; Gottfredson, in press).

IS INTELLIGENCE ANYTHING MORE THAN A SCORE ON AN IQ TEST?

Some critics assert that intelligence is no more than what intelligence tests measure, thus encouraging us to doubt that intelligence can be measured, if it exists at all. According to them, IQ tests trap us forever in an endless tautological loop going nowhere because, they suggest, the IQs calculated from a test simply summarize what testers themselves put into it. On the other hand, when testers respond that IQ tests measure something deeper, some phenomenon in its own right, how can we know what that phenomenon is apart from the tests they use to measure it? The fact that different intelligence tests correlate highly among themselves tells us nothing about what any of them measures. The scientific credibility of one test is not enhanced by pointing to others like it, because all could be similarly mistaken. This is the same tautology, just twice removed.

Other critics of intelligence testing suggest that we cannot know whether we have measured intelligence, let alone measured it well, until everyone agrees on a common, carefully specified, a priori definition of what it is. This would leave us worse off than before – with no tests of intelligence – as may be the critics' aim. Scholars certainly will never agree on what intelligence is before they have done the research necessary to learn what it is. Empirical phenomena are not defined into existence, but described once known.

How, then, do we even know that intelligence differences exist as a stable phenomenon to be investigated and measured? Some critics assert that testers find differences in intelligence only because they intend to, specifically, by developing tests that exaggerate minor differences or manufacture new ones (Fischer et al., 1996). They thus posit the ultimate tautology: IQ differences represent nothing but the intent by psychometricians to create the appearance of difference. By the critics' reasoning, there would be no differences absent such intent. This is akin to claiming that heat exists only because scientists have created thermometers to measure it.

Intelligence is, in fact, much like heat. Neither heat nor intelligence can be directly seen, touched, or held. We nonetheless notice differences in both as we go about our daily lives, often experiencing them as immediate and obvious. We might not understand them, but they clearly affect us regardless of whether we ever measure or define them. We have large vocabularies for each, itself indicating our ongoing concern with them, and we shape our lives somewhat in response to them. Both continua exist in nature, ready to be measured and scientifically explained. Psychometricians and other scholars of intelligence have steadily advanced against this measurement challenge, decade after decade, for over a century now (Bartholomew, 2004; Roberts, 2007).

WHAT IS INTELLIGENCE, AND HOW DO WE KNOW THAT IQ TESTS MEASURE IT?

The early intelligence tests might be likened to early thermometers – first efforts to measure a distinction long perceived as relevant to our lives, which are guided by our initial intuitions about that distinction. That is how Binet and Simon proceeded in 1906. Just as thermometer readings must not be influenced by humidity, much psychometric work since their time has gone into assuring that intelligence test scores are highly reliable and not influenced by irrelevant factors such as cultural bias (Jensen, 1980). Indeed, the margin of error in FSIQ scores is smaller than for many physical assessments, such as blood pressure readings, and their diagnostic sensitivity and specificity exceed that of many medical assessments. Researchers have tested competing notions about the structure of human cognitive abilities and of its stability and comparability across different ages and demographic groups. I am not aware of any important behavioral or psychological assessment with greater reliability, demonstrated construct validity, or predictive validity in many life arenas than a professionally developed intelligence test battery properly administered.

The century of research has also revealed a lot about what intelligence represents at the everyday behavioral level, as well as providing tantalizing glimpses of its manifestations in the brain. The most dramatic advance, in my view, has been to escape the tautology that "intelligence is what intelligence tests measure." In fact, as demonstrated shortly, psychometricians now have an independent means of determining *how well* different tests – indeed, any test or task – measure general intelligence.

What does the research reveal? Perhaps most importantly, it shows that global intelligence as measured by IQ tests is a highly organized system of interrelated mental abilities, all of which share a common core. Human intelligence is highly structured in this sense, not merely a collection of separate, independent abilities like marbles in a bag, where all that is required for an individual to be smart is to collect a large number of any type. There are many kinds of cognitive abilities, to be sure, but individuals who possess one tend to possess all others in good measure too. This observation is what led Charles Spearman (1904) to hypothesize a general factor of intelligence, g, and what has prompted so many decades of psychometric research aimed at charting the patterns of relatedness and overlap among seemingly different dimensions of cognitive variation.

These many abilities are best distinguished by their breadth of application, that is, by how domain-specific versus domain-general they are, and only secondarily by manifest content (verbal, quantitative, etc.). This structure of observed overlap and relatedness among abilities, based on factor analyses of their intercorrelations, is usually referred to as the hierarchical model of cognitive abilities. It is hierarchical because it classifies abilities into tiers according to their generality of application. The most general abilities are represented in the top tiers and the narrowest and most specific in the bottom tier. This model is useful for integrating all cognitive abilities into a single unifying framework where it can be seen, for example, that the narrower abilities are mostly composites of the broader ones. Carroll's (1993) Three-Stratum Model of cognitive abilities, developed from his re-examination of 500 prior studies, is currently the most influential model of the structure of human mental abilities.

More specifically, when batteries of diverse cognitive tests are factor analyzed, they reveal a smaller number of broad dimensions of ability, sometimes called primary abilities. There are positive correlations among all cognitive tests, as noted earlier, but certain subsets clump together as especially highly intercorrelated, as if they possess something else in common that the others do not. Carroll (1993) placed these broad factors in Stratum II of his model. He identified eight at this level of generality, including Fluid Intelligence, Crystallized Intelligence, General Learning and Memory, and Processing Speed. The four index scores of the WISC-IV represent abilities of comparable breadth: Verbal Comprehension Index (VCI), Perceptual Reasoning Index (PRI), Working Memory Index (WMI), and Processing Speed Index (PSI). The 12 WISC subtests from which they are calculated represent Stratum I abilities in Carroll's model. It is from these sorts of broad Stratum II abilities that school psychologists and vocational counselors construct ability profiles for individuals. A spatial tilt, for example, is often associated with interest in and aptitude for technical work in the physical sciences and the skilled crafts. Everyday intuition tells us that people are not equally intelligent or unintelligent in all respects, and the somewhat uneven profiles of Stratum II abilities in general populations confirm that. Specific learning disabilities such as dyslexia represent highly unusual disparities in abilities that normally move in tandem.

These broad abilities are themselves strongly intercorrelated, indicating that they are not separate, independent abilities but reflect some deeper commonality – that is, some yet more generalizable ability, a common core, that enhances performance across all the content domains they represent, from verbal reasoning to spatial and auditory perception. When the Stratum II ability factors are themselves factor analyzed, they yield a single higher-order factor of mental ability – called g, for the general mental ability factor. The g factor typically accounts for more of the common variance among tests than do all the other derived factors combined. In essence, most tests of specific abilities measure mostly g plus one or more specific additives. Carroll, for example, referred to Stratum II ability factors as differently flavored forms of the same g. The large core of g in all Stratum I and II cognitive abilities helps to explain why dedicated efforts to develop useful tests of them that do not correlate appreciably with IQ have all failed. g certainly cannot be said to encapsulate the whole of intelligence as many conceive it, but it does fit well what most experts and laymen alike think of as general intelligence: a general purpose tool for learning and reasoning well, spotting and solving problems, and using abstract ideas.

The g factor is not an artifact of factor analysis, but has been independently confirmed by biological, genetic, and other sorts of non-psychometric evidence (Jensen, 1998; Deary, 2000). This thick web of empirical correlations involving highly g-loaded tests also clarifies what intelligence is *not*, regardless of whether we use the label exclusively for g or to encompass the entire structure of cognitive abilities. Intelligence is not, as sometimes claimed, just a narrow academic ability, test-taking smarts, aptness with paper-and-pencil tests (the best IQ tests rely on neither), or a collection of narrow, independent skills. g is certainly not a thing or a place in the brain. It may not even be an ability as such, but a property of the brain – a sort of cerebral wattage, mental horsepower, or overall efficiency that tones up all parts of the brain and all aspects of cognitive functioning. Whatever g turns out to be at the physiological level, for most practical purposes the FSIQ is an excellent, albeit imperfect, measure of it at the psychometric level.

One side benefit of the integrative hierarchical model has been to clarify the different senses in which the term intelligence is often used – and confused. Some of us restrict the term to the single factor, g, found at the top of the Three-Stratum Model, although prefacing it with the adjective "general." Others apply the term intelligence to the small collection of broad abilities at the Stratum II level. This is presumably where the more cognitively oriented of Gardner's (1983) proposed multiple intelligences would show up were he to measure them (linguistic, logical-mathematical, spatial, and musical). Other scholars extend the term to include the entire hierarchy or, like Gardner, outside the cognitive realm to include a wide variety of non-cognitive skills and traits, ranging from physical coordination (Gardner's bodily kinesthetic intelligence) to motivation and conscientiousness, on the grounds that these human attributes also are culturally valued or adaptive.

g is a far more precise referent for the major construct which IQ tests measure than is the term intelligence. The distinction between g and IQ, on the other hand, is not merely semantic. It is a conceptual distinction whose importance cannot be overstated. The IQ is a reading from a measurement device, but g is a theoretical construct that transcends the particulars of any test or population (Jensen, 1998). The power to now separate the two – the yardstick from what it measures – is precisely what allows us to study the empirical phenomenon that IQ tests measure independent of the particular devices commonly used to measure it – in other words, to convincingly repudiate the false claim that "intelligence is what intelligence tests measure." All tests and tasks can now be characterized according to their degree of g loading, and the resulting patterns of g loadings across tests, jobs, subjects, ages, times, places, and settings allow us to test alternative hypotheses about the phenomenon they prod into greater or lesser action.

At the behavioral level, the g factor represents a general proficiency at learning, reasoning, thinking abstractly, and otherwise processing information efficiently and accurately almost without regard to type of the information being processed. g is a highly general ability because its practical value in enhancing performance is not restricted to any particular content domain: it is generalizable across many. Because cognitive tests of all types tend to measure g more than anything else, tests in one content domain generally predict performance in their own domain little better, if at all, than tests meant for other content domains. This fact, which has been known for decades (e.g., Jencks et al., 1979), is referred to as validity generalization in the personnel selection literature.

Some critics nonetheless still point to specific item attributes or item content on IQ tests to argue that they cannot possibly measure what we already know they do, namely, a general learning or reasoning ability, as if intelligence would necessarily mirror the superficialities of the items used to activate it. Based on their reading of these superficialities, critics usually posit some narrow facility at esoteric or highly structured tasks with no relevance to real life. Perhaps ironically, the most striking observation about intelligence tests such as the WISC-IV and WAIS-III and -IV is that they include such a great variety of items and those items are not similar in any obvious way. The items may use words, numbers, shapes, pictures, or blocks; require specific cultural knowledge or only universal concepts such as up/down and large/small; use language, paper, or pencils – or not.

This brings us to the key question: what, in fact, do IQ items share in common that allows them to activate so effectively the same general ability? Put another way, what is the chief active ingredient in IQ tests that allows them to call g forth on demand to be observed and measured? The answer: the complexity of the information to be processed. The more complex the test item or task, the more highly the quality of its performance correlates with individual differences in IQ (the more g *loaded* it is). Any number of elements can increase a task's complexity: amount of information to be integrated, presence of irrelevant information, abstractness, uncertainty and ambiguity, inferences required, and the like. Task complexity is the active ingredient in IQ test items, the source of differential item difficulty on adult literacy tests, the chief barrier to comprehension of health education materials, and the reason why cognitive tests predict job performance successively better in successively more complex jobs (Gottfredson, 1997, 2004). As discussed later, this knowledge also provides leverage to school psychologists, health workers, and others in their clinical work with individuals with cognitive deficits.

HOW ARE INDIVIDUALS DISTRIBUTED ALONG THE IQ CONTINUUM?

To the uninitiated, any distribution might seem plausible. The distribution of IQs within a population might conceivably resemble its distribution of income.

In most societies, mean income is much higher than median income because a small proportion of individuals make many multiples the typical income. Alternatively, the distribution might be rectangular, that is, evenly populated from low to high across the so-called normal range of IQ 70–130. On the other hand, if general intelligence is labile, then perhaps the distribution of IQs is unpredictable and fluctuates over time. In actuality, mental test performances appear to be fairly normally distributed at any given age (even before being statistically "normalized"), as are many biological traits. This alone is an interesting fact about general intelligence.

All populations manifest a g continuum of cognitive differences, and, as we can best discern, the members within each are normally distributed in IQ. The continuum itself seems isomorphic across all populations examined thus far, but they commonly differ in where along the IQ continuum they are centered or how spread out they are along it, that is, their means and standard deviations tend to differ somewhat. Small to moderate differences by both racial and ethnic heritage appear to be the rule, not the exception, both within and outside the United States and Europe (Frisby & Reynolds, 2005).

There are other striking regularities in the distribution of IQ scores within populations and hence, presumably, of g itself. At least in developed nations, IQs are fairly stable from late childhood to late adulthood. For example, IQ at age 11 correlated about 0.7 with IQ near age 80 in a Scottish cohort born in 1921 (Deary et al., 2004). Stability refers to maintaining similar rank within one's age group, because IQs are calculated as deviations from the average of one's age cohort. (The average IQ is set to 100 at every age.) The stability of IQ scores thus does not by any means suggest that intelligence level is "fixed," but only that individuals within an age cohort tend to retain the same rank in IQ as their age cohort rises or declines in average ability in absolute terms. If IQs were not stable in this sense, cognitive tests would not predict later outcomes nearly as well as they do.

Lacking ratio-level measurement, we cannot yet measure an individual's change in absolute ability level from one age to the next, but there is sufficient evidence to gauge general trends by age. General mental horsepower, as indexed by fluid g, increases rapidly in childhood, peaks in early adulthood, and then gradually declines into old age, though it may fall precipitously shortly before death. Very general language skills and cultural knowledge, indexed by crystallized g, are more robust and tend not to decline substantially until later in life. There is variation around these trend lines, of course, but they seem quite regular in the populations studied thus far.

Overall cognitive proficiency clearly changes over the lifetime, first rising and then declining. Whether it is malleable, that is, amenable to intentional change, is a different question. Adoption studies and interventions to raise low IQs have both been somewhat disappointing on this score, though many scholars would say the jury still out (Neisser, 1998; Williams, 2000; Flynn, 2007). It is fair to say, however, that there is as yet no effective and feasible means of substantially enhancing general intelligence in any significant proportion of the population, except perhaps in the most malnourished regions of the world. There is some evidence that it may be possible, however, to forestall some of the cognitive declines with advancing age. But saying that intelligence may be improvable or recoverable does not mean that it is equalizable across a population. Evidence for the former is sometimes mistaken as evidence for the latter.

The stability of IQ is commonly regarded as a problem to be solved. It is most certainly a problem for low-g individuals and a constraint on the ease and effectiveness with which families and organizations can intervene to improve performance in schools, work, health self-care, and other important life arenas. Yet, from some perspectives, the stability of general intelligence might be considered a blessing. It is hard to imagine how human intelligence could ever have evolved had it not been robust in the face of adverse circumstances – which must have been the lot of humankind throughout evolution.

In summary, intelligence tests reveal that phenotypic (observed) differences in general intelligence (g) are systematically patterned and probably a highly regular and predictable feature of human populations the world over.

WHAT IS THE PERSONAL AND SOCIAL IMPORT OF DIFFERENCES IN GENERAL INTELLIGENCE (g)?

Diverse sorts of research have confirmed the common intuition that differences in general intelligence have considerable practical importance in our lives, individual and collective (Jencks et al., 1979; Herrnstein & Murray, 1994; Ceci, 1996; Gottfredson, 1997a; Sternberg & Grigorenko, 2002; Lubinski, 2004). Most studies to date have focused on how higher intelligence levels improve the life chances of individuals, but the controversy over intelligence testing stems primarily from the societal-level waves generated by the resulting socioeconomic inequalities. The depth, strength, and patterning of those waves depend, in turn, primarily on the distribution of g because it overwhelms all other cognitive abilities at the population level.

I focus below on the real-world consequences for individuals of variation in g, whether or not it is ever measured. Using test scores to make decisions about individuals and organizations obviously can affect their well-being, but that is not the issue here. Making decisions based on test results constitutes social intervention rather than an empirical finding about the attribute being measured.

First, IQ/g is the best single predictor of a wide variety of outcomes in modern life, from performance on jobs and standardized achievement tests, to level of income and occupation, to law-abidingness, bearing children within marriage, and health self-care. IQ typically outperforms standard measures of socioeconomic advantage. Specific abilities add little incremental validity, as evidenced the fact that a whole battery of cognitive tests does little better than *g* alone in predicting differences in such outcomes.

The prognostic value of *g*/IQ differs greatly, however, by kind of outcome. That is, *g* affects a person's odds of success far more in some arenas than others. Moreover, these gradients of effect reflect the psychometric properties of everyday life (Gordon, 1997). For example, when everyday life is conceptualized as an IQ test writ large, its separate demands can be characterized by how *g* loaded they are, the extent to which outcomes depend exclusively on the person's own independent efforts, and how reliably and objectively the outcomes are evaluated. Because demands differ predictably in these regards, so do *g*'s gradients of effect.

Correlations with IQ (corrected for range restriction) extend, roughly, from about 0 for happiness, to -0.2 for delinquency, 0.3–0.4 for income (correlations rise by mid-career), 0.6 for education and occupation level attained, and 0.8 for standardized academic achievement. The odds of unfavorable outcomes on dichotomous measures also differ greatly by kind of outcome. Consider, for instance, the steadily greater odds for unfavorable outcomes of the following sort when comparing adults whose IQs are somewhat below average (IQs 75–90) to those who are somewhat above average (IQs 110–125): unemployed or getting divorced within 5 years (3:2), women bearing an illegitimate child (4:1), living in poverty (5:1), and mothers going on welfare after birth of first child (5:1) or being a chronic welfare recipient (8:1; Gottfredson, 1997, Table 10). Differences in *g* are not solely responsible for such differences, but they account for many of the upstream problems, such as school failure, contributing to them. The new fields of cognitive epidemiology and health literacy are also documenting pervasive differences in morbidity and mortality by level of IQ or aptness in learning, reasoning, and problem solving (Deary et al., 2004; Gottfredson, 2004), regardless of income or access to health care. Evidently, material resources do not substitute for mental resources in health either.

The differences in tightness of linkage of IQ with socio-economic outcomes arise in part because institutional practices often limit the control that individuals have over certain kinds of performance or whether their performance counts toward advancement (e.g., pay scales and promotions based on seniority), and partly because other personal traits and circumstances can make a big difference in some outcomes (e.g., conscientiousness for job performance, and family background for educational opportunities). In general, *g* predicts best when tasks are instrumental rather than socio-emotional and when individuals perform them independently of co-workers. This includes most work in school, training, jobs, health – and cognitive tests.

When individuals have reasonable control over their own performance, *g* predicts performance best when the tasks to be performed are more complex, as was noted earlier. Task complexity best explains, for example, why the correlations between mental test scores and job performance (corrected for range restriction) increase from about 0.2 in the simplest, most routine, and highly supervised factory and service jobs, to 0.5 in much clerical, crafts, and protective services work, to nearly 0.8 in highly demanding executive-level and professional jobs. Job analyses chart the increasing variety, fluidity, cognitive complexity, and learning demands of the task constellations comprising jobs higher up the occupational ladder. Higher-level jobs are like more difficult intelligence tests. Both civilian and military studies show that higher g typically overtakes the advantages of longer experience within several months to several years on the job.

Conversely, the distribution of task complexities in a setting allows us to forecast when and where differences in worker performance will be largest and smallest. Schools, for example, pose an increasingly complex set of cognitive tasks for students to master as they ascend in grade level, which gives an increasing edge in performance to brighter pupils and creates an increasingly grueling if not punishing experience for low-g individuals. And as pointed out in Chapter 1 (Weiss, Beal, Saklofske, Pickiam-Alloway, & Prifitera, 2008), learning also becomes more autonomous, instructions lengthier, and visual aids fewer in number as lessons become more complex – all of which can serve to widen the gap between children of average abilities and those with impairments. There is no more prolonged, relentless, highly public de facto test of general intelligence than that which the public schools administer on a daily basis in the normal course of instruction. As psychometricians know, the longer a test is, the better it will discriminate between individuals of low and high cognitive ability. In this case, the increasing discrimination by ability level manifests itself in widening gaps in academic achievement (except, of course, where achievement levels are artificially capped by limiting opportunities for brighter students to advance in the curriculum).

We can be grateful that g level does not correlate with happiness (subjective well-being), but higher levels of g do confer greater resilience in the face of adversity. Brighter children are better able to weather destructive rearing circumstances, and brighter soldiers are less susceptible to post-traumatic stress syndrome. As described in the accident literature, spotting hazards and avoiding accidental injury are quintessentially cognitive tasks, and research is beginning to confirm that a lower IQ increases risk of preventable injury and death. Demands for learning and reasoning are not limited to the classroom or workplace.

Finally, although it may be the single most useful mental tool in the larger human toolkit, g, like any tool, yields good results only when used diligently and wisely. High g allows for high levels of achievement but never guarantees them. General intelligence is not an achievement, but the mental capacity for it. Certain other personal traits, such as conscientiousness, also have general utility. They cannot compensate for low g when the situation requires apt learning and reasoning, but they can somewhat buffer the consequences of low g. For example, sociability and agreeableness allow individuals who are mildly mentally retarded to elicit more assistance, sustain a network of friends, and sometimes pass as "normal."

A corollary is that we, as professionals, ought to use wisely our knowledge about *g* when seeking to assist these and other individuals at risk. We know that intelligence is a general facility for learning and reasoning which becomes increasingly advantageous as learning and reasoning tasks become more complex. This means, conversely, that complex tasks pose bigger cognitive barriers to individuals who learn and reason poorly. We simply cannot expect all individuals to master complex learning tasks equally well when given the same amount of time and support to do so. Tasks that seem mindlessly simple to many people may be prohibitively difficult for some. That is why health educators advocate limiting the complexity of informational materials to the equivalent of a Grade 5 reading level – to provide low-literacy patients cognitive access to critical information.

Neither employers nor schools can reduce instruction to the lowest common dominator (nor should the health system, for that matter). Studies in both settings indicate, however, that learning is enhanced for all when the complexity of instruction is tailored to meet learning needs at different levels of the IQ continuum (Cronbach & Snow, 1977; Snow, 1994). To illustrate, between IQs 70 and 80, individuals tend to profit most from instruction that is highly concrete, step by step, involves much repetition and feedback, is tightly focused on the bare essentials, and is delivered one on one (Gottfredson, 1997). In the neighborhood of IQs 90–105, individuals typically profit most from programmed or mastery learning approaches that provide ample time and hands-on training experiences. This contrasts with individuals at the high end of the IQ distribution, say, above IQ 115, who in many ways are self-instructing. They are able to gather and synthesize information on their own, as well as independently analyze and draw inferences from the often confusing, swirling mass of information enveloping us in daily life and work. High IQ individuals profit from instruction in theory, but low-IQ individuals do not. Low-IQ individuals require massive scaffolding of instruction, but that interferes with learning at high IQ levels.

A focus on task complexity also reveals much needless complexity in instructional settings, whose elimination can make the difference between failure and success for children with cognitive impairments, specific or general. Consider, for example, the suggestions for intervention in Part II of Chapter 1. Many focus on paring away non-essential complexity, often mirroring the strategies developed independently by health educators and work literacy researchers seeking to enhance learning among low ability patients (Doak et al., 1996) and military recruits (Sticht, 1975): eliminate distractions, reduce visual clutter, include more white space on written materials, use simple words and short sentences, break tasks into a clear sequence of steps, pace them to avoid overwhelming the student, use lots of repetition and feedback, allow extra time, use physical manipulatives and visual aids where helpful, limit the need for drawing inferences, and limit the task to its most critical elements (e.g., allow oral rather than written responses). Others constitute a "metacurriculum" (Snow, 1996) in the sorts of mental self-regulation and reflection that allow learners to deploy those resources more efficiently, such as by using memory aids, outlines, advance organizers, and strategies for parsing tasks and self-pacing. Techniques for reducing cognitive load are especially important for children with generalized intellectual deficits (low g). But they also help children with specific impairments, say, ones involving visualization or memory, by freeing up mental resources for deployment in their area of impairment.

Better tailoring the complexity of learning tasks to the ability levels of learners clearly does not result in equal amounts learned at all ability levels, but it does result in *more* learning for everyone. This happy pedagogical result comes with a political downside, however, which may help explain schools' reluctance to pursue it. Namely, interventions that succeed in raising average levels of performance generally increase the spread (standard deviation) of performance levels (Ceci & Papierno, 2005; see also Fuchs & Young, 2006, on responsiveness to instruction). In common parlance, variance around the mean is described as inequality, and inequality is perceived as a bad thing to be eradicated.

Together, the foregoing generalizations allow us to predict with clockwork-like accuracy the ramifications of intelligence differences across social and political life. For instance, employee selection psychologists can predict the amount of disparate impact (racial disparities in test results) they will observe in different sorts of applicant pools if they administer selection batteries with certain combinations of cognitive and non-cognitive assessments rather than others (Schmitt et al., 1997). They want this information to determine which batteries of valid unbiased tests would, if implemented, put companies at greatest risk of employment discrimination lawsuits. These generalizations could also have been used to foresee the impact of the US Congress's 2001 *No Child Left Behind Act*, which mandates that the public schools eliminate achievement gaps between social groups by raising all children to a high level of academic proficiency by the year 2014. They forecast not just the Act's certain failure but also its side-effects, including the distorted testing and teaching strategies to which schools are turning to appear to satisfy it without actually doing so.

WHERE DO INTELLIGENCE DIFFERENCES ORIGINATE AND RESIDE?

Research on the physiology and genetics of intelligence helps to explain the regularity and stability of phenotypic differences in cognitive abilities. Perhaps ironically, it also allays common fears about what a sturdy biological basis for many individual differences would mean.

Individual differences in IQ are firmly but not entirely rooted in the genetic differences among individuals (Sternberg & Grigorenko, 1997; Plomin et al., 2001). This fact has been known far longer than it has been widely accepted. In fact, some behavior geneticists are concluding that variation in *all* human traits – abilities, personality, attitudes, interests, sexual preference, and so on – must now be presumed to be at least somewhat heritable until proved otherwise. The broad Stratum II abilities are somewhat less heritable than g, but their phenotypic correlations with g seem to be entirely genetic. That is, to the extent that they correlate with g, they arise from the same genetic sources. Neither shared nor non-shared environments contribute to their overlap with g.

Most of the broad abilities that behavioral geneticists have analyzed so far – but especially memory – are also influenced, though to a far lesser degree, by genes specific to that ability and not shared by g. This is not surprising because, unlike g, primary abilities such as verbal and spatial ability can be associated with particular regions of the brain. Differences in g, on the other hand, correlate with cross-brain attributes such as joint mobilization of particular Brodmann's Areas across the brain, volume of white and gray matter, dendritic branching, and such. The pre-frontal lobes may be especially important to g, but they are not the seat of it. A useful analogy is that g is like a giant turbine which powers an array of small motors, each devoted to different specialized activities. Consistent with findings in neuropsychology, the smaller motors do not necessarily work with equal efficiency and any one of them could be knocked off-line without materially affecting the turbine powering them all.

More surprising are several findings that even the behavior geneticists did not expect, and which help to explain the empirical regularities involving phenotypic g. One is that the heritability of IQ increases, not decreases, with age: from perhaps 0.2 in infancy (to the extent g can be measured at that age), to 0.6 by adolescence, to 0.8 by middle to late adulthood in typical Western research populations. That is, our phenotypic differences in intelligence line up more closely with our genotypic differences as we become more independent and freer to select and shape our own learning opportunities.

A second surprise is that the only non-genetic influences on general intelligence that last into adolescence originate in our non-shared environments. These are the influences that affect siblings one by one, not uniformly as members of the same household – say, an illness rather than parental education. Both unexpected findings mean that our IQs actually become less similar to those of parents and siblings as we age, because the shared environmental influences that boosted our similarities in childhood fade away as we become independent adults. The IQs of biological relatives remain moderately similar for genetic reasons, however, because we share exactly half of our genes with each parent and half, on average, with biological siblings. An important societal-level consequence of the 50% genetic *dissimilarity* among biological parents and children, combined with the high heritability of IQ, is that it generates considerable intergenerational social mobility (up and down) in societies allowing individuals to rise on the basis of their own merits rather than family advantage.

Also a surprise to many, but not to behavior geneticists, is the finding that personal environments and life events are also somewhat heritable, especially those over which we exercise obvious control such as having serious marital or financial troubles. Not surprisingly, then, the phenotypic correlations between

IQ, academic achievement, and years of education completed turn out to be mostly genetic in nature, but those for occupation and income successively less so (Rowe et al., 1998). The environment is not just "out there" but is perceived, shaped, and exploited differently depending on our own genetically conditioned proclivities and capabilities (Dawkins, 1999). For instance, the same classroom with the same teacher does not constitute the same environment or exert the same influence on genetically diverse students. Some students will be more willing or able to exploit the learning opportunities in that classroom. Some will build warm relations with their teachers, but others will consistently behave in a manner that engenders hostility among peers and teacher alike. Students are not identical lumps of clay which teachers can mold and remold in ways that we or they might wish. Children are born neither fungible nor passive, but ineradicably individual, self-constructing, and resistant to fundamental redesign according to the dictates of others. That seems mostly a good thing, even if sometimes frustrating to parents and teachers.

None of this should be taken to mean, as is sometimes mistakenly suggested, that school achievement is fixed by intelligence level or that we should give up on low-g individuals. Far from it. As already noted, intelligence is not achievement itself, but a mental capacity that facilitates many forms of achievement. Everyone can learn more than they currently do and apply their knowledge more effectively. That is, we can always improve achievement to some degree without changing g at all. Behavior genetic research has already revealed that academic achievement, unlike g itself, is permanently influenced to some extent by shared environmental factors. In fact, such research may provide the most efficient and effective methodology for ferreting out which specific environments and experiences account for the *non-genetic* influences on academic achievement.

Perhaps the most surprising but illuminating genetic finding is this. Despite high hopes and a decade of large-scale studies, no gene (to my knowledge) has yet been unambiguously identified that influences intelligence level within the normal range. Single gene mutations and chromosomal anomalies tend to send individuals straight to the low end of the IQ continuum, so they are easier to identify. The failure to locate genes for normal variation along the IQ continuum suggests that it originates in the actions of many genes with only small individual effects on the phenotype. Evincing this expectation, geneticists now pin their hopes on finding genes that account for at most 0.5% of the variance in IQ – and they do not seem terribly optimistic about that either.

Their challenge seems consonant with the growing body of results from research on the electrical, chemical, metabolic, structural, and functional properties of the human brain. They suggest that all elements of the brain are correlated with IQ differences to some extent: rate of glucose metabolism (negatively), complexity of EEG waves, size of various regions of white and gray matter, and so on (Vernon, 1993; Bock et al., 2000; Deary, 2000; Jung & Haier, 2007). Moreover, these phenotypic correlations turn out to be mostly genetic when the necessary data are available to investigate the matter. There are probably no genes for intelligence as such, but rather for many particulars in the brain, such as degree of nerve myelination and amount of dendrite branching at the end of nerve axons. Myelination shows the same developmental course as does IQ (it increases during childhood and decreases in adulthood), and dendritic branching correlates with differences in IQ.

The brain is also responsive to non-genetic influences, partly for genetic reasons. The genome operates more like a playbook than a blueprint, with contingencies for all manner of environmental conditions. Biologic factors such as drugs and lack of sleep can cause large day-to-day fluctuations in mental efficiency. Other posited non-genetic influences may have longer term although not necessarily permanent effects, such as intensive training and practice, malnutrition, or serious illness (Sternberg & Grigorenko, 2001). Socio-educational interventions to raise low IQs have not borne much fruit, but perhaps we have been looking in the wrong places for leverage in toning up intelligence and exploiting people's unused potential.

Some scholars wonder whether biologic factors such as these might explain the secular increase in IQ scores observed during the 20th century and throughout much of Europe and North America (Neisser, 1998). This steady increase of three IQ points per decade, dubbed the Flynn effect, is usually attributed to entirely socio-cultural influences, but this seems implausible in view of the fact that average heights have risen in tandem with IQs. I see no evidence that the rise in IQs is actually a rise in g itself, because the increases seem almost random with regard to the g loadings of the subtests on which scores have risen the most and least (Matrices and Similarities way up, but Vocabulary, Information, and Arithmetic not). Moreover, the heritabilities for IQ have not, to my knowledge, fallen as would be expected with the hypothesized injection of new environmental influences. This peculiar pattern of change and lack of change might be consistent, however, with potential biologic effects on the brain regions or specific abilities contributing variance (beyond g) to the subtests most responsible for boosting overall IQ. These localized effects could also be genetic, the effect of heterosis (hybrid vigor) resulting from individuals increasingly marrying outside their villages and small towns (Mingroni, 2007).

The puzzle of the Flynn effect remains unsolved in large part because intelligence tests lack ratio-level measurement, that is, a scale that starts at zero quantity and counts in equal-size units from there. Without that capability, we cannot know whether the observed secular rise in average IQ reflects an absolute change in the level of any of the constructs captured by IQ tests, either in g itself or some normally inconsequential source of variance in the composite IQ score. Critics often implicitly assume that IQ scores can register changes in absolute ability level when they criticize intelligence tests. A currently popular critique in this vein is that the Flynn effect disproves what had come to seem incontrovertibly true, namely, that IQ tests measure a stable, heritable, psychometrically unitary general intelligence. Their argument is that g cannot at once be heritable, unitary, and yet some subtest scores increase dramatically over time. Flynn (2007), for example, argues that the rise has "shattered g." It obviously has not. The problem is not with our conception or measurement of g, but with our measurement technology not yet allowing us to measure absolute rather than just relative positions along any ability continuum. This is the severest limitation of current IQ tests, yet to be overcome (Jensen, 2006), but it does nothing to invalidate the construct of g or the utility of current IQ tests for many diagnostic, selection, placement, training, and treatment purposes.

OF WHAT VALUE IS TESTING FOR INTELLIGENCE?

Intelligence testing is a highly sophisticated technical enterprise for measuring human cognitive diversity, itself perhaps the most socially consequential, genetically conditioned individual difference in modern life. Statistically and theoretically, testing has advanced tremendously since its Model-T days generations ago. Used with skill and responsibility, intelligence tests yield information of great value and precision not otherwise available to administrators, clinicians, and scientists. They can be misused, and they are often misunderstood or wrongly maligned (Gottfredson, in press). They are imperfect yardsticks, yet far superior to most others in the social sciences. If they and their results sometimes rouse controversy, it is usually because they have done their job all too well – illuminated human differences that are important to us. As this book shows, however, intelligence tests can be used to fashion more humane and constructive responses to those differences.

REFERENCES

Bartholomew, D. J. (2004). *Measuring Intelligence: Facts and Fallacies.* Cambridge: Cambridge University Press.

Bock, G. R., Goode, J. A., & Webb, K. (Eds.) (2000). *The Nature of Intelligence.* Novartis Foundation Symposium 233. Chichester, UK: Wiley.

Campbell, J. P., & Knapp, D. J. (Eds.) (2001). *Exploring the Limits of Personnel Selection and Classification.* Mahwah, NJ: Erlbaum.

Carroll, J. B. (1993). *Human Cognitive Abilities.* Cambridge: Cambridge University Press.

Ceci, S. J. (Ed.) (1996). Special theme: IQ in society. *Psychology, Public Policy, and Law,* 2(3/4), 403–645.

Ceci, S. J., & Papierno, P. B. (2005). The rhetoric and reality of gap closing – When the "Have-Nots" gain but the "Haves" gain even more. *American Psychologist,* 60(2), 149–160.

Cronbach, L. J., & Snow, R. E. (1977). *Aptitudes and Instructional Methods: A Handbook for Research on Interactions.* New York: Irvington.

Dawkins, R. (1999). *The Extended Phenotype: The Long Reach of the Gene.* Oxford: Oxford University Press.

Deary, I. J. (2000). *Looking Down on Human Intelligence: From Psychometrics to the Rain.* Oxford: Oxford University Press.

Deary, I. J., Whiteman, M. C., Starr, J. M., Whalley, L. J., & Fox, H. C. (2004). The impact of childhood intelligence on later life: Following up the Scottish Mental Surveys of 1932 and 1947. *Journal of Personality and Social Psychology*, 86, 130–147.

Doak, C. C., Doak, L. G., & Root, J. H. (1996). *Teaching Patients with Low Literacy Skills* (2nd ed.). Philadelphia, PA: Lippincott.

Fischer, C. S., Hout, M., Jankowski, M. S., Lucas, S. R., Swidler, A., & Voss, K. (1996). *Inequality by Design: Cracking the Bell Curve Myth*. Princeton, NJ: Princeton University Press.

Flynn, J. R. (2007). *What is Intelligence? Beyond the Flynn Effect*. Cambridge: Cambridge University Press.

Frisby, C. L., & Reynolds, C. R. (Eds.) (2005). *Comprehensive Handbook of Multicultural School Psychology*. New York: Wiley.

Fuchs, D., & Young, C. L. (2006). On the irrelevance of intelligence in predicting responsiveness to reading instruction. *Exceptional Children*, 73(1), 8–30.

Gardner, H. (1983). *Frames of Mind: The Theory of Multiple Intelligences*. New York: Basic Books.

Gordon, R. A. (1997). Everyday life as an intelligence test: Effects of intelligence and intelligence context. *Intelligence*, 24(1), 203–320.

Gottfredson, L. S. (Ed.) (1997a). Intelligence and social policy. *Intelligence*, 24(1), 1–320 (special issue).

Gottfredson, L. S. (1997b). Why *g* matters: The complexity of everyday life. *Intelligence*, 24(1), 79–132.

Gottfredson, L. S. (2004). Intelligence: Is it the epidemiologists' elusive "fundamental cause" of social class inequalities in health? *Journal of Personality and Social Psychology*, 86, 174–199.

Gottfredson, L. S. (in press). Logical fallacies used to dismiss the evidence on intelligence testing. In R. Phelps (Ed.), *The True Measure of Educational and Psychological Tests: Correcting Fallacies About the Science of Testing*. Washington, DC: American Psychological Association.

Herrnstein, R. J., & Murray, C. (1994). *The Bell Curve: Intelligence and Class Structure in American Life*. New York: Free Press.

Jencks, C., et al. (1979). *Who Gets Ahead? The Determinants of Economic Success in America*. New York: Basic Books.

Jensen, A. R. (1980). *Bias in Mental Testing*. New York: Free Press.

Jensen, A. R. (1998). *The g Factor: The Science of Mental Ability*. Westport, CT: Praeger.

Jensen, A. R. (2006). *Clocking the Mind: Mental Chronometry and Individual Differences*. Amsterdam: Elsevier.

Jung, R. E., & Haier, R. J. (2007). The parieto-frontal integration theory (P-FIT) of intelligence: Converging neuroimaging evidence. *Behavior and Brain Sciences*, 30, 135–187.

Lubinski, D. (Ed.) (2004). Cognitive abilities: 100 years after Spearman's (1904) "General Intelligence, Objectively Determined and Measured" (Special section). *Journal of Personality and Social Psychology*, 86, 96–199.

Mingroni, M. A. (2007). Resolving the IQ paradox: Heterosis as a cause of the Flynn effect and other trends. *Psychological Review*, 114(3), 806–829.

Neisser, U. (Ed.) (1998). *The Rising Curve: Long-term Gains in IQ and Related Measures*. Washington, DC: American Psychological Association.

Plomin, R., DeFries, J. C., McClearn, G. E., & McGuffin, P. (2001). *Behavioral Genetics* (4th ed.). New York: Worth.

Roberts, M. J. (Ed.) (2007). *Integrating the Mind: Domain General Versus Domain Specific Processes in Higher Cognition*. New York: Psychology Press.

Rowe, D. C., Vesterdal, W. J., & Rodgers, J. L. (1998). Herrnstein's syllogism: Genetic and shared environmental influences on IQ, education, and income. *Intelligence*, 26, 405–423.

Schmitt, N., Rogers, W., Chan, D., Sheppard, L., & Jennings, D. (1997). Adverse impact and predictive efficiency of various predictor combinations. *Journal of Applied Psychology*, 82.

Snow, R. E. (1994). Abilities in academic tasks. In R. J. Sternberg, & R. K. Wagner (Eds.), *Mind in Context: Interactionist Perspectives on Human Intelligence* (pp. 3–37). Cambridge: Cambridge University Press.

Snow, R. E. (1996). Aptitude development and education. *Psychology, Public Policy, and Law*, 2(3/4), 536–560.

Spearman, C. (1904). "General intelligence," objectively determined and measured. *American Journal of Psychology*, 15, 201–293.

Sternberg, R. J., & Grigorenko, E. L. (Eds.) (1997). *Intelligence, Heredity, and Environment*. Cambridge: Cambridge University Press.

Sternberg, R. J., & Grigorenko, E. L. (Eds.) (2001). *Environmental Effects on Cognitive Abilities*. Mahwah, NJ: Lawrence Erlbaum Associates, Publishers.

Sternberg, R. L., & Grigorenko, E. L. (Eds.) (2002). *The General Intelligence Factor: How General Is It?* Mahwah, NJ: Erlbaum.

Sticht, T. G. (Ed.) (1975). *Reading for Working: A Functional Literacy Anthology*. Alexandria, VA: Human Resources Research Organization (HumRRO).

Vernon, P. A. (Ed.) (1993). *Biological Approaches to the Study of Human Intelligence*. Norwood, NJ: Ablex.

Weiss, L. G., Beal, A. L., Saklofske, D. H., Pickiam-Alloway, T., & Prifitera, A. (2008). Interpretation and intervention with WISC-IV in the clinical assessment context. In A. Prifitera, D. Saklofske, & L. G. Weiss (Eds.), *WISC-IV Applications for Clinical Assessment and Intervention* (pp. 1–66). Amsterdam: Elsevier.

Williams, W. M. (Ed.) (2000). Special themes: Ranking ourselves: Perspectives on intelligence testing, affirmative action, and educational policy (Special issue). *Psychology, Public Policy, and Law*, 6(1), 1–252.

INDEX